CONTEMPORARY
Black
Biography

ISSN 1058-1316

CONTEMPORARY
Black
Biography

Profiles from the International Black Community

Volume 5

Barbara Carlisle Bigelow, Editor

 **Gale Research Inc.** · *DETROIT* · *WASHINGTON, D.C.* · *LONDON*

STAFF

Barbara Carlisle Bigelow, *Editor*

Sonia Benson, L. Mpho Mabunda, Mary K. Ruby, *Associate Editors*

Marilyn Allen, *Editorial Associate*

Michael J. Tyrkus, *Assistant Editor*

Robin Armstrong, Alison Carb Sussman, John Cohassey, Ed Decker, Harvey Dickson, Liza Featherstone, Simon Glickman, Nina Goldstein, Joan Goldsworthy, Joyce Harrison, Anne Janette Johnson, Mark Kram, Joe Kuskowski, Michael L. LaBlanc, Ondine E. Le Blanc, Cathleen Collins Lee, Glen Macnow, Jonathan Martin, Gordon Mayer, Louise Mooney, Michael E. Mueller, Rob Nagel, Jomel Nichols, Nicholas S. Patti, James J. Podesta, Isaac Rosen, Julia M. Rubiner, Jeffrey Taylor, Jordan Wankoff, Elizabeth Wenning, Gillian Wolf, *Contributing Editors*

Peter M. Gareffa, *Senior Editor, Contemporary Biographies*

Jeanne Gough, *Permissions Manager*
Margaret A. Chamberlain, *Permissions Supervisor (Pictures)*
Pamela A. Hayes, Keith Reed, *Permissions Associates*
Susan Brohman, Arlene M. Johnson, Barbara A. Wallace, *Permissions Assistants*

Mary Beth Trimper, *Production Director*
Mary Kelley, *Production Assistant*
Cynthia Baldwin, *Art Director*
Barbara J. Yarrow, *Graphic Services Supervisor*
C. J. Jonik, *Desktop Publisher*
Jeanne M. Moore, *Cover Designer*

Victoria B. Cariappa, *Research Manager*
Mary Rose Bonk, *Research Supervisor*
Reginald A. Carlton, Clare Collins, Andrew Guy Malonis, Norma Sawaya, *Editorial Associates*
Laurel Sprague Bowden, Rachel A. Dixon, Eva Marie Felts, Shirley Gates, Doris Lewandowski, Sharon McGilvray, Dana R. Schleiffers, Amy B. Wieczorek, *Editorial Assistants*

∞™ This book is printed on acid-free paper that meets the minimum requirements of American National Standard for Information Sciences— Permanence Paper for Printed Library Materials, ANSI Z39.48-1984.

ISBN 0-8103-8557-0
ISSN 1058-1316

10 9 8 7 6 5 4 3

I(T)P™
The trademark ITP is used under license.

Contemporary Black Biography
Advisory Board

Contents

Introduction

Contemporary Black Biography provides informative biographical profiles of the important and influential persons of African heritage who form the international black community: men and women who have changed today's world and are shaping tomorrow's.

Contemporary Black Biography covers persons of various nationalities in a wide variety of fields, including architecture, art, business, dance, education, fashion, film, industry, journalism, law, literature, medicine, music, politics and government, publishing, religion, science and technology, social issues, sports, television, theater, and others.

In addition to in-depth coverage of names found in today's headlines, *Contemporary Black Biography* provides coverage of selected individuals from earlier in this century whose influence continues to impact on contemporary life. *Contemporary Black Biography* also provides coverage of important and influential persons who are not yet household names and are therefore likely to be ignored by other biographical reference series.

Designed for Quick Research *and* Interesting Reading

- **Attractive page design** incorporates textual subheads, making it easy to find the information you're looking for.

- **Easy-to-locate data sections** provide quick access to vital personal statistics, career information, major awards, and mailing addresses, when available.

- **Informative biographical essays** trace the subject's personal and professional life with the kind of in-depth analysis you need.

- **To further enhance your appreciation** of the subject, most entries include photographic portraits.

- **Sources for additional information** direct the user to selected books, magazines, and newspapers where more information on the individuals can be obtained.

Helpful Indexes Make It Easy to Find the Information You Need

Contemporary Black Biography includes cumulative Nationality, Occupation, Subject, and Name indexes that make it easy to locate entries in a variety of useful ways.

Available in Electronic Formats

Diskette/Magnetic Tape. *Contemporary Black Biography* is available for licensing on magnetic tape or diskette in a fielded format. Either the complete database or a custom selection of entries may be ordered. The database is available for internal data processing and nonpublishing purposes only. For more information, call (800) 877-GALE.

Online. *Contemporary Black Biography* is available online through Mead Data Central's NEXIS Service in the NEXIS, PEOPLE and SPORTS Libraries in the GALBIO file.

We Welcome Your Suggestions

The editors welcome your comments and suggestions for enhancing and improving *Contemporary Black Biography.* If you would like to suggest persons for inclusion in the series, please submit these names to the editors. Mail comments or suggestions to:

The Editor
Contemporary Black Biography
Gale Research, Inc.
835 Penobscot Bldg.
Detroit, MI 48226-4094
Phone: (800) 347-GALE
FAX: (313) 961-6815

Photo Credits

Hank Aaron

1934—

Retired professional baseball player, business executive

Professional baseball may never see another slugger as great as Hank Aaron. Aaron's career record of 755 home runs in 23 years is by far the best in the history of the game. He also holds top honors for runs batted in and total bases and has been a member of the Baseball Hall of Fame since 1982. Aaron was a highly regarded but relatively unknown star of the Atlanta Braves (prior to 1966, the Milwaukee Braves) for nearly two decades before he became an American hero in 1973 and 1974 It was during those seasons that he chased, and finally surpassed, Babe Ruth's famed career home run record. When Aaron hit his 715th home run on April 8, 1974, amidst a near-melee in the Braves' home ballpark, he achieved a "superhuman accomplishment, as mysterious and remote as Stonehenge, and certain to stand forever," to quote Tom Buckley in the *New York Times Magazine*. Remarkably, that milestone came not at the end, but rather in the middle of an extraordinary baseball career.

Stardom never rested easily on Aaron's shoulders. By nature a reserved individual, he chafed under the public accolade that accompanied his record-breaking performance. In fact, Aaron spent the last years of his playing career in a constant state of uneasiness. Breaking the home run record brought him

legions of new fans, but it also exposed an ugly vein of racism in society. As he edged past Ruth in the record books, Aaron faced death threats and other forms of hate from some angry whites who saw his performance as a challenge to their cherished ideas of supremacy. "What does it say of America that a man fulfills the purest of American dreams, struggling up from Jim Crow poverty to dethrone the greatest of Yankee kings . . . yet feels not like a hero but like someone hunted?" asked Mike Capuzzo in *Sports Illustrated*. "The Home Run King is a grandfather now, and by tradition he should be lionized, a legend in the autumn of his life. But Henry Aaron takes no comfort in baseball immortality, in lore and remembrance."

Breaking the Color Barrier

Aaron was born and raised in a segregated neighborhood in Mobile, Alabama. The house where he and his seven siblings grew up did not have plumbing, electricity, or glass windows. He was born in 1934, in the midst of the Great Depression, and his parents struggled to keep ahead of the bills. Aaron's father worked at the Alabama Dry Dock and

At a Glance...

Born Henry Louis Aaron, February 5, 1934, in Mobile, AL; son of Herbert (a shipyard worker) and Estella Aaron; married Barbara Lucas, October 6, 1953 (divorced); married Billye Suber, November 1973; children (first marriage): Gail, Hank, Lary, Gary (deceased), Dorinda; (second marriage) Ceci.

Professional baseball player, 1952-76; baseball executive, 1976—; vice-president with Turner Broadcasting System, 1990—. Began baseball career with Indianapolis Clowns (Negro League), 1952; joined Milwaukee Braves organization (later became Atlanta Braves), 1952; made parent team, 1954. Traded to Milwaukee Brewers, 1975. Returned to Braves as vice-president for player development, 1976-89; named senior vice-president, 1989. Active in numerous charity concerns, including Easter Seal Society and Hank Aaron Scholarship Fund. Author, with Lonnie Wheeler, of autobiography *I Had a Hammer: The Hank Aaron Story*, Harper, 1991.

Selected awards: Spingarn Medal from the NAACP, 1976. Holds lifetime records for most home runs (755), most runs batted in (2297), most long hits (1477), and most total bases (6856). Named to National League All-Star roster 24 times; named National League Most Valuable Player, 1957; elected to Baseball Hall of Fame, 1982.

Addresses: c/o Atlanta Braves, P.O. Box 4064, Atlanta, GA 30302.

Shipbuilding Company. The job was steady, but so was the verbal abuse from white co-workers. Herbert Aaron rarely complained to his children, but he did encourage them to excel in school. Young Henry was a good student, but from an early age he knew he wanted to play professional baseball.

Aaron spent most of his spare time at Carver Recreational Park, a neighborhood playground a block from his home. There he played sandlot baseball, essentially teaching himself the game. When his parents realized that he was intent on pursuing sports, they advised him to "play a lot better than the white boy," according to Capuzzo.

When Aaron was a young teenager, professional baseball slowly began to integrate with the arrival of Jackie Robinson, the first black to play in the major leagues. While Robinson was enduring taunts and death threats in the majors, Aaron was making a name for himself in Mobile. His high school did not have a baseball team, so he played in local amateur and semi-pro leagues. Early teams included the Pritchett Athletics and the Mobile Black Bears.

Aaron was recruited by the Black Bears to help win an exhibition game against a professional Negro League team, the Indianapolis Clowns. The young man's talents attracted the attention of Syd Pollock, the Clowns' owner. In 1952, the Clowns offered Aaron a contract—$200 a month to play in the Negro League during baseball season. He was thrilled, and at that time he thought the salary was a small fortune. Armed with two sandwiches and two dollars his mother gave him, he embarked for Indianapolis by train. Capuzzo wrote of Aaron in those days: "He was skinny as a toothpick, batted cross-handed because no one had told him not to, [and] feared white pitchers because he'd heard they were a superior race."

After only a short time in the Negro Leagues, Aaron was recruited by the Milwaukee Braves. He joined the Braves' system in 1952 and was sent to the minor leagues. There he became one of the first black players to break the color line in the Deep South—a dangerous proposition in the last, desperate days of segregation that was legally enforced by Jim Crow laws. After one season in Wisconsin, Aaron found himself playing for a Jacksonville, Florida team in the South Atlantic League. Fans insulted him constantly, and even some of his teammates hurled racial slurs at him. Hotels and restaurants were closed to him because he was black. The situation was only tolerable because Aaron showed such talent, and because he was young. "I was only 19 in the [South Atlantic] League," he told *Sports Illustrated*. "It was like sending a 19-year-old into war. What did I know about death? What did I know about the world? It didn't matter so much then. Later, it mattered."

Somehow the heightened tension inspired Aaron. During his year with the South Atlantic League, he led the circuit in batting average, doubles, runs scored, total bases and runs batted in. He was voted League Most Valuable Player for 1953. The following year, a key injury opened a roster spot with the Braves in Milwaukee. Aaron won the position in spring training and joined the team for the 1954 season.

One Team, Many Records

As the Braves' starting right fielder, Aaron turned in a superb rookie year. He batted .280 and hit 13 home runs in an injury-shortened season. The following year he more than doubled his home run tally, hitting 27 with a .314

average. Aaron was also an able outfielder and a threat to steal. His speed and power quickly earned him a reputation in the National League. With his help, the Braves advanced to the 1957 World Series against the New York Yankees.

Aaron still remembers a crucial home run he hit in 1957 as one of the highlights of his career. On September 24, 1957, the Braves faced the second-place St. Louis Cardinals in a game that would clinch the National League pennant for one of the teams. The score was tied 2-2 into the 11th inning. Aaron smacked a homer to win the game and the pennant for the Braves. As he rounded the bases, his teammates gathered at home plate to carry him off the field. The Braves went on that year to beat the Yankees in the World Series. Aaron hit three home runs and a triple for 7 runs batted in as the Braves took the Series in seven games.

The Braves returned to the World Series in 1958, this time losing to the Yankees. By then Aaron was a bona fide baseball star, even if he did little to promote himself. His batting average stood at .326, and he was just beginning a hitting streak that would bring him more than 30 home runs a season almost every year until 1974. Aaron—who had once feared white pitchers—was now himself an object of terror in the National League. One hurler commented that getting a fast ball past Hank Aaron was like trying to get the sun past a rooster. Another said that trying to fool him was like slapping a rattlesnake. Yet after 1958, Aaron's talents were hidden on a Braves team that failed to make postseason play year after year.

People began counting, though, as Aaron passed the ten-year mark in his playing career. Three times—in 1957, 1963, and 1966—Aaron hit 44 home runs in a season. In 1971 he smacked 47. His lowest season total before 1974 was 24, in 1964. (The average major leaguer might consider himself blessed with 18 home runs each year.) Aaron inched toward the record with a batting stance and running style that defied logic, a carryover from his self-taught youth. At the age where most major league ball players retire, he was still maintaining his superb conditioning and his unique hand-eye coordination. He played throughout the 1960s in Milwaukee and Atlanta—the Braves moved South in 1966—and, in 1973, brought his home run totals to the verge of a new record.

Media attention began to build in 1970, when Aaron became the first player to combine 3000 career hits and 500 home runs. The countdown began for a run on Ruth's record of 714 homers. By 1973 Aaron had closed the gap considerably, and at the end of that season he had 713. The fame he had never particularly courted found him. Letters—most of them congratulatory—came from all over the world. He was offered lucrative endorsement contracts from Magnavox electronics and was honored

with a candy bar called "O Henry!" Charities like the Easter Seals Foundation and Big Brothers vied for his time. His second marriage in November of 1973 made international headlines. Aaron could not bask in the glory, however. He was afraid for his life, and the lives of his children.

Fame in a Racist Society

Among the 930,000 pieces of mail Aaron received in 1973 were numerous hate letters. One, printed in *Sports Illustrated,* read: *"Dear Hank Aaron, I got orders to do a bad job on you if and when you get 10 from B. Ruth record. A guy in Atlanta and a few in Miami Fla don't seem to care if they have to take care of your family too."* Many others contained similar threats. A few threatened Aaron's college-age daughter. Under siege, Aaron hired a personal bodyguard. The Federal Bureau of Investigation (FBI) investigated many of the threats and uncovered still other plots to harm the ballplayer.

On the surface Aaron seemed undaunted by the persecution. If anything, the hate mail increased his desire to break the record and set a new one that no one could possibly surpass. Aaron hit 40 home runs in 1973 and began the 1974 season by tying the Ruth record during an Opening Day game in Cincinnati. *Sports Illustrated* correspondent

> "Baseball needs me because it needs somebody to stir the pot, and I need it because it's my life. It's the means I have to make a little difference in the world."

Ron Fimrite commented: "Through the long weeks of on-field pressure and mass media harassment, [he] had expressed no more agitation than a man brushing aside a housefly. Aaron had labored for most of his 21-year career in shadows cast by more flamboyant superstars, and if he was enjoying his newfound celebrity, he gave no hint of it. He seemed to be nothing more than a man trying to do his job and live a normal life in the presence of incessant chaos."

The chaos came to a climax on April 8, 1974 in a home game in Atlanta. Aaron hit a monstrous home run off Dodger pitcher Al Downing, and the fans went wild. Aaron was greeted at the plate by his teammates and his mother. Play was suspended for fifteen minutes while he acknowledged the roar of the crowd. During the following weeks, he received more than 20,000 telegrams.

An Executive and Spokesperson

Aaron left the Atlanta Braves at the end of the 1974 season and finished his playing days with the Milwaukee Brewers. He retired in 1976 with a record 755 home runs and 2297 runs batted in. One week later he began a new phase of his career, as director of player development for the Braves. His duties included scouting new prospects for the team and overseeing the coaching of minor leaguers. The farm system Aaron directed provided the Braves with such talents as Dale Murphy, Tom Glavine, Mark Lemke, and Andres Thomas. Aaron worked hard to improve the Braves' chances of pennant contention, and he was successful. Once a forgotten franchise, the Atlanta Braves today offer one of the strongest teams in the National League.

Aaron was one of the first blacks hired in a major league front office. Throughout his tenure with the Braves' management, he has called for more black participation in the business end of baseball. The subject of minority hiring is still a priority for Aaron. He told *Sports Illustrated:* "They say we [African Americans] don't have the 'mental necessities' to sit behind the desk, we just have God-given talent. But, man, I had to work hard, too. I had to think. I didn't have any more natural talent than Ted Williams or Joe DiMaggio. I played the game 23 years, and that tells me I had to study some pitchers pretty well. But no—I was a dumb s.o.b. It's racism. These things really anger me."

The Home Run King gets angry, too, when the subject turns to his records and his stature in baseball history. "Funny how Babe Ruth's 714 home runs was the most impressive, unbreakable record in sports until a black man broke it," he commented in *Sports Illustrated.* "Then it shifted. Now it's DiMaggio's hitting streak."

Aaron's full schedule includes duties for the Braves, where he is now a senior vice president, and appearances on the behalf of national charities. He rarely takes part in the lucrative autograph-signing business that provides income for other retired baseball superstars, preferring to spend his spare time at his well-guarded estate near Atlanta with his wife, children, and grandchildren. "I wonder if I really need baseball anymore . . . and if it really needs me," Aaron concluded in his autobiography, *I Had a Hammer.* "But whenever I wonder about it, I usually come to the conclusion that I do, and it does—at least for the time being. Baseball needs me because it needs somebody to stir the pot, and I need it because it's my life. It's the means I have to make a little difference in the world."

Sources

Books

Aaron, Hank, and Lonnie Wheeler, *I Had a Hammer: The Hank Aaron Story,* Harper, 1991.
Plimpton, George, *One for the Record: The Inside Story of Hank Aaron's Chase for the Home-Run Record,* Harper, 1974.

Periodicals

Jet, February 23, 1987, p. 47; September 28, 1987, p. 50.
Look, May 15, 1956, p. 122.
Newsweek, June 15, 1959, p. 94; April 22, 1974.
New York Times Magazine, March 31, 1974, p. 22.
Sports Illustrated, April 15, 1974, pp. 20-23; December 7, 1992, pp. 80-88.
Time, July 29, 1957, p. 45; September 24, 1973, pp. 73-77.

—*Mark Kram*

Ali Mahdi Mohamed

1940—

Somali politician

For quite some time, Somalia has been a nation in chaos. Anarchy rules as armed citizens use brute force to survive. Children die for lack of proper food and medicine. Humanitarian aid and the military presence of the United States Army have not helped to restore an efficient government. The situation in this African country has been compared to that of America during the lawless days of the Wild West.

Somalia's nominal president, Ali Mahdi Mohamed, has fought to retain his precarious position since being named interim president by the United Somali Congress (USC) in January of 1991. According to the U.S. State Department, neither the United States nor any other government recognizes Ali Mahdi as the *official* leader of Somalia, but his presence as a contender for succession to the helm of a legitimate national government cannot be denied. A former businessman from the capital city of Mogadishu, Ali Mahdi commands some 4,000 troops and actually controls only a small portion of northern Mogadishu. Since taking power he has faced almost constant opposition from another powerful Somali military leader, Mohamed Farrah Aidid. Each man claims to be the ruler of Somalia, and their inability to reconcile is one of the primary forces destabilizing the nation. *New York Times* reporter Jane Perlez called Aidid and Ali

Mahdi "the strongmen of Somalia's chaotic, clan-based society, each with the ability to call on more fighters, money and ammunition than anyone else in the land."

The country at stake in this pitched battle is an east African coastal nation that juts out into the Indian Ocean and is bordered on the north by the Gulf of Aden. While never particularly prosperous, Somalia has provided a subsistence living for its six million inhabitants from farming and herding of cattle and camels. For more than two decades the nation was run by dictator Mohamed Siad Barre and members of his clan. Siad Barre and those in his inner circle enjoyed an opulent lifestyle at the expense of the ordinary citizen, and some observers feel that Ali Mahdi and General Aidid are attempting to achieve that kind of economic and political control for themselves; at the very least, each one accuses the other of holding that goal.

Many African nations contain tribes of people with different languages and cultures. Somalia is an exception. Almost all of its citizens speak the same language, Somali, and share the same religion, the Sunni branch of Islam. Legend says the entire populace descends from a mythical founder named Samaale. Ironically, the uniting factors of language and religion have been offset by a complicated system of clan loyalty, with six major clan groups divided into numerous sub-clans and extended families. This loyalty to a small clan unit once contributed to social stability in Somalia, as clan elders ran their communities and united for common causes. Tragically, the clan system has not provided a workable solution for the current social deterioration in Somalia.

Since Somalia is a coastal country, it has played host to European and Arabic colonizers who ruled with varying degrees of severity. In the nineteenth century, the country was divided between a British protectorate in the north and an Italian protectorate in the south. The Italians controlled most of Somalia into the twentieth century.

The Roots of Armed Struggle

In the late 1950s, the United Nations engineered independence for Somalia. The former British and Italian colonies were united under one government that became the country of Somalia on July 1, 1960. Under its first constitution, Somalia had a parliamentary government consisting of a president, a prime minister, and a national assembly. Somali citizens elected the president and the members of the assembly. One of the early members of the Somali parliament was Ali Mahdi Mohamed. He lived in Mogadishu and was a member of the Abgal sub-clan and the Hawiye clan. The Abgal people comprised the merchant middle class in Mogadishu and retained power and prestige by

maintaining strong family ties. For his part, Ali Mahdi ran a posh hotel whose clients included heads of state and members of the British royal family.

In 1969, the second president of Somalia was assassinated as part of a military coup. When the coup ended, General Mohamed Siad Barre became president, backed by the military and police forces. Siad Barre consolidated his power with help from the former Soviet Union. The Somali parliament was eventually disbanded and opposition parties were declared illegal. Throughout the mid-1970s, Ali Mahdi maintained his hotel business and began working with his fellow Hawiye clansmen to undermine the Siad Barre regime.

The process was dangerous and frustrating. Siad Barre imported sophisticated weaponry from the Soviet Union and Eastern Europe and sent his deputies there for military training. The dictator instituted a "One Somalia" policy dedicated to ending clan loyalties, but he also used the entrenched clan system to create friction between groups that might oppose him. He was more successful in stirring clan rivalries than he was in curbing the clan system. *Africa Report* correspondent Richard Greenfield noted that as the 1980s progressed, Siad Barre "was increasingly driven back [by] unpopular and unrealistic reliance on his own small Marehan clan. . . . He also came to rely more and more on his wider family, including his in-laws and those of his clansmen who were military men rather than politicians or bureaucrats."

Human rights violations in Somalia increased dramatically as Siad Barre attempted to hold onto power. In one instance, a 1988 revolt by the Isaaq clan in the north led to indiscriminate aerial bombing of the town of Hargeisa. Many of the buildings there still have not been repaired. Countrywide, more and more businesses came under the control of mafia-like clan-based cartels. Government corruption was widespread, and a portion of each foreign aid and development donation sent to Somalia fell into private pockets. When the Soviet bloc withdrew support for the Siad Barre regime, the dictator begged for help from the United States.

By 1990, Siad Barre's own brutal tactics began to backfire. Greenfield wrote: "Regardless of clan affiliation, there developed an absolute consensus that change had to be brought about and that Siad had to go." By spring of the same year, Ali Mahdi and more than 100 other prominent Somalis signed an open letter denouncing the existing regime. Ali Mahdi's urban Hawiye clan helped to fuel the opposition, providing both fighters and equipment for a revolution. "In the capital, demonstrations, explosions, looting—mainly by Barre's own guard—and indiscriminate killings became commonplace," Greenfield continued. As the situation deteriorated, prosperous Somali citizens fled, refugees poured into neighboring African nations, and famine loomed.

United Somali Congress Appointed Ali Mahdi President

Ali Mahdi was not trained as a military leader, but he lent his considerable political and economic muscle to the United Somali Congress (USC), a rebel group composed primarily of Hawiye clansmen. In January of 1991, the USC managed to bring the rebellion against Siad Barre right into Mogadishu. The dictator attempted a last, desperate defense by shelling the city, destroying homes at random and killing scores of citizens. This final act of casual brutality inflamed the populace, and on January 26, Siad Barre fled for his life as a mob attacked and ransacked his compound.

The death toll reached 20,000 as mobs looted the city, the deserted embassies, and the seaport installations. "As the city descended into complete anarchy, looting became a way of life and a means of survival for thousands of people with their plethora of newly acquired weapons, carried openly on the streets," observed Peter Biles for *Africa Report.* "Weeks after Barre had fled and the USC had established a caretaker government, I saw booty still being carted away by men pushing rickety wheelbarrows, piled high with every moveable asset, including on one occasion, the proverbial kitchen sink." Biles added: "What future awaits a nation which was plundered by its own people, torn apart by years of civil strife and insolvable inter-clan rivalries, and which has lost all strategic interest to the superpowers?"

The first step the USC took to restore order was to name Ali Mahdi interim president of Somalia. The appointment was made only a few days after the ouster of Siad Barre and was accomplished without consultation with some of Somalia's other armed political movements. At his installation ceremony, with his right hand on the Koran, Ali Mahdi swore "in the name of God Almighty to work without fear or favor in the interests of the Somali people," as quoted in the *Boston Globe.* He invited the other rebel groups to join in running the country and promised to seek international aid to restore the shattered economy.

The tide of clan warfare could not be stemmed, however. Siad Barre loyalists continued to make trouble in the southern portion of Somalia. Some powerful rebel groups refused to support Ali Mahdi's administration, while others supported him for a short term. Worse, the Hawiye clan itself split into factions, with fellow Hawiye Mohamed

Farrah Aidid emerging as a military leader in armed opposition to Ali Mahdi. Whatever peace might have been possible was scuttled within months, as forces loyal to Ali Mahdi or Aidid battled in the streets of Mogadishu. *Washington Post* contributor Keith B. Richburg noted that the dual between Ali Mahdi and Aidid "has been brutally played out in the streets of the capital. They have carved up the city into warring camps. Artillery shells have wrecked streets and buildings. Burned-out and mangled cars litter largely empty highways. In the absence of any kind of authority, armed militias have taken to roaming the streets in jeeps outfitted with rockets, mortars and antiaircraft guns."

Ali Mahdi found himself restricted to a region of Mogadishu only a few blocks wide as the fighting raged. His opponent could not press the advantage, however, because both sides were well-armed and motivated by self-interest. Several cease-fire attempts lasted for weeks or months at a

> "I swear in the name of God Almighty to work without fear or favor in the interests of the Somali people."

time but eventually fell apart. In the meantime, Ali Mahdi was unable to enact any measures to curb the violence in Somalia's countryside and the other major cities. "In the current tragedy of Mogadishu, it is difficult to tell between the president and the general who is the democrat and who the would-be dictator," wrote Richburg.

Sporadic but intense fighting continued in Mogadishu throughout 1992 as Somalia plunged into famine. Ali Mahdi formed a coalition of rebel factions into an anti-Aidid alliance, but the stalemate continued. Efforts by the United Nations and the United States to unite the two warlords failed to provide a lasting settlement. As the months dragged on, neither leader could prove that his side had earned wide support in Somalia.

In *Africa Report,* Alex de Waal and Rakiya Omaar offered a reason for Ali Mahdi's ineffectiveness as a leader. "Many members of opposition groups are interested essentially in control of the state, as governmental office amounts to a license to print money," wrote the reporters. "Thus the interim government of President Ali Mahdi, while controlling only a few square miles of north Mogadishu, has a cabinet of over 80 ministers—each clinging to his fictitious position in the anticipation of having his hand in the honeypot if the government obtains recognition."

Operation Restore Hope

Conditions in Somalia became so desperate by December of 1992 that then-U.S. President George Bush approved an American military operation with the objective of providing humanitarian aid. Operation Restore Hope began on December 9, 1992, and continued into 1993 in an attempt to save the lives of an estimated two million people at risk of starvation. Acting president Ali Mahdi welcomed the intervention by the United States and United Nations forces. He told *Newsweek* that he has been fighting for "the restoration of democracy and free elections," adding, "Americans are the fathers of democracy, so I hope Somalis can become like Americans."

"The world can provide short-term humanitarian aid to Somalia, but it cannot rebuild a nation that appears set on a path of self-destruction," wrote Peter Biles in *Africa Report* as the crisis continued. "National reconciliation is proving more and more elusive, if not impossible." Like all other would-be leaders in Somalia, Ali Mahdi faces the daunting task of reigning in a populace that has become accustomed to rule by lethal force. The chaotic violence, black marketeering, and clan rivalry that was nurtured throughout the Siad Barre regime has become a way of life. In spite of the fact that Ali Mahdi and Aidid announced in early 1993 an official end to the division of Somalia's capital into separate sectors, few people, if any, seemed willing to lay their weapons down and forge peaceful solutions to the nation's ills.

Then, in June of 1993, Aidid ordered an attack that left 23 UN peacekeepers from Pakistan dead and prompted fierce retaliation from UN troops. According to a Somali journalist quoted in *Time,* "The UN attacks [may] have made [Aidid] even more important as a spokesman for the Somalis against foreign aggression." Still, the degree of public support for either Ali Mahdi or Aidid remained unclear.

Ali Mahdi himself had stated earlier in the *Washington Post:* "I don't like to be president," but he quickly added that his rivals want to be dictators in the Siad Barre mold. Ali Mahdi added that he will continue to try to establish himself as a recognized national leader, despite the obvious dangers of his position. He is not afraid. "As a Muslim," he said, "I know my fate is predestined."

Sources

Books

Africa South of the Sahara: 1993, 22nd edition, Europa, 1992.

Periodicals

Africa Report, March-April 1991, pp. 14-18; May-June 1991, pp. 56-59; November-December 1991, pp. 35-37; January-February 1992, pp. 58-61; July-August 1992, pp. 31-33; November-December 1992, pp. 62-64; March-April 1993, pp. 21-28.
Atlanta Constitution, January 30, 1991, p. A3.
Boston Globe, January 30, 1991, p. 13; November 27, 1991, p. 10; July 21, 1992, p. 9.
Christian Science Monitor, January 30, 1991, p. 3.
Los Angeles Times, January 30, 1991, p. A20; January 31, 1991, p. B6.
Newsweek, February 22, 1993, p. 37.
New York Times, October 4, 1992, p. 1.
Time, January 11, 1993, pp. 24-25; June 28, 1993, pp. 46-48.
Washington Post, January 11, 1992, p. A1.

Additional information for this profile was obtained from the U.S. State Department.

—Anne Janette Johnson

Ella Baker

1903-1986

Social activist

A leader in the fight to end discrimination against African Americans, Ella Baker inspired several generations in struggles against racism, poverty, and injustice throughout the world. Baker had a gift for organizing people. For nearly twenty years, she worked for the National Association for the Advancement of Colored People (NAACP). She then cofounded the Southern Christian Leadership Conference (SCLC), the Student Nonviolent Coordinating Committee (SNCC, often pronounced "snick"), and the Mississippi Freedom Democratic Party (MFDP). All of these groups made historic gains in the struggle for civil rights for black Americans.

Baker was born in Norfolk, Virginia, in 1903. She grew up in North Carolina, in a small, rural community where working together and looking after others was seen as a natural part of daily life. As documented in Ellen Cantarow's *Moving the Mountain: Women Working for Social Change,* Baker recalled: "We had a big garden, much too big for the size of the family. I'd pick a bushel or more and we didn't need them, so you'd give them to the neighbors that didn't have them. That's the way you did it. It was no hassle about it." She was raised, as she put it, in "a kind of family that was concerned about people."

Furthermore, Baker's family instilled in her a sense of pride in her heritage and respect for all men and women, especially her elders. In the 1981 film *Fundi: The Story of Ella Baker,* the activist described her mother, Georgianna, as someone "you didn't talk back to." Being raised by a woman who commanded respect helped Baker later on in her life, when she would occupy leadership positions in civil rights organizations run almost exclusively by men.

Baker's grandfather also had a profound effect on how she viewed the world. She remembered him in *Fundi* as a "very tall, very black man who was very proud of being black." Consequently, from the time she was a child, she refused to be treated as anyone's inferior; when she was six years old and a white boy called her a nigger, she reportedly hit him in the face.

In 1927 Baker graduated from Shaw University in Raleigh, North Carolina, at the top of her class. At that time, teaching was the only profession open to most educated southern black women. Baker's mother wanted her to become a schoolteacher, but Ella had different goals. Her education had been quite rigid, and she commented in *Fundi* that she did not see schools as places where one was necessarily "free to express

At a Glance. . .

Born December 13, 1903, in Norfolk, VA; died December 13, 1986, in New York City; daughter of Blake (a ferryboat waiter) and Georgianna (a teacher) Baker. *Education:* Shaw University, B.A., 1927.

American West Indian News, editorial staff member, 1929-30; *Negro National News,* office manager and editorial assistant, 1932; Young Negroes' Cooperative League, national director, c. 1932-38; Works Progress Administration (WPA), consumer education project teacher, 1936-38; National Association for the Advancement of Colored People (NAACP), assistant field secretary, 1938-42, national field secretary and director of branches, 1942-46, president of New York City branch, 1954-56; American Cancer Society, Harlem branch, founder and staff member, 1947-54; Montgomery bus boycott adviser, 1955-56; In Friendship, cofounder, 1956; Southern Christian Leadership Conference (SCLC), Atlanta, GA, associate director, 1958-59, interim director, 1959-60; Student Nonviolent Coordinating Committee (SNCC), cofounder and adviser, beginning in 1960; Young Women's Christian Association (YWCA), Atlanta, human relations consultant, 1960-63; Southern Conference Educational Fund (SCEF), staff member, 1963-65, adviser, beginning in 1965; Mississippi Freedom Democratic Party (MFDP), keynote speaker at convention in Jackson, MS, Washington office organizer, and adviser, all beginning in 1964; Mass Party Organizing Committee, vice-chair, beginning in 1972; adviser to numerous liberation and human rights groups, including the African National Congress and the Puerto Rican Solidarity Committee, 1972-86.

Selected awards: Candace Award for outstanding achievement from the Coalition of 100 Black Women.

an opinion," something she was very anxious to do.

Baker wanted to be a medical missionary, a sociologist, or a social worker, but she did not have the money for foreign travel, medical school, or graduate school, so she moved to New York City to find work. At first, in spite of her education, she could only get waitressing and factory work. She also worked for newspapers, first an American West Indian newspaper, then the *Negro National News*. In the late 1920s and

early 1930s, New York City was home to many radical activists and intellectuals. Baker was eager to learn as much as she could and attended all sorts of political discussions.

"Began to Identify With the Unemployed"

Living in New York City during the Great Depression, Baker saw a great deal of economic suffering; many people were out of work and struggling to meet basic survival needs. The prevalence of economic hardship greatly influenced her politics: "With the Depression, I began to see that there were certain social forces over which the individual had very little control," she explained, as related in Paula Giddings's *When and Where I Enter: The Impact of Black Women on Race and Sex in America,* adding "I began to identify . . . with the unemployed."

In 1932 Baker was moved to start the Young Negroes' Cooperative League with George Schuyler, a leading black newspaper writer. She and Schuyler saw that, through pooling resources and working together, people with very little money could buy more with what they had. They formed groups called cooperatives, which were different from regular grocery stores because they were owned by the customers. Baker served as an adviser to many of these new businesses. Shyrlee Dallard's *Ella Baker: A Leader Behind the Scenes* quoted Baker's description of her work with the Young Negroes' Cooperative League: "The major job was getting people to understand that they had something within their power that they could use."

Through her affiliation with the league, Baker learned how to buy quality goods for less money. She became so good at it that the Works Progress Administration (WPA) hired her to teach buying classes. She taught for the WPA for three years in the late 1930s.

Twenty Years With the NAACP

In 1938 Ella Baker went to work for the National Association for the Advancement of Colored People (NAACP), an organization that was fighting against the Jim Crow laws that legally enforced segregation in the South. Serving as a field organizer who traveled to different southern NAACP offices recruiting new members and raising money, she was away from New York for six months of every year, sometimes visiting a different city every day. Baker was a powerful organizer because she could talk to poor and middle-class African Americans alike; wherever she went, people felt she was one of them. "You start where the *people* are," she was quoted as saying in *Moving the Mountain*.

In 1942 Baker became nationwide director of branches for

the NAACP. Four years later, she resigned her post because she had taken on the responsibility of raising her eight-year-old niece, Jackie Brockington. Aside from the fact that she could no longer spend much time away from home, Baker believed that the organization was becoming too bureaucratic and removed from the needs of ordinary black Americans. But when Jackie turned sixteen in 1954, Baker returned to the NAACP, this time as president of the New York City branch. She became involved in the struggle to integrate New York City's public schools. Her dissatisfactions with the NAACP, however, did not go away. She felt that the organization was too "wrapped up in legalism," she proclaimed in *Fundi.* "If people weren't willing to do what [was] necessary to move beyond a given spot, you were stuck." By "legalism," she meant that the NAACP was trying to change society through the courts. Baker had come to feel that this was not enough.

Joined the Bus Boycott

Not everyone in the country was "stuck," however, and it did not take Baker long to find people who were, indeed, willing to "move beyond" established, conventional ways of achieving political ends. In 1955 thousands of African Americans in Montgomery, Alabama, stopped riding public buses for 381 days. This action, known as the Montgomery bus boycott, was initiated by a civil rights organization called the Montgomery Improvement Association (MIA), in order to protest laws that forced blacks to sit in the backs of buses. Baker went down to Alabama to advise the leaders of the MIA and together with civil rights activists A. Philip Randolph, Bayard Rustin, and Stanley Levison founded a group called In Friendship, which raised money for the boycott. Ultimately, the protest was successful; in 1956 the Supreme Court ruled that the bus company and the city of Montgomery had to allow black passengers to sit wherever they wished.

"They Haven't Ever Had a Woman Say No to Them"

After such a triumph, Baker and other boycott leaders were anxious not to lose momentum. In 1957 they called a meeting of southern black ministers who were active in civil rights organizing. Out of that meeting, the Southern Christian Leadership Conference (SCLC) was formed. Dr. Martin Luther King, Jr., the man whose leadership was in many ways responsible for the triumph of the Montgomery bus boycott, was chosen to lead the new organization. The SCLC's purpose was to keep the black church-based movements in touch with one another so that they could work together. But their purposes went far beyond legal and political reform; members of the SCLC were on a

mission to, in their words, "redeem the soul of America," reported Adam Fairclough in his 1987 book—titled *To Redeem the Soul of America: The Southern Christian Leadership Conference and Martin Luther King, Jr.,* after their creed.

Baker directed the SCLC from 1958 through 1960, but her relationship with the organization was not always an easy one. The majority of members were men and ministers, and they were not always ready to listen to an opinionated woman who was not part of the clergy. Eleanor Holmes Norton, an early member of SNCC who later became the District of Columbia's congressional representative, recalled in *Fundi* that, as a woman in a leadership position, Baker "had too much talent for that time to be accepted by the ministers."

Baker also remembered her own refusal to be intimidated: "I wasn't one to say yes, just because [ideas or directives] came from Dr. Martin Luther King, Jr," she told Cantarow. Reminiscing about it with some amusement in the film *Fundi,* she admitted: "I was difficult. I was not an easy pushover. . . . I could talk back a lot. Not only could, but did. It's a strange thing about men, . . . if they haven't ever had a woman say no to them, they don't know what to do sometimes."

Godmother of the SNCC

Meanwhile, throughout the South, students were holding sit-in demonstrations to protest the unequal treatment of blacks at lunch counters, movie theaters, libraries, courthouses, and full-service restaurants. Baker and some of the student leaders thought that these protests could be even more effective if the various student groups were working together. In 1960 Baker called a conference of all the student leaders. This meeting led to the formation of the Student Nonviolent Coordinating Committee (SNCC), a group that was at the forefront of student civil rights activism of the 1960s.

Many of the representatives of older organizations who were at the conference wanted the students to join their groups, but Baker believed that the young activists could be a stronger force on their own. She encouraged the SNCC to cooperate with other groups toward common ends, but to stay separate. Julian Bond, an early member of SNCC, noted in a segment of *Fundi,* "She insisted that we had something special."

Baker guided SNCC through many hard decisions without trying to take the organization out of the students' hands. As Baker put it in the film: "I had always considered that my role was to facilitate. . . . I did not need to be a leader . . . so they felt they could trust me." Endowed with a talent for organizing and communicating with young people,

Baker valued her work with them above everything else. She admired young activists because "they acted as though this [equality] was their right. No 'would you please.'" The respect was mutual; youth of all races looked up to Baker. Soon after her death, students at the University of Michigan in Ann Arbor honored that special relationship by naming a campus antiracism organizing center after her.

Gave Keynote Speech at MFDP's Jackson Convention

The SNCC led voter registration drives in parts of the rural South where, at that time, African Americans who tried to vote were often risking their lives. In 1964 the SNCC organized the Mississippi Freedom Democratic Party (MFDP) so that blacks in Mississippi would have an alternative to the regular Democratic party, which they felt excluded them. That year, the MFDP held a convention in Jackson, Mississippi, at which Baker was the keynote speaker. She then went to Washington, D.C., to set up the party's national office. As Baker indicated in *Fundi,* she believed that there was "no way of effecting a basic change without political clout. The one way blacks could do that was through the ballot."

In the Mississippi primary the MFDP received more votes than the regular Democratic party, yet, at the convention in Atlantic City, the national party would not seat the MFDP's delegates. President Lyndon B. Johnson turned them down because he was afraid of losing his white southern support. In the ensuing years, however, many MFDP candidates were elected to local and state offices. The MFDP had won support all over the nation, and was, no doubt, partly responsible for the passage of the Voting Rights Act of 1965, which made it illegal to deny any adult U.S. citizen the right to vote and guaranteed federal protection of that right. The passage of this law was a major achievement for the civil rights movement.

Soon after the Voting Rights Act was passed, Baker moved back to Harlem, where she continued to advise the SNCC, SCLC, and MFDP. In the late 1960s, these groups became less active; Baker did not. She devoted her energies to community organizations and human rights movements all over the world, particularly the African National Congress, the Puerto Rican Solidarity Committee, and liberation groups in Zimbabwe.

They Called Her "Fundi"

Those who knew Baker called her "Fundi", which is a Swahili word for a person who masters a craft with the help of his or her community, practices it, then teaches it to the next generation. Baker's craft was organizing people to work together for social change. Gospel singer and historian Bernice Johnson Reagon wrote a song about her called "Ella's Song," which celebrates her role as "Fundi" to the American civil rights movement: "That which touches me most is that I had the chance to work with people / Passing on to others that which was passed on to me."

Baker died in 1986 on December 13, her eighty-third birthday. Shortly before her death, she was asked what had kept her going in her lifelong struggle against injustice. As quoted in *Moving the Mountain,* Baker answered in the spirit of a "Fundi": "I don't claim to have a corner on an answer, but I believe that the struggle is eternal. Somebody else carries on."

Sources

Books

Cantarow, Ellen, and others, *Moving the Mountain: Women Working for Social Change,* Feminist Press, 1980.
Dallard, Shyrlee, *Ella Baker: A Leader Behind the Scenes,* Silver Burdett Press, 1990.
The Eyes on the Prize Civil Rights Reader, Penguin, 1991.
Fairclough, Adam, *To Redeem the Soul of America: The Southern Christian Leadership Conference and Martin Luther King, Jr.,* University of Georgia Press, 1987.
Giddings, Paula, *When and Where I Enter: The Impact of Black Women on Race and Sex in America,* Morrow , 1984.
Powledge, Fred, *Free At Last? The Civil Rights Movement and the People Who Made It,* Little, Brown, 1991.

Periodicals

Christian Century, January 7-14, 1987.
Essence, February 1990.
Facts on File, December 19, 1986.
Jet, January 19, 1987.
Ms., May/June 1980.

Other

Baker was the subject of a documentary film titled *Fundi: The Story of Ella Baker,* Icarus Films, 1981, and the musical composition "Ella's Song," written and performed by Bernice Johnson Reagon, 1981.

—Liza Featherstone

Charles Barkley

1963—

Professional basketball player

Charles Barkley, the talented and controversial star of the Phoenix Suns, was voted the 1992-93 Most Valuable Player in the National Basketball Association (NBA). For years, the outspoken, combative Barkley languished in relative obscurity as his former team, the Philadelphia 76ers, failed to advance in NBA playoff competition. But his inclusion on the 1992 United States Olympic Team and his 1992 trade to the Suns provided Barkley with a national audience for both his fabulous basketball talents and his legendary attitude.

Coplon described Barkley as "a wild child who will say or do whatever crosses his trip-wired mind." *Philadelphia Inquirer* columnist Bill Lyon characterized the volatile player as "a newly cork-popped magnum of champagne [who] spills all over the court, frothing and foaming."

In an era when sports superstars find it fashionable to shun the media, Barkley is a sound-bite darling. After any game, win or loss, he can be counted upon to offer opinions on just about everything from his performance to his teammates' abilities to current political events. From time to time his comments cause a tempest, but he rarely apologizes or reconsiders anything he says. Barkley is adamant on one point: he does *not* consider himself a role model for youngsters. Political correctness is for government officials, not basketball players, in his opinion. "I believe in expressing what you feel," he told the *New York Times Magazine*. "There are people who hide everything inside—and it's guys like that who kill whole families."

At six-foot-five and 250 pounds, Barkley is short and stout by NBA standards, but that has not stopped him from becoming one of the premier power forwards in the league. Known in his early years as the "Round Mound of Rebound"—a cunning allusion to both his weight and his ability—Barkley has progressed through a decade of professional basketball while appearing to become stronger and more dominant each year. In 1991 *New York Times Magazine* reporter Jeff Coplon wrote that Barkley had "reached the stage where he can outrun, outjump, outwork, outsmart or outmuscle anyone who lines up against him." At the same time, "Sir Charles" developed a vast reputation for speaking his piece and exercising his temper both on and off the basketball court.

Charles Wade Barkley was born in rural Leeds, Alabama (population under 10,000), ten miles outside of Birmingham. At birth he weighed just six pounds. He suffered from anemia and required a complete blood transfusion at the tender age of six weeks. Barkley's parents were very young when he was born. They separated and divorced while Charles was still a baby. He was raised by his mother, grandmother, and a stepfather. Then, when Barkley was in grade school, his stepfather was killed in an automobile accident.

Aimed High

The emotional and financial setbacks the family faced did nothing to dampen Barkley's childhood ambitions. Coplon wrote: "In the 10th grade, when Barkley stood a chunky 5-10 and failed even to make his high school varsity, he vowed to anyone who'd listen that he was bound for the NBA. He shot baskets by himself into the night, seven nights a week; he jumped back and forth over a 4-foot high chain-link fence, for 15 minutes at a stretch." Barkley's mother, Charcey Glenn, told the *Philadelphia Daily News:*

"Other kids were getting new cars and nice clothes, but Charles never complained. He'd say, 'One of these days, mama, I'll buy you everything you want.' I'd ask him how and he'd say, 'Basketball.' Other boys signed on at the cement plant down the road, but Charles said he wasn't gonna do that kind of work. He said he was gonna make it in the NBA, nothing was gonna stop him, and he meant it."

As a high school junior, Barkley was named a reserve on the varsity team at his high school. Then, during the summer before his senior year, he grew from five-foot-ten to six-foot-four, from 220 pounds to 240 pounds. As a senior, Barkley starred for the Leeds High team, averaging 19.1 points and 17.9 rebounds a game and leading his team to a 26-3 record and the state semifinals. Nevertheless, the only college scholarship offer came from tiny Snead Junior College.

Heads began to turn during the state high school semifinal, when Barkley scored 26 points playing against Alabama's most highly recruited player, Bobby Lee Hurt. An assistant to Auburn University coach Sonny Smith happened to be at the game. The assistant quickly phoned Smith to report his discovery—"a fat guy . . . who can play like the wind," to quote Smith in the *Washington Post.*

Smith recruited Barkley, who majored in business management at Auburn. With his unusual shape and style, Barkley was an immediate sensation. "People concentrated on how much I weighed, not how well I played," Barkley remembered in *People.* "I led the conference in rebounding for three years, but nobody knew it. I was just a fat guy who could play basketball well." The relationship between Barkley and Smith began amicably enough but became rocky as the budding star rebelled against the coach's strict discipline. When Smith scolded, Barkley pointed to the bottom line: as a junior he was named Southeastern Conference Player of the Year while helping Auburn to its second-best win-loss record in 25 years.

In 1984 Barkley was invited to the Olympic trials, where he earned a spot on the preliminary squad before it was cut from 20 to 16 players. His flashy style and his 360-degree spinning dunks did not entertain Olympic coach Bobby Knight. Barkley was cut before the team left for Los Angeles and the Olympic games. At that point he decided to leave Auburn one year early to turn pro, applying for the NBA's hardship draft.

Drafted by the NBA in 1984

The 1984 NBA draft was one of the best in years. The first four players picked were Akeem Olajuwon, Sam Bowie, Michael Jordan, and Sam Perkins. The Philadelphia 76ers took the All-American Barkley with the fifth pick. At the news conference announcing the pick, Sixers general manager Pat Williams joked of Barkley, "He's so fat, his bath tub has stretch marks." More seriously, Williams told the *Los Angeles Times:* "We were concerned about his weight and his work habits. He had a reputation for being hard to coach. He should have made the Olympic team, but he couldn't get along with Knight. There were people who said he'd eat himself out of the league. But we went for the bottom line. We asked one question: 'Can this guy play?' The unanimous answer was yes. Fine, we'd start with that. The other stuff we could deal with later."

Barkley joined a fine, competitive 76ers team with a veteran core of Moses Malone, Julius Erving and Maurice Cheeks. He was thrilled at the opportunity to play with such renowned superstars. Their talents deflected pressure and publicity from Barkley's first season, when he averaged 14 points and 8.6 rebounds in part-time play and exasperated coaches and teammates with his aggressive on-court antics. Within months of his arrival Barkley was feuding with 76ers coach Billy Cunningham and alienating all but Philadelphia's fans with his nonstop commentary during and after games. Even then Sir Charles firmly asserted his right to be himself. "I don't have to please the public to win, I just have to do my job," he said in the *Philadelphia Daily News.* "Like [Larry] Bird. He's the most obnoxious man I ever played against. I never saw a player so cocky, but he backs it up. I can respect that. Even the fans who get on me, I think, respect me as a player. If they don't . . . well, you know, some people are just ignorant."

Tensions Mounted with the 76ers

Barkley's insistence on freedom of expression soon marked him for controversy. As the 76ers slid toward mediocrity in the late 1980s, he made headlines for lashing out against his teammates. In 1987 he called the Sixers "a bad team that has to play perfect to win." Enraged management fined him $3,000 for the remark. He was also fined—for a slightly more substantial amount—after he spit on a young fan during a game. On that occasion, Barkley had been heckled from the stands by opposing fans until he retaliated by spitting in their direction. He missed the hecklers and hit a girl, to whom he later apologized. Barkley answered his critics in the *Sporting News:* "If I play with emotion I'm a hotdog. That's okay, because I know if I don't play with emotion, I won't play anywhere near my ability. If I play nonchalantly, I can't play right. Am I not supposed to play with emotion?"

That "emotion" enabled Barkley to evolve into a power forward who could muscle past much taller opponents, a player who remained among the league's top rebounders through several seasons. Even the declining fortunes of the 76ers did not mask Barkley's stunning ability to dominate

games. He was determined to play his very best, both for his team and for himself. *Esquire* correspondent Mike Lupica wrote: "There will always be a lot of mouth to Charles Barkley. But there is also a lot of talent, the kind of talent only a handful of players will ever have."

Hot Shot with the "Dream Team"

In 1992 Barkley was given a second opportunity to represent America at the Olympic Games. He was a member of the first United States Olympic men's basketball team that featured professional players. The so-called "Dream Team," composed of the NBA's top stars, was the premier attraction in the 1992 Summer Games, and as usual Barkley drew the lion's share of publicity. As Jack McCallum noted in *Sports Illustrated,* Barkley was "the only member of the Dream Team to have elbowed an Angolan, drawn a technical [foul] for talking to the crowd, received gentle yet unmistakable rebukes from his teammates, been called on the carpet by the [United States Olympic Committee] and gotten alternately cheered and jeered in the pregame introductions." McCallum added:

> "If I play with emotion I'm a hotdog. That's okay, because I know if I don't play with emotion, I won't play anywhere near my ability."

"Barkley has earned a difficult and quite curious double distinction in Barcelona. He has become, at once, America's greatest Olympic ambassador and its greatest potential nightmare, a man who can turn a grimace into a smile—or vice versa—in an instant." Barkley was a scoring leader for a Dream Team that easily captured the Olympic gold medal.

The controversy continued in Philadelphia when Barkley returned to his pro game. He was unhappy with the lackluster 76ers and was anxious to be traded to a team that might qualify for high-level playoff action. At the same time, the 76ers front office had grown wary of the volatile superstar, whose statements were beginning to have embarrassing repercussions for the entire team. The Sixers might not have advanced far in post-season play in the NBA in the 1990s, but most Americans recognized Charles Barkley. He drew the wrath of feminists by describing one particular game as the kind that "if you lose, you go home and beat your wife and kids." Statements like that—as well as his outspoken views on racism in sports, front office management, and his own worth—assured Barkley plenty of ink in the nation's newspapers.

More Than Ready for Trade to Phoenix

At the end of the 1991-92 basketball season, Barkley was traded to the Phoenix Suns. Nearing the end of his own career, he was overjoyed to find himself on a talented squad with real championship potential. Asked what he planned to contribute to the Suns, Barkley gave his characteristic blunt answer in *Sports Illustrated:* "I'm not as good as I was . . . but nobody is as good at 30 as they were at 27. I mean, I'm the only guy I know who could be top 10 in scoring, top 10 in rebounding and top 10 in field goal percentage and have a bad year."

Barkley meshed well with his new team and earned his first Most Valuable Player citation for the 1992-93 season. McCallum suggested in *Sports Illustrated* that Barkley won the MVP award not only because of his considerable talent and his stellar 1993 performance, but also because of the impact he had on the Suns as a team. Barkley proved to be *the* pivotal player Phoenix needed to advance to the NBA championships. He helped to motivate the other players, and he himself performed like a man with something important to prove. According to McCallum, Barkley took "a successful team and made it a championship contender."

But even as the Suns made their push to the finals in 1993, Barkley was suggesting that he was ready to retire. "I feel the end coming," he told *Sports Illustrated.* "I've had enough limelight, and I've got enough money." No one seemed to take Barkley's threats very seriously. Suns coach Paul Westphal said in 1993 that he hoped Barkley would play at least until 1996 and perhaps longer.

The 1993 NBA Playoffs

The Suns faced the Chicago Bulls in the 1993 NBA playoff finals, with the spotlight on Barkley and his friend and opponent, Michael Jordan—the "bad boy" of the Bulls who is generally considered to be the greatest player in basketball. The Bulls won the first two games of seven and seemed intent on sweeping the championships, but, largely through the efforts of Barkley, the Suns managed to pull off two victories before losing the NBA title to Chicago in game six. The loss, which gave the Bulls their third championship title in a row, was hard for Barkley to take. "It's just really difficult, you just hurt," he was quoted as saying in an Associated Press report.

Even without the NBA title, though, the Most Valuable Player award serves as a fine cap to Charles Barkley's unusual career. Lambasted for his weight, criticized for his brash statements, feared on court for his aggressive play, and heckled just about everywhere, Barkley has emerged as the one thing he never wanted to be: a role model for the rugged individualists of the 1990s. "The majority of people in the world don't do what it takes to win," Barkley told the *New York Times Magazine.* "Everyone is looking for the easy road. . . . I made up my mind a long time ago to be successful at whatever I did. If you want to be successful, can't nobody stop you."

Sources

Books

Barkley, Charles, and Roy Johnson, Jr., *Outrageous* (autobiography), 1991.

Periodicals

Associated Press reports, June 19, 1993; June 20, 1993; June 21, 1993.
Boston Globe, November 9, 1984.
Chicago Tribune, February 15, 1987; February 1, 1988.
Esquire, March 1992.
Hartford Courant, December 22, 1987.
Jet, May 25, 1987.
Los Angeles Times, May 8, 1985; February 22, 1987; January 10, 1988; January 17, 1988.
Newsweek, May 24, 1993, pp. 64-65.
New York Times, April 24, 1984.
New York Times Magazine, March 17, 1991, p. 26.
People, April 27, 1987, p. 76.
Philadelphia Daily News, May 13, 1986; May 14, 1986; May 15, 1986; December 22, 1987.
Philadelphia Inquirer, June 20, 1984; April 28, 1985; April 18, 1986; May 1, 1986; February 1, 1987.
Sporting News, January 18, 1988.
Sports Illustrated, March 12, 1984; March 24, 1986, p. 32; January 11, 1988; August 10, 1992; November 9, 1992, cover story; March 8, 1993, pp. 25-27; April 12, 1993, p. 83; May 3, 1993, pp. 78-89; June 7, 1993, pp. 16-17; June 14, 1993, p. 84.
Time, June 14, 1993, p. 68.
Washington Post, April 23, 1984; February 2, 1987.

—Glen Macnow and Mark Kram

Jean-Michel Basquiat

1960-1988

Artist

No single artist represented the contemporary art scene of the 1980s more than Jean-Michel Basquiat. He rose from an anonymous, homeless graffiti artist spraying cryptic social messages on building walls around New York City's SoHo and East Village in the late 1970s to become, within five years, one of the first African American artists to receive international recognition, with sales of his works grossing millions of dollars. Basquiat's was a life of improbable contradictions and myths. His frenetic and prodigious artistic output—he produced thousands of paintings and drawings over a seven-year span—was often arrested by periods of heroin-induced stupor. During his career, he threw lavish parties, treated crowds to dinners at expensive restaurants, and painted in suits by Italian fashion designer Giorgio Armani. When he died from a cocaine-heroin overdose, he was alone and facedown on his bedroom floor on a hot August afternoon in 1988. He was 27.

Assessment of Basquiat's art is diverse and often as tumultuous as the works he created. His admirers claim he was a genius, an untutored primitive whose drug addition provided internal connections among various mental states necessary to his creations. Other views spiral downward from there; while some believe he was a gifted black artist overwhelmed by the pressures of a greedy white art establishment, others feel he was a talented artist who knew and desired too well the price of fame. Finally, his detractors assert that he represented everything that was wrong with the art explosion of the 1980s: a little raw, malnourished talent that was exploited, hyped, and ultimately heated beyond any recognizable value. "His work," Roberta Smith nonetheless wrote in the *New York Times,* "is one of the singular achievements of the '80s."

Much of the growing legend surrounding Basquiat was self-generated. That he was raised on the streets of the ghetto, ignorant of art and its history, is false; his was an ordinary middle-class upbringing. He was born in Brooklyn, New York, on December 22, 1960. His father was an accountant and would bring home scrap paper for his four-year-old son to paint and draw on. Since that age, Basquiat wanted to do nothing else. "He was like no other kid," the elder Basquiat explained to Phoebe Hoban in *New York.* "He was always so bright, absolutely an unbelievable mind, a genius. . . . He wanted to paint and draw all night." The young Basquiat's artistic inclinations were further spurred on by his mother, who took him to various museums around Brooklyn and Manhattan, his growing artistic sensibilities informed by the

At a Glance...

Born December 22, 1960, in Brooklyn, NY; died of a cocaine-heroin overdose August 12, 1988, in New York City; son of Gerard (an accountant) and Matilde Basquiat. *Education:* Attended City as School, Brooklyn, NY.

Began painting SAMO graffiti messages on walls around SoHo, 1977; sold painted sweatshirts and postcards and performed in the experimental band Gray, New York, 1977-80; paintings exhibited in first group show, "New York/New Wave," New York, 1981; first one-man show, Modena, Italy, 1981; first one-man show in the U.S., Annina Nosei Gallery, New York, 1982; became youngest artist ever included in prestigious international survey of contemporary art, "Documenta," Kassel, Germany, 1982; paintings included in Museum of Modern Art's re-opening exhibition, "International Survey of Painting and Sculpture," New York, 1984; Basquiat-Warhol collaborative show, Tony Shafrazi Gallery, New York, 1985; first museum retrospective, Whitney Museum of American Art, 1992. Paintings and drawings exhibited in 37 galleries (group and one-man shows) throughout the U.S. (including New York, Los Angeles, Dallas, Atlanta, St. Louis, Norfolk, and Boca Raton) and worldwide (including Paris, Tokyo, Amsterdam, Berlin, Zurich, Bologna, Montreal, and Seoul), 1981-88.

works of Pablo Picasso, Jasper Johns, Jean Dubuffet, and other modernist masters.

Another early influence was not a painter but a book—*Gray's Anatomy.* When he was six, Basquiat was hit by a car; his spleen had to be removed. While recovering, he was given a copy of the medical textbook by his mother. The diagrams, labels, and skeletal structures—the integration of pictures and words—that would come to characterize his art found their genesis here.

Although his surroundings were ordinary, Basquiat was not. "A kid that bright thinks for some reason he is above the school system and teachers and rebels against it," his father told Hoban. Basquiat attended both private and public schools but could not be disciplined. He had already formed his own vision. At 15, he ran away from home, shaved his head, and retreated to Washington Square Park. When his father found him a few days later, as the elder Basquiat related to Hoban, he said, "Papa, I will be very, very famous one day."

While at the progressive City as School in Brooklyn, Basquiat's last attempt at structured schooling, he entertained thoughts of becoming a cartoonist and illustrated the school paper. "His drawings, executed in a bright Peter Max style," Andrew Decker observed in *ARTnews*, "sympathetically depicted the homeless and sarcastically mocked bourgeois values." They were portentous.

Created Graffiti Alter Ego SAMO

Just before he left school and his home at 17, Basquiat and fellow classmate Al Diaz began spray painting graffiti on walls and bridges around lower Manhattan. Unlike ordinary graffiti, either brightly colored murals or vacuous expletives, theirs was a mixture of strange symbols and social commentary, often poetic. Signed with the name "SAMO," representing both a corporate logo and the phrase "same old shit," the messages "were far more cerebral and literate than the merely vibrant work of some of the pure graffitists," Decker noted. Phrases like SAMO AS AN ALTERNATIVE TO GOD and PAY FOR SOUP, BUILD A FORT, SET IT ON FIRE soon captured attention.

What Basquiat desired, however, was a certain type of attention from a certain type of people. SAMO messages soon appeared on walls near important art galleries and nightclubs. Although anonymous, the young artist sought recognition. Sleeping in Washington Square Park or on the floors of friends' apartments, Basquiat made money by selling handmade postcards and hand-painted sweatshirts on street corners. He also helped form a "noise" band called Gray, in which he played guitar with a file. "I was inspired by [modern American composer] John Cage at the time—music that really wasn't music," he explained to Cathleen McGuigan in the *New York Times Magazine.* "We were trying to be incomplete, abrasive, oddly beautiful."

What was even more purely abrasive and oddly beautiful were the images and words Basquiat was putting on anything he could find: refrigerators, table tops, lab coats, foam rubber, typewriters. He sold several of his postcards to the Museum of Modern Art, and his other works were displayed in clubs where his band played and at other popular late-night spots where influential people in the art community gathered. His work was getting noticed; he made sure of that. "He knew the most people on the scene," Gray bandmember Michael Holman recalled to Hoban. "He knew what was going on."

Graffiti Led to Painting

Sometime around 1980, the phrase "SAMO IS DEAD" began to appear around SoHo. Basquiat killed off his alter ego after a disagreement with Diaz. But it had served its evolutionary purpose. He turned increasingly to his art, encouraged by individuals such as curator, critic, and artist Diego Cortez, whom Basquiat had met in 1979. "He looked like a combination of a fashion model and a nineteen-year-old Bowery bum," Cortez related to Hoban, describing his first meeting with Basquiat. "I was convinced from the first that he was very talented."

Although a section of a SAMO wall had been displayed at the "Times Square Show" in 1980, garnering Basquiat critical notice, it was Cortez's alternative presentation "New York/New Wave" in January of 1981 that was Basquiat's launching pad. His exhibited works—"generally spare, childlike scrawls in crayon or paint on unprimed canvas," as Decker described—came to the attention of three important dealers: Bruno Bischofberger, a Swiss dealer who would represent Basquiat in Europe beginning in 1982; Emilio Mazzolli, a dealer from Modena, Italy, who would give Basquiat his first one-man show in Europe in the spring of 1981; and Annina Nosei, a SoHo dealer who would take Basquiat on as a gallery artist later that year.

Cloistered in the basement of Nosei's gallery, Basquiat turned out a vast amount of work. Nosei would often bring collectors to see his projects while he painted; she frequently sold them before he thought they were finished. But in this "hothouse" Basquiat's work evolved and flourished. His drawings and symbols, annotated with lists of words, were more detailed and colorful than his previous offerings. In a review of his one-man show at Nosei's gallery in 1982, Lisa Liebman wrote in *Art in America*, "What has propelled him so quickly is the unmistakable eloquence of his touch," adding that his "mock-ominous figures—apemen, skulls, predatory animals, stick-figures—look incorporeal because of the fleetness of their execution, and in their cryptic half-presence they seem to take on shaman-like characteristics."

Lived High Life

Basquiat rose to prominence. After two years his works were selling for $2,000 to $10,000, and by the time the artist was 24, his efforts earned $10,000 to $25,000 from private collectors and graced museums such as the Whitney Museum of American Art. In February of 1985 he made the cover of the *New York Times Magazine*. But the intensity of his artistic success was matched by that of his economic excess. Basquiat's lifestyle became extravagant. He spent thousands of dollars on designer suits, only to ruin them by painting in them. He staged elaborate parties and dinners. He gave away paintings and money to friends and to people he didn't even know. "He always clung to

the notion of making a name for himself," William Wilson wrote in the *Los Angeles Times*. "He started out wanting to be a cartoonist and wound up wanting to be a Star. Fatal desire."

"Since I was 17," Basquiat explained to *New York Times Magazine* contributor McGuigan, "I thought I might be a star. I'd think about all my heroes, Charlie Parker, Jimi Hendrix. . . . I had a romantic feeling of how people had become famous." These romantic notions were often unrestrained and contradictory. In 1978 he told a *Village Voice* reporter, as related by *New York*'s Hoban, that New York was "crawling with uptight, middle-class pseudos trying to look like the money they don't have; status symbols. . . . It's like they're walking around with price tags stapled to their heads. People should live more spiritually."

> "Since I was 17, I thought I might be a star. I'd think about all my heroes, Charlie Parker, Jimi Hendrix. I had a romantic feeling of how people had become famous."

But within a few years Basquiat would himself spend tens of thousands of dollars on televisions, stereo equipment, recording systems, and suits. He would fill his refrigerator with expensive French pastries, only to let them spoil. He would spend $150 a day on health food.

And he was spending $2,000 a week on cocaine and heroin. "He had a real romantic myth of heroin and of being a junkie," Lee Jaffe, a musician and friend of Basquiat, told Hoban. "He saw himself as painting's Charlie Parker." Indeed, some critics detected similarities between the ill-fated jazz saxophone great and the young painter. "Jazz was more than pleasant, syncopated patterns to Basquiat . . . it was an analogue of life," Kay Larson proposed in *New York*. "His style is one fierce don't-look-back pulsation of words, diagrams, screeching colors, and over-the-edge bravado, much like that of his hero Charlie Parker."

Relationship With Warhol

One who helped rein in Basquiat's excesses was Andy Warhol. Since his days of selling postcards on street corners, Basquiat had idolized and sought out the 1960s pop-art icon. The close relationship the two men developed beginning in 1983 was symbiotic; from Basquiat, Warhol drew energy and a link to the contemporary art scene. In return, Warhol gave his colleague business advice and a healthy-living spirit. He encouraged Basquiat to exercise and helped wean him from his heavy drug use. The two artists began to work together; but after a 1985 collaborative show that was critically panned and from which only one piece was sold, Basquiat cooled relations with Warhol. Many critics felt Basquiat's work suffered from Warhol's slick Factory influence. And the art community, which only a few years earlier had reveled in Basquiat's neo-expressionism, began to change its mind. At that time, Basquiat's "wasn't a raw, screeching line," dealer Guillaume Gallozzi told Decker. "If you came really close to it, you could see where it quivered. He was vamping himself, turning out works *á la manière de* Jean-Michel Basquiat." He did not exhibit in New York again until 1987.

"It was, in every sense, a triumphant return," Decker noted. "The works—which returned with a vengeance to the densely written style, most influenced by graffiti, that Basquiat had been using less and less—had a heavily layered, hieroglyphic feeling to them, and there was modest use of color." But the resurgence would not last. Warhol's death in February of 1987 unleashed any remaining tethers on Basquiat's emotional lid. He became reclusive. He produced many works, but his heroin intake increased. He rebounded slightly in 1988 with three shows, two of them abroad. Reviews were mixed. That summer Basquiat traveled to Hawaii for a retreat. He returned to New York in August, planning on seeking a cure for his heroin addiction—but not before one final "binge."

In retrospect, some felt "he was too concerned about prices and money," Mary Boone, one of Basquiat's many dealers, explained to Hoban. "He was too conscious of his place in the world and who he had dinner with and everything that implies. He was too externalized; he didn't have a strong enough internal life." Art critic Robert Hughes, writing in *Time,* agreed: "Basquiat had talent— more than some of the younger painters who were his contemporaries, though this may not be saying much. The trouble was that it did not develop; it was frozen by celebrity, like a deer in a jacklight beam."

Others contend, however, that Basquiat—in spite of the hype and the pressures of the 1980s art world—was a force of and for his time. Like any artist of depth, he saw and responded with both anger and vitality. And in his career there was an "often astounding sense of growth and maturation," Smith concluded in the *New York Times,* "a freewheeling physical inventiveness, . . . and an agile curious mind. Basquiat's rich tapestry of subject matter ranges through the history and culture of the world, of America and of black America, tying things together in fresh ways."

Selected writings

Basquiat Drawings, edited by John Cheim, Bulfinch/ Little, Brown, 1990.

Selected works

Irony of a Negro Policeman, 1981.
Charles the First, 1982.
Pater, 1982.
St. Joe Louis Surrounded by Snakes, 1982.
Tar and Feathers, 1982.
Hollywood Africans, 1983.
Brown Spots, 1984.
Gold Griot, 1984.
MP, 1984.
Glassnose, 1987.
Eroica II, 1988.
Riding With Death, 1988.

Sources

Books

Marshall, Richard, *Jean-Michel Basquiat,* Whitney Museum of American Art/Abrams, 1992.

Periodicals

Art in America, October 1982, p. 130.
ARTnews, January 1989, pp. 96-101.
Los Angeles Times, September 4, 1988, sec. CAL, pp. 5, 79.
New Republic, November 21, 1988, pp. 34-36.
Newsweek, November 9, 1992, p. 67.
New York, September 26, 1988, p. 36; November 9, 1992, pp. 74-75.
New Yorker, November 9, 1992, pp. 137-39.
New York Times, November 9, 1990, sec. C, p. 26; July 22, 1991, sec. C, pp. 13-14; October 23, 1992, sec. C, pp. 1, 20.
New York Times Book Review, February 9, 1992, p. 18; February 7, 1993, p. 22.
New York Times Magazine, February 10, 1985, p. 20.
Time, November 16, 1992, pp. 88-90.
Vanity Fair, November 1992, p. 124.

Additional information for this profile was obtained from a January 24, 1993, broadcast of *CBS Sunday Morning.*

—*Rob Nagel*

Ralph S. Bell

1934—

Evangelist

Dr. Ralph S. Bell is an associate evangelist with the Billy Graham Evangelistic Association. One of three Christian ministers handpicked by Dr. Graham to help lead the Billy Graham crusades, Bell assists in every aspect of the popular mass Christian meetings. He also holds city-wide and single-church crusades of his own and addresses Christian topics on radio and television shows. Since 1965 Bell has been directly involved in every major Billy Graham crusade, and since 1980 he has led more than 30 smaller crusades himself.

Like Graham, Bell does not believe that the message of a crusade begins and ends during the brief period when the well-known leaders come to town. Instead he urges a galvanization of Christians in all communities to continue the fight against such problems as racism, divorce, homelessness, poverty, and crime—and to seek converts to the Christian faith. Reverend James Fitzhugh of the Billings, Montana Evangelical United Methodist Church told *Decision* magazine that Dr. Bell "preaches the Gospel with great balance, presenting a personal relationship to the Lord and social issues."

Bell himself told the *Montgomery Advertiser* that he likes to go "right into the lion's den" to preach. Indeed, his best-known work as both an individual evangelist and a Billy Graham associate has been his dedication to prison ministry. During the weeks before and after a major crusade, he may visit as many as two prisons a day to preach. "If you can help one or two [inmates], and then they get a job and develop a stable family life, it's worth it," Bell told the *Syracuse Herald-Journal.* Nor does Bell shun controversial topics. He has used the pulpit to condemn the nation's soaring divorce rate and other social ills. "No nation can be secure if the family is deteriorating," Bell said in the *El Reno Daily Tribune.* "The church determines the stability of the family life and if there is no spiritual foundation in the home then it cannot survive."

A Promising Athlete Takes Another Path

Like the Reverend Graham before him, Ralph Bell dreamed of becoming a major league athlete. Bell was born in St. Catharines, Ontario, Canada in 1934. He spent much of his youth there honing his athletic ability, especially in baseball. As a teenager he was a member of a high school team that advanced to the all-province finals and then played for a Canadian national title. Baseball scouts lured

At a Glance...

Born May 13, 1934, in St. Catharines, Ontario, Canada; son of Archiebald and Cecilia Bell; married Jean Overstreet, 1957; children: Ralph S., Christian Eugene. *Education:* Attended Moody Bible Institute, Chicago, IL, 1954-57; Taylor University, B.A., 1959; Fuller Theological Seminary, Pasadena, CA, M.Div., 1963; attended pastoral clinical training, Metropolitan State Mental Hospital, Los Angeles, CA, 1963-64. *Religion:* Christian.

Pastor of West Washington Community Church, Los Angeles, CA, 1960-65; began intermittent association with Billy Graham Crusade in 1963, became associate evangelist of the Billy Graham Crusade, 1965. Has also worked as a professor at Los Angeles Bible Training School and as chaplain at the Los Angeles County Jail. Leader or associate leader of evangelical crusades in the United States, Canada, Europe, Australia, New Guinea, and Korea. Author of *Soul Free,* Baptist Publishing House.

Awards: Honorary degrees, including D.H. from Richmond College, Toronto, 1978, and D.D. from Indiana Christian University, 1981.

Addresses: *Home*—Bellvue, CO. *Office*—Ralph Bell Crusades, Billy Graham Evangelistic Association, P.O. Box 9313, Minneapolis, MN 55440-9313.

the talented youngster, and at sixteen Bell left home against his parents' wishes to play professionally with a minor league team.

While still in his teens, Bell had an experience that changed the direction of his life. He heard an evangelistic church sermon and realized that something was wrong. "As I listened I realized God was talking to me," he told the *Montgomery Advertiser.* "I was a sinner and needed a savior. . . . God came into my life."

Bell's newfound zeal in the Christian faith led him to Chicago's Moody Bible Institute, where he studied from 1954 until 1957. After marrying in 1957, he finished studies for his bachelor's degree at Taylor University in Upland, Indiana. By 1960 he was working as pastor of the West Washington Community Church in Los Angeles.

His evolution as an evangelist was gradual over the next three years, but in 1963 he was galvanized by the preaching of Dr. Graham, who visited Los Angeles for a crusade.

As one of the organizers for that crusade, Bell began a relationship with Graham that deepened over the ensuing two years. In the meantime, Bell earned a master's degree in divinity from the Fuller Theological Seminary and studied pastoral counseling at Los Angeles's Metropolitan State Mental Hospital.

In 1964 Bell took the challenging job of chaplain at the Los Angeles County Jail. That position convinced him to take his ministry community-wide, and he became a featured evangelist at ecumenical meetings and revivals. "It seems like I was out of church more than in it," he remembered in the *Montgomery Advertiser.* On the other hand, his ministry for the benefit of prisoners, the mentally ill, the homeless, and others on the fringe of society further endeared him to Billy Graham.

A Worldwide Calling

Bell was honored in 1965 when Dr. Graham asked him to join the Billy Graham crusades as an associate evangelist. Bell became a sort of right-hand-man to Graham and traveled with the popular television preacher all over the world. A dynamic speaker in his own right, Bell continued his prison ministry, this time visiting jails as part of the overall crusade goal. He felt his special calling was to develop a strategy for meeting the spiritual needs of both church members and the community at large.

While some other television ministries have foundered amidst allegations of corruption and fiscal mismanagement, no such charge has ever been leveled at a Billy Graham or a Ralph Bell crusade. Financial arrangements for the crusades are overseen by executive committees staffed completely by residents of the community in which the crusade is held. Local profits on crusades are forwarded to the Billy Graham Associate Crusades offices in Minneapolis. Bell himself earns an annual salary determined by the Minneapolis office. It is a modest sum. "I don't make as much as a garbage man in New York City," the minister told the *Montgomery Advertiser.*

But Bell does not labor for the financial rewards: he gains satisfaction in helping people to find answers to life's perplexing problems. His work as Dr. Graham's associate has taken him to all corners of the globe, and his solo crusades have been conducted in many parts of the United States and Canada. In preparation for crusades, Bell travels to the crusade location and spends weeks and months helping local pastors to mobilize congregations in order to reach out with aid and fellowship. Bell told the *Montgomery Advertiser:* "I have developed a strong belief in the important role the local church should play in meeting the needs of the sick, elderly, disadvantaged, and handicapped in the community."

The Continuing Goal of Evangelism

Illness has forced Dr. Graham to curtail his preaching in recent years, and from time to time Bell has taken the podium for his ailing friend. Like Graham, Bell urges Christians old and new to find a church in which they can be comfortable, no matter what the denomination. Bell himself is a member and minister with the Evangelical Free Church of America.

Bell's sermons follow a standard evangelical style, in which the minister challenges the audience to seek a personal relationship with God and Jesus Christ and then invites listeners toward the podium to make a public confession of faith. Many thousands have responded to Bell's call, and his ministry has been praised for its special outreach to indigenous American and minority populations.

The Message

Bell told *Decision* that his message is simple but important. "Death is the great leveler of mankind," he said. "It is also a great separator. . . . You may be successful in life, but that is no guarantee that you will be successful in death. You have to ask yourself, 'Where will I go? Where will I spend eternity?' Maybe your life is all mixed up, and you can't find a way out. . . . Level with God, and you will discover that he is able to give you a brand new beginning."

Sources

Decision, October 1987.
El Reno Daily Tribune (Oklahoma), March 24, 1992.
Montgomery Advertiser (Alabama), April 6, 1991; April 9, 1991.
Mountaineer (Colorado), May 22, 1991.
St. Louis Review, July 10, 1991.
Syracuse Herald-Journal (New York), March 3, 1989.

Additional information for this profile was supplied by the Billy Graham Evangelistic Association.

—*Anne Janette Johnson*

Lerone Bennett, Jr.

1928—

Writer, editor

Writer and editor Lerone Bennett, Jr., glides gracefully between the worlds of scholarship and journalism, tackling with equal vigor the history of race relations in the United States and the current political environment in which African Americans continue to strive for equality. In his many books and articles, Bennett proves himself not merely an insightful observer of society's racial injustices, but an activist articulating the ways in which people of color can overcome bigotry and a history of subjugation. Bennett has trained his sharp, analytical eye to spot lessons from history that others might overlook or dismiss narrow-mindedly. And he uses a spirited writing style laced with drama and punch to ensure that his insights enliven rather than depress the debate over the nature of race in America.

He was born in the fall of 1928, in Clarksdale, Mississippi, the son of Lerone and Alma Bennett. After taking a bachelor's degree in 1949 from Morehouse College—a predominantly black school in Atlanta about which he would later write and which he would always place at the center of his intellectual development—Bennett served as a reporter and then city editor at the now defunct *Atlanta Daily World* newspaper. In 1954, armed with a newsman's crisp writing and golden sense of story, Bennett became an associate editor at *Ebony,*

a picture and news magazine directed mainly at a black audience. *Ebony* had been founded in 1945 by pioneering black publisher John H. Johnson, who would always encourage Bennett's book writing and academic forays. Except for a one-year visiting professorship at Northwestern University, Bennett has consistently used *Ebony* as his home base. In 1958 he became senior editor at the magazine, and his sweeping articles have become one of the publication's literary signatures.

Out of a series of articles written for *Ebony* emerged Bennett's first book, 1962's *Before the Mayflower: A History of Black America, 1619-1962,* which, as he wrote in the preface, "is a history of 'the other Americans' and how they came to North America and what happened to them when they got here. . . . The story deals with the rise and growth of slavery and segregation and the continuing efforts of Negro Americans to answer the question of the Jewish poet of captivity: 'How shall we sing the Lord's song in a strange land?'"

With a reporter's thirst for drama and an inclination to place the story in a big-picture context, Bennett sets the stage for the black experience in *Before the Mayflower* by invoking the landing of the first Africans on American shores. "A year before the arrival of the celebrated 'Mayflower,' 113 years before the birth of George Washington, 244 years before the signing of the Emancipation Proclamation, this ship sailed in to Jamestown, Virginia, and dropped anchor into the muddy waters of history," he recounted in his book. "It was clear to the men who received this 'Dutch Man of War' that she was no ordinary vessel. What seems unusual today is that no one sensed how extraordinary she really was. Few ships, before or since, have unloaded a more momentous cargo."

Before the Mayflower takes the reader on a historical journey through the American revolution, the Civil War, postwar Reconstruction, the birth of the Jim Crow laws that legally enforced segregation, and into the tumultuous 1960s—the era of the civil rights movement in the United States. With a characteristic mixture of optimism and pessimism, Bennett lauds black accomplishment and the promise for the future but bemoans the political and economic alienation of blacks in a country passing itself off as a great melting pot.

Bennett's treatise, praised for its lucid writing, comprehensive vision, and masterful handling of both primary and secondary sources, sealed his reputation as a first-class popular historian. "*Before the Mayflower* does not purport to present information hitherto uncovered or to furnish new perspectives," Benjamin Quarles wrote in *American Historical Review.* "But whether or not one is familiar with the book's content, he may well be moved by its unusual ability to evoke the tragedy and the glory of the Negro's role in the American past."

Criticized Both Black and White Establishment

In subsequent books, Bennett continued to document the historical forces shaping the black experience in America but offered more of a sociological perspective as well, concentrating on the emergence of the civil rights movement and its effect on the foundations of the American political system in the 1950s and 1960s. His 1964 book *What Manner of Man,* a biography of Morehouse classmate Martin Luther King, Jr., was welcomed as an even-handed analysis of the black leader's life and his role in fundamentally changing the nature of racial dynamics in the United States. Paul Schlueter wrote in a 1965 *Christian Century* review that although the book on one level is a "sensitive account of the Negro-white confrontation of our time," it also serves to dispel "claims that only active and overtly violent behavior can effectively change the course of history."

Also in 1964, Bennett published *The Negro Mood,* a collection of essays that demonstrated a sharper editorial bite than his previous works. Probing such issues as the failed integration of blacks into American life and the ways in which blacks are denied the fruits of society, Bennett takes aim at the white liberal establishment for ignoring the accomplishments of African Americans and for just mouthing the words of racial justice rather than performing the actions that might remedy it. He argues that white liberals have not changed the political system they repeatedly label as unfair, and that their reaction to black violence, for example, dramatically illustrates the dangerous hypocrisy of their political positions. "White violence, though deplorable, is endurable, and white liberals endure it amazingly well," Bennett wrote. "But Negro violence creates or threatens to create a situation which forces white liberals to choose sides; it exposes their essential support of things as they are."

But Bennett is equally critical of the black establishment. In his 1965 publication *Confrontation: Black and White,* the author points to the mixed messages of various black leaders—ranging from support of nonviolent social action to the promotion of more aggressive black power tactics—as a source of divisiveness in the black community. In addition, he criticizes the leadership of the black power structure—including the National Association for the Advancement of Colored People (NAACP) and the Urban League—for being out of touch with the black masses who experience daily the prejudice and institutional discrimination that the organizations were ostensibly created to combat. Bennett also rebukes the "talented tenth" theory that an elite core of African Americans can lead the rest; instead, he argues for large-scale political organization, embracing people of color from all economic and social stations, to effect meaningful social change.

Writings Capture Drama

As much as Bennett's clarity of thought and precision of analysis make him, according to Harry Hansen in the *Saturday Review,* "a master of exposition," what gives his work spark is the liveliness of the writing, the talent he has for putting faces and personalities behind names, for capturing the spirit of an event or person, for using anecdote and setting to highlight the drama of the unfolding of history. For example, in describing Nat Turner, the slave who led a violent revolt against whites in Virginia in 1831, Bennett wrote in *Before the Mayflower:* "A mystic with blood on his mind, a preacher with vengeance on his lips, a dreamer, a fanatic, a terrorist, [he] was a fantastic mixture of gentleness, ruthlessness, and piety. Of middling stature, black in color, in demeanor commanding and bold, Nat was five feet, six inches tall, a little dumpy perhaps, running to fat around the middle, with a mustache and a little tuft of hair on his chin. Early in life, Nat came to the view that God had set him aside for some great purpose."

Underlying the literary texture and suspense that grace his books and magazine pieces is the talent Bennett has for finding a good story and tapping it for all its worth. That is what drew him to the case of black sprinter Jesse Owens, the son of a sharecropper and grandson of slaves who at the 1936 Berlin Olympics squashed German leader Adolf Hitler's boasts of Nazism by beating Germany's premier Aryan athletes. "Thirty-seven years later," Bennett wrote in *Ebony,* "a panel of major sports writers would call Jesse Owens' Olympic triumph the most important sports story of the century. But this story, which will be told as long as men and women celebrate grace and courage, was more than a sports story. It was politics, history even, played out on an international stage with big stakes riding on every

contest." Bennett added that when Owens died in 1980, his golden moment of 1936 "became a living memorial, giving imperishable testimony on the limits of tyranny and the swiftness and grace of the human spirit."

Discussed Black Accomplishments in the Face of Adversity

Throughout Bennett's work is the proposition, either implicitly or explicitly stated, that African Americans will enjoy equality and triumph over discrimination only if they understand the lessons of history. The author contends that is in the suffering and also the accomplishments of yesterday's blacks that youths of today can find the self-confidence to withstand the vicious stereotypes of discrimination. So in listing the ten most dramatic events in black

> "Blacks and whites must meet and know each other as brothers in a marriage of visions, as co-conspirators in the making of a dream, as fellow passengers on a journey into the unknown."

history for an *Ebony* article, Bennett covers the sadness—the forced importation of blacks into this country, the assassination of Dr. King—but focuses mostly on the successes: the 1954 *Brown vs. Board of Education* Supreme Court decision, which rejected the separate but equal defense of segregated public education; the Montgomery bus boycott that was forged by the heroic actions of Rosa Parks; the emergence of brilliant leaders like Booker T. Washington and W. E. B. Du Bois; the founding of the first black newspaper; and President Abraham Lincoln's Emancipation Proclamation, the 1863 statement of freedom for all slaves, which Bennett called "a downpayment on the redemption of the American soul."

Blacks and whites, Bennett wrote in *The Negro Mood,* must turn their backs on racial stereotypes and celebrate the contributions blacks have made to the United States despite the odds. "America would not have been America without the Negro and America cannot become America until it confronts not only the Negro but the gifts the Negro bears. What is required now is an act of the spirit. We must abandon our shallow trenches and confront each other as co-inheritors of a common land, which is to say that we must meet and know each other as brothers in a marriage of visions, as co-conspirators in the making of a dream, as fellow passengers on a journey into the unknown.''

Selected writings

Before the Mayflower: A History of Black America, 1619-1962, Johnson Publishing Company, 1962.
The Negro Mood, Johnson Publishing Company, 1964.
What Manner of Man: A Biography of Martin Luther King, Jr., Johnson Publishing Company, 1964.
Confrontation: Black and White, Johnson Publishing Company, 1965.
Black Power U.S.A.: The Human Side of Reconstruction, 1867-1877, Johnson Publishing Company, 1967.
Pioneers in Protest, Johnson Publishing Company, 1968.
The Challenge of Blackness, Johnson Publishing Company, 1972.
The Shaping of Black America: The Struggles and Triumphs of African Americans, 1619-1990s, Johnson Publishing Company, 1975, reprinted, Viking Penguin, 1993.
Wade in the Water, Johnson Publishing Company, 1979, reprinted as *Great Moments in Black American History.*

(With John H. Johnson) *Succeeding Against the Odds,* Amistad Press, 1993.

Sources

Books

Bennett, Lerone, Jr., *Before the Mayflower: A History of Black America, 1619-1962,* 4th edition, Johnson Publishing Company, 1969.
Bennett, Lerone, Jr., *The Negro Mood,* Johnson Publishing Company, 1964.
Bennett, Lerone, Jr., *What Manner of Man: A Biography of Martin Luther King, Jr.,* Johnson Publishing Company, 1964.

Periodicals

American Historical Review, July 1963.
Christian Century, September 22, 1965.
Ebony, September 1988; November 1990; February 1992.
Saturday Review, October 16, 1965; March 23, 1968.

—*Isaac Rosen*

Les Brown

1945—

Motivational speaker, author

Les Brown has a dream, and he is living it. In 1986, broke and sleeping on the cold linoleum floor of his office, he began to pursue a career as a motivational speaker. By the early 1990s, he was one of the highest paid speakers in the nation, with his company, Les Brown Unlimited, Inc., earning $4 million a year from his speaking tours and the sale of motivational tapes and materials. Brown's audience is wide: from Fortune 500 companies to automobile workers to prison inmates to special-education classes to ordinary individuals. His mission "is to get a message out that will help people become uncomfortable with their mediocrity," he explained to a reporter for *Ebony*. "A lot of people are content with their discontent. I want to be a catalyst to enable them to see themselves having more and achieving more."

Brown's message works because "he kindles the warmth, humor, and well being in a society that's seen the gradual disintegration of families and mounting technology and alienation in industry," Maureen McDonald wrote in the *Detroiter*. Brown knows the function of the able individual in a worn community: he delivers not only nurturing words but money as well, donating 20 percent of his business revenues to fund drug prevention programs. His message also works, and for a stronger reason, because he is not an outsider, an academic who offers a theoretical prescription. "I can't lecture on something unless I am living it," Brown wrote in his 1992 bestseller *Live Your Dreams*. He connects with other people's lives—their misfortunes and missed opportunities—because he has been through it all and triumphed.

Leslie Calvin Brown and his twin brother, Wesley, were born on February 17, 1945, on the floor of an abandoned building in Liberty City, a low-income section of Miami, Florida. Their birth mother, married at the time to a soldier stationed overseas, had become pregnant by another man and went to Miami secretly to give birth to her sons. Three weeks later, she gave them away. At six weeks of age, both boys were adopted by Mamie Brown, a 38-year-old unmarried cafeteria cook and domestic. The importance of her entrance into his life, Brown concludes, was immeasurable. "Everything I am and everything I have I owe to my mother," he told Rachel L. Jones of the *Detroit Free Press*. "Her strength and character are my greatest inspiration, always have been and always will be."

The confidence that Brown's adoptive mother had in him, the belief that he was capable of greatness, was not shared by his teachers. As a child he found excitement in typical boyhood misadventures. He liked to have fun, and he liked attention. Overactive and mischievous, Brown was a poor student because he lacked concentration, especially in reading. His restlessness and inattentiveness, coupled with his teachers' insufficient insight into his true capabilities, resulted in his being labeled "educably mentally retarded" in the fifth grade. It was a label he found hard to remove, in large part because he did not try. "They said I was slow so I held to that pace," he recounted in his book.

A major lesson Brown imparts early in *Live Your Dreams* is that "there comes a time when you have to drop your burdens in order to fight for yourself and your dreams." It was another significant figure in Brown's early life who awakened his listless consciousness and brought about this awareness: LeRoy Washington, a speech and drama instructor at Booker T. Washington High School in Miami. While in high school, Brown "used to fantasize being onstage speaking to thousands of people," he related to Jones, "and I used to write on pieces of paper, 'I am the world's greatest orator.'"

But it wasn't until he encountered Washington that he truly learned of the sound and power of eloquent speech to stir and motivate. Brown related in his book that when he once told Washington in class that he couldn't perform a task because he was educably mentally retarded, the instructor responded, "DO NOT EVER SAY THAT AGAIN! Someone's opinion of you does NOT have to become YOUR reality." Those words provided Brown's liberation from his debilitating label. "The limitations you have and the negative things that you internalize are given to you by the world," he wrote of his realization. "The things that empower you—the possibilities—*come from within.*"

First Dream Was in Radio

Employed after high school as a city sanitation worker but determined to achieve what he desired—perhaps for the first time in his life—Brown pursued a career in radio broadcasting. He had been enthralled throughout his life with the almost music-like patter of disc jockeys, so he repeatedly bothered the owner of a local radio station about a position until the owner relented. Having no experience, Brown was hired as a gofer. Firmly intent on becoming a deejay, he learned all he could about the workings of a radio station. One day, when a disc jockey became drunk on the air and Brown was the only other person at the station, he filled in at the microphone. Impressed, the owner of the station promoted Brown to part-time and then full-time disc jockey.

In the late 1960s, Brown moved to Columbus, Ohio, where he had a top-rated radio program, and was eventually given added duties as broadcast manager. Here his world widened. He became more socially conscious and more of an activist, urging his listeners to political action. Part of the motivation behind this fervor came from Mike Williams, the station's news director and an activist who would, in some 15 years, come to oversee Brown's motivational speaking tours and programs. "I thought he was a master communicator," Williams told Cheryl Lavin of the *Chicago Tribune.* "I knew it was a gift. I saw him as an international figure. I saw him in very large situations, moving audiences." But the owners of the radio station thought Brown was becoming too controversial of a figure. He was fired.

Ventured into Politics and Youth Training

Urged on by Williams, Brown ran for the Ohio State Legislature, winning the seat of the 29th House District. In 1976, his first year, he passed more legislation than any other freshman representative in Ohio legislative history. In his third term, he served as chair of the Human Resources Committee. But he had to leave the state house in 1981 to care for his ailing mother in Florida. While in Miami, continuing his focus on social matters, Brown developed a youth career training program and held community meetings, speaking out on social injustice.

Again, controversies arose around him. The Dade County state's attorney general investigated his handling of the youth program. Finally after a year, during which time Brown openly invited any inquiry, the case was dropped: no improprieties were found. The motivating factor behind the criticisms, Brown believed, was jealousy. "A lot of people felt threatened and offended because I came on very strong," he told Jones, "and I had an instant following they couldn't get." This effect was not lost on Brown. Urged on again by Williams and by a chance encounter with motivational millionaire Zig Zigler, who, Brown learned, was earning $10,000 for one-hour talks, Brown decided to become a professional motivational speaker.

"Didn't Want to Get Soft"

"Life takes on meaning when you become motivated, set goals, and charge after them in an unstoppable manner," Brown wrote in *Live Your Dreams*. It is a maxim he learned well. When he entered the motivational speaking arena in the mid-1980s, he had virtually nothing, having moved to Detroit with his clothes and just one tape of his motivational speeches. He rented an office that he shared with an attorney. He worked hard and always seemed to be the first one there in the morning and the last one there at night. Indeed, he never left the office; Brown was forced to sleep on the cold floor because he could not afford an apartment. But he welcomed this ascetic lifestyle. "I didn't even want a blanket or a pallet on the floor," he explained to Jones. "I wanted it to be hard and cold so it would motivate me to keep striving. I didn't want to get soft."

Brown read books on public speaking and studied the habits of established speakers. He first spoke to grade school students, then high school students. Clubs and organizations followed. Less than four years later, in 1989, he received the National Speakers Association's highest award—the Council of Peers Award of Excellence—becoming the first African American to receive such an honor. He was known in professional circles as "The Motivator."

"Victories can become obstacles to your development if you unconsciously pause too long to savor them," Brown wrote in his book. "Too many people interpret success as sainthood. Success does not make you a great person; how you deal with it decides that. You must not allow your victories to become ends unto themselves." His goal was not just to win awards, but to inspire people to pursue their own goals.

In 1990 Brown reached for a wider audience by recording the first in a series of motivational speech presentations for the Public Broadcasting Service (PBS-TV). He conducted motivational training sessions not only for executives of

---

"Life takes on meaning when you become motivated, set goals, and charge after them in an unstoppable manner."

---

corporations such as American Telephone and Telegraph, General Electric, and Procter & Gamble, but also for prison inmates and—remembering his own background—for special education students in high schools. "We all have a responsibility to give something back," he told a reporter for *Upscale*. "I am who I am because of the relationships I have developed, because of the people who have enriched my life."

Teaches by Example in *Live Your Dreams*

Brown details his life and the relationships that have helped shape it in his book *Live Your Dreams*. Much more than a simple autobiography, the book, which is divided into ten chapters followed by written exercises in a built-in workbook, focuses on areas of personal deficiency—such as fear, inattentiveness, and laziness—as well as on areas of personal value—such as self-knowledge, courage, and dreams. Brown makes vague, personal faults understandable and ambitious virtues attainable by elaborating on them through personal or historical narratives that are almost parable-like. He moves easily between the ordinary and the extraordinary to emphasize his point. For instance, a discussion about a boy who was scared of a bulldog that constantly chased him until he realized the dog lacked teeth might be followed on the next page by a discussion of how basketball superstar Michael Jordan handles the pressures of being a public persona.

Often to prove a maxim, Brown links the worldly with the mundane in *Live Your Dreams,* as in the retelling of the stories of Terry Anderson, the Associated Press correspondent held hostage for seven years by Shiite Muslims, followed by the tale of an anonymous young boy who had to fight a neighborhood bully on a school bus. For further reinforcement, Brown sprinkles quotes throughout from historical figures such as former U.S. president Theodore Roosevelt, American nature writer Henry David Thoreau, and German poet Johann Wolfgang von Goethe, and from personal figures such as teacher LeRoy Washington and his own mother, Mamie.

The book's idealistic tone is tempered by an acceptance of life's realities. "You will be cruising along, knocking them dead, in full synchronization—and then you'll hit the speed bumps," Brown wrote. "You miss a bus. Your paycheck bounces. Your car won't start. That's life. Maybe it is set up that way so that we learn and grow." Brown knows this firsthand and that is his point: he has faced life's obstacles and has been inspired to overcome them in quest of his own dreams, so he tries to inspire those whose dreams are similarly thwarted by life's misadventures.

"I am intrigued by the concept of selling people on their own greatness with the same fervor that Madison Avenue sells them on the wondrous attributes of Nike athletic shoes, Chevy trucks, and Calvin Klein jeans," Brown wrote in *Live Your Dreams.* "What if our young people heard encouragement to dream and strive as many times a day as they are exhorted to drink Dr. Pepper or to go to the land of Mickey Mouse?" Brown got his chance to answer this question and share his philosophies with his widest audience ever when his own television talk show, the *Les Brown Show,* debuted in the fall of 1993. The program, which is Brown's most ambitious goal to date, is syndicated by King World, the same company that distributes *Oprah.* "I think people are ready to be entertained and inspired and I want to make them feel good about themselves," he

explained to Jefferson Graham of *USA Today.* "I want to use TV in a way in which it's never been used before—to empower people."

Selected writings

Live Your Dreams, Morrow, 1992.

Sources

Books

Les Brown, *Live Your Dreams,* Morrow, 1992.

Periodicals

Chicago Tribune, December 10, 1991, sec. 5, p. 7; April 13, 1992, sec. 5, pp. 1-2.
Detroiter, September 1991, p. 7.
Detroit Free Press, November 5, 1992, pp. G1-4.
Ebony, October 1990, pp. 96-98.
EM, May 1992, p. 54.
Essence, March 1993, p. 63.
Herald-News (Joliet, IL), May 13, 1990.
Upscale, August/September 1992, p. 97.
USA Today, January 25, 1993, p. D3.

Additional information for this profile was obtained from a press release distributed by Les Brown Unlimited, Inc., February 1993.

—Rob Nagel

Ron Brown

1941—

Member of the U.S. Cabinet

Ron Brown made history in 1989 when he became the first African American chosen to lead a major U.S. political party. From 1989 through 1992, Brown served as the highly visible deputy chairman of the Democratic National Committee (DNC). Prior to that, he was Jesse Jackson's manager at the 1988 Democratic National Convention. But Brown's liberal roots go even deeper: he was earlier the National Urban League's chief Washington lobbyist, the deputy campaign manager for U.S. Senator Edward (Ted) Kennedy's 1980 presidential bid, and a chief counsel for the Senate Committee on the Judiciary. Brown's confirmation in 1993 as President Bill Clinton's secretary of Commerce, however, focused the nation's attention on him even further.

As a boy growing up in the Theresa Hotel in Harlem managed by his father—boxer Joe Louis and actor Paul Robeson were guests there—Ronald Harmon Brown learned early to straddle two worlds. The Theresa, near the famed Apollo Theater, was an oasis for the black entertainment and professional classes of the day. Brown, whose parents were graduates of Howard University, was bused to exclusive preparatory schools and attended the virtually all-white Middlebury College in Vermont. Because of such a background, Brown, unlike many black political leaders of his generation, had for the most part no involvement in the civil rights movement of the 1960s. While Jesse Jackson led 278 students arrested at sit-ins over civil rights at all-black North Carolina A&T State University, Brown was fulfilling ROTC responsibilities at his private rural college.

One instance of activism came far from the beaten paths of Southern civil rights battlefields but would characterize his later skill at nonconfrontational negotiations. The only black student in his freshman class at Middlebury, Brown was rushed by white classmates from the Sigma Phi Epsilon fraternity, the campus "jock house." But the national organization objected because of an exclusionary clause that barred blacks. As the debate dragged on, reported *Time* magazine, "Brown let it be known that he was unwilling to finesse the issue by accepting house privileges without full membership." Finally, fraternity members rallied to his side, provoking their expulsion by the national chapter leaders. Middlebury then barred all exclusionary charters from campus. Brown became a trustee at the mostly white school.

After college Brown served as the only black officer at his U.S. Army post in West Germany. Back home, he earned a law degree, worked as an inner-city social worker, and then joined the National Urban League—considered the most moderate of civil rights groups—as its Washington lobbyist. Later, he became the first African American attorney at the high-powered Washington law firm of Patton, Boggs & Blow.

Political Savvy Paid Off

Brown's election as head of the Democratic party came despite his carrying all the wrong credentials as far as many party regulars were concerned: he had served as Jesse Jackson's campaign manager in the 1988 bid for the party's presidential nomination. Brown's ties to the aggressive and somewhat controversial Jackson made some

observers feel he was too volatile for the job, but his role as peacemaker between the Jackson and Michael Dukakis camps during the 1988 Democratic Convention helped cement his reputation as a suave negotiator. Jackson, who knew his '88 bid for the Democratic nomination was out of gas, at least wanted respect from Dukakis.

Such respect, however, was hard to elicit from the Dukakis camp, since it seemed to have the nomination—if not the 1988 general election against the Republicans—all wrapped up. Divisiveness within the party could have been a disaster for the Democrats, with even worse repercussions than Dukakis's eventual defeat against George Bush. But Brown helped to avoid an irreparable split in the party along color lines. "He is not bragging when he says that his conciliation efforts 'played a part in turning a potential disaster into a love-in,'" wrote David Broder in the *Washington Post.* And Donna Brazile, a Democratic activist aligned with Michael Dukakis in the 1988 election campaign, told the *Atlanta Journal and Constitution,* "If Ron was a pop singer, he would have crossover appeal."

Brown is the consummate Washington insider who learned how to work the levers of power by being a team player. Before becoming party chairman, he served on the DNC's Executive Committee as deputy chairman and chief counsel for the party and worked for Ted Kennedy and other Democrats in Congress. "His political formation is within national political processes and not within ethnic political processes," Harvard professor Martin Kilson told the *Washington Post.* "Brown is the new black transethnic politician." Soon after his election to the DNC in 1989, Brown made a vow to the committee, stating, as reprinted in the *Washington Post,* "I promise you, my chairmanship will not be about race, it will be about the races we win."

Brown's political savvy was evident in his engineering of his own election as party chairman. He began the campaign as just one of five candidates for the post, but he deployed his lobbying skills early. One call Brown made looking for support went to his former boss, Senator Kennedy, chair of the crucial Labor Committee. Soon after the call, the AFL-CIO endorsed Brown. The *New York Times* wrote, "Mr. Brown's election, the product of a meticulously organized campaign, gave him such an overwhelming advantage that his four competitors dropped out of the contest weeks before the voting."

However, Brown faced scrutiny for trying to be too many different things to too many people. "If you asked people in the Fifties and Sixties what it was to be a Democrat, they could easily tell you," Brown told *Gentleman's Quarterly.* "Somehow in recent years, it has become harder and harder. If we continue to let our opponents . . . define us . . . there's no way we're going to win elections." But some critics feel that Brown's own self-analysis betrays just that weakness. When the magazine asked him to define his own beliefs, Brown replied, "Let's see, what did we come up with? I'm a mainstream progressive Democrat . . . meaning I embrace the traditional values of the Democratic party, but I'm progressive."

Success as Chairman of the Democratic National Committee

The role of Democratic National Committee chairman became increasingly important during the dozen years between 1980 and 1992 when Democrats were out of the White House. As party chairman, Brown was successful in raising funds against the odds and helping to elect approved candidates. The 1989 off-year elections were, in Brown's own words, "a slam dunk," according to the *New York Times*. Democrats registered two firsts: a black governor in Virginia and a black mayor in New York City. Just as significantly, the Democrats picked up four congressional seats in special elections, including winning former Vice-President Dan Quayle's seat in heavily Republican Indiana. Brown remarked to the *New York Times,* "What the party does over here and over there should be strategically connected. The voter registration, the redistricting, the state party building and the campaigns— everything should be connected to winning elections." That the party, and Brown, succeeded in that to a good degree is made even more impressive given President Bush's sky-high approval ratings during that period.

Still, potentially thorny racial questions—exactly the kind that could alienate jumpy white Southern Democrats— always threatened to grab headlines. There too, though, Brown found a way to defuse the many pressures facing him. In the Chicago mayoral election of 1989, for instance, Brown dodged a tricky, racially-charged issue—whether to support white Democratic nominee Richard Daley, son of the late mayor, over black alderman Tim Evans, a Jackson ally running as an independent. He vowed to toe the party line and back the Democratic nominee, Daley.

But there was nowhere to escape to, no corner of America in which Brown could hide, when the political theater expanded from local elections to the presidential campaign of 1992. After the Persian Gulf War with Iraq, President Bush was enjoying high favorability ratings with the American electorate, and it appeared the Democratic party would again face an uphill battle to wrest White House control from the Republicans. Initially, because of Bush's popularity, Brown had difficulty raising money for the Democratic National Committee. Another problem was that, in the eyes of some Jewish contributors, Brown had not sufficiently distanced himself from Jesse Jackson, whose anti-Semitic remarks several years earlier were still a festering sore spot in Jewish/African American relations.

Worked for Democratic Unity in the 1992 Presidential Election

But Brown's greatest challenge, in terms of attracting dollars and, ultimately, the votes of Americans, was to remold the image of the party, shedding the "tax and spend" label that the Republicans had successfully applied to democratic candidates in the past. "We need to define ourselves as a party," Brown was quoted as telling *Black Enterprise*. "When you allow your adversaries to define you, you can be assured that the definition is going to be a very unpleasant one and that you find yourself on the defensive trying to dig yourself out of a hole. We can't let that happen again."

The answer, as many political observers had long known, lay in the middle. Brown understood that for the party to reclaim the so-called Reagan Democrats, it would need a candidate with fiscally conservative economic policies that would not adversely affect the struggling middle class.

> "I embrace the traditional values of the Democratic party, but I'm progressive."

While he could not keep liberals such as Iowa senator Tom Harkin out of the primaries, Brown did muzzle the potential candidacy of Jesse Jackson, who, Brown feared, would unwittingly tarnish the new, moderate image that the party desperately needed.

Brown's plan was to minimize any acrimony among the primary candidates, hoping to focus their disparate voices on the need to unseat the Republican president. Bush, meanwhile, had suffered a precipitous fall in popularity, as his success in the Persian Gulf was overshadowed by a lingering recession in the United States. At a time when the citizenry had grown tired of politics as usual and were calling on the U.S. president to focus on domestic affairs, the Democratic party became the agent of "change."

In addition to nudging the party toward the center of the political spectrum, Brown's plan was to throw the party's support behind its candidate early in the political season. Indeed, one primary candidate, former California governor Jerry Brown, accused the party chairman of coddling then-Arkansas governor Bill Clinton, who was emerging as the leading democratic figure, in spite of several personal and professional scandals in the Clinton camp that might have led to yet another Democratic loss in the general elections.

At the Democratic National Convention in July of 1992,

Clinton won the nomination despite the various controversies surrounding him, and Brown, having calmed many of the voices of dissent, earned widespread praise for a smooth democratic crowning whose central messages were unity and enthusiasm for the party candidate. "Ron sensed what he had to do right from the start," former DNC chairman Paul G. Kirk was quoted as saying in the *New York Times*. "He knew the party had to show it could govern itself before it could hope to govern the country." Brown's public trumpeting about a redefined Democratic party, and his behind-the-scenes maneuvering to generate support for Clinton, were seen as key to the first democratic presidential victory since 1976.

Named Secretary of Commerce

Brown's departure from the DNC was as controversial as his election as its chairman. In what some skeptics viewed as a political payback and an effort to create a racially diverse cabinet, Clinton nominated Brown as secretary of Commerce. Immediately, Brown's past experience as a lobbyist took on the weight of a political liability. As secretary, he would make administrative and policy decisions that might affect his former clients, to whom, it was feared, he would feel some sort of allegiance. Moreover, several political commentators found it ironic that Clinton, who had campaigned against the status quo and the government-insider lobbyist crowd, had nominated Brown, the Washington power broker who played the political game with expert finesse. Illustrative of the ethical questions raised by Brown's nomination was a celebration in his honor that several of the largest American and Japanese corporations had planned. These companies, whose financial interests are impacted by decisions of the Commerce secretary, were to have donated $10,000 each for the gala, which was abruptly canceled by Brown after Clinton expressed disapproval. Despite these setbacks, Brown was confirmed by the U.S. Senate in 1993 as the nation's first African American secretary of Commerce. He has pledged to make the department more responsive to the country's needs and concentrate on the promotion of American business interests both at home and in the international arena. As he told Frank McCoy in *Black Enterprise*, "By helping to create jobs, [the Commerce Department] is going to be a key factor in economic renewal."

Sources

Atlanta Journal and Constitution, January 7, 1989; February 12, 1989; May 22, 1989.

Black Enterprise, March 1992, p. 48; June 1993, pp. 223-26.

Boston Globe Magazine, October 22, 1989.

Business Week, February 13, 1989, p. 54; June 18, 1990, p. 30; January 11, 1993, p. 31.

Gentleman's Quarterly, July 1989.

Nation, February 20, 1989.

Newsweek, February 6, 1989, p. 20.

New York Times, February 11, 1989; March 28, 1992, p. A9; July 20, 1992, p. A11; January 14, 1993, p. A1.

New York Times Magazine, December 12, 1989.

Oakland Press (Oakland County, MI), December 13, 1992, p. A12.

Time, January 30, 1989, p. 56.

Wall Street Journal, January 8, 1993, p. A14.

Washington Post, February 5, 1989; February 11, 1989.

—Harvey Dickson and Isaac Rosen

Grace Bumbry

1937—

Opera and concert singer

Ancient Egypt, Macbeth's Scotland, Spain—singer Grace Bumbry has been transporting opera fans to such exotic worlds for more than 30 years. Initially trained as a mezzo-soprano, she switched to the slightly higher soprano register in 1970. Both repertoires have always shown a voice of silken purity that teams with a vibrant ability to bring operatic characters to life.

Bumbry's schedule is filled a year in advance, but every couple of months between tours she manages to fit in visits with her family. In addition, she finds time to guide young singers and lecture to disadvantaged teenagers about the undisputed benefits of concentration and hard work.

Grace Bumbry was born in 1937 in St. Louis, Missouri, to a freight handler for the Cotton Belt Route railroad and his wife, a Mississippi schoolteacher who had once dreamed of becoming a singer herself. A religious, middle-class couple, Benjamin and Melzia Bumbry taught their three children to count their riches in music. There were always neighborhood kids rehearsing at the house after school; there was singing around the piano in the evenings; and there was warbling around the washtub on Saturdays, when the family did the laundry. Every Thursday night, the parents went off to rehearse with their church choir, while their sons, Benjamin and Charles, sang in

the youth chorus. Too young to stay home alone, Grace tagged along with her brothers, who eventually persuaded their choir master to let her join the group, even though she was younger than the other members.

The choir soon became the focus of her life. Though unenthusiastic about the piano lessons she took with her mother, she lost no opportunity to practice singing her songs, which were already drawing admiring applause from church audiences when she was eleven years old.

Bumbry entered Sumner High School with her eyes already fixed on the concert stage. Determined to learn as much as she could as fast as possible, she practiced constantly, often storming home from music lessons in tears when dissatisfied with her own performance. The first of several important mentors, no-nonsense voice teacher Kenneth Billups, guided her carefully, pacing his lessons to her developing voice and reining her in when she wanted to leap ahead.

Bitter Blessing

In 1954 St. Louis radio station KMOX held a teenage

At a Glance. . .

Born Grace Ann Bumbry, January 4, 1937, in St. Louis, MO; daughter of Benjamin James (a freight handler for a railroad company) and Melzia (a schoolteacher) Bumbry; married Edwin Andreas Jaeckel, 1963 (divorced 1972). *Education:* Studied at Boston University, Northwestern University, and with Lotte Lehmann at the Music Academy of the West, Santa Barbara, California.

Opera singer. Paris Opera debut, March 1960, as Amneris in Verdi's *Aïda;* first black artist to appear at Bayreuth, debuting as Venus in Wagner's *Tannhäuser,* July 1961; Metropolitan Opera debut, 1965; changed to soprano repertoire from mezzo-soprano in 1970; sang title role in Richard Strauss's *Salome,* Covent Garden, 1970; sang role of Abigaille in Verdi's *Nabucco,* 1981, Bess in Gershwin's *Porgy and Bess,* 1985, and Cassandra in Berlioz's *Les Troyens,* 1990.

Awards: John Hay Whitney Award, 1957; Marian Anderson Scholarship, 1957; Metropolitan Opera Auditions of the Air, semifinalist, 1958; Richard Wagner Medal, 1963; honorary degrees from St. Louis University, Rockhurst College, Kansas City, and University of Missouri.

Addresses: *Agent*—Columbia Artists Management, attention Zemsky-Green, 165 West 57th St., New York, NY 10019.

talent contest. Billups encouraged his 17-year-old student to enter, sharing her pleasure when she won. Grace was now the proud possessor of a $1,000 war bond, a free trip to New York, and a $1,000 scholarship to the St. Louis Institute of Music.

The scholarship proved to be a bitter blessing; it slammed her up against the ugly reality of a prejudiced board of trustees who offered her segregated private lessons at the institute in lieu of admission alongside other students. Rosalyn Story, in her book *And So I Sing,* recalled Melzia Bumbry's parting shot after an acrimonious meeting with institute trustees: "It may be YOUR school, but it's MY daughter," she said, and stalked out.

A crisp revenge came by way of embarrassed KMOX executives, who did their best to neutralize Grace's pain by arranging for her to sing on Arthur Godfrey's nationally televised *Talent Scouts* program. According to a 1962

Ebony magazine feature, opera buff Godfrey was moved to tears by her interpretation of the aria "O Don Fatale" from nineteenth-century Italian composer Giuseppe Verdi's *Don Carlos.* "Her name will be one of the most famous names in music one day," he declared. "Beautiful! Just beautiful!"

Godfrey was not alone in his opinion. Soon scholarship offers began to pour in from colleges—several of them known for training far superior to that found at the St. Louis Institute of Music.

Someone to Flatten the Stone

Bumbry was still a high school senior when a second mentor entered her life. Contralto Marian Anderson had been a musical legend for many years. Scheduled to appear in 1955 as the first black member of the Metropolitan Opera Company, Anderson experienced bittersweet triumph over prejudice. Anderson's brush with bigotry had come in 1939, when the Daughters of the American Revolution had barred her appearance in Washington's Constitution Hall. Undaunted, she sang instead for a 75,000-strong Easter Sunday audience on the steps of the Lincoln Memorial, a venue that displayed her magnificent voice and dignified bearing to perfection.

A woman of pragmatic intelligence, Anderson was quick to acknowledge that impresario Sol Hurok had been a wise and steadfast friend on her journey to fame. "My mother taught me you can't do anything by yourself," Anderson told *Ebony* magazine in 1982. "There's always somebody to make the stone flat for you to stand on."

Having reached the pinnacle of her own fame, Marian Anderson gladly made the stone flat for a promising high-school senior when a tour brought her to St. Louis in 1954. She took time out to put a dazzled Bumbry at ease, to listen intently while she sang her good luck aria "O don fatale," and to report her opinion of the young singer's "magnificent voice" to Sol Hurok.

A longtime representative of such artists as pianist Arthur Rubinstein and violinist Isaac Stern, Hurok knew that much hard work still lay between Grace Bumbry and any guidance he could provide. At present he simply kept an eye on her, noting that she had picked the Boston University scholarship from the many offers the appearance on Arthur Godfrey's show had brought.

Unfortunately Boston was not a success. Wanting an indefinable "something extra," Bumbry transferred to Northwestern University in Chicago. She has never been able to explain why Northwestern beckoned so insistently, but she readily admits that the decision to go there transformed her life by introducing her to yet another invaluable mentor.

Enter Madame Lotte Lehmann

Lotte Lehmann had been one of opera's immortals since her debut in 1909. She swiftly matured into the type of singer whose performance becomes a standard for others. Lehmann had retired from the stage in 1951 but continued to contribute to opera by passing her own interpretative techniques on to young singers with promising futures.

Bumbry and Lehmann arrived at Northwestern simultaneously—Bumbry as a student, Lehmann to offer masterclasses. Bumbry presented some meticulously prepared operatic scenes and songs for Madame Lehmann's criticism and was thrilled to receive an invitation to spend a summer at her Musical Academy of the West in Santa Barbara, California. Eager to see that nothing stood in the way, Lehmann even arranged a scholarship, which was partly funded by comedian Anna Russell.

Bumbry worked so hard in Santa Barbara that the original summer stretched to three and a half years of study. Still aiming for a career as a concert artist, she studied with a fierce intensity, taking piano lessons; lessons from Lehmann in how to analyze every piece of music down to its skeletal essence; lessons in French, German and Italian, so she could sing the works of the world's best-known composers; and lessons in musical theory.

She also took lessons with voice teacher Armand Tokatyan, who categorized her voice as a dramatic soprano. Lehmann disagreed. Bumbry's voice was a mezzo-soprano, she said, and should be trained as one. It was a significant difference of opinion. A mezzo-soprano's range is lower than that sung by a soprano, and the voice itself, usually darker and more richly textured, covers a different repertoire of roles. Equally qualified to judge, Lehmann and Tokatyan never compromised; their disagreement ended only with Tokatyan's death in 1960.

Lehmann continued to train Grace Bumbry as a mezzo-soprano. Overcoming her student's shyness about acting, she coaxed her into learning songs needing drama to round them out. She tempted her into learning operatic arias and lent her books on the historical periods in which certain operas were set. Then, Lehmann persuaded Bumbry to refocus her career goal towards opera itself.

Bumbry was still in California when she began to build a reputation promising enough to merit the Marian Anderson Scholarship and the John Hay Whitney Award for 1957, plus a joint first prize with soprano Martina Arroyo the next year in the Metropolitan Opera Auditions of the Air. Her prize money mounted, allowing her to spend a summer in Europe studying the French art song.

Bayreuth

By 1960 Bumbry's career was clearly on its way. She made her debut at the Paris Opera as Amneris in Verdi's *Aïda,* and signed a two-year contract with the Opera House of Basel, Switzerland. However, these events were but preliminaries to the big break, which came later that year.

Bumbry happened to be in Cologne, Germany, when conductor Wolfgang Sawallisch of Bavaria's Bayreuth Festival was searching for a possible Venus for Richard Wagner's opera *Tannhäuser.* She sang for him and was invited to audition for Wieland Wagner, director of Bayreuth and grandson of the composer.

Wagner had definite ideas about the ideal Venus. He was planning an avant-garde production, and he wanted a mezzo-soprano who could tempt Tannhäuser the Wanderer into her citadel of love with an elegant mixture of mystery and controlled sexuality. Despite the fact that Venus had previously been sung only by white singers, Wagner offered Bumbry the part.

Immediately, Bayreuth began to buzz with angry letters and unwelcome press coverage. "A cultural disgrace!" blared the neo-Nazi German Reich Party. "If Richard Wagner knew this," wrote another correspondent in a letter quoted in *Newsweek,* "he'd be turning in his grave! Why does Venus have to be black? We've always known her as pink."

Bayreuth's director kept his head. Wieland Wagner was uncomfortably aware that his composer-grandfather had been such a notorious racist and anti-Semite that black GIs who had liberated the city during World War II had paraded sarcastically through the streets dressed in Wagner opera

> "When I heard Grace Bumbry I knew she was the perfect Venus."
> —*Wieland Wagner*

costumes. He was now determined to erase the Aryan stigma that still hung over Bayreuth. So he answered his critics very carefully, stating, as recounted in Rosalind Story's *And So I Sing:* "I shall bring in black, brown and yellow artists if I feel them appropriate for productions.

When I heard Grace Bumbry I knew she was the perfect Venus. Grandfather would have been delighted."

Bumbry kept away from the fracas and concentrated on bringing the bewitching temptress to life. Her effort brought its reward on opening night in 1961. Dressed in a spectacular gold costume, she sang the role of Venus with self-assured radiance. It was an unforgettable performance all around. The curtain came down to thunderous applause that rocked the theater for 30 minutes and brought the cast back for 42 curtain calls.

Bumbry has often remarked that racial prejudice is not a great problem in opera. Far more important are technical perfection and musicality—the ability to interpret the composer's wishes while adding an individual stamp to any role. Yet the question of skin color is one that a black singer must face. For instance, there are certain times when members of an operatic cast play a fictional family, and an opera's realism may be considerably compromised if these family members do not have similar skin tones. The solution, of course, is to use the right makeup.

At Bayreuth, Bumbry's skin color issue had been easily solved with gold body paint to match Venus's golden gown. But the question came up again later in the year, when she had to look Russian for a Basel production of Tchaikovsky's *Evgeny Onegin*. The company makeup artist experimented but came up with a formula that turned the diva's face yellow and did nothing to emphasize her huge doe eyes. Bumbry began to learn the intricacies of personalized stage makeup and came up with a formula so successful that the company adopted it to broaden the color palette for other artists.

This triumphant year was in its full midsummer bloom in August, when impresario Sol Hurok left his watchful place in the shadows to summon Bumbry to London. She signed a five-year, $250,000 contract for recordings, television appearances, and opera and concert engagements. Hurok also outlined plans for an American tour in November of 1962 and made arrangements to bring her back to Washington D.C. in February, where she sang for President and Mrs. Kennedy and other dignitaries at the White House.

Bumbry's tour at the end of 1962 marked her as one of America's most distinguished artists. Lasting nine exhausting weeks, it consisted of a Carnegie Hall concert debut as well as 25 performances in 21 other cities, including St. Louis, where she sang for a packed 3,000-strong house in the same auditorium in which Marian Anderson had thrilled her eight years earlier. She reveled in the first family Christmas she had enjoyed in years and also visited her alma mater, Sumner High School, where she sat in on one of Mr. Billups's classes. The sight of the mentor who had set her on the road to stardom reportedly moved her to tears.

The Day of the Diva

Since she was now part of the opera company in Basel, Switzerland, Bumbry bought a villa in nearby Lugano. Other new acquisitions included apartments in New York and California, plus a Mercedes Benz, a Jaguar, and a bright-orange Lamborghini that she used for her new hobby—auto-racing.

Nineteen sixty-three was a big year for the singer. Covent Garden audiences were introduced to Bumbry in *Don Carlos,* and Chicago's Lyric Opera featured her in *Tannhäuser.* She was also married that year to Erwin Andreas Jaeckel, a Polish-born tenor she had met in Basel. Jaeckel soon gave up his career to manage hers and was thus able to take care of her 1965 Metropolitan Opera debut.

The 1970s brought several changes. One of the most important was Bumbry's decision to concentrate on soprano roles rather than the mezzo-soprano repertoire. Her first soprano role was that of Salome, which she sang at Covent Garden in 1970. Feeling sure of her ability to handle this new challenge, she gave in to a mischievous urge and "let slip" to the press that the end of the "Dance of the Seven Veils" would show her stripped "to her jewels and her perfume." On opening night, sure enough, the jewels were much in evidence—securely attached to a flesh-colored bikini. *Salome* was an absolute sensation, as she told *Ebony* magazine in 1973. "Covent Garden had never before rented so many opera glasses. When I started dancing everything else on stage stopped and I could see the glasses going up en masse."

Salome became an enduring success, which was soon joined by other dramatic soprano roles in operas such as *Macbeth,* Vincenzo Bellini's notoriously difficult *Norma,* and, in 1975, Paul Dukas's *Ariane and Bluebeard* in a revival staged especially for her. The switch to the soprano range, it seemed, had been a perfect career move.

Jaeckel, however, still thought of his wife as a mezzo-soprano and could not accept that she had reached the decision to change her register independent of his judgment. The disagreement rankled, and along with too much togetherness, was a major factor in the couple's 1972 divorce. With Jaeckel's departure went much of the flamboyant lifestyle, including the orange Lamborghini.

Bumbry in Bloom

As the decade wore on, two other major mentors passed away. Lotte Lehmann died at age 88, and Sol Hurok, reverently eulogized by Marian Anderson, passed away at age 85. Anderson herself, the "stone-flattener" who had given Grace Bumbry her first close-up look at fame, was then still in good health. In February of 1982, then 80 years old, she was honored by Bumbry and African American soprano Shirley Verrett with a Carnegie Hall concert that took a year to arrange.

Not all events were as happy. The previous year, Bumbry had returned to the United States to sing the role of Abigaille in Beverly Sills's New York City Opera production of *Nabucco,* by Verdi. Despite acknowledgement that Abigaille is one of opera's most taxing characters, the production itself met with lukewarm reviews.

The Metropolitan Opera's 1985 production of *Porgy and Bess* was much more successful. Incredibly, this was the 50-year-old opera's first appearance at the Met, since it had previously been regarded as part of the popular, rather than the classical, musical repertoire. American composer George Gershwin had carved this niche for *Porgy and Bess;* adamant that all American productions be played by black artists rather than by white singers in blackface, he chose to unveil it on Broadway, where black singers were more readily available.

At first, feeling that the opera represented a period of history most African Americans preferred to forget, Bumbry was unenthusiastic about the project. But once tempted into accepting it, she threw herself into the work with her usual zest and resurrected Bess in a performance that ended in ten triumphant curtain calls on opening night.

The diva from St. Louis achieved an unshakable artistic maturity with the beginning of the 1990s. Along with the poise that is her longtime trademark, this trait proved invaluable during the 1990 production of French composer Hector Berlioz's *Les Troyens* that opened the brand new Bastille Opera in Paris. The opening night was an ongoing disaster of malfunctioning props, unpopular costumes, and scenery that one critic suspected was unfinished. But Bumbry, along with conductor Myung Whun Chung, was highly praised for heroically holding the performance together. Bumbry had matured into an artist capable of "flattening the stone" for less experienced colleagues to stand on.

Selected discography

Verdi, Giuseppe, *Aïda,* RCA, 1971.
Wagner, Richard, *Tannhäuser,* Philips, 1992.

Bumbry's recordings have been released by Deutsche Grammophon, Angel, London, and RCA labels and include Handel's *Messiah,* with Joan Sutherland; *Orfeo; Carmen;* and *Il trovatore,* among others.

Sources

Books

Harries, Meirion, and Susie Harries, *Opera Today,* St. Martin's Press, 1986.
International Dictionary of Opera, St. James Press, 1993.
Rosenthal, Harold, and John Warrack, *The Concise Oxford Dictionary of Opera,* 2nd edition, Oxford University Press, 1979.
Story, Rosalyn, *And So I Sing: African American Divas of Opera and Concert,* Warner Books, 1990.

Periodicals

Ebony, May 1962, p. 91; December 1973, p. 66; May 1982, p. 48.
New York Times, July 22, 1961, p. 12; July 24, 1961, p. 16; August 14, 1961, p. 28; December 10, 1967, sec. 2, p. 21; June 13, 1970, p. 22; March 3, 1974, p. 32; March 7, 1974, p. 42; August 27, 1976, p. 1; February 1, 1982, p. C13; March 20, 1990, p. C13.
Look, February 26, 1963, p. 66.
Newsweek, November 19, 1962, p. 73.
Opera, June 1970, p. 506.
Opera News, October 1981, p. 11.
Village Voice, February 26, 1985, p. 78.
Wall Street Journal, March 20, 1990, p. A12.

—*Gillian Wolf*

Ralph J. Bunche

1904-1971

Political scientist, diplomat, United Nations official

With quiet dignity and a deep-rooted commitment to world peace, the late Nobel laureate Ralph Bunche ascended the ladder of government service to become the highest ranking black and American in the United Nations (UN), an international organization of more than 150 member nations that serves to monitor political activity and mediate disputes throughout the world. Bunche is credited with having used his disarming diplomatic skills to broker peace among warring factions that many observers believed would never even negotiate with each other.

Although he began his career as a scholar, garnering a string of notable academic firsts, Bunche's principal contribution to history lies in his pacifying heated political tempers in the Middle East, the Congo, Greece, and other hot spots around the world. In his later years, Bunche was criticized by some elements of the conservative right wing in the United States, and, more scathingly, by members of the militant wing of the black civil rights movement, who charged that he was an "Uncle Tom" more interested in serving his white superiors and resolving international conflicts than in addressing the plight of blacks in his own segregated backyard. He graciously answered this criticism by pointing to his history of commitment to civil rights and, on a broader level, by arguing that

efforts made toward world peace would help the United States maintain peace at home as well.

Ralph Johnson Bunche's life was, in the eyes of many, the stuff of legend. He was born August 7, 1904, in Detroit, Michigan, the only son of Fred Bunche, an itinerant barber, and the former Olive Agnes Johnson, an amateur pianist. He was not, as has often been said, the grandson of a slave, but Bunche did grow up in a ghetto racked by poverty, a condition that he would rise above by virtue of his sharp mind.

In 1914, in the hope that dryer air and a warmer climate would improve Olive's tuberculosis, the Bunches moved to Albuquerque, New Mexico. The ride to the southwestern United States provided young Ralph's first exposure to a Jim Crow train in which blacks were relegated to the cars carrying luggage.

Disease claimed his parents' lives when he was 12, and Bunche, along with his sister, moved to Los Angeles, California, where they were taken in and reared by their maternal grandmother, Lucy Johnson. She taught the importance of self-respect, integrity, and hard work, and Bunche excelled in his studies, emerging as the class valedictorian at Jefferson against the offer, and Bunche, with the help of an athletic scholarship, enrolled instead at the University of California at Los Angeles.

Studied Colonialism, U.S. Race Relations

Studying for a degree in international relations, Bunche refined the worldview that his grandmother first had instilled in him, a perspective that was manifested in the optimism and goodwill with which he carried out his life. The *New Yorker* quoted a 1925 academic paper in which Bunche rejected the theory of philosopher Thomas Hobbes that human beings are naturally brutish, self-serving, egotistic animals. "It is true that man has these qualities in him, but I contend that these base characteristics are in part counteracted by good ones. I have a deep-set conviction that man *must* have an inherent notion of right and wrong, a fundamental moral structure and a simple sense of individual obligation, whether he be in a natural state or in society."

In 1927 Bunche graduated at the head of his class and in his commencement address urged his fellow graduates to dedicate their lives to human fellowship and peace. He earned a scholarship to pursue graduate studies at Harvard University in Massachusetts, and, lacking train fare and money for expenses, was given $1000 by a black women's social club convinced of his talent and potential. He received his master's degree in 1928 and traveled to western Africa to complete his dissertation on French colonial rule in Togoland (now Togo and Ghana) and Dahomey (now Benin). In 1934 Bunche became the first black American to receive a doctorate in political science.

Bunche helped establish the political science department at the all-black Howard University, became codirector of the Institute of Race Relations at Swarthmore College, and from 1936 to 1938, engaged in postdoctoral work in anthropology at Northwestern University, the London School of Economics, and the University of Capetown in South Africa. From 1938 to 1940, armed with an expertise in colonialism and field research, Bunche collaborated with the eminent Swedish sociologist Gunnar Myrdal on *An American Dilemma,* a monumental study of race relations and prejudice in the United States. In one incident, while trying to gather comprehensive information on black-white relations in the deep South, Bunche and Myrdal were chased through Alabama by a mob of whites angered by questions about interracial sex.

Became Leading United Nations Official

During World War II, in which he could not serve because of a sports injury, Bunche launched his career of public

High School. He worked for a time as a carpet layer, and his boss offered to send him to the prestigious Massachusetts Institute of Technology to study the chemistry of dyes. But his grandmother, wary of his being beholden to anybody, advised

Bunche reads his Nobel Peace Prize Diploma moments after receiving the award in Oslo, Norway, on December 10, 1950.

service by joining the National Defense Program's Office of the Coordinator of Information (which later became the Office of Strategic Services). As senior analyst of Africa and the Far East, he studied colonial areas of possible strategic importance to the United States. He went on to become chief of the office's Africa section and subsequently worked at the U.S. State Department, where he participated in the initial conferences that laid the groundwork for the United Nations and wrote a section of the UN charter dealing with the administration of former colonies of countries defeated in the war. In 1946 Bunche was the only African American to serve on the U.S. delegation to the first General Assembly of the United Nations, and a little more than a year later he was hired by then-UN secretary-general Trygve Lie to serve as director of the Trusteeship Department. He rose to the position of undersecretary-general—the highest U.S. official at the United Nations—and would become the valued right-hand man of Lie, as well as of future UN heads Dag Hammarskjold and U Thant.

It was at the United Nations that Bunche found the perfect fit of his commitment to world peace, his belief that the good qualities of people can triumph over the bad, and his optimism that conflict, no matter how entrenched and bitter, can be resolved. "I have a number of very strong biases," a 1972 *Ebony* article quoted Bunche as having once said. "I have a deepseated bias against hate and intolerance. I have a bias against racial and religious bigotry. I have a bias against war, a bias for peace. I have a bias which leads me to believe in the essential goodness of my fellow man, which leads me to believe that no problem in human relations is ever insoluble. And I have a strong bias in favor of the United Nations and its ability to maintain a peaceful world."

Won Nobel Peace Prize

Bunche's first major diplomatic challenge validated the hopes he had pinned on the United Nations. In 1948 Lie asked him to accompany United Nations-appointed mediator Count Folke Bernadotte of Sweden to the Middle East in an effort to peacefully resolve the Arab-Israeli conflict over the birth of a Jewish state and the partitioning of Palestine. The UN mission in the Holy Land was perilous, as the conflict touched not only on political states and geographic borders, but on fundamental and divisive religious animosities. The cars in which the UN negotiators rode were often fired on by snipers, and one of the chauffeurs driving Bunche was killed.

When Bernadotte was assassinated by Israeli terrorists in late 1948, the UN Security Council entrusted Bunche with the task of brokering a peace. Recognizing that the factions refused to sit face to face at the negotiating table, Bunche worked night and day organizing and leading small committees that discussed particular points, lest they be distracted by the enormity of the problem as a whole. Marshaling a strong personality and an objectivity that demonstrated his fairness, Bunche earned the trust of both the Israelis and the Arabs and succeeded in negotiating a truce, then an armistice, and, in 1949, the end of the conflict.

Bunche was awarded the 1950 Nobel Peace Prize, the first black to be so honored, and brought new respect to the organization that he had long championed. A UN colleague was quoted as telling the *New Yorker,* "I've known him and worked with him since 1946, and his devotion to the UN—I must say, greatly to his own cost—has been single-minded. He's usually the first into a dangerous situation and the last out. He regards life with the calm and compassion of a selfless man devoted to a great task."

While most famous for the 1949 agreement, Bunche is said to have considered his proudest accomplishment his

1956 role in directing the 6000-man UN Emergency Forces that helped sustain peace for 11 years in Egypt when the Suez crisis seemed on the brink of a catastrophic war. "For the first time we have found a way to use military men for peace instead of war," Bunche was quoted in *Time* as having said.

Bunche's most difficult assignment, by his own admission, was keeping the peace in the Congo (now Zaire) in 1960, when Belgium granted independence to the African country and pulled out, leaving a vacuum of political leadership and skilled personnel. Bunche was called in to lead a 20,000-man UN force to prevent the collision of a leaderless military and a province threatening to secede. After two months of negotiations, Bunche successfully shaped a political environment in which the fledgling country of Zaire was afforded a promising, peaceful opportunity to survive.

Because of his commitment to peace and his successes in the art of diplomacy, Bunche was offered the position of assistant secretary of state in the administration of Harry Truman, then the highest U.S. post ever offered an African American. However, Bunche declined the offer, saying, according to *Time,* "It is well known that there is Jim Crow in Washington. It is equally well known that no Negro finds Jim Crow congenial. I am a Negro."

Criticized by Militant Blacks *and* Right Wing Conservatives

Ironically, Bunche was accused by some factions of trying to escape his race. As many whites proclaimed Bunche the quintessential successful black man, some militant civil rights activists charged that, in trotting around the globe to foster world peace, he had turned his back on the bitter struggle blacks were waging for equality in a segregated United States. But Bunche, who understood the personal and cultural impact of bigotry, answered that he had not only studied prejudice against blacks; more importantly, he had lived it. He walked his first picket for the National Association for the Advancement of Colored People (NAACP) in 1937, demonstrated with Dr. Martin Luther King, Jr. at the Lincoln Memorial in Washington in 1963, and took part in the civil rights marches on Selma and Montgomery, Alabama, two years later.

Furthermore, Bunche argued during the Vietnam War that if the United States were serious about combating and eliminating racism, the government would take the funds and energy it was investing in Southeast Asia and channel them into a domestic war against the black ghettos. As a citizen of the world, he also saw for the troubled United States an educational example in the way former European colonies in Africa were beginning to stand on their own two feet. "They sit in the international councils on an equal basis with their former mother countries and rulers," he noted in *Newsweek.* "I have come to believe that what is good for the world is good for my country."

A more predictable source of criticism was the far right. For instance, the *National Review,* a conservative mouthpiece, editorialized in 1962 that Bunche was an unapologetic Marxist [advocate of the social and economic doctrine of nineteenth-century German intellectual Karl Marx, centering on the establishment of a classless society and common ownership of production] and had told "bald lies" concerning the United Nations' involvement in the Congo. "It had

---

> "I have come to believe that what is good for the world is good for my country."

---

been our intention to leave Dr. Bunche alone, having dismissed him as, essentially, a UN mercenary, a man with an undistinguished mind and rather bad personal manners," the magazine said. "It becomes necessary under the circumstances . . . to go on just a little bit further, and say that Mr. Bunche's judgment is very poor indeed, and that this should be kept in mind in evaluating his assessments of the tangled affairs of our disintegrating world."

Bunche, whom President Lyndon Johnson had beseeched not to resign from the UN in 1966, remained undersecretary-general until just before his death in 1971. He always maintained that his diplomatic successes were a testimony to the vision behind the United Nations and argued that persisting, seemingly insoluble crises, such as that in the Middle East, would be more productively addressed by negotiation rather than by war.

Echoing the thoughts of many world leaders, former British UN ambassador Lord Caradon was quoted as saying in *Newsweek,* "Of all the people I have worked with in my life, there is no one I respect more. He has always been my great hero. He represents everything I admire in international affairs and public life. Of all his great qualities—and he had so many—the one that I would choose is that of determined optimism. Never did he give up. Never did he despair. He is certainly one the great Americans."

Selected writings

A World View of Race, Association of Negro Folk Education, 1936.
Peace and the United Nations, Leeds University, 1952.

The Political Status of the Negro in the Age of FDR (interviews), University of Chicago Press, 1973.

An African American in South Africa: The Travel Notes of Ralph J. Bunche, 28 September 1937-1 January 1938, edited by Robert R. Edgar, Swallow, 1992.

Sources

Books

Cornell, Jean G., *Ralph Bunche: Champion of Peace,* Garrard, 1976.

Jakoubek, Robert, *Ralph Bunche,* Chelsea House, 1989.

Kugelmass, J. Alvin, *Ralph J. Bunche: Fighter for Peace,* Messner, 1962.

Mann, Peggy, *Ralph Bunche: UN Peacemaker,* Coward, McCann & Geoghegan, 1975.

Periodicals

Christian Century, December 29, 1971.

Ebony, February 1972; September 1992.

Holiday, April 1970.

Nation, December 17, 1971.

National Review, May 22, 1962.

Newsweek, October 11, 1971; December 20, 1971.

New Yorker, January 1, 1972.

New York Times, December 10, 1971.

Time, December 20, 1971.

—*Isaac Rosen*

Stokely Carmichael

1941—

Activist, lecturer, author

"Flailing at the white society he condemns, the young man galvanizes his audience with the strident call for 'Black Power.'" Such was the sensational portrait of Stokely Carmichael offered by *Life* magazine in the late 1960s. Considerable emphasis was placed on Carmichael's "stridency," and the fear of this incendiary speaker, organizer, and author was palpable in much mainstream rhetoric about him. Over many years of organizing and activism, Carmichael moved from the peaceful integrationist doctrine of the civil rights marchers to a more radical pro-revolutionary position, eventually inspiring so much hatred from U.S. institutions that he opted for self-imposed exile in Guinea, West Africa. And decades after his first inflammatory speeches, he demonstrated only a deepened commitment to revolutionary politics.

After the dovish sermons and speeches of the Reverend Martin Luther King, Jr., whites were unprepared for the uncompromising demands of black militants such as the Black Panthers and the All Afrikan People's Revolutionary Party, and Carmichael was an important figure in both organizations. Carmichael himself has been credited for the "Black Power" slogan, which frightened whites and turned off even activists like King. Fellow militant Eldridge Cleaver quoted

Carmichael's strategy: "The civil rights movement was good because it demanded that blacks be admitted into the system. Now we must move beyond the stage of demanding entry, to the new stage of changing the system itself." "Black Power," wrote James Haskins in 1972's *Profiles in Black Power,* "has become the philosophy of the black revolution, and because of that Stokely Carmichael is assured a place in history."

Carmichael was born in Port-of-Spain, Trinidad, in 1941. His carpenter father, Adolphus, moved with Stokely's mother, Mabel, to the United States when their son was two years old, leaving him in the care of two aunts and a grandmother. Adolphus—who had been swept up by the cause of Trinidadian independence but left his homeland to better his family's economic fortunes—moonlighted as a cab driver, while Mabel found work as a maid. Stokely attended Tranquility Boys School, learning, he would recall angrily years later, the mentality of the colonized. "I remember that when I was a boy," he wrote in "What We Want," which originally appeared in a 1967 issue of the *New York Review of Books* and was later reprinted in *Chronicles of Black Protest,* "I used to go to see Tarzan movies on Saturday. White Tarzan used to beat up the black natives. I would sit there yelling, 'Kill the beasts, kill the savages, kill

At a Glance. . .

Born June 29, 1941, in Port-of-Spain, Trinidad; immigrated to U.S., 1952; immigrated to Guinea, 1969; son of Adolphus (a carpenter) and Mabel (also known as Mae Charles) Carmichael; married singer Miriam Makeba, 1968 (divorced). *Education:* Howard University, B.A., 1964.

Civil rights activist and organizer; organizer with Student Nonviolent Coordinating Committee (SNCC, also known as Student National Coordinating Committee), Atlanta, GA, 1964-66, chairman, 1966-67; director of civil rights activities, Mississippi Summer Project, 1964; organizer for All Afrikan People's Revolutionary Party; honorary prime minister of Black Panther party, 1967-69; began self-imposed exile in Conakry, Guinea, 1969, and changed name to Kwame Ture; lecturer and author. Member of "Agenda for Black Power" panel sponsored by Knopf Publishing Group, 1993.

Awards: Honorary LL.D. from Shaw University.

Addresses: *Home*—Conakry, Guinea. *Publisher*—Random House, Inc., 201 East 50th St., New York, NY 10022.

'em!' I was saying: Kill me. It was as if a Jewish boy watched Nazis taking Jews off to concentration camps and cheered them on." Carmichael joined his parents in New York City's Harlem when he was 11, later attending the Bronx High School of Science after his parents moved to the Bronx. He had been the only black member of a street gang called the Morris Park Dukes but settled down after discovering the lure of intellectual life. His status as a foreigner and self-described "hip" demeanor assured him of popularity among many of his liberal, affluent white schoolmates, he said in an interview with *Life;* he dated white girls and attended parties on swank Park Avenue.

Carmichael was interested in politics even then, especially the work of black socialist Bayard Rustin, whom he heard speak many times. "Bayard played a crucial role in my life," Carmichael told *Fire in the Streets* author Milton Viorst. "He was one of the first people I had direct contact with that I could really say, 'That's what I want to be.' He was so at ease with all the problems. I mean, he was like Superman, hooking socialism up with the black movement, organizing blacks." At one time Carmichael volunteered to help his mentor organize

black workers in a paint factory. But the friendliness—doctrinal and otherwise—of Rustin and other black intellectual leftists with the white liberal establishment would eventually alienate Carmichael.

Joined Civil Rights Movement

Before beginning college, Carmichael had become aware of the flowering of the civil rights movement in the South and the injustice experienced by blacks and others who challenged segregation. "Suddenly I was burning," he told *Life's* Gordon Parks. Soon he joined antidiscrimination pickets in New York and sit-ins in Virginia and South Carolina. He began his studies at Howard University in Washington, D.C., in 1960. "Several white schools offered me scholarships," he informed Parks, "but Howard seemed "a natural. It was black. I could keep in touch with the movement there."

While at Howard, Carmichael met members of the Student Nonviolent Coordinating Committee (SNCC; often pronounced "snick"), an Atlanta-based organization that received funds from the Southern Christian Leadership Conference (SCLC). During his freshman year he participated in the first of the famous "Freedom Rides" sponsored by the Congress of Racial Equality, traveling south and getting beaten and arrested in Jackson, Mississippi, for his activism. It was the first of many incarcerations in the career of a confrontational activist.

In 1964 Carmichael graduated from Howard with a bachelor's degree in philosophy, but he intended to stay very much involved in the civil rights movement. That summer saw six civil rights workers murdered in the South, in addition to many arrests, beatings, and other indignities and harassment. Carmichael soon became an organizer for SNCC and participated in the group's drive to register black voters—the first of these well-publicized efforts—in Lowndes County, Alabama. SNCC helped start the Lowndes County Freedom Association, a political party that chose a black panther as its symbol to fulfill a state requirement that all parties have visual symbols to assist voters. The panther was indigenous to Alabama and seemed both a dignified symbol for empowered blacks and an effective response to the white rooster that symbolized the Alabama Democratic party. In his book *Freedom Bound,* historian Robert Weisbrot related that Carmichael and other SNCC activists, despite their differences with the SCLC and Martin Luther King's resolute nonviolence, continued to associate themselves with King because older black Alabamans regarded the Reverend, in Carmichael's own words, "like a God."

Standing atop an automobile, Carmichael stokes the crowd with his fiery visions of "Black Power" during a rally at Florida A & M University.

Turning From Nonviolence

A turning point in Carmichael's experience came, however, as he watched from his locked hotel room, while outside, black demonstrators were beaten and shocked with cattle prods by police. The horrified Carmichael began to scream and could not stop. As Carmichael's activism deepened, however, and as he saw the violence doled out to violent and nonviolent resisters alike, he began to distance himself from King's tactics. In 1965 he replaced the moderate John Lewis as head of SNCC and began to trumpet the message of "Black Power." White members of the group were not encouraged to stay, and Carmichael and other SNCC leaders began to talk about "revolution."

Carmichael's articulation of "Black Power," evidenced by his 1967 book of that title (co-written with Charles V. Hamilton), and his article "What We Want," advanced the idea that mere integration was not the answer to American racism, and that America formed only a piece in the puzzle.

Carmichael and Hamilton linked the struggle for African-American empowerment definitively to economic self-determination domestically and the end of imperialism and colonialism worldwide. "What We Want" described the need for black communal control of black resources—"Ultimately, the economic foundations of this country must be shaken if black people are to control their lives"—but also delved into the crippling psychological effects of racism. "From birth," Carmichael wrote, "black people are told a set of lies about themselves," concluding, "We are oppressed not because we are lazy, not because we're stupid (and got good rhythm); but because we're black."

The term "Black Power," however disconcerting to moderate black leaders, absolutely terrified mainstream whites; it was not interpreted to mean "empowerment" but rather black domination and possibly even race war. Journalists demanded repeatedly that Carmichael define the phrase, and the activist soon came to believe that no matter what his explanation, they would continue to make it sound sinister. *Life's* Parks, a black journalist, pressed Carmichael and received a somewhat exasperated reply: "*For the last time,* Black Power means black people coming together to form a political force and either electing representatives or forcing their representatives to speak their needs," rather than relying on the established parties. "Black Power doesn't mean anti-white, violence, separatism or any other racist things the press says it means. It's saying, 'Look, buddy, we're not laying a vote on you unless you lay so many schools, hospitals, playgrounds and jobs on us." Nonetheless, as Haskins recorded in *Profiles in Black Power,* Carmichael gave the term a different spin when he spoke to black audiences: "When you talk of 'black power,' you talk of building a movement that will smash everything Western civilization has created."

International Focus

As the revolutionary fervor of the 1960s deepened, SNCC became a "Black Power" vehicle, more or less replacing the hymn-singing integrationism of earlier days. Yet Carmichael had gone as far as he could with the organization, deciding not to run for reelection as its leader in 1967, just before SNCC fell apart. Carmichael's political emphasis had shifted as well; he began speaking out not only against the war in Vietnam but against what he called U.S. imperialism worldwide. *Time* reported with supreme disdain that Carmichael had traveled the world denouncing his adopted country, speaking to cheering throngs in Cuba, and declaring, "We do not want peace in Vietnam. We want the Vietnamese people to defeat the United States." The magazine called him a purveyor of "negritude and nihilism" and noted that many U.S. politicians wanted to jail him for sedition on his return to the country he called "hell."

When he did return, in 1968, U.S. marshals confiscated Carmichael's passport. Meanwhile, the radical Oakland, California-based Black Panther party made him honorary prime minister; he would resign from the position the following year, rejecting Panther coalitions with white activists. He based himself in Washington, D.C., and continued to speak around the country. In March of 1968 he announced his engagement to South African singer-activist Miriam Makeba; they were wed two months later. The Tanzanian ambassador to the United States hosted their reception. Carmichael and Makeba were permitted to honeymoon abroad after they agreed not to visit any "forbidden" countries; even so, many nations refused them entrance. In 1969 Carmichael left the U.S. for Conakry, Republic of Guinea, in West Africa. He moved

there in part to assist in the restoration to power of the deposed Ghanaian ruler Kwame Nkrumah, who lived in Guinea and served as an exponent of the sort of anti-imperialist, pan-African empowerment Carmichael had espoused in the United States.

While in Guinea, Carmichael took the name Kwame Ture. Over the ensuing decades he solidified his commitment to revolution as the answer to racism and injustice. In 1993, speaking at Michigan State University, he made it clear that he still considered capitalism the source of most of the problems he had been studying during his career as an activist. "Those who labor do not enjoy the fruits of their labor," he said, as quoted in the *Michigan Chronicle.* "We

> ### "From birth, black people are told a set of lies about themselves. We are oppressed not because we are lazy, not because we're stupid, but because we're black."

know that to be slavery." But Carmichael's 1992 afterword to a new edition of *Black Power* showed that he felt real progress had been made in certain respects in the U.S.— "From 1965 to 1992, no one could deny that change has occurred," he acknowledged in the *Chronicle*—and that a "coalition of oppressed minorities plus poor whites represents the real force for change. The 1992 Los Angeles rebellion [civil unrest following the acquittal by a white jury of the four police officers who had been videotaped beating black motorist Rodney King] reflects this reality; other oppressed nationalities joined the rebellion in mass character." He told the crowd at Michigan State that the riots "were good for us." He insisted in his conclusion to the *Black Power* afterword that "mass political organization on a Pan African scale is the only solution. Thus, Black Power can only be realized when there exists a unified socialist Africa."

Steeped in the civil rights struggle, Stokely Carmichael emerged as one of the firebrands of the black militant movement of the 1960s, and unlike many of his compatriots from that time, he has in the intervening years experienced neither burnout nor conversion; the years have only refined the flame of his convictions. "Since we shed blood continually and sporadically and in a disorganized manner for reforms," he insisted in his 1992 afterword to *Black Power,* "let us permanently organize ourselves and make Revolution."

Selected writings

(With Charles V. Hamilton) *Black Power: The Politics of Liberation in America,* Random House, 1967, revised edition, 1992.

"What We Want," in *Chronicles of Black Protest,* edited by Bradford Chambers, New American Library, 1968.

Stokely Speaks: Black Power Back to Pan-Africanism, Random House, 1971.

Sources

Books

Eldridge Cleaver: Post-Prison Writings and Speeches, edited by Robert Scheer, Random House, 1969.

Haskins, James, *Profiles in Black Power,* Doubleday, 1972.

Johnson, Jacqueline, *Stokely Carmichael: The Story of Black Power,* Silver Burdett Press/Simon & Schuster, 1990.

Viorst, Milton, *Fire in the Streets: America in the 1960s,* Simon & Schuster, 1979.

Weisbrot, Robert, *Freedom Bound: A History of America's Civil Rights Movement,* Norton, 1990.

Periodicals

Life, May 19, 1967, pp. 76-80.

Michigan Chronicle, February 24, 1993, p. 1.

New York Times, August 5, 1966.

Time, December 15, 1967, p. 28.

—*Simon Glickman*

Kenneth B. Clark

1914—

Psychologist, educator, writer

Kenneth Bancroft Clark is among the most prominent black social scientists of the twentieth century. For many years a professor of psychology at City College of New York (now City College of the City University of New York), Clark achieved national recognition when his work was cited by the U.S. Supreme Court in its 1954 ruling that racially segregated schools were inherently unequal and therefore unconstitutional. That decision was a catalyst for the civil rights movement of the 1960s, and Clark went on to author a series of highly influential books about ghetto life, education, and the war on poverty. After retiring from teaching in 1975, Clark established a consulting firm to assist corporations and other large employers with their racial policies and minority hiring programs.

Clark was born in 1914 in the Panama Canal Zone, the son of Miriam Clark and Arthur Bancroft Clark, a native of the West Indies who worked as a superintendent of cargo for the United Fruit Company. Despite the family's relatively comfortable situation in Panama, Miriam Clark, a Jamaican woman of stubborn courage, insisted that the Clark children should be raised in the United States, where they would get better education and employment opportunities than in Panama. Kenneth and his sister, Beulah, accordingly moved with their mother to the Harlem district of New York City when Kenneth was four and a half; their father, however, refused to relocate to a country where his color would prevent him from holding a job similar to his position with United Fruit. Undeterred, Miriam Clark found work in Harlem as a seamstress and proceeded to raise the children on her own.

In later life, Clark became famous as an uncompromising advocate of integrated schooling, and it is not surprising that his own education took place in the culturally diverse setting of 1920s Harlem. At that time Harlem was home to immigrants of various nationalities, especially those of Irish and Jewish origin, and was also the center of a rapidly growing black population.

Attending classes in New York City schools, young Clark was held to the same high standards as his fellow students, most of whom were white. As he told *New Yorker* magazine many years later, "When I went to the board in Mr. Ruprecht's algebra class, . . . I had to do those equations, and if I wasn't able to do them he wanted to find out why. He didn't expect any less of me because I was black." That is a capsule description of the educational philosophy Clark would maintain for the rest of his life: schools must be open to students of

At a Glance...

Born Kenneth Bancroft Clark, July 24, 1914, in Panama Canal Zone; son of Arthur Bancroft (a cargo superintendent for United Fruit) and Miriam (a seamstress; maiden name, Hanson) Clark; married Mamie Phipps (a psychologist), April 14, 1938 (died, 1983); children: Kate Miriam, Hilton Bancroft. *Education:* Howard University, B.A., 1935, M.S., 1936; Columbia University, Ph.D., 1940. *Religion:* Episcopalian.

Howard University, Washington, D.C., psychology instructor, 1936; Hampton Institute, Hampton, VA, psychology instructor, 1940; worked for U.S. Office of War Information, 1941-42; City College of New York (now City College of the City University of New York), instructor, 1942-49, assistant professor, 1949-1960, professor, 1960-70, distinguished professor of psychology, 1970-75, professor emeritus, 1975—; chairman of board of directors, Harlem Youth Opportunities Unlimited (HARYOU), 1962-64; president, Metropolitan Applied Research Center, Inc. (MARC Corp.), 1967-75; president and chairman of the board, Clark, Phipps, Clark & Harris, Inc. (consulting firm), beginning 1975.

Awards: Rosenwald fellow, 1940-41; Spingarn Medal, National Association for the Advancement of Colored People, 1961; Franklin Delano Roosevelt Four Freedoms Award, Franklin and Eleanor Roosevelt Institute, 1985. Honorary degrees from Columbia University, Johns Hopkins University, Princeton University, and others.

Addresses: *Publisher*—University Press of New England, 17 Lebanon St., Hanover, NH 03755.

every race, and teachers must expect the same performance from each child. In such an environment, some students will naturally perform better than others, but not according to racial categories.

Educational Experience Sparked Interest in Psychology

When he finished the ninth grade, Kenneth Clark was faced with a critical juncture in his education. School counselors advised most black youths to attend vocational

high school, where they could learn skills appropriate to the limited employment opportunities available to blacks. When Clark's mother heard of this plan she went directly to the counselor's office and told him that under no circumstances would her son go to trade school; she had not come all the way from Panama to raise a factory worker.

Instead, Kenneth was sent to George Washington High School, where he excelled in all subjects and grew especially fond of economics. He had thoughts of becoming an economist until he was denied an award for excellence in economics by a teacher who apparently could not bring himself to so honor a black student. Clark remembers this as his first direct experience of discrimination, and it may well have prepared the ground for his subsequent decision to study psychology, particularly the psychology of racism.

Upon entering Howard University in 1931, Clark originally intended to become a medical doctor. In his second year at the all-black institution he took a class in psychology taught by Francis Sumner that changed forever the course of his studies. "What this professor showed me," Clark told the *New Yorker,* "was the promise of getting some systematic understanding of the complexities of human behavior and human interaction, . . . the seemingly intractable nature of racism, for example." Clark determined that he would follow the example of Sumner in the field of psychology, and after receiving a master's degree in 1936, he joined the faculty of Howard for a year of teaching.

At that point Clark came to another critical fork in his career. He could have remained at Howard, teaching with either his master's degree or a doctorate, but at the urging of his mentor Sumner and a number of other outstanding faculty members, Clark went on to Columbia University with the express purpose of obtaining his doctorate and teaching at an integrated college. He became the first black doctoral candidate in psychology at Columbia and completed his degree in 1940.

Brown v. Board of Education

Clark was married in 1938 to Mamie Phipps, a fellow psychology student at Howard who would coauthor many of the articles that later made the couple famous. After graduating from Columbia, Clark taught briefly at Hampton Institute in Virginia, a very traditional black college whose most famous alumnus was Booker T. Washington. Hampton was far too conservative a school for Clark, who left after one term rather than teach a form of psychology based on the subjugation of blacks. Following a two-year stint with the U.S. Government's Office of War Information, Clark joined the faculty of City College of New York in 1942, becoming an assistant professor seven years later and, by 1960, a full professor—the first black academic to be so honored in the history of New York's city colleges.

As a black psychologist, Clark had always been deeply concerned with the nature of racism, and in the 1940s he and his wife, Mamie, began publishing the results of their research concerning the effects of segregated schooling on kindergarten students in Washington, D.C. Between 1939 and 1950 the Clarks wrote five articles on the subject and became nationally known for their work in the field.

In 1950 Kenneth Clark wrote an article for the Midcentury White House Conference on Children and Youth, summarizing his own work and other psychological literature on segregation. This report came to the attention of the National Association for the Advancement of Colored People (NAACP) during its post-World War II campaign to overturn legalized segregation. In its landmark 1954 decision declaring such segregation unconstitutional, the U.S. Supreme Court cited the Clark report as representative of "modern authority" on the subject.

Clark was intimately involved in the long legal struggle which culminated in *Brown v. Board of Education,* as the court's 1954 desegregation decision was titled. He testified as an expert witness at three of the four cases leading up to the Supreme Court's review of *Brown,* and his report on the psychology of segregation was read carefully by the justices. Psychological findings were critical to the NAACP's case, in which they asked the court to overturn its earlier decision (*Plessy v. Ferguson,* 1896) that "separate but equal" schooling for the two races did not violate individual rights under the Constitution.

In *Plessy v. Ferguson,* the court had held that as long as separate schools were of equal quality, they did not inherently "deny . . . the equal protection of the laws" guaranteed by the Fourteenth Amendment. The NAACP challenged the Plessy decision by asserting that, in reality, separate meant unequal for blacks—especially black schoolchildren. In his testimony before one of the lower courts, Clark defined the harmful effects of segregated schooling as "a confusion in the child's own self esteem—basic feelings of inferiority, conflict, confusion in his self-image, resentment, hostility toward himself." Such effects would be felt, Clark and the NAACP argued, regardless of the relative merits of the schools involved; or, as the court eventually stated, "Separate educational facilities are inherently unequal."

Brown v. Board of Education was not only a milestone in the modern civil rights movement, it also made Kenneth Clark into something of an academic superstar. Clark went on to become the most influential black social scientist of his generation. He received honorary degrees from more than a dozen of the nation's finest colleges and universities, but his larger goal of integrated, adequate schooling for blacks had not become a reality even four decades after the announcement of the monumental court decision.

Dark Ghetto: The Frustrations of Kenneth Clark

America's schools did not suddenly integrate themselves the day after *Brown v. Board of Education;* in most urban areas the growth of black ghettoes only reinforced the segregation of black and white schoolchildren. Clark understood that in order to improve the education of students of color, the African American community as a whole needed to lobby for a massive infusion of capital and commitment from the federal government and from private citizens. After sparring unsuccessfully with the New York City Board of Education during the late 1950s over issues of segregation, Clark was given a unique opportunity to effect a wholesale reformation of the school system in

> "We have not yet made education a process whereby students are taught to respect the inalienable dignity of other human beings."

Harlem. As part of the "Great Society" plans inaugurated by the administrations of President John F. Kennedy and his successor, Lyndon B. Johnson, federal funds were provided in 1962 to create Harlem Youth Opportunities Unlimited (HARYOU), the task of which was to study and suggest remedies for the causes of juvenile delinquency in the Harlem area.

Clark was appointed chairman of HARYOU, which over the next two years produced a 620-page report recommending, among other things, the "thorough reorganization of the schools" in Harlem. This would include increased integration, a massive program to improve reading skills among students, stricter review of teacher performance, and, most importantly, a high level of participation by the residents of Harlem in implementing these changes. HARYOU was the first example of what would later be known as a community-action program.

HARYOU was sabotaged by political power bargaining in New York, and few if any of its recommendations were followed. As Clark commented in the *New Yorker,* "As it turned out, all we did at HARYOU was to produce a document." Clark's community-based approach inspired many subsequent programs in the "War on Poverty," but with few exceptions they too fell victim to the complexities of urban politics. Although his experience with HARYOU must be counted as a failure in terms of political reality, it did spur Clark to write the book for which he is best known, *Dark Ghetto: Dilemmas of Social Power.* In this work, Clark goes beyond his HARYOU research to write what he describes in the introduction as "no report at all, but rather the anguished cry of its author"—an overview of black ghetto life that has become required reading in sociology classes around the country.

In 1967 Clark formed and presided over a nonprofit corporation known as MARC Corp. (the Metropolitan Applied Research Center), composed of a group of social scientists and other professionals who hoped to identify and solve problems of the urban poor. MARC's most significant work was undertaken in 1970, when the school board of Washington, D.C., asked Clark and his associates to design a new educational program for the city's 150,000 schoolchildren, 90% of whom were black and the majority of whom were poor.

In an era of radical social and political experimentation, the Washington, D.C. school system offered Clark the chance to test his theories of education on a large scale and under ideal conditions. Clark outlined a program similar to the HARYOU program for New York, calling for a massive and immediate upgrading of reading skills, teacher evaluation based on student performance, and community involvement in the schooling process.

Once again, however, real life proved far more complex than theory: the Washington, D.C. teachers refused to make their pay and position dependent on the outcome of student tests, and a new superintendent of schools (elected in 1971) refused to cooperate with the plan and even challenged Clark's central thesis that children of the ghetto could and should be expected to perform at "normal" levels. Ghetto life, argued this administrator, was anything but normal, and it would be unfair to hold teachers and schools responsible for the performance of students handicapped by living in the ghetto.

Continued to Argue for Integration in Education

Such a claim flew in the face of everything Kenneth Clark had learned and fought for since he was a grade school student. It also contradicted the findings of *Brown v. Board of Education:* if ghetto children could not be held to the same standards as other children, then the schools they were attending were obviously *not* "equal." Clark's defeat at the hands of political reality did not dampen his belief in integrated schooling, however; nor did he cave in to the demands of the politically fashionable black separatist movement in the late 1960s and early 1970s. He opposed

the creation of any organization based on racial exclusivity, including such projects as a black dormitory at the University of Chicago and Antioch College's Afro American Institute. As a result, Clark was attacked as a "moderate" at a time of black radicalism, in some instances receiving personal threats for his adamant rejection of racial separatism.

After his retirement from City College in 1975, Clark and his wife and children founded a consulting firm called Clark, Phipps, Clark & Harris, Inc., helping large corporations design and implement minority hiring programs. The firm flourished, attracting prestigious clients such as AT&T, Chemical Bank, and Consolidated Edison, and Clark remained active in the burgeoning field of minority concerns in the 1990s workplace.

Back in 1982, Clark admitted in the *New Yorker* that the educational outlook was poor for children of color. "Things are worse. In the schools . . . more black kids are being put on the dung heap every year." His wife, Mamie, was even more frank, stating: "More people are without hope now. . . . I really don't know what the answer is." Viewing this discouraging prospect eight years later, Clark admitted that even he was beginning to doubt the possibility of racial harmony through integration. "I look back and I shudder," he told the *Washington Post,* "and say, 'Oh God, you really were as naive as some people said you were.'"

With the commitment of U.S. president Bill Clinton's administration to equalize opportunities for all Americans, Clark continued to voice his outrage over the country's lack of educational progress—in academic, social, and psychological terms—but offered a mandate for change in the nineties. In a 1993 essay for *Newsweek* titled "Unfinished Business: The Toll of Psychic Violence," Clark commented: "We have not yet made education a process whereby students are taught to respect the inalienable dignity of other human beings. . . . [But] social sensitivity can be internalized as a genuine component of being educated. This is nonviolence in its truest sense. By encouraging and rewarding empathetic behavior in all of our children—both minority and majority youth—we will be protecting them from ignorance and cruelty. We will be helping them to understand the commonality of being human. We will be *educating* them."

Selected writings

Prejudice and Your Child, Beacon Press, 1955, reprinted, University Press of New England, 1988.
(With Lawrence Plotkin) *The Negro Student at Integrated Colleges,* National Scholarship Service and Fund for Negro Students, 1963.
The Negro Protest: James Baldwin, Malcolm X, Martin Luther King Talk with Kenneth B. Clark, Beacon

Press, 1963, published as *King, Malcolm, Baldwin: Three Interviews,* University Press of New England, 1985.

Dark Ghetto: Dilemmas of Social Power, Harper, 1965, reprinted, University Press of New England, 1989.

Social and Economic Implications of Integration in the Public Schools, U.S. Department of Labor, 1965.

(Editor with Talcott Parsons) *The Negro American,* Houghton, 1966.

(With Jeannette Hopkins) *A Relevant War Against Poverty: A Study of Community Action Programs and Observable Change,* Harper, 1969.

(With Harold Howe) *Racism and American Education: A Dialogue and Agenda for Action,* Harper, 1970.

(Editor with Meyer Weinberg) *W. E. B. Du Bois: A Reader,* Harper, 1970.

Pathos of Power, Harper, 1974.

Author, with wife, Mamie Phipps, of a series of articles on the effects of school segregation. Also author of numerous articles published in journals of psychology and sociology.

Sources

Books

Clark, Kenneth B., *Dark Ghetto: Dilemmas of Social Power,* Harper, 1965.

Clark, Kenneth B., *Pathos of Power,* Harper, 1974.

Periodicals

Commentary, November 1971.

New Yorker, August 23, 1982.

Newsweek, January 11, 1993.

Washington Post, March 4, 1990.

—Jonathan Martin

Eldridge Cleaver

1935—

Political activist, author

"As the charismatic Information Minister of the Black Panther Party, Eldridge Cleaver was one of the most dazzling and controversial fixtures of the '60s," judged an *Ebony* magazine contributor. "For more than a decade, the Arkansas-born writer-activist mesmerized audiences with his calls for revolutionary violence against the agents of racism, capitalism and Christianity." Cleaver was an early leader of the Black Panthers, a political union of disenchanted African Americans that eventually attracted nationwide membership. From the pages of his bestselling book *Soul on Ice* as well as from public platforms, Cleaver urged blacks and whites alike to oppose repression, police brutality, and unequal economic opportunity. To racist whites, Cleaver represented a clear threat: he eloquently advocated extreme measures to assure the overthrow of a society that discriminated against minorities.

Cleaver told *People* magazine that during the late 1960s he felt "there was no hope of effecting real freedom within the capitalistic system. I was the guy who demanded we go down shooting." Cleaver's rhetoric caught up with him in 1968 after a gun battle between the Black Panthers and the San Francisco police. Fleeing a federal warrant for his arrest, he took refuge in Cuba, Algeria, and later Paris in an exile that lasted almost a decade. The first-hand experience of life in communist nations dramatically transformed Cleaver's thinking on his American homeland. Since his return to the United States in 1976, he has pursued a more conventional political agenda. "During the eight years that I was absent from the United States, I underwent a change in my whole philosophy based on my observations," Cleaver told *Ebony*. "I stopped being a communist or socialist and developed an understanding and respect for free enterprise and the democratic political system. . . . I found the systems of dictatorships and communism to be absolutely unacceptable. Living in those countries put an end to my advocacy of communism."

Eldridge Cleaver was born in 1935 in Wabbaseka, a small Arkansas town near Little Rock. His father, Leroy, worked as a waiter and entertainer in a Little Rock nightclub, and his mother taught elementary school. While Cleaver was still young, his family moved to Phoenix, Arizona, because Leroy Cleaver had gotten a job in the dining car of the Super Chief, a train running between Chicago and Los Angeles. Eventually the Cleavers moved on to the Watts neighborhood of Los Angeles. There Cleaver's parents separated, and his mother

At a Glance...

Born Leroy Eldridge Cleaver, August 3, 1935, in Wabbaseka, AR; son of Leroy (a dining car waiter) and Thelma (a teacher and janitor) Cleaver; married Kathleen Neal (a law professor), December 1967 (divorced, 1987); children: Maceo (son), Joju (daughter). *Education:* Attended junior college; also educated in Soledad Prison.

Ramparts (magazine), assistant editor and contributing writer, 1966-68; Black Panther Party, Oakland, CA, minister of information, 1967-71; U.S. presidential candidate, Peace and Freedom Party, 1968; lived in exile in Algeria, Cuba, and Paris, 1968-76; returned to United States, 1976. Writer, 1966—; public speaker, 1976—; political activist based in California. Men's clothing designer and marketer, 1978; artist and owner of a recycling business in Berkeley, CA, 1988—.

Selected awards: Martin Luther King Memorial Prize, 1970, for *Soul on Ice.*

Addresses: c/o Bantam/Doubleday/Dell, 666 5th Ave., New York, NY 10103.

supported the children by serving as a janitor at a junior high school.

Cleaver's first brush with the law came just as he entered junior high. After a conviction on bicycle theft, he was sent to a California reform school. Released in 1953, he was arrested again for selling marijuana. This time he was remanded to the Preston School of Industry for a year. At the end of his sentence, he was arrested yet again for selling marijuana and was sent to the California State Prison at Soledad. Cleaver spent the lion's share of his teen years behind bars in one institution or another. He earned his high school degree at Soledad and read widely, including the works of such authors as Thomas Paine, Karl Marx, Richard Wright, and W. E. B. Du Bois.

The Rage of a Convict

In *Soul on Ice*, Cleaver writes that a youth spent in prison filled him with rage. Upon his release from Soledad, he began selling marijuana again and then engaged in increasingly violent acts. Once again the law caught up with Cleaver, and he was convicted of assault with intent to murder and remanded to San Quentin and Folsom prisons.

Further incarceration gave Cleaver an opportunity to examine his life and to seek the source of his rage and despair. In an effort to understand himself and his society, he began to write essays and snatches of autobiography. He became a disciple of the Black Muslim movement founded by Elijah Muhammad and was moved by the fiery speeches of Malcolm X. Attempts to win converts to the faith among his fellow convicts were punished by long stints in solitary confinement. Cleaver used these periods of isolation to write and to study the Bible, the only book he was allowed to take with him.

Cleaver spent eight years in prison before he became eligible for parole in 1965. In an effort to secure his freedom, he wrote to civil liberties lawyer Beverly Axelrod in San Francisco. Axelrod took his case and showed his manuscripts to left-wing writer Edward M. Keating. Keating published a Cleaver essay, "Notes on a Native Son," in *Ramparts* magazine and promised Cleaver a job at the magazine should he receive parole. Subsequent Cleaver essays in *Ramparts* attracted the support of Maxwell Geismar, Norman Mailer, and other influential writers. Cleaver was granted parole in November of 1966.

The Black Panther Party

Eldridge Cleaver literally leaped from confinement in a tough, maximum-security prison to a high-profile life among West Coast intellectuals and African American community leaders. He served as an editor and contributor to *Ramparts* and, in his spare time, helped to start Black House, a San Francisco cultural center for African American youth. At Black House in the early months of 1967, Cleaver met Huey Newton and Bobby Seale, the founders of the Black Panther Party. From a base in neighboring Oakland, the Black Panther Party offered urban blacks the possibility of aggressive self-defense and self-determination. A chief concern of the Panthers was police brutality. Members would follow law officers through the ghetto to guard against the use of undue force or the false arrest of black citizens. As a paroled felon, Cleaver ran a great risk by becoming involved with the Panthers, but his zeal for the cause outweighed his caution.

Cleaver was named minister of information for the Black Panther Party. As a top Panther official, he made speeches and sought new members for the growing organization. Within a year the group had attracted followers in most major American cities, and the black leather-clad Panthers became symbolic of a new, vocal menace to white supremacy. Tensions mounted as the Federal Bureau of Investigation (FBI) and local law enforcement sought to undermine the movement and its leadership.

On April 6, 1968, Cleaver was wounded in an armed confrontation between the Black Panthers and the San Francisco police. *New York Times Magazine* correspondent T. D. Allman described the incident: "Cleaver and a companion, Black Panther Treasurer Bobby Hutton, were holed up in a house with a rifle and a few pistols. The police poured thousands of rounds of ammunition into the house. Though some fire was returned, no policemen were wounded. Hutton, however, was shot dead, apparently while trying to surrender." Arrested at the scene, Cleaver faced another stint in prison. A local judge ruled that the charges against him were politically motivated, however, and for some months he was allowed to go free. Cleaver used the time to continue his agenda with the Panthers and to run for president of the United States on the radical Peace and Freedom Party ticket.

Late in 1968, a higher court ruled that Cleaver should return to jail for parole violation *and* face new charges stemming from the April shoot-out incident. Cleaver became a fugitive, traveling to Cuba by way of Canada. "When Cleaver dropped out of sight, he was Black Panther minister of information, a potent force in an exploding people's movement," wrote Laile E. Bartlett in *Reader's Digest*. "Under his leadership, the Black Panthers had developed from a local Oakland organization into an international movement being copied by liberationists around the world. As a writer—his *Soul on Ice* was a bestseller—Cleaver was both symbol and spokesman for a public that transcended race and class. His enemies had good reason to want him out of the way."

The Education of an Exile

Cleaver was accorded a warm welcome in Cuba. He met Cuban leader Fidel Castro and the senior ministers of the Cuban Communist party. After some time there, he moved on to Algeria, where he became a sort of foreign ambassador for the Black Panthers. Throughout the communist empire Cleaver was greeted as a revolutionary hero. He discovered, however, that the very government systems he had admired for so long were repressing citizens more forcefully than anything he had encountered in America.

"I came to see that there is a fundamental mistake contained in the Marxist-Leninist ideologies, where they make the distinction between idealism and materialism," Cleaver told *Reader's Digest*. "Everything dealing with the spirit or with religious subjects is lumped under 'idealism' and condemned as being 'the opium of the people.' I came to feel that there is not only room but a necessity for us to address ourselves to morality and the relationship between people. What made Marxism-Leninism unworkable was that there was no humanity in it, no love." He added: "So I was wrong, and the Black Panthers were wrong. We had a totally political and economic approach, without giving any consideration to the more civilizing influences. Materialism, racial separation, destructive negativism, hate—they won't do the job. I can see that, now."

The transformation in Cleaver's thinking was a gradual process, fueled by the isolation he felt because he could not

> "There is a necessity for us to address ourselves to morality and the relationship between people. Materialism, racial separation, destructive negativism, hate— they won't do the job."

speak any foreign languages. He lived abroad for eight years with his wife and two children, eventually moving to Paris. By December of 1975 he was ready to return to America, even if it meant going back to prison. "I'd rather be in jail in America than free anywhere else," he told *Reader's Digest*.

At first, Cleaver was incarcerated, but his conservative political philosophy and blossoming Christian faith found him powerful supporters from among the very people he once scorned the most. By 1978 he was cleared of charges and was a sought-after speaker at universities, religious gatherings, and political rallies. Some of his former associates questioned his conversion to Americanism and Christianity, but Cleaver steadfastly maintained that he had the right to change if he wanted to. "They try to make it look like I'm doing flip-flops all over the ocean," he said in *Ebony*. "I have a very good track record of being ahead of other people in understanding certain truths and taking political positions far in advance of the crowd and turn out to be vindicated by subsequent experience. Yet, when I take these experiences, I have been attacked for taking them."

Since 1980 Cleaver has lived in Berkeley, California. He has run for various political offices there, including city council in 1984, the U.S. Senate in 1986, and the San

Francisco Regional Transit Board in 1992. He has not won any of the seats he has sought. Financially Cleaver has almost always been on shaky ground, since the Internal Revenue Service staked a claim on the earnings he might have received from *Soul on Ice,* which has sold more than two million copies. In the late 1980s, he began running a recycling pickup service and making ceramic pottery for sale.

Cleaver broke from the Black Panthers even before he returned to the United States in 1976. However, he does not disavow his actions from those days or the ultimate aims of the Panthers. "The Black Panthers? That's not where I am now, but it's where I learned," he told *Reader's Digest.* "*Soul on Ice?* Those are not my words now, but they were honest at the time." In fact, Cleaver told *Ebony,* "the Black Panther Party played a very positive role at a decisive moment toward the liberation of Black people in America." Cleaver said in *People* that his outlook on life now is not the result of mellowing as he becomes a senior citizen. "That implies your ideas have changed because of age," he concluded. "I've changed because of new conclusions."

Selected writings

Soul on Ice, McGraw, 1968, reprinted, Dell, 1992.
Eldridge Cleaver: Post-Prison Writings and Speeches, Random House, 1969.
Eldridge Cleaver's Black Papers, McGraw, 1969.

Soul on Fire, Word, Inc., 1978.

Sources

Books

Cleaver, Eldridge, *Soul on Ice,* McGraw, 1968, reprinted, Dell, 1992.
Cleaver, Eldridge, *Soul on Fire,* Word, Inc., 1978.
Contemporary Literary Criticism, Volume 30, Gale, 1984.
Oliver, John A., *Eldridge Cleaver: Ice and Fire!* Bible Voice, 1977.

Periodicals

Ebony, March 1988, pp. 66-68.
Entertainment Weekly, February 12, 1993, p. 68.
Jet, February 24, 1986, p. 25; May 19, 1986, p. 12; October 26, 1987, p. 38.
Life, February 6, 1970, p. 20.
Newsweek, March 17, 1975, p. 40; December 1, 1975, p. 42.
New York Times Magazine, January 16, 1977, p. 10.
People, March 22, 1982.
Playboy, May 1968.
Reader's Digest, September 1976, pp. 65-72.
Washington Post, August 1, 1992, p. A12.

—*Mark Kram*

Johnnetta B. Cole

1936—

Educator, anthropologist, writer

Spelman College is the oldest, most respected institution of higher learning for black women in the United States. It is somewhat ironic, therefore, that 107 years of the school's history passed before a black woman filled its presidential office. Johnnetta Cole is that woman, and since taking responsibility for Spelman in 1987, she has proven to be a dynamic administrator, an energetic fund-raiser, and a source of inspiration to both faculty and student body. At a time when historically black colleges have been deemed obsolete by some commentators, Cole has emerged as one of their most passionate advocates. Discussing Spelman with an interviewer from *Dollars & Sense,* Cole stated: ''I think that our students are being pulled here by the ambiance, by the affirming environment, by our insistence that African American women can do anything that they set out to do.''

Higher education and high standards of achievement are traditions in Cole's family. In 1901 her great-grandfather, Abraham Lincoln Lewis, cofounded the Afro-American Life Insurance Company of Jacksonville, Florida. That business grew and thrived, eventually employing both of Cole's parents, each of whom had graduated from a black college. Her mother had worked as an English teacher and registrar at Edward Waters College prior to becoming a vice-president of Afro-American Life Insurance, and it was assumed that Johnnetta would also join the family business after completing her education.

Johnnetta was precocious, finishing high school by the age of fifteen. She earned outstanding scores on an entrance examination for Fisk University's early admissions program and began studying there in the summer of 1952. Her stay at Fisk was brief, yet pivotal. While there, a world of intellectual endeavor far beyond anything she'd experienced in Jacksonville's segregated schools was revealed to her. She had frequent contact with Arna Bontemps, the noted writer who also held a job as Fisk's librarian. Seeing this respected author in a work setting was important to her because, as she later wrote in a *McCall's* column, ''When our . . . heroes are portrayed as bigger than life, living, working, accomplishing beyond the realm of the normal, when they are depicted as perfect human beings, . . . they are placed so far from us that it seems impossible that we could ever touch them or mirror who they are in our own lives.''

After just one year at Fisk, Cole was eager to move on to new horizons. In 1953 she transferred to Oberlin College, where her sister was majoring in music. Seventeen-year-old Johnnetta was by then tightly focused on a career in medicine, but an

At a Glance...

Born Johnnetta Betsch, October 19, 1936, in Jacksonville, FL; daughter of John, Sr. (an insurance company employee) and Mary Frances (an educator, registrar, and insurance company vice-president; maiden name, Lewis) Betsch; married Robert Cole (an economist), 1960 (divorced, 1982); married Arthur Robinson, Jr. (a public health administrator), December 1988; children: (first marriage) David, Aaron, Ethan Che. *Education:* Oberlin College, B.A., 1957; Northwestern University, M.A., 1959, Ph.D., 1967.

Washington State University, assistant professor of anthropology and director of Black Studies, 1967-70; University of Massachusetts—Amherst, professor of anthropology and Afro-American Studies, 1970-83; provost of undergraduate education, 1981-83; Hunter College of the City University of New York, Russell Sage Visiting Professor of Anthropology, 1983, professor of anthropology, 1983-87, director of Latin American and Caribbean Studies, 1984-87; Spelman College, Atlanta, GA, president, 1987—; writer. Member of board of directors, American Council on Education, Global Fund for Women, and Points of Light Initiative Foundation, among others.

Member: National Council of Negro Women, American Anthropological Association (fellow).

Selected awards: Elizabeth Boyer Award, 1988; Essence Award in Education, 1989; inducted into Working Woman Hall of Fame; Jessie Bernard Wise Woman Award and American Woman Award, 1990; Sara Lee's Frontrunner Award, 1992; numerous honorary degrees.

Addresses: *Office*—Office of the President, Spelman College, 350 Spelman Ln. SW, Atlanta, GA 30314.

anthropology course (taken to fulfill a liberal arts requirement) and its enthusiastic instructor changed her direction permanently. "On my own little track, I would have simply taken my science courses, and never would have taken a class with George E. Simpson. This white American professor played Jamaican cult music in the classroom, jumping up and down, beginning to hyperventilate, talking about African retentions in the New World! 'This is what anthropologists try to

understand,' said he. 'Good-bye, premed and hello, anthropology!' said I," she was quoted as saying in a *Ms.* magazine article by Susan McHenry.

After earning her bachelor's degree in anthropology at Oberlin in 1957, Cole went on to graduate study at Northwestern University. There she worked under noted anthropologists Paul J. Bohannan and Melville J. Herskovits. To her surprise, she also fell in love with a white graduate student in the economics program. "It was not my plan to fall in love with Robert Cole," she remarked in *Ms.* "And I doubt seriously that this man coming from an Iowa dairy farming family . . . intended to fall in love with a black woman from Jacksonville, Florida." Nevertheless, the two were married. Robert Cole shared his wife's fascination with Africa, and after their wedding day, they traveled to Liberia to work cooperatively on research that would form the basis of both their dissertations.

Conducted Anthropological Studies Abroad

She did anthropological field studies in villages while he conducted economic surveys of the area. Cole has stated that the experience of living in Africa imparted a unique perspective to her and her husband that helped their interracial marriage endure for more than twenty years, despite the fact that they returned to the United States at the beginning of the black power movement. It was "a time when for many *black* folk interracial marriage was a problem," she was quoted as saying in *Ms.* "But perhaps because I was working largely in an academic setting, with students, it was not just manageable, it was all right."

By 1967 Cole had completed her dissertation, "Traditional and Wage Earning Labor in Liberia," received her Ph.D. from Northwestern, and joined her husband as a faculty member at Washington State University. Beginning as an assistant professor of anthropology, she went on to become a key player in the creation of the school's Black Studies program, also serving as director of the program. In 1970, Cole and her husband moved to New England, where she had been offered a tenured position at the University of Massachusetts at Amherst. She spent thirteen productive years there, developing the existing Afro-American Studies program, increasing the interaction between her school and the others in the Connecticut River valley, teaching courses in anthropology and Afro-American studies, and serving as provost of undergraduate education.

Cole's marriage ended in 1982, and the following year she moved on to Hunter College of the City University of New York. She remained on the staff of the anthropology department until 1987 and was director of the Latin American and Caribbean Studies program. She also continued her field work, which since her days in Liberia had encompassed studies of households headed by women, the lives of Caribbean women, Cape Verdean culture in the United States, and racial and gender inequality in Cuba.

Wrote on Issues of Culture, Race, and Gender

Cole's focus on cultural anthropology, Afro-American studies, and women's issues all came together in a groundbreaking book published in 1986. *All-American Women: Lines That Divide, Ties That Bind* was cited by numerous reviewers for its perceptive synthesis of issues concerning race, class, gender, and ethnicity. Cole remarked in *Ms.* that her field work has definitely influenced the administrative side of her career: "I tend to look at problems in ways that I think are very, very much in the anthropological tradition. Which means, first of all, one appreciates the tradition, but second, one also at least raises the possibility that there are different ways of doing the same thing. And it's in that discourse where interesting things can happen."

When Spelman College began looking for a new president in 1986, finding a black woman for the job was a top priority. When the school was founded in 1880 by white abolitionists from New England, it was conceived as a missionary school where emancipated slave women could learn literacy, practical skills, and Christian virtues. Its first four presidents were white women; the first black to fill the office, Albert Manley, was not hired until the 1950s. When he left in the mid-1970s, a small but very vocal group of students demanded a black woman president for this black woman's school. The search committee had three excellent candidates that fit the criteria, but two of them withdrew from the selection process before it was completed. The third was offered the job, but had already accepted another. Donald Stewart, former associate dean at the University of Pennsylvania, was hired. A group of Spelman students reacted angrily to the announcement, locking the trustees in their boardroom for twenty-six hours.

Became President of Spelman College

When Stewart left office ten years later, Cole was clearly the standout choice of all the applicants for the vacancy, not just because of her race and sex but because of her strong background as a scholar, a feminist, and a student of black heritage. "Her credentials were not only impeccable, but her incredible energy and enthusiasm came through during the personal interview. She showed certain brilliance in every sense of the word," Veronica Biggins, co-vice-chair of Spelman's board of trustees, was quoted as saying in *Working Woman*. "Cole's charismatic personality, cooperative leadership style, and firm 'black womanist' attitude . . . raise[d] expectations for an exciting new era at Spelman," according to a *Ms.* article published shortly after Cole took office. "While [she] is a highly qualified, purposeful, serious-minded individual, she is also a thoroughly warm and unpretentious *sister*—in both the black and feminist senses of the term."

Cole's presidency had an exciting kickoff—during her inauguration, Bill and Camille Cosby announced a gift of $20 million to Spelman. Delighted with the donation, Cole

> "African American women can do anything that they set out to do."

was nevertheless quick to point out that there is never enough money. She estimates that fund-raising takes up 50 percent of her time. The other half is divided between teaching (one class per term), building up academics, and starting new traditions such as her Mentorship Program, in which CEOs of six major Atlanta corporations are paired with promising students from Spelman. She is committed to building and maintaining a powerful liberal arts program at the school, for it is her belief that a good liberal arts education is the proper foundation for any career. "I tell my students to write, to learn to think, and the rest will fall in place," she told *Working Woman* contributor Audrey Edwards.

Looking to the Future

Cole firmly believes that black colleges are vital to black success. She has frequently quoted statistics showing that although only 17 percent of black students enter black colleges, 37 percent of those who make it to graduation were attending black colleges, and a full 75 percent of black professional women are graduates of black colleges. She is convinced that these schools give black students more opportunities to excel, to discover their heritage, and to see role models in their own image. "I am obviously not an objective soul. I happen to think that this school is the greatest women's college in America," she told an interviewer for *Dollars & Sense*. When asked what lies ahead, she responded: "I would like to think that Spelman has in her future a good deal of continuity and some intriguing changes. . . . Tradition is important at this institution, not just for its own sake, but because it works."

In her 1993 book *Conversations: Straight Talk with America's Sister President,* Cole broadens her call for a new order, targeting "a multiplicity of audiences" with her message of equality. Mixing enthusiastic discourse on race, gender, and learning with ruminations on her own experiences as a black woman, she argues for the eradication of racist and sexist views through education, tolerance, and expanded social awareness. While reaching readers of both sexes and all races, Cole marshals the forces of young black women in the United States to act for change, stating, "We African American women must cure whatever ails us."

Selected writings

All-American Women: Lines That Divide, Ties That Bind, 1986.
Conversations: Straight Talk with America's Sister President, Doubleday, 1993.

Editor of *Anthropology for the Eighties* and *Anthropology for the Nineties.* Contributor to numerous magazines and journals. Member of editorial board of *Anthropology and Humanism Quarterly, Black Scholar, Emerge,* and *SAGE: A Scholarly Journal on Black Women.* Columnist for *McCall's.*

Sources

Books

Bateson, Catherine, *Composing a Life,* Atlantic Monthly Press, 1989.
Cole, Johnnetta, *Conversations: Straight Talk with America's Sister President,* Doubleday, 1993.

Periodicals

Art in America, September 1990.
Change, September/October 1987.
Dollars & Sense, March 1992.
Ebony, February 1988.
Essence, November 1987; July 1990.
McCall's, October 1990; February 1991.
Ms., October 1987.
People, May 10, 1993.
Publishers Weekly, July 13, 1992; November 30, 1992.
SAGE: A Scholarly Journal on Black Women, Fall 1988.
Working Woman, June 1989; November 1991.

—*Joan Goldsworthy*

Ellis Cose

1951—

Journalist, author

Ellis Cose was a Chicago newspaper columnist before he was old enough to vote, and from that brilliant beginning has gone on to build successful careers in three related fields. A respected journalist, Cose has worked as reporter and columnist for several major newspapers and went on to become editor of the *New York Daily News*'s editorial page; he is the author of a number of well-received books; and he has also served with government and university think tanks as an expert in journalism and the politics of energy. At an age when most journalists are still struggling to establish their credentials, Ellis Cose has already secured a place among the leaders of his profession.

Cose was born in Chicago on February 20, 1951, the son of Raney and Jetta Cose. He grew up in one of Chicago's high-rise public housing projects—an environment notorious for perpetuating crime and stunting lives—and he might well have remained there if not for the political upheavals and rising black consciousness of the 1960s. By the time Cose reached high school the civil rights movement and Vietnam War had given a political edge to his youthful dissatisfactions, and after demonstrating an early interest in mathematics, he found his voice as a writer. As he told *Publishers Weekly* in a

1992 interview, "In the midst of everything blowing up, the big riots and [Martin Luther] King [Jr.] getting killed [in 1968], I got this notion that I had something worthwhile to say."

Like many other budding authors, however, Cose found his high school English classes more of a hindrance than a help to his development. After drifting through three years of indifferent work, in his senior year Cose met a teacher named Mrs. Klinger who encouraged him to write about whatever interested him. In short order, Cose turned out two hundred pages of essays on a variety of social and racial topics, so impressing Klinger that she forwarded his work to Gwendolyn Brooks, the famed black poet laureate of Illinois. Brooks congratulated Cose on his precocious talent and invited him to join her circle of writers, an honor for which the rebellious Cose had little use. "I'm seventeen in with these guys in their thirties and forties," he recalled in *Publishers Weekly*. "I didn't stay very long." More to his taste was a novel he completed soon thereafter and sold to a small publishing firm; the publisher promptly went bankrupt, however, and Cose went off to the University of Illinois at Chicago to study psychology.

While a student, Cose contributed regularly to the university

At a Glance. . .

Born February 20, 1951, in Chicago, IL; son of Raney and Jetta (Cameron) Cose. *Education:* University of Illinois at Chicago, B.A., 1972; George Washington University, M.A., 1978.

Chicago Sun-Times, columnist and reporter, 1970-77; Joint Center for Political Studies, Washington, D.C., senior fellow and director of energy policy studies, 1977-79; *Detroit Free Press,* Detroit, MI, editorial writer and columnist, 1979-81; resident fellow at National Academy of Sciences and National Research Council, 1981-82; special writer for *USA Today,* 1982-83; president of Institute for Journalism Education, University of California at Berkeley, 1983-86; Gannett Center for Media Studies fellow, Columbia University, New York City, 1987; *New York Daily News,* editorial page editor, 1991—.

Awards: First place newswriting award from Illinois United Press International, 1973; Stick-o-Type Award from Chicago Newspaper Guild, 1975; Lincoln University National Unity Award for best political reporting, 1975 and 1977.

Addresses: *Office*—Editorial Page Editor, *New York Daily News,* New York News Inc., 220 East 42nd St., New York, NY 10017.

the establishment's leading journals, all while completing his degree in psychology at the University of Illinois. It was the kind of pressure-filled situation journalists thrive upon, and Cose proved to be a born journalist. He continued writing columns for the *Sun-Times* for seven years, during which time he completed both his bachelor's degree and a master's from George Washington University in science, technology, and public policy.

In 1977 Cose was named senior fellow and director of energy studies at the Joint Center for Political Studies in Washington, D.C. Energy and the politics of its distribution became matters of great concern for Americans after the oil crisis of 1973-1974, and Cose spent much of the later 1970s researching and writing about the politics of energy. The fruit of this labor took the form of several books, culminating in the 1983 publication of *Decentralizing Energy Decisions: The Rebirth of Community Power.*

Documented U.S. Energy Concerns

In *Decentralizing Energy Decisions,* Cose addresses the growing awareness by Americans of the country's critical shortage of energy sources. The frustration and helplessness felt by many consumers following the 1973 oil crisis prompted a wave of resolutions calling for energy management on the level of local communities, together with a general sentiment that "small is better" in all aspects of economic and social life. Cose describes the efforts of communities both large and small to remedy what he calls the "loss of control many Americans feel over important parts of their lives." He analyzes the contradictions inherent between the desire for local control of resources and the realities of modern energy production and distribution, and he concludes that while local empowerment is possible and in some cases a reality, few communities are willing to pay the price for such control. As the author succinctly put it in his book, community activists need "to realize that even a 'quiet revolution' is not free."

After his stint at the Joint Center for Political Studies, Cose resumed his career in journalism as a columnist and editorial writer for the *Detroit Free Press* between 1979 and 1981. He later joined the staff of the newly created *USA Today* as a special reporter on management and labor issues, remaining there until 1983 when he was named president of the Institute for Journalism Education at the University of California at Berkeley.

newspaper, sharpening his skills as a political commentator. On a momentary inspiration he sent a collection of his work to Ralph Otwell, managing editor of the Chicago *Sun-Times.* Otwell liked what he saw and asked Cose to write a column for the paper's school edition. In 1970, when Cose was still only nineteen years old, Otwell and *Sun-Times* editor Jim Hoge invited him to contribute a column to the regular edition of the *Sun-Times,* making him the youngest columnist in the history of Chicago newspapers.

Became Spokesperson for Blacks in Chicago

The exalted position brought with it a huge responsibility for Cose, who suddenly found himself a major spokesperson for Chicago's black population at a time of extreme social tension. While radical black organizations such as the Black Panthers were attacking the foundations of the so-called "establishment," Cose was given the task and honor of articulating the needs of black people in the pages of one of

Gained Attention with *The Press*

Cose's three-year tenure at the institute led to the 1989

publication of *The Press: Inside America's Powerful Newspaper Empires—From the Newsrooms to the Boardrooms,* his first book to receive widespread notice. In this ambitious book Cose attempts to chronicle the changes at five of the leading U.S. newspapers between the early 1960s and late 1980s. (The five papers studied are the *New York Times, Los Angeles Times, Washington Post,* and the Knight-Ridder and Gannett chains.)

The Press focuses on a period during which these mostly family-owned newspapers came under increasing pressure from business advisers to diversify and enlarge their non-news holdings—to become more like other large corporations and less like the traditional ideal of an independent, "above the fray" observer of the national scene. Cose provides thumbnail sketches of each of the paper's origins as background for his tale of boardroom battles and generational change and for the most part concludes that the papers have avoided the conflicts of interest possible in diversified asset holdings by confining their growth to the media business.

Studied Immigration in America

Following a year with the Gannett Center for Media Studies at Columbia University, Cose spent several years researching and writing another substantial book, *A Nation of Strangers: Prejudice, Politics, and the Populating of America.* Here Cose provides a history of America's ambivalent attitude toward the waves of immigration that have contributed to its population during the last three centuries. The United States was created by immigrants, as Cose points out, yet each generation of citizens has feared and opposed the arrival of certain groups of later immigrants. At various times, Americans have been worried about the increasing numbers of Catholic, Irish, Jewish, Chinese, and Hispanic individuals in this country, to name only a few of the religious and ethnic groups singled out for hostility. As Cose wrote in the epilogue to *Nation,* "For while it is true America's history is one of absorbing successive waves of immigrants, it is also a history of intermittent outbreaks of anti-immigrant hysteria." Cose decries the existence of such discrimination but sees little hope that it will soon end.

In August of 1991 Cose became editor of the *New York Daily News*'s editorial page. He enjoys shifting between the realm of authorship, which allows him greater leisure to consider issues in all their complexity, and the hustle-bustle of daily journalism. In the latter arena, as Cose described in *Publishers Weekly,* "If you criticize something the mayor does, he gets rattled."

Selected writings

Energy and the Urban Crisis, Joint Center for Political Studies, 1978.
(Editor) *Energy and Equity: Some Social Concerns,* Joint Center for Political Studies, 1979.
Decentralizing Energy Decisions: The Rebirth of Community Power, Westview, 1983.
The Press: Inside America's Most Powerful Newspaper Empires—From the Newsrooms to the Boardrooms, Morrow, 1989.
A Nation of Strangers: Prejudice, Politics, and the Populating of America, Morrow, 1992.

Sources

Books

Cose, Ellis, *Decentralizing Energy Decisions: The Rebirth of Community Power,* Westview, 1983.
Cose, *The Press: Inside America's Most Powerful Newspaper Empires—From the Newsrooms to the Boardrooms,* Morrow, 1989.
Cose, *A Nation of Strangers: Prejudice, Politics, and the Populating of America,* Morrow, 1992.

Periodicals

Newsweek, June 3, 1985.
Publishers Weekly, March 23, 1992.
Time, November 27, 1989.

—*Jonathan Martin*

Benedita da Silva

1942—

Brazilian politician

"Three times a minority" in a country where people are only beginning to admit racism is a force to be reckoned with, Benedita da Silva came from the bottom of society to assume a position of leadership in Brazilian politics.

Brazil is an ethnically diverse country in eastern central South America. An estimated 10 percent of its 150 million people are of African descent, and an additional third of the population is racially mixed. Yet in a nation with more blacks than any other except Nigeria, only nine elected members of Brazil's congress, the Chamber of Deputies, are black. Of the chamber's 569 members, only 25 are women. In addition, blacks and people of mixed racial descent make up a disproportionate percentage of the country's lower class population.

In an interview with the *New York Times* in 1987, da Silva called herself "three times a minority": black, a woman, and poor. Many city dwelling people of color like da Silva, who is the granddaughter of a slave, grow up and live out their lives as squatters in shantytowns called *favelas*. Da Silva is from Chapeu Mangueira, one of several hundred *favelas* that surround Rio de Janeiro, built on the steep cliffs that overhang Rio's Copacabana Beach.

The youngest of 12 children, da Silva was born to a priestess of the Umbanda Afro-Brazilian religion who worked as a laundress; her father was a carwasher. By the time she was five, da Silva had her first job, delivering laundry for her mother and other Chapeu Mangueira laundresses. She started working at a belt and pocketbook factory when she was just 11. Five years later, shortly after her mother died, da Silva's family married her off to her first husband. The couple held a variety of jobs: she worked as a maid, a cook, and a street vendor, and he peddled biscuits and painted houses. Occasionally they would be homeless for several days with their five children, only two of whom survived.

In the 1960s, da Silva became a community activist, fighting to get Rio's city government to provide the area with basic services such as electricity, running water, and a primary school—all at a time when few people spoke out on any controversial issues. Brazil was then ruled by an oppressive military government that even burned down Rio's Praia do Pinto *favela* in 1971.

By the 1970s, da Silva had joined the Brazilian Democratic Movement, an opposition political party formed to seek

At a Glance...

Born in 1942 in Chapeu Mangueira, Rio de Janeiro, Brazil; married in 1958 (husband died, 1980); married Aguinaldo Bezerra dos Santos; children (first marriage) Nilcea (daughter), Pedro Paulo (son).

Member of Brazilian Democratic Movement briefly in the early 1970s; cofounder and member of Worker's party of Brazil, beginning 1980; served on Rio de Janeiro City Council, 1982-87; elected to Chamber of Deputies, Brasilia, 1987—; ran for mayor of Rio de Janeiro, 1992.

Addresses: *Office*—Camera dos Deputados, Praca dos 3 Poderes, Anexo No. 2, Brasilia DF 70000.

protection from the country's strong-armed government, but she soon left the party because its leaders were uninterested in grassroots community activism. She continued to fight for her community, winning a municipal health center for Chapeu Mangueira, and at the end of the decade, although she had sworn never to rejoin a political organization, she helped found the leftist Worker's party when the government relaxed political controls. In 1982, da Silva won an election to Rio's city council in the first free election following the end of military rule; before her term was up, the party slated her for a seat on congress. She has since served two terms as a deputy in the Brasilia, the nation's capital, and in 1992 she ran for mayor of Rio de Janeiro.

Exception to the Rules

"I am the exception to every established rule in this country," da Silva told a *Christian Science Monitor* reporter in September of 1987, shortly after her election to the congressional Chamber of Deputies. Religion is a case in point. Brazil is the largest Catholic nation in the world, and the man da Silva names as one of her most important influences is Dom Helder Camara, the Auxiliary Bishop of Rio and later Archbishop of Recife and Olinda. But da Silva converted to the pentecostal Apostolic Church of God at the age of 26. Since then she has ceased to smoke, drink, or dance—a sharp contrast to her role as Carnival samba queen in her youth in a country where Carnival, the celebration of Fat Tuesday during Lent, is a national event.

Da Silva was also influenced by her family's slave heritage. Her grandmother, Maria Rosa, was a former slave in Brazil's mining and farming state of Minas Gerais. Brazil was colonized by the Portuguese, who sent slaves there

from Africa during the 16th and 17th centuries. The country gained independence in 1822 but didn't abolish slavery until 1888, becoming the last country in the Americas to do so. On Brazilian Abolition Day, celebrated every May 13, da Silva's whole family would gather and "speak of the importance of our being Black, of the need to go forward and never to be turned around," she recounted in *Essence* magazine.

Da Silva was plagued by blatant racism both as a young girl and as an adult, but having hailed from a family known for its pride and determination in the face of adversity, she was able to cope with the various indignities she endured in her time. As a child, for instance, her teachers actually told her that her hair was ugly and that she would never be as intelligent as her white classmates; later in life, she became a victim of discrimination in the workplace when, after responding to an advertisement for an "administrative job," in a Catholic high school, she was told that she would have to wash the school's floors.

Entered Politics

Da Silva ventured into politics, since the political forum offered her the greatest chance to improve conditions for her people. "The worst thing I could do is run away from [my blackness]," she told the *Washington Post*. The Worker's party she helped form in 1980 rejected military rule for the country but stopped short of endorsing Soviet-style Communism for Brazil. In the first round of free elections in nearly 20 years, she became a member of Rio's city council in 1982. Several years later, federal elections for deputy were held. She ran for office as a representative from the state of Rio de Janeiro in a campaign that relied more on word of mouth than on an elaborate campaign organization or television promotions—she was on the air once for only 30 seconds. Still, da Silva's appeal as a candidate was remarkable, and her supporters in the *favelas* and around the city came to know her as "Bene," a familiar version of her given name.

In 1987 the Worker's party won 285,000 votes, giving da Silva and one other Worker's party candidate seats in the Chamber of Deputies. Da Silva was the first elected black woman deputy in Brazil. Ironically, one of her fellow freshman deputies, Marcia Kubitschek, had been a former laundry client of da Silva's mother 25 years before.

Helped Draft Constitution

Da Silva arrived in the congress just in time to take part in the drafting of a new constitution for Brazil. She was instrumental in adding to the 1988 constitution a section codifying the rights and benefits due to domestic workers.

Unlike provisions for other employees in the Brazilian economy, previous laws had extended little or no coverage to maids and other domestics. Da Silva also headed a commission of inquiry into the heated debate over women's sterilization and investigated the murder of some seven thousand street children a year in Brazil—out of an estimated seven million children with no permanent home. Other causes she championed included land reform, the restructuring of public education, and limitations on the role of multinational corporations in Brazilian policymaking. In addition, da Silva was one of the first to call for the impeachment of former President Fernando Collor de Mello on corruption charges. Collor was eventually ousted for taking millions of dollars in personal profits from the Brazilian government.

In 1991 da Silva was part of a committee that invited African National Congress leader Nelson Mandela to visit Brazil. Mandela began a one-day visit to the country believing that people of color had achieved an enviable level of equality in Brazil. After he talked with da Silva—who had not been invited to any of the ANC leader's official activities—Mandela reevaluated his understanding of Brazilian racial policies. By the end of the visit, he was telling Brazilian blacks to take their share of political power in the country.

Ran for Mayor

Acting on Mandela's advice, da Silva ran for mayor of Rio de Janeiro in 1992. From a slow start with four percent of the vote, she swept the primaries in October of 1992, defeating six other candidates with 800,000 votes. Her opponent in a November 15th run-off was Cesar Maia, a white university professor and businessman of the Democratic Movement party. Shortly before the election, six polls were taken; three pegged Maia as the winner, and the other three reported da Silva in the lead.

Race became an important issue in the campaign, and the mayoral election brought to the fore racial prejudices that had previously lurked in the background of Brazilian life. Voters debated whether da Silva, a deputy and former councilwoman, would be capable of managing the city's 130,000 employees. The country's largest newspaper, O Globo, accused her of nepotism, revealing that she had her two children and a stepdaughter transferred from other city jobs to the permanent staff of the city council while she was an elected member of the group. And her son admitted to falsifying a high school diploma in order to get a better salary.

The key issue in the election for a majority of voters was security. Maia waged a war on crime, saying he would call out federal troops to keep beaches secure. Rio's solid citizens were unconvinced by da Silva, who called for more jobs and other opportunities for the gang members who frightened the city. The perception of Rio's *favelas* as havens of crime often run by drug lords also hurt her campaign. In the end she lost with 38 percent of the vote to Maia's 48 percent.

Although she lost the election, da Silva retained her deputy's seat. It is unlikely that she will stop fighting any time soon. During the mayoral campaign, she visited Washington, D.C. to meet with Mayor Sharon Pratt Kelly and U.S. congressional delegate Eleanor Holmes Norton. *Washington Post* columnist Donna Britt wrote in August of 1992 that the forces of racism against which da Silva was struggling were nearly overwhelming. But da Silva claims that "those forces are simply not that strong. If they were," she concluded, "we would not be here after 500 years of oppression."

Sources

Books

Baer, Werner, *The Brazilian Economy: Growth and Development,* 2nd edition, Greenwood, 1983.
Chacel, Julian, *Brazil's Economic and Political Future,* Westview, 1988.
Conniff, Michael L., and Frank D. McCann, *Modern Brazil: Elites and Masses in Historical Perspective,* University of Nebraska Press, 1989.
De Onis, Harriet, translator, *The Mansions and the Shanties: The Making of Modern Brazil,* by Gilberto Freyre, University of California Press, 1986.
Perlman, Janice E., *The Myth of Marginality: Urban Poverty and Politics in Rio de Janeiro,* University of California Press, 1976.
Wesson, Robert, and David Fleischer, editors, *Brazil in Transiton,* Greenwood, 1983.

Periodicals

Chicago Tribune, December 28, 1990, sec. 1A, p. 19.
Christian Science Monitor, September 24, 1987, p. 1.
Essence, June 1991, p. 36.
New York Times, February 17, 1987, p. A4; November 14, 1992, p. A3.
Washington Post, August 4, 1992, p. B1; November 15, 1992, p. F1.

—Gordon Mayer

Jaye Davidson

1967(?)—

Actor

"What makes a good actor?" Jaye Davidson asked *Rolling Stone* interviewer Jeff Giles rhetorically. "It's not a question of being theatrical, is it? It's a question of being real." The costar of the 1992 sleeper hit *The Crying Game* relied on a natural presence to play a film character whose "real" identity comes as a surprise to most audience members. "The movie is about how you just never know. You never know what you will be attracted to—or who you will love—until it happens to you," Davidson ruminated in *Rolling Stone*. The well-kept secret of *The Crying Game*—that the woman Davidson plays in the film turns out to be a man—was nearly shattered when he received an Oscar nomination for best supporting actor. *Entertainment Weekly* called Davidson's portrayal "the most talked-about *not*-talked-about performance of the year."

His English accent notwithstanding, Davidson was born in Riverside, California, to a white English mother and a father of African descent; he was, however, raised in Hertfordshire, England. The actor is cagy about discussing his parents, especially his late father: "We shan't even mention him. My mother would be very annoyed," he noted in the *Rolling Stone* interview. Davidson did, however, emphasize his "fabulous relationship" with his mother. "We've both got a great sense of self-worth," he explained. "And when we find something that we want to do, we do it hammer-on. We really *do* it. My mother's very correct and very beautiful. She's to be admired. She brought three children up and worked full time and ran a house—all on her own."

After high school, Davidson worked for Walt Disney's London offices—inside a life-sized Pluto costume—and later became a fashion assistant. "I bought the fabric," he told Giles. "I made sure that everything was smooth in the workroom. And I scrambled all over London on the Tube [subway], looking for buttons. It was great." When asked if, after tasting the world of cinema and achieving stardom, he could see himself as a fashion assistant for the rest of his life, he replied in the affirmative: "I don't want the responsibility of making a picture of a bloody dress. I want to make [the designer's] vision real."

Chosen for Pivotal Role in *The Crying Game*

Acclaimed Irish writer-director Neil Jordan addresses

At a Glance...

Born c. 1967 in Riverside, CA; raised in Hertfordshire, England; son of an English businesswoman.

Worked as employee of Walt Disney corporation and as fashion assistant for David and Elizabeth Emmanuel; actor in film *The Crying Game,* 1992.

Awards: Voted best newcomer by National Board of Review, 1993; Oscar nomination for best supporting actor, Academy of Motion Picture Arts and Sciences, 1993.

Addresses: c/o Miramax Films, 375 Greenwich St., New York, NY 10013.

issues of politics, race, gender, and identity in *The Crying Game,* a film that turns on the compelling relationship that develops between an IRA (Irish Republican Army) captor and his prisoner, a black British soldier. Jordan told *Time*'s Richard Corliss that for the key role of the hairdresser Dil (the British soldier's love interest), he "needed a man with a very particular kind of femininity." Producer Stephen Wooley admitted to *Entertainment Weekly* that the filmmakers "combed London" looking for the right person. "We tested and tested for that role." The twenty-five-year-old Davidson was spotted by a casting assistant who saw him at a wrap party for British filmmaker Derek Jarman's *Edward II.*

Offered an audition, Davidson—by his own admission rather inebriated—refused. "I said no and staggered off," he told Janet Maslin of the *New York Times.* "Afterward, I didn't even remember any of it happening." Even so, the film's casting personnel, unsatisfied by the parade of transvestites seeking the part, kept after him. Though he had been working for fashion designers David and Elizabeth Emmanuel, he soon found his employers' business going under. At last Davidson relented and read for the role; his unstudied poise and integrity appealed to Jordan, and he was offered the part.

Acting Posed New Challenges

"When I was told I had got the part," Davidson recalled in *Time,* "I just put the phone down and laughed my head off. But when I saw the whole script, I thought, dear God, how am I going to do this?" Jordan noted that "at first Jaye was shaking. But an extraordinary quality came through: an

elegance, a sense of inner dignity, an emotional purity. And a beautiful woman." Costar Stephen Rea, who also received an Oscar nomination for his portrayal of Fergus, the IRA terrorist who falls for Dil, told *Rolling Stone,* "If Jaye hadn't been a completely convincing woman, my character would have looked stupid. Everyone would have said, 'That's one *sick* Paddy.'"

Davidson was concerned about the intense demands of the role but decided to entrust himself entirely to Jordan. "I just thought, 'I've got to be really professional, these people are paying me,'" Davidson told Maslin. Jordan managed in turn to evoke Davidson's "sad, elfin, ambiguous, direct, unique screen charisma," according to Corliss. And David Ansen of *Newsweek* called Davidson "startling good as a woman ready to give all for love." The National Board of Review voted Davidson the most auspicious newcomer of the year for his performance in *The Crying Game.* "I think it's so strange that certain people think they know you because you've been in a film," the new star observed in *Entertainment Weekly.* "It's very flattering, but it's also very scary. I mean, why on earth do they want to know *me*?"

Problematic Fame

Davidson returned to the United States late in 1992 to shoot a Gap advertisement with legendary photographer Annie Leibovitz and to grant two major interviews: one with Maslin and one with *Rolling Stone*'s Giles. Maslin's piece is a *tour de force* of gender-neutral language, passively maintaining—with the help of photos from the film featuring a gorgeous Dil—the pretense that Davidson is a woman. Giles, however, talks openly with the actor about his real identity, his oddly marginal position as a "feminine" gay man, and other deeply personal matters. Davidson insisted to Giles that he had only dressed in drag once prior to the making of the film: "It was during a Trinidadian carnival [in London]—in 1989, I think," and involved "a white, silk-crepe, baby-doll dress. I had my hair up, and I had lilies in my hair. It was a fierce look and all that, but it was too much hard work."

The Crying Game opened as an art-house import and quickly earned the approval of film buffs. The mostly superlative reviews by U.S. critics displayed obvious pleasure in maintaining the principal secret of the film: Dil's sexual identity. Therefore, when the film moved into the mainstream, garnering further laurels, much word-of-mouth appeal, and finally a slew of Oscar nominations, the filmmakers were concerned that Davidson's newfound publicity—especially his nomination for best supporting actor—could adversely affect *The Crying Game*'s momentum.

"Amazed" by Academy Award Nomination

The actor related his sense of shock after his nomination for an Academy Award when interviewed by Maslin. "You could've said to me yesterday that I would wake up and be part of the royal family, and I would have been less surprised," he said. "The Oscars are [Hollywood stars like] Joan Crawford, Jack Nicholson, Elizabeth Taylor; the Oscars aren't me." Describing the experience as resembling "something out of a 50's movie," he explained, "I really can't express how amazed I am. And I am not an unsophisticated person." Even so, he insisted in *People* magazine: "To me, an Oscar nomination is irrelevant," and then claimed to "hate publicity" as well.

Given the nature of his role and the dearth of public knowledge about him, Davidson's nomination inspired a round of media speculation. Steve Pond of *Entertainment Weekly* noted that the allegedly publicity-shy Davidson "didn't seem fragile" during a brief pre-Oscars interview "as much as shy, soft-spoken, and genuinely uninterested in all the hoopla."

As it happened, Gene Hackman, the veteran character actor who costarred in Clint Eastwood's western epic *Unforgiven*, took the Academy Award home. "I'm not a Hollywood person," Davidson reflected to Pond, "and if they gave it [the Oscar] to me, it would be very insulting for the other people, who are *actors*." In an interview with Leeza Gibbons for *Entertainment Tonight*, Davidson claimed to be unfazed by the film industry and somewhat uninterested in pursuing a film career: "I never really wanted to be in the papers. I came from oblivion. I wasn't famous before. I didn't grown up thinking God, I really want to be famous."

Sources

Entertainment Weekly, February 12, 1993, pp. 16-21; March 26, 1993, p. 43; April 9, 1993, p. 10.
Los Angeles Times, March 28, 1993, p. 28.
New York Times, December 17, 1992; February 18, 1993.
Newsweek, November 30, 1992.
People, March 29, 1993, p. 72.
Rolling Stone, April 1, 1993, p. 36.
Time, January 25, 1993, p. 63; March 1, 1993, p. 57.

Additional information for this profile was taken from a taped interview with Davidson by Leeza Gibbons for *Entertainment Tonight,* broadcast on ABC-TV, April 30, 1993.

—*Simon Glickman*

Angela Davis

1944—

Activist, educator, author

Political activist, writer, and public speaker Angela Davis has never wavered in her quest for women's rights and the eradication of poverty and oppression. The energetic Davis became embroiled in controversy in California at the end of the 1960s and emerged as an international symbol of a proud, defiant African American woman under political siege. Davis was fired from a prestigious professorship because she was a Communist and later was jailed for sixteen months for crimes she did not commit. For a time in the early 1970s she was on the Federal Bureau of Investigation's "Ten Most Wanted List," a distinction that brought her worldwide recognition as a victim of political repression. As Melba Beals put it in *People,* "In the idol-seeking rebellion of the American '60s, Angela Davis became a lightning rod almost in spite of herself." Subsequent decades have found Davis to be an impassioned worker for the causes of nationalized health care, civil rights, and nuclear disarmament.

"Angela is one of the most well-known women in the United States—and one of the busiest," wrote Cheryll Y. Greene in *Essence* magazine. "She is active in five organizations, among them the Communist Party [of the] U.S.A., in which she is the major Black figure and plays a leading role. . . . She travels extensively both in the United States and abroad, lecturing to diverse audiences, from college students to white male union members. In 1980 and 1984 she ran for vice-president of the United States on the Communist Party ticket."

Davis admitted in *Essence* that she is "always amazed" that she is invited to give so many speeches even now, decades after young people demonstrated on her behalf with "Free Angela" placards. "I *know* I wouldn't have sought this kind of public life—if it had been something that I could have chosen," she said. "I didn't choose to be where I am now. I didn't choose to be the target of the repression at that time. It just happened that way. It was, in a sense, a historical accident that I was the one. But I feel that I should accept that role for what it can accomplish for all of us." She added: "I try never to take myself for granted as somebody who should be out there speaking. Rather, I'm doing it only because I feel there's something important that needs to be conveyed."

Angela Davis was born in 1944 in Birmingham, Alabama, one of four children of B. Frank and Sallye E. Davis. Her parents were both schoolteachers, but her father left the profession and bought his own gas station. The family lived in a segregated neighborhood, and Davis attended segregated public schools. As a youngster she had ample opportunity to

At a Glance...

Born Angela Yvonne Davis, January 26, 1944, in Birmingham, AL; daughter of B. Frank (a teacher and businessman) and Sallye E. (a teacher) Davis. *Education:* Attended the Sorbonne, University of Paris, 1963-64; Brandeis University, B.A. (magna cum laude), 1965; graduate study at University of Frankfurt (Germany), 1965-67; University of California, San Diego, M.A., 1968, doctoral study, 1968-69. *Politics:* Communist.

University of California, Los Angeles, assistant professor of philosophy, 1969-70; activist and author of books on civil rights, women's issues, and global policy, 1970—. Communist Party candidate for vice-president of the United States, 1980 and 1984. Professor at San Francisco State University, 1979-91, and University of California at Santa Cruz, 1992—.

Member: Communist Party of the U.S.A. (member of Central Committee), National Alliance Against Racist and Political Repression (founder and co-chairperson), National Political Congress of Black Women (national board member), National Black Women's Health Project (national board member), Phi Beta Kappa.

Addresses: *Office*—c/o History of Consciousness, University of California at Santa Cruz, 218 Oakes College, Santa Cruz, CA 95064; or c/o Communist Party of the U.S.A., 235 W. 23rd St., 7th Floor, New York, NY 10011.

observe the effects of racism on the lives of her neighbors and friends.

While she was still a young girl, Davis began to attend civil rights demonstrations in Birmingham with her mother. The white majority responded to the demonstrations with clandestine hostility. So many homes in Davis's neighborhood were bombed by marauding white supremacists that the area became known as "Dynamite Hill." Attempts by Davis and some of her friends to conduct interracial study groups were disbanded by police. The racially motivated violence and the unfair laws governing blacks' behavior in public places helped to instill in Davis a sense of social purpose, as well as a deep resentment of the white power structure.

Davis's mother spent summers working toward a master's degree at New York University. Often Davis spent the summers in Manhattan too, and after her sophomore year of high

school in Birmingham she earned a scholarship to attend Elizabeth Irwin High, a private school in Greenwich Village. A straight-A student at home in Birmingham, Davis had to struggle to achieve the same grades in New York. She added summer courses to her schedule and repeated some of her hardest classes. In 1961 she graduated and accepted a scholarship to Brandeis University.

Activism Fueled by Education

At Brandeis, Davis majored in French literature. She spent one school year abroad studying at the Sorbonne. There she met students from Algeria and other African nations who had grown up under colonial rule. Their stories of discriminatory conditions in their homelands deepened her commitment to radical social change. She was further inflamed when news reached her of a bombing of a Birmingham church that killed four children she had known. Davis returned to Brandeis in search of some political philosophy that could mandate changes in the treatment of blacks—not only in America, but on the international level.

Her search brought her to the classroom of Herbert Marcuse, a Marxist professor of philosophy. Marcuse directed Davis to the tenets of socialism and communism. In her autobiography, *Angela Davis,* the activist wrote: "The *Communist Manifesto* [by nineteenth-century German philosopher and political economist Karl Marx] hit me like a bolt of lightning. I read it avidly, finding in it answers to many of the seemingly unanswerable dilemmas which had plagued me. . . . I began to see the problems of Black people within the context of a large working-class movement. . . . What struck me so emphatically was the idea that once the emancipation of the proletariat became a reality, the foundation was laid for the emancipation of all oppressed groups in society."

Davis graduated from Brandeis with top honors in 1965 and attended graduate school at the University of Frankfurt in Germany. She continued her studies of philosophy there, mastering the German language as well as the theories of knowledge set forth by German philosophers Immanuel Kant and Georg Wilhelm Friedrich Hegel. Although her professors were impressed with her scholarship, they could not persuade her to stay in Germany as the social situation deteriorated in America. In 1967 Davis returned to the United States to finish work on her master's degree at the University of California, San Diego.

"Free Angela"

In California Davis finished her master's degree and began

work toward her doctorate. She also joined a number of activist groups, including the Student Nonviolent Coordinating Committee (SNCC) and the Black Panthers. Her most important affiliation came in June of 1968, when she formally joined the Communist Party and became involved with the Che-Lumumba Club, an all-black Communist collective in Los Angeles. As a member of Che-Lumumba, she helped to organize militant demonstrations and protests designed to focus public attention on the plight of minorities. And thus her troubles began.

The University of California at Los Angeles had hired Davis as an assistant professor of philosophy in 1969. She taught four courses: "Dialectical Materialism," "Kant," "Existentialism," and "Recurring Philosophical Themes in Black Literature." Quickly she became a popular teacher on the UCLA campus, but an ex-FBI informer leaked the news that Davis was a member of the Communist party. The information made the newspapers, and UCLA's board of regents—which included then-governor Ronald Reagan—dismissed her from her post. The situation bore an uncanny resemblance to the deplorable "Red Scare" in the 1950s. Fellow faculty members and even the university president overwhelmingly condemned the regents' action as illegal and an infringement on academic freedom. Davis was reinstated by court order, but when her contract expired the following year she was dismissed again.

By that time Davis had become actively involved in the cause of the Soledad Brothers, a group of inmates at California's Soledad Prison who were treated especially harshly because they had tried to organize a Marxist group among the prisoners. Davis led demonstrations and gave speeches calling for parole of the young black prisoners. When one of the prisoners was shot by a guard in an incident ruled "justifiable homicide" by the warden, Davis grew even more strident in her demands. Her public exhortations drew anonymous threats by telephone and by mail, so she purchased several weapons and stored them in the headquarters of the Che-Lumumba Club.

On August 7, 1970, a teen-aged sibling of one of the Soledad Brothers used the firearms Davis had purchased to stage a dramatic prisoner rescue and hostage-taking attempt at California's Marin County Courthouse. The attempt was foiled in a barrage of gunfire that killed a county judge. Quickly the firearms were traced to Davis, and she fled into hiding. The FBI responded by placing her on the "Ten Most Wanted List" and undertaking a massive search for her. Two months later they found her in New York City and extradited her to California, where she was held in prison for over a year.

Once a tireless crusader for the incarcerated, Davis soon found herself behind bars, a victim and—in many minds—a political prisoner. "That period was pivotal for me in many respects," Davis told *Essence*. "I came to understand much more concretely many of the realities of the Black struggle of that period." Davis's case became an international issue, especially in the Soviet Union, and demonstrations on her behalf were held on both sides of the Atlantic. "Free Angela" picket signs and lapel pins became a catchword for the mistreatment of blacks by an overzealous federal law enforcement system.

Davis was taken to trial on charges of kidnapping, conspiracy, and murder in the spring of 1972. Her defense was able to prove that she did not help to plan or execute the incident at the Marin County Courthouse, and a jury of eleven whites and one Mexican American acquitted her of

> "I wouldn't have sought this kind of public life—if it had been something that I could have chosen. I didn't choose to be the target of repression. But I feel that I should accept that role for what it can accomplish for all of us."

all charges. Finally free, Davis embarked on a national lecture tour and visited the Soviet Union, where she was accorded a hero's welcome. As the 1970s progressed, she became a well-known lecturer and writer who demanded a total reassessment of attitudes about the black family, an overhaul of repressive prison systems, and a black-white coalition for the formation of a socialized state.

The Communist Party of the United States has benefitted from Davis's talents for decades. Her presence in the party helped to change the African American perception of communism and bolster black membership. In 1980 and again in 1984 the party nominated her as its vice-presidential candidate. *Progressive* magazine contributor Julius Lester has commented that, with Davis, "one is left with the impression of a woman who lives as she thinks it necessary to live and not as she would like to, if she allowed herself to have desires. She seems to be a woman of enormous self-discipline and control, who willed herself to a total political identity. Her will is so strong that, at times, it is frightening."

Addresses Issues of Race, Gender, and Culture

The years have not dimmed Davis's ardor for her causes,

nor have they softened her philosophy. As a teacher at such colleges as San Francisco State University and the University of California at Santa Cruz, she has developed courses on women's issues from a global perspective. Her ideas on the subject are presented in two collections of essays, *Women, Race & Class* and *Women, Culture & Politics*. Davis told *Essence:* "Something happened during the period of my persecution by the government and the FBI and others. When I was underground, enormous numbers of Black women were arrested and harassed. I came to realize the government feared the political potential of Black women—and that that was a manifestation of a larger plan to push us away from political involvement." Davis said that knowledge helped to empower her and other black women as well. "A new collective consciousness was emerging. I think that during that very compressed historical moment we managed to formulate many of the issues that were of concern to us. And to formulate responses to the propagandistic assault, which are still valid 20 years later. That is what is so fascinating to me, to recognize that 20 years have gone by, yet many of the ideas raised during that period have not become historically obsolete."

A self-avowed "soldier of freedom," Davis is encouraged by a strain of militancy she sees in young Americans. She calls for multicultural coalitions and global strategies to achieve equality for all peoples. "It is no longer possible for various groups to live and function and struggle in isolation," she told *Ebony.* "While we may specifically be involved in our own particular struggles, our vision has to be that we understand how our own issues relate to the issues of others. My consciousness has grown so that when I speak and write, I make a point of discussing the need for understanding how Native Americans, Latinos, and other people of color are marginalized in this society."

As the 1990s progressed, Angela Davis remained on the front line, fighting for women's rights, for a global peace plan including nuclear disarmament, for enhanced opportunities for workers, and especially for affordable health care for all American women. "Black women have no choice but to force the government to take responsibility for all its citizens," she told *Essence.* "The budget cutting of the Reagan administration that abolished many programs vital to the poor must be restored. Ultimately, the economic system will have to be changed. I don't think that under this system we will ever achieve economic power or equality. Some Black people, yes. But the majority still suffer now more than ever before." Also in *Essence,* Davis concluded on behalf of women of color everywhere: "It's about time, the decade of the nineties—as we prepare for a new century—to claim our voice and to demand that our community give us the respect that we have given it for as many decades and centuries as we have been present on this continent."

Selected writings

(With others) *If They Come in the Morning: Voices of Resistance,* Third Press, 1971, reprinted, Okpaku Communications, 1992..

Angela Davis: An Autobiography, Random House, 1974, reprinted, International Publications, 1988.

Women, Race & Class, Random House, 1983.

Women, Culture & Politics, Random House, 1989.

Sources

Books

Ashman, Charles R., *The People vs. Angela Davis,* Pinnacle Books, 1972.

Davis, Angela, *Angela Davis: An Autobiography,* International Publications, 1988.

Davis, Angela, and others, *If They Come in the Morning: Voices of Resistance,* Okpaku Communications, 1992.

Smith, Nelda J., *From Where I Sat,* Vantage, 1973.

Periodicals

Ebony, July 1990, p. 56.
Emerge, April 1991, cover story.
Essence, August 1986, p. 62; January 1988, p. 67; June 1989, p. 24; May 1990, p. 92.
New Statesman, August 14, 1987, p. 16.
Newsweek, June 5, 1972, p. 40.
Parade, November 29, 1992, p. 2.
People, January 23, 1978, p. 22.
Progressive, February 1975.
Sepia, December 1970, p. 9.
Time, October 17, 1969, p. 64.

Additional information on Angela Davis is available from the sound recording *Angela Davis Speaks,* Folkways, 1974; the Oceana microfilm of *The Angela Davis Trial,* 1974; and the student-produced documentary *Portrait of a Revolutionary.*

—Anne Janette Johnson

Ossie Davis

1917—

Actor, writer, director, producer

With the build and vitality of an NFL lineman, Ossie Davis hardly looks like the grand old man of black theater. Known to younger audiences as Ponder Blue on television's *Evening Shade* and as "the mayor" in filmmaker Spike Lee's *Do the Right Thing,* Davis made his Broadway debut in 1946. He directed the landmark film *Cotton Comes to Harlem* in 1970 and wrote and starred in *Purlie Victorious,* the 1961 play that was eventually revived as the smash Broadway musical *Purlie.*

Davis was born on December 18, 1917, in tiny Cogdell, Georgia. The oldest of five children, he grew up in a family of poor but inspired preachers and storytellers, an environment that provided him good grounding for the stage. "Acting and preaching are essentially the same—unabashedly so," Davis told Florida's *Palm Beach Post*. "The theater is a church and I consider myself as part of an institution that has an obligation to teach about Americanism, our culture and morals."

Though neither his father, Kince Charles Davis, a railway construction worker, or his mother, Laura, ever learned to read, they nevertheless, through the oral tradition, taught Davis the importance of education. "I was just caught up in the wonderful stories mom and dad would tell," he told the

Palm Beach Post. "They weren't children's stories, but humorous tales of their own escapades. They took life and broke it up in little pieces and fed it to us like little birds. I think I always knew what I wanted to do. I went to school to learn to write."

Like many blacks growing up in the 1920s, Davis managed to find good role models despite a resource-poor environment. "My mentors were real and unreal," he told *American Visions*. "My mentors were Brer Rabbit and High John the Conqueror, and even animals to whom I could talk when I was a boy. My mentors were friends who could tell jokes faster than me. Of course, I had organized mentors, too. Regular teachers in school and out. And there were mentors on the stage itself. People like [singers] Paul Robeson, Lena Horne, and [trumpet player] Louis Armstrong."

But while a lack of resources could not prevent him from wanting to learn, they almost prevented him from getting an education. Though Davis's parents were full of pride when he won a scholarship to Tuskegee Institute in Alabama, he had to turn it down because they had no money to pay for his living expenses. In 1935, though, things took a turn for the better; two aunts living in Washington, D.C., agreed to house him

At a Glance...

Born December 18, 1917, in Cogdell, GA; son of Kince Charles (a railway construction worker) and Laura Davis; married Ruby Ann Wallace (Ruby Dee; an actress), December 9, 1948; children: Nora, Guy, Lavern (Hasna). *Education:* Howard University, B.A., 1939.

Member of Rose McClendon Players, 1938-1941; stage actor, 1946—; made Broadway debut in *Jeb*, 1946; other stage appearances include *Anna Lucasta, A Raisin in the Sun, Wisteria Trees, Purlie Victorious,* and *I'm Not Rappaport;* film appearances include *Gone Are the Days,* 1963, *Do The Right Thing,* 1989, and *Jungle Fever,* 1991. Television appearances include roles in the teleplays *The Emperor Jones* and *Teacher Teacher;* guest spots in *The Defenders, The Fugitive,* and *Bonanza;* regular roles in series *With Ossie and Ruby* (and co-producer), and *Evening Shade;* photodocumentary *Lincoln* (voice of Frederick Douglass), ABC-TV, 1992; *The American Experience* (narrator), PBS, 1993; and roles in miniseries *Queen,* CBS, 1993, and film *The Ernest Green Story,* Disney Channel, 1993. Radio appearances include the *Ossie Davis and Ruby Dee Story Hour,* 1974-78. Director of films, including *Cotton Comes to Harlem,* 1970, *Kongi's Harvest,* 1970, and *Gordon's War,* 1973; producer of *Martin Luther King: The Dream and the Drum* and *A Walk Through the 20th Century With Bill Moyers. Military service:* U.S. Army, 1942-1945.

Awards: Emmy nomination for performance in *Teacher Teacher,* 1969; inducted into NAACP Image Award Hall of Fame, 1989.

Addresses: *Agent*—The Artists Agency, 10,000 Santa Monica Blvd., Ste. 305, Los Angeles, CA 90067.

while he attended Howard University. "My parents found enough money to buy me lunch one day and I hitchhiked to Washington to live with my aunts and attend Howard University," he told the *Palm Beach Post.* "There I met a number of people who were very important to my career."

Chief among Davis's influences at Howard was Alain Locke. Called "the philosophical midwife to a generation of younger artists, writers and poets" by *American Visions,* Locke, a drama critic and professor of philosophy, encouraged Davis, who already wanted to write for the theater, to move to

Harlem and join the Rose McClendon Players. Locke suggested that Davis, who had never seen live actors, would benefit from acting and learning what it takes to put on a play. Davis accepted the idea but only as a way to further his writing ambitions. "I never, never intended to become an actor," he told *Newsday.*

Arrived in New York City

Davis arrived in Harlem in 1938 and worked odd jobs while studying acting. It was a difficult period; at times he was reduced to sleeping in parks and scrounging for food. In 1941 he made his stage debut in the McClendon Players presentation of *Joy Exceeding Glory.* When the U.S. entered World War II, Davis joined the Army. He began his service as a surgical technician in Liberia, West Africa. Later, he was transferred to the Special Services Department, where he wrote and produced stage works to entertain military personnel. Among these was *Goldbrickers of 1944,* which was first produced in Liberia.

After the war Davis returned to Georgia but was soon contacted by McClendon director Richard Campbell, who convinced him to come to New York and audition for *Jeb,* a play by Robert Ardrey. At age 28, Davis won the lead role and made his Broadway debut. He earned favorable reviews as a disabled veteran attempting to succeed as an adding-machine operator in racist Louisiana, but the play itself was panned and lasted only nine performances. Though it bombed at the box office, *Jeb* was far from a total loss; it put Davis on the theatrical map, and it was in the cast of *Jeb* that Davis met Ruby Ann Wallace, whose stage name was Ruby Dee. The two became close and took roles with the touring company of *Anna Lucasta.* They were married on December 9, 1948. "Ruby was my colleague," Davis told *Newsday,* "and then she became my friend and eventually my wife."

After his marriage, Davis continued to appear in plays and, as time progressed, he took roles in television and films. Presentations like *Stevedore* and *No Time for Sergeants* paid the bills while others, like *No Way Out*—the powerful film about racial violence with Sidney Poitier and Ruby Dee—Lorraine Hansberry's *A Raisin in the Sun,* and Kraft Theater's 1955 television presentation of Eugene O'Neill's *The Emperor Jones* provided roles into which Davis could sink his teeth. Later, he remembered what an all-encompassing political and social—as well as professional—life the theater was. "In our day, theater was a serious commitment," he told the *Milwaukee Journal.* "That was the style of the times. . . . In New York City, you acted in the theater, and afterward, you went to a [civil rights movement] party for a lynching victim later that evening. [Actor Marlon] Brando was in one corner and [actor-director] Orson Welles was in the other corner. It was the same at home. I was born in the South, and my parents were always involved in something, raising money for this cause or that protest."

Frustrated by Limited Roles for Blacks

Despite some good roles, Davis was not happy with his treatment or that of blacks in general. "I knew I was going to be rejected so I had very low expectations," he revealed in *Blacks in American Film and Television*. "But rejection did sting. In the theater it took a peculiar form—of having to compete with your peers, like I did for *The Green Pastures* on Broadway, to fight to say words you were ashamed of. Ruby and I came along at a time when being black was not yet fashionable. There was little in the theater for us except to carry silver trays."

But Broadway was not the only place in which Davis could exercise his considerable talents. "We have always been involved in black theater, in the way that we saw [it]," Davis told *American Visions*. "Ruby and I took our notebooks and created our own theater. We went out into the marketplace, then to churches, to the schools and did what we could theatrically. Our relationship with black theater has always been continuous. It is just that we had to sometimes define what it is we meant by black theater." Davis and Dee's commitment to the black community went beyond staging dramas; in 1963 they acted as official hosts for the legendary civil rights March on Washington. Throughout the 1950s and '60s they stayed in constant contact with African American activists such as Malcolm X (at whose funeral Davis delivered the eulogy), Paul Robeson, and W. E. B. Du Bois.

Davis and Dee made every effort to build a normal family life for their three children, Hasna, Guy, and Nora. Living in a working-class neighborhood of Mount Vernon, New York, they preserved the family unit, which is so often distorted by the pressures of show business. "I think if there is anything to be said, our children were able at all levels and at all times to participate fully in the life we led," Davis told *American Visions*. "We didn't live a life away from them. There wasn't a career outside of the house from which they were barred. We managed to function as a family—with a sense of 'us-ness.'"

Considered Himself Primarily a Writer

Davis, who had never ceased to regard himself primarily as a writer, continued writing and shopping his plays and screenplays to producers throughout the 1950s and '60s. His play *Alice in Wonder* appeared in New York in 1952.

The drama, which recreated the Senator Joe McCarthy era of Cold-War communist-hunting, was revised and expanded the following year as *The Big Deal* but was dimly received. It was not until 1961 that Davis's writing abilities brought him real success. *Purlie Victorious* premiered September 28, 1961, at New York City's Cort Theatre. A comedy about an itinerant black preacher who attempts to claim his inheritance and establish an integrated church, *Purlie Victorious* enjoyed a long and interesting life; it ran more than seven months in New York City and was later revived first as a motion picture called *Gone Are the Days* and then as the Broadway musical *Purlie*. Despite its relatively long run in its first incarnation, *Purlie Victorious* made little money. Whites did not attend it and without white support, a black theater of that era could not succeed in New York.

Davis spent much of the 1960s earning his bread and butter in movies and in episodes of television shows like *The Defenders, The Doctors, The Fugitive,* and *Bonanza*. It was not the kind of work he relished. "I'm not a great actor," he told *Blacks in American Film and Television*. "I've never devoted myself to my craft with the intensity Ruby has. I've always felt I'd rather be a writer. But we had to make a living." Despite this self-criticism, Pauline Kael, film critic for the *New Yorker,* wrote that Davis, "in such movies as *The Hill* and *The Scalphunters,* brought a stronger presence to his roles than white actors did, and a deeper joy. What a face for the camera. He was a natural king."

> "I can move between different disciplines because I am essentially a storyteller, and the story I want to tell is about black people. I always want to share my great satisfaction at being a black man at this time in history."

As the 1960s progressed, Davis began receiving the kind of attention he deserved; in 1968 his play *Curtain Call, Mr. Aldridge, Sir* was produced at the University of California at Santa Barbara and in 1969, he received an Emmy nomination for his performance in the teleplay *Teacher Teacher*. By 1970 he had become one of the busiest African Americans in the entertainment industry. He made his debut as a film director with *Cotton Comes to Harlem,* adapted Nigerian writer Wole Soyinka's *Kongi's Harvest* for the screen, and his play *Purlie Victorious* returned to Broadway as the musical smash *Purlie*.

Cotton Comes to Harlem

Cotton Comes to Harlem was a landmark of black cinema. One of the first black films to make money from a mainstream audience, it opened the way for a wave of pictures about blacks now known as "blaxploitation" films. Unlike that of later, darker movies like *Shaft,* Davis's vision was more comic. Donald Bogle, author of *Blacks in American Film and Television,* attested of *Cotton,* "A joyousness ran through the film that lured audiences around the country into the theaters." Clive Barnes of the *New York Times* called *Purlie,* which opened at the Broadway Theater on March 15, 1970, "by far the most successful and richest of all black musicals," describing the production as "strong" and "so magnificent" and praising "the depth of the characterization and the salty wit of the dialogue."

Through the mid-1970s Davis continued to direct. While his films—*Black Girl, Gordon's War,* and *Countdown at Kusini*—were received unevenly, there was a significance to his work that critics could not ignore. Bogle commented that "in a strange way . . . Davis could be called one of the more serious black directors of his era; political undercurrents [ran] throughout much of his work. He . . . never settled for simply making a standard action movie. . . . [He] hoped to take black American cinema into a new, more politically oriented direction [and] for that he has to be commended."

Davis spent the remainder of the 1970s pursuing diverse interests. From 1974 until 1978 he and his wife co-hosted the *Ossie Davis and Ruby Dee Story Hour* on radio. In 1976 he appeared in the film *Let's Do It Again.* Also that year, his play *Escape to Freedom: A Play About Young Frederick Douglass* was produced at New York City's Town Hall. In 1981, he and Ruby began appearing in *With Ossie and Ruby* on PBS. Through their company, Emmalyn II Productions, they co-produced the show with two public television stations. The program, which presented a broad mix of material, ran for three years. "It was one of the highlights of our lives because it gave us the opportunity to do shows by authors we respect," Dee told the *Greensboro News and Record.*

With their children, Davis and Dee worked in the context of Emmalyn II through much of the 1980s, producing a variety of programs including *Martin Luther King: The Dream and the Drum* and *A Walk Through History* for PBS. Far from withdrawing from acting, though, Davis continued working on the stage, in film, and on television. In 1986 he starred in a production of Tony Award-Winning American dramatist Herb Gardner's *I'm Not Rappaport* at actor Burt Reynolds's Jupiter Theater in Florida. Davis appeared in Spike Lee's 1988 film *School Daze* and in 1989, he played "the mayor" in Lee's controversial and acclaimed *Do the Right Thing.* It was a role in which he presided not only over the street where the film's action took place but over the coming of age of a new generation of black filmmakers.

Past 70 and in the public eye more than ever for his stunning performance as the Good Reverend Dr. Purify in Lee's *Jungle Fever,* as well as for his regular spot as Burt Reynolds's best friend on television's *Evening Shade,* Davis reflected on his career, telling *American Visions,* "I was able to hang on to the gifts of my childhood longer than normal, to daydream, to think of things in the imagination, to play and be a play actor." In 1992 Davis exercised his gifts as a novelist when he published a story for young adults called *Just Like Martin.* Centered on the activities of a small-town Alabama church congregation during the civil rights movement, Davis's first foray into fiction is "an attempt to recapture some sense of the black church as a political and moral base in the fight against racism," according to *Publishers Weekly* contributor Calvin Reid. Of his decision to move in this direction, Davis told Reid, "I can move between these different disciplines because I am essentially a storyteller, and the story I want to tell is about black people. Sometimes I sing the story, sometimes I dance it, sometimes I tell tall tales about it, but I always want to share my great satisfaction at being a black man at this time in history."

Selected writings

Plays

(And director) *Goldbrickers of 1944* (produced in Liberia), 1944.
Alice in Wonder (produced at Elks Community Theater, 1952; revised and produced as *The Big Deal* at New Playwrights Theater, New York City, 1953).
Purlie Victorious (produced at Cort Theatre, New York City), 1961.
Curtain Call, Mr. Aldridge, Sir (produced at University of California at Santa Barbara), 1968.
(With Philip Rose, Peter Udell, and Gary Geld) *Purlie* (produced at Broadway Theater, New York City), 1970.
Escape to Freedom: A Play About Young Frederick Douglass (produced at Town Hall, New York City), 1976.
Langston: A Play, Delacorte, 1982.

Film and television

Gone Are the Days (film), Trans Lux, 1963.
(With Arnold Perl; and director) *Cotton Comes to Harlem* (film), United Artists, 1970.
(And director) *Kongi's Harvest* (film; adapted from work by Wole Soyinka), Calpenny Films Nigeria Ltd., 1970.

Today Is Ours, CBS-TV, 1974.

Fiction

Just Like Martin, Simon & Schuster, 1992.

Contributor to periodicals, including *Negro History Bulletin, Negro Digest,* and *Freedomways.*

Sources

Books

Bogle, Donald, *Blacks in American Film and Television,* Garland, 1988.

Funke, Lewis, *The Curtain Rises—The Story of Ossie Davis,* Grosset & Dunlap, 1971.

Periodicals

American Visions, April/May 1992.
Greensboro News and Record (North Carolina), August 17, 1989.
Los Angeles Times, July 6, 1989.
Milwaukee Journal, June 9, 1991.
Newsday, March 24, 1987.
New York Times, June 30, 1989.
Palm Beach Post (Florida), May 10, 1988.
Publishers Weekly, December 28, 1992.

—Jordan Wankoff

Ulysses Dove

1947—

Choreographer, teacher, dancer

"I am interested in passion," internationally acclaimed dance choreographer Ulysses Dove told Sally Sommer of *Connoisseur* magazine when speaking about his work. "In *every* embrace, *every* second of life [should be] lived so fully that there can be no regrets, no retreats, no looking back." His modern and ballet dance pieces—which have been called sexually charged, bold, powerful, and strikingly original—ardently reflect this theme while celebrating the freedom of full self-expression.

tributor commented that the performance of *Bad Blood* was "terrifically danced by a cast of seven . . . around a theme of male-female confrontation. . . . Dove managed a lively, sometimes even a wryly humorous exchange between couples in terms of physical challenges laid down and picked up with gusto by both parties. There's lots of hard, taut body-contact . . . as well as some ingenious, even gasp-provoking, solutions to the puzzles presented by bodies interlocked in improbable complexes."

A South Carolina-born globetrotter who was well known in Europe before he began garnering recognition in the United States in the early 1990s, Dove has produced a dozen forceful and contemporary dance pieces that often reach audiences on a visceral level. Through dance Dove conveys a sense of the larger social world, and his pieces, from *Bad Blood* to *Vespers* to the award-winning *Episodes,* reflect his overall concern about human behavior, however unsettling that behavior might be.

Specifically, Dove presents the shifting balance of power between men and women. In some of his pieces men submit to women's demands; in others women submit to men's. Concerning this theme, a *Musical America* con-

About the quality of Dove's work, Gus Solomons, Jr., observed in *Dance Magazine,* "He translates emotion into movement with stunning clarity: His works resonate with emotional truth. *Episodes* epitomizes the character of Dove's choreography. It is a suite of searing encounters between men and women caught in diagonal corridors of light. They hurl themselves against one another in passionate embraces that could at once signify love or hate. High-flung limbs whip the air like blades. Women wrap themselves weblike around the men, only to be shed with shuddering vehemence. The moving bodies become the emotion itself, as they attract and repulse each other at whizzing speeds with courageous assurance."

Having performed with legendary dance masters Merce Cunningham and Alvin Ailey, Dove is said to have been influenced by both. Wrote William Harris in the *New York Times,* "Within his steps, one can see . . . the precise coolness of Cunningham and the dramatic, sweaty energy of Ailey." Alan M. Kriegsman further observed in the *Washington Post* that Dove, along with Bill T. Jones and other fledgling black choreographers, was a "beneficiary of Ailey's vision and largess." But the road toward self-expression was not an easy one for Dove to travel.

Born in Jonesville, South Carolina, to Ulysses and Ruth Lee Dove on January 17, 1947, Dove grew up in a non-artistic family. Rebelling against the discipline of his Catholic elementary school, Dove spontaneously made up "interpretive" dances that he performed before his classmates and his parents. "Sometimes that dance would get me sent to bed early," he said during an interview with Peter Barton, author of the book *Staying Power: Performing Artists Talk About Their Lives.* Though his parents were intrigued by his youthful performances, the idea of a male dancing unsettled them, according to Dove.

By the time he was ready for college Dove decided to please his family and study medicine. He enrolled at Howard University in Washington, D.C. as a pre-medical student. But he wasn't happy. "It didn't take me long to figure out that that would never do," he told Barton. After seeing the Martha Graham Dance Company perform for the first time Dove was exhilarated and decided on a dance career. "There was no separation between me and the stage," he recalled to Barton. "I was up there. Rather than thinking, 'Ahh,' I thought, 'I can do that! The only thing that lies between me and that is training.'"

Despite his parents' objections he transferred from Howard to Wisconsin University in Milwaukee, where he studied dance on a scholarship. Later, he attended Bennington College on a dance fellowship and graduated from there with a B.A. in 1970. During his college years, Dove studied ballet and modern dance with teachers who made a lasting impression on him, including Carolyn Tate, Judith Dunn, and Mary Hinkson. After college he moved to New York City, where he danced with different companies, among them those of Jose Limon, Mary Anthony, Pearl Lang, and Anna Sokolow.

Danced With Cunningham's Company, Then Ailey's

When he received a scholarship to study with Merce Cunningham, Dove ended up performing with that company for three years. "I went to Merce Cunningham for classes to get in shape, so I could audition for Alvin Ailey," he told Barton. "But my audition with Alvin was disastrous. . . . They couldn't come to a decision. Meantime, Merce asked me to join his company. I thought: 'You can't say no to this guy. He's a genius.'" About Merce Cunningham, Dove later told Sommer in *Connoisseur,* "He made me understand space and time. He taught me about having integrity and belief in what you are dancing."

Still, after three years with Cunningham, Dove felt artistically constrained because he was performing dances by the same choreographer. "I thought, either I have to stay here and become a Cunningham dancer, or I'll have to keep going on this journey to find different aspects of dance that fit me," he reminisced in the interview with Barton. Confused about what to do next, Dove returned home to Columbia, South Carolina, in 1973 and debated giving up dance altogether. But a couple of months later he was back in New York auditioning again for Alvin Ailey's company, which performed dances by different choreographers. This time he was accepted. He remained with the company for seven years, performing pieces and eventually choreographing his first dance, *I See the Moon . . . and the Moon Sees Me,* in 1979.

"Since the first piece I did, Alvin believed in my work," he told Solomons. "He would take the time to argue with me, because he knew I would just not accept anything unless I really believed it. . . . The crazier my stuff got, the more I found my own voice, the more he liked it." Dove has credited Ailey with having a more personal impact on him than Cunningham. "He taught me about humanity," Dove continued, adding, "His heart beat once for himself and once for the rest of the world."

Stopped Performing and Focused on Choreography

In 1980 Dove stopped performing and focused on creating dances. On commission he developed a solo dance called *Inside* for Judith Jamison of the Ailey company. Three other dances by Dove have since been presented by the Ailey company, including *Vespers,* which the company continues to perform. Then Dove became involved with the experimental division of the Paris Opera Ballet, the Groupe de Recherche Choréographique de l'Opéra de Paris, as an assistant director, teacher, and choreographer. But after Rudolf Nureyev took charge of the Paris Opera Ballet in 1983, Dove departed, apparently because Nureyev did not want him concentrating on choreography.

Since 1983 Dove has worked in Europe and the United States as a free-lance choreographer for international ballet and modern dance companies. His works include: *Bad Blood* (1984), performed by Les Ballets Jazz de Montreal; *Vespers* (1986), danced by the Dayton Contemporary Dance Company and the Alvin Ailey American Dance Theater; *Episodes* (1987), presented by the London Festival Ballet and the Ailey company; and *Serious Pleasures* (1992), performed by the American Ballet Theatre. In addition, Dove choreographed a dance for an operatic saga called *Civil Wars,* which was performed as part of the New Wave Festival at the Brooklyn Academy of Music in 1986.

Controversy Generated by Overt Sexuality in Dances

Dove's dance pieces have generated controversy because of their overt sexuality and perceived aggression. Initial performances of *Bad Blood* produced mixed reactions. One of these was a commentary by Hal de Becker in *Dance Magazine* about Dove's theme of warring sexes: "Ulysses Dove's *Bad Blood* gave considerable amplitude to the dancers' abilities and possessed many original choreographic ideas. But his female characters were treated with so little tenderness and subjected to so much arrogance and roughness by their male partners . . . that many in the audience grew offended by what seemed to be a pervasive abuse of women."

His 1986 piece *Vespers* was praised for the very thing that *Bad Blood* reportedly lacked. It realistically and sympathetically portrays the trials of women, and black women in particular. Janice Ross of the Oakland *Tribune* lauded *Vespers* for its "harsh spectacle of a mad matriarchy of fierce women." Camille Hardy, writing in *Dance Magazine,* described the piece this way: "*Vespers* by Ulysses

> "I am interested in passion . . . in every embrace, every second of life being lived so fully that there can be no regrets, no retreats, no looking back."

Dove is as powerful as it is stark. Danced by six women in simple black dresses with no props except half a dozen wooden chairs . . . Dove has limited the movement vocabulary to a terse selection of spirals, single hands pointing upward, and arabesques that slice like arrows into your heart. . . . Grief and determination—unvarnished and unadorned—propel the cast . . . through a dance of black women that is, quite simply, a knockout."

Episodes, one of Dove's most energetic and accomplished pieces, dramatically expresses his war-between-the-sexes theme. In the *New York Times,* Anna Kisselgoff summed it up as "a tough-minded dance piece . . . full of energy, sexual connotations and technical polish from dancers who seem shot out of a cannon . . . the kind of choreography that propels young audiences to their feet and sets them screaming." She continued, "The work is a visceral turn-on, testimony to Mr. Dove's incontrovertible gift for exciting the senses, for exploiting a physical and kinetic impact to its utmost. Young viewers identify with its transient street-smart courtships. Older spectators . . . may admire the piece more than actually like it." Nevertheless, for her it showed "the complexity of human relationships."

Career Received Boost After Performance of *Episodes*

Many critics have suggested that Dove's career received a boost after the 1989 U.S. performance of *Episodes* by the Ailey company. Later, *Episodes* was shown on television as part of PBS-TV's *Dance in America* series. It also won a "Bessie" choreography award. Still, during the 1980s and early 1990s Dove had not really made a big splash in his own country. "I wanted to come back and do all the major New York companies," he told Martha Southgate of *Essence* in 1992. By the time his piece *Serious Pleasures* was performed for the first time by the American Ballet Theatre in Chicago that year, Dove's notoriety at home seemed assured. Though Dove said in *Essence* that the piece is about "love in the age of AIDS" and is "serious business," some reviewers criticized it for being trendy and superficial. "Rather than come to intimate terms with his own vision," wrote Laura Jacobs in the *New Leader*, "[Dove] has chosen to play it cool."

Criticism notwithstanding, Dove has high expectations of his pieces and his dancers. "If I weren't so particular about what I do," he told Harris in the *New York Times*, "I could be working all the time. But I don't want to be the . . . special of the month. . . . I'm not easy to work with, because I want a lot." Above all, his main concern is how his dancers convey the intense passion that has become the signature of his work. "You have to be there even before the music starts," he told the dancers rehearsing *Serious Pleasures* before it premiered. "You're already alive . . . and you have to show that to the audience."

Sources

Books

Barton, Peter, *Staying Power: Performing Artists Talk About Their Lives,* Dial Press, 1980, pp. 126-137.

Periodicals

Connoisseur, April 1991, p. 60.
Dance Magazine, April 1987, pp. 20, 24; April 1988, pp. 38-39; April 1990, pp. 64-65; June 1991, p. 79; May 1992, pp. 54-56.
Essence, March 1992, p. 46.
Musical America, May 1987, pp. 31-32; May 1990, pp. 14-15.
New Leader, June 29, 1992, p. 23.
New York Post, December 14, 1989; December 7, 1990.
New York Times, December 3, 1989, sec. 2, p. 32; December 14, 1989.
Tribune (Oakland, CA), February 24, 1989.
Washington Post, June 1, 1990.

—Alison Carb Sussman

Marian Wright Edelman

1939—

Attorney, administrator, social activist

Marian Wright Edelman, the leading advocate for children in the United States and the founder of the Children's Defense Fund, can trace her commitment to serve others directly back to her own childhood in the southern United States. Her father, Arthur Wright, was a Baptist preacher who raised his five children to believe that it was their Christian duty to help others and to try to make the world a better place. Although people of color were treated unfairly in their segregated South Carolina hometown, he urged the community to follow the self-help philosophy of African American labor leader A. Philip Randolph and do what it could for itself. Edelman remembers that when blacks were barred from the public parks in her neighborhood, her father helped build a park and roller-skating rink behind his church for them to use. "That taught me, if you don't like the way the world is, you change it," she told *Time*. "You have an obligation to change it. You just do it one step at a time."

Since those early days, Edelman has taken many steps toward her goal of making the world a better place, especially for the poor and for minorities. She served as a civil rights lawyer in Mississippi at the height of the civil rights movement in the 1960s; she brought the plight of the desperately poor families of the Mississippi Delta to the attention of Senator Robert Kennedy; and she helped begin and operate a Head Start program in Mississippi, designed to give underprivileged children a boost before entering the formal education system.

Born in 1939 in segregated Bennettsville, South Carolina, Edelman was a teenager when the Supreme Court's historic *Brown v. Board of Education* decision banned school segregation and ignited the fledgling civil rights movement in the United States. As reported in *Parade* magazine, the dying words of Arthur Wright to his daughter, then only 14 years old, were: "Don't let anything get in the way of your education." In 1956, Edelman enrolled at Spelman College in Altanta, a straightlaced, liberal arts school for black women. As the winner of a Merrill scholarship, she was able to spend her junior year abroad in Geneva, Switzerland, and then traveled the following summer to the Soviet Union under a Lisle Fellowship. "That year gave me the confidence that I could navigate in the world and do just about anything," she said in the *New Yorker*.

Returning to college in 1959, Edelman plunged into the early civil rights movement. She often heard Martin Luther King, Jr., speak on the Spelman campus and helped organize other students to participate in sit-ins in Atlanta to protest laws of

At a Glance...

B orn June 6, 1939, in Bennettsville, SC; daughter of Arthur Jerome (a Baptist minister) and Maggie (Bowen) Wright; married Peter B. Edelman (an attorney and professor of law), July 14, 1968; children: Joshua, Jonah, Ezra. *Education:* Studied in Paris, France, and Geneva, Switzerland, 1958-59; Spelman College, B.A., 1960; received law degree from Yale University Law School, 1963. *Religion:* Baptist.

NAACP Legal Defense and Education Fund, New York City, staff attorney, 1963-64, director of office in Jackson, MS, 1964-68; partner in Washington Research Project of Southern Center for Public Policy, 1968-73; director of Harvard University Center for Law and Education, 1971-73; Children's Defense Fund (CDF), Washington, DC, founder, 1973, and president, 1973—. Member of numerous professional and civic organizations.

Selected awards: Louise Waterman Wise Award, 1970; Whitney M. Young Award, 1979; leadership award from National Women's Political Caucus, 1980; Black Women's Forum Award, 1980; MacArthur fellow, 1985; Martha May Eliot Award from American Public Health Association, 1985; John W. Gardner leadership award, independent sector, 1985; Grenville Clark Prize, 1986; A. Philip Randolph Award, 1987; William P. Dawson Award from Congressional Black Caucus, 1987; Ronald McDonald Children's Charities Award, 1988; Gandhi Peace Award, 1989; Fordham Stein Prize, 1989; Murray-Green-Meany Award from AFL-CIO, 1989; Frontrunner Award from Sara Lee Corporation, 1990; Jefferson Award from American Institute for Public Service, 1991; many honorary degrees.

Addresses: *Office*—Office of the President, Children's Defense Fund, 122 C St. NW, Washington, DC 20001.

She was accepted at Yale Law School, where she met Bob Moses, a pioneering member of the Student Nonviolent Coordinating Committee (SNCC) who worked from time to time with the Yale-based Northern Student Movement. He was staunchly committed to breaking the cycle of racist intimidation that denied people of color their right to vote, and he fought to increase black voter registration in Mississippi, which was then considered a dangerous place for civil rights activists to work. Regardless of the hazards, Edelman went to Mississippi on a mission to recruit and register black voters during spring break of her third year at law school.

After graduating from Yale Law School in 1963, she spent one year in New York as a staff attorney for the NAACP Legal Defense and Education Fund before returning to Mississippi, where she headed the fund's Jackson office for four years. The first black woman lawyer to practice in the state, she defended many African Americans who were arrested during the voter registration efforts of the 1960s. In the summer of 1964, the Ku Klux Klan rocked the South with their brutal white supremacist acts. But Edelman learned to live with violence and fear. "That summer, I very seldom got a client out of jail who had not been beaten, who didn't have broken bones or missing teeth," she told the *New Yorker.* "One young boy I represented had been shot and killed in jail, and I had to take his parents to the funeral home to view the body. . . . It was [one] of those watershed experiences—I had nightmares for weeks, but afterward I felt I could face anything."

Edelman also became involved in efforts to establish a Head Start program for poor children in Mississippi and helped in the fight to keep it funded year after year. At the same time, mechanization of the cotton industry had created tremendous poverty in Mississippi, but few people outside the state were aware of it. Edelman helped bring the problem to national attention when she testified before a Senate subcommittee holding a public hearing in Jackson in 1967. Later she took two of the senators, Robert Kennedy and Joseph Clark, both Democrats, on a tour of Mississippi Delta slum areas where families lived without heat, light, or running water. During this trip she became acquainted with Peter Edelman, a white, Jewish lawyer who was then serving as Senator Kennedy's legislative assistant.

From Mississippi to Washington, D.C.

Edelman moved to Washington, D.C., in 1968. "Peter was one reason," she told Terry in *Parade*—within months the couple was married—but Edelman also knew that she could be more effective in her quest for social justice if she were based in the nation's capital. That same year, the United States was sent into a tailspin by the deaths of civil rights leader Martin Luther King, Jr., and Senator Kennedy, both at the hands of assassins.

segregation. As a volunteer worker at a local office of the National Association for the Advancement of Colored People (NAACP), Edelman realized that impoverished African Americans had almost no one to represent them. Instead of pursuing graduate work in Russian and entering the foreign service as she had planned, she decided to study law. "I had no aptitude or interest in law. I simply thought about what was needed," she told Wallace Terry in *Parade.*

Shortly after Edelman relocated to Washington, King's Poor People's Campaign—a mass demonstration for social and economic equity—arrived in the capital with plans of carrying on their slain leader's work. Their shock and grief over King's death, combined with a lack of Washington savvy, made it impossible for the group to coordinate their crusade. Edelman, who had learned the Washington ropes through her work for Head Start, stepped in to help pull the campaign together. She also began working on other important issues, like child care legislation, and laid the foundation for the establishment a few years later of the Children's Defense Fund.

The Edelmans went on to have three sons and instilled in them a sense of pride in the richness of their mixed racial background and a deep respect for both Jewish and Christian religious traditions. Raising three children while pursuing a very demanding vocation has given Edelman a personal perspective on the problems of working parents. "I who have everything am hanging in there by my fingernails," she told *Ms.* "I don't know how poor women manage."

Edelman's work to help "poor women manage" a little more easily intensified in the early 1970s. In 1971, she helped put together a broad coalition of groups in support of a comprehensive child development bill. It sailed through both the U.S. House and the Senate but was vetoed by President Richard Nixon. Although Edelman was disappointed, she claimed that the effort marked an important beginning for her. She had been struggling for years to get more federal help for the poor and minorities. But the child care issue helped her realize that by focusing on the needs of children—all children—she could cut across class and race to gain broader support. "I was absolutely shattered [by the veto]," she told the *New Yorker.* "But that whole experience was very useful to me. I'd learned the importance of being highly specific in my goals. I'd got the idea that children might be a very effective means for broadening the base for change. The country was tired of the concerns of the sixties. When you talked about poor people or black people, you faced a shrinking audience."

Founded the Children's Defense Fund

In 1973 Edelman founded the Children's Defense Fund (CDF) to protect the interests of the country's children. Supported entirely by private foundations, the CDF studies and documents conditions affecting children and lobbies intensively for legislation it believes will help them. Through the CDF, Edelman called attention to many issues on the national agenda that had previously been ignored—from foster care to teen pregnancy to child care. She has also expressed many of her views in her books *Families in*

Peril: An Agenda for Social Change and *The Measure of Our Success: A Letter to My Children and Yours.*

Edelman is consulted by both lawmakers and journalists on virtually any issue relating to children. Senator Edward Kennedy has called her "the 101st senator on children's issues." "She has real power in congress, and uses it brilliantly," Kennedy told *Time.* One of the sources of Edelman's credibility is the CDF's respected documentation of the status of American children. Many find it hard to

> "Investing in children is not a national luxury or a national choice. It's a national necessity."

argue with the organization's overwhelming statistics. According to the CDF, one-fifth of all American children—twelve and a half million—live in poverty. "If recent trends continue," Edelman was quoted as saying in *Parade* in 1993, "by the end of the century, poverty will overtake one in every four children."

In addition, the United States has one of the highest infant mortality rates among the 20 leading industrialized countries. And every year almost half a million teenage girls give birth. As child psychiatrist Robert Coles told the *New Yorker,* Edelman "has built up a major American institution that is *sui generis* [unique]. Of course, this country has always been fascinated by children because of its own youthfulness and hopefulness. But she educates us about them. She organizes a body of knowledge—statistical, investigative, observational and analytic—and she puts it together in astonishing ways. One of the major achievements of the Children's Defense Fund is its documentation. There's a faith in knowledge . . . that the truth will somehow prevail, and so they are constantly educating us."

Although the administrations of presidents Nixon, Gerald Ford, and Jimmy Carter were often opposed to increased spending for social services, Edelman lobbied, often successfully, for more support for the handicapped, Head Start programs, foster care, and health and nutrition for poor women and children. Congress did enact a child welfare bill in 1980, but when other programs for poor families were slashed under President Ronald Reagan, Edelman struggled to at least keep fundamental legislation in place.

In the mid-1980s, as poverty and homelessness increased, Congress began to restore some funding for social programs. In 1984 the CDF successfully lobbied for increased Medicaid coverage for poor children. On this, as on many other issues, Edelman argued for the importance of what she calls preventive investment: "One dollar up front prevents the spending of many dollars down the road," she explained in *Ms*. In this case, she showed that increasing health services to children leads to lower doctor and hospital bills later on.

Focused on Child Care and Pregnancy Prevention

In the late 1980s Edelman felt the United States was ready to address the child care issue. After consulting with 170 groups all over the country, the CDF put together a multibillion-dollar program that would put some money toward helping low and moderate income families pay for child care and some money toward improving child care for all families. It also established strict health, safety, and quality guidelines. Although the bill had wide support, it foundered in the last days of the Reagan administration and was reintroduced in the 101st Congress.

Edelman's concerns about child welfare extend to the rampant problem of teen pregnancy, which plays a major role, she says, in perpetuating poverty. "I saw from our own statistics that fifty-five and a half percent of all black babies were born out of wedlock, a great many of them to teenage girls," she said in the *New Yorker*. "It just hit me over the head—that situation insured black poverty for the next generation." To combat the problem, which affects proportionately more black teens, but many more white teens overall, the CDF has sponsored an annual pregnancy prevention conference that brings together social workers and community and church leaders from all over the country. By emphasizing pregnancy prevention, the group has sidestepped the issue of abortion and attracted broad support. The CDF has also tried to reach teens and their parents through publicity campaigns. One of the organization's posters featured a pregnant teenage girl and asked the question, "Will your child learn to multiply before she learns to subtract?"

On all these issues, from child care to teen pregnancy to Head Start, Edelman has a reputation not only for concern and vision, but for formidable political skill as well. Peter Edelman, himself a Georgetown University law professor, told the *New Yorker* that his wife has "an absolutely super strategic and tactical sense, a real smell for how to get things done. . . . She understands how the system works. She's as tough and determined as anyone can be, but always within the rules of the system." Her friend Robert Coles sees another side to Edelman. "There's still . . . a kind of lovely innocence [about her]," he remarked in the *New Yorker*. "It's a mixture of gentleness and personal dignity and savvy, and maybe even southerness. She didn't fall prey to arrogance or smugness. She had good judg-

ment, a sharp, active mind and she knew how to stay connected to the ordinary people of the region."

The 1990s and Beyond

Under Edelman, the CDF has ballooned in size—to a staff of over 100 child care, welfare, and educational specialists, and an annual budget of approximately $9 million. More importantly, in the decades since its founding, the agency has become a central organ of hope for the 13.4 million American children who live in poverty. Possessing the commitment of a missionary and the tactical skills of a seasoned Washington insider, Edelman, as a voice of conscience, has challenged politicians and everyday citizens to make good on their professed dedication to the well-being of the nation's youth.

In Edelman's eyes, ignorance is the explanation for the empty lip service paid to an issue as critical as child welfare. "There's ignorance in people who just don't know that we have a national child emergency," she told *Black Enterprise*. "And there are a lot of people who are conveniently ignorant—they don't want to know." Edelman's educational crusade, involving her tactical placement of the CDF at the center of many high-profile policy debates, has been a battle against common yet mistaken assumptions that threaten many of the CDF's basic initiatives. Edelman, for example, must frequently tell people that the majority of poor children in the United States are white and from rural and suburban areas, thus correcting the impression that her agency's programs benefit only inner-city blacks on welfare. To those who loudly bemoan the throwing of public funds at social programs, Edelman answers that it is wiser to spend some money on preventive medicine, such as prenatal care, rather than huge amounts on the treatment of low-birth-weight babies whose parents may not be able to foot the hospital bills.

Most of Edelman's child-betterment sermons have been delivered in Washington, where her faith in government has endured despite years of cuts to many of the CDF's pet programs. Speaking on the benefits of government spending, notably President Lyndon Johnson's "Great Society" domestic programs of the 1960s, Edelman was quoted in the *New York Times* as saying, "The fact is we made dramatic progress in the 1960's in eradicating hunger and improving the health status of children, and then we just stopped trying." Her attempts to re-energize this public sector activism were rewarded in 1990 with the passage of a child care bill through Congress and in 1992 with a $200 million boost for Head Start funding. The child care go-around spawned a controversy involving Edelman, who publicly lambasted two representatives for, in her view, self-servingly leading a war against the legislation. This bitter attack, according to some observers, weakened the

CDF's effectiveness, but Edelman countered, saying her agency, unlike other lobbying organizations, represents a silent constituency—children—that is too precious for compromises and political games.

As much as Edelman understands her role as a government prod, she is aware that politics can never deliver all the answers, particularly in the area of child rearing, which is well beyond the bounds of legislation. In this vein, she has urged parents to reevaluate the messages they teach their children and to pay keen attention to the cultural signals—the images of sex and violence on television, for example—that frame the mindset of children and therefore play a central role in the development of the adults of tomorrow. "I think we've had a breakdown in values in all of our society," she noted in *Newsweek*. It is as a celebratory ode to family that Edelman wrote her 1992 bestseller *The Measure of Our Success: A Letter to My Children and Yours.* Hailed as a "profound and moving book" by *Library Journal* reviewer Angela Washington-Blair, the slim volume is a doctrinal overview of the moral values Edelman absorbed as a child—beliefs that have endured through her experiences as a mother and powerbroker. In it, she warns that "the 1990s struggle is for America's conscience and future—a future that is being determined right now in the bodies and minds and spirits of every American child."

Close Ties to Clinton Administration

When Bill Clinton was elected U.S. president, it was understood that Edelman, as a friend and intellectual soulmate of First Lady Hillary Clinton (who had earlier served as chairman of the CDF), would command a level of attention within the new administration that had been absent during the tenures of presidents Bush and Reagan. There were rumors that Edelman would join the cabinet, but she was quick to reaffirm her role as an advocate who relishes her independence. "I need to work outside government, on my own," she was quoted as saying in the *New York Times.* "I love what I do, and I think I am making a difference."

Edelman has estimated that it may cost as much as $47 billion to accomplish the goals articulated by the CDF in its "Leave No Child Behind" campaign, which began in 1992. The goals cover full-funding of Head Start, proper medical insurance for every child and pregnant mother, vaccinations for every child, and an expanded children's tax credit for parents.

Although the issues and the strategies have changed somewhat over the years, Edelman has maintained through it all the sense of commitment and hope with which she was raised. Through the CDF, she continues to address a wide range of issues relating to children—and to insist that the needs of children be taken seriously. "Investing in [children] is not a national luxury or a national choice," she told the *New Yorker.* "It's a national necessity. If the foundation of your house is crumbling, you don't say you can't afford to fix it while you're building astronomically expensive fences to protect it from outside enemies. The issue is not are we going to pay—it's are we going to pay now, up front, or are we going to pay a whole lot more later on."

Selected writings

Families in Peril: An Agenda for Social Change, Harvard University Press, 1987.
The Measure of Our Success: A Letter to My Children and Yours, Beacon, 1992.

Sources

Black Enterprise, May 1992, p. 67.
Christianity Today, March 17, 1989, p. 35.
Christian Science Monitor, November 5, 1987, p. 27; May 30, 1989, p. 19.
Ebony, July 1987, p. 60; August 1988, p. 128.
Essence, September 1980, p. 70; May 1988, p. 65.
Glamour, December 1990, p. 96.
Library Journal, May 1, 1992, p. 103.
Mother Jones, June 1990, p. 6; May/June 1991, p. 31.
Ms., July/August 1987, p. 98.
Nation, July 24-31, 1989.
Newsweek, June 8, 1992, p. 27; February 15, 1993, p. 20.
New Yorker, March 27, 1989, p. 48.
New York Review of Books, December 3, 1987, p. 26.
New York Times, January 5, 1990, p. A20; January 29, 1991, p. A18; May 19, 1991, sec. 1, p. 28; October 8, 1992, p. C1.
New York Times Book Review, June 7, 1987, p. 12.
Parade, February 14, 1993, p. 4.
People, July 6, 1992, p. 101.
Rolling Stone, December 10-24, 1992, p. 126.
Time, March 23, 1987, p. 27.
U.S. News & World Report, March 26, 1990, p. 22.

—*Cathleen Collins Lee and Isaac Rosen*

Duke Ellington

1899-1974

Pianist, bandleader, composer

Duke Ellington was a distinctive and pivotal figure in the world of jazz. While many critics agree that his flair for style far exceeded his raw musical talent, few dispute the significance of his impact on the music scene in the United States and abroad. A prolific composer, Ellington created over two thousand pieces of music, including the standard songs "It Don't Mean a Thing (If It Ain't Got That Swing)" and "Sophisticated Lady" and longer works like *Black, Brown, and Beige* and *The Liberian Suite.* With the variously named bands he led for more than fifty years, Ellington was responsible for many innovations in the jazz field, such as the introduction of "jungle-style" musical variations and the manipulation of the human voice as an instrument—singing notes without words. During the course of his long career, Ellington was showered with many honors, including the highest civilian award granted by the United States, the Presidential Medal of Freedom, which was presented to him by President Richard M. Nixon in 1969. "No one else in the . . . history of jazz," concluded critic Alistair Cooke in a 1983 issue of *Esquire,* "created so personal an orchestral sound and so continuously expanded the jazz idiom."

Born Edward Kennedy Ellington in Washington, D.C., on April 29, 1899, "Duke" earned his nickname at an early age to suit his aristocratic demeanor. He was brought up in a cultured, middle-class household: his father made blueprints for the U.S. Navy and served as a White House butler for extra income, and his mother, who hailed from a respected Washington family, set a dignified tone for the family to follow. "Ellington's parents lived by the ideal of Victorian gentility until they died," noted James Lincoln Collier in *Duke Ellington,* "and they raised Duke to it. . . . The view that he was special was cut into Duke's consciousness when he was very young. . . . [He] came into his teens, then, as a protected and well-loved child, growing up in an orderly household where decorous behavior was simply part of the air he breathed; he was confident in manner and sure that he had . . . been born to high estate."

But Ellington matured at a time when attitudes and values were changing in America. The Harlem Renaissance—a period of heightened pride, interest, and activity in black arts and culture—was beginning to dawn. Rigid self-discipline was cast aside, and people began to indulge in the satisfaction of a variety of earthly desires. This newfound freedom to enjoy "good times," as Collier put it, had a profound influence on American music. The syncopated rhythms of ragtime, a wildly popular precursor of jazz that flourished in the late 1800s,

At a Glance...

Born Edward Kennedy Ellington, April 29, 1899, in Washington, DC; died of lung cancer, May 24, 1974, in New York City; son of James Edward (a butler, carpenter, and blueprint maker) and Daisy (Kennedy) Ellington; married Edna Thompson, July 2, 1918; children: Mercer. *Education:* Left high school in his senior year; later received honorary diploma.

Worked in a soda shop and as a sign painter, c. 1914-17; began playing in jazz bands, c. 1917; served as a U.S. Navy and State Department messenger during World War I; formed his first band, 1918; performed in Washington, DC and New York City during the 1920s; toured Europe in the 1930s; appeared many times at Newport Jazz Festival; concert performer and recording artist (primarily on Reprise and RCA labels) with his various bands until his death in 1974. Appeared in and/or wrote scores for films, including *Check and Double Check,* 1930, *Murder at the Vanities,* 1934, *Anatomy of a Murder,* 1959, *Paris Blues,* 1961, and *Assault on a Queen,* 1966.

Selected awards: Spingarn Medal from the National Association for the Advancement of Colored People, 1959; Academy Award nomination for the score of *Paris Blues,* 1961; Lifetime Achievement Award from the National Academy of Recording Arts and Sciences (NARAS), 1966; Grammy Awards in several categories, including jazz composition and jazz performance—big band, 1966, 1967, 1968, 1971, 1972, 1976, and 1979; Presidential Medal of Freedom from Richard M. Nixon, 1969; inducted into NARAS Hall of Fame, 1990; elected to the National Institute of Arts and Letters.

is above all a total freedom to express oneself," he concluded, as quoted by Stanley Dance in Peter Gammond's *Duke Ellington: His Life and Music.*

A Late Bloomer

Both his father and his mother could play the piano, and Ellington was exposed to music at an early age. The Ellingtons were strongly religious and hoped that if their son learned piano he would later exchange it for the church organ, but at first he showed little interest in music. He proved to be an uncooperative student of his ironically named piano teacher—Miss Clinkscales—and managed to wrangle his way out of lessons after just a few months.

As he grew older, Ellington became interested in drawing and painting. He won a prize from the National Association for the Advancement of Colored People (NAACP) for a poster he created, and was eventually offered a scholarship to the prestigious Pratt Institute in Brooklyn to study commercial art. But a latent interest in music kept him from pursuing a career in art. According to some biographers, Ellington's motivations to make it in the music world were far from pure: he apparently felt that he could earn more money as a bandleader than as an artist, and he noticed that pretty girls tended to flock around piano players.

Ellington lacked the self-discipline to engage in the formal study of the piano. However, he did begin to take the piano more seriously as a high school student, learning harmonies from his school's music teacher, Henry Grant. But Ellington never really learned to read music, and he could never play a musical selection for piano on demand. Ellington's son, Mercer, was quoted in Collier's *Duke Ellington* as having said: "The greater part of his knowledge was self-taught, by ear, and gradually acquired." Collier suggested that Duke's pride and stubbornness were at the root of his roundabout musical education. "This was the hard way of doing it, but it was the way [he] preferred, even if it would take him more time and cost him more energy."

Despite his unorthodox training, Ellington achieved the power to leave an audience spellbound. In an essay dated September 1957 in *Duke Ellington: His Life and Music,* Hughues Panassié noted, "Duke might not be one of the most agile or brilliant technicians of the keyboard, but what a great stylist he is!. . . He [puts] so much of his own spirit into the band. . . . He is an outstanding creator who puts all that is humanly possible into the greatest of jazz orchestras."

Formed His Own Band

Around 1914, while working after school in a soda shop,

gave way in the early 1900s to the blues of the Mississippi Delta area. New Orleans, Louisiana is generally regarded as the hot spot in music history where ragtime, blues, and other forms coalesced, giving birth to jazz.

But, according to Collier, "it was not until 1915, when a cadre of white musicians brought it to Chicago, that [jazz] made a significant splash. The stir it created there encouraged an entrepreneur to bring . . . the Original Dixieland Jazz Band to New York, where it also made a hit. . . . [Their] records became best-sellers, and the jazz boom began." And so the 1920s came to be known as the Jazz Age. The independent-minded Ellington fell in love with the sounds of the time. "Jazz

Ellington wrote his first jazz song, "Soda Fountain Rag." He later dropped out of school to pursue his musical career, playing in jazz bands by night and supplementing his income by painting signs during the day. Often he managed to persuade club owners to let him paint the signs announcing the group's engagement. Around the same time, Ellington married schoolmate Edna Thompson, who had become pregnant with their son, Mercer.

Influenced by the style of earlier jazz artist Doc Perry, Ellington continued to work on his piano playing and, after the end of World War I, formed his own band. Critics contend that it was his band, rather than his piano, that was his true instrument. He composed not so much with a particular instrument in mind, but rather thinking of the current band member who played that instrument, suiting the music to the style of the player. The turnover rate in Ellington's band was not high, but due to the band's longevity many musicians and singers played with Ellington over the years, among them: saxophonists "Toby" Otto Hardwick, Harry Carney, Johnny Hodges, and Paul Gonsalves; trumpeters Artie Whetsol, Bubber Miley, and Cootie Williams; banjo players Elmer Snowden and Sterling Conaway; drummer "Sonny" William Greer; clarinet and sax player Barney Bigard; bass player Wellman Braud; trombonist Joe Nanton; vocalist Adelaide Hall; and pianist-composer Billy Strayhorn.

Ellington and his band, then known as the Washingtonians, began playing local clubs and parties in Washington, D.C., but during the early 1920s moved to New York City, where they secured steady work at the midtown Kentucky Club and, later, a three-year engagement at the popular Cotton Club. His notable compositions during this period included "Black and Tan Fantasy" and "Love Creole," both of which became jazz standards.

During the 1920s and 1930s, Ellington branched out into writing musical revues, such as *Chocolate Kiddies,* a success in Germany; playing in Broadway musicals, such as Florenz Ziegfeld's 1929 *Show Girl;* and appearing with his band in motion pictures, including the 1930 Amos and Andy feature *Check and Double Check.* Ellington's 1931 long piece, titled *Creole Rhapsody,* offered "confirmation of [his] emergence as a major composer," according to Collier. He soon added to the band's popularity with the legendary cuts "It Don't Mean a Thing (If It Ain't Got That Swing)" and "Sophisticated Lady."

Throughout the 1930s, Ellington also played the hot, primitive sounds of so-called "jungle music" and began experimenting with the infusion of Latin American elements into jazz. In 1939 Strayhorn joined Ellington's band, beginning a composition partnership that would last until the former's death in 1967. Strayhorn is perhaps best known for writing the band's theme, "Take the 'A' Train." The band's horizons expanded geographically in the 1930s

as well—Ellington was well received on tours throughout the United States and in Europe.

In 1943 Ellington helped set up an annual jazz concert series at New York City's Carnegie Hall that lasted until 1955. Ellington was deeply involved with it each year and used the event to premier new, longer works of jazz that he

> ## "Jazz is above all a total freedom to express oneself."

composed. For the first concert, he introduced *Black, Brown, and Beige,* a piece in three sections that represented symphonically the story of blacks in the United States. "Black" concerned people of color at work and at prayer, "Brown" celebrated black soldiers who fought in American wars, and "Beige" depicted the African American music of Harlem. Other Carnegie Hall debuts included *New World a-Comin',* about a black revolution to come after the end of World War II, and *Liberian Suite,* commissioned by the government of Liberia to honor its centennial.

"Blew the Joint Away" at Newport

The band's triumph at the Newport Jazz Festival of 1956 did much to broaden Ellington's audience. That year, Ellington's band was set to close the bill on the night of July 7th. Due to delayed starting times for earlier acts, the group did not take the stage until 11:45 p.m.—just 15 minutes before the concert was scheduled to end. Some members of the audience were already starting to leave. After performing an elaborate suite and a few standard works, Ellington led the band into "Diminuendo and Crescendo in Blue," highlighted by the improvisations of tenor saxophonist Paul Gonsalves.

The piece brought listeners to their feet. "It was solid jazz, blazing hot," proclaimed Collier. "Four men went out and played . . . for six minutes and blew the joint away. . . . [The audience was] shaken by the music, and those who were there would never forget it. . . . Within weeks Ellington's picture was on the cover of *Time.* The record of the Newport concert sold in the hundreds of thousands and became Ellington's biggest seller."

The 1960s: Musician, Historian, Lecturer

Ellington continued to compose throughout the 1960s, writing scores for various motion pictures and garnering an

Academy Award nomination for the score of the 1961 film *Paris Blues,* which featured Paul Newman and Sidney Poitier as lovestruck musicians in Paris. Two years later, Ellington was appointed by President John F. Kennedy's Cultural Committee to represent the United States on a State Department-sponsored tour of the East, including Syria, Jordan, Afghanistan, India, Ceylon, Pakistan, Iran, Iraq, and Lebanon. Aside from performing in concert on the tour, Ellington lectured on the history of jazz, famous jazz musicians, and the state of American race relations.

During the mid-1960s Ellington and his band, ever innovative, started to perform jazz-style sacred-music concerts in large cathedrals throughout the world. The first was in San Francisco's Grace Episcopal Cathedral in 1965 and included *In the Beginning God.* Ellington featured another lineup of sacred songs at his 1968 concert in New York City's Episcopal Cathedral of St. John the Divine and went on to perform at St. Sulpice in Paris, Santa Maria del Mar in Barcelona, and Westminster Abbey in London.

Duke Ellington was active as a performer and composer until his death from lung cancer on May 24, 1974, in New York City. His compositions such as "Mood Indigo" and "In a Sentimental Mood" remain jazz standards more than half a century after their introduction. Following Ellington's death, his son, Mercer, who had been serving as the band's business manager and trumpet player, took over its leadership. But as Phyl Garland, writing in *Ebony* magazine, put it, the elder Ellington will always be remembered for "the daring innovations that came to mark his music—the strange modulations built upon lush melodies that ramble into unexpected places; the unorthodox construction of songs. . . ; the bold use of dissonance in advance of the time."

Selected compositions

Shorter works

"Black and Tan Fantasy," 1927.
"Creole Love Call," 1927.
"Hot and Bothered," 1928.
"Mood Indigo," 1931.
"It Don't Mean a Thing (If It Ain't Got That Swing)," 1932.
"Sophisticated Lady," 1933.
"Drop Me Off at Harlem," 1933.
"In a Sentimental Mood," 1935.
"Diminuendo and Crescendo in Blue," 1937.
"Caravan," 1937.
"Empty Ballroom Blues," 1938.
"Concerto for Cootie," 1939.

Other compositions include "Soda Fountain Rag," "Soli-

tude," "I Got It Bad and That Ain't Good," "When a Black Man's Blue," "Rockin' in Rhythm," and "The Blues Is Waitin'."

Longer works

Creole Rhapsody, 1931.
Black, Brown, and Beige, 1943.
New World a-Comin', 1945.
The Deep South Suite, 1946.
The Liberian Suite, 1947.
The Tattooed Bride, 1948.
Harlem, 1950.
Night Creature, 1955.
Festival Suite, 1956.
My People, 1963.
The Far East Suite, 1964.

Selected discography

Afro-Bossa, Reprise, 1963.
Happy Reunion (recorded 1957-1958), Sony, 1991.
At Newport, Columbia House Legends of Jazz Program, 1993.
The Beginning (recorded 1926-1928), Decca.
The Best of Duke Ellington, Capitol.
(With the Boston Pops) *Duke at Tanglewood,* RCA.
Early Ellington, Everest Archives.
The Ellington Era (two volumes), Columbia.
Fantasies, Harmony.
Hot in Harlem (recorded 1928-1929), Decca.
The Indispensable Duke Ellington, RCA.
In My Solitude, Harmony.

Sources

Books

Collier, James Lincoln, *Duke Ellington,* Oxford University Press, 1987.
Dance, Stanley, *The World of Duke Ellington,* Da Capo, 1980.
Ellington, Duke, *Music Is My Mistress,* Doubleday, 1973.
Ellington, Mercer, and Stanley Dance, *Duke Ellington in Person,* Houghton Mifflin, 1978.
Frankl, Ron, *Duke Ellington,* Chelsea House, 1988.
Gammond, Peter, editor, *Duke Ellington: His Life and Music,* Da Capo, 1977.
Jewell, Derek, *Duke: A Portrait of Duke Ellington,* Norton, 1977.

Rattenbury, Ken, *Duke Ellington: Jazz Composer,* Yale University Press, 1991.

Periodicals

Crisis, January 1982.
Ebony, July 1969, p. 29.
Esquire, December 1983.
Newsweek, May 12, 1969.
New York Times Magazine, September 12, 1965, p. 64.
Progressive, August 1982.

Reader's Digest, November 1969, p. 108.

A permanent exhibit titled *Duke Ellington: American Musician* was installed at the Smithsonian's Museum of American History, Washington, DC, in the late 1980s; a larger exhibit, *Beyond Category: The Musical Genius of Duke Ellington,* was scheduled for display at the Museum of American History from April through September of 1993 before traveling throughout the United States.

—*Elizabeth Wenning and Barbara Carlisle Bigelow*

John Hope Franklin

1915—

Historian, educator, writer

When John Hope Franklin arrived at the North Carolina state archives in 1939 to conduct research for his Harvard doctoral dissertation, he had to wait three days for a separate room to be prepared to segregate him from white scholars who were working there. The archive's director even gave Franklin keys to the manuscript collection so the white assistants would not have to fetch documents for him. But another special office was waiting when Franklin returned for an extended visit in 1967, leading a delegation of his University of Chicago graduate students. This time it was intended as a tribute to one of America's leading historians. "I was something of a hero," he told *People* magazine. "They didn't want me to be inconvenienced."

For more than 50 years Franklin has successfully pursued dual roles as academic scholar and social activist. Author of about a dozen books on various aspects of Southern history, including *From Slavery to Freedom: A History of Negro Americans,* the first modern survey of the important role blacks played in American history, he has edited nine other books and taught at some of the country's most prestigious universities—like Harvard, Cornell, Duke, Chicago, and the University of California at Berkeley, as well as at England's Cambridge University and institutions in Australia and New Zealand.

Along the way he has received more than 90 honorary degrees.

Franklin became the first black historian to hold a full-time position at a predominantly white institution when he was appointed chairman of the history department at Brooklyn College in 1956. He was the first African American to deliver a paper before the Southern Historical Association, later becoming its president. He also has served as president of the American Historical Association, the Organization of American Historians, the American Studies Association, and the United Chapters of Phi Beta Kappa.

Actively involved in the civil rights struggle, Franklin provided invaluable historical research for Thurgood Marshall and the National Association for the Advancement of Colored People (NAACP) legal defense team that won the landmark *Brown v. Board of Education* school-desegregation case before the Supreme Court in 1954. In addition, he joined Martin Luther King, Jr.'s 1965 march from Selma to Montgomery, Alabama, to protest the denial of black voters' rights, and in 1987 he testified before the Senate Judiciary Committee in opposition to Judge Robert Bork's nomination to the Supreme Court.

At a Glance. . .

Born January 2, 1915, in Rentiesville, OK; son of Buck Colbert (a lawyer) and Mollie (a schoolteacher; maiden name, Parker) Franklin; married Aurelia E. Whittington (a librarian), June 11, 1940; children: John Whittington. *Education:* Fisk University, B.A., 1935; Harvard University, M.A., 1936, Ph.D., 1941. *Politics:* Democrat.

Instructor in history, Fisk University, 1936-37; professor of history, St. Augustine's College, 1939-43, North Carolina College, 1943-47, and Howard University, 1947-56; chairman of Department of History, Brooklyn College, 1956-64; University of Chicago, professor of American history, 1964-82, chairman of Department of History, 1967-70, John Matthews Manly Distinguished Service Professor, 1969-82, professor emeritus, 1982; Duke University, James B. Duke Professor of History, 1982-85, professor emeritus, 1985—, professor of legal history at Duke University Law School, beginning 1985. Pitt Professor of American History and Institutions, Cambridge University, England, 1962-63; visiting professor of history at Harvard and Cornell universities and the universities of Wisconsin, Hawaii, and California at Berkeley.

Member: American Historical Association, Southern Historical Association, Organization of American Historians, American Studies Association, American Academy of Arts and Sciences, American Philosophical Society, Association for the Study of Afro-American Life and History.

Selected awards: Clarence L. Holte Literary Prize, 1986; Britannica Award, 1990; more than 90 honorary degrees.

Addresses: *Office*—Department of History, Duke University, 208C East Duke Building, Box 90719, Durham, NC 27708; or c/o Louisiana State University Press, P.O. Box 25053, Baton Rouge, LA 70894-5053.

Though a strong believer in the meaningful role that scholarship can play in social change, Franklin has always stressed maintaining objectivity and established standards in all historical research. As he wrote in his preface to *Race and History:*

Selected Essays 1938-1988: "While a black scholar has a clear responsibility to join in improving the society in which he lives, he must understand the difference between hard-hitting advocacy on the one hand and the highest standards of scholarship on the other. If the scholar engages in both activities he must make it clear which role he is playing at any given time."

Early Years

"I could not have avoided being a social activist even if I wanted to," Franklin wrote in his autobiographical essay, "John Hope Franklin: A Life of Learning," included in *Race and History.* Racism and financial distress would plague him throughout his childhood and adolescence.

His parents had moved to the all-black town of Rentiesville, Oklahoma, "to resign from the world dominated by white people," after his lawyer father had been expelled from a courtroom solely because of his race. In this town of less than 200, Franklin's father worked as a lawyer, justice of the peace, postmaster, farmer, and president of the Rentiesville Trading Company to make ends meet. Born there in 1915 where the quality of life was "as low as one can imagine," Franklin grew up without electricity, running water, indoor plumbing, a park, playground, or library.

But as compensation, he was introduced to the world of learning at an early age. With no one to take care of him at home, he spent his early years sitting in the rear of his schoolteacher mother's classroom, learning to read and write by the age of four. At night his father read and wrote at home. Following this example, Franklin's constant nighttime reading by the light of a kerosene lamp apparently caused the poor eyesight that led to his first pair of glasses when he was five years old.

"My parents would never voluntarily accept segregation," Franklin recalled in "A Life of Learning." Still, growing up in segregated Oklahoma, there was no escaping it. On one shopping trip out of town, he and his mother were ejected from a train for sitting in a white coach and had to trudge home on foot through the woods.

In 1921 Franklin's father moved to Tulsa alone, hoping to make a better living there at law. The family was to follow in six months. That June, a race riot burned down much of the city's segregated black section. Franklin's father was unharmed, but the property he had contracted to buy for his law office was destroyed. He practiced law from a tent for several months while fighting a new city ordinance that aimed to exclude poor blacks permanently by requiring all new buildings to be constructed of expensive brick and stone. Appealing all the way to the state supreme court, he won the case. Four years later the family finally joined him.

Racism continued to haunt Franklin through his teens. He received a scholarship and moved to Nashville in 1931 to attend Fisk University, a historically black college founded after the Civil War. An abusive streetcar company clerk called him a nigger for paying the fare with a $20 bill, and gave him $19.75 worth of dimes and quarters for change. After that Franklin seldom went into town, and when he did was never alone. Trouble came to Fisk instead when a young black man out riding his bicycle struck and slightly injured a white child. A white mob dragged him from his university-owned home on the edge of campus and lynched him. As president of the student government, Franklin protested to the mayor, the governor, and even President Franklin Delano Roosevelt. Nothing was done.

Seduced by History

To Franklin, college at first was merely a way station en route to law school and joining his father in practice. But in his first quarter, Professor Theodore S. Currier, the white chairman of the school's history department, delivered the most exciting lectures he had ever heard for a course on contemporary civilization. During his sophomore year, Franklin took two courses from Professor Currier, while forming a close personal relationship that developed into a deep friendship. Soon his law school plans were forgotten, replaced by a desire to study, write, and teach history.

Currier became the most important influence in Franklin's life. To stimulate and train his prize pupil, the professor offered new courses and seminars. He encouraged Franklin to apply for graduate study at Harvard, where he had gone. Franklin was admitted after graduating from Fisk in 1935, apparently the first time a student from a historically black institution was allowed to attend without first proving himself with some undergraduate work at Harvard itself. The university, however, did not offer him a scholarship.

In the depths of the Great Depression, Franklin's family was unable to offer him more than a token amount of money to attend Harvard in far away Massachusetts. He thought of attending the University of Oklahoma close to home, but that school would not admit a black to graduate study. Professor Currier took matters into his own hands, borrowing $500 from a Nashville bank to send Franklin on his way. "It was a good investment," the late professor once told *People* magazine.

There were few other blacks at Harvard. Franklin took a room with a local black family and a job washing dishes for his evening meals. He received his master's degree in nine months and won fellowships to complete his Ph.D. requirements. Finding the course of study "far from extraordinary," he left Harvard in 1939 to teach at St. Augustine's College in Raleigh, North Carolina. Two years later he completed his dissertation on free blacks in North Carolina and received his doctoral degree.

War-Time Disillusionment

Shortly thereafter the Japanese bombed Pearl Harbor and the United States was drawn into World War II. Hearing that the U.S. Navy desperately needed volunteers to handle office work, Franklin went to its Raleigh recruiting office. Despite his qualifications (three gold medals in typing, six years secretarial experience in college and graduate school, a course in accounting, and shorthand experience) and the wartime emergency, he was lacking in one important qualification—the right color skin. Rejected, he turned to the War Department, then assembling a staff of historians to record the definitive history of the conflict. Several whites without advanced degrees had already been signed up, but Franklin, with a book in press, never had his application answered.

At the physical ordered by his draft board in 1943, he was not permitted to enter the doctor's office and was told to wait outside by the fire escape. Concluding that the government obviously did not need his services, Franklin spent the remainder of the war outwitting the military by taking a teaching position at North Carolina College for Negroes in Durham, whose president was on the local draft appeal board.

Two later incidents confirmed his judgment about the extent of racial discrimination in the United States. First, while standing in the overcrowded black half coach of a North Carolina train in 1945, he noticed only six men in the adjoining whites-only full-sized coach. Asking the conductor if the two groups could switch coaches, he was told the men were German prisoners of war and could not be moved. Later, when visiting the Louisiana state archives following V-J Day, he learned that blacks were not permitted entry. But since the archives were closed for a week to celebrate victory over the totalitarian Nazis and Japanese, he was unofficially allowed inside to pursue his research.

Legitimizing African American History

An editor at the New York publishing house of Alfred A. Knopf first approached Franklin in the mid-1940s to write a history of black Americans. But Franklin, engaged in research on the South's militant culture, turned him down. The editor persisted, even visiting Franklin in North Carolina, finally convincing him to write the book. Now in its sixth edition, *From Slavery to Freedom: A History of Negro Americans* has sold more than two million copies since appearing in 1947 and has been translated into French, German, Japanese, Portuguese, and Chinese.

"When I began to write in 1945, there were few courses in black history and hardly any materials," Franklin recalled 45 years later in *Southern Living*. "Now it's a respectable area of intellectual inquiry." To write his groundbreaking history of African Americans, Franklin found it necessary "to retell the story of the evolution of the people of the United States in order to place the Negro in his proper relationship and perspective," he wrote in the book's preface. *From Slavery to Freedom* complemented the country's changing intellectual climate and growing sentiment for equal rights for blacks. It legitimized the academic study of African American history and remains "the Bible of the field," according to Professor Louis Harlan of the University of Maryland. Before the book appeared, "black history was being ignored," Harlan said in a 1990 *U.S. News & World Report* article. "That was hard to do after Franklin marshaled overwhelming evidence of the role blacks played in American history."

Revising Southern History

Despite his success at propelling the study of black history into the academic mainstream, Franklin maintained his identification as a Southern historian. "It's often assumed I'm a scholar of Afro-American history, but the fact is I haven't taught a course in Afro-American history in 30-some-odd years," he told the *New York Times Book Review* in 1990. "My specialty is the history of the South, and that means I teach the history of blacks and whites."

Franklin accepted a professorship at Howard University, a prestigious black institution in the nation's capital, in 1947. Continuing his research on Southern history and publishing a steady stream of articles, he coped as best he could with segregated seating in archives and libraries and exclusion from toilets, hotels, and even restaurants near the Library of Congress well into the 1950s. But for him, "a Negro scholar searching for truth, the search for food in the city of Washington was one of the minor inconveniences," Franklin wrote in "The Dilemma of the American Negro Scholar," published in *Race and History*. In the same essay he confessed to channeling his emotions into unpublished articles to keep his fury at racism from intruding on his scholastic pursuit of the truth.

His published work on various aspects of Southern history sought "a better understanding of the entire South and all

of its people," Franklin wrote in *Race and History*. It also attacked the historical status quo. *The Militant South, 1800-1860,* appearing in 1956, was a pioneering examination of the Southern psyche—a search to find answers to why the South invariably reacted violently to crisis situations. "If America in general has been a land of violence, it was the South that institutionalized it and bestowed on it an aura of respectability," Franklin wrote. He identified the region's peculiar economic and social institutions, particularly slavery, as the reasons. "Throughout their history, many Southerners have continued to invoke the rule of personal judgment as to what the law was," he argued. "Keeping this tradition alive and making it a part of the apparatus for maintaining white supremacy became a way of life in the South." Though some traditionalists called the book "a Negro view" of the Old South, it is

---

> ## "I could not have avoided being a social activist even if I wanted to."

---

now considered "a point of departure" for Southern scholars according to Carol Blesser, a historian from Clemson University, as quoted in *U.S. News & World Report.*

His next book, *Reconstruction After the Civil War,* published in 1961, exposed earlier historical fallacies about this era. There was no long Northern military occupation of the South; no seizure of vast political power by incompetent blacks; and too large a role previously given to carpetbaggers. In fact, Franklin pointed out, "Radical Republican" rule in the South lasted less than a decade in all but three states and was not marked by excessive black misconduct or poor government, a view now widely accepted.

Other books followed, including *The Emancipation Proclamation* in 1963 and *A Southern Odyssey: Travelers in the Antebellum North* in 1976. That same year, Franklin delivered the National Endowment for the Humanities Jefferson Lecture in three parts in three different cities during the American bicentennial. In his lecture, published as *Racial Equality in America,* he confronted the country's persistent disparity between the goal of racial equality and the facts of discrimination.

Civil Rights Activist

Franklin's prominence as a historian aided him in his role

as racial pioneer. His appointment as chairman of a department of 52 white historians at Brooklyn College in 1956 became front-page news in the *New York Times*. Still, it took him more than a year and the help of a shrewd lawyer to locate, buy, and finance a home in the neighborhood surrounding the college.

To counter such discrimination, Franklin frequently aided the NAACP's legal efforts to achieve equality. He served as an expert witness in *Lyman Johnson v. The University of Kentucky* in 1949, a case that successfully challenged that state's "separate but equal" graduate education system. In 1953 he spent two months commuting between Washington and New York for the upcoming *Brown v. Board of Education* case that would overthrow "separate but equal" grade schools the following year. Franklin worked with the lawyers, wrote historical essays, and provided a historical setting for their legal questions. "Using one's skills to influence public policy seemed to be a satisfactory middle ground between an ivory tower posture of isolation and disengagement and a posture of passionate advocacy that too often deserted the canons of scholarship," he later wrote in *Race and History*.

In 1962 Franklin became the first African American ever elected to membership in Washington D.C.'s exclusive Cosmos Club. The following year, serving as Pitt Professor of American History at the University of Cambridge, he appeared on British television to explain the civil rights movement—in particular black student James Meredith's attempts to enter the University of Mississippi and 1963's historic March on Washington—to viewers.

Back in the United States, he joined Martin Luther King's 1965 march from Selma to Montgomery with 30 other historians. More recently, he testified against Robert Bork's nomination to the Supreme Court before the Senate Judiciary Committee in 1987. In an *Ebony* magazine article in 1990, he described himself as "living two separate lives—one as a historian, carefully guarding the limits that one can go in that area, and another as an activist citizen, trying to change things in society."

Throughout his career, Franklin has remained committed to integration. "He has never bowed to the pressure of fashions and the propaganda of black nationalism," Yale historian C. Vann Woodward told *U.S. News & World Report*. After joining the University of Chicago in 1964, Franklin opposed student attempts to establish a separate black studies program.

Continuing Passion

Franklin later served as chairman of the University of

Chicago's history department from 1967 to 1970 and became the school's John Matthews Manly Distinguished Service Professor in 1969. He moved to Duke University in 1982 as James B. Duke Professor of History, becoming professor emeritus in 1985 when he joined Duke's law school as professor of legal history.

In 1990 he and his wife, Aurelia, celebrated their golden wedding anniversary. They met in 1931, married in 1940, and became parents of their only child, John, twelve years later. Franklin is also a world traveler, avid fisherman, and orchid grower. His custom-built greenhouse holds more than 1,000 of the flowers, including *Phalaenopsis John Hope Franklin,* a white-and-red hybrid recognized by Britain's Royal Horticultural Society.

Well past retirement age, Franklin's passion for history remains strong. "I love to teach. I love to write. And I love to lecture to the public on historic subjects," he told *Ebony* magazine in 1990. "These things—individually and together—are exciting to me. They make my existence worthwhile."

Perhaps nothing better illustrates Franklin's drive than his 40-year quest to write a biography of *George Washington Williams,* author of the first scholarly account of American blacks. In his essay "Stalking George Washington Williams," Franklin conveys his astonishment and elation at discovering this early black historian's two-volume *History of the Negro Race in America from 1619 to 1880* in 1945. Determined to write Williams's biography, Franklin set out to learn more about this elusive figure. In his brief 42 years, Williams had fought in two wars, served as a pastor in several churches, been a lawyer, an editor, the first black in the Ohio Legislature, and a world traveler.

Following Williams's trail to Boston, Washington, Cincinnati, Zaire, Belgium, Germany, and England, Franklin reached countless dead ends, but was unwilling to give up. He found the key at the Syracuse University Library in the uncatalogued papers of railroad magnate Collis Huntington, a patron of Williams's later life. In 1975, 30 years after beginning his quest, Franklin laid a wreath at Williams's unmarked grave in Blackpool, England. Ten years later, *George Washington Williams: A Biography* was published and the pioneering historian memorialized with a black granite tombstone.

Summing up 50 years of historical writing, Franklin collected 27 of his essays, including his brief autobiography, in *Race and History: Selected Essays 1938-1988.* Looking back over his career in the book's preface, Franklin reflected on the "enormous satisfaction to this historian who seeks to mine the various quarries of the past in the belief that good history is a good foundation for a better present and future."

Selected writings

The Free Negro in North Carolina, 1790-1860, University of North Carolina Press, 1943.

From Slavery to Freedom: A History of Negro Americans, Alfred A. Knopf, 1947.

The Militant South, 1800-1860, Belknap, 1956.

Reconstruction After the Civil War, University of Chicago Press, 1961.

The Emancipation Proclamation, Doubleday, 1963.

(With John W. Caughey and Ernest R. May) *Land of the Free,* Benziger, 1965.

(With the editors of Time-Life Books) *Illustrated History of Black Americans,* Time-Life, Inc., 1970.

A Southern Odyssey: Travelers in the Antebellum North, Louisiana State University Press, 1976.

Racial Equality in America, University of Chicago Press, 1976.

George Washington Williams: A Biography, University of Chicago Press, 1985.

Race and History: Selected Essays 1938-1988, Louisiana State University Press, 1990.

The Color Line: Legacy to the Twenty-first Century, University of Missouri Press, 1993.

Editor

The Civil War Diary of James T. Ayers, Illinois State Historical Society, 1947.

(With Isadore Starr) *The Negro in the Twentieth Century,* Random House, 1967.

Color and Race, Houghton, 1968.

Reminiscences of an Active Life: The Autobiography of John R. Lynch, University of Chicago Press, 1970.

(With August Meier) *Black Leaders of the Twentieth Century,* University of Illinois Press, 1982.

Also editor of Albion Tourgee's *Fool's Errand,* 1961; T.W. Higginson's *Army Life in a Black Regiment,* 1962; and W. E. B. Du Bois's *Suppression of the African Slave-Trade,* 1969.

Sources

Books

Franklin, John Hope, *George Washington Williams: A Biography,* University of Chicago Press, 1985.

Franklin, John Hope, *The Militant South, 1800-1860,* Belknap, 1956.

Franklin, John Hope, *Race and History: Selected Essays 1938-1988,* Louisiana State University Press, 1990.

Periodicals

Ebony, February 1990; November 1990.

Journal of American History, September 1990.

New Republic, April 30, 1990.

New York Times Book Review, June 3, 1990.

People, October 29, 1979.

Southern Living, June 1990.

U.S. News & World Report, September 17, 1990.

—James J. Podesta

Samuel L. Gravely, Jr.

1922—

Retired U.S. naval officer

At the peak of his career, Samuel L. Gravely, Jr. was the highest ranking African American officer in the U.S. Navy, a three-star vice admiral. Even after his retirement, he maintained the commanding presence that he had honed during his 38 years in the military. Throughout his long career, Gravely was not only the first African American officer to become an admiral, but was also the first to serve on—and later command—a fighting ship. His many decorations, honors, and awards attest to his success.

Born in 1922 in Richmond, Virginia, Gravely came from a family committed to government service. His father, Samuel L. Gravely, Sr., was a postal worker, and his siblings worked at various government posts with the Veterans Administration and the Internal Revenue Service. After a short stint at the post office himself, Gravely responded to the call to arms issued during the Second World War and joined the U.S. Navy.

Interrupting his education at Virginia Union University, Gravely enlisted in the U.S. Naval Reserve in 1942. He quickly rose to officer rank. After boot camp at the Great Lakes Naval Training Station in Illinois, he attended Officer Training Camp at the University of California at Los Angeles, and then midshipman school at Columbia University. He was the first

African American to reach the rank of captain, and when he boarded his first ship in May of 1945, he became its first black officer.

After serving as a communications, electronics, and personnel officer, Gravely left the navy in 1946 to get married and return to school; in 1948, he earned a degree in history from Virginia Union University. He had no immediate plans to return to the navy. After graduation, he told Ebony, "I planned to teach and coach, but took a job in the post office instead. I guess the urge for government service was just that overpowering." The same year he graduated, 1948, President Harry S Truman issued an executive order to integrate the armed forces. The following year, the U.S. military stepped up recruitment of African Americans. In 1952, Gravely returned to active duty on board the USS Iowa.

Gravely's tenure in the naval service was tainted by the difficulties of racial discrimination. He learned early on that he was, as he told Ebony magazine, "saving America for democracy, but not allowed to participate in the goddamn thing." As a new recruit, he was trained in a segregated unit; as an officer, he was barred from living in the Bachelor's Officers Quarters. As far back as 1945, when his first ship reached its berth in Key West Florida, he was specifically forbidden entry

At a Glance...

Born Samuel Lee Gravely, Jr., June 4, 1922; son of Samuel L. (a postal worker) and Mary George Gravely; married Alma Bernice Clark, 1946; children: Robert (deceased), David, Tracy. *Education:* Attended Officer Training Camp at the University of California, Los Angeles, and midshipman school at Columbia University; Virginia Union University, B.A., 1948.

U.S. Navy, career military officer, 1942-80; became vice admiral; commander USS *Falgout,* 1962; commander of the third fleet, 1976-78; director of Defense Communications Agency, 1978-80; Armed Forces Communications and Electronics Associations (AFCEA), executive director of education and training, 1984-87.

Selected awards: Named Distinguished Virginian by Governor Holton, 1972; Communications Award from the Los Angeles Chapter of the National Association of Media Women, 1972; Major Richard R. Wright Award of Excellence, Savanna State College, 1974; Prince Hall Founding Fathers Military Commanders Award, Scottish Rite Prince Hall Masonic Bodies of Maryland, 1975; San Diego Press Club Military Headliner of the Year, 1975. Military awards: Legion of Merit with Gold Star, Bronze Star Medal, Meritorious Service Medal, Joint Services Commendation Medal, Navy Commendation Medal, World War II Victory Medal, Naval Reserve Medal for 10 years of service in the U.S. Naval Reserve, American Campaign Medal, Korean Presidential Unit Citation, National Defense Medal with one bronze star, China Service Medal, Korean Service Medal with two bronze stars, United Nations Service Medal, Armed Forces Expeditionary Medal, Vietnam Service Medal with six bronze stars, and the Antarctic Service Medal.

Addresses: *Home*—15956 Waterfall Rd., Haymarket, VA 22069.

into the Officers Club on the base. President Truman's executive order prohibited segregation, but it could not eliminate racism and hypocrisy among military staff members. Long after Truman's executive order, the unofficial policy in the navy was to have as few blacks as possible on any ship. Furthermore, African American officers were limited to work on large ships.

Surviving Discrimination in the U.S. Military

Gravely had received a very friendly reception when he reported for duty aboard the battleship USS *Iowa* in 1952, but he later found a letter from the Bureau of Naval Personnel to the *Iowa*'s commanding officer, instructing the commander to brief the ship's personnel before Gravely's arrival. Gravely knew that the briefing pertained to his race, and he later told *Ebony:* "I gave the letter to my roommate and suggested that it be returned to the ship's office. When he saw that I had read the letter, he immediately began to tell me about the briefing, how delighted everyone was with my being assigned, and how I must have been a fine guy to have earned a commission. He added: 'There was one problem. No one wanted to live with you, so I volunteered.'"

Gravely survived the indignities of racial prejudice and displayed unquestionable competence as a naval officer. He eventually earned a reputation as an expert in naval communications. Early in his career, Gravely served with distinction as a radio specialist aboard the *Iowa*, where the ship's communications officer was more interested in his qualifications than his color: "I don't care if he's black, white, or green, all I want is a radio officer!" the senior officer once declared, according to *Ebony.* (This man later became godfather to Gravely's eldest child.) Several years later, on board the USS *Seminole*, a visitor to the ship remarked that Gravely, then working as operations officer, was "colored." *Ebony* reported that the ship's captain replied with a completely straight face: "Is that right? What color is he?"

First African American to Command a Ship

In 1961 Gravely became temporary skipper of the USS *Theodore E. Chandler*, making him the first black naval officer to command a ship. A few months later, in January of 1962—having achieved the rank of lieutenant commander—he was assigned to the USS *Falgout*, the first fighting ship to be commanded by an African American officer. As a full commander, he again made naval history in 1966 as the first black commander to lead a ship—the USS *Taussig*—into direct offensive action.

The crew of the *Taussig* was skeptical at first. "I think," Gravely told *Ebony* magazine, that "initially they [were] interested in two things: can the Old Man take the ship out, and can he get it back in port." After proving himself, he was accepted by his staff. In fact, they quickly grew to like his style of command, because he gave officers more responsibility than they were usually allowed. One crew member noted in *Ebony,* "It makes a big difference in morale. There is a much freer atmosphere when junior officers can perform certain tasks. If junior officers never get a chance to run the ship, pretty soon they are senior officers and they still don't know how." Gravely said in the same article, "You have to have faith in your executive officers and department heads, and they have to have it in their junior officers."

Gravely also demanded very high standards from his crew. In a 1977 address to navy officers, as quoted in *Ebony,* he stated: "We must improve our individual understanding of our fundamental warfare skills. We must improve the performance and productivity of our people. And we must continue to stress the very rudiments of our profession—smartness, appearance, seamanship, and most importantly, pride. Pride in ourselves! Pride in our ships! And pride in our Navy!"

Increasing Responsibilities

In 1976 Gravely became the commander of the entire third fleet. He was in charge of over 100 ships, 60,000 officers, and oversaw more than 50 million square miles of ocean, or about one-fourth of the earth's surface. His 32 official duties included protecting the western sea approaches to the United States, guarding merchant ships in the area, and providing emergency search and rescue aid. He also developed and improved fleet tactics, organized and scheduled ship movements and port visits, and conducted antisubmarine warfare operations. The stress of these responsibilities was inescapable, but he fought to relieve them through exercise when he had the time. He was also known to drink up to thirty cups of coffee a day and chainsmoke.

In 1978 Gravely became the director of the Defense Communications Agency and was able to move home to Virginia from his base in Hawaii. After his official retirement in 1980, he kept active as a military adviser and corporate consultant. Between 1984 and 1987, Gravely served as the executive director of education and training for the Armed Forces Communications and Electronics Associations (AFCEA). A year later, he became an adviser to Potomac Systems Engineering. He continues to travel the world, speaking at conferences on leadership. "I still do things for the military," he told *Ebony* in 1990. "I still have great affection for the military. The military gave me an opportunity to do some things that I thoroughly enjoyed." He does plan to retire fully someday and spend time fishing, gardening, and raising pigeons.

As a trailblazer for African Americans in the military arena, Gravely fought for equal rights quietly but effectively, letting his actions speak for him. After four decades of service in the U.S. Navy, he holds no illusions about the status of race relations in the military but, according to *Ebony,* readily admits: "I basically grew up in the military. . . . The military did a lot for me, and hopefully, I did some things for it."

Sources

Chicago Tribune, July 8, 1973.
Crisis, December 1973; March 1983.
Ebony, July 1966; September 1977; November 1985; December 1990.
Jet, February 5, 1970; June 5, 1975; August 28, 1980.

—*Robin Armstrong*

Dennis Green

1949—

Professional football coach

Dennis Green assumed head coaching responsibilities for the Minnesota Vikings early in 1992. Only the second black head coach in modern professional football, he brings a wealth of experience to the Vikings, a franchise in need of a strong leader. Few would argue that Green's ascent in the National Football League (NFL) has anything to do with his race—he has worked his entire professional life as either an assistant or head coach for a number of teams, including the difficult programs of Northwestern University and Stanford. His career includes long periods of association with legendary San Francisco 49ers coach Bill Walsh, and he is credited with developing the talents of future Football Hall of Famer Jerry Rice. Minneapolis/St. Paul *Star Tribune* reporter Steve Aschburner pointed out that Green "is known as a hard worker and a fair man but one who expects most of a player's motivation to come from within. . . . And he has a habit of taking on tasks that others might have considered overwhelming."

A high-energy, hardworking optimist, Green predicted that he would take the lackluster Vikings to the 1992 playoffs, and he did just that. Aschburner noted: "If Dennis Green were a doctor, he would work in an intensive care unit. The man has shown an ability, and a willingness, to pump life into the most ailing, weakened football operations. Where others might have pulled plugs, he has ordered transfusions. Only St. Jude has taken on more lost causes than Green." And *San Jose Mercury News* correspondent Nancy Gay maintained that Green is absolutely consumed by "the Herculean job he [was] hired to do—whipping the Vikings, a legendary band of underachieving malcontents, into contenders."

For his own part, Green told the *San Jose Mercury News* that he sees no task as impossible, especially in football. "Very few guys think there's a job they can't do. No matter how big the obstacles," he said. "If there's one way to sum up myself, I just like to get the job done. I don't care if I'm coaching receivers or whatever, I'm going to take the responsibility to make sure our guys do right." Asked about how his race has shaped his career, Green told the *Star Tribune*: "I don't think anybody considers me a black coach. I don't think a player is concerned what my race is. I think he wants someone who will teach him something."

"I see challenges, even problems, as opportunities," Green explained in the *Star Tribune*. Even the most overwhelming coaching obstacles seem insignificant to a man who has experienced some of life's more lasting misfortunes. Green

At a Glance...

Born February 17, 1949, in Harrisburg, PA; son of Penrose (a postal worker) and Anna (a beautician) Green; married Margie Shindler, c. 1967; children: Patti, Jeremy. *Education:* University of Iowa, B.S., 1971.

Professional player/coach, British Columbia Lions (Canadian Football League), 1971; worked for a sheet metal shop in Iowa City and as a volunteer assistant coach at the University of Iowa, 1972; running backs and receivers coach, University of Dayton, 1973; receivers coach, University of Iowa, 1974-76; running backs coach, Stanford University, 1977-78; special teams coach, San Francisco 49ers, 1979; offensive coordinator, Stanford University, 1980; head coach, Northwestern University, 1981-85; wide receivers coach, San Francisco 49ers, 1986-88; head coach, Stanford University, 1989-92; head coach, Minnesota Vikings, 1992—.

Head coaching record: 10-45 at Northwestern, 16-18 at Stanford, 11-5 at Vikings (1992 regular season).

Selected awards: Named "Big Ten Coach of the Year," 1982.

Addresses: *Office*—Minnesota Vikings, 9520 Viking Drive, Eden Prairie, MN 55344.

was born and raised in a blue-collar section of Harrisburg, Pennsylvania. His father was a postal worker and his mother a beautician. "We didn't live in the projects," he remembered, "but we lived where people who had just moved from the projects lived." Tragedy struck when Green was still a boy. His father died of a ruptured appendix in 1960, and then— only two years later—his mother succumbed to cancer.

Even though he lost both parents by the time he was thirteen, Green carried their lessons of integrity and discipline with him into adulthood. He told the *Star Tribune* that his father "was a special guy who was his own man. I don't think there was ever a time when he felt like he was going to take any crap out of anybody. I'd say he had a lot of pride in that. . . . His pride always came first."

Taking the Game Seriously

For the remainder of his school years, Green lived with an older brother who left the U.S. Air Force in order to care

for the family. By that time, football was a strong lure for Green. He recalled in the *Star Tribune* that he admired the players who were ahead of him in school and sought to be like them. "Everybody respected them," he said. "In contrast to all the guys who talked a good game, they actually went to practice. They were doing something significant." When he joined the varsity squad at John Harris High School, he added, the coaches "instilled the love of football in me. They said, 'This is football and we're going to do this better than anybody.' It didn't matter whose dad had a job and whose didn't. It didn't matter if you could afford new clothes. We were a football team."

Football competition is especially fierce in central Pennsylvania, and college recruiters find it a fertile talent pool. Green was recruited by Frank Gilliam, a football staff member from the University of Iowa who went on to become director of player personnel for the Minnesota Vikings. Asked to describe the teenaged Dennis Green for the *St. Paul Pioneer Press*, Gilliam noted that the future coach was "a hard-nosed, tough slashing running back whose personality was straight forward and eager. Playing football was very important to him." Even as a youth, Green perceived that he would have opportunities denied his grandfather and father, and even his older brothers. "I'm a product of the '60s. I graduated from high school in 1967. . . . It was . . . a window of opportunity. If you were a black athlete and you took care of business, you could go to school anywhere you wanted." Green told Rick Telander in *Sports Illustrated*. Green made the most of that "window of opportunity" at each step of his career.

Green was a three-year starter for the University of Iowa Hawkeyes, playing two seasons at tailback and one at flanker. Gilliam, who was Iowa's assistant coach during those years, told the *Star Tribune*: "[Green] blocked, he ran, he was real versatile. I can't say I knew then he'd be a coach, but he approached the game real seriously." Green graduated from Iowa in 1971 with a degree in recreation education. His only stint as a professional football player came later that year with the British Columbia Lions of the Canadian Football League. Even there he showed his budding talents for coaching. He left the Lions after one season.

Rising in the Ranks

Green returned to the University of Iowa as a volunteer graduate assistant to the football program. To support his wife and two children, he took a full-time job driving a truck for a sheet metal business. By 1973 he landed a paying post within collegiate football that made other work unnecessary. He became coach of running backs and receivers at the University of Dayton. After a year there, he went back to Iowa, this time as receivers coach.

In 1977 Green was invited to join the football coaching staff at Stanford University. The head coach at that time was Bill Walsh, a man who would soon become world-famous for his work with the San Francisco 49ers. Even in his Stanford days, Walsh was careful to surround himself with people who were as dedicated and hardworking as he was. He and Green worked very well together—so well that when Walsh was called to coach the 49ers in 1979, he took Green along to lead the special teams unit. At the tender age of thirty—younger, indeed, than some of the players—Green found himself coaching in the NFL.

Greater responsibilities beckoned Green back to the college ranks in 1980. He became offensive coordinator at Stanford under Paul Wiggin, serving in that position for one year. In 1981, Green was offered his first head coaching job. Northwestern University, a school that hadn't won a conference game in five years, presented the challenge of a lifetime to the fledgling coach. As part of the Big Ten, hapless Northwestern played regularly against football giants like the University of Michigan, Ohio State University, and the University of Illinois. Green was realistic: he knew he could not turn Northwestern into a giant, but he saw room in the program for vast improvement. He accepted the job and became the first black coach in Big Ten history.

When Green arrived at Northwestern, the team had won only three of its last 75 games. In his first year coaching the team, Northwestern continued its losing ways, but in 1982 he guided the squad to three victories. That feat was enough to earn him the Big Ten "coach of the year" award in 1982. His fellow Big Ten coaches saw in Northwestern's modest gains nothing less than a major turnaround. And while Green was not able to build further on those gains, he did bring Northwestern more victories in his five seasons there than the team had in recent history. By the end of the 1985 season Northwestern had a 10-45 record under Green.

Walsh beckoned Green back to the professional ranks in 1986. Green rejoined the 49ers, this time as wide receivers coach. Walsh had one prospect in particular that he wanted Green to tutor—a young player named Jerry Rice. *St. Paul Pioneer Press* reporter Ray Richardson noted that Green "played a key role in the development of one of the best wide receivers ever to wear an NFL uniform," namely Rice. Green and Rice worked together closely, and Rice leaped into national notoriety for his stellar performance in the 49ers' offense. "I would say he taught me everything I know," Rice recalled in the *St. Paul Pioneer Press*. "When he told me something I was doing wrong, it was only because he wanted me to get better, and it's paying off for me now."

In 1989, Stanford University offered Green the head coaching job that had once been Walsh's. The salary for the three-year contract was reported to be $200,000 per year. *San Jose Mercury News* correspondent Mark Purdy heralded Green's choice as "the best for Stanford" and added: "Here is an intelligent, glib, 39-year-old who's had the world by the tail for most of his life. . . . Green doesn't deserve this job because he's black. He deserves this job because his background proves he's capable of handling any mine field you can erect in his path." During his first months on the job, Green was faced with a player revolt that had ousted his predecessor, demands by disgruntled alumni, and challenges to find top-rank players who could satisfy Stanford's tough admission requirements. He also had to assemble a staff of nine assistants—all before his team played a single game.

Similarities abound between the programs at Northwestern and Stanford. Both colleges put a premium on academics, allowing only the best scholar-athletes to attend. Even so they attract promising players who can, under the right guidance, perform at high levels. Green let it be known at

> **"I just like to get the job done."**

Stanford that he expected top-level play from his team. Slowly the Cardinals began to improve. After finishing 3-8 in 1989, they went 5-6 in 1990 and 8-4 in 1991. Green became a bona fide Stanford hero, loved by the players and the fans alike.

Into the Limelight with the Vikings

Green's success in California did not go unnoticed. NFL front office personnel in search of new coaches realized that he had proven himself as a motivator and that he had learned coaching techniques from possibly the best source available in the 1980s, Bill Walsh. One such NFL manager was Minnesota Vikings president Roger Headrick. The Vikings presented a special challenge at the dawn of 1992. Once a young, aggressive team, the players had aged and become cynical. Newcomers were overlooked on a squad heavy with All-Pro talent. *Sports Illustrated* contributor Paul Zimmerman declared that former coach Jerry Burns had allowed a "creeping lethargy" to envelop the team. Having finished 8-8 in 1991, the Vikings did not make the playoffs.

Green took over as head coach of the Vikings on January 10, 1992. His four-year contract with an option for a fifth year paid an estimated $350,000 the first year with significant raises for future seasons. Wasting no time, Green initiated tougher training regimes and stern lectures about substance abuse and attitude problems among his players. He maintained that the Vikings could reach the playoffs *if* they worked hard. He traded a few established stars and gave younger players opportunities. As his first season drew to a close with a much-anticipated wild card playoff game, Green told the *San Jose Mercury News* that he and his staff "were going to run a tight ship. We weren't going to allow three guys to project the wrong image for the 45 other players."

The Vikings became an exciting team again under Green. Their schedule brought them into conflict with Green's former team, the 49ers—and a coach who had worked with Green there—as well as with the Green Bay Packers, headed by another former Green associate, Mike Holmgren. Many observers felt that the Vikings' strong showing of 11 victories and five losses for the regular season was due in large part to the standards set and enforced by Green. "More than anything else . . . Green's emotional, tough-but-fair style of management is what has turned around the Vikings," commented Telander.

In the 1992 playoffs, the Vikings met the Washington Redskins and were favored to win the wild card game. Unfortunately, Green and his team found themselves outplayed by a seasoned Redskins unit that won 24-7. Knocked out of the playoffs early, the Vikings still have much to be optimistic about for the future. Sports analysts agree that Green's abundant energy and proficient football knowledge will give Minnesota a needed catalyst in its run for the 1993 Super Bowl. Vikings tight end Steve Jordan told the *San Jose Mercury News:* "When [Green] came in, he was very focused on what he wanted to have happen.

One thing he's really helped us to do is focus on what's happening on the field, focus on winning games."

Dennis Green is perceived as a workaholic who spends long hours overseeing every aspect of his team's performance. His wife, Margie, told the *San Jose Mercury News* that Green "thinks sleep is a waste of time, and he only does it because he needs to." Few people in any business take their responsibilities more seriously than does Green. The coach noted in the *Star Tribune:* "We've got our work cut out for us, but we're making some inroads, because people are starting to talk about the Vikings again on a positive note. . . . It's my job to make sure if we say we're going to do something, we do it."

Sources

Newsweek, November 23, 1992, pp. 67-68.

St. Paul Pioneer Press, January 11, 1992, pp. 1A and 1C; September 3, 1992, p. 1C; September 6, 1992, p. 1C; December 10, 1992, p. 1F; December 13, 1992, p. 1C.

San Jose Mercury News, March 25, 1986, p. 1F; January 4, 1989, p. 1C; January 8, 1989, p. 1D; December 13, 1992, p. 1D.

Sports Illustrated, September 24, 1992, p. 24; December 14, 1992, p. 33.

Star Tribune (Minneapolis/St. Paul), January 11, 1992, p. 4C; January 12, 1992, p. 1C; April 10, 1992, p. 1C; September 6, 1992, p. 7C; December 12, 1992, p. 1C.

—Mark Kram

Rosa Guy

1925(?)—

Author

Award-winning novelist Rosa Guy was born in the West Indies and grew up in New York City's Harlem. "I'm a storyteller," Guy said in a speech entitled "Children's Writing Today for Tomorrow's Adults," which she gave at the 1984 *Boston Globe* Book Festival. "I write about people. I want my readers to know people, to laugh with people, to be angry with people, to despair of people, and to have hope. . . . I want my readers . . . to care just a little bit more, when they put down a book of mine." Guy has primarily written about young black people whose experiences often resemble her own. Like authors June Jordan, Louise Meriwether, and Toni Morrison, she has been praised for creating memorable black protagonists. Her books have also attracted criticism for addressing controversial subjects in an often harshly realistic way.

Guy has published nine young adult novels, three adult novels, and three children's books. She has also written and edited nonfiction essays and contributed to periodicals. Chiefly a fiction writer for young adults, Guy began by chronicling the lives of young black women but later expanded her focus to include mysteries involving young black men. Her young adult novels describe the obstacles black teenagers face in America. Through the experiences of largely adolescent protagonists

living in Harlem and elsewhere, Guy has explored themes of individual and community survival, friendship, and social acceptance.

These novels are also informed by the cultural differences between native-born black Americans and people of Caribbean descent living in the U.S. In *The Friends,* for instance, Phyllisia, a West Indian girl much like Guy, is ostracized at her Harlem school because of her island origins. The only classmate who tries to befriend her is the poor, sloppy Harlemite Edith. Observes Phyllisia, "Edith always came to school with her clothes unpressed, her stockings bagging about her legs with big holes, which she tried to hide by pulling them into her shoes but which kept slipping up, on each heel, to expose a round, brown circle of dry skin the size of a quarter." Phyllisia rejects her, explaining, "I pulled myself tall in my seat, made haughty little movements with my shoulders and head, adjusted the frills on the collar of my well-ironed blouse, touched my soft, neatly plaited hair and pointedly gave my attention to the blackboard." Later, though, Phyllisia learns she needs tough Edith's friendship.

On a broader scale, Guy's works have focused on race and class prejudice and economic discrimination. In arguing for racial, social, and sexual tolerance, she has raised questions

At a Glance...

Surname pronounced "Gee"; born Rosa Cuthbert, September 1, 1925 (some sources say 1928), in Diego Martin, Trinidad; immigrated to U.S., 1932; daughter of Henry and Audrey (Gonzales) Cuthbert; married Warner Guy (separated, 1950); children: Warner Guy, Jr. *Education:* Attended New York University, 1940s; studied writing with Viola Brothers Shaw.

Writer, 1940s—; wrote plays and short stories at night while working days in a factory, 1940s-1950s; play *Venetian Blinds* produced at Topical Theater, New York City, 1954; published first adult novel, 1966; published nonfiction anthology *Children of Longing,* 1971; published first young adult novel, *The Friends,* 1973; worked on trilogies, 1976-87; adapted and translated Senegalese story into first children's book, *Mother Crocodile,* 1981; *The Friends* adapted as a Thames television documentary, 1984; third adult novel, *My Love, My Love or The Peasant Girl,* 1985, made into award-winning Broadway musical *Once on This Island.*

Awards: American Library Association Best Book for Young Adults awards, 1973, for *The Friends,* 1976, for *Ruby,* 1978, for *Edith Jackson,* 1979, for *The Disappearance,* and 1981, for *A Mirror of Her Own;* Coretta Scott King Award, 1981, for *Mother Crocodile;* Parents' Choice Award for Literature, 1983, for *New Guys Around the Block;* Children's Rights Workshop Other Award, 1987, for *My Love, My Love or The Peasant Girl;* New York Times Outstanding Book of the Year awards for *The Friends* and *The Disappearance.*

Member: Harlem Writers Guild (cofounder; president, 1967-1978); American Negro Theater; Committee for the Negro in the Arts.

Addresses: *Home*—New York, NY. *Agent*—Ellen Levine Literary Agency, Inc., 15 East 26th St., Ste. 1801, New York, NY 10010.

never count unless you decide to break the rules, take hold of your life, and make yourself count."

Guy's first young adult trilogy—*The Friends* (1973), *Ruby* (1976), and *Edith Jackson* (1978)—is probably her best-known work. Each installment was named an American Library Association (ALA) best book for young adults, and the series is often used as a learning tool in schools throughout the United States and England. *The Friends* was later made into a television documentary.

Guy later wrote another trilogy—this time of young adult mystery stories based on the adventures of an inner-city sleuth named Imamu Jones. The first book of the series, *The Disappearance* (1979), also won "best book" from the ALA. It was followed by two others, *New Guys Around the Block* (1983) and *And I Heard a Bird Sing* (1987). Guy's outlook is reflected in what she wrote about the series for her publisher, Delacorte Press: "Believing as I do that the world's survival rests with the young, I like to think that my contribution as a writer to their understanding of the world lies in exposing a segment of society often overlooked, ignored, or treated with contempt."

Guy also has written adult novels, among them *My Love, My Love or The Peasant Girl.* In addition, she has written stories for children and has adapted and translated a Senegalese tale from French into English. A result of her West Indian heritage, Guy speaks Creole and French. Her longtime interest in African history and culture has taken her to Haiti to observe life there, as well as to Africa. Some of her books grew out of these trips.

Endured Difficult Childhood

Rosa Cuthbert Guy was born in Trinidad on September 1, 1925, though some sources put her year of birth at 1928. After immigrating to the United States with her family in 1932, she lived in Harlem with her parents, Henry and Audrey (Gonzales) Cuthbert, and her older sister, Ameze. Family tragedy forced Guy to grow up fast: her mother died when she was nine and her father died six years later. She and her sister lived in institutions and foster homes. Not surprisingly, many of Guy's characters suffer parental loss and life among strangers. Guy was 14 when her sister became ill. She quit school and went to work in a factory in the garment district to support them both. By the age of 16, she was married to Warner Guy and the mother of a son, Warner Guy, Jr.

Later, Guy developed an interest in creative pursuits and took acting classes at the American Negro Theater. After she and her husband separated in 1950, she became involved with the Committee for the Negro in the Arts. She even performed in a play she wrote, *Venetian Blinds,*

about what she terms society's "old prejudices" and "fixed ideas." And she has encouraged young people to change their circumstances. In *Edith Jackson,* for example, a teenaged orphan girl living in a foster home is told by a lawyer, "You will which was produced at a small Off-Off-Broadway theater in 1954. Frustrated by the lack of roles available to black actors, Guy told Jerrie Norris in her biography, *Presenting Rosa Guy,* "It was a one-shot deal and after[wards] I started writing short stories."

She had spent years honing her literary skills, studying writing with Viola Brothers Shaw and at New York University in the 1940s. In the early 1950s Guy and other young black writers, including John Killens, who encouraged her to keep writing, formed the Harlem Writers Guild, a workshop in which writers shared and critiqued their work. "What we wanted to do," she told Norris, "was to have a group that really projected the . . . type of writing . . . that could only come from the black experience in the United States. . . ." She served as the Guild's president from 1967 to 1978.

Published First Novel

Guy published her first novel, *Bird at My Window,* in 1966. Powerful and intense, it was written for adults about adults. The author was moved in part to write the book following the shocking murder of her husband in 1962 and her subsequent trip to Haiti, which gave her an opportunity to sort out her feelings on violence in American society. Thomas L. Vince said of its main character in *Best Sellers,* "When first encountered, Wade Williams is recovering in the psychopathic ward of a New York hospital. . . . Unlike the bird at his window, thirty-eight-year-old Wade has never been free and . . . one is given a stunning insight into the forces that hampered his freedom, discouraged his talent, and crushed his spirit." Brooks Johnson of the *Negro Digest* praised the novel for its "evocation of Harlem" and the "amoralization of a black man." According to him and other critics, Guy's writing showed great promise.

In 1968, after race riots, civil rights protests, and the assassinations of Malcolm X and Martin Luther King, Jr., Guy traveled across the nation interviewing young black adults about their reactions to these events. She edited their comments, and they were published in 1971 in her first book of nonfiction, *Children of Longing.* The social concerns and compelling voices of the youths represented in this book later appeared in Guy's young adult fiction.

Because of her unflinching treatment of the effects of racism and discrimination, her sophisticated subject matter, and the obvious anger and pain in her work, Guy's young adult books have elicited a variety of reactions. Author Alice Walker praised *The Friends* as a "heart-slammer" in the *New York Times Book Review* and

observed, "The struggle that is the heart of this very important book [is] the fight to gain perception of one's own real character; the grim struggle for self-knowledge and the almost killing internal upheaval that brings the necessary growth of compassion and humility and courage, so that friendship (of any kind, but especially between those of notable economic and social differences) can exist." *Times Literary Supplement* contributor Brian Baumfield wrote of *Edith Jackson,* "This is a vigorous, uncompromising novel by Rosa Guy, [whose] characters, especially Edith, live and breathe and are totally credible. . . . It is a raw novel of urgency and power"

Some reviewers, though, thought Guy's subsequent young adult novel, *The Disappearance,* was too adult for young readers. It introduces Imamu Jones, a tough Harlem street youth acquitted of murder, who becomes a sleuth. When he is adopted by a black middle-class Brooklyn family and they suspect him of being connected with the disappearance of their daughter, Imamu learns that their prejudice is just as damaging as that of white middle-class families.

> "I'm a storyteller. I write about people. I want my readers to care just a little bit more, when they put down a book of mine."

Katherine Paterson wrote in the *Washington Post Book World,* "This is a harsh book, but not a hopeless one. It is a book which cries to its readers to resist being sucked into crushing and being crushed."

School Library Journal praised *New Guys Around the Block* (1983), as reprinted in the 1992 Delacorte Press catalog, for being "dramatic and moving." This sequel to *The Disappearance* follows Imamu as he leaves his middle-class foster home to return to Harlem to care for his ailing alcoholic mother. There he solves the mystery of a "phantom" burglar in the white neighborhood nearby after he and other black men in his area automatically become suspects.

The *Bulletin* of the Center for Children's Books praised Guy's last installation of this series, *And I Heard a Bird Sing* (1987), for having "some strong black characters" but also noted that "too often" they become "sounding boards for ideas that seem grafted on . . . rather than emerging naturally." The book revisits Imamu, who is living with his recovered mother in Brooklyn. While delivering groceries to the estate of a wealthy white woman he becomes a prime suspect in a murder and solves the crime to prevent his arrest.

Expanded Focus

During the 1980s Guy wrote about teenagers and their families from a new perspective. In *A Mirror of Her Own* (1981), by some accounts her least successful young adult novel, Guy describes a white family living in wealthy suburban surroundings and convincingly portrays the effects of racial discrimination on white *and* black people. A better-received second novel for adults followed, titled *A Measure of Time*. Here Guy returns to a Harlem setting but also writes about Montgomery, Alabama. She depicts the Harlem of the 1920s, '30s, and '40s, rather than her usual time frame of the 1970s and '80s. In this ironic story, Dorine Davis is born to a poor Alabama family and molested as a child by her boss, "Master Norton," while working for him as a maid. Dorine eventually becomes an upscale shoplifter but winds up vindicated as a wealthy woman in Harlem three decades later. *Los Angeles Times* reviewer Stuart Schoffman described *A Measure of Time* as "a black *bildungsroman* [novel of education] in the tradition of Claude McKay, Ralph Ellison and James Baldwin [and] a sharp and well-written meld of storytelling and sociology." He observed, "The writing is impressive, smelling of truth, hard and cutting and coarse, completely appropriate for such a sassy narrator as Dorine."

Guy's first venture into the world of children's books was also a success. While visiting Senegal, Guy discovered a folktale by the Senegalese writer Birago Diop and adapted and translated it from French into English. Titled *Mother Crocodile*, it was published as a children's book in 1981 and won the Coretta Scott King Award. Marguerite Feitlowitz of the *New York Times Book Review* wrote, "Guy is at her best in the lyrical passages, in leisurely descriptions of mythical landscapes. She has a good ear, and her prose has pleasing rhythms." In 1984 Guy wrote another children's book, *Paris, Pee Wee and Big Dog*, about three street-smart boys.

A year later, Guy drew on her knowledge of the Caribbean to retell a fable set there in *My Love, My Love or The Peasant Girl*, on which the Broadway musical *Once on This Island* was based. In the tale, a poor peasant girl falls in love with a boy whose differences from her in color and social standing necessitate great sacrifice on her part, and her action provokes the island's temperamental voodoo gods. This philosophical, spiritual adult story also illuminates Guy's favorite themes of race and class.

Guy has continued to write about class conflict and color distinctions among African Americans, as typified by *The Music of Summer,* her 1992 young adult novel about a poor, dark teenager who clashes with her lighter-skinned upper-middle-class friends during a summer on Cape Cod. Guy has also pursued the themes of friendship and family life in children's stories like *Billy the Great* (1992), which revolves around a boy who teaches his parents about choosing one's own friends. Spring of 1993 found the author working on a new novel for adults.

Selected writings

Young adult fiction

The Friends, Holt, 1973.
Ruby: A Novel, Viking, 1976.
Edith Jackson, Viking, 1978.
The Disappearance, Delacorte, 1979.
A Mirror of Her Own, Delacorte, 1981.
New Guys Around the Block, Delacorte, 1983.
And I Heard a Bird Sing, Delacorte, 1987.
The Ups and Downs of Carl Davis III, Delacorte, 1989.
The Music of Summer, Delacorte, 1992.

Adult fiction

Bird at My Window, Lippincott, 1966, Schocken, 1985.
A Measure of Time, Holt, 1983.
My Love, My Love or The Peasant Girl, Holt, 1985.

Children's fiction

(Adaptation and translation) Birago Diop, *Mother Crocodile: An Uncle Amadou Tale From Senegal,* Delacorte, 1981.
Paris, Pee Wee and Big Dog, Gollancz, 1984, Delacorte, 1985.
Billy the Great, Delacorte, 1992.

Contributor

Ten Times Black, edited by Julian Mayfield, Bantam, 1972.
Sixteen: Short Stories by Outstanding Writers for Young Adults, Delacorte, 1984.

Other

Venetian Blinds (one-act play; produced at Topical Theater, New York City), 1954.
(Editor), *Children of Longing* (nonfiction anthology), Holt, 1971.

Also author of essays and contributor to periodicals, including *Cosmopolitan, New York Times Magazine, Redbook,* and *Freedomways.*

Guy's *My Love, My Love or The Peasant Girl* was adapted by Lynn Ahrens and Stephen Flaherty for a stage musical titled *Once on This Island.*

Sources

Books

Black Writers, Gale, 1988.
Contemporary Literary Criticism, Volume 26, Gale, 1983.
Dictionary of Literary Biography, Volume 33: *Afro-American Fiction Writers After 1955,* Gale, 1984.
Guy, Rosa, *The Friends,* Holt, 1973.
Norris, Jerrie, *Presenting Rosa Guy,* Twayne, 1988.
Notable Black American Women, Gale, 1992.
Something About the Author, Volume 14, Gale, 1978.

Periodicals

Best Sellers (University of Scranton), January 15, 1966.
Bulletin (Center for Children's Books), April 1987.
Essence, October 1979; November 1991.
Los Angeles Times, August 24, 1983.
New York Times, December 4, 1979; October 9, 1983.
New York Times Book Review, November 4, 1973; December 2, 1979; October 4, 1981; August 28, 1983.
Publishers Weekly, October 5, 1992.
Times Literary Supplement, December 14, 1979; July 18, 1980.
Washington Post Book World, November 11, 1979.

Additional information for this profile was obtained from an audiotape of the speech "Children's Writing Today for Tomorrow's Adults," given at the *Boston Globe* Book Festival, 1984, and a Delacorte Press catalog, 1992.

—*Alison Carb Sussman*

Gordon Henderson

1957—

Fashion designer

Gordon Henderson first made a splash in the fashion world with his practical, sensibly priced line of sporty clothing. Awarded the fashion industry's Perry Ellis Award for best new talent in 1990, Henderson garnered considerable acclaim for designs that mix style, color, and affordability. That same year, *People* magazine deemed him "fashion's man for the woman who works." By late 1992, Henderson had secured an exclusive contract with Saks Fifth Avenue to market his newest designs throughout the United States.

path. In 1981, he transferred to New York City's Parsons School of Design, considered by many to be the premier preparatory school for Seventh Avenue fashion designers. Henderson graduated in 1984 and eventually landed a job as an assistant to Calvin Klein, a fashion industry guru. The budding designer gleaned much of his fashion finesse from Klein. "I learned everything there," Henderson told Martha Duffy in *Time*. "[Klein] gives you consistency, and he's so clean and precise; it's almost ridiculous. He can take a good idea and go on with it forever."

The California native's interest in fashion started early. In his second grade class picture, he reportedly wore flannel dress pants, an oxford shirt, and a scarf tied like an ascot. As he grew older, Henderson often watched his mother, a single parent, sew her own dresses from *Vogue* patterns as a matter of economy. "I knew he had a special eye, and I would consult him," Henderson's mother, Yvonne Simmons, told *People*. By the time he reached high school, Henderson was stitching his own jackets, pants, and shirts.

After high school, Henderson considered becoming a doctor, taking pre-med classes at the University of California at Davis. But his love of fashion eventually led him to a different career

With Klein's influence, Henderson developed his own unique style. "Klein's influence shows," Duffy asserted, adding, "Henderson's nifty, sporty outfits are never fussy. But they aren't Calvin rip-offs either, partly because Henderson has avoided the beige-and-black neutral shades that dominate Klein's sportswear."

Henderson started his own fashion designing firm after serving a six-month apprenticeship with Klein. The young designer's popularity grew rapidly. In his first two shows, Henderson did very well, winning approval from both the press and retail buyers. "His intelligent affordable sportswear . . . eschews the flamboyant, crowd-pleasing styles that make

At a Glance. . .

Born in 1957 in San Joaquin Valley, CA; son of Gordon Henderson and Yvonne Simmons. *Education:* Attended University of California at Davis; graduated from Parsons School of Design, New York City, 1984.

Apprenticed with Calvin Klein; started his own fashion design business and held first show, 1988; launched new clothing line, "But Gordon," 1990; embarked on exclusive marketing venture with Saks Fifth Avenue, 1992.

Awards: Perry Ellis Award for best new fashion design talent, 1990.

Addresses: *Office*—450 West 15th St., New York, NY 10011.

good newspaper pictures but do not sell," noted Woody Hochswender in the *New York Times.*

Henderson's focus on affordable clothing stemmed from his early experience working in menswear retail stores in San Francisco and New York, where he saw that customers wanted inexpensive, practical clothes that looked good. "I don't believe in this whole yuppie, nouveau, riche spending thing," Henderson told Hochswender. "It's not smart. The '90s are about giving, not taking away. How can a designer be in fashion when no one can afford you? Then there's really no excitement. I'm trying to make clothes more compatible with people's pocketbooks."

Focused on Affordable Fashions

Filling the gap between pricey clothes and no-frills sportswear, Henderson became known for designing simple, unconstructed shapes in fine linen instead of silk or cashmere, or cotton twill rather than wool gabardine—all in an effort to keep his clothing affordable. In addition, he assumed a very active role in the day-to-day operations of his business, even pricing clothes himself.

Versatility has been another key to the success of Henderson's fashion designs. "Though Henderson's designs, like most clothes, look best on slim young things, individual pieces can be mixed and matched and worn with style by a middle-aged woman who wears a size 12," commented Nina Darnton in *Newsweek.* "You can take the clothes and put them together for career women," Henderson told Darnton, "or combine them for weekend or evening.

That's what the '90s are about—servicing your customer in the way she needs."

"But Gordon!"

In 1990, Henderson introduced a new clothing line called "But Gordon," inspired by a line from conversations he had with his customers. He explained in *Time* that clients would say things like, "But Gordon, I want something new," or "But Gordon, can't you deliver sooner?" or even "But Gordon, I want it all." Henderson's customer service approach has paid off. His 1991 sales exceeded $6 million, according to *People* magazine.

Henderson's financial success did not affected his casual way of living. Usually clad in a white T-shirt and jeans, he does not look like a stereotypical fashion designer. "Whatever I wear, even a tuxedo, has to be comfortable. Being comfortable brings out the best of beauty. There is always an element of the unexpected in beauty," Henderson mused in *People.* "What I look for is inner confidence, a sense of style rather than the outer shell."

For fashion inspiration, Henderson studies old movies. "[His] facility lies in translation, turning mid-century nostalgia into 90's gear," noted Duffy in *Time.* The final outfit modeled in one of his early fashion shows was a pair of white silk pajamas. "I wanted [the model] to be like Audrey Hepburn or Doris Day when they were stuck in the apartment. They looked so fantastic," Henderson told Duffy. The designer's use of color has also caused a stir in the fashion world, with shades of gold, copper, and plum becoming his signature in the early 1990s. "I like fruit tones, wood, stones," he told *Time.* "I keep beautiful rocks around, and I dry flowers to see which shades will emerge."

New Venture with Saks Fifth Avenue

Henderson's fresh approach to fashion has made a definite mark on the fashion industry. His "commitment to great looking clothes that women really love to wear" made him a winner in the fashion business at a time when a nationwide recession—coupled with women's growing sense of fashion independence—made clothing design a "risky business," reported *Essence* magazine.

With the success of his early fashions behind him, Henderson went on to break new ground in the industry, solidifying his name in fashion circles as a bold and talented businessman. As the United States began to emerge from depressed economic times in the early 1990s, upscale retailer Saks Fifth Avenue embarked on an exclusive, unprecedented agreement with Henderson, becoming the first retailer to serve as a designer's financial backer. No longer involved with other retail chains, the designer launched his new "Gordon Henderson" line in late 1992, marketing it solely through Saks Fifth Avenue stores.

Sources

Boston Globe, August 18, 1990, p. 14.
Essence, November 1991, p. 74.
Los Angeles Times, March 30, 1990, p. E1.
Mademoiselle, March 1990, p. 204.
Newsweek, November 20, 1989, p. 87.

New York Times, April 16, 1989; November 2, 1989; November 28, 1989, p. B10; September 17, 1990; March 26, 1992, p. C1.
People, March 19, 1990, p. 80.
Time, February 26, 1990, p. 61.
USA Today, January 15, 1990, p. D6.
Vogue, September 1989, p. 192.
Wall Street Journal, September 18, 1990, p. A1; November 3, 1992, p. B6.

—*Jomel Nichols*

Anita Hill

1956—

Lawyer, social activist, educator

On October 6, 1991, Anita Hill's life was dramatically and irrevocably changed when her charges of sexual harassment against a former employer, Clarence Thomas, were made public on the eve of his confirmation as a U.S. Supreme Court justice. In the ensuing days, Hill was grilled by the Senate Judiciary Committee about the graphic details of the alleged harassment and about her personal life. Her compelling testimony before the committee was broadcast live around the globe, sweeping her from the quiet obscurity of her life as a professor of law at the University of Oklahoma. Her charges produced a stunning collision of race and gender issues, and reactions to her and her story were highly polarized; some viewed her as a hero and a martyr, while others vilified her as mentally unstable, a liar, and even a racist.

In the end, the U.S. House and Senate chose to dismiss her allegations, and as a result, Thomas was given a seat on the highest court in the nation. Yet, Hill's appearance in Washington, D.C., was by no means without far-reaching effects. Her testimony, and the committee's reaction to it, have since been credited with revitalizing feminism, greatly increasing the public's awareness of sexual harassment, inspiring women to run for office in record numbers, and significantly increasing the numbers of women willing to speak out publicly about their own experiences of sexual harassment when they might otherwise have suffered in silence.

Nothing in Anita Hill's upbringing could have prepared her for the glare of international publicity she would eventually face. The youngest in a family of 13 children, she was raised in a deeply religious atmosphere on her parents' farm in rural Morris, Oklahoma, located some 45 miles south of Tulsa. Sundays were spent at the Lone Pine Baptist Church, while the rest of her week was filled with farm chores and schoolwork. She attended Okmulgee County's integrated schools, where she earned straight As and graduated as class secretary, valedictorian, and a National Honor Society student. After graduation, she attended Oklahoma State University, where she continued her outstanding academic performance and graduated with a degree in psychology and numerous academic honors.

An internship with a local judge had turned her ambitions to the field of law, and she sought and won admission into Yale University's demanding School of Law, where she was one of 11 black students in a class of 160. After graduation, she took a full-time job as a professional lawyer with the Washington

At a Glance...

Born Anita Faye Hill, July 30, 1956, in Morris, OK; daughter of Albert (a farmer) and Irma Hill. *Education:* Oklahoma State University, B.S., 1977; Yale University School of Law, LL.D., 1980. *Religion:* Baptist.

Lawyer with the firm of Ward, Harkrader, and Ross, Washington, DC, 1980-81; personal assistant to the head of the Office of Civil Rights at the Education Department and the chairman of the Equal Employment Opportunity Commission, Washington, DC, 1981-83; Oral Roberts University School of Law, Tulsa, OK, civil rights professor, 1983-86; University of Oklahoma School of Law, Norman, professor of law, 1986—.

Awards: Ida B. Wells Award from the National Coalition of 100 Black Women, 1991; named one of *Glamour* magazine's 10 Women of the Year, 1991.

Addresses: *Office*—University of Oklahoma School of Law, 300 Timberland Rd., Norman, OK 73019.

law firm of Ward, Harkrader, and Ross and worked there during the summer between her second and third years of law school.

Association with Clarence Thomas

In 1981, after working with the firm for about a year, Hill accepted a job as the personal assistant to Clarence Thomas, who was then head of the Office of Civil Rights at the Education Department in Washington. It was at this time, according to her sworn testimony, that he made repeated advances toward her and, when she rebuffed him, began to make vulgar remarks to her and to describe in vivid detail various hard-core pornographic films he had seen. When he began dating someone else, Hill stated, the harassment stopped, and she accepted an offer to follow him to a better job when he was made chairman of the Equal Employment Opportunity Commission. The alleged harassment began again, however, according to Hill's version of the events. In 1983, after being hospitalized with stress-related stomach problems, she left Washington to accept a position as a civil rights professor at Oral Roberts University in Tulsa. As a faculty member of this conservative religious school, Hill took an oath that said in part: "I will not lie, I will not steal, I will not curse, I will not be a talebearer."

In 1986, the university was reorganized, and the law school moved to the state of Virginia. Because she preferred to be near her family in Oklahoma, Hill declined to move with the school and instead sought employment at the University of Oklahoma, where she became a specialist in contract law. Six years of teaching are usually required before tenured status is granted to a professor there, but Hill was tenured after only four years. In addition to her teaching duties, she served on the faculty senate and was also named the faculty administrative fellow in the Office of the Provost, which made her a key voice in all major academic policy decisions.

Call from the Senate

Such was the state of Hill's life on September 3, 1991, when she was approached by the Senate Judiciary Committee and asked to supply background information on Clarence Thomas, who was then being considered as a replacement for Supreme Court Justice Thurgood Marshall. In a news conference given at the University of Oklahoma by Hill, which was excerpted at length in the *New York Times,* Hill elaborated: "They asked me questions about work that I had done there, and they asked me specifically about harassment and issues involving women in the workplace. Those questions, I have heard, were prompted by rumors that individuals who had worked at the agency had understood that I had been subject to some improper conduct . . . while at the agency." Hill, who had never filed a complaint against Thomas, found herself reluctant to go public with her story some ten years after the fact.

Initially, she decided to protect herself and her privacy by remaining silent. On further reflection, however, she apparently felt an obligation to tell the truth as she knew it, no matter how difficult that might be. "Here is a person [Thomas] who is in charge of protecting rights of women and other groups in the workplace and he is using his position of power for personal gain for one thing," she said in an interview with National Public Radio, also quoted by the *New York Times.* "And he did it in an very ugly and intimidating way."

By September 9, Hill had decided to cooperate in the investigation of Thomas on the condition that her identity be kept confidential. But she was informed on September 20 that the Judiciary Committee could not be told her story unless Thomas was notified of her identity and given a chance to respond to her allegations. Furthermore, if she agreed to cooperate, she and Thomas would both be questioned by the FBI. Hill pondered these new facts as the confirmation hearings for Thomas, already underway, drew near their close. On September 23, she agreed to allow her name to be used in an FBI investigation. She also requested permission to submit a personal statement to the committee.

Hill has since criticized the handling of her complaint, in part because copies of the FBI report were given to just two committee members, and her personal statement also failed to reach all those who should have seen it. Thomas, meanwhile, had issued a sworn statement forcefully denying all of Hill's allegations against him. In his version of the events, he had simply asked Hill out for dates a few times. He and his supporters characterized her eleventh-hour appearance as a ploy designed to keep him off the bench, engineered by liberals opposed to his appointment to the court. Hill answered such suggestions in her press conference at the University of Oklahoma: "There is absolutely no basis for that allegation, that I am somehow involved in some political plan to undermine the nominee. And I cannot even understand how someone could attempt to support such a claim. . . . This has taken a great toll on me personally and professionally, and there is no way that I would do something like this for political purposes."

Televised Hearings

After considerable debate, the U.S. Senate decided that new hearings on Thomas's confirmation would be held and that Hill would be called to Washington to testify before the Senate Judiciary Committee—which was made up of 14 white, male legislators. The televised hearings, which included Hill's and Thomas's appearances, drew an audience of millions, who were riveted by the drama of race and sex unfolding on the screen. Hill remained dignified and composed throughout the proceedings—in the face of repetitive questioning by the senators. Her credibility and character were vehemently attacked by some observers, who questioned why she maintained a speaking relationship with Thomas after the alleged incidents occurred and why she never filed a formal complaint. Republican legislator Arlen Specter went so far as to imply that Hill had fantasized the whole scenario; others suggested that she was acting out of jealousy because Thomas had failed to provide her the attentions she secretly desired from him.

Racial issues were in evidence during the hearings and influenced reaction among both the general public and the Judiciary Committee. Thomas himself fueled that fire when he denounced the proceedings as a "high-tech lynching," effectively accusing Hill of participating in a racist plot to keep him out of the Supreme Court because he is black. In the book *Race-ing Justice, En-gendering Power,* essayist Carol M. Swain discussed another race-related phenomenon that turned the tide of black opinion against Hill: "For African Americans generally, the issue was not so much whether Hill was credible or not; she was dismissed because many saw her as a person who had violated the

code . . . which mandates that blacks should not criticize, let alone accuse, each other in front of whites."

In the Aftermath

The nomination of Clarence Thomas was confirmed on October 16, 1991. Hill, who had by then returned to Oklahoma, accepted the news with the composure that had marked her appearance before the committee. Disregarding all the racial, political, and feminist implications of the decision, she told Roberto Suro of the *New York Times:* "For me it is enough justice getting it heard. I just wanted people to know and understand that this had happened. . . . You just have to tell the truth and that's the most anyone can expect from you and if you get that opportunity, you will have accomplished something."

Many of Hill's detractors had predicted that she would capitalize on her experience by making high-paid speaking appearances, writing a book, or even selling her story as a television movie-of-the-week, but in the months following her testimony, she proved them wrong. She resumed her

> "Cooperating in the investigation of Clarence Thomas has taken a great toll on me personally and professionally, and there is no way that I would do something like this for political purposes."

usual teaching duties and returned to her regular routine as nearly as was possible, given the reporters and others who constantly sought her out. In time she took a sabbatical from teaching, using the interlude to study the sociology and psychology of sexual harassment. Aside from an appearance on the CBS News program *60 Minutes,* and, much later, one on the *Today* show, she turned down all interview requests. She made carefully selected appearances on the speaking circuit, often for no fee, and at such appearances, she declined to talk in detail about the hearings or her own personal experience, focusing instead on the larger issues of sexual harassment and discrimination in general.

Following the hearings, former Minnesota House representative Gloria M. Segal approached Hill with a plan to establish an endowed fund for a special professorship in her name—devoted to the study of sexual harassment and workplace equity—at the University of Oklahoma. In spite of the fact that half of the $250,000 needed for the project was easily raised, by mid-1993 work on establishing the professorship had stalled, due mainly to the adverse publicity and political fallout felt at the University of Oklahoma. The future of the fund remains in doubt, although several other colleges and universities across the country have reportedly expressed an interest in assuming control of the money and following through on the institution of the professorship.

The Thomas-Hill hearings continued to resonate long after the headlines had faded. Public opinion polls taken at the time of the Senate hearings showed that a majority of those polled discredited Hill's story. Yet a poll taken one year later showed that twice as many people had come to believe her version of the events. Then, in the spring of 1993, investigative journalist David Brock published his controversial book *The Real Anita Hill,* in which he claims to offer hard evidence that Hill lied about her relationship with Thomas. Conservative political commentator George F. Will commented in *Newsweek:* "To believe that Hill told the truth you must believe that dozens of people, with no common or even apparent motive to lie, did so. Brock's book will be persuasive to minds not sealed by the caulking of ideology." However, several reviews of the book questioned the reliability of Brock's assertions. As Jacob Weisberg put it in *Entertainment Weekly, The Real Anita Hill* "has yet to produce many converts."

Still, Anita Hill has, for many, become a symbol of a new and powerful wave of feminism. Women's groups continue to credit Hill's appearance before the Senate Judiciary Committee with vastly increasing the public's awareness of sexual harassment and making it much less tolerated in the workplace. In an Associated Press news story dated October 11, 1992, Helen Neuborne, executive director of the NOW Legal Defense and Education Fund, stated: "A lot of women had felt so isolated and perhaps couldn't even define sexual harassment. . . . The hearings made an enormous difference even though they were horrible."

The Equal Employment Opportunity Commission, where Hill and Thomas once worked, reported a 50 percent increase in complaints filed for harassment in the year following Hill's testimony. Additionally, in the aftermath of the hearings, numerous women ran for and won election to government office for the first time, citing their dissatisfaction with the all-male Senate Committee's response to Hill's allegations as their primary reason for doing so. And debate about the truth or falsity of Hill's allegations went on. Tonya Bolden, a *Black Enterprise* contributor commenting on the various analyses of the Hill-Thomas affair, suggested that the entire incident may have sparked a vital understanding of broader issues. As she put it in the April 1993 issue: "At the end you care less about who was lying and more about what you can do to counter racism and sexism."

Sources

Books

The Black Scholar staff, editors, *Court of Appeal: The Black Community Speaks Out on the Racial and Sexual Politics of Thomas vs. Hill,* One World/Ballantine, 1992.

Brock, David, *The Real Anita Hill,* Free Press, 1993.

Morrison, Toni, editor, *Race-ing Justice, En-gendering Power: Essays on Anita Hill, Clarence Thomas, and the Construction of Social Reality,* Pantheon, 1992.

Periodicals

American Spectator, March 1992.

Associated Press wire report, October 11, 1992.

Black Enterprise, April 1993, p. 12.

Entertainment Weekly, June 18, 1993, p. 53.

Essence, March 1992, pp. 55-56, 116-17.

Ms., January-February 1992.

Nation, November 4, 1991.

National Law Journal, January 20, 1992.

Newsweek, December 28, 1992, pp. 20-22; April 19, 1993, p. 74.

New York Times, October 7, 1991; October 8, 1991; October 9, 1991; October 10, 1991; October 11, 1991; October 14, 1991; October 16, 1991; October 17, 1991; November 2, 1991; December 18, 1991; February 3, 1992; April 26, 1992; October 7, 1992; October 17, 1992; October 19, 1992.

New York Times Book Review, October 25, 1992.

Oakland Press (Oakland County, MI), October 11, 1992; April 24, 1993, p. A4.

Time, October 21, 1991; October 19, 1992; June 28, 1993.

U.S. News & World Report, November 2, 1992.

Working Woman, September 1992, p. 21.

—*Joan Goldsworthy*

Natalie Hinderas

1927-1987

Pianist, educator

In the rarefied world of classical music performance, artists are often judged by their interpretive ability and degree of skill in transmitting the artful expression of the composer. Classical pianist Natalie Hinderas, possessed of a profoundly diverse musical expression, was viewed through another spectrum: her place in the classical music world was reflected not by the shadings that infused the notes she played, but by the color of her skin.

At the time of her death in 1987, Hinderas was recognized as "one of the first black artists to establish an important career in classical music," as was reported in her *New York Times* obituary. Throughout her life, she strove to advance the works of black composers and performers. But of equal importance for Hinderas was the indoctrination of young people to the unbiased artistic pleasures and human scope of classical music, the very attributes that guided her into the field.

Natalie Leota Henderson was born on June 15, 1927, in Oberlin, Ohio, into a family with a deep musical heritage. Her great-grandfather had been a bandleader and teacher in South Carolina; her father was a jazz pianist who toured Europe with his own group; and her mother was a classically trained piano teacher who served on the faculty of the

Cleveland Institute of Music. Both parents were graduates of the Oberlin Conservatory. "I grew up with music," Hinderas later understated to Raymond Ericson of the *New York Times.* "I listened to my mother practice. I still remember her playing [Arthur] Rubinstein's D minor Concerto and [César] Franck's Prelude, Choral, and Fugue."

This attention to the art of classical music was not lost on the young Hinderas. Indeed, she began playing the piano at age three. Her inherent talents matured under her mother's tutelage, and at the age of eight, she gave her first full recital on the piano. Immediately afterward, she was accepted into Oberlin Conservatory's Special Student's School. Hinderas's orchestral debut, playing Edvard Grieg's Piano Concerto, came with the Cleveland Women's Symphony in 1939. She was 12.

When Hinderas received her degree in music with honors from Oberlin in 1945, she became the conservatory's youngest graduate and one of its most prominent—her senior recital had attracted one of the school's largest audiences. She subsequently won an audition for advanced study at the Juilliard School of Music in New York City. There she was guided by the distinguished concert pianist and instructor Olga Samaroff, who educed from Hinderas's playing a warm, romantic feeling. Samaroff (who had changed her surname from Hickenlooper, and who convinced her student to change hers from Henderson to the more exotic Hinderas) recognized Hinderas's potential for greatness but was also realistic in her view of the young pianist's future in the classical world. "She used to say," Hinderas related to Shirley Fleming in *High Fidelity/Musical America,* "'My dear, you're going to have a hard time.'" Previously, Hinderas had been judged—and praised—solely on her talents. Samaroff's forewarning, however, would unfortunately prove prophetic.

After Samaroff's death in 1948, Hinderas continued her studies for the next five years with Edward Steuermann at the Philadelphia Conservatory of Music. Steuermann deepened her ability to handle the arduous technical and intellectual demands of classical music's more exacting compositions. At this time she also studied composition with Vincent Persichetti.

In the early 1950s, Hinderas's career seemed to be blossoming. While continuing her studies with both Steuermann and Persichetti, she made her European debut and signed a contract with NBC-TV to make appearances on network programs, both classical and variety shows. A Cleveland television station broadcast Hinderas in concert in 1953. One year later, she debuted at New York City's Town Hall.

Debut Promised Exceptional Career

With a program featuring Wolfgang Amadeus Mozart's Sonata in F, Maurice Ravel's *Alborado del Gracioso* and *Jeux d'eau,* Alban Berg's Piano Sonata, Paul Hindemith's Sonata No. 1, and Frédéric Chopin's F minor Ballade, Hinderas demonstrated to a *New York Times* reviewer that she had "honest musical instincts. Very often she shaped a phrase with real authority, leaving no doubt that a strong controlling force was engaged." Although this critic found fault with some of her execution—a certain lack of musical maturity in the Hindemith and Chopin pieces—he nonetheless foresaw Hinderas, after a few more years of experience, taking her place as a world-class pianist accompanied by world-class orchestras.

Hinderas did gain valuable artistic insight in the following years. She traveled around the United States on a recital tour, performed with the National Symphony, and gave concerts in the British West Indies. During 1957 and 1958, she gave televised recitals in Austria, England, Germany, Holland, and Italy. In 1959 she won an award from the Leventritt Foundation, which sponsored subsequent performances with numerous orchestras. None of these, however, was recognized as world-class.

But Hinderas remained tireless in her quest to expose audiences to the classical repertoire, producing two series on classical music for a Philadelphia radio station in 1959. That year she also began a four-month world tour under the auspices of the U.S. State Department, visiting Sweden, Yugoslavia, Iran, Jordan, Taiwan, and the Philippines and giving lecture/recitals on American music and fostering cultural goodwill. In 1961 she appeared on behalf of the American Society for African Society at the opening of a cultural center in Lagos, Nigeria. A second State Department tour took place in 1964. This time she traveled to Sweden, Poland, Yugoslavia, and England, and, in addition to her recitals and seminars, performed with the Dubrovnik and Skopje Symphony Orchestras.

Even after these performances on the world's stages, Hinderas was not given the opportunity to perform with the best orchestras in the United States. "Orchestras simply wouldn't hire a black woman—this was in the days when there weren't even black players in the orchestras," Hinderas told Fleming. "People used to say to me, 'You're the only black musician around.' And I think I was until André Watts—he broke the barrier. Before that I felt like a freak; it was a terrible sense of responsibility."

Sought to Reach All Audiences

A more self-centered musician might have been deterred by the lack of exposure with a renowned orchestra, but Hinderas, devoted to the art of classical music, instead sought to reach an audience for the art's sake, not her own. In 1966 she joined the faculty of Temple University's College of Music and began lecturing and performing at various colleges and music festivals around the country. The college lecture/recital became a calling for Hinderas. She explained why to Fleming: "Young people are an untapped source—they can be a good audience because they're less inhibited, less structured than older people, though of course they have their own form of 'structure' and that can be limiting too. But I talk to them about the importance of music, how it is an enunciation of one's life, really the expression of what they're living. I try to set up a dialogue and ferret out their questions and doubts."

Hinderas also sought to reconcile the black community to her art, fighting the idea, as she told *New York Times* contributor Ericson, that "classical music is white man's music." To this end, she began touring southern black colleges in 1968, performing the music of black classical composers and lecturing on the history of black classical musicians in the United States. "I'm trying to change the jazz- and gospel-oriented image," she told Fleming. "People have never associated us with the classics."

To dispel this notion, not only for the black community but for the global community as well, Hinderas recorded *Natalie Hinderas Plays Music by Black Composers* for the Desto label in 1971. The two-record set featured the works of nine composers: R. Nathaniel Dett, Thomas H. Kerr, Jr., William Grant Still, John W. Work, George Walker, Arthur Cunningham, Stephen A. Chambers, Hale Smith, and Olly Wilson. The significance and necessity of the recording was confirmed by Leslie Gerber in a review for *American Record Guide*: "It is hardly possible to be unaware of the tremendous contributions made by black musicians to American folk, popular, and jazz music; but one may sometimes wonder what blacks have achieved in the more academic forms of the tonal art." This anthology showed Gerber exactly what some of them had achieved, and his highest praise was bestowed on Hinderas. "I would welcome the opportunity to hear her in works from the classical repertoire," he wrote. "Of all the musicians whose acquaintance I have made through these records, she is the

one who has made the most thoroughly favorable impression on me."

Recognition At Last

That impression was felt elsewhere as well, and Hinderas's talent was finally fully recognized in the fall of 1971 when conductor Eugene Ormandy invited her to play Alberto Ginastera's Piano Concerto No. 1 with the Philadelphia Orchestra. With this debut, she became the first black woman ever to appear as an instrumental soloist in the regular series of any major symphony. Another first was the selection of music. In this setting, a work by Grieg or Chopin would traditionally have been offered. But Ormandy and Hinderas chose instead to feature the Argentine composer's 1961 work, which would highlight Hinderas's

> "Orchestras simply wouldn't hire a black woman—this was in the days when there weren't even black players in the orchestras. People used to say to me, 'You're the only black musician around.' I felt like a freak."

strengths as a pianist. James Felton, reviewing the concert for *High Fidelity/Musical America,* lauded the choice, remarking, "Like some writhing marine animal, the work seemed to ripple over cross rhythms and asymmetrical bars, handled at the keyboard with tensile strength. Miss Hinderas was now leader, now follower, now a full partner in forceful tuttis that reinforced a recurrent percussive wallop."

Immediately afterward, Hinderas was engaged to play with major orchestras across the nation: the New York Philharmonic, the Cleveland Symphony, the Los Angeles Philharmonic, the Atlanta Symphony, the Chicago Symphony, the San Francisco Symphony, the Pittsburgh Symphony. She found her appearance with the Los Angeles Philharmonic at the Hollywood Bowl particularly satisfying; she explained to Ericson that early in her career a manager had told her, "You know, Natalie, a little colored girl like you can't play in the Hollywood Bowl."

Again, an artist of lesser character might have been content to sit and accept the laurels. But Hinderas remained committed to developing the public's recognition and appreciation of classical music. She believed a greater understanding could be achieved through the media, specifically television. "It is time we changed the total direction of classical music in this country and got support from the public media," she declared to *High Fidelity/Musical America* contributor Fleming. "The major TV networks are molding our minds and they have the responsibility to further the arts. You can lead people into anything if you know how to."

The music Hinderas created was large and physically exuberant, but it took the world almost 20 years to notice it. She fought for and gained recognition and respect not only for herself as a performer, but also for the contributions of black musicians and composers to the world of classical music, a world where color is only a shading of a note. "To begin with, of course, she is a pianist." So began Fleming's 1973 profile of Hinderas. In a more colorblind society, this would have been the initial standard by which Hinderas was measured.

Selected discography

Natalie Hinderas Plays Music by Black Composers, Desto, 1971, reissued as *Natalie Hinderas: Piano Music by African American Composers,* CRI, 1993.

Natalie Hinderas Plays Sensuous Piano Music, Orion.
George Walker's Piano Concerto, Columbia.

Sources

Books

Abdul, Raoul, *Blacks in Classical Music,* Dodd, Mead, & Co., 1977.

Periodicals

American Music Teacher, January 1975; February/ March 1975.
American Record Guide, April 1971.
Ebony, February 1993.
High Fidelity/Musical America, February 1972; October 1973.
New York Times, November 14, 1954; November 10, 1972; July 23, 1987.
Saturday Review, December 26, 1970; December 16, 1972.

—*Rob Nagel*

bell hooks

1952—

Social activist, feminist theorist, educator, writer

Writer, professor, and social critic bell hooks is undeniably one of the most successful "cross-over" academics of the late twentieth century. Her name, as well as the criticisms of racism and sexism that she has penned, are central to many current academic discussions, and they are also read widely outside of the educational arena. Her 1992 publication *Black Looks: Race and Representation,* was described by *Publishers Weekly* as "imbued with hooks's theoretical rigor, intellectual integrity, breadth of knowledge and passion" and "a necessary read for anyone concerned with race in America."

Her other books, five of which were on the market before 1992, similarly analyze the functions of race and gender in contemporary culture, taking as their subjects movies, television, advertising, political events, socioeconomic conditions—anything that reflects social inequality. In the introduction to *Black Looks,* which includes essays about Madonna, Spike Lee, and the Anita Hill-Clarence Thomas hearings, hooks explained the fundamental political purpose of her cultural criticism: "It struck me that for black people, the pain of learning that we cannot control our images, how we see ourselves (if our vision is not decolonized), or how we are seen is so intense that it rends us. It rips and tears at the seams of our efforts to construct self and identify."

The essayist and teacher known to her readers as bell hooks was born Gloria Jean Watkins on September 25, 1952. The sense of community that would become so significant a note in hooks's work grew out of her early life in a black neighborhood in Hopkinsville, a small, segregated town in rural Kentucky. She recalled her neighborhood as a "world where folks were content to get by on a little, where Baba, mama's mother, made soap, dug fishing worms, set traps for rabbits, made butter and wine, sewed quilts, and wrung the necks of chickens." In the same essay, "Chitlin Circuit," hooks explained how the hardships created by racism could be turned by this community into a source of strength: "A very distinctive black culture was created in the agrarian South, by the experience of rural living, poverty, racial segregation, and resistance struggle, a culture we can cherish and learn from. It offers ways of knowing, habits of being, that can sustain us as a people."

Gloria was one of six siblings: five sisters and a baby brother. Her father worked as a janitor, and her mother, Rosa Bell Oldham Watkins, worked as a maid in the homes of white families, as did many of the black women in town. Although

At a Glance. . .

Born Gloria Jean Watkins, September 25, 1952, in Hopkinsville, KY; daughter of a janitor and mother, Rosa Bell (a domestic laborer; maiden name, Oldham) Watkins. *Education:* Stanford University, B.A., 1973; University of Wisconsin, M.A., 1976; University of California at Santa Cruz, Ph.D., 1983.

Worked as a telephone operator during college; lecturer at University of Southern California, 1976-79, University of California at Riverside, 1978, Occidental College, 1980, San Francisco State University, 1981, and University of California at Santa Cruz, 1981-84; first book, *Ain't I a Woman,* published by South End Press, 1981; assistant professor of African American Studies and English Literature at Yale University, beginning 1985; associate professor in American Literature and Women's Studies at Oberlin College, 1988—; teacher of courses in black studies at City College of New York, 1993.

Awards: Before Columbus Foundation's American Book Award, 1991, for *Yearning: Race, Gender and Cultural Politics.*

Addresses: 222 Elm Street, Oberlin, OH 44074; or c/o South End Press, 116 St. Botolph Street, Boston MA 02115.

integration to Kentucky. Looking back on her sophomore year of high school in "Chitlin Circuit," she recalled, "What I remember most about that time is a deep sense of loss. It hurt to leave behind memories, schools that were 'ours,' places we loved and cherished, places that honored us. It was one of the first great tragedies of growing up."

The neighborhood where she grew up provided young Gloria with the affirmation that fostered her resistance to racism, but it also provided her with the negative and positive experiences that would shape her feminism, which she discussed in the essay "Ain't I a Woman: Looking Back": "I cannot recall when I first heard the word 'feminist' or understood its meaning. I know that it was early [in my] childhood that I began to wonder about sex roles, that I began to see and feel that the experience of being 'made' female was different from that of being 'made' male; perhaps I was so conscious of this because my brother was my constant companion. I use the word 'made' because it was obvious in our home that sex roles were socially constructed—that everyone could agree that very small children were pretty much alike, only different from one another physiologically; but that everyone enjoyed the process of turning us into little girls and little boys, little men and little women, with socially constructed differences."

Learned to "Talk Back"

Although Gloria was supposed to become a quiet, well-behaved young woman, she became instead a woman who "talked back." This phenomenon, for which hooks eventually named a volume of essays, actually refers to the development of a strong sense of self that allows black women to speak out against racism and sexism. In the introduction to *Talking Back: Thinking Feminist, Thinking Black,* a collection published in 1989, hooks emphasized the importance of this trait in her personality: "Folks who know me in real life and in the unreal life of books can bear witness to a courageous openness in speech that often marks me, becomes that which I am known by." In the essay of the same name, hooks noted the origin of this outspokenness: "I was always saying the wrong thing, asking the wrong questions. I could not confine my speech to the necessary corners and concerns of life."

Young Gloria's personality was a mix of this disobedient curiosity and a painful reserve; she explained, in retrospect, that "safety and sanity were to be sacrificed if I was to experience defiant speech. Though I risked them both, deep-seated fears and anxieties characterized my childhood days."

She wasn't, however, afraid of writing or of books; she used both to further develop her voice. In "'When I Was a Young Soldier': Coming to Voice," hooks explained that poetry—an element of particular importance in the growth

hooks—writing in the essay "Keeping Close to Home" from *Black Looks*—described her father as "an impressive example of diligence and hard work," she paid the most tribute to her mother's care; in "Homeplace" she explained, "Politically, our young mother, Rosa Bell, did not allow the white supremacist culture of domination to completely shape and control her psyche and her familial relationships." The author further described how this role applied to mothers in black communities in general: "Black women resisted by making homes where all black people could strive to be subjects, not objects, where we could be affirmed in our minds and hearts despite poverty, hardship, and deprivation, where we could restore to ourselves the dignity denied us on the outside in the public world."

As a student at segregated public schools such as Booker T. Washington Elementary and Crispus Attucks High, hooks was taught by a dedicated group of teachers, mostly single black women, who helped to shape the self-esteem of children of color. But the late 1960s brought forced school of her voice—first captured her attention at church "with reading scripture with those awkward and funny little rhymes we would memorize and recite on Easter Sunday." By the time she was ten, she had begun writing her own poetry and soon developed a reputation for her ability to recite verse. She described the way poetry figured into her early life in "When I Was a Young Soldier": "Poetry was one literary expression that was absolutely respected in our working-class household. Nights when the lights would go out, when storms were raging, we would sit in the dim candlelight of our living room and have a talent show. I would recite poems: [William] Wordsworth, James Weldon Johnson, Langston Hughes, Elizabeth Barrett Browning, Emily Dickinson, Gwendolyn Brooks. Poetry by white writers was always there in schools and on family bookshelves in anthologies of 'great' works sold to us by door-to-door salesmen. . . . Poetry by black writers had to be searched for."

Although hooks has continued to write poetry and has published some, she gained notoriety as a writer of critical essays on systems of domination. In order to do this work, she found herself needing to develop a different voice, a different name. In an essay called "To Gloria, Who Is She: On Using a Pseudonym," hooks noted: "Gloria was to have been a sweet southern girl, quiet, obedient, pleasing. She was not to have that wild streak that characterized women on my mother's side."

She first used her pseudonym—her maternal great-grandmother's name—for a small book of poems; another woman in her community was named Gloria Watkins, and she wanted to avoid confusion. But a different purpose gradually developed, as she noted in "Talking Back": "One of the many reasons I chose to write using the pseudonym . . . was to construct a writer-identity that would challenge and subdue all impulses leading me away from speech into silence." This writer-identity, represented by the pseudonym bell hooks, grew out of the reputation that the original bell hooks had in Gloria's community and, consequently, the sense of self that it could make for Gloria: "I was a young girl buying bubble gum at the corner store when I first really heard the full name bell hooks," she remembered in "Talking Back." "I had just talked back to a grown person. Even now I can recall the surprised look, the mocking tones that informed me I must be kin to bell hooks—a sharp-tongued woman, a woman who spoke her mind, a woman who was not afraid to talk back. I claimed this legacy of defiance, of will, of courage, affirming my link to female ancestors who were bold and daring in their speech."

Found Racism in Women's Studies

To a southern black girl from a working-class background who had never been on a city bus, who had never stepped on an escalator, who had never traveled by plane, leaving the comfortable confines of a small town Kentucky life to attend Stanford University was not just frightening, it was utterly painful. In "Keeping Close to Home: Class and Education," hooks described her difficult first journey out of Hopkinsville, which she made to begin her undergraduate education at Stanford, a white, Ivy League institution.

Accepting the scholarship that would take her to northern California, hooks gave up the affirmation of her black community but hoped to find a place that would affirm a woman's voice talking back. Initially, as she acknowledged in "Ain't I a Woman: Looking Back," she found some of the intellectual and political affirmation that she had anticipated: "I eagerly responded to the fervor over the contemporary feminist movement on campus. I took classes, went to meetings, to all-women's parties." But one of the significant weaknesses of that women's movement quickly became apparent to her: "It was in one of my first Women's Studies classes, taught by Tillie Olsen, that I noticed the complete absence of material by or any discussion about black women. I began to feel estranged and alienated from the huge group of white women who were celebrating the power of 'sisterhood.'"

That initial disillusionment would eventually fuel hooks's major contribution to mainstream feminism—her critique of its persistent racism. In "Feminism: a Transformational Politic," she translated that early experience in Women's

> "Moving from silence into speech is for the oppressed a gesture of defiance that heals, that makes new life and new growth possible."

Studies into broad political insight: "Within the feminist movement in the West, [there exists] the assumption that resisting patriarchal domination is a more legitimate feminist action than resisting racism and other forms of domination." It became hooks's main work to change that assumption.

The unspoken racism she witnessed in the classroom reflected the racism embedded in the academy at large, where an institution run largely by middle-class, white men actively worked to limit the movement of the few people of color who were present. In "Black and Female: Reflections on Graduate School," hooks recalled the racism that began in her undergraduate education: "We were terrorized. As an undergraduate, I carefully avoided those professors who made it clear that the presence of any black students in their classes was not desired. . . . They communicated their message in subtle ways—forgetting to call your name when reading the roll, avoiding looking at you, pretending they do not hear you when you speak, and at times ignoring you altogether.''

She encountered further obstacles when she pursued her study of literature later in graduate school. Several professors at the University of Southern California and the University of Wisconsin were determined to stop hooks—a black woman—from earning the graduate degree that she needed to become a university professor. Neither of these programs nor her final degree program at the University of California at Santa Cruz had black women on the faculty. Persisting against the racism, hooks completed her dissertation titled *Toni Morrison's Fiction: Keeping "A Hold on Life,"* in 1983. Although she would go on to teach African American literature, hooks only submitted this work for publication in the early 1990s. As early as 1981, however, she already had a major publication to her credit, *Ain't I a Woman: Black Women and Feminism.*

Wrote First Book at Nineteen

In the early 1970s, in order to combat the racism that permeated her world, hooks turned to the same strategy that had served her so well in childhood: talking back. She was experiencing, every day, as she recorded in *Ain't I a Woman,* "a social reality that differed from that of white men, white women, and even black men." She tried to find texts that would explain that difference and validate her recognition of the injustice. The impetus to write her own text finally came from a black male friend who was her lover at the time: "When I could not find sources, when I expressed mounting bitterness and rage, he encouraged me to write this book that I was searching for." In *Breaking Bread: Insurgent Black Intellectual Life,* she summarized the fundamental idea she needed to capture in that first book: "What I wanted so much to do . . . was to say there is a history that has produced this circumstance of devaluation. It is not something inherent in Black women that we don't feel good about ourselves, that we are self-hating. Rather it is an experience which is socially circumscribed, brought into being by historical mechanisms."

Despite the full-time studies she was pursuing at Stanford when she began *Ain't I a Woman* at the age of nineteen, hooks took a job as a telephone operator. Finding time for her writing was a challenge, but hooks also found that the job offered her something she didn't have in school at the time—a community of working-class, black women: "They provided support and affirmation of the project," she wrote, "the kind of support I had not found in a university setting. They were not concerned about my credentials, about my writing skills, about degrees. They, like me, wanted someone to say the kinds of things about our lives that would bring change or further understanding."

The author went through several drafts of the manuscript over the next six years before she had one that satisfied her. A large part of the process, as she reconstructed it in "'When I Was a Young Soldier': Coming to Voice," was once again about discovering a voice that was strong enough to talk back: "The initial completed manuscript was excessively long and very repetitious. Reading it critically, I saw that I was trying not only to address each different potential audience—black men, white women, white men, etc.—but that my words were written to explain, to placate, to appease. They contained the fear of speaking that often characterizes the way those in a lower position within a hierarchy address those in a higher position of authority. Those passages where I was speaking most directly to black women contained the voice I felt to be most truly mine—it was then that my voice was daring, courageous." It was at this moment that the persona of bell hooks truly rescued Gloria Watkins.

At first hooks had considerable trouble publishing her work: some publishers would release works on racism, and a number of feminist presses were printing anti-sexist books, but no one wanted to take a risk on a book that treated the two topics together. Eventually, hooks was directed to her future publisher, South End Press, while giving a talk at a feminist bookstore in San Francisco. Once published in 1981, *Ain't I a Woman* became central to discussions of racism and sexism. Eleven years later, *Publishers Weekly* ranked it among the "20 most influential women's books of the last 20 years." Much of the response, as hooks characterized it in "Talking Back," was shockingly negative: "The book was sharply and harshly criticized. While I had expected a climate of critical dialogue, I was not expecting a critical avalanche that had the power in its intensity to crush the spirit, to push one into silence."

Most of the criticism came from the academic community, both because hooks's form defied academic convention and because her subject matter pressed vulnerable points with established white feminists. The author explained in *Breaking Bread* that she received her most important feedback from her non-academic readers: "When *Ain't I a Woman* was first published I would get dozens of letters a week, where, say, a Black woman from a small town, out in the middle of nowhere, would tell me that she read my book at the public library and it transformed her life.

A Career in Higher Education

While *Ain't I a Woman* made bell hooks a vital name in

feminist debate, Gloria Watkins continued her work. With a Ph.D. in English literature, she embarked on her teaching career. It was in her role as a teacher that hooks felt she was doing her most important work, as she explained in "On Being Black at Yale: Education as the Practice of Freedom": "Fundamentally the purpose of my knowing was so I could serve those who did not know, so that I could learn and teach my own—education as the practice of freedom." She knew that for a people historically and legally deprived of the right to education, teaching was one of the most substantial forms of political resistance she could choose.

After holding various lectureships at Santa Cruz in the early 1980s, hooks left for Yale when she had the opportunity to teach in African American Studies, stating: "I would not have accepted a job solely in the English Department. I believed that I would find in African American Studies a place within the university wherein scholarship focusing on black people would be unequivocally deemed valuable—as necessary a part of the production of knowledge as all other work." In 1988, she joined the faculty at Oberlin College in Ohio, where she would teach in Women's Studies, a program that now offered the critique of racism that was absent during her undergraduate years.

Along with her teaching, hooks has continued to write and publish at a rate that is astonishing even for an academic. She published *Feminist Theory: From Margin to Center* while still lecturing at Santa Cruz in 1984 and followed it in 1989 with *Talking Back: Thinking Feminist, Thinking Black*. She then produced three books in three years: *Yearning: Race, Gender and Cultural Politics* in 1990; *Breaking Bread: Insurgent Black Intellectual Life,* which she wrote with Cornel West, in 1991; and *Black Looks: Race and Representation* in 1992. Her essays frequently appear in a publications that range from the *Journal of Feminist Studies in Religion* to *Essence.* In 1992 she also submitted volumes of poetry and fiction to publishers.

It is clear that hooks intends to hold fast to the goal she described in "Talking Back": "Moving from silence into speech is for the oppressed, the colonized, the exploited, and those who stand and struggle side by side a gesture of defiance that heals, that makes new life and new growth possible. It is that act of speech, of 'talking back,' that is no mere gesture of empty words, that is the expression of our movement from object to subject—the liberated voice."

Selected writings

And There We Wept (poems), Golemics, 1978.
Ain't I a Woman: Black Women and Feminism, South End Press, 1981.
Feminist Theory: From Margin to Center, South End Press, 1984.
Talking Back: Thinking Feminist, Thinking Black, South End Press, 1989.
Yearning: Race, Gender and Cultural Politics, South End Press, 1990.
(With Cornel West) *Breaking Bread: Insurgent Black Intellectual Life,* South End Press, 1991.
Black Looks: Race and Representation, South End Press, 1992.
A Woman's Mourning Song, Harlem River Press, 1992.

Sources

Books

hooks, bell, *Talking Back: Thinking Feminist, Thinking Black,* South End Press, 1989.
hooks, bell, *Yearning: Race, Gender and Cultural Politics,* South End Press, 1990.
hooks, bell, and Cornel West, *Breaking Bread: Insurgent Black Intellectual Life,* South End Press, 1991.
hooks, bell, *Black Looks: Race and Representation,* South End Press, 1992.

Periodicals

Essence, July 1992, p. 124.
Publishers Weekly, June 15, 1992, p. 95.

—*Ondine E. Le Blanc*

Lena Horne

1917—

Singer, actress, activist

"She is one of the incomparable performers of our time," Richard Watts, Jr., wrote of Lena Horne in the *New York Post* in 1957. This assessment continued to hold true decades later: Lena Horne, the beautiful, elegant, and talented singer and actress has become a legend. Horne encountered adversity throughout her career: first from her family, who disapproved of her choice of occupation; then from white audiences and managers, who were uncomfortable with her assertiveness; and even from other African American performers, who felt threatened by her refusal to accept stereotypical roles. But her strong sense of her own identity, of justice, and of dignity forced her to struggle against this adversity—and allowed her to triumph.

Lena Mary Calhoun Horne was born on June 30, 1917, in the Bedford-Stuyvesant neighborhood of Brooklyn, New York, to Edwin "Teddy" Horne and his wife, Edna. Horne's parents separated by the time she was three years old, and she lived for several years with her paternal grandparents, Cora Calhoun and Edwin Horne. Her early life was nomadic: Horne's mother, who was a fairly unsuccessful stage performer, took the young Lena on the road with her, and they lived in various parts of the South before returning to Horne's grandparents' home in Brooklyn in 1931. After her grandparents died, she

was sent to live with her mother's friend Laura Rollock. Shortly thereafter, her mother married Miguel "Mike" Rodriguez, and Horne moved in with them.

Horne had early ambitions to be a performer—against the wishes of her family, who believed that she should aspire to greater heights. The Hornes were an established middle-class family, with several members holding college degrees and distinguished positions in organizations such as the National Association for the Advancement of Colored People (NAACP) and the Urban League. Nevertheless, Horne persisted, and in 1933 she began her first professional engagement—at the Cotton Club, the famed Harlem nightclub. She sang in the chorus, and though only sixteen years old, held her own among the older and more experienced cast members. She soon left high school to devote herself to her stage career.

Performed in New York and Hollywood

In 1934 Horne had a small role in an all-black Broadway show called *Dance with Your Gods.* The next year, she left the Cotton Club and began performing as the featured singer with Noble Sissle's Society Orchestra under the

Is Tops. In 1939 she had a role in the musical revue *Blackbirds of 1939* at the Hudson Theatre in New York City; it ran for only eight nights. Before her marriage to Jones ended in divorce, she had two children, Gail and Edwin ("Teddy").

Horne left Jones in 1940, taking a job as a singer with Charlie Barnet's band and going out on tour with him. Horne was the only black member of the ensemble, and the kind of racial discrimination she encountered from audiences, hotel managers, and others was so unsettling that she decided to quit the band. In 1941, she began performing at the Café Society Downtown, a club in New York City that catered to intellectuals and social activists, both black and white.

At the Café Society, Horne learned about black history, politics, and culture, and developed a new appreciation for her heritage. She rekindled her acquaintance with Paul Robeson, whom she had known when she was a child. In her autobiography entitled *In Person: Lena Horne,* she said that through her conversations with Robeson, she realized "that we [African Americans] were going forward, and that knowledge gave me a strength and a sense of unity. Yes, we were going forward, and it was up to me to learn more about us and to join actively in our struggle." From this point on, Horne became a significant voice in the struggle for equality and justice for blacks in America.

Landed Film Contract with MGM

In the summer of 1941, Horne moved to California after getting an offer to appear at an as-yet-unbuilt club on the Sunset Strip in Hollywood called the Trocadero. Although the plans for the Trocadero fell through, another, smaller club, the Little Troc, opened in February of 1942, and Horne was featured there. In the same year, she signed a seven-year contract with MGM—the first black woman since 1915 to sign a term contract with a film studio. "They didn't quite know what to do with me," she told Leonard Maltin of *Entertainment Tonight* regarding the studio's resulting dilemma: she wasn't sufficiently dark skinned to star with many of the African American actors of the day, and her roles in white films were limited, since Hollywood wasn't ready to depict interracial relationships on screen. Her first film under contract was *Panama Hattie,* a 1942 motion picture version of Cole Porter's Broadway musical, in which she had a small singing role in one scene.

Several of Horne's roles in subsequent films were similar. James Haskins, in his book *Lena: A Personal and Professional Biography of Lena Horne,* wrote: "The image of Lena, always elegantly gowned, singing while draped around a marble column in a lavishly produced musical sequence, would become virtually standardized. Only her ability to

name "Helena Horne," which Sissle thought more glamorous than "Lena." In 1937 Horne quit her tour with the Sissle Orchestra to marry Louis Jones, a friend of her father, and live with him in Pittsburgh, Pennsylvania. During this short and troubled marriage, Horne went to Hollywood to appear in an all-black film called *The Duke* appear enigmatic prevented her from being completely exploited in these stock sequences; she managed to carry them off with a dignity that, coupled with her aloof and detached delivery, enhanced both her mystery and her audience appeal." The sad footnote to this is that Horne's scenes were purposely constructed so that they could be cut out with ease when the films were shown to white audiences in the South.

The Struggle for Equality Continued

Horne appeared in the all-black film musicals *Cabin in the Sky* and *Stormy Weather,* both released in 1943, but she refused to take on any roles that were demeaning to her as a woman of color. This led to an uproar among the black Hollywood "extras," who represented what Horne's daughter, in her book *The Hornes: An American Family,* called "a kind of stock company of stereotypes." These actors felt threatened and accused Horne of being a tool of the NAACP. In her own defense, Horne wrote in her 1965 autobiography *Lena:* "I was only trying to see if I could avoid in my career some of the traps they had been forced into."

During World War II, Horne went on USO tours along the West Coast and in the South. She appeared on the Armed Forces Radio Service on programs such as *Jubilee, G.I. Journal,* and *Command Performances* and helped Eleanor Roosevelt press for antilynching legislation. After the war, she worked on behalf of Japanese-Americans who faced discrimination because Japan had been an enemy of the United States.

In the fall of 1947, Horne went to Europe with Lennie Hayton, a white musician she had met in Hollywood. They were married in December in Paris because interracial marriages were against the law in California. Back in Hollywood, she appeared in more film musicals, among them, *Till the Clouds Roll By* in 1946, *Words and Music* in 1948, and *The Duchess of Idaho* in 1950.

Blacklisted in the 1950s

In the early 1950s, Horne, along with many of her colleagues, was a victim of the anti-Communist "witch hunts" that successfully blacklisted performers who were thought to have ties to Communist organizations or activities. The blacklisting hurt Horne's career and kept her from appearing on radio and television. By the mid-1950s, though, Horne was cleared of these charges. In 1956, she signed a recording contract with RCA Victor. Her albums included *Stormy Weather, Lena Horne at the Coconut Grove,* and *Lena Horne at the Waldorf-Astoria.* The latter became the top-selling recording by a female artist in

RCA's history. In 1957 Horne was featured in *Jamaica,* a Broadway musical with an all-black cast. The show had a successful run, closing in the spring of 1959.

In the 1960s, Horne was involved in the American civil rights movement, participating in the March on Washington in 1963, performing at rallies in the South and elsewhere, and working on behalf of the National Council for Negro Women. During the same period she appeared

> "African Americans were going forward, and that knowledge gave me a strength and a sense of unity. Yes, we were going forward, and it was up to me to learn more about us and to join actively in our struggle."

on various television programs, including several performances on the popular Ed Sullivan and Perry Como variety shows, and her own special, *Lena in Concert,* in 1969. In the same year she appeared in a nonsinging role in the western *Death of a Gunfighter.*

The 1970s began tragically for Horne: her son, Teddy, died of kidney disease in 1970, her father died in the same year, and Lennie Hayton died of a heart attack in 1971. However, the decade offered a variety of opportunities for Horne to perform. She appeared on Broadway with Tony Bennett in 1974 in a show called *Tony and Lena* and was featured in several television commercials. In 1978, she played the role of Glinda, the Good Witch, in the film version of *The Wiz,* the all-black musical based on *The Wizard of Oz.*

One-Woman Broadway Show Was a Sensation

In the summer of 1980, Horne launched a "farewell tour," but her greatest success of the decade was her one-woman show, *Lena Horne: The Lady and Her Music,* which opened in May of 1981 at Broadway's Nederlander Theatre. The show ran for two years and was a tremendous success—so much so that Horne was given a special Tony Award for her performance. She also received a Drama Desk Award and a special citation from the New York Drama Critics' Circle. The soundtrack to the show, produced by Quincy Jones, won two Grammy awards. In *Lena: A Personal and Professional Biography,* Haskins noted that the show was "not only the longest-running one-woman show in the history of Broadway but the standard against which every future one-person show would be measured." Horne herself, in an article she wrote for *Ebony* magazine in 1990, described the show as "the most rewarding event in my entire career."

In the 1990s, Horne cut back on performing, but she continued to be a favorite of audiences throughout the world. Her pride in her heritage and her refusal to compromise herself, combined with an innate ability to project elegance, grace, and dignity, have made her a legendary figure. Some observers consider her most important role to be that of a catalyst in the elevation of the status of African Americans in the performing arts. But Horne laments the sluggishness of progress in Hollywood; if given the chance to do it all again, she told Leonard Feather of *Modern Maturity,* "I'd be a schoolteacher."

Selected discography

(With the Lennie Layton Orchestra) *Lena Goes Latin,* recorded in 1963, DRG, 1987.
(With Sammy Davis and Joe Williams) *The Men in My Life,* Three Cherries, 1989.
Stormy Weather: The Legendary Lena, 1941-1958, Bluebird, 1990.
Lena Horne, Royal Collection, 1992.
At Long Last Lena, RCA, 1992.
Greatest Hits, CSI, 1992.
The Best of Lena Horne, Curb, 1993.
Stormy Weather, RCA Victor.

Lena Horne at the Coconut Grove, RCA Victor.
Lena Horne at the Waldorf-Astoria, RCA Victor.

Sources

Books

Buckley, Gail Lumet, *The Hornes: An American Family,* Alfred A. Knopf, 1986.
Haskins, James, and Kathleen Benson, *Lena: A Personal and Professional Biography of Lena Horne,* Stein & Day, 1984.
Horne, Lena, as told to Helen Arstein and Carlton Moss, *In Person: Lena Horne,* Greenberg, 1950.
Horne, Lena, and Richard Schickel, *Lena,* Doubleday, 1965.
Wormley, Stanton L., and Lewis H. Fenderson, editors, *Many Shades of Black,* William & Co., 1969.

Periodicals

Ebony, May 1980; November 1990.
Modern Maturity, February/March 1993, p. 28.
New York Post, November 1, 1957.
New York Times, May 4, 1981.

Additional information for this profile was obtained from Leonard Maltin's interview with Lena Horne, broadcast on *Entertainment Tonight,* ABC-TV, March 22, 1993.

—*Joyce Harrison*

Rex Ingram

1895-1969

Actor

When Rex Ingram returned to the stage after what seemed to be a final tumble from the heights of his career, his audience welcomed him back with a memorable, glorious reception. In his essay, "I Came Back from the Dead," published in *Ebony,* Ingram recalled his first opening night since the beginning of his absence three years earlier: "It came and I stepped out on that stage with a cold sweat breaking out all over me. I will never forget the reception that audience gave me. It was deafening. They roared, clapped, cheered, and whistled for nearly two minutes, yelling 'come on, REX.' I felt good. I was crying inside but couldn't show it in my eyes. When the cheering stopped I began my lines. . . . I knew then that I was not dead."

That night in 1951 in the Las Palmas Theater in Los Angeles, Ingram began acting once again. Before his swift fall, he had established himself as a favorite among both black and white audiences of his time. Throughout his career, he struggled to eradicate the stereotypical roles usually given to African American actors both in the theater and particularly in Hollywood. His resources in the struggle to broaden the range of parts for blacks were his forceful acting style and his increasingly selective standards for his own roles as he gained fame and notoriety. "For black audiences of that time [the 1930s and 1940s], he was clearly an emblem of pride and assertion," wrote Donald Bogle in his 1988 book *Blacks in American Film and Television.*

Ingram met with brilliant success on screen. He gained an early and enduring fame with his portrayal of De Lawd in the 1936 film *The Green Pastures,* which became a box office hit and remained Hollywood's most successful film with an all-black cast for many years. Bogle, however, criticized the film as a "fraud" in its claims to represent genuine black folk culture. The film depicts an all-black heaven that, Bogle wrote, "ultimately becomes a perpetual Negro holiday, a church picnic, one everlasting weekend fish fry." The critic added that the religion represented in the film amounts to a caricature of the religion of people of color. Furthermore, the humor of the film depends on the assumption that early twentieth-century blacks—with their "lowly language and folkways"—were out of place in the high, classical, biblical world before the flood. Nevertheless, *The Green Pastures* proved to be a successful career advance for Rex Ingram, who played the lead role of God in heaven, as well as two other roles. Bogle wrote that "the actors . . . transcend[ed] the trash," and added that Ingram interpreted De Lawd as stately, bringing "substance, weight, and durability" to the role.

At a Glance. . .

Born October 20, 1895, on a houseboat on the Mississippi River near Cairo, IL; died of a heart attack, September 19, 1969, in Hollywood, CA; son of Robert E. Lee (a fireman on the steamer); twice married, with children. *Education:* Received degrees from Northwestern University.

Began acting career with role in *Tarzan of the Apes,* 1918; appeared in silent films *The Ten Commandments,* 1923, and *The Big Parade,* 1925; major screen roles in motion pictures, including *The Green Pastures,* 1936; *Adventures of Huckleberry Finn,* 1939; *The Thief of Bagdad,* 1940; *Sahara,* 1943; *Cabin in the Sky,* 1943; *Moonrise,* 1949; and *Anna Lucasta,* 1958. Roles in stage productions, including *Lulu Belle,* Broadway, 1929; *Porgy,* Broadway; *Stevedore,* The Theater Union, 1933; *The Emperor Jones,* Suffern, 1933; *Haiti,* Federal Theater Project, 1938; *Waiting for Godot,* Broadway, 1957; and a number of plays in San Francisco, Los Angeles, and other regional theaters. Roles on television shows, including *Daktari, I Spy, Gunsmoke,* and *The Bill Cosby Show.*

Member: Phi Beta Kappa.

Fought Against Racial Stereotypes in Film

Early Hollywood was racist to the core and offered virtually no opportunities for black actors or actresses. Although *The Green Pastures* and 1934's *Imitation of Life*—two early Hollywood films that focused on black life—had been box office successes, Hollywood still did not produce another major film about black culture and people until World War II.

From the beginnings of the film industry through the 1920s, the roles available to African American actors and actresses replicated common racial stereotypes, including "gentle Toms, doomed mulattoes, comic coons, over-stuffed mammies, and mean, menacing, violent black bucks," Bogle commented. To the extent to which any of these roles could be considered important, the more significant roles were played by white actors "in black-face." There was the exception of notable film director Erich Von Stroheim, who in defiance of the censors cast a black actor as a priest delivering the last rites to a dying white woman in an African brothel; but aside from this one casting decision, black actors were excluded from all but the most stereotypical, insignificant roles. Films from the period that are serious about racial issues can be found in abundance only from the host of relatively low-budget, independent black film companies, which, despite their limited resources, provided the beginnings of an ongoing tradition of quality films by black artists about black life.

Not until the 1930s, after the advent of sound pictures and the all-black musical, did black actors begin to appear regularly on screen, although still in slurred, formulaic roles. Bogle credited these actors with altering the character of their roles, however: "Through style the black actors turned their cheap, trashy, demeaning stereotyped roles inside out, refining, transforming, and transcending them. The great black performers did not simply play characters. Rather they played *against* their roles." In this context, even if the God of *The Green Pastures* inhabited a heaven based on a caricature of religious belief, the role still might afford an actor like Ingram the opportunity to influence the perception of African Americans in film.

In *The Green Pastures,* the role of De Lawd provided ample scope to elevate the character to stateliness. Ingram aspired to play the role since he had seen it performed on stage by Richard B. Harrison with "majestic presence and beautiful sincerity," he wrote in the *Ebony* essay. Also, while working on the part, Ingram gained faith in his own abilities as an actor and in his potential power as an individual. He recalled his work on this role in these words: "My faith in my own ability to portray God as a fictional character gradually rose. When it was all over I found that I had come through a remarkable spiritual experience. It was the most wonderfully moving thing that has *ever* happened to me."

His success in *The Green Pastures* led him to more challenging film roles. Through his forceful acting style, Ingram championed improved race relations and offered a powerful call for black liberation. His role as Jim in the 1939 MGM production *Adventures of Huckleberry Finn* "spelled out in theatrical terms the powerful message of human brotherhood," the actor noted in *Ebony.* The following year, he played the Genie of the Lamp in the British technicolor production of *The Thief of Bagdad.* In that part, Ingram as the Genie exclaims his joy at being freed after centuries of entrapment in the bottle. Bogle reported that this exclamation for freedom struck a chord among black audiences "that went beyond the bounds of the movie." Ingram was also compensated well for the role, earning $2,500 each week for fourteen months from 1940 to 1941.

In Hollywood in 1943, Ingram played a heroic Sudanese soldier sacrificing his life for the troops in the film *Sahara.* That same year, he also portrayed the mischievous Lucifer, Jr., who schemes the downfall of Eddie "Rochester"

Anderson in *Cabin in the Sky*. Finally, in *Moonrise* in 1949, Ingram played a wizened outcast who helps a young white man grow to maturity. Bogle championed Ingram's ability to "act against" his roles throughout his entire film career: "In all these films [*The Green Pastures, Thief of Bagdad, Sahara, Cabin in the Sky,* and *Moonrise*] and so many more, Rex Ingram seems to stand apart from the Hollywood system, repeatedly refusing to let himself be demeaned by a role."

Fame and Dignity on Stage

If Rex Ingram was able to achieve relative success in struggling for dignity through his film roles, his stage roles afforded him much more room for expression. *New York Times* critic Brooks Atkinson's review of Ingram's performance in a Federal Theater Project play was quoted in the paper's obituary for Ingram years later. The actor had played the leading role of Christophe, the Black Napolean, in the 1938 Federal Theater Project play *Haiti*, which depicted the black Haitian insurrection of 1802. Atkinson wrote, "Mr. Ingram has been a good actor for a long time. It is not very often, however, that he finds a heroic part like that of Christophe, the leader of a cause. Mr. Ingram gives a rattling good performance." In 1938, Ingram had by then acted in *The Green Pastures* and in a few Broadway plays, but not yet in his other major film roles. His meatiest early parts, however, were for the stage.

Ingram had made his Broadway debut in the 1929 show *Lulu Belle,* produced by a leading figure in American theater, David Belasco. After his debut, Ingram appeared as Crown in DuBose Heyward's play *Porgy,* upon which the later *Porgy and Bess* was based, and then in *Stevedore,* a Theater Union production, in 1933. These parts were not particularly heroic and did not entirely escape from common stereotypes of the day, but in his later stage roles—as the Emperor in the 1933 touring production of Eugene O'Neill's *The Emperor Jones* and as Christophe in *Haiti*—Ingram found opportunities to portray heroic characters who exploded common racial stereotypes. The actor was quoted in the *New York Times* as having praised his role in *The Emperor Jones* as his favorite among all he had ever acted. "I'd rather play the emperor than any other part ever written. I can get way into that part and give it the gun. You know, I love a good fight and anything that's blood and thunder," he said.

Struggling for his Principles

After acting in the parts of the Emperor and De Lawd and gaining self-confidence from each experience, Ingram decided not to work again in roles that he considered demeaning to African Americans. In the *New York Times* in 1938, he described his watershed personal decision: "I decided [two years ago] to help our cause to the best of my ability. I wouldn't take parts which didn't at least do us justice." No longer would he play every kind of porter and butler and native, as he had since his beginnings in 1918 as an actor in a variety of films, including the original *Tarzan of the Apes.* As a result of this decision—even after having played the lead in the successful film *The Green Pastures*—Ingram found himself unemployed for the following two years. He went bankrupt and was dispossessed of all his belongings. After persisting in his decision through this difficult time, however, he was offered the part of Christophe in *Haiti,* followed soon after by major roles in British and American mainstream film and continuing

> "I decided to help our cause to the best of my ability. I wouldn't take parts which didn't at least do us justice."

opportunities in the theater in New York, San Francisco, and across the United States. Ingram did not merely transcend whatever role he was given; as soon as his career gained steam, he *chose* the roles he would transform and enliven.

Troubled Personal Life Threatened Career

In 1948, Ingram's career was interrupted once more, although this time not for decisions based on noble principles. This time he pleaded guilty to charges under the Mann Act that he transported a 15-year-old girl from Kansas to New York "for immoral purposes." He served over nine months in prison before being released on parole from an 18-month sentence. In his *Ebony* essay, Ingram set out his side of the story: "My trouble arose from a casual, genuinely warm friendship with a young woman. That friendship was distorted and misunderstood. Because the woman happened to be white I was persecuted and made a target of charges and innuendoes." Still he perceived the event as his mistake: "Like anybody else I made a few mistakes; a couple might be termed major ones. We have to pay for our mistakes in this life and I have certainly paid for mine." Instead of specifying his mistake, however, he continued to offer a defense of this "casual, genuinely warm friendship." Ingram's career suffered a devastating blow as a result.

The actor's personal life had been somewhat turbulent

before: his wife had divorced him when he went bankrupt during an earlier period of unemployment. He had also been arrested twice in Harlem on assault charges and had served a brief jail sentence in New Jersey for multiple driving violations. None of this earlier personal turbulence had interrupted his career, however.

Determined to the End

It was after his 1948 indiscretion, the subsequent jail term, and his three-year absence from the entertainment industry that Rex Ingram received the glorious welcoming reception back to the stage from the Los Angeles theater audience in 1951. From then on, Ingram continued to work on stage, screen, and later on television. His most notable achievement in this last phase of his career was his portrayal in 1957 of Pozzo in an all-black stage production of Samuel Beckett's *Waiting for Godot.* He appeared in a number of television shows in the 1960s, including *Daktari, I Spy, Gunsmoke,* and *The Bill Cosby Show.* He also starred as an incestuous father in the 1958 film *Anna Lucasta,* an adaptation of the earlier Broadway show.

Bogle believed Ingram's part in *Anna Lucasta* to be his final major film role, stating in *Blacks in American Film and Television* that in this and subsequent roles, Ingram's characterizations seemed to reveal "the pressure and perhaps the disillusionment, too" of the professional and personal stresses the actor had experienced through the course of his life. Bogle reprinted at length the lavish praise Ingram received from *Variety* for his creation of the old man in *Anna Lucasta:* "Ingram as old Joe Lucasta is excellent from start to finish. As the story develops, it is made clear that under his pretense of detesting a daughter who has become a streetwalker, he is also fighting off his own temptations, for Joe is in love with his own daughter. Fogged by age and alcohol, stubborn and stern, Ingram creates a vivid portrait of the old man, and to a large extent he steals the show."

Ingram kept acting into 1969, the year of his death at age 73. The 1976 edition of *The Oxford Companion to Film* esteemed Ingram, along with the legendary Paul Robeson, as "the only black actors to attain a degree of stardom in the thirties and forties and to escape, to some extent, the permissible racial stereotype."

Sources

Books

Bawden, Liz-Anne, editor, *The Oxford Companion to Film,* Oxford University Press, 1976.
Bogle, Donald, *Blacks in American Film and Television: An Encyclopedia,* Garland Publishing, 1988.

Periodicals

Ebony, March 1955, pp. 48-58.
New York Times, July 24, 1938; September 20, 1969, p. 29.

—*Nicholas S. Patti*

Roy Innis

1934—

Activist, organization official

A controversial figure in the civil rights movement, Roy Innis has guided the Congress of Racial Equality (CORE) since the summer of 1968. His stormy career has been marked by radical rhetoric, shifts in ideology, and financial and legal troubles. Nevertheless, his prominent position with CORE—an organization dedicated to the political and economic advancement of people of color—has established him as a significant figure on the front line of American activism.

smart.''

Innis attended the prestigious Stuyvesant High School in New York City, and in 1950, when he was 16 years old, he lied about his age and joined the U.S. Army. It was two years before his superiors found out he was underage and discharged him. On returning to New York, Innis earned his high school diploma and majored in chemistry at the City College of New York. Subsequently, he worked as a researcher for the Vicks Chemical Company and had three children with his first wife, Violet.

Innis was born June 6, 1934, in St. Croix, Virgin Islands. He was six years old when his father died, but it was not until 1947 that he moved to the United States, following his mother, who was sending for her children as money became available. The shock of moving from the racially tolerant and predominantly black Virgin Islands to Harlem in New York City was tremendous. At that time discrimination against black Americans was commonplace, and the continually reinforced message of white supremacy led some blacks to question the intellect and competence of their own race. ''My father was a cop [back in St. Croix],'' Innis told Ebony, ''the symbol of authority. . . . The judge was black and had a kind of basic confidence in the ability of black people. But I used to notice how Harlem blacks would be surprised if other blacks were smart. They seemed to feel that only whites were

After his first marriage ended, Innis fell in love with and married civil rights activist Doris Funnye. Funnye was active in the Harlem chapter of CORE, an organization from which Innis had previously shied away. ''Too many white people were directing traffic,'' he told Ebony. Because of Funnye, Innis joined CORE—first to be near her and later because he felt he could make a difference in the organization.

By 1963 he was one of the more active members of CORE's Harlem chapter. Later called ''the very soul of the civil-rights movement'' by Jesse Jackson, the Congress of Racial Equality had been founded in 1942 by six young Chicagoans as an interracial passive resistance organization. Led by longtime

At a Glance...

Born Roy Emile Alfredo Innis, June 6, 1934, in St. Croix, Virgin Islands; immigrated to the United States, 1947; son of Alexander (a police officer) and Georgianna Thomas Innis; married first wife, Violet (divorced); married Doris Funnye; children: Alexander (deceased), Roy (deceased), Cedric, Patricia, Corinne, Kwame, Niger, Kimathi. *Education:* Attended City College of New York, 1952-56.

Vicks Chemical Company, research chemist, 1958-63; Montefiore Hospital, New York City, research assistant in cardiovascular research laboratory and hospital union official, 1963-67; Congress of Racial Equality (CORE), chairman of Harlem chapter, 1965-67, named associate national director, December 27, 1967, national director, 1968-81, and national chairman, 1981—. Resident fellow, Metropolitan Applied Research Center, New York City, 1967; Harlem Commonwealth Council, executive director, 1967-68; coeditor, *Manhattan Tribune. Military service:* Served in U.S. Army, 1950-52.

Addresses: *Office*—National Chairman, Congress of Racial Equality, 2111 Nostrand, Brooklyn, NY 11210.

chairman James Farmer, CORE began by protesting discrimination in Chicago restaurants and grew to lead sit-ins at lunch counters in the South and sponsor the famous Freedom Rides that tested compliance with federal orders to desegregate bus lines.

While a member of CORE's Harlem chapter, Innis was part of a minority whose aims did not coincide with CORE's stated goal of integration. Innis and his allies sought to promote the notion of "economic competition" while devaluing the idea of integration for blacks. "When I first started hanging around CORE, I didn't dig the operation," he told *Ebony.* "I thought people didn't know what they were talking about. But I saw sincerity and a lot of energy and drive. I thought if you could harness it, it would be a useful force. I thought their ideology of integration was out of it. I was a black nationalist."

Leadership of CORE's Harlem Chapter

Innis tried to obtain control of CORE's Harlem chapter and ran for chairman several times before gaining the post in 1965 over the staunch objection of moderates. During his

two years as head of the Harlem branch, he more than any other figure was instrumental in moving the organization from a strategy of nonviolent social change to a strategy of nationalistic self-defense.

In 1966 James Farmer retired from the post of national chairman amid charges that he was too conservative. Reflecting these sentiments, the CORE convention led by Innis and the Harlem chapter elected Floyd McKissick to the vacated position. McKissick moved CORE toward an all-black membership and eliminated the word "multiracial" from its constitution.

On December 27 of the following year, McKissick appointed Innis to the post of associate national director. Critics claimed that the appointment was illegal, since McKissick never consulted with CORE's decision-making body, the National Action Council. According to some observers, Innis had relied on both charisma and scare tactics to further his agenda while serving as chairman of the Harlem chapter.

But while Innis was moving upward in the CORE hierarchy, tragedy struck his family. On April 15, 1968, his 13-year-old son, who was playing with his brother outside a Bronx apartment house a short distance from his mother's house, was shot by an irate postal worker. "It was a very sad thing to have to explain to a father," the detective who informed Innis of the shooting told the *New York Times.* "The kids were just playing. They were just horsing around."

On July 8 of the same year, Chairman McKissick, himself under fire from CORE's more radical elements, took a leave of absence from the chairmanship. As associate national director, Innis assumed power, pledging to tighten up the organization and give it direction. According to the *Saturday Review,* he also proclaimed CORE "once and for all . . . a black nationalist organization." Disillusioned with the minimal progress made after the passage of the Civil Rights Act of 1964 and with failed efforts to desegregate schools in America's cities, Innis concluded: "Integration as an end in itself is as dead as a doornail."

Became National Director of CORE

At the CORE convention the following September, 47 disgruntled delegates walked out before others formally elected Innis and adopted a new constitution that centralized power and advocated black nationalism. According to the *New York Times,* Innis remarked: "For the first time, CORE is one team working together. . . . We are moving away from separate little baronies."

Although the turn to black nationalism led to a severe decline in membership—making CORE what *Ebony* called "a shadow of its former self"—Innis's early leadership of the organization was marked by seemingly dramatic action. He founded the Harlem Commonwealth Council, an agency designed to create black-owned businesses and black-directed economic institutions in Harlem, and he served as co-editor of the *Manhattan Tribune,* a weekly New York tabloid stressing the affairs of Harlem and the upper West Side.

His black nationalist viewpoint converged with conservative ideas and received wide play in conservative magazines such as *National Review* and *U.S. News & World Report.* Innis explained black nationalism in *Life* as "the philosophy of self-determination, the philosophy of an oppressed people. . . . One solution to such oppression is assimilation—in essence, the loss of one's self. . . . That won't work for us. We have to devise a philosophy applicable to our own dilemma. We must rehabilitate blacks as people. We must control the institutions in our areas."

"Integration should not be an end in itself," Innis stated in *U.S. News & World Report.* "It should be a means to an end—toward true equality and justice. But if it's obvious that integration is not achieving those ends, then you seek other means." An advocate of community power, Innis told the magazine after the 1968 presidential election: "[Richard M.] Nixon should support the concept of community control of schools, welfare, sanitation, fire, police, health and hospitals and all other vital institutions operating in the so-called ghettos." Innis's view of school desegregation coincided with both his desire for community control and the philosophy of segregationists. "I say let us create two districts—one predominantly white and one predominantly black—where you now have one district," he was quoted as saying in *U.S. News & World Report.* "Each district will create its own board to manage the school system. Each will hire a superintendent. Each will be autonomous and truly equal."

Judgment Questioned, Legal Issues Raised

But while Innis was making a splash with his ideas, some members of CORE were dropping out, charging that he was running the organization as a one-man show. In addition, Innis became involved in questionable affairs that many considered beyond the realm of CORE's stated goals. In 1973 Innis toured Uganda and visited murderous dictator Idi Amin, conferring upon him a life membership in CORE. On returning to the United States, Innis told the *Saturday Review:* "General Amin will lead a liberation army to free those parts of Africa still under the rule of white imperialists." Innis's interest in African affairs was not limited to Uganda. In 1976 he claimed to have recruited between 300 and 1,000 black American veterans

to fight as mercenaries in the Angolan civil war on the side supported by western countries and South Africa. Denounced as an "anti-African reactionary group," by the Organization of African Unity, CORE never actually sent soldiers to Africa.

Innis defended his junkets to Angola and Uganda as vital to solving the problems of oppressed people of color throughout the world. When questioned about his use of CORE funds for activities that went beyond the interests of the organization, the *Saturday Review* reported that he answered: "The monies of CORE are my money and CORE is my organization and I'll run it the way I see fit."

In December of 1978, New York State assistant attorney general William Lee charged Innis and two of his subordinates with misuse of charitable contributions. According to

"Our No. 1 problem today is black crime."

the *Saturday Review,* the three were accused of unlawful fund-raising practices, maintaining nonexistent "paper programs," putting the organization's funds to questionable use, and perpetuating Innis's one-man directorship of CORE. Specifically, the affidavit stated that CORE employed a "technique of fear and apprehension" in soliciting funds for its *Equal Opportunity Journal* and added that CORE had become "an organization whose sole *raison d'etre* had degenerated to the acquisition of more and more money, none of which ever reached the intended beneficiaries, the disadvantaged minority members."

Harry Zehner of the *Saturday Review* went on to claim that though the organization was raising in excess of four million dollars a year from corporate contributions, its editorial, community renewal, child day care, prison reform, tutorial reading, media communication, job bank, housing, employment referral, and Operation Self Help programs had "no more than paper existence."

Following the filing of charges, an injunction preventing CORE from raising funds was filed. The case, however, never went to trial, and on December 30, 1981, CORE and the state attorney general reached an out-of-court settlement that did not require CORE to admit any wrongdoing but did require Innis to contribute $35,000 to the organization over the following three years.

In November of 1980, in the midst of Innis's financial and legal troubles, a group of 200 dissident CORE members met in Columbia, South Carolina, and voted to dismiss him from the post of national director. According to the *New*

York Times, CORE member and South Carolina state representative Theo Mitchell said the organization "ha[d] been used for personal gain, egotism and grandiose plans." The same meeting elected Waverly Yates, head of CORE's Washington office and one of the organization's founders, to replace Innis. When Innis refused to hand over the chairmanship, Yates and others filed a lawsuit that was ultimately ruled in Innis's favor.

A Change in Philosophy

While Innis's political philosophy had always been marked by conservative tendencies, he took an overt swing to the right during the 1980s. In October of 1984 he took the stand as a character witness for perennial right-wing presidential candidate Lyndon La Rouche, who was eventually convicted of tax evasion. The following month he urged African Americans to desert Democrat Walter Mondale's presidential candidacy, saying black voters "had nothing to lose and everything to gain" by supporting Republican candidate Ronald Reagan over Mondale. "The successful desegregation of the Republican Party," he told the *New York Times* "can be one of the most important and healthy political developments for the black community and for the country at large."

Looking to exploit his popularity on the political right, Innis told a 1985 New York Republican gathering that he would run for a Brooklyn seat in the House of Representatives the following year and that, though politics necessitated he run as a Democrat, he would sit with the Republicans if he won. A month before the election—which he lost—the IRS fined him $56,000 in back taxes plus $28,000 in civil fraud penalties. According to the *Wall Street Journal,* "The IRS . . . claimed he got $116,000 in unreported income from CORE in 1975 and 1976, [which] he allegedly spent . . . on travel, apartment rent, jewelry, furniture, entertainment, and other personal items."

Innis gained considerable exposure in 1988 when his appearances on television talk shows degenerated into bizarre skirmishes. On August 9 of that year, he appeared with the controversial Reverend Al Sharpton in a taping of the *Morton Downey Jr. Show.* When Sharpton questioned Innis's abilities and authority as a black leader, a shouting match began. The show's producer told the *Chicago Tribune:* "Innis stood up and was basically telling Sharpton to let him speak. . . . [He] towered over him." Then, the story went on, "as the rotund Sharpton started to get up, Innis pushed him. Rev. Sharpton fell into the chair and toppled over backward onto the floor."

In November of the same year, Innis appeared with white-supremacist Tom Metzger on the *Geraldo Rivera Show.* According to the *New York Times,* Innis attacked Metzger after Metzger offended him with an inflammatory, racially motivated remark. A scuffle ensued, and soon members of the audience joined in, with chairs, punches, and insults being hurled in all directions. Later, Innis told the *Times,* "I was just trying to cool things down quickly and end the verbal assault against me. I wanted to avoid a Sharpton-like confrontation."

Focused on Black Crime

In the late 1980s, Innis focused on issues in addition to racism that affected the black community. Crime became an important topic. In a *Christian Science Monitor* interview, he noted, "Crime is bigger and more destructive than racism. . . . Crime affects our community, its business, education, jobs, health. Senior citizens can't walk the streets without endangering their health."

Innis remained in the public eye throughout the early 1990s. In a 1991 *Wall Street Journal* editorial, "Gun Control Sprouts From Racist Soil," he argued that banning handguns would keep guns out of the hands of black families in high crime areas who needed protection. He stated in an interview with Robert Santiago for *Emerge* that "CORE is the only group with the courage to admit the obvious—that black folks, minority folks, folks in high-crime areas need to arm themselves legally."

All controversy aside, Innis continues to be an important voice on the American civil rights scene. He, along with a group of other prominent African American leaders, was called to the White House as a consultant after the Los Angeles riots of 1992, linked to anger about perceived police brutality toward blacks. He commented in the *Emerge* interview that CORE's agenda for the future involves battling the sources and effects of crime within the black community: "CORE and Roy Innis were the first to jump on the question of black crime. . . . Our No. 1 problem today is black crime. If the white man goes away tonight, we still have black crime."

Sources

Chicago Tribune, August 10, 1988.
Christian Science Monitor, March 26, 1987.
Ebony, October 1969.
Emerge, August 1992, p. 11.
Life, December 13, 1968.
National Review, February 11, 1969.
New York Times, July 24, 1966; April 16, 1968; June 26, 1968; November 14, 1968; April 1, 1980; November 23, 1980; December 31, 1981; November 4, 1984; November 25, 1985; November 4, 1988.
Saturday Review, April 28, 1979.

U.S. News & World Report, November 25, 1968; March 2, 1970.

Village Voice, July 12, 1988.

Wall Street Journal, October 8, 1986; November 21, 1991.

—Jordan Wankoff

Mahalia Jackson

1911-1972

Gospel singer

Throughout her celebrated career, gospel singer Mahalia Jackson used her rich, forceful voice and inspiring interpretations of spirituals to move audiences around the world to tears of joy. In the early days, as a soloist and member of church choirs, she recognized the power of song as a means of gloriously reaffirming the faith of her flock. And later, as a world figure, her natural gift brought people of different religious and political convictions together to revel in the beauty of the gospels and to appreciate the warm spirit that underscored the way she lived her life.

The woman who would become known as the "Gospel Queen" was born in 1911 to a poor family in New Orleans, Louisiana. The Jacksons' Water Street home, a shotgun shack between the railroad tracks and the levee of the Mississippi River, was served by a pump that delivered water so dirty that cornmeal had to be used as a filtering agent. Jackson's father, like many blacks in the segregated south, held several jobs; he was a longshoreman, a barber, and a preacher at a small church. Her mother, a devout Baptist who died when Mahalia was five, took care of the six Jackson children and the house, using washed-up driftwood and planks from old barges to fuel the stove.

As a child, Mahalia was taken in by the sounds of New Orleans. She listened to the rhythms of the woodpeckers, the rumblings of the trains, the whistles of the steamboats, the songs of sailors and street peddlers. When the annual festival of Mardi Gras arrived, the city erupted in music. In her bedroom at night, young Mahalia would quietly sing the songs of blues legend Bessie Smith.

But Jackson's close relatives disapproved of the blues, a music indigenous to southern black culture, saying it was decadent and claiming that the only acceptable songs for pious Christians were the gospels of the church. In gospel songs, they told her, music was the cherished vehicle of religious faith. As the writer Jesse Jackson (not related to the civil rights leader) said in his biography of Mahalia, *Make a Joyful Noise Unto the Lord!,* "It was like choosing between the devil and God. You couldn't have it both ways." Mahalia made up her mind. When Little Haley (the nickname by which she was known as a child) tried out for the Baptist choir, she silenced the crowd by singing "I'm so glad, I'm so glad, I'm so glad I've been in the grave an' rose again. . . ." She became known as "the little girl with the big voice."

At 16, with only an eighth grade education but a strong

ambition to become a nurse, Jackson went to Chicago to live with her Aunt Hannah. In the northern city, to which thousands of southern blacks had migrated after the Civil War to escape segregation, she earned her keep by washing white people's clothes for a dollar a day. After searching for the right church to join, a place whose music spoke to her, she ended up at the Greater Salem Baptist Church, to which her aunt belonged. At her audition for the choir, Jackson's thunderous voice rose above all the others. She was invited to be a soloist and started singing additionally with a quintet that performed at funerals and church services throughout the city. In 1934 she received $25 for her first recording, "God's Gonna Separate the Wheat from the Tares."

Tempted by the Blues

Though she sang traditional hymns and spirituals almost exclusively, Jackson continued to be fascinated by the blues. During the Great Depression, she knew she could earn more money singing the songs that her relatives considered profane and blasphemous. But when her beloved grandfather was struck down by a stroke and fell into a coma, Jackson vowed that if he recovered she would never even enter a theater again, much less sing songs of which he would disapprove. He did recover, and Mahalia never broke that vow. She wrote in her autobiography, *Movin' On Up:* "I feel God heard me and wanted me to devote my life to his songs and that is why he suffered my prayers to be answered—so that nothing would distract me from being a gospel singer."

Later in her career, Jackson continued to turn down lucrative requests to sing in nightclubs—she was offered as much as $25,000 a performance in Las Vegas—even when the club owners promised not to serve whisky while she performed. She never dismissed the blues as antireligious, like her relatives had done: it was simply a matter of the vow she had made, as well as a matter of inspiration. "There's no sense in my singing the blues, because I just don't feel it," she was quoted as saying in *Harper's* magazine in 1956. "In the old, heart-felt songs, whether it's the blues or gospel music, there's the distressed cry of a human being. But in the blues, it's all despair; when you're done singing, you're still lonely and sorrowful. In the gospel songs, there's mourning and sorrow, too, but there's always hope and consolation to lift you above it."

Reigned as "Gospel Queen"

In 1939 Jackson started touring with renowned composer Thomas A. Dorsey. Together they visited churches and "gospel tents" around the country, and Jackson's reputation as a singer and interpreter of spirituals blossomed. She returned to Chicago after five years on the road and opened a beauty salon and a flower shop, both of which drew customers from the gospel and church communities. She continued to make records that brought her fairly little monetary reward. In 1946, while she was practicing in a recording studio, a representative from Decca Records overheard her sing an old spiritual she had learned as a child. He advised her to record it, and a few weeks later she did. "Move On Up a Little Higher" became her signature song. The recording sold 100,000 copies overnight and soon passed the two-million mark. "[It] sold like wildfire," Alex Haley wrote in *Reader's Digest*. "Negro disk jockeys played it; Negro ministers praised it from their pulpits. When sales passed one million, the Negro press hailed Mahalia Jackson as 'the only Negro whom Negroes have made famous.'"

Jackson began touring again, only this time she did it not as the hand-to-mouth singer who had toured with Dorsey years before. She bought a Cadillac big enough for her to sleep in when she was performing in areas with hotels that failed to provide accommodations for blacks. She also stored food in the car so that when she visited the segregated south she wouldn't have to sit in the backs of restaurants. Soon the emotional and resonant singing of the "Gospel Queen," as she had become known, began reaching and appealing to the white community as well. She appeared regularly on famous Chicagoan Studs Terkel's radio show and was ultimately given her own radio and television programs.

On October 4, 1950, Jackson played to a packed house of blacks and whites at Carnegie Hall in New York City. She recounted in her autobiography how she reacted to the jubilant audience. "I got carried away, too, and found myself singing on my knees for them. I had to straighten up and say, 'Now we'd best remember we're in Carnegie Hall and if we cut up too much, they might put us out.'" In her book, she also described a conversation with a reporter who asked her why she thought white people had taken to her traditionally black, church songs. She answered, "Well, honey, maybe they tried drink and they tried psychoanalysis and now they're going to try to rejoice with me a bit." Jackson ultimately became equally popular overseas and performed for royalty and adoring fans throughout France, England, Denmark, and Germany. One of the most rewarding concerts for her took place in Israel, where she sang before an audience of Jews, Muslims, and Christians.

Involved in the Civil Rights Movement

In the late 1950s and early 1960s, Jackson's attention turned to the growing civil rights movement in the United States. Although she had grown up on Water Street, where black and white families lived together peacefully, she was well aware of the injustice engendered by the Jim Crow laws that enforced racial segregation in the South. At the request of the Reverend Martin Luther King, Jr., Jackson participated in the Montgomery bus boycott, the groundbreaking demonstration that had been prompted by Alabaman Rosa Parks's refusal to move from a bus seat reserved for whites. During the famous March on Washington in 1963, seconds before Dr. King delivered his celebrated "I Have a Dream" speech, Jackson sang the old inspirational, "I Been 'Buked and I Been Scorned" to over 200,000 people.

Jackson died in 1972, never having fulfilled her dream of building a nondenominational, nonsectarian temple in Chicago, where people could sing, celebrate life, and nurture the talents of children. *Christian Century* magazine reported that at the funeral, which was attended by over six thousand fans, singer Ella Fitzgerald described

Jackson as "one of our greatest ambassadors of love . . . this wonderful woman who only comes once in a lifetime."

Jackson considered herself a simple woman: she enjoyed cooking for friends as much as marveling at landmarks around the world. But it was in her music that she found her spirit most eloquently expressed. She wrote in her autobiography: "Gospel music is nothing but singing of good tidings—spreading the good news. It will last as long as any music because it is sung straight from the human heart. Join with me sometime—whether you're white or colored—and you will feel it for yourself. Its future is brighter than a daisy."

Selected discography

Amazing Grace, CBS Records, 1977.
Mahalia Jackson, Bella Musica, 1990.
Gospels, Spirituals, and Hymns ("Gospel Spirit" series), Columbia/Legacy, 1991.
Nobody Knows the Trouble I've Seen, Vogue, 1991.
Best Loved Hymns of Dr. Martin Luther King, Jr., Columbia.
Bless This House, Columbia.
Come On, Children, Let's Sing, Columbia.
The Great Mahalia Jackson, Columbia.
Great Songs of Love and Faith, Columbia.
I Believe, Columbia.
In the Upper Room, Vogue.
Let's Pray Together, Columbia.
Mahalia Sings, Columbia.
Mahalia Jackson—The World's Greatest Gospel Singer and the Falls-Jones Ensemble, Columbia.
Mahalia Jackson's Greatest Hits, Columbia.
Make a Joyful Noise Unto the Lord, Columbia.
Newport, 1958, Columbia.
The Power and the Glory, Columbia.
Silent Night, Columbia.
Sweet Little Jesus Boy, Columbia.
You'll Never Walk Alone, Columbia.

Sources

Books

Goreau, L., *Just Mahalia, Baby,* Pelican, 1975.
Jackson, Jesse, *Make a Joyful Noise Unto the Lord!,* G.K. Hall & Co., 1974.
Jackson, Mahalia, and Wylie, Evan McLeod, *Movin' On Up,* Hawthorne Books, 1966.

Schwerin, Jules, *Got to Tell It: Mahalia Jackson, Queen of Gospel,* Oxford, 1992.

Periodicals

Christian Century, March 1, 1972.
Ebony, March 1972, April 1972.
Harper's, August 1956.
Reader's Digest, November 1961.
Saturday Review, September 27, 1958.

—Isaac Rosen

James Weldon Johnson

1871-1938

Writer, lyricist, lawyer, consul, civil rights activist, educator

James Weldon Johnson's boundless energy and concern for the plight of African Americans combined to produce an extraordinary career. As a poet, journalist, social activist, and educator, Johnson sought new standards for the treatment of blacks in the early decades of the twentieth century. He was simultaneously a mainstream American writer, a leader of the National Association for the Advancement of Colored People (NAACP), and a collector of the most poignant songs and poems produced by black Americans prior to 1930. In *Black Poets of the United States: From Paul Laurence Dunbar to Langston Hughes*, Jean Wagner called Johnson "doubtless one of the most distinguished and influential personalities the black world has ever known."

Johnson was a "Renaissance man" before the term was popular. He overcame enormous obstacles presented by white prejudice, earning a college degree, becoming certified as a Florida attorney, serving the U.S. government as a consul to foreign nations, and leading the NAACP in its determined opposition to lynchings and to Jim Crow legislation, which legalized segregation. He is also well remembered as a poet and a lyricist whose hymn "Lift Every Voice and Sing" became known as the "Negro National Anthem." In his own

time, Johnson was admired for his intellectual breadth, self-confidence, and leadership qualities. More than half a century after his death, he is recognized for his original contributions to American letters, his preservation of essential African American songs and poems, and his temperate civil rights agitation. Eugene Levy noted in an essay for *Black Leaders of the Twentieth Century:* "In both roles [as literary figure and activist] Johnson fought to move beyond the severe constraints set by racial prejudice and discrimination to shape the attitudes and actions of both black and white Americans."

Johnson was born in 1871 in Jacksonville, Florida. His parents had moved to the city from the North two years before his birth, and both had found jobs there. Johnson's father worked as the headwaiter at a posh resort hotel, and his mother was a schoolteacher and part-time musician. Young James therefore grew up amidst financial security in a family that stressed the dual goals of hard work and education. Wagner contended that in his home circle, Johnson "learned to avoid both excessive fear of the white man and the tendency to esteem him too highly."

Even in a relatively tolerant city such as Jacksonville, Johnson

At a Glance...

Born James William Johnson, June 17, 1871, in Jacksonville, FL; changed middle name to Weldon, 1913; died of injuries suffered in an automobile accident, June 26, 1938, in Wiscasset, ME; buried in Greenwood Cemetery, Brooklyn, NY; son of James (a restaurant headwaiter) and Helen Louise (a schoolteacher; maiden name, Dillet) Johnson; married Grace Nail, February 3, 1910. *Education:* Atlanta University, A.B., 1894, A.M., 1904; graduate study at Columbia University.

Poet, novelist, editor, lyricist, civil rights leader, diplomat, lawyer, and teacher. Worked in Jacksonville, FL, as school principal, newspaper editor, teacher, and attorney, 1894-1901; moved to New York City, 1901, and wrote lyrics for musical theater in partnership with brother, John Rosamond Johnson, and Bob Cole; named U.S. consul to Venezuela, 1906, and to Nicaragua, 1909; retired from foreign service, 1913; writer for *New York Age* (newspaper), 1914-24; National Association for the Advancement of Colored People (NAACP), New York City, field secretary, 1916-20, executive secretary, 1920-30; professor of creative literature and writing at Fisk University, Nashville, TN, 1931-38.

Member: NAACP, American Society of Composers, Authors, and Publishers, Academy of Political Science.

Selected awards: Spingarn Medal from NAACP, 1925; Harmon Gold Award for *God's Trombones;* Julius Rosenwald Fund grant, 1929; W. E. B. Du Bois Prize for Negro Literature, 1933. Johnson appeared on a 22-cent postal stamp as part of the "Black Heritage USA" series of the 1970s.

lighter popular songs of the day. Johnson's involvement with music would eventually broaden his horizons and take him far from the dusty Southern city of his birth.

When Johnson graduated from college, he returned to Jacksonville as a teacher and principal of Stanton, where he began to demonstrate the enormous energy and social consciousness that would mark most of his adult life. First he expanded Stanton's curriculum to include high school studies. Then, in 1895, he founded and co-edited the *Daily American*, the first black-oriented daily newspaper in America. The venture began bravely but folded after eight months. Nevertheless, the ambitious project—with its agenda of black empowerment—caught the attention of prominent national leaders such as W. E. B. Du Bois and Booker T. Washington.

Meanwhile Johnson decided to study law. With the help of a white attorney in Jacksonville, he prepared to take the Florida bar examinations. When he passed the bar on his first attempt in 1898, he became the first black attorney in the state of Florida since the days of Reconstruction. The last years of the nineteenth century found Johnson teaching, practicing law in Jacksonville, speaking for the black community's interests, and writing poems and songs.

"Lift Every Voice and Sing"

Late in 1899 Johnson was invited to give a speech at a local celebration of Abraham Lincoln's birthday. Instead, he wrote a hymn for the occasion, and his brother, John Rosamond Johnson, composed the music. Their composition, "Lift Every Voice and Sing," was first performed by 500 Jacksonville school children in February of 1900. The song offers a moving and faithful cry from free blacks for a future of hope in America. Johnson is said to have considered the composition of the lyrics for "Lift Every Voice and Sing" to be the most satisfying accomplishment of his life.

Although Johnson and his brother did little to promote the song at first, it took on a life of its own. Soon it could be heard throughout the South in churches and on festive occasions. By 1920 it was so popular that the NAACP adopted it as a theme song. It was the best-known anthem of black America at least until the 1960s, when civil rights demonstrators popularized "We Shall Overcome."

In 1901, Johnson and his brother left Jacksonville for New York City, where they sought work writing songs for the musical theater. They formed a partnership with Bob Cole and over the next five years composed some two hundred songs for Broadway and burlesque shows. Success came rapidly, and by 1904 the Johnson brothers and Bob Cole were well known in entertainment circles. Shows they had written toured America and Europe, giving them an opportunity to see the world. At home in New York they were

could only attend the segregated Stanton Central Grammar School where his mother taught. The school was not equipped to teach high school courses, so Johnson was forced to travel to Atlanta, Georgia, to complete his studies. He attended Atlanta University, eventually earning a secondary school diploma and then, in 1894, a bachelor's degree. A decade later, he completed his master's degree at the same institution.

Johnson's mother had encouraged him to enjoy music, so from his childhood onward, he sang, played guitar, and performed songs. In Atlanta he appeared with the Atlanta University quartet, entertaining audiences with spirituals and minor celebrities. Even during this period, though, Johnson continued more scholarly pursuits. He took graduate courses at Columbia University and wrote poetry, some of it in black dialect, after the manner of his friend and fellow poet Paul Laurence Dunbar.

Early 20th Century Political Activity

Johnson had always been interested in politics. In 1904 he helped to found a Colored Republican Club in New York City, and he worked actively for the election of Republican presidential candidate Theodore Roosevelt. One of his contributions to the campaign was a spirited song he wrote for Roosevelt. The song—and Johnson's other activities on behalf of the Republican party—strengthened his ties to those in political power. One of Johnson's friends, social activist and Tuskegee Institute founder Booker T. Washington, helped him to earn an official position with the Roosevelt administration as U.S. consul in Puerto Cabello, Venezuela. Johnson began his duties there in 1906.

With few official chores in his tropical posting, Johnson had plenty of time to write. He completed numerous poems and his only novel, *The Autobiography of an Ex-Coloured Man,* during his three years in Venezuela. Some of his poetry was published in monthly magazines back in America, and the novel appeared in print without Johnson's name as early as 1912. *The Autobiography of an Ex-Coloured Man* is a melancholy fictional memoir of a light-skinned black man who reluctantly chooses to "pass" for white after witnessing a brutal lynching in the rural South. Johnson's subject matter was not new, but his story managed to bring depth to its main character and address perplexing moral questions. When the novel was published under Johnson's name in 1922, some people believed it was truly an autobiography. That led the author to write his *real* life story, *Along This Way,* in 1933.

In 1909, Johnson was promoted to a consular post in Corinto, Nicaragua. There he found himself in a turbulent political climate that culminated in the landing of United States troops in Corinto in 1912. That same year, Woodrow Wilson, a Democrat, took office as president. Johnson felt little hope of advancement under the new administration, so he resigned from the civil service in 1913.

He returned to New York City and found a job as editorial writer for the *New York Age,* a prestigious and well-established black newspaper. According to Levy, "Johnson developed in his early columns a call for action by examining such issues as residential segregation, lynching, and the need for racial pride, making known to his readers that he believed in forthright, explicit protest." Specifically, Johnson urged blacks to use the power of the press as a weapon in the fight for equality. Levy quoted him as having said: "The greatest thing the American Negro gained as a result of the Civil War and the amendments to the Constitution was the right to contend for his rights."

Politically, however, Johnson was a conservative who shunned the notion of black separatist movements. "As much as he extolled black culture and achievements," wrote Levy, "he did not believe blacks could gain both their full rights and economic opportunity without the aid of whites."

Became NAACP Leader

That belief would be tested as the years passed. In 1916 Johnson accepted the newly created post of field secretary of the NAACP. His duties included investigating incidents of racial discrimination and organizing new NAACP branches across the country. The organization grew tremendously between 1917 and 1930 and provided a nucleus of opposition to the growing trend toward white supremacist legislation and brutal lynchings.

From 1920 until 1930 Johnson served as the first black executive secretary of the NAACP, replacing white chief executive John R. Shillady, who suffered considerable psychological trauma after being beaten by a mob of bigoted whites in Austin, Texas, because of his work on behalf of blacks. Johnson's deft skills of communication—with both blacks and whites—served him well in his new

> "The greatest thing the American Negro gained as a result of the Civil War and the amendments to the Constitution was the right to contend for his rights."

position. Membership in the NAACP continued to grow, and the organization gained influence in both judicial and legislative arenas. Johnson worked fervently to get a bill passed by the federal government that would end lynching, and he oversaw challenges to Jim Crow laws that moved to the U.S. Supreme Court. Still, for all the advances he made, little actual progress was made for black civil rights in the national halls of justice during Johnson's tenure with the NAACP. In fact, the demise of his federal anti-lynching bill caused him to become disillusioned with the American political system in general and led to his break with the Republican party.

The 1920s proved to be a difficult time for black Americans. The Ku Klux Klan attracted vast membership in the North as well as the South, and "separate but equal" became state law in many places. These setbacks helped to move Johnson toward his more radical political philosophy. From the podium and from the pages of magazines he urged blacks to organize and vote in strength. He continued to call for more and better education for black citizens. Most important, however, he began to use black poetry and song as a means to communicate to the white majority. Wagner stated: "[Johnson's] most eminent services to his race were his labors to make known the cultural achievements of the Negro past. In this way he also had a decisive influence on the development of the Negro Renaissance."

A Preserver of Culture

Johnson collected verse in an important work called *The Book of American Negro Poetry*. Then he turned to spirituals—black Christian hymns, some of them quite old—and published *The Book of American Negro Spirituals* in 1925 and *The Second Book of American Negro Spirituals* the next year. He encouraged young poets and novelists and was himself identified with the flowering of black creative writing in the 1920s known as the Harlem Renaissance. His essays for mainstream periodicals such as the *New York Times, Harper's,* and the *Nation* won him the recognition of the leading journalists of the time, including H. L. Mencken and Mark Van Doren.

Johnson's groundbreaking creative work *God's Trombones* was published in 1927. The book consists of free verse sermons in the style of black evangelistic ministers' discourse, written not in dialect but conventional English. Johnson claimed that *God's Trombones* was his attempt to preserve an essential artistic form—the black sermon— for future generations of readers. In a review for *Phylon* magazine in 1960, Eugenia W. Collier wrote of *God's Trombones:* "The sensitive reader cannot fail to hear the rantings of the fire-and-brimstone preacher; the extremely sensitive reader may even hear the unwritten 'Amens' of the congregation."

In 1930 Johnson retired from his demanding post at the NAACP and took a part-time teaching position at Fisk University in Nashville, Tennessee. During the later years of his life, he taught creative writing at both Fisk and at New York University. He also published his autobiography, *Along This Way;* a serious study of black art and music called *Black Manhattan;* and another volume of poetry, *Saint Peter Relates an Incident.* The title poem of the latter work concerns the opening of the Tomb of the Unknown Soldier on Judgment Day. A crowd waits to see the honored but unknown military hero buried there and is astonished when a black man emerges. Johnson wrote the poem in response to unfair treatment accorded the mothers of deceased black soldiers on a nationally sponsored trip to Europe.

A Legacy of Hope

Johnson died in 1938 when an automobile in which he was riding was struck by a train in rural Maine. More than 2000 mourners attended his Harlem funeral. He was buried in Brooklyn's Greenwood Cemetery holding a copy of *God's Trombones* in his hands.

Throughout his long and busy life, Johnson strove to end discrimination in America. By example and exhortation, he encouraged African Americans to become educated, to express themselves creatively, and to work hard for political power. Above all else, he was a staunch advocate of black pride, empowerment, and self-assertion, but he simultaneously called for interracial communication and cooperation. "Johnson was not the man to throw down the gauntlet to America," wrote Wagner. "He preferred to appeal to its reason and to persuade it that, since blacks and whites are irrevocably destined to live in association, the welfare of one group can only be maintained through assuring the welfare of another."

That idea forms the theme of many of Johnson's poems and songs, especially "Lift Every Voice and Sing." It is one of the many lasting contributions to black America made by James Weldon Johnson, songwriter, poet, civil rights leader, and shining example of advancement against phenomenal odds.

Selected writings

The Autobiography of an Ex-Coloured Man (novel), 1912, reprinted, Viking Penguin, 1990.
Fifty Years and Other Poems, Cornhill, 1917.
(Editor) *The Book of American Negro Poetry,* Harcourt, 1922, reprinted, 1969.
(Editor) *The Book of American Negro Spirituals,* Viking, 1925.
(Editor) *The Second Book of American Negro Spirituals,* Viking, 1926.
God's Trombones: Seven Negro Sermons in Verse (poetry), Viking, 1927, reprinted, Viking Penguin, 1990.
Black Manhattan (nonfiction), Knopf, 1930, reprinted, Da Capo, 1991.
Along This Way: The Autobiography of James Weldon Johnson, Viking, 1933, reprinted, Viking Penguin, 1990.
Negro Americans, What Now? (nonfiction), Viking, 1934, reprinted, Da Capo, 1973.
Saint Peter Relates an Incident (poetry), Viking, 1935.

Lyricist for numerous songs, including "Lift Every Voice and Sing," 1900, published by Walker and Company, 1993. Contributor to numerous newspapers and magazines.

Sources

Books

Black Literature Criticism, Gale, 1992.

Black Writers, Gale, 1989.

Bone, Robert A., *The Negro Novel in America,* Yale University Press, 1958.

Bronz, Stephen H., *Roots of Negro Racial Consciousness,* Libra, 1964.

Fleming, Robert E., *James Weldon Johnson,* Twayne, 1987.

Franklin, John Hope, *An Illustrated History of Black Americans,* Time-Life Books, 1970.

Franklin, John Hope, and August Meier, editors, *Black Leaders of the Twentieth Century,* University of Illinois Press, 1982.

Johnson, James Weldon, *Along This Way: The Autobiography of James Weldon Johnson,* Viking Penguin, 1990.

Levy, Eugene, *James Weldon Johnson: Black Leader, Black Voice,* Chicago University Press, 1973.

Logan, Rayford W., and Michael R. Winston, editors, *Dictionary of American Negro Biography,* Norton, 1982.

Smythe, Mabel M., editor, *The Black American Reference Book,* Prentice Hall, 1976.

Tolbert-Rouchaleau, Jane, *James Weldon Johnson,* Chelsea House, 1988.

Wagner, Jean, *Black Poets of the United States: From Paul Laurence Dunbar to Langston Hughes,* translated from original French by Kenneth Douglas, University of Illinois Press, 1973.

Periodicals

Crisis, June 1971.

Nation, July 2, 1938.

Newsweek, July 4, 1938.

New York Times, June 28, 1938, p. 18.

Phylon, December 1960.

Time, July 4, 1938.

—*Mark Kram*

Jackie Joyner-Kersee

1962—

Track and field athlete

Jackie Joyner-Kersee is "the greatest multi-event track and field athlete of all time," announced Randy Harvey in the *Los Angeles Times*. An Olympian to be reckoned with since 1984, Joyner-Kersee is the first American ever to win a gold medal in the long jump and the first woman in history to earn more than 7,000 points in the grueling seven-event heptathlon. Joyner-Kersee has won three Olympic gold medals, one silver, and one bronze, and she established a world record in the heptathlon in 1986. Her achievements are so astounding—and her personality so engaging—that she has become one of America's favorite track athletes.

According to Kenny Moore in *Sports Illustrated,* Jackie Joyner-Kersee, "like her name, is a blend. Her years of hard, thoughtful training are the Kersee part, the expression of her husband-coach Bob Kersee's hatred of talent lying fallow. The Joyner half is Jackie in competition. She wants to win, but having won, wants to go on. She wants to impress, but having performed gloriously, still wants to go on. The Joyner gift is her open joy in practiced, powerful movement, in improvement for its own sake, and it causes observers to presume, in error, that what she does is without personal cost."

Indeed, Joyner-Kersee has often found herself in competition with only the clock and the yardstick, having left her competitors in the dust. Not satisfied just to win, she struggles for records, for solid recognition that she dominates her sport. She has won championships—Olympic and otherwise—with hamstring injuries, has broken world records in heat that would stagger a camel, and has managed through it all to maintain a stable relationship with her husband-coach Bob Kersee. As Ken Denlinger put it in the *Washington Post,* Joyner-Kersee "smokes the world's playgrounds as no other female athlete in history."

Before Joyner-Kersee set her sights on it, the heptathlon was a virtually unknown event in America. It has since become a track and field favorite, especially during the Olympics. For the heptathlon, athletes amass points by running a 200-meter dash, completing both high and long jumps, throwing a javelin and a shot put, running the 100-meter hurdles, and finishing an 800-meter run, all in the space of two days. The seven-event series demands skills in a variety of areas that most athletes choose as specialties.

Joyner-Kersee has been a star in the heptathlon since 1984, when she won a silver medal after losing the 800-meter run

At a Glance...

Born Jacqueline Joyner, March 3, 1962, in East St. Louis, IL; daughter of Alfred (a railroad employee) and Mary (a nurse's assistant) Joyner; married Bob Kersee (a track and field coach), January 11, 1986. *Education:* Attended the University of California, Los Angeles, 1980-84.

Track and field athlete, 1973—. Has competed in national and international track events since 1980, including the 1984, 1988, and 1992 Olympic Games; the Goodwill Games in Moscow and the Olympic Festival in Houston, both 1986; the Pan American Games in Indianapolis, 1987; and the World Championships in Rome, 1987 and Tokyo, 1991.

Selected awards: Olympic silver medal in heptathlon, 1984; athlete of the year citation from *Track & Field News* and Jesse Owens Award, both 1986; established world record in heptathlon competition, 1986; Sullivan Award for best amateur athlete, 1986 and 1987; amateur sportswoman of the year award from McDonald's, 1987; Olympic gold medals in heptathlon and long jump, 1988; honorary doctorate from University of Missouri, 1989; Olympic gold medal in heptathlon and bronze medal in long jump, 1992; first woman athlete ever to score more than 7,000 points in a heptathlon competition.

Addresses: *Home*—Box 21053, Long Beach, CA 90801. *Office*—c/o United States Olympic Committee, One Olympic Place, Colorado Springs, CO 80909.

by a fraction of a second. In the 1988 and 1992 Olympics she won a gold in the event. Even more remarkable, she has managed to single out one specialty—the long jump—and win Olympic medals in that event as well. In 1988 she earned a gold medal for a jump, and in 1992 she settled graciously for a bronze. A drug-free athlete sometimes faced with steroid-enhanced competitors, Joyner-Kersee is the first American woman ever to win an Olympic long jump competition.

"Making It Out" of a Life of Poverty

Born in 1962, Joyner-Kersee grew up in East St. Louis, Illinois, a poverty-stricken city on the Mississippi River.

Her parents, Alfred and Mary Joyner, were barely in their teens when they got married. Mary was only 14 when her first child, Al, was born and just 16 when she gave birth to Jackie in 1962. Both parents worked hard to provide for their growing family, Alfred in construction and on the railroads and Mary as a nurse's aid. The couple's salaries were hardly adequate, and the Joyners knew real desperation. *Sports Illustrated* correspondent Kenny Moore wrote: "Their house was little more than wallpaper and sticks, with four tiny bedrooms. During the winters, when the hot-water pipes would freeze, they had to heat water for baths in kettles on the kitchen stove. Their great-grandmother (on their father's side) lived with them until she died on the plastic-covered sofa in the living room while Jackie was at the store buying milk."

The Joyner family—especially Jackie—wished desperately for better circumstances. A grandmother had named her Jacqueline, after Jacqueline Kennedy Onassis, the wife of former U.S. president John F. Kennedy, hoping that the youngster would someday be "first lady" of something. Joyner-Kersee's brother Al, himself an Olympic gold medalist, told *Sports Illustrated:* "I remember Jackie and me crying together in a back room in that house, swearing that someday we were going to make it. Make it out. Make things different."

Their mother encouraged—and even bullied—Al and Jackie to improve themselves. Having been a teenaged parent herself, Mary Joyner told the children they could not date until eighteen and spurred their interest in other activities. As a child, Jackie began to study modern dance at the local Mary Brown Community Center. One day she saw a sign advertising the center's new track program. She decided to give it a try.

At first Joyner-Kersee lost every race, but soon she was winning. In 1976 she watched the Summer Olympics on television and later recalled in the *Chicago Tribune,* "I decided I wanted to go. I wanted to be on TV, too." After that she tried harder and became a tremendously versatile athlete at a very tender age. The first competitor she beat regularly was her older brother, Al. The two siblings began to spur one another on to greater and greater achievements, growing very close in the process.

At the age of 14, Joyner-Kersee won the first of four straight national junior pentathlon championships. Track and field events were only part of the weapons in her arsenal, however. In high school she was a state champion in both track and basketball. Her Lincoln High School basketball team won games by an average of 52.8 points during her senior year. Joyner-Kersee also played volleyball and continued to encourage her brother in his sporting career. Her athletic achievements notwithstanding, she was an excellent student who finished in the top ten percent of her graduating class.

Joyner-Kersee was heavily recruited by high-ranking colleges and chose the University of California at Los Angeles. She began school there in 1980 on a basketball scholarship. Tragedy struck in her freshman year when her mother developed a rare form of meningitis and died at the age of 37. Stunned by the sudden and unexpected loss, both Jackie and Al Joyner dedicated themselves to athletics with new resolve.

Athletic Talents Nurtured at UCLA

Having returned to UCLA, Jackie became a starting forward for the Bruins and worked with the track team as a long jumper. She was rather surprised to find herself singled out by an intimidating assistant track coach named Bob Kersee, who detected untapped possibilities in the young collegian. "I saw this talent walking around the campus that everyone was blind to," he told *Sports Illustrated*. "No one was listening to her mild requests to do more. So I went to the athletic director and made him a proposition." Kersee literally put his own job on the line, demanding to coach Jackie Joyner in multi-events, or he would quit. The university athletic department agreed to his plan. The coach remarked in *Sports Illustrated,* "By 1982, I could see she'd be the world record holder."

Joyner-Kersee was already a powerhouse in the long jump and the 200-meter sprint. She was also a top-scoring forward on the basketball team, so her endurance was excellent. Al Joyner taught her how to run the hurdles and to throw the javelin—a type of spear—and the shot put—a heavy palm-sized metal ball. By 1983 Joyner-Kersee qualified for the world track and field championships in Helsinki, Finland. Her first chance to be a world champion ended in disaster, however, when she pulled a hamstring muscle and could not complete the heptathlon. Ironically, her brother Al was also present, and he too was injured. Al Joyner told *Sports Illustrated* that he consoled his sister by telling her, "It's just not our time yet."

Silver Medalist at the 1984 Olympic Games

In 1984 both Jackie and Al Joyner qualified for the U.S. Olympic team. Having recovered from her injuries, Jackie was a favorite to win the heptathlon. Al, on the other hand, was not considered likely to win his event, the triple jump. Confounding all predictions, Jackie won the silver medal in the heptathlon, missing the gold by only .06 seconds in her final event, the 800-meter run. Meanwhile, Al Joyner became the first American in 80 years to win the Olympic triple jump. The tears Jackie shed at the end of the day were not for her hair's-breadth loss, but rather for joy at her brother's victory. Both of them knew that Jackie would be back to compete another day.

Exhausted yet elated, Joyner-Kersee smiles during the victory lap after winning her second Olympic heptathlon at 1992's Barcelona Games.

The depths of Joyner-Kersee's potential began to be apparent in 1985, when she set a U.S. record with a long jump measuring 23 feet 9 inches. By then she had quit playing basketball and was devoting herself exclusively to track, under the guidance of Bob Kersee. Their relationship became romantic after years spent working together as friends, and they were married on January 11, 1986. When Al Joyner was wed to a sprinter named Florence Griffith, the stage was set for the emergence of a track and field "family" of champions: Jackie Joyner-Kersee and Florence Griffith Joyner. The two women were among an elite cadre of track stars coached by Bob Kersee in preparation for the 1988 Olympic Games.

Back in 1985 Joyner-Kersee was ranked third in the world heptathlon. She changed that ranking forever at the Goodwill Games in Moscow in 1986. There she set a new world record in the event with 7,148 points—more than 200 points higher than her nearest competitor *in history*. Just three weeks later she broke her own record with a score of 7,161 points in Houston, Texas, where temperatures reached 100 degrees during competition. Her devotion to the heptathlon was recognized by numerous awards, including the 1986 Sullivan Award for best amateur athlete and the coveted Jesse Owens Award.

Triumph at the '88 Games

Joyner-Kersee's performance at the 1988 Olympics was nothing short of phenomenal. Not only did she win a gold in the heptathlon, she also took the gold medal in the long jump, flying 24 feet 3.5 inches. Her heptathlon score of 7,291 points was her fourth world record, and it will probably stand for many years to come. Joyner-Kersee's achievement in the 1988 Olympics was particularly exciting because multi-event track competitions and the long jump had long been dominated by countries of the former Soviet Bloc, where steroid use among athletes was acceptable. Joyner-Kersee became not only the first American woman to win a gold medal in the Olympic long jump, she also became the first athlete in 64 years to win in a gold in both a multi-event and a single event.

Much attention has been focused over the years on the relationship between Jackie Joyner-Kersee and her coach/ husband, Bob. The pair have been spotted quarreling during competition, and Kersee is an exacting man who makes his demands well known. The coach told the *Chicago Tribune* that he and his wife try not to take their disagreements home with them at night. "We want to make it in terms of the coach-athlete relationship, and we want to stay married for the rest of our lives," he said. "So we've got rules in terms of our coach-athlete relationship and our husband-wife relationship." He added: "I'm surprised it works as well as it does, and I'm happy it does for both of us. We enjoy sport so much, and we enjoy one another so much, it would be a shame if we let track and field get in the way of our personal life, or our personal life get in the way of track and field."

Another Gold in the '92 Heptathlon

Joyner-Kersee has not been able to break her 1988 Olympic heptathlon record. Since then she has reinjured her hamstring and had moments when she lacked the resolve to continue. The incessant prodding of Kersee has kept her at the top of the world standings, however, and in the 1992 Olympics she sought to become the fourth

woman in Olympic history to win four gold medals. Her performance in the heptathlon earned her another gold, but she could only turn in a bronze medal performance in the long jump. The 30-year-old Joyner-Kersee was gracious about her defeat in the long jump, because the winner was her close friend, Heike Drechsler, of Germany. Joyner-Kersee told the *Los Angeles Times* that she was thrilled for her rival. "With other athletes, even though you're fierce competitors, you get a sense of them as people, whether they're nice," she said. "You still want to beat them, but when the competition is over, you realize that there's more to life than athletics."

Los Angeles Times reporter Randy Harvey wrote of Jackie Joyner-Kersee: "She is one of the warmest, most even-tempered persons in athletics. The next bad word that anyone who knows her, including her competitors, says about her will be the first." Joyner-Kersee has combined the ability of a natural athlete with the resolve of a fierce competitor. She has passed the age of 30 but still plans to compete in track and field as long as she can. After that, she says, she may try her hand at other sports. (She plays both tennis and golf with relish when her training schedule allows.) But in *Parade Magazine,* Joyner-Kersee stated that her primary intention is to complete her Olympic career "on U.S. soil," adding, "I started in 1984 in Los Angeles, and I'll end up in Atlanta [in 1996.]"

Sources

Books

The Olympics Factbook: A Spectator's Guide to the Winter and Summer Games, Visible Ink Press, 1992.

Periodicals

Chicago Tribune, September 25, 1988.
Ebony, October 1986; April 1992; October 1992.
Los Angeles Times, September 14, 1988; September 29, 1988; February 17, 1990; June 22, 1992; August 8, 1992.
Parade Magazine, June 13, 1993, p. 14.
Philadelphia Daily News, August 7, 1992.
Sports Illustrated, April 27, 1987; September 14, 1987; October 10, 1988.
Washington Post, February 26, 1987; July 17, 1988; September 25, 1988.

—*Mark Kram*

Jomo Kenyatta

1891(?)-1978

Former President of Kenya

On December 12, 1963, the flag of independent Kenya billowed over the capital city of Nairobi for the first time. Flanked by thousands of other Kenyans, Jomo Kenyatta watched the unfolding of a 50-year-old dream that had sent him overseas to Europe, landed him in jail, and earned him the hushed admiration of his fellow-Kikuyu tribesmen. An astute politician known to his people as "Mzee," or "The Wise Elder," Kenyatta became the country's first president in 1964. History remembers him as a brilliant communicator who stressed the importance of black African rule in Kenya and conveyed his message with stunning effectiveness to both his supporters and his opponents.

Jomo Kenyatta never knew the exact year of his birth—only that he was born sometime in the 1890s into a tribe that had always counted people's ages according to their initiation groups. This custom, part of a long tradition, had kept the group members loyal to each other even after the burgeoning Kikuyu population expanded into new territory during the nineteenth century. However, unchanging tradition could not barricade the people against outside events; it was powerless against both the drought of 1889-1890 and the evils of smallpox and cattle disease that sent Kikuyu fleeing back to their ancestral stronghold in the fertile highlands around Mount Kenya. On their homecoming, they met yet another disaster: foreigners had claimed their vacant land after Kenya became the British East Africa Protectorate in 1895. Furthermore, these foreigners could support their claims with 99-year Crown leases that virtually turned the Kikuyu into squatters on their own land, tolerated only as a source of cheap labor.

By 1902 Kikuyu lands were divided again, this time by the Uganda Railway built by the British to connect the Kenyan port of Mombasa with Lake Victoria. The railroad shattered tribal isolation forever, enticing the people into the new era with trading posts and introducing them to European missionaries bearing the messages of Christianity and education for their children.

The future president of Kenya enrolled in a Scottish-run mission school in Kenya's Central province around the year 1909. Naked except for three wire bracelets plus a strip of cloth around his neck, he is said to have given his name as Kamau wa Ngengi. There was little about him to hint at his future role as Jomo Kenyatta: he abandoned academic life for a carpentry apprenticeship in 1912, though he stayed at the mission long enough to undergo both the traditional Kikuyu initiation into manhood and entry into Christianity, taking the

At a Glance. . .

Born Kamau wa Ngengi, c. October 20, 1891 (birth date is uncertain; some sources say 1890, 1893, or 1897), in Ngenda, Kiambu District, British East Africa Protectorate (now Kenya); took the name Johnstone Kamau, 1914; later known as Jomo Kenyatta; died August 22, 1978, on Mombasa, Kenya; son of Muigai (a farmer and herdsman) and Wambui; married Grace Wahu, Edna Clarke, Jane (daughter of Chief Koinange), and Ngina (four wives; no divorces, since Kikuyu society was polygamous); children: eight. *Education:* Attended University College, London; studied in Moscow, 1932; postgraduate study in anthropology, London School of Economics, 1937. *Politics:* Conservative Pan-Africanist. *Religion:* Christian.

Store clerk and water works maintenance employee for Nairobi Municipality, 1921-26; Kikuyu Central Association (KCA), secretary, beginning 1928 (organization banned in May 1940), KCA representative in England intermittently between 1929 and 1945; also worked as a teacher, farm laborer, and lecturer while abroad; co-organizer of 5th Pan-African Congress, 1945; Independent Teachers' College, Githunguri, Kenya, vice principal, beginning 1946, became principal; president, Kenya African Union (KAU; political party), 1947-52 (also president in absentia, beginning 1944); imprisoned by British Government for alleged role in Mau Mau terrorism, 1953-61; president, Kenya African National Union (KANU; political party), 1960-78 (first year in absentia); Government of Kenya, minister for Internal Security, Defense and Foreign Affairs, 1963-64; prime minister of Kenya, December 12, 1963-December 12, 1964; president of Kenya, December 12, 1964-August 22, 1978.

Awards: Knight of Grace, Order of St. John of Jerusalem, 1972; LL.D. from University of East Africa; Order of the Golden Ark, bestowed by the World Wildlife Fund, 1974.

baptismal name of Johnstone.

The end of World War I found Johnstone Kamau settled in Nairobi, attending evening mission classes and working as a water meter reader. Generously paid, he was able to build a hut for his new wife and baby in his native Kiambu district. Johnstone is said to have made his hut big enough to accommodate a small general store, which he called "Kinyata" after the bead-strung leather strips he often wore as a belt.

Political Awareness Awakened

A social center as well as a place of business, the shop was an ideal place for customers to air grievances over the laws that were instituted after Kenya was declared a British colony in 1920. Several topics came up for discussion. A 1915 law extending white-held land leases from 99 to 999 years and placing all black-held land under the British Crown was hotly opposed, as was a registration act stating that all black males had to carry a *kipande*, or document listing their employment history and references. Taken together, these laws increased the squatter problem, especially when combined with a ban on profitable sisal (hemp) and coffee crops for black farmers. The Kikuyu resented this almost as much as they resented the hut tax now payable for each wife, complaining that tax money would be better spent on government-run schools.

Discontented rumblings found expression in a rash of government-opposed societies. Kenyatta joined the fledgling Kikuyu Central Association (KCA) in 1925, later becoming secretary. Successful at increasing member support in rural areas, he soon earned himself an official reputation as a troublemaker by helping to shape a petition to the British government, asking, among other things, for permission to grow coffee and for publication of all laws in the Kikuyu language.

By 1929 the KCA had not received a response from local government about either these grievances or the issues of land rights and the hut tax. Disregarding the local authorities' assurances that they would have no success as an unofficial organization that did not represent all the Kikuyu, the KCA scraped together the funds to send Johnstone to England to consult the Colonial Office.

His Mission in England

From London, Johnstone wrote to the British Colonial Office frequently. While he waited for a response, he took the opportunity to visit Europe and Russia, despite a shortage of money so acute that his landlord impounded his possessions in lieu of rent. Ignored by the authorities, he returned to Kenya in 1930 but was soon sent back by the KCA to protest a threatened federation of Tanganyika (now Tanzania), Uganda, and Kenya that would tighten Britain's colonial grip. Johnstone ventured back to England eagerly, lingering only to send his wife two bunches of bananas by way of acknowledging the birth of his second baby. Once in England, however, neither frequent letters to the Colonial Office nor impassioned pleas to several parliamentary committees brought any response on the federation question.

Nevertheless, he gained a chance to make himself heard, for the Kikuyu land loss complaint had at last found a British response. In 1932 the government appointed the Carter Commission to walk the precarious claims tightrope teetering between the powerful, wealthy settlers and the impoverished, aggrieved Kikuyu. Sir Morris Carter took statements from Kenyatta and others, then went to Kenya to inspect the lands. Finding that the ancestral territory around Mount Kenya had indeed been cut, he compromised by ruling that the Kikuyu be moved and compensated with less desirable land reclaimed from the thin strip of forest separating them from the Masai tribes. The white settlers were permitted to remain in the fertile area that would henceforth be known as the White Highlands.

Having infuriated the Kikuyu by removing them from their ancestral stronghold, the might of the law moved on to the neighboring Wakamba. Outraged by the devastating effects of Carter's dictums on their cattle-raising tradition, 3,000 Wakamba tribesmen marched to see the governor in Nairobi. Denied entry, they protested by swelling KCA membership rolls, which reached 10,000 by 1938.

These explosive events were faithfully relayed to Johnstone in England. In turn, he publicized the Wakamba and Kikuyu complaints both in lectures given all over England and in articles published in the Manchester *Guardian*. The Colonial Office, however, refused to acknowledge him, though they had begun to keep a list of all his activities. Meticulously documented were Johnstone's 1932 visit to Moscow, where he attended an institute for revolutionaries; his job teaching Kikuyu language at London University's School of African and Oriental Languages; and a bit part he played in a movie called *Sanders of the River,* which brought him a friendship with the world-renowned singer and activist Paul Robeson. Also noted were details of Johnstone's association with left-wing intellectuals who introduced him to the possibilities of Kenyan independence and black majority rule.

Facing Mount Kenya

In 1936, despite the fact that he lacked a college degree, Johnstone went to the London School of Economics to take a postgraduate level class in anthropology from the distinguished Bronislaw Malinowski. Around the same time, he wrote a study of Kikuyu life called *Facing Mount Kenya,* depicting a complex African society that had developed free from European influence. To illustrate his pride in the uncorrupted Kikuyu culture, he was photo-

graphed for the book's cover in tribal dress consisting of a borrowed monkey-fur cloak and a spear made from a sharpened plank. He also rejected the missionary-given name of Johnstone, deciding that "Jomo," meaning "burning spear," might be more appropriate. By way of a last name, he adopted "Kenyatta," reminiscent of his little store in Kiambu. His book sold only 517 copies but was well received in academic circles.

The outbreak of World War II prevented Kenyatta's return to Kenya but did not leave his Colonial Office dossier incomplete. The list now included his job as a farm laborer in an English town, his 1942 marriage (Kenyan family notwithstanding) to an Englishwoman named Edna Clarke, and the birth of a son the following year. The record ended in 1946, when he finally returned to Kenya, leaving Edna behind.

Returned to Kenya

Sixteen years abroad had changed both Kenyatta and his country. Fiftyish, highly educated, and well-traveled, he received an ecstatic welcome from his supporters. Kenya now had a booming economy, fueled mainly by exports of food to a hungry, wartorn Europe. Wealth, in turn, had

> Flanked by thousands of other Kenyans, Jomo Kenyatta watched the unfolding of a 50-year-old dream of independence that had sent him overseas to Europe, landed him in jail, and earned him the hushed admiration of his fellow-Kikuyu tribesmen.

brought thousands of settlers streaming from India on the eve of its partition from Britain. By 1948, the white population in Kenya stood at around 30,000, many of whom needed cheap labor to work their growing lands.

But Kenyatta's keen eye saw that the country's labor force would not be easy to manage. Blacks who had spent the war years in Kenya had learned about free education and territorial security from British Broadcasting Corporation (BBC) news bulletins. Those who had gone overseas with the 75,000-strong fighting forces had left the racial discrimination of their colonial-run homeland behind, only to return at war's end to the usual problems of work documents and confiscated land. With no means of livelihood, these highly trained veterans had drifted into the rapidly swelling new slums of Kenya's cities, where the crime rate had begun to soar.

Kenyatta was dismayed to see the traditional honor of the Kikuyu besmirched by dishonesty and violence. Despite government restrictions that made meetings difficult to arrange, he harangued his huge audiences with pep talks on the necessities for hard work, fair trade in the cities, and an immediate end to tribal violence.

Ideas of Independence Take Root

Kenyatta was a staunch opponent of white rule for Africans, and he introduced the idea of independence for his country's people through the Kenya African Union (KAU). Formed in 1944, the multitribal organization declared him its president in absentia and rallied for racial equality by law, voting privileges for blacks, and the restoration of land ownership rights to native Kenyans. Noting that urban blacks were more comfortable with the move towards independence than their conservative rural counterparts, Kenyatta made a decision that led to disaster: he chose to spur black allegiance with traditional oath-taking.

Oaths had always been part of the Kikuyu moral code. Underscoring loyalty to initiation groups, they were also a familiar part of each land sale, proving the seller's ownership before new boundaries were marked by the stomach contents of a ceremonially-slaughtered ram. But Kikuyu acceptance did not automatically guarantee backing for oaths from tribes unfamiliar with the practice. Distrustful of the unknown, they withdrew their support. White Kenyans, citing Kenyatta's enormous following and his familiarity with Communism, demanded that he be followed constantly by the Special Branch Bureau of Criminal Investigation. Kenyatta proceeded to reject oathing as a rural canvassing measure, but not soon enough to stop it from spreading in a perverted and most virulent form.

Terror Stalked the Land

In 1948 Kenya began to experience a terrorist threat called Mau Mau. Its architects, both Kikuyus, were British army veteran Bildad Kaggia and trade unionist Fred Kubai. Like Kenyatta, they were bent on Kenyan independence; unlike him, they were committed to using any means necessary—no matter how forceful—to achieve it. Determined to force the whites out of Kenya, the men swiftly organized fighting cells in the Kikuyu-held forests girdling Mount Kenya and the Aberdare Range of mountains. Mau Mau raiders left

behind them trails of strangled dogs and cats, disembowelled cattle with amputated legs, and human victims who had been burned alive or hacked to pieces with machetes. During the late 1940s and early 1950s, the Mau Mau is believed to have murdered a small number of white settlers and more than 11,000 blacks suspected of collaborating with the white regime.

Many political observers agree that Kenyatta knew about Mau Mau. However, he always disclaimed connection with it on the simple grounds that he opposed its brutality. Asked by the British government to denounce Mau Mau in his home district of Kiambu, he gladly did so, thereby bringing Mau Mau assassination threats down on his head. Still, the government banned the KAU in 1952 as a suspected Mau Mau front and then declared a state of national emergency.

Imprisoned as Mau Mau Organizer

Kenyatta and several Mau Mau committee members were arrested in October of 1952 and tried in a remote little town called Kapenguria. Found guilty of organizing the terrorist group, Kenyatta spent the following six years in Laukitaung Prison, cooking for the other convicts, reading books on comparative religion sent to him by his daughter, and piecing together news of his home district, where his farm had been destroyed on government orders.

Kenyatta completed his prison sentence in April of 1959. Opposition to colonialism in Kenya continued, and the government was reluctant to release him immediately. The turning point came after eleven hardcore Mau Mau supporters were slaughtered in an alleged disciplinary action that embarrassed the British government and caused the resignation of the colonial secretary.

The Cell Door Opened

The new colonial secretary was Iain MacLeod, a man firmly committed to Kenyan independence and black majority rule. Moving briskly, by mid-1960 MacLeod had encouraged the formation of two political parties: the Kenya African National Union (KANU) was a coalition between the dominant Kikuyu and runner-up Luo tribes, while the Kenya African Democratic Union was made up of smaller tribes fearing Kikuyu domination. Once again in absentia, Kenyatta was nominated the president of KANU.

MacLeod also authorized a press conference for Kenyatta, who had been transferred to another town. Now about 70, Kenyatta appeared before selected journalists fit and alert, and armed with a crisp three-point statement: he declared that he had not been the organizer of Mau Mau; he expressed his belief that black Kenyans must rule their country; and he emphatically denied any Communist connections, assuring the journalists that he had merely been to the former Soviet Union for educational purposes. Kenyatta went back to Kiambu in August of 1961 to a rebuilt farm packed with 10,000 well-wishers. The greeting was a triumphant boost to the beginning of his successful KANU campaign.

Kenyan Independence

Kenya became Africa's 34th independent state at the end of 1963. Honored guests at the celebration included Britain's Prince Philip, actor Sidney Poitier, and U.S. Supreme Court Justice Thurgood Marshall. Also present were several truckloads of Mau Mau, all of whom had been promised feasts of oxen, jobs, and generous loans for land purchase. (Their euphoria, however, was shortlived. On learning that the loans would have to be repaid, many of them returned to lives of crime in the forests.)

Kenyatta was now the country's prime minister, and "Harambee!" ("Let us all pull together!") was the motto of new independence. By December of 1964, Kenyatta had become the first president of Kenya, with business in the one-party state getting off to a brisk and pragmatic start. The new order swept away tribal rivalries in favor of nationalism for the benefit of all Kenyans.

Kenyanization became the new economic watchword. A British-financed Land Transfer Program eased government efforts to buy out white farmers so that blacks could purchase their land; reluctant sellers, especially if they were noncitizens, were warned of "severe action" if they refused to comply. As a result, despite the doctrine of forgiveness and nonviolence that had always been Kenyatta's creed, 5,000 of the 45,000 white farmers in Kenya had already left the country by the time it became a republic at the end of 1964.

Still, Kenyanization was progressing more slowly than Kenyatta had expected. Nearly six dozen American companies, including Union Carbide, Colgate-Palmolive, and Caltex, had established ties with Kenya, but the president was troubled by and determined to curb the considerable economic influence of Asians who gained prominence in Kenya since the days of the Uganda Railway.

Cracks in the Facade

Anxious to avoid claims of Kikuyu favoritism, Kenyatta had

carefully selected his first cabinet from each population group. Nevertheless, cracks in party loyalty began to appear early. Vice President Oginga Odinga, a self-confessed Communist, was later shown to have campaigned for anti-government support among the Mau Mau. Odinga resigned from Kenyatta's government in 1966 and formed a new party called the Kenya People's Union, which gained considerable support in the late 1960s. Kenyatta's aura of invincibility was threatened by the opposition of Odinga and the Kenya People's Union. He met the challenge with a grim warning later published in *Time* magazine's November 7, 1969 issue: "We will crush you into flour. Anyone who toys with our progress will be crushed like locusts." His first example was Odinga, who was placed under immediate house arrest.

The 1970s: Money and Murder

As the 1970s advanced, the Kenyatta ranks split further. Rumors of government-sanctioned corruption abounded, with officials of the Kenyatta regime—and even members of the president's family—implicated as key players in incidents of poaching, deforestation, ivory exportation, and land grabbing.

A courageous and popular politician named Josiah Kariuki began to speak out against the corruption surrounding the aged president. "Kenya does not need ten millionaires and ten million beggars," he declared in a speech quoted by the London *Times* in 1975. Soon afterwards, Kariuki was abducted from the Nairobi Hilton, tortured, and murdered, his body lying unclaimed in a mortuary for more than a week before one of his wives identified it. Kenyatta made his position on the murder clear: he warned that further opposition would bring further bloodshed.

When Jomo Kenyatta died in his sleep on August 22, 1978, Vice President Daniel arap Moi, a handpicked successor, assumed smooth control of the government. In spite of the controversy and charges of corruption that surrounded him during his lifetime, Kenyatta remains in death the father of Kenyan independence and a key figure in the struggle to promote black rule and economic autonomy throughout Africa.

Selected writings

Facing Mount Kenya: The Tribal Life of the Gikuyu, Secker & Warburg, 1938.
My People of Kikuyu and the Life of Chief Wangombe, United Society for Christian Literature, 1942.

Harambee! (speeches), Oxford University Press, 1964.
The Challenge of Uhuru (speeches), East African Publishing House, 1971.

Sources

Books

Cox, Richard, *Kenyatta's Country,* Hutchinson, 1965.

Delf, George, *Jomo Kenyatta,* Doubleday, 1961.

Edgerton, Robert B., *Mau Mau: An African Crucible,* Free Press, 1989.

Farson, Negley, *Last Chance in Africa,* Gollancz, 1950.

Kenyatta, Jomo, *Facing Mount Kenya,* Vintage Books, 1965.

Lineberry, William P., editor, *East Africa: The Reference Shelf,* volume 40, number 2, 1968.

Murray-Brown, Jeremy, *Kenyatta,* Dutton, 1973.

Nelson, Harold D., editor, *Kenya: A Country Study,* American University, 1983.

Periodicals

Nation, August 11, 1969.

Newsweek, September 4, 1978.

New York Times, October 29, 1952; June 9, 1953; July 2, 1953; May 13, 1963; December 11, 1963; July 16, 1964; April 3, 1965; April 15, 1966; May 2, 1966; January 11, 1970; February 11, 1970; October 17, 1975.

Phylon, volume 14, number 4, 1953.

Time, June 11, 1965; November 7, 1969; September 4, 1978.

Times (London), August 10, 1975; August 17, 1975; August 24, 1975.

—Gillian Wolf

Vincent Lane

1942—

Public housing administrator, business executive

Unlike most wealthy real estate developers in the United States, Vincent Lane has spent his career working on both the private and public sides of the low-income housing business. While continuing his own highly successful development firm, Lane became a figure of national importance in 1988, when he assumed control of the Chicago Housing Authority (CHA), the nation's second largest provider of public housing. Since then, Lane has become a renowned consultant on housing issues throughout the country and served as part of the advisory committee that chose Henry Cisneros as President Bill Clinton's secretary of Housing and Urban Development.

The CHA had a long and well-deserved reputation as one of the worst-run housing authorities in the country, many of its 46,000 apartments located in high-rise monstrosities infamous as centers of crime, drugs, and gang warfare. Lane was given virtually no chance of successfully turning around this massive urban disaster—indeed, many experts believe that all such high-rise public housing should be torn down. But in the first five years of his tenure at the CHA, Lane brought to his job a combination of energy and new ideas that has given tens of thousands of public housing residents in Chicago some hope for a better future. And at the same time, Lane has

quietly become one of the nation's largest landlords, his private business concerns now owning or managing upwards of 40,000 residential units nationwide.

Lane often explains his ability to gain the confidence and respect of poor Chicagoans by describing himself as a "country person," as he told Jorge Casuso of the *Chicago Tribune*. Lane was born March 29, 1942, in the small Mississippi town of West Point, where his father, Doyle, worked at a sawmill and his mother Berthe Lee ran a strict household. It was Berthe Lee who first thought of moving her three sons to Chicago, since factory jobs were plentiful there during World War II and daily life was not officially segregated by race. In July of 1942, when Vincent Lane was just four months old, Berthe led the Lane family to the South Side of Chicago and a new life far removed from the one they had known in rural Mississippi.

Doyle Lane soon found work in a copper smelting factory, and the Lanes moved into an apartment above a grocery store near Comiskey Park. Across the street from their flat was Wentworth Gardens, an example of Chicago's recent commitment to provide housing for citizens too poor to afford it otherwise. As a young boy, Lane remembered envying the

At a Glance. . .

Born March 29, 1942, in West Point, MS; son of Doyle (a factory worker) and Berthe Lee Lane; married, c. 1965 (divorced, 1971); children: three sons. *Education:* Roosevelt University, B.S., 1966; University of Chicago, M.B.A., 1973.

U.S. Immigration and Naturalization Service, became supervisor, mid-1960s; worked variously in the accounting departments of institutions including Mt. Sinai Hospital, International Harvester, and U.S. Steel; Woodlawn Community Development Corporation, Chicago, senior vice-president, 1972-1976; president and general manager of Urban Services and Development, Inc., and LSM Venture Associates (housing management companies), 1976-88; Chicago Housing Authority, executive director, 1988-91, chairman, 1988—; American Community Housing Associates, Inc., Chicago, chief executive, 1991—. Member of the board of directors of many Chicago organizations, included United Charities, Goodman Theatre, Hispanic Housing Development Corporation, and National Association of Severely Distressed Public Housing.

Awards: Housing and Urban Development (HUD) Regional Award for minority developer of the year, 1986; HUD certificate of special achievement, 1989; named by *U.S. News & World Report* as one of its "National Heroes of 1991."

Addresses: *Office*—Chicago Housing Authority, 22 West Madison, Chicago, IL 60602; or, American Community Housing Associates, Inc., 343 South Dearborn, Suite 1500, Chicago, IL 60604.

residents of Wentworth Gardens their tidy and relatively comfortable homes; at that time, the CHA was a small organization able to screen the backgrounds of its multiethnic clients before awarding them one of its new apartments or semi-detached homes. As a result, public housing such as Wentworth Gardens was highly sought after and generally free of crime. "Wentworth parents," Lane recalled in an interview with Paul Glastris for *U.S. News & World Report*, "were the type who showed up at PTA meetings."

That situation changed rapidly in the 1950s. With the city's swelling population of impoverished minorities, the CHA was forced to admit virtually anyone who applied, housing many in new high-rise structures that have remained a plague on the city ever since. To escape their deteriorating neighborhood, the Lanes moved farther south to the city of Englewood in 1957, when Vincent was fifteen years old. His father was able to buy and renovate a number of apartment buildings there, and Vincent became familiar with the ins and outs of routine construction techniques and the economics of housing.

A Budding Entrepreneur

While pursuing a degree in business from Chicago's Roosevelt University, Lane worked at the U.S. Immigration and Naturalization Service, eventually becoming a supervisor; after finishing his degree in 1966, he held important positions in the accounting departments of Mt. Sinai Hospital, International Harvester, and U.S. Steel. But the ambitious young Lane felt thwarted in the corporate world by subtle forms of discrimination. "I could speak better than they could, I could write better, I carried a bigger load," Lane noted in the *Chicago Tribune*. "Skin color was the only difference."

Lane proved to be a born entrepreneur. He attended night classes at the University of Chicago's prestigious business school, receiving an M.B.A. in 1973, and took a job as senior vice-president of the Woodlawn Community Development Corporation. Woodlawn Development, part of the Woodlawn Organization founded by the famed social activist Saul Alinsky, was involved in the development of nonprofit housing in and around the university's Hyde Park location on the city's South Side. The African American-run company allowed Lane to work in an atmosphere free of social handicaps, and he took pride in the low-cost housing developed by Woodlawn. The combination of social responsibility and capitalist incentives proved to be irresistible for Lane, who in 1976 formed his own housing management company, Urban Services and Development.

Created in partnership with two other investors, Urban Services became a specialist in the politically complex development of federally subsidized housing projects. Such undertakings usually involved the coordination of government funds (under the Department of Housing and Urban Development [HUD]) and a private contractor/manager such as Urban Services, which would build or manage a low-income housing complex for a stated fee. Lane also formed a second company called LSM Venture Associates, which along with Urban Services developed ten large, federally financed real estate projects between 1976 and 1988. Lane's work as a developer made him a millionaire and gave him backroom experience at HUD, the key organization for anyone interested in public housing in the United States.

Became Head of the Chicago Housing Authority

Chicago remained the center of Lane's activities, and the center of Chicago public housing remained the Chicago Housing Authority. When Eugene Sawyer, then acting mayor of the city following the death of Mayor Richard J. Daley, began searching for a new CHA chief in 1988, the agency had used up eight directors in the preceding five years and was widely perceived as a corrupt, inefficient bureaucracy. High-rise complexes such as Cabrini-Green and the Robert Taylor Homes were recognized nationally as examples of urban decay in its most advanced state. HUD was threatening to take control of the CHA, so badly managed were its 40,000 apartments, and a growing number of observers believed that most of its buildings should simply be torn down.

In the spring of 1988, Vincent Lane was nominated by Mayor Sawyer to become executive director of the CHA, with former Illinois governor Richard Ogilvie to be chairman. On May 10, however, Ogilvie died of a heart attack, and Lane lobbied for both titles and a free hand to restore order in the CHA system. Support for Lane was so strong that arrangements were made that allowed him to assume his new duties while continuing to run his private companies, which in many instances received funds from the CHA.

"Operation Clean Sweep"

Once his nomination was approved by the city council, Lane gave early notice that his reign would be unlike those of previous CHA directors. He selected what was probably the worst of all CHA sites, the Rockwell Gardens development, where rival street gangs were in the midst of a war for control of the buildings, and in September of 1988 led a force of 60 police officers and a handful of CHA employees on what he called a "security sweep" of the largest building. A single, temporary entrance was put up in the development, and officers combed the building room by room for drugs and weapons. All legal residents of the building were issued photo IDs, and all others were escorted out. The raid made headlines in Chicago as a dramatic example of Lane's commitment to cleaning up the projects. "Operation Clean Sweep," as it came to be called, also resulted in a substantial decrease in robberies and murders in the Rockwell Gardens development.

After agreeing with the American Civil Liberties Union to limit the scope of the searches, Lane's men went on to "sweep" 55 of the CHA's 155 high-rise buildings in the next three years, in the process winning national recognition for Lane. The director made a similar assault on the CHA's sluggish bureaucracy, firing many upper-level administrators and transferring or firing many managers of the organization's 19 largest complexes, some of whom had become tools of the local gangs. In addition, Lane's staff tightened accounting procedures and made every effort to cut costs. In recognition of its new discipline, HUD has increased federal grants to the CHA every year since Lane's arrival. Although his policies have been widely praised, some critics believe that Lane is "the captain of the Titanic," as Ed Marciniak told the *Tribune*. "While he turns one development around, four or five are going down the tubes."

Lane, however, argues that he will succeed in cleaning up *all* of Chicago's public housing. He told *Prime Time Live* correspondent Judd Rose that he plans to push the heavily armed gangs and druglords out of the housing projects and into "Lake Michigan" or, better yet, "into suburbia," where the problems of drugs and violence will gain immediate national attention and be eradicated instead of tolerat-

---

"This country has a standard for normal people, and a lower standard for poor people."

---

ed. At the root of the housing project nightmare is the fact that "this country has a standard for normal people, and a [lower] standard for poor people," Lane explained to Rose. Lane feels compelled to devote his life's work to improving those standards for the disadvantaged.

Unveiled Lake Parc Place

In 1992 Lane showcased a $17 million experimental project in mixed-income housing: Lake Parc Place contains nearly 300 apartments that have been divided among both the unemployed poor and working class families, with all applicants carefully screened before admittance. Lane believes that working families can be attracted to such a development by low rents and quality building, and once there will serve as both an inspiration and a peacekeeping force to the poorer residents. Forcing tenants to take responsibility for their building, he makes neighborhood patrols and grounds upkeep a mandatory part of each rental agreement and sees to the enforcement of curfews for the project's children.

In addition to his groundbreaking work for the CHA, Lane expanded his private business concerns in 1991, becoming chief executive of American Community Housing Associates, a newly formed for-profit company. American Community Housing struck a deal with a California company to buy some or all of its 40,000 low-income residential units in 26 states, an acquisition that would make Lane's firm the largest black-owned real estate company in the United States.

But Lane realizes that his other concern, namely the problems of the Chicago Housing Authority, remain far from over. In October of 1992, for instance, seven-year-old Cabrini-Green resident Dantrell Davis was shot and killed by a sniper's bullet while walking to school with his mother. And so Lane continues to struggle with the grim realities of public housing in Chicago.

Sources

Business Week, October 28, 1991.
Chicago Tribune, July 22, 1990.
Fortune, November 20, 1989.
Newsweek, August 19, 1991; March 15, 1993.
U.S. News & World Report, August 26/September 2, 1991.

Additional information for this sketch was obtained from a December 17, 1992 broadcast of ABC-TV's *Prime Time Live*. Lane was also profiled on ABC's *World News Tonight* in July of 1992.

—*Jonathan Martin*

Spike Lee

1957—

Filmmaker

"Fight the power," the theme song to his 1989 film *Do the Right Thing,* could easily be Spike Lee's personal motto. From his earliest days as a student filmmaker to his $33-million epic *Malcolm X,* Lee has shown a willingness to tackle prickly issues of relevance to the black community—and has savored every ounce of controversy his films invariably produce. "Spike loves to fight," the filmmaker's friend and business associate Nelson George told *Vanity Fair.* "There's a gleeful look he gets, a certain kind of excitement in his eyes when shit is being stirred up." "I guess you could call me an instigator," Lee admitted in an interview with *Vogue.*

Although the bane of Hollywood executives, Lee's delight in playing the provocateur has not only made his own films bankable, but has also created an industry-wide awareness of an untapped market niche. Following the unforseen box office success of Lee's earliest films, Hollywood's gates have opened to a new generation of young African American filmmakers. "Spike put this trend in vogue," Warner Bros. executive vice president Mark Canton told *Time.* "His talent opened the door for others." Lee relishes his role as path-paver. "Every time there is a success," he explained to *Ebony,* "it makes it easier for other blacks. The industry is more receptive than it

has ever been for black films and black actors. We have so many stories to tell, but we can't do them all. We just need more black filmmakers."

Shelton Jackson Lee was born in Atlanta, Georgia, on the eve of the civil rights era. He grew up in Brooklyn, New York, an area that would figure largely in his work as a mature filmmaker. Lee's awareness of his African American identity was established at an early age. His mother, Jacquelyn, infected her children with a schoolteacher's enthusiasm for black art and literature. "I was forced to read Langston Hughes, that kind of stuff," Lee told *Vanity Fair.* "And I'm glad my mother made me do that." His father, Bill, an accomplished jazz musician, introduced him to African American jazz and folk legends like Miles Davis and Odetta.

By the time he was old enough to attend school, the already independent Lee had earned the nickname his mother had given him as an infant, Spike—an allusion to his toughness. When he and his siblings were offered the option of attending the predominantly white private school where his mother taught, Lee opted instead to go the public route, where he would be assured of the companionship of black peers. "Spike used to point out the differences in our friends,"

At a Glance...

Born Shelton Jackson Lee, March 20, 1957, in Atlanta, GA; son of William (a musician and composer) and Jacquelyn (a teacher; maiden name, Shelton) Lee. *Education:* Morehouse College, B.A., 1979; New York University, M.F.A., 1982.

Screenwriter, director, actor. Directed *Joe's Bed-Stuy Barbershop: We Cut Heads,* 1982; launched Hollywood career with low-budget, black-and-white film *She's Gotta Have It,* 1986; also director of music videos and commercials for Nike, Levi-Strauss, and Diet Coke. Opened film production studio 40 Acres and a Mule, 1987, and first Spike's Joint promotional outlet, 1990.

Awards: 1983 Motion Picture Arts and Sciences' Student Academy Award for *Joe's Bed-Stuy Barbershop: We Cut Heads;* Cannes Film Festival's Prix de Jeunesse, 1986, for *She's Gotta Have It;* two Academy Award nominations for *Do the Right Thing.*

Addresses: *Office*—40 Acres and a Mule Filmworks, 124 DeKalb Ave., Brooklyn, NY 11217.

recalled his sister Joie, who was a private school student. "By the time I was a senior," she told *Mother Jones,* "I was being channeled into white colleges." Lee chose to go to his father's and grandfather's all-black alma mater, Morehouse College, where he majored in mass communication.

Pursued Film Career

It was at Morehouse that Lee found his calling. Following his mother's unexpected death in 1977, Lee's friends tried to cheer him with frequent trips to the movies. He quickly became a fan of directors Bernardo Bertolucci, Martin Scorsese, and Akira Kurosawa. But it wasn't until he had seen Michael Cimino's *Deer Hunter* that Lee knew the die was cast. His friend John Wilson recalled their conversation on the ride home from the film in an interview with *Vanity Fair.* "John, I know what I want to do," Lee had said. "I want to make films." But not just any films: Lee wanted to make films that would capture the black experience, and he was willing to do so by whatever means necessary. "Spike didn't just want to get in the door of the house," Wilson explained. "He wanted to get in, rearrange the furniture—then go back and publicize the password."

Lee pursued his passion at New York University, where he enrolled in the Tisch School of Arts graduate film program. One of only a handful of African American students, he wasted no time incurring the wrath of his instructors with his affinity for "rearranging the furniture." As his first-year project, Lee produced a ten-minute short, *The Answer,* in which a black screenwriter is assigned to remake D.W. Griffith's classic film *The Birth of a Nation. The Answer* was panned. Although the film program's director, Eleanor Hamerow, told the *New York Times,* "it's hard to redo *Birth of a Nation* in ten minutes," Lee suspected that his critics were offended by his digs at the legendary director's stereotypical portrayals of black characters. "I was told I was whiskers away from being kicked out," he told *Mother Jones.* "They really didn't like me saying anything bad about D.W. Griffith, for sure."

Hardly deterred, Lee went on to produce a 45-minute film that won him the 1983 Motion Picture Arts and Sciences' Student Academy Award, *Joe's Bed-Stuy Barbershop: We Cut Heads.* Although the honor enhanced his credibility as a director, it didn't pay the bills. Faced with the reality of survival, Lee worked for a movie distribution house cleaning and shipping film while hustling funds for a semi-autobiographical film, *The Messenger.*

A coming-of-age story about a young bicycle messenger, *The Messenger* was aborted prematurely when sufficient funding failed to materialize. "We were in pre-production the entire summer of 1984, waiting on this money to come, and it never did," Lee told *Vanity Fair.* "Then, finally, I pulled the plug. I let a lot of people down, crew members and actors that turned down work. I wasn't the most popular person. We were devastated." But all was not lost; Lee had learned his lesson. "I saw I made the classic mistakes of a young filmmaker, to be overly ambitious, do something beyond my means and capabilities," he said. "Going through the fire just made me more hungry, more determined that I couldn't fail again."

Scored a Surprise Hit with *She's Gotta Have It*

When he filmed *She's Gotta Have It* a year later, Lee's determination payed off. Made on a shoestring $175,000 budget in just twelve days, the black-and-white picture was shot on one location with a limited cast and edited on a rented machine in Lee's apartment. By the time it was completed, Lee was so deeply in debt that his processing lab threatened to auction off the film's negative.

After Island Pictures agreed to distribute it, *She's Gotta Have It* finally opened in 1986. A light comedy centering on sex-loving artist Nola Darling and her relationships with three men, the film pokes fun at gender relations and offers an insightful spin on stereotypical macho male roles. It packed houses not only with the black audience Lee had anticipated, but also with a crossover, art-house crowd. Grossing over $7 million, the low-budget film was a surprise hit.

With the success of *She's Gotta Have It,* Lee became known in cinematic circles not only as a director, but also as a comic actor. Mars Blackmon—one of Nola's rival lovers, played by Lee—won an instant following with his now-famous line, "Please baby, please baby, please baby, baby, baby, please." "After *She's Gotta Have It,* Spike could've gone a long way with Mars Blackmon," the film's co-producer Monty Ross told *Mother Jones.* "He could've done *Mars Blackmon the Sequel, Mars Blackmon Part 5.*" Not anxious to be typecast, though, Lee "said to the studios 'Mars Blackmon is dead.'"

School Daze: A Microcosm of Black Life

With a major hit under his belt and the backing of Island Pictures, Lee had more latitude with his next film, a musical called *School Daze.* An exposé of color discrimination within the black community, *School Daze* draws on Lee's years at Morehouse. "The people with the money," he told the *New York Times,* "most of them have light skin. They have the Porsches, the B.M.W.'s, the quote good hair unquote. The others, the kids from the rural south, have bad, kinky hair. When I was in school, we saw all this going on." This black caste system, Lee explained to *Newsweek,* was not a limited phenomenon. "I used the black college as a microcosm of black life."

School Daze created a brouhaha in the black community: while many applauded Lee's efforts to explore a complex social problem, others were offended by his willingness to "air dirty laundry." Everyone agreed that the film was controversial. When production costs reached $4 million, Island Pictures got hot feet and pulled out. Within two days, Lee had arranged a deal with Columbia Pictures that included an additional $2 million in production costs. But Columbia, then under the direction of David Puttnam, apparently misunderstood the film's true nature. "They saw music, they saw dancing, they saw comedy," Lee told *Mother Jones.* By the time *School Daze* was released in 1988, Puttnam had been ousted. Despite the fact that the studio's new management failed to promote it, the film grossed $15 million.

Explored Racial Tensions in *Do the Right Thing*

School Daze established Lee's reputation as a director ready to seize heady issues by the horns. *Do the Right Thing,* released in 1989, confirmed it. The story of simmering racial tension between Italian and African Americans in the Bedford-Stuyvesant section of Brooklyn, the film becomes a call to arms when violence erupts in response to the killing of a black man by white police

> "No other Black contemporary entertainer can claim to enlighten so many young Black people."
> —*John Singleton*

officers. It ends on a note of seeming ambiguity with two irreconcilable quotes: Martin Luther King's, "The old law of an eye for an eye leaves everyone blind." followed by Malcolm X's, "I am not against violence in self-defense. I don't even call it violence when it's self-defense. I call it intelligence."

The meaning of "the right thing," Lee told *People,* is not ambiguous. "Black America is tired of having their brothers and sisters murdered by the police for no reason other than being black." "I'm not advocating violence," he continued. "I'm saying I can understand it. If the people are frustrated and feel oppressed and feel this is the only way they can act, I understand."

Critical response to the film was both enthusiastic and wary. Media critic Roger Ebert called it "the most honest, complex and unblinking film I have ever seen about the subject of racism." Others voiced warnings of possible violence. *New York* magazine said, "Lee appears to be endorsing the outcome, and if some audiences go wild he's partly responsible."

Striking a Balance: *Mo' Better Blues*

Despite the fact that *Do the Right Thing* failed to inspire the predicted violence, Lee chose a lighter topic for his next film—a romance. The saga of a self-centered jazz trumpeter, Bleek Gilliam, whose personal life plays second fiddle to his music, "*Mo' Better Blues* is about relationships," Lee explained to *Ebony.* "It's not only about man-woman relationships, but about relationships in general—Bleek's relationship to his father and his manager, and his relationship with two female friends. Bleek's true love is music, and he is trying to find the right balance."

Bleek's character was inspired by Lee's jazz-musician

father, Bill Lee, who wrote the film's score. "Bleek is my father's nickname," Lee told *People*. The character's dilemma—the need to temper the obsessive nature of the creative act—however, has universal relevance. That theme, *Newsweek* suggested, is one with which the director himself can readily identify.

Although recognized for its technical mastery and snappy score—partially the result of a $10 million budget—*Mo' Better Blues* received tepid reviews. "The movie is all notions and no shape," said the *New Yorker,* "hard, fierce blowing rather than real music." And more than one critic took offense at Lee's shallow treatment of female characters and ethnic stereotyping of Jewish jazz club owners Moe and Josh Flatbush.

Examined Interracial Love in *Jungle Fever*

In his next film, *Jungle Fever,* Lee explored the theme of romance further—but this time, from a more provocative slant. Inspired by the 1989 murder of black teenager Yusuf Hawkins by a mob of Italian-American youths, *Jungle Fever* examines the sexual mythology that surrounds interracial romance. "Yusuf was killed because they thought he was the black boyfriend of one of the girls in the neighborhood," Lee told *Newsweek*. "What it comes down to is that white males have problems with black men's sexuality. It's as plain and simple as that. They think we've got a hold on their women."

Jungle Fever looks at issues of race, class, and gender by focusing on community response to the office affair of a married, black architect and his Italian-American secretary. Lee concludes that interracial relationships are fueled by culturally based, stereotypical expectations. "You were curious about black . . . I was curious about white," the architect explains when the couple parts ways. But Lee insisted in an interview with *Newsweek* that the film does not advocate separatism. The characters aren't meant "to represent every interracial couple. This is just one couple that came together because of sexual mythology."

Although it received mixed reviews, *Jungle Fever* succeeded in whetting the appetite of Lee groupies for further controversy. *Malcolm X,* Lee's pièce de résistance, satisfied even the most voracious.

Malcolm X

Sparking controversy from the moment of its inception, the making of *Malcolm X* became a personal mission for Lee, who had long been an admirer of the legendary black leader. Vowing to cut no corners, Lee planned a biographical film of epic proportions that required months of research, numerous interviews, and even an unprecedented trip to Saudi Arabia for authentic footage of Malcolm's pilgrimage to the holy city of Mecca; taken shortly before his assassination in 1965, this journey that is said to have brought on a significant transformation in Malcolm's ideology.

The final product, a three-hour-and-21-minute production, traces Malcolm X's development from his impoverished, rural roots to his final years as an ever-evolving activist. "I knew this was going to be the toughest thing I ever did," Lee told *Time*. "The film is huge in the canvas we had to cover and in the complexity of Malcolm X."

Lee fought tooth and nail to win the right to direct the film and to defend his vision of Malcolm X from the start. When he learned of plans by Warner Bros. to make *Malcolm X,* Norman Jewison had already been chosen as its director. After Lee told the *New York Times* that he had a "big problem" with a white man directing the film, Jewison agreed to bow out.

Lee, however, faced considerable resistance to his role as director of the film. Led by poet and activist Amiri Baraka (formerly LeRoi Jones), an ad hoc group that called itself the United Front to Preserve the Memory of Malcolm X and the Cultural Revolution voiced its opposition to Lee's direction in an open letter. "Our distress about Spike's making a film on Malcolm is based on our analysis of the [exploitative] films he has already made," *Ebony* quoted the group as saying.

But Lee's spat with Baraka was only a momentary setback. He still had to deal with reworking an unsatisfactory script, which had been started by African American novelist James Baldwin shortly before his death and completed by writer Arnold Perl. And when Lee first locked horns with Warner Bros. over *Malcolm X's* budget, he was bracing for another prolonged battle.

Initially, the director had requested $40 million for the film—an amount that was necessary, he claimed, in order to accurately portray all of the phases of his subject's life. The studio countered with a $20-million offer, prompting Lee to raise an additional $8.5 million by selling foreign rights to the film, kick in a portion of his own $3-million salary, and, to make up the difference, acquire the backing of a host of black celebrities, including Bill Cosby, Oprah Winfrey, Michael Jordan, Janet Jackson, and Prince—much to the studio's embarrassment. "It didn't look good for Warner Bros. that Spike had to go to prominent African Americans to finish the movie," noted *Entertainment Weekly*. When the film was completed, Barry Reardon, the studio's president of distribution, conceded, "Spike did a fabulous job. He knows theaters, he's very smart. This is Oscars all the way."

Although *Malcolm X* received no Oscars, the film played a significant role in the elevation of the black leader to mythic status; it also spawned a cultural phenomenon often referred to as "Malcolm-mania." By the time the movie was released, its logo, a bold "X," was pasted on everything from a ubiquitous baseball cap to posters, postcards, and T-shirts. What's more, a plethora of spin-off products was born, ranging from serious scholarly studies to a plastic Malcolm X doll, complete with podium and audio cassette. Promotional merchandise for the film was marketed by Lee himself through Spike's Joint, a chain of stores that comprise a portion of the director's growing business empire.

Lee is quick to defend himself against charges of commercialism. In fact, he says, Malcolm X's philosophy—that African Americans need to build their own economic base—is the motivation for his business investments. "I think we've done more to hold ourselves back than anybody," Lee told *Esquire.* "If anybody's seen all my films, I put most of the blame on our shoulders and say, 'Look, we're gonna have to do for ourselves.'. . . I feel we really have to address our financial base as a people."

Lee's innate ability to "do for himself," his father suggested in an interview with *Mother Jones,* is the key to his success as a filmmaker. "Spike was kind of chosen," he explained. "I think there was something spiritual about it. He inherited it from his family. [The ability] to make a statement." Fellow filmmaker John Singleton, writing in *Essence,* said of Lee, "No other Black contemporary entertainer can claim to enlighten so many young Black people." But, as he stated in the *New York Times,* Lee wants even more to prove "that an all-black film directed by a black person can still be universal."

In mid-1993 Lee began shooting his seventh feature film, *Crooklyn,* a comic tribute to his childhood memories of life in Brooklyn in the 1970s.

Selected writings

Films: Screenwriter and director

Joe's Bed-Stuy Barbershop: We Cut Heads, 1982.
She's Gotta Have It, released by Island, 1986.
School Daze, released by Columbia, 1988.
Do the Right Thing, released by Universal Pictures, 1989.
Mo' Better Blues, released by Universal Pictures, 1990.
Jungle Fever, released by Universal Pictures, 1991.

(Coauthor) *Malcolm X,* released by Warner Bros., 1992.

Other writings

Spike Lee's Gotta Have It: Inside Guerilla Filmmaking, Simon & Schuster, 1987.
(With Lisa Jones) *Uplift the Race: The Construction of School Daze,* Simon & Schuster, 1988.
Do the Right Thing: The New Spike Lee Joint, Simon & Schuster, 1989.
Mo' Better Blues, Simon & Schuster, 1990.
By Any Means Necessary: The Trials and Tribulations of Making Malcolm X, Hyperion, 1992.

Sources

America, August 19, 1989; September 15, 1990; August 10, 1991.
American Film, July/August 1989; September 1989.
Ann Arbor News, October 30, 1992; November 18, 1992.
Commonweal, November 8, 1991.
Detroit News, January 26, 1992.
Ebony, November 1991.
Emerge, November 1991, pp. 28-32.
Entertainment Weekly, November 27, 1992.
Esquire, August 1991.
Essence, November 1991, p. 64.
Film Comment, July/August 1989.
Jet, June 10, 1991.
Maclean's, February 17, 1992, p. 60.
Mother Jones, September 1989.
Ms., September/October 1991.
Newsweek, February 15, 1988; August 6, 1990; June 10, 1991; February 3, 1992, p. 30; November 16, 1992, pp. 67-72.
New York, June 17, 1991.
New Yorker, August 13, 1990; June 17, 1991; October 12, 1992.
New York Times, August 9, 1987; November 15, 1992; November 29, 1992; December 6, 1992.
People, July 10, 1989; March 5, 1990; August 13, 1990; June 22, 1992.
Rolling Stone, November 26, 1992, pp. 36-40, 80-81.
Time, June 17, 1991; March 16, 1992.
Upscale, October/November 1992.
Vanity Fair, June 1991, pp. 70, 80-92.
Video, February 1990; February 1991.
Vogue, August 1990.

—Nina Goldstein

Hughie Lee-Smith

1915—

Artist, educator

Like his paintings, artist Hughie Lee-Smith is generally perceived as being somewhat enigmatic. Although his works have been exhibited at museums, schools, and galleries around the United States, have earned him many honors and awards, and have even hung on the set of *The Cosby Show* on national television, Lee-Smith did not enjoy a major solo exhibition of his work until fifty years after he began painting. His first retrospective exhibit—at the New Jersey State Museum in Trenton in 1988—came when he was 73 years old.

Unlike his contemporary, painter Jacob Lawrence, New Jersey-based Lee-Smith didn't get wide notice as a young man. Slowly, however, he gained national recognition while turning out a steady stream of oil paintings. In addition, he has done commissioned murals for the U.S. Navy, as well as an impressive series of lithographic prints. Lee-Smith's works, which often feature the fantastic elements of magical realism and surrealism, are well known for their hard-hitting social commentary. Many critics have observed that his paintings bear a resemblance to the stylings of Italy's Giorgio de Chirico and American artist Edward Hopper.

Attention has not come quickly to Lee-Smith for a variety of reasons. First, his paintings often confront viewers with a world where black and white people maintain a cautious or uneasy distance from one another. Second, his work has mainly been shown in African American art exhibits and for many years remained largely unrecognized in mainstream art circles. Third, he chose to paint figuratively at a time when abstract expressionism was at its height.

Despite a lack of acclaim for half a century, Lee-Smith's past credits are impressive. In the 1980s alone he was awarded a day in his honor in Cleveland, Ohio; the key to the city of Hartford, Connecticut; honors from the Maryland Commission on Afro-American History and Culture; and prizes from the National Academy of Design and Audubon Artists. His works are included in the Evans-Tibbs collection in Washington, D.C., and have been displayed in museums such as the Cleveland Museum of Art, the Whitney Museum of American Art, and the Museum of Modern Art in New York City, as well as in galleries, including New York's June Kelly Gallery.

The selected works shown at the New Jersey State Museum retrospective in 1988 ranged from Lee-Smith's depictions of alienated youth in the 1940s through his desolate landscapes of the 1950s and sixties, to later scenes of isolated black and

At a Glance...

Born September 20, 1915, in Eustis, FL; son of Luther and Alice (Williams) Lee-Smith; married Mabel Louise Everett, 1940 (divorced, 1953); married Helen Nebraska, 1965 (divorced, 1974); married Patricia Thomas-Ferry, 1978; children: (first marriage) Christina. *Education:* Graduated from Cleveland Institute of Art, 1938; Wayne State University, B.S., 1953.

Worked for the Ohio Works Progress Administration and the Ford Factory at River Rouge during the 1930s and 1940s; did a series of lithographic prints; painted murals at the Great Lakes Naval Station in Illinois; taught art at Karamu House, Cleveland, late 1930s, the Grosse Pointe War Memorial in Michigan, 1955-56, Princeton Country Day School, NJ, 1963-65, Howard University, Washington, DC, 1969-71, the Art Students League, New York City, 1972-87, and elsewhere. Works shown in museums, schools, galleries, and collections across the U.S., including the American Negro Exposition, Chicago; Southside Community Art Center; Snowden Gallery; Detroit Artists Market; Cleveland Museum of Art; Whitney Museum of American Art; Museum of Modern Art; the June Kelly Gallery, New York City; and the Evans-Tibbs collection, Washington, DC. Council member, National Academy of Design, 1986-89. Had first retrospective show at the New Jersey State Museum, Trenton, 1988. *Military service:* Served in the U.S. Navy during World War II.

Selected awards: Bronze Plaque, Maryland Commission on Afro-American History and Culture, 1981; October 19, 1984 declared Hughie Lee-Smith Day, Cleveland, OH; key to Hartford, CT, 1984; awarded the Ralph Fabri, 1982, the Binny & Smith, 1983, the Emily Lowe, 1985, and the Len Everette Memorial, 1986, all from Audubon Artists, Inc.; National Academy of Design's Clarke Prize, 1959, and Ranger Fund Purchase, 1963 and 1977.

Addresses: c/o June Kelly Gallery, 591 Broadway, New York, NY 10012.

According to some art critics, what makes Lee-Smith unique is his ability to fuse the black experience in America with his own brand of surrealism. In her essay for the *Hughie Lee-Smith Retrospective Exhibition* catalogue, Lowery S. Sims, an associate curator in the department of twentieth-century art at the Metropolitan Museum of Art, wrote of the settings and images used in the artist's works: "Lee-Smith's dramas unfold on desolate beaches, or vacant lots bordering on a lake, or tenement buildings and disengaged, crumbling walls. Balls, balloons, ribbons, wires, poles, antennae, rotten piers, bricks and rocks, labyrinths and, more recently, antique sculpture fragments and mannikins [sic] are the accoutrements that charge these scenes with metaphorical and allegorical content that eludes definitive interpretations."

Elsa Honig Fine, writing in *The Afro-American Artist: A Search for Identity*, described the artist's work as "captur[ing] the loneliness and alienation of contemporary urban life through the emotive devices associated with the Surrealists—a sharply converging perspective and an 'ambiguous sense of nearness and distance' between figure and background. Lee-Smith's people are alienated from each other and from the space that encloses them." And in *American Artist* magazine, Carol Wald characterized Lee-Smith's paintings as "haunting" and "memorable," adding, "Figures in them move silently across the stage of a barren universe and seem to be teetering on the very edge of another kind of reality . . . perhaps that of sleep. Often the subject is a desolate, dark landscape occupied by one or a few solitary figures related somehow by their proximity but nevertheless adrift in separate worlds of being and action."

Whatever qualities may be attributed to Lee-Smith's paintings, the artist offered his own analysis of his work in *American Artist:* "I think my paintings have to do with an invisible life—a reality on a different level." And in an interview with Inga Saffron for the *Philadelphia Inquirer*, he said that his paintings "deal with alienation, which is a fact of life . . . separation of the races . . . and of races coming together."

Lee-Smith's paintings also reflect his childhood experiences. After his birth in Eustis, Florida, on September 20, 1915, his family moved to Atlanta and then to Cleveland. His parents divorced when he was still quite young, and his mother raised him during the Great Depression. "I was already aiming at perfection," he told Wald, "at being good at whatever I was doing. . . . I drew all the time, and it became a natural thing. I breathed it; I dreamed it. Art was my whole being, and I knew from an early age that it was my mission." Lee-Smith's mother encouraged him in his artistic pursuits and helped him gain admission to a class for gifted children at the Cleveland Museum of Art. From then on he was hooked.

When he was twenty years old, Lee-Smith won a *Scholastic* magazine competition that enabled him to study on a one-year scholarship at the Art School of the Detroit Society of

white men and women confronting or refusing to confront one another. While allusions to the isolation of African Americans are present, the paintings also portray the universality of human beings' inability to make contact with each other.

Arts and Crafts. Later, he taught art at Karamu House in Cleveland and studied at the Cleveland Institute of Art on another scholarship, this time from the Gilpin Players, the resident company of the Karamu Theatre.

In addition to attending the Cleveland Institute of Art, from which he graduated in 1938, Lee-Smith also studied at Wayne State University in Detroit, where he received his bachelor's degree in art education in 1953. His early works were shown mostly in Chicago and Detroit, at the Southside Community Art Center, the Snowden Gallery, and the Detroit Artists Market. His work was also displayed at a 1940 exhibit of art at the American Negro Exposition in Chicago.

Gravitated Toward Artistic Group in 1940s

Lee-Smith was still a child during the Harlem Renaissance, a period of heightened literary and artistic activity among blacks centered in New York City's Harlem during the 1920s. As a young man in the 1940s, however, he gravitated toward an artistic group that met at the Southside Community Art Center in Chicago. It included painter Rex Goreleigh, as well as poet Gwendolyn Brooks. Around the same time, Lee-Smith met artist Joseph Hirsch, who had seen the young painter's work in Chicago and later saw to his admission to the prestigious National Academy of Design. Lee-Smith would serve on the academy's council over forty years later.

To support himself as an artist during the 1930s and 1940s, Lee-Smith worked for the Ohio Works Progress Administration (WPA) and the Ford Factory at River Rouge while turning out a series of lithographic prints. He received an award from the Cleveland Museum for freehand drawing in 1938 and for his lithographs in 1939 and 1940. Commenting on the style of the lithographs, James Porter wrote in *Modern Negro Art,* "Lee-Smith takes huge delight in his expert ability as a draftsman, and for him line and form are the essence of the picture. Into this mold he pours all the exciting experience that his mind can call up—sometimes with startling results."

Painted Murals on African Americans in History for U.S. Navy

Lee-Smith continued working on his art while serving as a seaman in the U.S. Navy during World War II. The Works Progress Administration assigned him to paint murals with patriotic subjects at the Great Lakes Naval Station in Illinois. "They were on the theme of the Negro in U.S. history [and] were intended to build morale with black recruits," he recalled in the *Chicago Free Weekly.* Having spent his time in the service stationed in the Chicago area, the city served as an inspiration for his early paintings. "I

have always thought that this part of the midwest affected the character of my palette," he added in the *Chicago Free Weekly.* "The climate, the weather—dark, dreary lugubrious days that darkened the colors. Those years in Chicago . . . also affected the way I see things politically, socially, philosophically."

Style Evolved From Realism to Surrealism

For Lee-Smith, art must reflect common daily life experiences. During the 1930s and 1940s he expressed himself through a kind of social realism, as illustrated by his dark, serious *Portrait of a Boy* (1938). From there his work became "primitivist," as reflected in his painting *Girl with Balloon* (1949-50), in which the elongated figure of a yearning girl stands in front of a simple shack. By the early 1950s, according to Sims, Lee-Smith's style underwent the change that still remains in his work today—the use of surrealist devices much like those used by Giorgio de Chirico.

> "Art was my whole being, and I knew from an early age that it was my mission."

Sims observed that such paintings as *The Scientist* (1949), *Impedimenta* (1958), and *Woman in Green Sweater* (1950s) "evoke de Chirico's celebration of the enigma." Elizabeth Ness of the *Village Voice* reacted to the riddle Lee-Smith presents in *The Scientist* as follows: "A black man . . . wearing sunglasses and a raincoat, stands alone near a coffin-size hole, as if he were the last man on earth; the sky threatens to burst into a storm. Is this man an agent of social change or social control? The artist wants us to consider the alternatives."

From the 1950s through the 1980s, Lee-Smith divided his time between the Midwest and Northeast, teaching art in Michigan, New Jersey, Washington, D.C., and New York City. His works were exhibited at various galleries, academic institutions, and museums, including the Museum of Modern Art and the Whitney Museum. Meanwhile, he steadily amassed awards, among them several from the National Academy of Design and Audubon Artists.

Brush Captured Racial and Urban Isolation

Before and during the civil rights movement of the 1960s, Lee-Smith often painted black figures set against the backdrop of inner cities. Such is the case in *Boy with a Tire*

(1952), *The Walls* (1952), *Slum Song* (1962), and *Ball-player* (1970). Aside from the more obvious symbols of racial separation in America, his paintings from this period portray subtle psychological tensions between blacks and whites. About one, *Man with Balloons* (c. 1960), *Village Voice* contributor Ness observed: "A black man holding a bouquet of pastel balloons is being followed by a white man who does not seem friendly, but isn't exactly threatening."

Before 1970 Lee-Smith was known as an elder statesman of black art. He told Douglas Davis of *Newsweek*, "We are concerned with communications, with glorifying our heroes, contributing to black pride. We look upon this as our historical mission." However, Lee-Smith has mixed feelings about art shows that contain only the works of African American artists. "There was a time during the 1960s when it was necessary to bring the reality of black artists into the consciousness of the mainstream. But there's a time limit on that sort of thing," he explained to Joy Hakanson Colby of the *Detroit News*. "If you're black, people can see that. But I guess that kind of label is part of the American racial fabric, and I just don't allow it to hinder me in any way."

Throughout the 1980s, Lee-Smith's works often focused on blacks and whites attempting to relate to each other. In *Counterpoise II* (1989), a puzzled, angry young black woman is left standing on a stage while a white woman walks away from her and blends in with the set in the background. In *End of Act One* (1987), a black woman walks away from a white counterpart, leaving her with a headless mannequin. Other paintings from both this phase in Lee-Smith's career and earlier periods highlight the artist's ongoing use of solitary figures to depict loneliness and alienation in contemporary life.

While there have been no major changes in Lee-Smith's style since the 1950s, several art critics contend that subtle variations have emerged in his works from the late 1980s and beyond. Vivien Raynor wrote in *ARTnews*: "He seems to stand closer to his subjects, incorporating more foliage and architectural detail; and perhaps there is more menace in his mystery. The color may be colder and harsher, too. But the imagery continues to be beautiful and the mood fatalistic." As for what Lee-Smith thinks about his style, he told Colby, "I've always felt a need to communicate on an emotional level with people. My paintings don't tell stories. they are about expressing emotion by means of form and color."

Selected works

Paintings

Portrait of a Boy, 1938.

The Scientist, 1949.
Girl with Balloon, 1949-50.
Bouquet, 1949.
Boy with a Tire, 1952.
The Walls, 1952.
The Piper, 1953.
Landscape with Black Man, 1953.
Impedimenta, 1958.
Woman in Green Sweater, 1950s.
Interval, 1960.
Man with Balloons, c. 1960.
Slum Song, 1962.
The Juggler #1, c. 1964.
Man Running, 1965.
The Other Side, 1960s.
Man Standing on His Head, 1970.
Ballplayer, 1970.
Trio, 1973.
Hard Hat, 1980.
Industrial Landscape, c. 1980.
Acropolis II, 1984.
Merry Go Round I, 1984.
Desert Elegy, 1987.
End of Act One, 1987.
Waiting, 1987.
Silent Riddle, 1988.
Curtain Call, 1989.
Counterpoise II, 1989.
Crossroads, 1991.
Temptation, 1991.
A Summer Spell, 1992.

Commissioned works

Idyllic Landscape (mosaic tile mural), Prudential and Deansbank Investment Corporation, McPherson Building, Washington, DC; *Cityscape* (mural painting), New Jersey State Council on the Arts, New Jersey State Commerce Building, Trenton; and *Navy Black History* (oil painting), U.S. Navy, Washington, DC, 1974.

Sources

Books

African-American Artists 1880-1987: Selections from the Evans-Tibbs Collection, Smithsonian Institution Traveling Service, in association with the University of Washington Press, 1989, pp. 78, 80, 120.
Cederholm, Theresa D., *Afro-American Artists: A Bio-Bibliographical Directory,* Boston Public Library, 1973, pp. 174-76.
Fine, Elsa Honig, *The Afro-American Artist: A Search*

for Identity, Holt, Rinehart & Winston, 1973, pp. 97-98, 142-45, 280.

Hedgepeth, Chester M., Jr., *Twentieth-Century African American Writers and Artists,* American Library Association, 1991, pp. 193-95.

Locke, Alain, *The Negro in Art: A Pictorial Record of the Negro Artist and of the Negro Theme in Art,* Associates in Negro Folk Education, 1940, pp. 126, 135.

Porter, James A., *Modern Negro Art,* Dryden Press, 1943, pp. 160-64.

Sims, Lowery S., essay in *Hughie Lee-Smith Retrospective Exhibition* (catalogue), New Jersey State Museum, 1988, pp. 1-35.

Periodicals

American Artist, October 1978, pp. 48-53, 101.
Art in America, February 1990, p. 168.
ARTnews, December 1987, pp. 156, 158; March 1989, pp. 124-31; March 1990, p. 176.
Arts New Jersey, Summer 1987.
Black Enterprise, December 1986, pp. 86, 88, 92.
Chicago Free Weekly, February 24, 1989, sec. 1, p. 6.
Detroit News, October 15, 1989, pp. 1M, 4M.
Ebony, May 1986, p. 50.
Emerge, May 1992.
Newsweek, June 22, 1970, pp. 89-90.
New York Times, October 17, 1987; December 4, 1988; March 12, 1989, p. 34; July 28, 1989.
Philadelphia Inquirer, December 19, 1988, pp. 1E, 4E.
Time Off, January 21, 1987, p. 21; October 3, 1990; October 24, 1990.
Village Voice, June 21, 1988.

—*Alison Carb Sussman*

Joe Louis

1914-1981

Professional boxer

Joe Louis is widely regarded as the greatest fighter in the history of boxing, and he was the most popular black athlete of his time. Known as the "Brown Bomber," Louis was heavyweight champion of the world for nearly 12 years and was never defeated during his reign. He defended his title 25 times, a total greater than the eight heavyweight champions before him combined. Of those defenses, 21 were won by knockout.

Louis possessed neither great speed of foot nor craftiness in the ring. What he did wield, however, were two fists that moved with jackhammer quickness and landed with incredible power. He also wore a deadpan expression while fighting that never changed as he dispatched his opponents. Louis's 68 victories as a professional boxer (he lost only three times) included 54 knockouts, and five of his knockouts occurred in the first round.

Joseph Louis Barrow's starting point on his road to fame could hardly have been more humble. He was born in a sharecropper's shack in Lexington, Alabama, one of eight children. His father, Munn, was committed to a mental institution when Louis was two. Two years later the family was told that Munn had died, although in 1938 it was discovered that he was still alive. When Louis was seven, his mother, Lily,

married Patrick Brooks, a widower with five children of his own.

Money was scarce in Louis's extended family. The children slept three to a bed, and young Joe walked barefoot to school. In search of jobs in the growing automobile industry, the family moved to Detroit. Louis's inadequate schooling down South landed him in a class with much younger children up North. His resulting embarrassment made him withdraw, and he developed a stammer. For many years he kept to himself and talked little.

After teachers told Louis's parents that their son would have to make a living with his hands—a prophetic statement, to be sure—he attended Bronson Trade School to study carpentry. When his stepfather was put out of work, Louis helped out with odd jobs. His hauling of ice blocks for an ice-wagon driver gave him massive shoulder muscles, which he put to work as a sparring partner at a local gym. He quit school at age 17, then got a job pushing truck bodies at the Briggs Automobile Factory for a dollar a day as he continued honing his boxing skills. As quoted by James Cox in the *Smithsonian,* Louis's son, Joe Jr., recalled: "My aunts and uncles told me they were absolutely flabbergasted when he [Joe Louis]

At a Glance. . .

Born Joseph Louis Barrow, May 13, 1914, in Lexington, AL; died of cardiac arrest, April 12, 1981, in Las Vegas, NV; son of Munn (a sharecropper) and Lily Barrow; married Marva Trotter, 1935 (divorced); married second wife, 1949 (divorced); married Rose Morgan, 1955 (marriage annulled); married Martha Jefferson, 1959; children: (both with Trotter) Jacqueline, Joe Jr.

Boxer. Worked odd jobs, hauling ice blocks, sparring at a local gym, and pushing truck bodies at the Briggs Automobile Factory in Detroit, MI, all while a teenager. Won 50 of 59 bouts as an amateur boxer; turned professional, 1934. Youngest boxer (aged 23) of his time to become heavyweight champion, 1937; held heavyweight title longer than any other boxer; defended title 25 times and retired without a defeat as champion; finished professional career with a record of 68-3, with 54 knockouts. Brief stint as a professional wrestler and co-owner of food franchise in the 1960s. Official greeter at Caesar's Palace in Las Vegas, NV, 1970s. *Military service:* Served in the U.S. Army, 1942-45.

Awards: Golden Gloves light-heavyweight champion of Detroit, 1933; National Amateur Athletic Union (NAAU) light-heavyweight champion, 1934; heavyweight champion of the world, 1937-49; elected to boxing's Hall of Fame, 1954; honored with a U.S. postage stamp honoring the 55th anniversary of his victorious rematch with Max Schmeling, June 22, 1993.

became a boxer because he was so quiet and peaceful. He was the most tranquil kid on the block.''

Louis's boxing talent developed rapidly and made him a winner in 50 of 59 amateur bouts, with 43 knockouts. In 1933 he won the National light-heavyweight Golden Gloves crown, then won the light-heavyweight finals in the National Amateur Athletic Union (NAAU) tournament the next year. Louis turned professional in 1934 under the management of John Roxborough, a black Detroit businessman and king of the illegal numbers rackets in the city's black neighborhoods, and Julian Black, a black Chicago-based mortician who was also involved in illegal gambling. Roxborough dropped the Barrow from Louis's name because he thought Joe Louis Barrow was too long for the pro.

Meanwhile, Julian Black hired Jack Blackburn, a top Midwest trainer with whom Louis developed a close friendship. Seeing that Louis had no speed, Blackburn taught him the flat-footed shuffle that became a Louis trademark. Moving around the ring was so foreign to Louis that in training he practiced stepping to diagrams drawn on the ring floor, like someone learning the cha-cha.

Odds Tipped Against Black Fighters

The status of blacks in boxing had been dealt a severe blow by the controversial Jack Johnson, who held the world heavyweight title from 1908 to 1915. Johnson invited the wrath of whites by chattering away to opponents in the ring and gloating after he knocked them down. At the time, the white public was also outraged by his romancing of white women in public. Due to this sensitivity to the Johnson legacy, Louis felt obligated to set an exemplary standard and live down every black stereotype. His managers gave him strict instructions on how to act in public, insisting that he never drink, smoke, or be seen alone with a white woman. He was also told never to exult when he was victorious over white opponents and never to grin or show any emotion in front of the press.

The word was spread that Louis was a shy man who was loyal to his country, didn't rock the boat, and read the Bible every night. Actually, the image was only partially true. Although he was modest, generous, and didn't drink or smoke, Louis allegedly liked the night life, spent money recklessly, and had romantic liaisons with both black and white women. However, he was discreet in these activities and received no bad publicity.

During his string of 22 wins without a loss in his first year as a pro, Louis was dubbed the ''Brown Bomber of Detroit.'' U.S. media coverage during the 1930s revealed a racist streak that permeated society. Journalists of that time often nicknamed African Americans with a reference to color or a black stereotype, and Louis was called everything from ''Shufflin' Joe'' to the ''coffee-colored kayo king.'' Many articles discussed the fighter as if he were an animal from the African jungle. Cartoonists depicted him with huge lips, and he was quoted in an exaggerated ''Uncle Remus'' dialect.

Fight promoter Mike Jacobs put the national spotlight on Louis by arranging a bout for him against former champion Primo Carnera at Yankee Stadium. Louis sent Carnera to the floor in the sixth round in 1934, then dropped former champion Max Baer in 1935. Mere hours before the Baer bout, the fighter married Marva Trotter, a 19-year-old Chicago stenographer. At age 21, Joe Louis was the most famous African American in the United States.

Louis Versus Schmeling: A Victory for Nazi Propagandists

One of the most well-known bouts in boxing history was Louis's first fight against the German Max Schmeling in 1936. Schmeling knocked out Louis, even though the "Brown Bomber" was a 10-to-1 favorite. The victory was trumpeted by Adolf Hitler's Nazis as proof of Aryan superiority over blacks. Racism reared its ugly head in the States, too, as hundreds of Americans sent congratulatory telegrams to Schmeling. Many sportswriters, especially those in the South, reported that Louis was finished, nothing but a flash in the pan. Embarrassed and angered by the defeat, Louis whipped himself into better shape and won seven bouts over the next eight months. Then, on June 22, 1937, he knocked out heavyweight champion James J. Braddock and became the new world champion. Just 23 years old, Louis had become the youngest man ever to hold the heavyweight crown.

Meanwhile, a second bout with Schmeling was scheduled for 1938. With the Nazi menace looming more ominously on the international horizon, this grudge match became a symbol of good versus evil. Cox wrote in the *Smithsonian* that "Louis-Schmeling II was no longer just a championship boxing match. It was a prelude to World War II." President Roosevelt actually met with Louis and told him how vital it was to triumph this time. The "Bomber" was ready. Overwhelmed from the opening bell, Schmeling was knocked out by his swarming opponent in the first round.

As Louis's popularity soared in the 1930s, he became an important model for the black struggle against white injustice. Chris Mead wrote in *Champion:* "To downtrodden blacks, Louis came to be a hero of fierce revolutionary proportions—a black man who trounced white men in hand-to-hand combat before a national audience." Some thought that Louis was an "Uncle Tom" and not involved enough in the fight for equality for people of color, but the champion contributed generously to many black causes. He also helped integrate football and baseball teams in army camps while serving in the military and refused to sit in segregated camp buses.

A Series of Blows in Personal Life

While still winning in the ring, Louis ran into personal problems that he couldn't punch out of his life. His marriage began failing, and he lost thousands of dollars betting on the golf course. Throughout his career, he was continually buying expensive gifts for friends and family

Posing for the camera, the Brown Bomber strikes his famous fighting stance before winning yet another bout.

and supporting a large entourage of freeloaders. To make matters worse, his managers took 50 percent of his winnings, while all training expenses were taken out of Louis's share. Louis didn't clear up his debts with the government until the mid-1960s.

In 1941 Roxborough, still managing Louis, was put in jail for two-and-a-half years for running his numbers operation. Then in 1942, Louis's beloved trainer Blackburn died of heart disease. As he absorbed these blows, Louis was blindsided by the government's demand for $117,000 in back taxes. To escape this financial hole, he began his so-called "bum-of-the-month" campaign. From December of 1940 through 1941, he took on one challenger every month. No heavyweight champion had ever undergone such a punishing schedule. The going wasn't entirely easy, as Louis almost lost to Billy Conn in a tough fight at the Polo Grounds. When journalists told Louis before the fight that Conn was too quick for him, Louis uttered his famous line, "He can run but he can't hide."

The Later Years

After he was drafted into the U.S. Army in 1942, Louis staged 96 boxing exhibitions for his fellow soldiers. But he was in even worse financial shape after his discharge. When he announced his retirement and gave up his title on March 1, 1949, a few months before turning 35, he owed income taxes of well over $1 million that were compounded by penalties and interest. This financial distress brought Louis back into the ring for an attempted comeback in the early 1950s, but age had finally caught up with him. Consecutive losses to Ezzard Charles and Rocky Marciano closed the book on his boxing career. He tried pro wrestling, then got involved in sports and commercial promotions. In 1969 Louis and his former victim Billy Conn set up the Joe Louis Food Franchise Corporation in an attempt to operate an interracial chain of food shops. During his last years he was an official "greeter" at Caesar's Palace in Las Vegas, Nevada.

Louis collapsed on a Manhattan street in 1969 and was hospitalized for a "physical breakdown." Later he said that the collapse resulted from cocaine use and that he had been plagued by fears of a murder plot against him. In 1970 the former champ was hospitalized for five months due to paranoid delusions. His health worsening, Louis suffered a number of strokes and heart problems in his final decade. He was confined to a wheelchair in 1977 following surgery to correct an aortic aneurysm. Death from cardiac arrest came to him in 1981 at the age of 66, mere hours after he attended the heavyweight championship fight between Larry Holmes and Trevor Berbick at Caesar's Palace.

Joe Louis remains among the best loved and most talented boxers in the history of the sport. His popularity helped pave the way toward breaking the color barrier in other sports as well—including Jackie Robinson's legendary entry into major league baseball. As Arthur Ashe wrote in *A Hard Road to Glory,* "Much of the goodwill for black athletes generated in the dozen years leading to the end of the war was due to the positive image that Louis had created."

Sources

Books

Ashe, Arthur R., Jr., *A Hard Road to Glory,* Warner, 1988, pp. 11-18.
Bromberg, Lester, *Boxing's Unforgettable Fights,* Ronald Press, 1962.
Fleischer, Nat, *The Heavyweight Championship: An Informal History of Heavyweight Boxing from 1719 to the Present Day,* Putnam, 1949, revised, 1961.
Louis, Joe, *My Life Story,* Duell, Sloan & Pearce, 1947.
McGowen, Deane, essay in *The New York Times Book of Sports Legends,* edited by Joseph J. Vecchione, Times Books, 1991, pp. 171-183.
Mead, Chris, *Champion,* Scribners, 1985.
Nagler, Barney, *Brown Bomber,* World Pub., 1972.

Periodicals

Life, June 17, 1940, pp. 48-50.
Smithsonian, November 1988, pp. 170-196.
Sports Illustrated, September 16, 1985, pp. 82-100.
Time, November 25, 1985, pp. 117-118.

—*Ed Decker*

Bob Marley

1945-1981

Reggae singer, songwriter, guitarist

In his brief life, Bob Marley rose from poverty and obscurity to the status of an international superstar—the first Third World artist to be acclaimed to such a degree. Were it not for his charisma and ambition, reggae music might still be confined to Jamaica's ghettoes where it originated. Loved by millions for his musical genius, Marley was also a heroic figure to poor and oppressed people everywhere because of his passionate articulation of their plight and his relentless calls for political change. As Jay Cocks wrote in *Time,* "His music could challenge the conscience, soothe the spirit and stir the soul all at once."

Robert Nesta Marley was born to Cedella Malcolm when she was barely nineteen years old. The child was the result of her clandestine affair with Norval Marley, the local overseer of crown lands in the rural parish where she lived. Captain Marley, a white man more than twice Cedella's age, married the girl to make the birth legitimate, but he left the countryside the day after his impromptu wedding in order to accept a post in the city of Kingston. He had virtually no contact with his wife and son for several years, and Bob grew up as the pet of his grandfather Malcolm's large clan. He was known as a serious child and had a reputation for clairvoyance.

When Bob was about five years old, Cedella received a letter from her estranged husband, who asked that his child be sent to Kingston in order to attend school. Bob's mother reluctantly agreed and put her young son on the bus to Jamaica's largest city. Captain Marley met the child, but, for reasons unknown, he took him to the home of an elderly, invalid woman and abandoned him there. Bob was left to fend almost entirely for himself in Kingston's ghettos, generally considered some of the world's most dangerous. Months passed before Cedella managed to track down her child and bring him back to his country home. Before long, however, mother and child had returned to Kingston, where Cedella believed she had a greater chance of improving her life. She and Bob were joined by Bob's closest friend, Bunny Livingston, and Bunny's father, Thaddeus.

Jamaican society held very few opportunities for blacks at that time. Bob and Bunny grew up in an environment where violent crime was glorified by many young people as one of the few ways of getting ahead. Music was seen as another means of escape. Like most of their contemporaries, the two boys dreamed of becoming recording stars, and they spent their days coming up with songs and practicing them to the accompaniment of makeshift guitars, fashioned from bam-

At a Glance. . .

Born Robert Nesta Marley, February 6, 1945, in Nine Miles, Saint Ann, Jamaica; died of cancer, May 11, 1981, in Miami, FL; buried in Nine Miles, Saint Ann, Jamaica; son of Norval Sinclair Marley (a British Army captain) and Cedella Marley Booker (a shopkeeper, and later, a singer; maiden name, Malcolm); married Alpharita Constantia Anderson (known as Rita; a singer), February 10, 1966; children: (with wife) David (Ziggy), Cedella, Stephen, and Stephanie; (other legally recognized children with seven different women) daughters Karen and Makeda Jahnesta, and sons Rowan, Robbie, Kimani, Julian, and Damian. *Religion:* Rastafarian.

Worked as a welder, Kingston, Jamaica, briefly in 1961; lab assistant at Du Pont, forklift driver in a warehouse, and assembly-line worker at Chrysler, all in Delaware, 1966; owner of a record store, Wailin' Soul, Kingston, Jamaica, beginning 1966; formed Tuff Gong recording label, 1970; recording artist, 1962-81; founding member, with Peter Tosh and Bunny Wailer, of musical group the Wailers (originally known as the Teenagers, then as the Wailing Rudeboys, then the Wailing Wailers), early 1960s.

Awards: Special citation on behalf of Third World nations from United Nations, 1979; Jamaica's Order of Merit, 1981; May 11 proclaimed Bob Marley Day in Toronto, Canada.

boo, sardine cans, and electrical wire. By 1963, Marley's dream had come true—he'd released his first single, "Judge Not." Soon he and Bunny had teamed with another singer, Peter Macintosh (later known as Peter Tosh), to form a group known as the Wailers. Through talent shows, gigs at small clubs, and recordings, the Wailers became one of the most popular groups in Jamaica.

Their early success was based on popular dance hits in the "ska" music style. As time passed, they added social commentary to their lyrics and were instrumental in transforming the light, quick ska beat into the slower, bass-heavy reggae sound. The three men also came under the influence of Rastafarianism. This complex set of mystical beliefs holds that the now deceased Emperor Haile Selassie I of Ethiopia (whose given name was Ras Tafari) was the living God who would lead blacks out of oppression and into an African homeland. It was once considered the religion of outcasts and lunatics in

Jamaica, but in the 1960s it came to represent an alternative to violence for many ghetto dwellers. Rastafarianism lent dignity to their suffering and offered them the hope of eventual relief. Rejecting the standards of the white world that led many blacks to straighten their hair, Rastas let theirs mat up into long, ropy "dreadlocks." They follow strict dietary rules, abhor alcohol and drugs, but revere "ganja" (marijuana) as a holy herb that brings enlightenment to users. The Wailers soothed ghetto tensions with lyrical messages of peace and love, but at the same time, they warned the ruling class of "imminent dread judgement on the downpressors."

Wailers Gained Worldwide Popularity

For all their acclaim in Jamaica, the Wailers saw few profits from their early recording career, as unscrupulous producers repeatedly cheated them out of royalties and even the rights to their own songs. That situation changed in the early 1970s, after Marley sought an alliance with Chris Blackwell, a wealthy white Jamaican whose record company, Island, was the label of many major rock stars. At the time, reggae was still considered unsophisticated slum music that could never be appreciated by non-Jamaican audiences. Blackwell had a deep interest in the music, however, and because he felt that the Wailers were the one group capable of popularizing reggae internationally, he offered them a contract. He handled the marketing of their first Island album, *Catch a Fire,* just as he would have handled any rock band's product, complete with slick promotional efforts and tours of Britain and the United States. Slowly, the Wailers' sound began to catch on beyond the borders of Jamaica. An important catalyst to their popularity at this time was Eric Clapton's cover of Marley's composition, "I Shot the Sheriff," from the Wailers' 1973 album *Burnin'*. Clapton's version became a worldwide hit, leading many of his fans to discover the Wailers' music.

As their popularity increased, the original Wailers drew closer to a parting of the ways. Bunny Livingston (who had taken the name Bunny Wailer) disliked leaving Jamaica for extended tours, and Peter Tosh resented Chris Blackwell's efforts to make Bob the focus of the group. Each launched solo careers in the mid-1970s, while Marley released *Natty Dread* in 1974, which was hailed by *Rolling Stone* reviewer Stephen Davis as "the culmination of Marley's political art to this point." The reviewer continued: "With every album he's been rocking a little harder and reaching further out to produce the stunning effect of a successful spell. *Natty Dread* deals with rebellion and personal liberation. . . . The artist lays his soul so bare that the careful listener is satiated and exhausted in the end." *Rastaman Vibration* was released in 1976 to even more enthusiastic reviews. It was full of acid commentary on the worsening political situation in Jamaica, including a denouncement of the CIA's alleged involvement in island politics—a bold statement that brought Marley under the surveillance of the CIA and other U.S. intelligence organizations. His prominence in Jamaica reached messianic proportions, causing one *Time* reporter to exclaim, "He rivals the government as a political force."

Assassination Attempt Followed by Exile

Marley regarded all politicians with skepticism, considering them to be part of what Rastafarians call "Babylon," or the corrupt Western world. In the election for Prime Minister of Jamaica, however, he was known to favor Michael Manley of the People's National Party—a socialist group—over Edward Seaga, candidate of the right-wing Jamaican Labour Party. When Manley asked Bob Marley to give a "Smile Jamaica" concert to reduce tensions between the warring gangs associated with the two parties, the singer readily agreed.

Shortly before the concert was to take place on December 3, 1976, Marley's home was stormed by seven gunmen, suspected henchmen of the Jamaican Labour Party. Marley, his wife, Rita, and their manager Don Taylor were all injured in the ensuing gunfire. Yet despite the assassination attempt, the concert went on as scheduled. An audience of 80,000 people was electrified when Marley, bandaged and unable to strum his guitar, climbed to the stage to begin a blistering ninety-minute set. "At the close of his performance, Bob began a ritualistic dance, acting out aspects of the ambush that had almost taken his life," reported Timothy White in *Catch a Fire: The Life of Bob Marley.* "The last [the audience] saw before the reigning King of Reggae disappeared back into the hills was the image of the man mimicking the two-pistoled fast draw of a frontier gunslinger, his locks thrown back in triumphant laughter."

Immediately after the "Smile Jamaica" concert, Marley left the country, beginning a long term of self-imposed exile. After a period of recuperation, he toured the United States, Europe, and Africa. Reviewing his 1977 release, *Exodus,* Ray Coleman wrote in *Melody Maker:* "This is a mesmerizing album . . . more accessible, melodically richer, delivered with more directness than ever. . . . After an attempt on his life, Marley has a right to celebrate his existence, and that's how the album sounds: a celebration." But *Village Voice* reviewer Roger Trilling found that *Exodus* was "underscored by deep personal melancholy, a musical echo of the rootless wanderings that followed [Marley's] self-exile from Jamaica."

In 1978, Marley injured his foot during an informal soccer game. The painful wound was slow to heal and finally forced the singer to seek medical help. Doctors informed him that he was in the early stages of cancer and advised

amputation of his damaged toe. He refused, because such treatment was not in keeping with Rasta beliefs. Despite worsening health, Marley continued to write and perform until September, 1980, when he collapsed while jogging in New York's Central Park during the U.S. leg of a world tour. Doctors determined that tumors were spreading throughout his lungs and brain. He underwent radiation therapy and a controversial holistic treatment in the Bavarian Alps, but to no avail. After his death on May 11, 1981,

> "Marley was an inspiration for black freedom fighters the world over. . . . When his death was announced, the degree of devastation felt . . . was incalculable."
> —*Timothy White*

he was given a state funeral in Jamaica, which was attended by more than 100,000 people. Prime Minister Edward Seaga remembered Marley as "a native son . . . a beloved and departed friend." "He was a man with deep religious and political sentiments who rose from destitution to become one of the most influential music figures in the last twenty years," eulogized White in *Rolling Stone.* He was "an inspiration for black freedom fighters the world over. . . . When his death was announced, the degree of devastation felt . . . was incalculable."

Legal Battles over Estate

Throughout his life, Marley had always remained a man of the street. Even after earning millions of dollars, he would frequently return to the neighborhood where he grew up, leaving his BMW automobile unlocked at the curb while he visited old friends. His casual disregard for money and material possessions endeared him to the masses but gave rise to a monumental legal tangle after his death. Though his estate was worth an estimated $30 million at the time he passed away, he had scoffed at the idea of a will, believing that such a document showed an inappropriate concern with earthly matters.

Under Jamaican law, half of the estate of a man who dies intestate goes to his widow, while the remainder is divided equally among his children. When the court advertised for heirs, hundreds stepped forth claiming to be Marley's offspring. Marley's widow, Rita, became locked in a ten-year battle with the court-appointed administrator of the estate, a conservative lawyer who had not liked Marley when he was alive and who, after the singer's death, sometimes seemed bent on taking as much as possible from those who had been closest to the deceased. The administrator attempted to evict Marley's mother from a house her son had given her—on the grounds that the title had never been legally transferred; in a similar fashion, he tried to have property seized from Rita and accused her of illegally diverting royalty money that should have become part of the contested estate.

That royalty money represented a considerable sum. At the time of his death, Marley had sold about $190 million worth of albums and had an average annual royalty income of $200,000. Posthumous releases of his work were ranked high on *Billboard*'s music charts ten years and more after his death, pushing the annual royalty income to $2.5 million and leading many industry experts to rank Marley as one of the largest-selling recording artists of all time. Control of the rights to his music was as hotly disputed as the division of his estate, with rival record companies trying to wrest control from Rita Marley and Island Records.

Eventually, Rita Marley admitted in court that she had forged her husband's signature on backdated documents that transferred ownership of some of his companies to her. Showing a disregard for legalities similar to her husband's, she calmly told a *Newsweek* reporter that she had been acting on her lawyers' advice. Firm in her belief that Marley would have wanted her to protect herself and his rightful heirs—which were eventually determined to include his and Rita's four children, as well as seven other offspring with various women—she asked, "How can I steal from myself?" She was dismissed as an executor of the estate for this transgression but charged with no crime. The battle over Marley's fortune was finally settled late in 1991. The Jamaican Supreme Court ruled in favor of Rita Marley and Chris Blackwell's Island Logic Ltd., a company that had controlled the estate since 1989. Under the terms of the court ruling, the estate would be managed by Island Logic for ten more years before passing into the hands of Marley's widow and his 11 legally recognized children.

Enduring Cultural and Musical Legacy

Bob Marley's artistic output was so great that previously unreleased work of his has continued to appear on the market years after his death. In 1992, a 78-song package entitled *Songs of Freedom* was released, tracing his career from his first single, "Judge Not," to a version of his haunting "Redemption Song" recorded at his final concert in 1980. The tenth anniversary of his death was marked by several days of commemorative celebrations in Kingston, and *New York Times* writer Howard W. French noted that "whereas Marley's long-haired, ganja-smoking Rastafarian

sect was long seen by the staid Establishment [in Jamaica] as an embarrassing threat to tourism, the Jamaica Tourist Board sponsored the memorial [events]." Once shunned, Marley is now acknowledged as the person who, more than any other, has generated lasting interest in his native country.

Marley's musical legacy can be seen in the continuing popularity of reggae and its pervasive influence on mainstream music. The Melody Makers, arguably the most popular modern reggae group, was formed by Marley himself years ago; its members are his children, led by his oldest son, Ziggy. Yet no one, not even his son, has been able to touch Bob Marley's position as the undisputed "king of reggae." French commented on the musician's lasting popularity: "Marley's appeal succeeded remarkably in transcending an often-militant lyrical message explicitly centered on the ideal of cultural and spiritual redemption for black people. However racially based his core message, Marley's dreadlocked look of alienation, and his Old Testament-style prophecies promising the poor that their oppressors would soon 'eat the bread of sorrow,' carried strong germs of universality."

David Fricke summarized in *Rolling Stone:* "Since Jamaica's favorite musical son succumbed to the ravages of cancer, the search for a worthy successor—a 'new Marley' with comparable vision, personality and musical nerve, not to mention the magic crossover touch—has yielded only flawed contenders. . . . But looking for a new Marley is as pointless as looking for a new [Bob] Dylan or [Jimi] Hendrix. Bob Marley, like those other two originals, revolutionized pop music in his own singular image, transforming a regional mutant product of Caribbean rhythm, American R & B and African mysticism into a personalized vehicle for spiritual communion, social argument and musical daring."

Selected discography

Soul Rebel, Trojan, 1971.
Catch a Fire, Island, 1973.
Burnin', Island, 1973.
African Herbsman, Trojan, 1973.
Best of Bob Marley and the Wailers, Studio One, 1974.
Natty Dread, Island, 1974.
Rasta Revolution, Trojan, 1974.
Live! Bob Marley and the Wailers, Island, 1975.
Rastaman Vibration, Island, 1976.
Birth of a Legend, Calla, 1976.
Reflection, Fontana, 1977.
Exodus, Island, 1977.
Kaya, Island, 1978.
Babylon by Bus, Island, 1978.
In the Beginning, Psycho, 1979.
Survival, Island, 1979.

Bob Marley and the Wailers, Hammer, 1979.
Uprising, Island, 1980.
Crying for Freedom, Time-Wind, 1981.
Chances Are, Cotillion, 1981.
Soul Revolution, Part II, Pressure Disc, 1981.
Marley, Phoenix, 1982.
Jamaican Storm, Accord, 1982.
Bob Marley Interviews. . ., Tuff Gong, 1982.
Confrontation, Island, 1983.
Legend, Island, 1986.
Rebel Music, Island, 1986.
Bob Marley, Urban Tek, 1989.
Talkin' Blues, Tuff Gong/Island, 1991.
One Love, Heartbeat, 1992.
Songs of Freedom (three-disc retrospective), Tuff Gong/Island, 1992.

Sources

Books

Blackbook: International Reference Guide, 1993 Edition, National Publications, 1993, pp. 62-63.
Davis, Stephen, *Bob Marley,* Doubleday, 1985.
Davis, Stephen, *Reggae Bloodlines: In Search of the Music and Culture of Jamaica,* Anchor Press, 1979.
Goldman, Vivian, *Bob Marley: Soul-Rebel—Natural Mystic,* St. Martin's, 1981.
White, Timothy, *Catch a Fire: The Life of Bob Marley,* Holt, 1983.
Whitney, Malika Lee, *Bob Marley, Reggae King of the World,* Dutton, 1984.

Periodicals

Black Stars, July 1979.
Crawdaddy, July 1976; August 1977; May 1978.
Creem, August 1976.
Down Beat, September 9, 1976; September 8, 1977.
Encore, January 1980.
Essence, January 1976.
First World, Number 2, 1979.

Gig, June-July 1978.
Guitar Player, May 1991, p. 82.
Interview, August 1978.
Jet, December 30, 1992.
Los Angeles Times, May 5, 1990; July 16, 1991.
Melody Maker, May 1, 1976; May 14, 1977; November 18, 1978; September 29, 1979.
Mother Jones, July 1985; December 1986.
Newsweek, April 8, 1991, p. 57.
New York Times, May 13, 1991; September 3, 1992; December 13, 1992.
New York Times Magazine, August 14, 1977.
People, April 26, 1976; December 21, 1992.
Playboy, January, 1981.
Rolling Stone, April 24, 1975; June 1, 1978; June 15, 1978; December 28, 1978; January 11, 1979; March 18, 1982; May 27, 1982; June 4, 1987; March 7, 1991.
Sepia, March 1979.
Spin, June 1991.
Stereo Review, July 1975; September 1977; February 1982.
Time, March 22, 1976, pp. 83-84; December 20, 1976, p. 45; October 19, 1992, pp. 77-78.
Village Voice, June 27, 1977; April 17, 1978; November 5, 1979.
Washington Post, August 25, 1991.

Obituaries

Jet, May 28, 1981.
Maclean's, December 28, 1981.
Newsweek, May 25, 1981.
New York Times, May 12, 1981; May 21, 1981.
Rolling Stone, May 28, 1981; June 25, 1981.
Time, May 25, 1981, p. 76.
Variety, May 20, 1981.

Marley's life and musical career are chronicled in the documentary *Time Will Tell,* released in 1992 in combination with his retrospective CD package.

—*Joan Goldsworthy*

Quett Masire

1925—

President of Botswana

Lying between Zimbabwe and Namibia to the east and west, Angola and Zambia to the north, and South Africa in the south, Botswana is the picture of unspoiled Africa. Its enchanting countryside features stalactite-laden caves, exotic animals and birds, and scenic contrasts of the Kalahari Desert and Okavango Swamp areas that have long been the stuff of dramatic adventure novels.

But one look at the nation's capital, Gaborone, instantly dispels any impression that Botswana is a romantic backwater. Boasting all the electronics-driven accessories of the late twentieth century, the city is the nerve center of a modern state concerned with financial independence and technological advancement. Gaborone also houses a government unshakably committed to harmony between black and white citizens—an amicable way of life symbolized by the African zebra, with its black and white stripes.

Botswana's leader, Dr. Quett Ketumile Joni Masire, is a deft statesman who skillfully blends the principles of Western capitalism with an understanding of tribal tradition. Formerly the country's vice-president, he was unanimously voted into Botswana's top office in 1980, soon after the death of the first commander in chief, the revered Sir Seretse Khama. Widely regarded as a forthright, level-headed man, Masire has given wholehearted support to the newly independent African states beyond his borders; yet he dexterously maintains a mutually profitable economic relationship with South Africa, steering a neutral course through the explosive splinters of his closest neighbor's disintegrating apartheid policy.

Masire was born on July 23, 1925, into a minor headman's family in the southern Kanye district of a British colony called the Bechuanaland Protectorate. The president rarely discusses his youth; public knowledge covers only the fact that he was educated far away from home at Tiger Kloof College in what was later ruled to be South Africa, and that he completed his teacher training courses in 1949.

Zeroing In on the Problems

Masire returned to Kanye in 1950 to find that the British colonial service had deposed and exiled Seretse Khama, the hereditary chief of the dominant Bamangwato Tribe, for daring to marry a white Englishwoman. Khama's absence brought a waning of tribal influence that distressed the young schoolmaster. Perturbed by the possibility that

At a Glance. . .

Born Quett Ketumile Joni Masire, July 23, 1925, in Kanye, British Bechuanaland Protectorate (now Botswana); married Gladys Molefi Olebile, 1958; children: three sons, three daughters. *Education:* Attended Tiger Kloof College, South Africa; completed teacher training courses, 1949.

Founder and principal, Seepapitso Secondary School, Kanye, British Bechuanaland Protectorate, 1950-56; farmer, Kanye, 1956-58; *African Echo,* journalist, 1958-60, became director, 1960; elected member of Bechuanaland Protectorate Legislative Council (LEGCO) for Kanye South, 1960; cofounder of Botswana Democratic party (BDP), January 29, 1962, became BDP's secretary-general; editor of *Therisanyo* (Democratic party newspaper); appointed deputy prime minister, 1965, became vice-president and minister of finance and development planning, both upon Botswana's independence, 1966-80; president, Republic of Botswana, 1980—. Also president of Southern African Development Coordination Conference (SADCC).

Member: Botswana Society (president), International Committee Against Apartheid, Racialism and Colonialism in Southern Africa, Okavango Wildlife Society, Botswana Boy Scouts Association.

Awards: Honorary LL.D., St. John University, New York; United Nations award for famine management; Africa Prize for Leadership, 1989.

Addresses: *Office*—Office of the President, Private Bag 001, Gaborone, Botswana.

precious underground water. Thus frozen out, poorer farmers were forced to abandon independent efforts to support their families. Instead, they had to hire themselves out as laborers or leave their homes altogether for the South African mines.

Having become politically active in the 1950s, Masire fought for the rights of farmers as a Bangwaketse Tribal Council member. Determined to compare the status of subsistence farmers all over Southern Africa, he became a correspondent on the *African Echo,* the most widely read newspaper in the British Protectorate regions of Swaziland, his own Bechuanaland, and Basutoland. Masire's new career as a reporter gave him a wider perspective on the region's economic and political affairs; the knowledge stood him in good stead after he became a member of the newspaper's board of directors in 1960.

Democracy Dawns: Khama and Masire

Journalistic and political activities brought him into close working contact with Seretse Khama, who by 1960 had firmly reestablished his power in Botswana. Sharing Khama's view that the country's future should transcend tribal loyalties without erasing them, Masire became a member of the newly formed Bechuanaland Protectorate Legislative Council (LEGCO) and also helped Khama to found the Botswana Democratic Party (BDP). Elected to the post of secretary-general—a position, he would hold for the following 14 years—Masire's list of responsibilities included both party organization in the southern region and the editorship of *Therisanyo,* the Democratic party newspaper.

The competent and mutually respectful working relationship between Seretse Khama and Quett Masire helped to bring the Botswana Democratic party to victory in its 1965 debut. Mindful of the militant, headstrong independence movements budding throughout the country, the two men made sure that their party had something to offer everybody. Colonial government liked its moderation. Traditional tribal leaders were impressed with the way it favored alliance with them. At the same time, the party wooed voters in favor of a new order by supporting independence and absolute nonracialism. With consummate tact, Khama chose not to dwell on his six-year, racially motivated banishment, and instead expressed his country's gratitude for British strategic help during the democratization process. Britain bestowed on him the gift of a knighthood as reward for this wise moderation.

The former Bechuanaland Protectorate became the independent Republic of Botswana in 1966. As president, Khama lost no time in clarifying his regime's priorities. At the top of the list was an emphasis on interracial harmony, of which Khama's marriage was a shining example. He

the youth of his own Bangwaketse tribe would grow up with neither traditional values nor a Western education, Masire started the Seepapitso Secondary School in his hometown and stayed to head it for the following five years.

In 1956, the year that Seretse Khama returned to his people, Masire became a farmer. Around the same time, Masire discovered that his country's true power had fallen into the hands of a few wealthy landowners, who were grabbing the grazing areas of subsistence farmers by drilling boreholes beyond their own lands to capture the also took a strictly neutral stance toward the turmoil that was beginning to surface in South Africa and Zimbabwe. Underlining this neutrality was the offer of shelter in Botswana to political refugees from both governments, provided that they did not instigate militant activities against their countries of origin.

Masire Faced Challenges as Botswana's First VP and Minister of Finance

With the cultural direction of the country set, attention turned to financial matters. Elected the country's vice-president and minister of finance and development planning in 1966, Masire had a considerable challenge on his hands. Of Botswana's 830,000 inhabitants, about 60 percent were still subsistence farmers, completely dependent on plentiful rains to ensure adequate crops. Workers in the well-established beef exporting industry were also at the mercy of the weather and had suffered greatly just one year before, when the persistent drought of 1965 had wiped out 400,000 of the country's 1.3 million-strong cattle herd.

With the cooperation of the United Nations Food and Agriculture World Food Program, Masire devised a food-for-work scheme, whereby people in drought stricken areas could choose community projects on which to work in exchange for food. Nevertheless, the per capita income dwindled to only $75 per annum. In its year of independence, Botswana was known as one of Africa's poorest countries.

Managing the famine was not Masire's first experience with fiscal matters. In 1956 he participated in the formation of Botswana's first real economic outline, which consisted of a list of development schemes to be funded by grants from Britain's Colonial and Welfare Fund. Throughout the early 1960s he honed his fiscal skills, working alongside Britain's resident commissioner to draw a financial blueprint that would smooth the way to Botswana's independence. The resulting "1963-68 Development Plan," Botswana's first to be based on centralized strategy, concentrated on three vital areas; urban development, construction of a working government, and the growth of private sector business.

All of these objectives sprang to life in 1967, when the second largest diamond pipe the world had ever seen was discovered at Orapa, in central Botswana. The find brought the country into closer contact with South Africa, for the Botswana government borrowed money for a mining township and operations from De Beers, a subsidiary of the fabled mining empire called Anglo-American Corporation. Masire hoped that these mining operations might create enough jobs to make it unnecessary for the Batswana to work in the South African mines. But in the end only 2,000

extra jobs resulted, plus 400 in mining administration and sorting.

In 1970 Vice-President Masire announced a five-year economic plan of his own design. It focused on rural development, stating as its goal the slashing of reliance on the imported foodstuffs that were vital lifelines for drought stricken areas. The formal document delineated strategy for the installation of basic services for irrigation as well as for produce storage facilities, so that crops could be held and sold at the best prices available rather than being

> Masire is a deft statesman who skillfully blends the principles of Western capitalism with an understanding of tribal tradition.

rushed to market over fear of spoilage. Also featured was a roadbuilding plan for freight transport. Masire received both loans and grants from the United States, Denmark, Sweden, and Canada for water development, new agricultural techniques, and famine relief.

As the 1970s wore on, the finance minister steered an increasingly sophisticated urban economy, based mostly on mining. Orapa became operational in 1971, producing more than 2 million diamond carats per annum until 1977, when another diamond mine at Letlhakane added its own bounty. Additional mining activities centered around copper-nickel operations at Selebi-Pikwe and coal mining at Morupule, after the biggest coalfield in Southern Africa was discovered at the latter.

By the mid-1970s, Masire refined his economic plans with a "trickle-down" scheme, in which income from exports like beef and diamonds went into education and training, manufacturing and agriculture, and improved service in rural areas. At the same time, he introduced the country's own currency. Called the "pula," it reflects the Batswana reverence for water—the name means "let it rain." Masire also enticed foreign entrepreneurs with the prospect of attractive investment, giving them open access to markets in Swaziland, South Africa, and Lesotho.

Elected President of Botswana

In 1980 Sir Seretse Khama died of stomach cancer. Taking stock of his considerable achievements, the world press noted that Khama's legacy included a corruption-free government and one of the sturdiest economies in Africa. Mining activities and their attendant mineral exports had risen to $184 million from just $3.3 million in 1970, and per capita income had passed the $325 per-annum mark by 1975. The country's status as one of Africa's poorest nations was a long-gone memory.

Unanimously elected to the presidency in late 1980 by Botswana's National Assembly, Masire handed executive financial duties over to others. Yet he continued to set financial goals by means of five-year plans, constantly updating them to meet the diverse needs of the Batswana people. Among the 1.2 million-strong population exist a melange of cultural heritages. At one extreme are the !kung Bushmen of the Kalahari Desert, while the opposite end consists of sophisticated city dwellers who run the country's burgeoning mining and tourist industries. In between lie eight differing tribal groups, plus white agriculturalists, teachers, and business executives.

Bent on economic self-reliance for each of Botswana's families, Masire has wisely overseen a system of programs based on his people's present ways of life. One project is an agricultural course designed to teach farmers about water conservation techniques, record-keeping, and crop selection; another ensures that the nomadic Bushmen can earn financial independence by producing handcrafted hunting bags, bows, and arrows for export through the Botswanacraft Marketing Company that is based in Ghanzi, a desert town close to their home region.

Inevitably these well-meaning efforts have their downside. Sixty percent of the population is still enmeshed in poverty. The already huge number of single-parent households continues to rise, prompted in large part by the exodus of Batswana men for attractive jobs in South Africa's mines; the high adult illiteracy rate persists; and schools and social services are still desperately needed, especially in rural areas.

Bountiful exports could easily finance such projects. But basic social programs are not the president's only economic priority. Another issue jostling for attention is the transportation system, which is tied inextricably to both Zimbabwe and South Africa. Botswana's main railroad line starts its northward journey in South Africa but really belongs to Zimbabwe Railways. Professional training and an ongoing construction program for transportation in Botswana are vital but expensive stepping stones to firming up the country's industrial base.

Famine and Financial Fertility

Politically, Masire's policies are not too different from Khama's, although he is considered less conservative. Squarely sympathizing with nations wanting to escalate sanctions against South African apartheid (a policy of economic and political discrimination against blacks prac-

ticed by the white minority government), he nevertheless refuses to participate in any such confrontational activities for fear he might harm the Botswana economy, which still has strong trade ties with Pretoria, South Africa's administrative capital. In fact, he shows the same policy of inactive sympathy that he previously applied to SWAPO, the organization that eventually achieved the independence of Namibia.

By 1981, most urgent, day-to-day administration in Botswana was running smoothly. However, the country then entered a period of drought which was destined to linger—on and off—for the next seven years. Driest of all were 1983 and 1984, when the developing program of cattle improvement was severely affected.

Characteristically, Masire used the crisis as an opportunity to plan for the future by refining the country's famine relief program. He chose to institute a labor-based relief scheme in which village and district councils instituted projects such as road building, dam excavation, and land clearing. Then, local residents were employed in these projects for a few months for wages large enough to replace what the famine had withered away. So efficiently was this program managed that not one Batswana died of famine during these difficult years—an achievement that pleased Masire far more than the United Nations award of $100,000 he shared with Burkina Faso for famine management.

Another 1981 challenge involved foreign relations. Masire stepped into a three-year term of office as president of the Southern African Development Coordination Conference (SADCC), a new organization consisting of ten Southern African states. Botswana, Zambia, Angola, Malawi, Lesotho, and Swaziland were founding members of the group, and Namibia and Zimbabwe joined as soon as they had achieved independence. While the organization's expressed mission was to reduce economic dependence on South Africa, the SADCC sensibly ruled out military opposition, since South Africa's superiority was obvious. Instead, each country assumed responsibility for a single project—from a list that included food processing technology, wild life conservation, fisheries, famine aid, and technology—that could lessen their general dependence on South Africa for labor and transport.

In 1984 SADCC achievements were assessed. Reports revealed that because South African companies were heavily involved in manufacturing, mining, and other industries based in all the SADCC countries, trade between them and South Africa amounted to $1.3 billion, while intra-SADCC trade was only $245 million for the year. Furthermore, the transport problem had actually worsened with the growth of each country's external trade network; like Botswana, five other member states are landlocked, leaving port facilities available to the group only in Tanzania, Angola, and Mozambique. Therefore, though only half of

Botswana's regional overseas trade had passed through South Africa in 1981, by 1985 the figure had risen to 85 percent.

Strong Leadership in a Maturing Democracy

Now interested in charting his country's future on the international scene, Masire was unperturbed by this localized problem. In 1982 he had seen the opening of a third Botswana diamond mine called Jwaneng, which by the end of 1984 had helped to raise the annual diamond total to almost 13 million carats. Much of this yield was sold in London through the De Beers-controlled Central Selling Organization. Still, despite the fact that De Beers owns 50% of the equity in De Beers Botswana (Debswana), the Botswana government had stockpiled a large enough supply to sell outright to De Beers in 1987 for P430 million, thus gaining for Botswana a five percent share in De Beers itself, two directorships on the De Beers international board, and highly coveted inside information on De Beers' international decisions.

Botswana's tedious relationship with South Africa has also necessitated tact and skill on the part of the Masire administration. Increasingly vulnerable since Zimbabwe's 1980 independence, South Africa began to adopt an aggressive external stance towards its northern neighbors. Disturbed by increasingly loud anti-apartheid protests from the African National Congress (ANC), the South African Defense Force made several raids across the border in search of ANC supporters who had taken refuge in Botswana. In response to the raids, President Masire strongly reiterated his country's stance on political refugees—that they were welcome in Botswana as long as they did not initiate terrorist activities against their country of origin—but he could not deny that there was an official ANC representative living in the country. The raids made him uneasy about this official's safety, however, so he prudently asked him to leave.

Masire won a landslide victory in 1989, and since his reelection, the 1990s have brought international recognition to his able, corruption-free leadership. A newly minted civilian alliance with America is seen in the up-to-date Voice of America shortwave-transmitter outside Selebi-Phikwe (replacing one rendered inoperable by deteriorating conditions in Liberia), while a military friendship is evident in the new air base that houses Botswana's fledgling air force as well as several American spotter aircraft used against poachers. Further bonds are linking Batswana soldiers and their American counterparts: Masire's forces have recently learned American sniper techniques and have shared their traditional knowledge of desert tracking.

Other, less welcome developments are common to all rapidly industrializing countries. Unemployment is growing because the persistent drought is chasing farmers from the land; the fading of strict tribal behavior codes is producing a high rate of teenage pregnancy; and there are grumbles from the rising intellectual class about the number of foreign residents in vocational positions of authority. But Masire accepts the rough with the smooth, and his main concerns remain the financial self-reliance and peaceful democracy of his country. Above all, he prizes the harmonious mingling of his country's black and white citizens.

Sources

Books

Africa Today, London, Africa Books, Ltd., 1991.
Glickman, Harvey, editor, *Toward Peace and Security in Southern Africa,* Gordon & Beach, 1990.
Morton, Fred, and others, editors, *Historical Dictionary of Botswana,* Scarecrow Press, 1989.
Van Baren, L. editor, *New African Yearbook: 1991-1992,* Hunter Publishing, 1991.

Periodicals

Africa Diary, Sept. 23, 1980.
Africa Report, November-December 1980; July-August 1984; January-February 1987.
Africa Research Bulletin, July 15-August 15, 1980.
Africa Today (special issue titled "Botswana: Achievements and Challenges"), 1st Quarter, 1993.
Christian Science Monitor, August 17, 1989; April 2, 1991.
New York Times, Sept. 16, 1989; May 16, 1990; June 3, 1990; July 15, 1990.
Washington Post, April 15, 1991; April 30, 1992.

Additional information for this profile was obtained from various issues of the *Botswana Daily News,* 1980-81, and the "Republic of Botswana: National Development Plan, 1985-91."

—Gillian Wolf

Walter E. Massey

1938—

Physicist, educator, researcher, administrator

In 1954 Walter E. Massey had just completed the tenth grade. Although he had yet to take a single course in chemistry or advanced algebra or trigonometry, his precocious skills in mathematics earned him an immediate scholarship to college at the age of 16. Two weeks after arriving on the campus of Morehouse College in Atlanta, Georgia, Massey called his mother and pleaded with her to take him home; she refused.

He continued his schooling, persevered, and, guided by the wisdom and understanding of faculty mentors, achieved levels of success largely unimagined during his initial unfocused days as a college freshman: a doctorate in physics; full professorships at Brown University and the University of Chicago; directorship of Argonne National Laboratory, one of the nation's largest energy research and development laboratories; leadership positions in many professional scientific organizations; government administrative positions, including a seat on the U.S. President's Council of Advisors on Science and Technology and the directorship of the National Science Foundation, both under President George Bush; and appointment to the number two administrative post within the University of California system.

In choosing theoretical physics as his academic specialty,

Massey pursued a somewhat solitary discipline. Throughout his distinguished career, however, he has been anything but cloistered, working instead to open the world of science to others. As an educator, a scientist, and an administrator, Massey has advocated the need for academic mentors to help draw in and then support students—especially minorities and women—in pursuing a career in science and engineering. He has also pushed for a closer link between educational institutions and industry that would allow for the safe and speedy incorporation of technological advances into everyday life, as well as for a more pervasive and intensive science education in American schools that would raise individual literacy and enhance the country's economic competitiveness.

Born in 1938 in Hattiesburg, Mississippi, Massey displayed as a child an unusual aptitude for mathematics. He recalled to Tim Beardsley in *Scientific American,* "There was just something about sitting down and working through problems." His felicity with numbers earned him, in the middle of high school, a Ford Foundation fellowship to Morehouse College in Atlanta. He began studying theoretical physics because it gave him the chance to rise above the discrimination he had witnessed as a youth growing up in the segregated have foundered had he not been guided by Sabinus H. Christensen, a white physics instructor teaching at the traditionally black college. Christensen's tutorials and inspiration helped Massey earn a bachelor's degree in physics and mathematics. Later, in graduate school at Washington University in St. Louis, Missouri, Massey studied under Eugene Feenberg. Though tempted to quit the rigors of pursuing a doctoral degree, Massey found the courage, through Feenberg, to continue. "If he had not taken extraordinary care," Massey explained to Beardsley, "I would have quit. I was just lucky. That kind of effort he put forth is not common."

While finishing his doctoral studies, Massey began working in 1966 as a member of the research staff at Argonne National Laboratory, operated for the U.S. Department of Energy by a consortium of universities and then by the University of Chicago. While there, he focused on the study of the many-body theory of liquids and solids, which attempts to explain the properties of systems of interacting particles in various states. He also continued his own research, applying correlated basic functions to both liquid and solid helium. Two years later, his doctorate completed and his work at the laboratory continuing, Massey accepted an assistant professorship at the University of Illinois.

In 1970 Massey was offered an associate professorship at Brown University, where, according to Goodwin, he completed his most significant academic research, collaborating with Humphrey Maris on the study of changes in sound waves in superfluid helium. (Superfluid helium, which is liquid helium at temperatures below -271°C, is known for displaying unusual behavior such as the apparent defiance of the forces of gravity.) By 1975 Massey was a full professor at Brown.

Intellectual and Social Awareness Interact

"The life of the mind," Beardsley emphasized, "did not weaken Massey's commitment to social issues." He neither forgot nor ignored the social injustices that led him, in part, to study theoretical physics. Massey admitted that he took the University of Illinois post because he had been out of the mainstream during the height of campus protests at the end of the 1960s. On his first night on campus, Massey helped win the release of 264 jailed black students who had protested racial discrimination at the university.

But Massey's greater concern for black students then—as well as now—was their lack of education in mathematics and the sciences. At Illinois, he recruited minority students but found he had to tutor and counsel many. At Brown, he discovered the same discouraging condition. Remembering his own weak academic beginnings, Massey recounted to Norman M. Bradburn and David Rosen in *Science:* "At

South of the 1940s and 1950s. "So much depends on what people think of you," he related to Irwin Goodwin in *Physics Today.* "In theoretical physics, no one reading your papers would know if you were black or white. There's no such thing as black physics."

Mentors played an important role in Massey's academic life. Initially at Morehouse, he lacked direction and may well critical points in my life and in my academic career, mentors [gave] me the confidence and support without which it would have been impossible to carry on." He added, "Unfortunately, not everyone is so fortunate. Minority students, who perhaps need that support more than most other students, often find it unavailable."

While at Brown, Massey developed and directed the Inner City Teachers of Science program (ICTOS), through which undergraduates studying to become science teachers served as mentors and tutors in urban high school science classes. The achievement of this program earned Massey the distinguished service citation of the American Association of Physics Teachers in 1975.

Scientist Turned Administrator

Massey's administrative abilities, highlighted by his work with ICTOS and as dean of Brown's undergraduate college, were heralded in 1979 with the offer of the directorship of Argonne National Laboratory and a concurrent position as full professor at the University of Chicago. "As a scientist you're trained so early to look for things that excite you personally, and a lot of that is intellectual excitement," Massey explained to Lynn Norment in *Ebony*. "There becomes almost a need to be involved in problem solving, and it carries on through life."

His eagerness and ability to tackle problems could not have been put to better use at a better time. When Massey began directing Argonne, he assumed control of an annual budget of more than $250 million and a staff of almost four thousand. But he also assumed control of a nebulous public relations image. National laboratories at the time were highly suspect: their work was not being translated to industry. To the outside world, the laboratories lacked clear missions; on the inside, scientists and technicians lacked morale. D. Allen Bromley, President Bush's assistant for science and technology, explained in *Physics Today* one of the key methods Massey used to turn Argonne around in the early 1980s: "He introduced what can only be called participatory democracy, and in turn the scientists responded with a dazzling array of ideas for the lab's research efforts." Massey then responded to the lack of outside connections by helping formulate the Argonne National Laboratory-University of Chicago Development Corporation (ARCH), an organization that expedited the transfer of technologies created in the laboratory to industry and the marketplace.

While at Argonne and the University of Chicago, Massey also sought to improve the level of scientific education and awareness through the civic arena. In 1982 he headed the Chicago Mayoral Task Force on High-Technology Development and was the founding chair of the Chicago High-

Tech Association. He also served on the Illinois Governor's Commission on Science and Technology and was highly visible on two educational fronts, helping to organize the Illinois Science and Mathematics Academy, a high school developed for talented students, and serving as a trustee for the Academy for Mathematics and Science Teachers, which trained almost 17,000 Chicago public school teachers in those fields.

First African American President of the AAAS

Massey's influence extended far beyond the Chicago area. From 1978 to 1984 he was a member of the National Science Board, the policy-making body of the National Science Foundation, the governmental agency that funds basic science research, excluding medical and military research. In 1989 he became president of the American Association for the Advancement of Science (AAAS), an organization that lists over 140,000 members and 285 scientific societies. It was in this latter position that Massey—the first African American ever to hold that post—was able

> "If we look at the comparative performance of American students in science relative to that of their peers in other countries, we see that a great deal needs to be done."

to fully highlight the problems of science education on a national level. "We need to be concerned not only about attracting and retaining more students in areas of science and technology but also about the quality of education being received by all students," Massey stated in his presidential address to the AAAS, excerpted in *Science*. "If we look at the comparative performance of American students relative to that of their peers in other countries, we see that a great deal needs to be done."

Part of the AAAS's plan under Massey to improve science education in grades kindergarten through 12 was the sponsorship of Project 2061 (named after the projected date of the return of Halley's Comet), which attempts to structure curricula to emphasize major scientific concepts. "Unlike many of the programs, which were primarily about finding gifted students for the sciences, this one has a different focus," Massey explained to *Ebony*'s Douglas C. Lyons. "Its focus is to raise the science literacy level of all Americans." By doing so, Massey hoped to combat not only the United States' loss of economic competitiveness in the world market that began in the mid-1980s, but also to fight the health and environmental crises that affect the entire world.

Massey lamented in his address to the AAAS that, historically, the United States has put a national emphasis on science and technology only in times of war. In the late 1980s and early 1990s, "the energy crisis, the trade and budget deficits, acquired immunodeficiency syndrome [AIDS], and the greenhouse effect [became] profoundly serious and deeply troubling issues with long-lasting consequences, but not one has provided the coalescing influence concerning courses of action that wars provide," he pointed out.

Became Director of National Science Foundation

Massey was allowed the opportunity to forge a productive relationship between the science community and the U.S. government when President Bush nominated him in 1990 to become the new director of the National Science Foundation. When the nomination was announced, William Golden, then treasurer of the AAAS, typified the reaction of the scientific community. As quoted by Jon Van in the *Chicago Tribune,* Golden deemed the selection "brilliant," and added that Massey "can really make a case for funding scientific research and for the need to educate and train more young scientists and engineers. He'll also serve as an excellent role model for young people."

At the time of his selection, Massey was in Europe, studying how university and government laboratories were transferring technology to the marketplace in preparation for the possible reunification of the European Community in the early 1990s. After assuming control of the National Science Foundation, Massey told Curt Suplee of the *Wash-*

ington Post that developing connections between academia and industry would be a major part of the mission of the foundation, in view of world changes: "As Europe becomes more and more of an integrated community, they may find that they may not need us as much as they did in the past."

Completing the mission of the National Science Foundation, Massey believed, would be a strong movement toward science education—providing grants to university research centers and individuals and upgrading pre-college science education, with an emphasis on attracting more women and minority groups to careers in science. "The idea of what scientists are doing is just either very uninformed or, worse, very ill-formed," he told Lyons. "You certainly don't think of it as being fun, but most youngsters don't realize what a broad set of possibilities exists as a result of pursuing the study of science."

In the spring of 1993, when his tenure at the National Science Foundation was completed, Massey entered another new phase of his career, becoming provost and vice-president for academic affairs at the University of California system. Massey holds the number two administrative office in the university system, overseeing academic concerns at all of its nine campuses.

Sources

Chicago Tribune, September 15, 1990.
Ebony, November 1979; August 1989; August 1991.
New York Times, September 15, 1990; June 4, 1991.
Physics Today, October 1990.
Science, December 18, 1987; September 1, 1989.
Scientific American, June 1992.
Washington Post, September 15, 1990; April 1, 1991.

—*Rob Nagel*

Mark Mathabane

1960—

Writer

Mark Mathabane escaped a life of poverty and terror in South Africa and, recalling that life in print, has become a bestselling author in the United States. Mathabane's 1986 memoir, *Kaffir Boy,* "catapulted him to celebrity and respect as a voice for oppressed blacks," according to Lisa Anderson in the *Chicago Tribune.* In *Kaffir Boy,* the author recounts his childhood in the squalid black township of Alexandra and his determination not to accept the boundaries set for him by the white minority government of South Africa. In subsequent books, *Kaffir Boy in America* and *Love in Black and White,* Mathabane offers his perspective on race relations—personal and social—in modern America. *Los Angeles Times* correspondent Itabari Njeri called Mathabane a writer with "an intellect constantly refining itself; a man turning himself into a more astute receptor and generator of ideas."

As a child, Mathabane saw his parents victimized repeatedly by the barbaric South African system of apartheid. He witnessed violence, suffered malnutrition, and endured humiliation, emerging from a ruinous environment only because he dedicated himself to receiving an education. "There was a time when I thought that if life meant unending suffering and pain, there was no use living," Mathabane told *Time* maga-

zine. "At 10 years old, I contemplated suicide. What kept me going was my discovery of books. In the world of books I could travel around the world, go to the moon, do great things. That made it worthwhile to live another day."

Having resided in the United States since 1978, Mathabane has become a spokesperson not only for the oppressed people in his homeland but also for the plight of black Americans. "What was really shocking was discovering that the black world in America resembled the world I had left, the townships of South Africa—the poor buildings, the bad roads, the hopelessness, the rage, the frustration on the faces of the black boys and girls I met," he told *Time.* "These were the same emotions I felt when I was fighting for my life under apartheid. Everyone in this country is an accomplice to what is happening in the black ghettos of America." Mathabane feels that conditions could improve in the United States if a climate of racial communications could be nurtured. "My mother and grandmother, though illiterate, taught me what I have come to regard as the most important lessons in race relations," Mathabane commented in the *Los Angeles Times.* "There are good white people and bad white people, just as there are good black people and bad black people. Black racism is as reprehensible and corroding to the soul as white racism."

Mark Mathabane was born in 1960 in Alexandra township, a one-square-mile ghetto just outside Johannesburg, South Africa. Like 150,000 other black South Africans, the Mathabanes were forced to live in the township. Their only alternative was a desolate tribal reserve created for blacks in the countryside, a "homeland" from which Mathabane's father had emigrated in search of work. The author described the conditions in Alexandra in a piece for *Writer's Digest:* "The eldest of seven children—two boys and five girls—I lived with my parents and siblings in a shack made of crumbling bricks and rusted sheets of metal zinks. The shack measured roughly 15 by 15 feet. Till I was 10, my siblings and I slept on pieces of cardboard under the kitchen table."

Mathabane's father, a laborer, was a target of near constant harassment by the police. Once, when Mathabane was five, officers broke into the family shack in the middle of the night. Kicking young Mathabane aside savagely, they grabbed his father and interrogated him about his passbook, a document all blacks were forced to carry. "What a pitiful sight my father was, naked and begging for mercy," the author remembered in *People.* "That morning I began to learn the meaning of hate. Following the police as they carried my father away, I watched as dozens of people were herded into police vans because their passbooks . . . were not in order. My parents were regarded as 'undesirables' because they did not have the necessary permit to live together as husband and wife. My

father was arrested for that and for the crime of being unemployed, because he had recently lost his $10-a-week job as a menial laborer. My mother narrowly escaped arrest by hiding herself in our wardrobe."

Frequently arrested and detained for months at a time, Mathabane's father left the family to fend for itself in the bleak confines of Alexandra. Mathabane told *Writer's Digest* that he and his siblings "scavenged for half-eaten sandwiches thrown away by whites at the garbage dump. . . . There were many days when nothing was available to eat, and we would simply stare at each other, at the empty pots, and at the sun going down."

Creativity Fueled by Tradition

His mother worked to restore family spirits by telling stories she had learned from her own mother. "Her stories about black culture, traditions, magic, and heroes and heroines were the only books we had," the author recalled in *Writer's Digest.* "By sharpening my sensibilities and firing my curiosity and imagination, these stories, almost Homeric in their vividness, drama, and invention, became the seeds of my own creativity."

When Mathabane was seven, his mother took a job as a washerwoman for a large Indian family in order to earn the money to send her oldest son to school. Education was not compulsory for South African blacks—in fact, those who wished to attend school had to pay fees and purchase slates and books. The whole process of schooling was met with cynicism in the township because, as Mathabane noted in *Writer's Digest,* the program "was meant to reconcile us black children to our subjection and the status quo, to keep us ignorant of our fundamental rights as human beings, and to make us better servants of whites."

Mathabane was literally dragged to school on the first day, and when he returned home, he discovered that his mother and father had fought over the matter. "My father had beaten her badly for sending me to school, which he though was 'unmanly' and would only teach me how to be a slave," Mathabane told *People.* "To spite my father, I promised [my mother] I would go to school as long as she wanted."

The Path to Education and Opportunity

One day when Mathabane was eleven, his grandmother took him to the home of the white family she worked for. "It was like taking a leap into another galaxy," the author explained in *People.* Taunted by the white son of the family for his poor English, Mathabane became determined to master the language. He taught himself from discarded comic books and newspapers his grandmother brought him from her job. At thirteen he began to work on Saturdays for the white family and soon impressed them with his hunger for knowledge. They were the first in a string of white people who helped Mathabane escape from the township life that had nearly driven him to suicide at the tender age of ten.

"Granny's employer began giving me books that were only read in white schools," Mathabane remembered in *Writer's Digest.* "These 'revolutionary' books—*Treasure Island, David Copperfield* and other classics—changed my life. They convinced me that there was a world beyond that of the violence, poverty and suffering in which I was steeped. They helped emancipate me from mental slavery and taught me to believe in my own worth and abilities, despite apartheid's attempts to limit my aspirations and prescribe my place in life." The same employer also gave Mathabane another valuable gift—a used tennis racket and some tennis balls. Mathabane began to teach himself to play tennis, inspired by the example of American star Arthur Ashe.

In 1977 Mathabane defied a black boycott to play in an important tennis tournament in South Africa. Several Americans participated in the event, and although Mathabane lost his match in the first round, he did get to meet former Wimbledon champion Stan Smith. Smith took a personal interest in Mathabane, contacting American colleges on the young student's behalf. Within weeks of the tournament, Mathabane began to receive letters and scholarship offers from colleges in America. Mathabane left South Africa in the autumn of 1978, clutching copies of the United States Constitution and the Declaration of Independence as he boarded the plane for Limestone College in South Carolina. "Tennis became my passport to freedom in America," Mathabane wrote in the *Los Angeles Times.* "I continued to encounter white racists, but their bigotry failed to eradicate in me the reality that there were other whites who were different."

Mathabane quickly discovered that life in America could pose its own problems. A dedicated student, he was shocked by the drug and alcohol use among his classmates. Their lackadaisical attitude toward schoolwork ran counter to his own ambitious plan of study, and soon he found himself at odds with the college's tennis coach over the amount of time he spent with his books. Worse, he found that he had left apartheid behind only to find a subtler form of segregation at work in the United States. White and black students did not socialize or sit together at his college. They pursued different agendas and seemed to distrust one another. Mathabane challenged this system by talking to white *and* black students and by defending the liberal arts curriculum that leaned heavily toward white male authors.

"My attitude rankled some black students," Mathabane wrote in the *Los Angeles Times.* "Some felt that any black student who sat with whites in the cafeteria, worked with them on projects, shared with them black culture and socialized with them was a traitor. In their militant rage at white racism, these students apparently forgot that communicating with each other is one effective way of combatting the cancer of racism. Some white students felt uncomfortable with me because I did not fit their prejudiced view of what a black person is: those whites felt comfortable only around blacks who acted unintelligent and happy-go-lucky."

With Stan Smith's financial support, Mathabane eventually attended four colleges as an undergraduate. While at Quincy College in Illinois, he read *Black Boy,* the autobiography of Richard Wright. The work was a revelation to Mathabane, who immediately went to the library and

> "The most important thing I have to fight as a black person in an oppressive, racist society is what I think about myself."

checked out a dozen books by black American authors. Mathabane was elated to discover the sentiments of Eldridge Cleaver, James Baldwin, Richard Wright, and Maya Angelou, among others. Even better, the student felt he might contribute to this literary tradition by writing about his own childhood.

Made Famous by a Memoir

Mathabane graduated from Dowling College in 1983 and began work on his first book, a memoir about his childhood in South Africa. He called the story *Kaffir Boy,* using the slang equivalent of "nigger" from his native country. While writing the manuscript, he gave talks occasionally about conditions in South Africa, and one of these was attended by novelist Phyllis Whitney. She encouraged Mathabane to send the unfinished work to her agent. In the few weeks that followed, Mathabane met with a number of agents in New York City, finally choosing the same one who represented Arthur Ashe. The manuscript was received with great excitement by several major publishers, and Macmillan eventually won rights to publish it in hardcover.

Kaffir Boy, published in 1986, won the Christopher Award. For Mathabane, the book "gave me a feeling of being purged," he told *Writer's Digest.* "I was finally able to fully accept who I was and where I came from. In short, I wrote to heal myself as well as inform others."

Television talk show host Oprah Winfrey bought a paperback copy of *Kaffir Boy* and was so moved by the story that she invited Mathabane to appear on her show. She also flew Mathabane's mother and siblings to the United States for a reunion—he had not seen his family in nearly a decade and faced possible arrest if he dared enter South Africa. The television show provided further publicity for Mathabane's book, and soon it was on the bestseller lists. Encouraged by its reception, Mathabane moved on to other projects.

Called for Improved Race Relations

Kaffir Boy in America details Mathabane's culture shock in the American college system and his reaction to the dual experiences of freedom and racism in America. *Atlanta Constitution* reviewer Fredrick Robinson called the work "a perceptive, revealing and accurate comparison between the sharply drawn contradictions in American society and those of [Mathabane's] homeland. His ideas don't give way to simplicity and quick solutions—he recognizes the complexities of life—and the opinions expressed in his book clearly reflect this. What resonates so vividly in the book is his honesty, his love for knowledge and, above all, his tireless commitment to social justice."

Mathabane will not allow himself to be pigeonholed as a "voice of the oppressed." His third book, *Love in Black and White,* explores his marriage to a white woman and the hostility they have faced together from both blacks and whites. In his speeches and writings, Mathabane exhorts people to see past skin color to the character of the individual. He also makes a plea for genuine interaction between races, something he feels is sorely lacking in America. "It's amazing what happens when you finally free your mind of those mental shackles," he told the *Los Angeles Times.* "When you realize that the most important thing I have to fight as a black person in an oppressive, racist society is what I think about myself. It is so easy to fall into the state of saying, 'I am a victim.' It is formidable, but [African Americans] have to succeed in America despite racism. You have to, this is your fate. This is your lot. You belong here."

Selected writings

Kaffir Boy: The True Story of a Black Youth's Coming of Age in Apartheid South Africa, Macmillan, 1986.
Kaffir Boy in America, Scribner, 1989.
(With wife, Gail Mathabane) *Love in Black and White,* HarperCollins, 1992.

Sources

Books

Black Writers, Gale, 1989.
Mathabane, Mark, *Kaffir Boy: The True Story of a Black Youth's Coming of Age in Apartheid South Africa,* Macmillan, 1986.

Periodicals

Atlanta Constitution, June 15, 1989; February 23, 1992.
Chicago Tribune, June 21, 1989; March 15, 1992.
Los Angeles Times, April 29, 1989; July 7, 1989; February 10, 1992.
Newsweek, March 9, 1992, p. 62.
People, July 7, 1986, p. 67.
Time, November 12, 1990, pp. 16-19.
Washington Post, May 28, 1989; February 16, 1992.
Writer's Digest, November 1989.

—Anne Janette Johnson

Hattie McDaniel

1895-1952

Actress, entertainer

Hattie McDaniel's 1939 portrayal of Mammy in *Gone with the Wind* set the screen image of the loyal black maid serving a household of well-to-do white people. Known for her broad smile, ample proportions, and ebullient manner, the actress appeared in over 300 films during the 1930s and 1940s, almost without exception in the character of maid or cook, a role with which she became so identified after the success of *Gone with the Wind* that many of her fans and friends took to calling her Mammy.

McDaniel enjoyed a long and prosperous career in film and radio drama and in 1940 became the first African American to win an Academy Award; but because she was used exclusively in the role of a domestic, she became the object of intense criticism from progressive blacks in the 1940s. By the time she appeared in *Gone with the Wind,* McDaniel had broadened her portrait of the Mammy role, endowing the character with an earthy, all-knowing sensibility and delivering her lines with saucy self-assurance. But, caught between the demands of two cultures, McDaniel became embittered by the attacks on her integrity made by the black intelligentsia, and when she died in 1952 the role of Mammy pretty well died with her.

Hattie McDaniel was born in 1895, in Wichita, Kansas, the

thirteenth child in a family of performers. Her father, Henry McDaniel, led a varied life as a Baptist minister, carpenter, banjo player, and minstrel showman, eventually organizing his own family into a minstrel troupe. Henry married a gospel singer named Susan Holbert in 1875 and moved their growing family to Denver, Colorado, in 1901.

McDaniel was one of only two black children in her elementary school class in Denver. Racial prejudice was less virulent in the West than elsewhere in the United States, and she became something of a favorite at the 24th Street Elementary School for her talents as a singer and reciter of poetry. Even as a child, according to a letter written to Hattie years later by her teacher, "you had an outstanding dramatic ability, an ability to project to your listeners your strong personality and your ever present sense of humor." McDaniel sang at church, at school, and at home; she sang so continuously that her mother reportedly bribed her into silence with spare change. Before long she was also singing in professional minstrel shows, as well as dancing, performing humorous skits, and later writing her own songs.

In 1910 McDaniel left school in her sophomore year and became a full-time minstrel performer, traveling the western

At a Glance. . .

Born June 10, 1895, in Wichita, KS; daughter of Henry (a preacher, carpenter, and minstrel musician) and Susan (a gospel performer; maiden name, Holbert) McDaniel; died of cancer, October 26, 1952, in Woodland Hills, CA; buried at Rosedale Cemetery; married George Langford, 1922 (died that year); married Howard Hickman, 1938 (divorced 1938); married James Lloyd Crawford (a real estate broker), 1941 (divorced 1945); married Larry Williams (an interior designer), 1949 (divorced 1950). *Education*: Attended Denver East High School for two years; practical training with her father's minstrel troupe, 1911-16.

Stage, film, radio, and television actress; singer. Minstrel performer in western United States, 1910-20; member of Professor George Morrison's orchestra, 1920-1925; first radio performance, Denver station KOA, 1925; continued work on vaudeville circuits through 1929; ladies' room attendant, then vocalist, at Sam Pick's Club Madrid, Milwaukee, WI, 1929-31; first motion picture roles, 1931; first significant film roles in *Judge Priest,* 1934, and *The Little Colonel,* 1935; actress in *Gone with the Wind,* 1939; continued film career through late 1940s; starred as Beulah in *The Beulah Show,* CBS radio, 1947-1951.

Awards: Gold medal from Women's Christian Temperance Union, 1910; Academy Award for best supporting actress for *Gone with the Wind,* 1940.

states with her father's Henry McDaniel Minstrel Show and several other troupes. The minstrel shows, usually performed by blacks but sometimes by whites in blackface, presented a variety of entertainments based on caricatures of black cultural life for the enjoyment of mostly white audiences. With her father's troupe, which also featured a number of her brothers and sisters, she visited most of the major cities in the western United States while honing the skills that would later make her famous.

When her father retired around 1920, McDaniel joined Professor George Morrison's famous "Melody Hounds" on longer and more publicized tours. As recounted by Carlton Jackson in *Hattie: The Life of Hattie McDaniel,* she was unquestionably one of the stars of Morrison's troupe; of one concert, the *Portland Telegram* wrote that "the biggest show

stopper of them all was Morrison's orchestra and its Hattie McDaniel." She also wrote dozens of show tunes such as "Sam Henry Blues," "Poor Wandering Boy Blues," and "Quittin' My Man Today."

Broke into Radio and Film

In the 1920s McDaniel toured constantly with Morrison's troupe and other well-known vaudeville companies. A first marriage ended abruptly in 1922 when her husband of three months, George Langford, was reportedly killed by gunfire. Little is known of this or any of McDaniel's three subsequent marriages, except that they were all relatively short and unhappy. More heartening was the progress of her career, which included a first radio performance in 1925 on Denver's KOA station. McDaniel was one of the first black women to be heard on American radio, the medium in which she would always remain most comfortable.

In 1929, the booking organization for whom she was working went bankrupt at the onset of the Great Depression, stranding McDaniel in Chicago with little money and no job. On a tip from a friend, she went north to Milwaukee and found work at Sam Pick's Club Madrid—as a bathroom attendant. At that time, the Club Madrid engaged only white nightclub performers and had no use for a black minstrel/vaudeville entertainer such as Hattie McDaniel. True to her nature, however, McDaniel could not refrain from singing while she worked, and she became well known among the club's patrons for her unfailing good humor and obvious talent. After repeated promptings from McDaniel's fans, the club's owner gave her a shot at performing on his main stage, where her rendition of "St. Louis Blues" was a smash hit. She remained as a performer at the Club Madrid for about a year, until she was lured to Hollywood by the enthusiastic reports of her brother Sam and sister Etta, who had been living in Los Angeles for several years.

Sam and Etta McDaniel already had small roles in a number of motion pictures, but Hattie was forced to take menial jobs in order to support herself in Los Angeles. Opportunities for blacks in Hollywood were severely limited to a handful of stereotypic roles, and even these parts were hard to come by. Sam McDaniel had a regular part on LA's KNX radio show "The Optimistic Do-Nuts" and was able to get Hattie a small part, which she promptly turned into a big opportunity. McDaniel earned the nickname "Hi-Hat Hattie" after showing up for the first radio broadcast in formal evening wear. According to Jackson, "she instantly became a hit with black West Coast listeners," and eventually stole the show.

McDaniel landed her first movie role in 1931 as an extra in the chorus scenes of a routine Hollywood musical. The next year, she played in her first major motion picture—the Twentieth Century Fox film *The Golden West*—as a house servant. She continued to appear in a number of similar bit parts, receiving screen credit for none of them, until famed director John Ford cast her in the 1934 Fox production of *Judge Priest*. In this picture, McDaniel was given the opportunity to sing a duet with Will Rogers, the well-known American humorist, and her performance was well received by the press and her fellow actors alike.

In 1935 McDaniel played "Mom Beck" in *The Little Colonel,* which starred Shirley Temple and Lionel Barrymore and faithfully reflected the image then held by many white Americans of the happy black servant in the Old South. A number of black journalists objected to Hattie's performance in the film, charging that the character of Mom Beck implied that blacks might have been happier as slaves than they were as free individuals. This movie marked the beginning of McDaniel's long feud with the more progressive elements of the black community.

Won Oscar for *Gone with the Wind*

Once established in Hollywood, McDaniel found no shortage of work. In 1936 alone she appeared in twelve films, including the Universal release *Show Boat,* starring Paul Robeson. For the decade as a whole, her performances numbered about forty—nearly all of them in the role of maid or cook to a household of whites. As such, she was a leading candidate for the role of Mammy in David O. Selznick's 1939 production of *Gone with the Wind,* adapted from Margaret Mitchell's bestselling novel of the same name.

Gone with the Wind was dead certain to be a hugely successful film, and competition for parts was intense in Hollywood. McDaniel won the role of Mammy over several rivals, signing a contract with Selznick that gave him exclusive rights to her work for a number of years. Her salary for *Gone with the Wind* was to be $450 a week, which—while not in the same league as the pay of stars like Clark Gable and Vivien Leigh—was nevertheless a long way from what her real-life counterparts could hope to earn. Responding to a friend who objected to the limited scope of her film roles, McDaniel is often quoted as having said: "Hell, I'd rather play a maid than be one."

Gone with the Wind rewarded McDaniel with far more than a weekly salary, however. As the loving but occasionally sharp-tongued Mammy, Hattie McDaniel became known and loved by the millions of people who would eventually see the movie, one of Hollywood's all-time hits. Her performance as Mammy was more than a bit part, and it so impressed the Academy of Motion Picture Arts and Sciences that she was awarded the 1940 Oscar for best

supporting actress, the first ever won by an African American. In contrast to the widespread criticism she had received for some of her earlier roles, McDaniel's award-winning performance was *generally* seen by the black press as a symbol of progress for African Americans, although some members of the NAACP were still displeased with her work. At the least, her Oscar was a symbol of possible conciliation between the races, especially potent at a time when the country was preparing to do battle with fascist enemies such as German leader Adolf Hitler.

Feuds with NAACP

Gone with the Wind lifted McDaniel to the ranks of known film personalities and was unquestionably the high point of her career. In the wake of the film's great success, she spent much of 1940 touring the country as Mammy, and in the following year she appeared in three substantial film roles, earning no less than $31,000 for her efforts. She was married, for a third time, to James L. Crawford in 1941, and once released from her contract with Selznick in 1943, she became a free agent in the Hollywood markets.

During World War II, McDaniel worked with the Hollywood Victory Committee, entertaining black troops and encouraging Americans to buy war bonds. But the mid-1940s brought trying times for McDaniel, who experienced a heart-wrenching false pregnancy in 1944 and soon after became the victim of racist-inspired legal

> Her performance in *Gone with the Wind* so impressed the Academy of Motion Picture Arts and Sciences that she was awarded the 1940 Oscar for best supporting actress, the first ever won by an African American.

problems. At about the time the war ended, the actress found herself embroiled in a legal battle over a restrictive covenant system in Los Angeles that limited black land and home ownership rights. Having purchased a thirty-room house in the city back in 1942, McDaniel faced the possibility of eviction if the discriminatory restrictive covenant were enforced. She was one of several black entertainers who challenged the racist system in court, however, and won.

Still, throughout the 1940s, a growing number of activists

viewed McDaniel and all she represented as a detriment to the budding fight for civil rights. By the end of the war, the United States had entered a new phase in the struggle for equality between the races. Minstrel shows and the stereotyped roles heretofore allowed blacks were no longer acceptable to a growing community of intellectuals and activists, who demanded that films represent people of color as capable of greater accomplishments than those of cook, servant, and shoe shine boy. NAACP president Walter White pressed both actors and studios to stop making films that tended to degrade blacks, and he singled out the roles of Hattie McDaniel as particularly offensive. According to Jackson in *Hattie,* McDaniel was referred to as "that Twentieth Century Fox specialist in the bug-eye" by a reporter for the *New York Post,* and she appeared in all three of the films White described as excessively "anti-Negro" (*Gone with the Wind, The Little Colonel,* and *Maryland*).

In response, McDaniel defended her right to choose whichever roles she saw fit, adding that many of her screen personae, like Mammy in *Gone with the Wind,* had shown themselves to be more than the equals of their white employers. Jackson suggested that McDaniel "was a gradualist, 'inadvertent,' reformer, and she accomplished more in this capacity than many of those who had set out specifically to change the system. . . . Hattie's fight against restrictive covenants, and her straight playing of [black roles] influenced the [civil rights] revolution more than she or anyone around her realized. She . . . [proved] to listeners that a black person could have a comedic role without degradation. . . . She was able to instill a mood of rising expectations in young blacks on their way up in the entertainment and business worlds."

Renewed Success in Radio

By the late 1940s McDaniel found herself in a difficult position. She was nationally famous and loved as the personification of the hard-working, humble black servant yet was under attack for playing that character by many members of the black community; and, perhaps most difficult of all, such roles were disappearing in the changing racial climate of post-World War II America. Inevitably, McDaniel found her screen opportunities drying up even as she suffered insults from progressive blacks, and after her third marriage ended in divorce in 1945, she became increasingly depressed and confused as to her proper path.

Although her screen image was permanently linked to a now-outdated stereotype, McDaniel could still use her vocal talent on radio. In 1947 she won the starring role of Beulah on *The Beulah Show,* a CBS radio show about a black maid and the white family for whom she worked. *The Beulah Show* had been on the air for some years, but

always with white males taking the role of Beulah; when Hattie McDaniel took over the role, she became the first black to star in a radio program intended for a general audience. Beulah was an ideal role for the actress, allowing her to make use of her considerable comedic gifts while not being limited to a crude racial cliche. Moreover, the program was generally praised by the NAACP and the Urban League, along with the twenty million other Americans who listened to it every evening at the height of its popularity in 1950.

McDaniel's last marriage, to an interior decorator named Larry Williams, lasted only a few months. In 1951 she suffered a heart attack while filming the first few segments of a projected television version of *The Beulah Show.* Although she recovered enough to tape more than a dozen episodes of the *Beulah* radio show in the spring of 1952, by summer she was diagnosed with breast cancer. McDaniel died on October 26, 1952. She will always be remembered as Mammy of *Gone with the Wind,* a role that many critics find offensive, many others prize as the movie's finest performance, and most agree could have been played by no one but Hattie McDaniel.

Selected filmography

The Blonde Venus, Paramount Publix, 1932.
I'm No Angel, Paramount, 1933.
Judge Priest, Fox, 1934.
Babbitt, RKO, 1934.
The Little Colonel, Fox, 1935.
Alice Adams, RKO, 1935.
Show Boat, Universal, 1936.
Can This Be Dixie?, Fox, 1936.
Saratoga, MGM, 1937.
Nothing Sacred, United Artists, 1937.
Battle of Broadway, Fox, 1938.
The Mad Miss Manton, RKO, 1938.
Gone with the Wind, MGM, 1939.
Maryland, Fox, 1940.
The Great Lie, Warner, 1941.
In This Our Life, Warner, 1942.
Thank Your Lucky Stars, Warner, 1943.
Since You Went Away, United Artists, 1944.
Song of the South, Disney, 1946.
Family Honeymoon, Universal-International, 1948.

Selected radio performances

Optimistic Do-Nuts, KNX, Los Angeles, 1931.
(With Eddie Cantor) *Rudy Vallee Show,* NBC, 1941.
Blueberry Hill, CBS, 1943.
The Billie Burke Show, CBS, 1944.
Amos 'n' Andy Show, NBC, 1945.

The Beulah Show, CBS, 1947-1951.

Sources

Books

Bogle, Donald, *Toms, Coons, Mulattoes, Mammies and Bucks: An Interpretive History of Blacks in American Films,* Viking Press, 1973.

Bogle, Donald, *Brown Sugar: Eighty Years of America's Black Female Superstars,* Harmony Books, 1980.

Jackson, Carlton, *Hattie: The Life of Hattie McDaniel,* Madison Books, 1990.

Noble, Peter, *The Negro in Films: Literature of the Cinema,* Arno Press, 1970.

Periodicals

Amsterdam News (New York), November 19, 1949; November 1, 1952; April 28, 1979, p. 37.

Collier's, December 1939, pp. 20-21, 32.

Crisis, October 1937, p. 297.

Ebony, August 1948, p. 57; December 1949, p. 92.

Hollywood Studio Magazine, April 1977, pp. 19-20.

Journal of Popular Film, Fall 1973, pp. 366-71.

New York Times, March 7, 1948; October 27, 1952.

New York Times Magazine, December 10, 1939.

Our World Magazine, February 1952.

Village Voice, May 5, 1975.

—*Jonathan Martin*

Mark McEwen

1954—

Broadcast journalist

As the weather reporter and entertainment editor for *CBS This Morning,* Mark McEwen takes an enthusiastic approach toward his work and transcends his job description. While traveling the country to bring his viewers the latest forecast or entertainment report for the early-morning television news show, McEwen feels compelled to participate in events that are unique to the area that he is visiting. He has gone hang gliding in Kitty Hawk, North Carolina, toyed with bulls in a Jackson, Mississippi rodeo, and even strapped himself to the "gyro thing" at NASA's space camp in Florida, all in the name of television.

Yet, for many of McEwen's fans, it is not the zany stunts that make them tune in every morning. His cheery disposition and enthusiastic attitude are the attributes that make him stand out. "When the news is bleak," CBS producer Jay Kernis told Diane Goldner of *USA Weekend,* "Mark reminds you it's worth getting up." Even his friend and rival, Willard Scott, weatherman for NBC's *Today* show, admits that McEwen is "ebullient."

McEwen realizes that his role as weatherman is incidental to his real job. "Weather is what I do," he told Jane Marion of *TV Guide,* "but when I get out there, I'm just trying to entertain."

And he has plenty of experience to make his special brand of entertainment work.

Growing up as one of six children of a U.S. Air Force colonel, McEwen lived in Germany, Alabama, Texas, and Maryland before starting college at the University of Maryland. Though life as a military child provided him with many enriching experiences, it never gave him a clear path for the future. "I never knew what I wanted to be," he told Marion. "I just knew I wanted to be famous." After a few years of college, McEwen started on his search for fame.

McEwen's first job came in 1977 as a sports director and overnight disc jockey for WKTK-FM radio in Baltimore, Maryland. After working as "Midnight Mark" for a year, he moved to Detroit to take the job of music director for rock station WWWW-FM (known as W-4). It wasn't long before his duties were expanded and he was given his first big opportunity as an on-air personality—that of the coveted morning drive-time disc jockey. His success as one of the first black deejays on a rock station was almost immediate and proved to be long-lasting. In a review of McEwen's role as weatherman for *CBS This Morning, Detroit News* television reporter Jim McFarlin fondly remembered McEwen as "possibly Detroit's

At a Glance. . .

Born September 16, 1954, in San Antonio, TX; son of Alfred (an Air Force colonel) and Dolores (a bank officer) McEwen; married first wife (divorced); married Judith Lonsdale (an attorney), June 7, 1992. *Education:* Attended University of Maryland, College Park, 1972-75.

Weather reporter, music and entertainment editor, disc jockey, and comedian. Sports director and disc jockey, WKTK-FM, Baltimore, MD, 1977-78; music director and disc jockey, WWWW-FM, Detroit, MI, 1978-80; research director and disc jockey, WLUP-FM, Chicago, IL, 1980-82; disc jockey, WAPP-FM, New York City, 1982-83; disc jockey, WNEW-FM, New York City, 1983-86; weather reporter, *The Morning Program,* CBS-TV, New York City, 1987; weather reporter and music editor, *CBS This Morning,* New York City, 1987—, named entertainment editor, 1992. Performed as comedian in numerous nightclubs including The Improv and Catch a Rising Star. Made television appearances on various shows, including *Comedy Tonight, The Late Show,* and *Hollywood Squares.* Also host of *Steampipe Alley* (a live children's show), on WOR-TV, New York City, 1987, and *Wanna Bet?* (a game show), on CBS-TV, 1992.

Addresses: *Office—CBS This Morning,* CBS Inc., 524 West 57th St., New York, NY 10019.

best solo rock 'n' roll morning man when he worked for WWWW-FM."

Stations from across the country soon became aware of his talents. In 1980 McEwen left Detroit to accept a position at Chicago's WLUP-FM as a disc jockey for the 10 p.m. to 2 a.m. shift. McEwen summed up his departure from Detroit for McFarlin: "After two years here I was just ready for a bigger challenge, and I'm going to the hottest rock 'n' roll station in the country right now." Though he was only hired as an on-air personality, it wasn't long before the station recognized his managerial abilities. Soon after his arrival, McEwen was given the added responsibility of research director.

From Disc Jockey to Comic

While in Chicago, McEwen decided that he wanted to

break away from the traditional disc jockey role and dive into the world of comedy. Even though he trained with the Second City Players Workshop and appeared at various clubs around the area, including Byfield's and the Playboy Club, McEwen's listeners never got to experience his comedic talents. "I've never been a comedian on the air," he told Eric Zorn of the *Chicago Tribune.* "An audience has to see me to get what I'm doing."

What McEwen was doing was setting his sights on becoming a full-time actor and comic. Though he loved his job on the radio, he was beginning to enjoy his new sideline career. After catching his act at one of the local comedy clubs, Zorn offered *Tribune* readers a critique of McEwen. "McEwen engages his audience and does not talk down to them, preferring a folksy, mildly ironic delivery filled with lots of 'I-tell-ya's' and 'ya-knows.' He is among the few black deejays on an FM rock station in the country, but makes relatively few racially oriented or radio-oriented jokes, sticking instead to drugs, TV and sex."

McEwen's radio and comedy career continued to climb upward when he moved to New York City in 1982 to take a job at WAPP-FM. He also continued to fine tune his comedy routine at local comedy clubs—like Catch a Rising Star and The Improv—and even worked as the opening act for legendary comic George Burns. But McEwen was beginning to question his abilities as a stand-up comic. "I was too sensitive," he told Goldner in *USA Weekend.* "If the audience didn't laugh, I thought they didn't like me."

Broke into Television

A move to rival station WNEW-FM in 1983 would eventually lead McEwen to his big break. After working at the station for three years, he was fired due to the loss of a ratings war. At the same time, CBS was getting ready to launch *The Morning Program,* a new morning news show. When the program's executive producer read about the deejay's ouster in the *New York Daily News* and learned of his television aspirations, McEwen was given the job as weather reporter for the show.

Unfortunately, the show's popularity among viewers and critics alike was not good. "It's fluff and froth," wrote television critic Don Merrill in *TV Guide,* "which, with the occasional pauses for news, goes on for an hour and a half. It seems a lot longer. Of course much of television is fluff and froth. 'The Morning Program' is just fluffier and frothier—and earlier." It took less than a year for the network executives to cancel the show. Every on-air anchor for the program was fired, except for McEwen.

Landed Spot on *CBS This Morning*

When *CBS This Morning* debuted in November of 1987, McEwen was back on the air and excited to be a part of the new show. He explained his optimism to McFarlin at the time of the program's debut. "I'm really looking forward to the new one because now we have a 'big brother'—the news division is behind us. I think we'll get more of a commitment, and I think they'll allow the show to evolve."

McEwen was not only excited to be back on a morning news show with his old duties as weatherman, but he was equally excited to be given the chance to bring his music background into the picture. As the show's new music editor, McEwen was thrilled with the opportunity to interview music legends like Phil Collins, Quincy Jones, and Diana Ross. "McEwen relishes interviews with such music luminaries as Paul Simon and B. B. King—practice, perhaps, for the talk show he hopes to host someday," Goldner wrote. The producers of *CBS This Morning* were so impressed with his ability to profile music celebrities that they expanded his role to that of entertainment editor to include a wide range of stories on entertainment personalities and subjects.

It didn't take long for *CBS This Morning* to become competitive with its rival morning programs. The ratings climbed, thanks in part to the popularity of Mark McEwen. Once the show was clearly on solid ground, McEwen's responsibilities at CBS branched out to other areas, including serving as a fill-in host for *CBS This Morning,* a contributor to the CBS-TV news magazine *48 Hours,* and the host of the game show *Wanna Bet?* In addition, he was given the responsibility of "network announcer," doing voice-overs and promotional segues for prime-time programs on CBS. McEwen also appeared as a regular on the syndicated television series *Comedy Tonight,* a guest on *The Late Show,* and the first weatherman to be featured on *Hollywood Squares.*

McEwen claims that the secret to his success is that he doesn't put on any airs, he just tries to be himself. His marriage to attorney Judith Lonsdale in June of 1992 caused him to question the more dangerous stunts that he has done for the program, but it hasn't stopped them. His love of music, specifically his favorite album, Bruce Springsteen's *Born to Run,* sets the tone for his world view. "Life is not a sprint," he told Marion in *TV Guide.* "It's a marathon."

Sources

Chicago Tribune, July 26, 1982.
Detroit News, March 5, 1990; November 30, 1987; June 11, 1992; December 22, 1992.
TV Guide, April 11, 1987; September 30, 1989.
USA Today, April 20, 1993.
USA Weekend, May 15-17, 1992.

—*Joe Kuskowski*

Walter Mosley

1952—

Author

Photograph by Chester Higgins, Jr. / NYT PICTURES

Walter Mosley has broken new ground as a mystery writer by incorporating issues of race into novels that stand on their own as gripping detective fiction. His books *Devil in a Blue Dress, A Red Death,* and *White Butterfly* were all written from a black perspective. *Ebony* made the point clearly in its review of *White Butterfly,* saying that the novel had "a decidedly Black American point of view that greatly distinguishes it from any other work in the genre."

Critics have praised Mosley's writing for its realistic portrayal of street life in black neighborhoods of post-World War II Los Angeles. Sara M. Lomax wrote in *American Visions* that Mosley has "a special talent for layering time and place with words and ideas." *Library Journal*'s review of *A Red Death* noted, "As before, Mosley's inclusion of life in Watts, contemporary social attitudes, and colloquial speech contribute to the excellence and authenticity of plot and character portrayal."

Much of Mosley's success has been due to the powerful recurring character of Ezekiel ("Easy") Rawlins, one of the most innovative private investigators to appear in fiction. Unlike many detectives who populate the pages of hard-boiled prose, Rawlins is a multidimensional character who stumbled into his sleuthing career as a means to pay mounting

debts. Mosley has used Rawlins to expose the problems of getting by in a world where only a thin line lies between crime and business as usual. As Christopher Hitchens said in *Vanity Fair,* "Rawlins is more of a fixer than a hustler, a kind of accidental detective who gets pulled into cases because of his reluctantly acquired street smarts and savoir faire." D. J. R. Bruckner added in the *New York Times* that Easy Rawlins "is trapped into becoming a private detective, and the way he is trapped gives Mr. Mosley an opportunity to raise scores of moral questions in a novel of little more than 200 pages."

Walter Mosley was born in southeastern Los Angeles in 1952 and grew up in Watts and the Pico-Fairfax district. His father was an African American from the deep South, and his mother a white, Jewish woman whose family emigrated from Eastern Europe. This unique black/Jewish heritage made prejudice a major topic in the household. An only child, Mosley grew up hearing about the woes of life for blacks in the South, as well as the horrors of anti-Semitism across the Atlantic. However, he was also regaled by colorful accounts of partying and carrying on among his black relatives, along with tales of czars in old Russia.

At a Glance. . .

Born January 12, 1952, in Los Angeles, CA; son of LeRoy (a school custodian) and Ella (a school personnel clerk) Mosley; married Joy Kellman (a dancer and choreographer), 1987. *Education:* Attended Goddard College, 1971; Johnson State College, B.A., 1977; attended writing program at City College of New York, 1985-89.

Worked as a computer consultant for Mobil Oil, and as a computer programmer, potter, and caterer; became full-time writer, 1986.

Awards: John Creasey Memorial Award and Shamus Award, both for outstanding mystery writing; *Devil in a Blue Dress* was nominated for an Edgar for best first novel by the Mystery Writers of America, 1990.

Addresses: *Home*—New York City. *Publisher*—W. W. Norton & Co., Inc., 500 Fifth Ave., New York, NY 10110.

After earning a bachelor's degree at Johnson State College in 1977, Mosley drifted for a number of years in various jobs, even working as a potter and caterer. He and Joy Kellman, a dancer and choreographer, moved to New York City in 1982 and were married in 1987. The parents of Kellman, who is white and Jewish, reportedly didn't speak to their daughter for five years after meeting Mosley.

Mosley settled down into a career as a computer programmer in the 1980s, but his work left him unfulfilled. Meanwhile, he read voraciously, including mysteries by Raymond Chandler, Dashiell Hammett, and Ross MacDonald and existential novels such as *The Stranger* by Albert Camus. This blend of suspense and philosophy served him well in the mysteries he would later write.

Alice Walker Novel Triggered Interest in Writing

According to a profile in *People* magazine, Mosley's decision to become a writer was strongly influenced by his reading of *The Color Purple* by Alice Walker. That book rekindled the youthful urge to write that he had lost and made him feel that he could create the same kind of prose. He began writing feverishly on nights, weekends, and whenever he could find time. Intent on devoting himself totally to his craft, Mosley quit his computer programming

job in the mid-eighties and enrolled at the City College of New York to study with Frederic Tuten, head of the school's writing program. While in the program he also received instruction from writers William Matthews and Edna O'Brien.

Mosley's first book, a short psychological novel entitled *Gone Fishin'* that introduced the character of Easy Rawlins, was turned down by 15 agents. In 1989 Mosley showed *Devil in a Blue Dress*, which he had first written as a screenplay, to his writing teacher. The teacher showed the book to his agent, who sold it to the W. W. Norton publishing company.

When the novel came out in 1990, the *New York Times* said that it "marks the debut of a talented author." Rawlins's reappearance a year later in *A Red Death* caused *Publishers Weekly* to theorize that "Mosley . . . may well be in the process of creating a genre classic." *White Butterfly* was also greeted by critical acclaim, with *Cosmopolitan* saying that Mosley "brings it all so thoroughly, sizzlingly to life." The author's reputation soared when Bill Clinton said during his 1992 U.S. presidential campaign that Mosley was his favorite mystery writer.

Father's Background a Major Influence

Many characters in the Easy Rawlins novels are based on the experiences of Mosley's father, with similarities between LeRoy Mosley and Easy Rawlins especially apparent. After being treated like a hero abroad during World War II, LeRoy Mosley was dismayed to find that he was still a second-class citizen back in the States. This disillusionment was also felt by veteran Easy Rawlins in *Devil in a Blue Dress*. However, the war made it clear to Rawlins that the white man was not much different from himself. Early in the novel, the character ruminates: "I had spent five years with white men, and women, from Africa to Italy, through Paris, and into the Fatherland itself. I ate with them and slept with them, and I killed enough blue-eyed young men to know that they were just as afraid to die as I was."

In a commentary in the *Los Angeles Times*, Mosley asserted that "black soldiers learned from World War II; they learned how to dream about freedom." LeRoy Mosley's dream of freedom took him to California, where endless jobs and opportunities were rumored to be waiting for everyone, including African Americans. In the *Los Angeles Times*, Mosley described the Los Angeles of Easy Rawlins as "a place where a black man can dream but he has to keep his wits about him. Easy lives among the immigrants from the western South. He dreams of owning property and standing on an equal footing with his white peers. Deep in his mind he is indoctrinated with the terror of Southern racism. In his everyday life he faces the subtle, and not so subtle, inequalities of the American color line.''

Racism an Ever-Present Theme

Similar to the canon of Chester Himes, a black author who wrote Harlem-based crime novels in the 1940s and 1950s, Walter Mosley's works have consistently addressed social and racial issues. Drawing on his father's life and his own as a close observer of the Watts riots during the 1960s, Mosley shows in his books how racism infects the lives of inner city blacks. Double standards abound in *Devil in a Blue Dress,* in which a white man hires Rawlins to find a woman known to hang out in black jazz clubs. Easy was chosen because he was black and regarded as a bridge into a world where the white man dare not go. In *White Butterfly,* the police show a keen interest in the case of a murdered white cocktail waitress—after basically ignoring the murders of a series of black waitresses that occurred earlier.

Mosley has also tapped his Black/Jewish perspective to deal with Jewish suffering as perceived by blacks. In *Devil in a Blue Dress,* two Jewish liquor store owners in the black ghetto cause Easy Rawlins to remember when his unit broke open the gates of a Nazi extermination camp. This recollection leads to an understanding of similarities in the oppression suffered by blacks in America and Jews abroad.

The author has provided a loud voice on racial strife in the real world as well. He was particularly angered over the racially motivated riots that occurred in Los Angeles in 1992. The rioting was triggered by the ''not guilty'' verdicts handed down in the first trial of four white Los Angeles police officers involved in the brutal beating of African American motorist Rodney King. Mosley was outraged that racial tensions had led to blatant violence before people started to address the problems in urban black communities. As he stated in an editorial in the *Los Angeles Times,* ''The rioters sent out a message that is louder than a billion pleas over the past 400 years of beating, burning and death.''

This concern over the degeneration of black neighborhoods has been traced in Mosley's novels, each of which moves Easy Rawlins further into the future to confront changing racial and societal conditions. Nine novels in all have been planned for the Rawlins series, the final one bringing the protagonist into the early 1980s.

Moral Issues Raised Frequently

Mosley's novels have made it clear that morality cannot be

judged the same for blacks as it is for whites. The author wrote in the *Los Angeles Times* that ''Easy tries to walk a moral line in a world where he is not treated equally by the law. . . . He's a man who, finding himself with dark skin, has decided that he's going to live his life and do what's right, in that order.'' Mosley has used Easy's moral flexibility to force his hero back into the private eye business, as in *A Red Death* when Rawlins bought some buildings with stolen money. When the IRS threatened to look into his finances, Easy reluctantly agreed to spy on a suspected Jewish communist for an FBI man in exchange for protection from the taxman. As Mosley said in the *Los Angeles Times,* ''In Easy's world . . . you have to know what the law is but you also have to understand that the reality might be different.''

Mosley has found Greenwich Village, a noted haven for people in the arts, to be a good psychological base for him. ''It's hard to be conspicuous here,'' he was quoted as saying in *Vanity Fair.* While he may not want to be noticed, his writing has certainly put him on the literary map. Walter Mosley is an important voice in a new brand of African American fiction that has spawned memorable characters and plots. As Charles Champlin wrote in the *Los Angeles Times Book Review,* ''Mosley, who . . . knows Watts like an after-hours bartender, creates characters—men, women and children—who are vivid, individual and as honest as home movies.''

Selected writings

Devil in a Blue Dress (novel), Norton, 1990.
A Red Death (novel), Norton, 1991.
White Butterfly (novel), Norton, 1992.

Also author of the screenplay *Devil in a Blue Dress.*

Sources

American Visions, April/May 1992, pp. 32-34.
California, August 1990, p. 115.
Cosmopolitan, July 1991, p. 28; July 1992, p. 30.
Detroit Free Press, November 17, 1991, p. 6.
Ebony, September 1992, p. 21.
Essence, January 1991, p. 32; October 1992, p. 50.
Library Journal, June 1, 1991, p. 200; March 15, 1992, p. 68.
Los Angeles Times, May 5, 1992, pp. B7, E1, E5; May 14, 1992, p. 6.
Los Angeles Times Book Review, July 14, 1991. pp. 1-2, 9.
New Statesman & Society, April 19, 1991, p. 37.
Newsweek, July 7, 1990, p. 65.

New York Times, September 4, 1990, pp. C13, C16.
New York Times Book Review, August 5, 1990, p. 29.
People, September 7, 1992, pp. 105-106.
Publishers Weekly, May 17, 1991, p. 57.
Vanity Fair, February 1993, pp. 46, 48, 50.

—Ed Decker

Jessye Norman

1945—

Opera and concert singer

American soprano Jessye Norman is hailed as one of the world's greatest opera and concert singers and performers. Since the early 1970s she has starred at leading opera houses, concert halls, and music festivals throughout Europe, North America, and three other continents. She has also enjoyed a prolific recording career with over 40 albums and several Grammy Awards to her credit and is even recognized as the inspiration for the title character in the 1982 French film *Diva,* directed by Jean-Jacques Beineix.

Norman's voice has been resoundingly praised for its mastery of expression, technical control, and sheer power, while her diverse song repertoire spans standard and obscure operas to German lieder (classical songs), avant-garde works, and even popular ballads. As a performer, she is known for her magnetic and dramatic personality, and, with her imposing physical presence, cuts an impressive figure before audiences. According to Curt Sanburn in *Life,* Norman on stage creates the perception of one who "veritably looms behind her lyrics."

Born into a musical family in Augusta, Georgia, at the close of World War II, she was encouraged in her youth to be a singer.

Norman's mother, an amateur pianist, saw that all the children in the family took piano lessons, while her father, a successful insurance broker, sang frequently in the family's Baptist church. As a young girl Norman loved singing and performed wherever she had the opportunity—at church, school, Girl Scout meetings, even a supermarket opening; yet she never formally studied voice until college. "I was completely sure I would be a psychiatrist," she recalled in an interview with Charles Michener for *Vanity Fair.*

Norman fell in love with opera the first time she heard a Metropolitan Opera radio broadcast. "I was nine and I didn't know *what* was going on, but I just loved it," she told Michener. "After that I listened religiously." Soon after, Norman mastered her first aria, "My Heart at Thy Sweet Voice," from French composer Camille Saint-Saëns's *Samson and Delilah.* At 16 she traveled to Philadelphia with her school choral director for the Marian Anderson Scholarship competition and, while most of the participants were much older and she failed to win, received positive comments from the judges. On her return trip to Georgia she visited the music department at Howard University in Washington, D.C., and sang for Carolyn Grant, who would later become her vocal

At a Glance. . .

Born September 15, 1945, in Augusta, GA; daughter of Silas (an insurance broker) and Janie (a schoolteacher; maiden name, King) Norman. *Education:* Howard University, B.M. (cum laude), 1967; postgraduate study at Peabody Conservatory, 1967; University of Michigan, M.Mus., 1968. *Politics:* Democrat.

Opera and concert singer, 1969—; recording artist, 1971—. Opera credits include roles in *Tannhäuser; The Marriage of Figaro; Deborah; Idomeneo; L'Africaine; Aïda; Les Troyens; The Damnation of Faust; Ariadne auf Naxos; Bluebeard's Castle; Erwartung; Die Walküre; Don Giovanni; Hippolyte et Aricie; Gotterdämmerung; Dido and Aeneas; Oedipus Rex; Herodiade;* and *Les Contes d'Hoffmann.*

Numerous concert performances with orchestras around the world, including the Los Angeles Philharmonic, New York Philharmonic, London Philharmonic, Israel Philharmonic, Orchestre de Paris, Stockholm Philharmonic, Vienna Philharmonic, and Berlin Philharmonic; and numerous music festival performances, including Tanglewood, Aix-en-Provence, and Salzburg.

Selected awards: First prize in vocal competition from the National Society of Arts and Letters, 1965; Grammy Awards, 1980, 1982, and 1985; *Musical America's* Outstanding Musician of the Year Award, 1982; Commandeur de l'Ordre des Arts et des Lettres (France), 1984; member, Royal Academy of Music. Honorary degrees from Howard, Yale, Harvard, and Brandeis universities, the University of Michigan, and the Juilliard School of Music.

Addresses: *Office*—c/o Shaw Concerts Inc., 1995 Broadway, New York, NY 10023.

coach. After hearing Norman's voice, Grant recommended the budding soprano for a full-tuition four-year scholarship to the university when she came of college age.

Norman graduated from Howard with honors in 1967 and during her university career won many fans who heard her sing in the university choral group and local church choirs. She went on to complete a summer of postgraduate study at the Peabody Conservatory in Baltimore, Maryland, followed by her master's degree at the University of Michigan in Ann Arbor. While at Michigan, Norman worked with two re-

nowned teachers of voice, French baritone Pierre Bernac—a famous teacher of the art song—and Elizabeth Mannion. To finance her graduate school studies Norman auditioned for and received grants from various musical foundations and in 1968 received a scholarship from the Institute of International Education that allowed her to enter Bavarian Radio's International Music Competition in Munich, Germany. When Norman was on a U.S. State Department musical tour of the Caribbean and Latin America that year she received word that she had won the prestigious European contest. Subsequently, she received offers to perform and work in Europe and moved overseas in 1969, following the path of many American singers who began their careers in the celebrated concert and opera halls of Europe.

Gained International Acclaim Early in Career

Norman enjoyed rapid success in Europe. In December of 1969 she signed a three-year contract with the venerable Deutsche Oper in West Berlin and was a sensation in her debut—at the age of 23—as Elisabeth in German composer Richard Wagner's *Tannhäuser.* Norman thereafter received other primary roles with the opera company, in addition to numerous offers to sing concerts and operas throughout Europe. In 1970 she made her Italian debut in Florence in George Frideric Handel's *Deborah* and the following year her busy opera schedule included performances in Wolfgang Amadeus Mozart's *Idomeneo* in Rome, Giacomo Meyerbeer's *L'Africaine* in Florence, and Mozart's *Marriage of Figaro* at the Berlin Festival. Later in 1971 Norman auditioned for and won the opportunity to sing the role of the Countess in a Philips recording of *Figaro* with the BBC Orchestra under the direction of Colin Davis. The recording was a finalist for the prestigious Montreux International Record Award competition and brought Norman much exposure to music listeners in Europe and the United States.

In 1972 Norman performed in a Berlin production of Giuseppe Verdi's *Aïda,* a role in which she debuted later that year at the famed Italian opera stage, La Scala, in Milan. Also in 1972 she sang in a concert version of *Aïda* at the Hollywood Bowl in California, followed by a performance at Wolf Trap in Washington, D.C., with the National Symphony Orchestra, and an acclaimed Wagner recital at the prestigious Tanglewood Music Festival in Massachusetts.

Norman's triumphs of 1972 continued when she returned to Europe in the fall and debuted at the Royal Opera House in Covent Garden, England, as Cassandra in Hector Berlioz's *Les Troyens.* She also made her debut at the prestigious Edinburgh Music Festival that year. As a result of these victories, much acclaim and excitement awaited her first-ever New York City recital the following year when she appeared as part of the "Great Performers" series at Alice Tully Hall in Lincoln Center. Norman's performance, which included songs by European masters Wagner, Strauss, Brahms, and Satie, was hailed by Donald Henahan in the *New York Times* as one of "extraordinary intelligence, taste and emotional depth."

Took Temporary Leave of Opera

In the mid-1970s, wanting to more fully develop her vocal range, Norman made the decision to stop performing operas temporarily to concentrate on concert perform-ances. She told John Gruen in the *New York Times* of her desire to master a broad repertoire. "As for my voice, it cannot be categorized—and I like it that way, because I sing things that would be considered in the dramatic, mezzo or spinto range. I like so many different kinds of music that I've never allowed myself the limitations of one particular range."

The decision to take a half-decade leave from opera prompted criticism in concert circles. "I was considered difficult to deal with because I said 'No' so much," she noted in *Vanity Fair*. "But my voice was changing and it needed time to develop. It takes years to get that under-standing of how *your* voice works, years before you're able to divorce yourself from that horrible word we call 'tech-nique' and are able to release your *soul*."

Over the years Norman's technical expertise has been among her most critically praised attributes. In a review of one of her recitals at New York City's Carnegie Hall, *New York Times* contributor Allen Hughes wrote that Norman "has one of the most opulent voices before the public today, and, as discriminating listeners are aware, her performances are backed by extraordinary preparation, both musical and otherwise." Another Carnegie Hall ap-pearance prompted these words from Bernard Holland in the *New York Times:* "If one added up all the things that Jessye Norman does well as a singer, the total would assuredly exceed that of any other soprano before the public. At Miss Norman's recital . . . tones were produced, colors manipulated, words projected and interpretive points made—all with fanatic finesse."

Norman returned to the operatic stage in 1980 in a performance of Strauss's *Ariadne auf Naxos* in Hamburg, Germany, and in 1983 made her debut with New York City's Metropolitan Opera Company in its gala centennial season opener of *Les Troyens*. Norman shone among the star-studded cast, as Henahan wrote in his review. "Miss Norman . . . is a soprano of magnificent presence who commanded the stage at every moment," he declared. "As

the distraught Cassandra she sang grippingly and projects well, even when placed well back in the cavernous sets."

Although Norman has had great success performing in full-scale opera productions, her formidable physical stature has somewhat limited the availability of stage roles to her and she has increasingly directed her opera singing to condensed concert versions. One of the standards in her repertoire is "Liebestod" ("Love of Death"), the finale from Wagner's *Tristan und Isolde,* in which a despondent and soon-to-expire Isolde sings to her dead beloved, Tristan. Henahan reviewed Norman's performance of "Liebestod" at the 1989 New York Philharmonic season opener: "Although she has never sung the complete role on any stage, she has handled this fearsome 10-minute challenge with increasing vocal authority and dramatic insight. . . . Hers is a grandly robust voice, used with great intelligence and expression."

Inspired Lavish Ovations

Norman's performances have sparked seemingly endless ovations from audiences throughout the world—a report-ed 47 minutes in Tokyo in 1985 and 55 minutes in Salzburg the next year. Another pinnacle of her career came in 1987 with the Boston Symphony Orchestra at Tanglewood; her program of Strauss songs, which fea-tured the final scene from Strauss's opera *Salome,* prompted

> "It takes years to get that understanding of how *your* voice works, years before you're able to divorce yourself from that horrible word we call 'technique' and are able to release your *soul.*"

both critical acclaim and more than ten minutes of ap-plause from the audience. Michael Kimmelman wrote in the *New York Times* on the power of that particular performance: "Ms. Norman's voice seems to draw from a vast ocean of sound. . . . No matter how much volume Sieji Ozawa requested from his orchestra during the fiery scene from 'Salome,' it seemed little match for her voice. Yet, as always, what made the soprano's performance particularly remarkable was the effortlessness with which she could hover over long, soft notes. . . . And there is also the quality of sound she produces: even the loudest passages are cushioned by a velvety, seductive timbre."

Over the years Norman has not been afraid to expand her talent into less familiar areas. In 1988 she sang a concert performance of Francis-Jean-Marcel Poulenc's one-act opera *La Voix humaine* ("The Human Voice"), based on Jean Cocteau's 1930 play of the same name, in which a spurned actress feverishly pleads to keep her lover on the other end of a phone conversation. Although Henahan noted in the *New York Times* that Norman's "characteristic . . . style puts great emphasis on tragic dignity," and that the role perhaps called for less restraint, he nonetheless admired her as among those artists "driven to branch out into unlikely roles and whole idioms that stretch their talents interestingly, if sometimes to the breaking point."

Other of Norman's diverse projects have included her 1984 album *With a Song in My Heart,* which contains numbers from films and musical comedies, and a 1990 performance of American spirituals with soprano Kathleen Battle at Carnegie Hall. Norman told William Livingstone in *Stereo Review* that one of her objectives as a performer is "to communicate, to be understood in many ways and on many levels." In 1989 she was invited to sing the French national anthem—"La Marseillaise"—in Paris during the celebration of the bicentennial of the French Revolution. Norman, who sings nearly flawless French (in addition to German and Italian), was particularly honored by the opportunity. "It makes you feel really good that people at home think you are worth their interest, but it's incredible to be so warmly received in a foreign country," she told Livingstone. "I love watching the faces of the people who are listening as I sing these songs and know that they understand."

In the *New York Times* interview with Gruen, Norman described the reverence with which she approaches her work. "To galvanize myself into a performance, I must be left totally alone. I must have solitude in order to concentrate—which I consider a form of prayer. I work very much from the text. The words must be understood, felt and communicated. . . . If you look carefully at the words and absorb them, you're half-way home already. The rest is honesty—honesty of feeling, honesty of involvement. If a performer is truly committed, then the audience will be the first to know and will respond accordingly. Of course, love is the thing that propels us all. It's what carries us along—*that's* the fuel!"

Selected discography

Beethoven, Ludwig van, *Symphonie No. 6, op. 68: "Pastoral,"* Deutsche Grammophon, 1981.
Beethoven, *Symphony No. 9 in D minor,* London, 1987.
Berg, Alban, *Lulu Suite* [and] *Der Wein,* CBS Masterworks, 1979.

Berlioz, Hector, *Les Nuits d'été,* Philips, 1980.
Berlioz, *Les Nuits d'été* [and] *La Mort de Cléopâtre,* Deutsche Grammophon, 1982.
Berlioz, *Roméo et Juliette,* Angel, 1986.
Bizet, Georges, *Carmen,* Philips, 1989.
Brahms, Johannes, *Lieder,* Deutsche Grammophon, 1983.
Brahms, *A German Requiem,* Angel, 1985.
Bruckner, Anton, *Symphonie nr. 8 c-moll* [and] *Te Deum,* Deutsche Grammophon, 1981.
Bruckner, *Te Deum* [and] *Helgoland* [and] *150 Psalm,* Deutsche Grammophon, 1983.
Debussy, Claude, *L'Enfant prodigue* [and] *La Damoiselle élue,* Pro-Arte, 1982.
Faure, Gabriel Urbain, *Penelope,* Erato, 1982.
Gluck, Christoph Willibald, *Alceste,* 1982.
Haydn, Joseph, *La vera costanza,* Philips, 1977.
Haydn, *Armida,* Philips, 1979.
Mahler, Gustav, *Das Lied von der Erde,* Philips, 1982.
Mahler, *Symphony 2: "Resurrection,"* CBS, 1984.
Mozart, Wolfgang Amadeus, *The Marriage of Figaro,* Philips, 1971.
Offenbach, Jacques, *Les Contes d'Hoffmann,* Angel, 1988.
Purcell, Henry, *Dido and Aeneas,* Philips, 1986.
Ravel, Maurice, *Songs of Maurice Ravel,* CBS Masterworks, 1984.
Schubert, Franz, *Lieder,* Philips, 1973.
Schubert, *Lieder,* Philips, 1985.
Schumann, Robert, *Frauenliebe und Leben, op. 42* [and] *Liederkreis, op. 39,* Philips, 1976.
Strauss, Richard, *Four Last Songs,* Philips, 1983.
Strauss, *Lieder,* Philips, 1986.
Strauss, *Ariadne auf Naxos,* Philips, 1988.
Stravinsky, Igor, *Oedipus Rex,* Orfeo, 1983.
Verdi, Giuseppe, *Un giorno di regno,* Philips, 1974.
Verdi, *Il corsaro,* Philips, 1976.
Wagner, Richard, *Tristan und Isolde* [and] *Five Poems by Mathilde Wesendonk,* Philips, 1975.
Wagner, *Wesendonk Songs,* Angel, 1986.
Wagner, *Lohengrin,* London, 1987.
Wagner, *Scenes from Tristan und Isolde, Tannhäuser, Der fliegende Holländer, Gotterdämmerung,* EMI, 1988.
Wagner, *Die Walküre,* Deutsche Grammophon, 1988.
Weber, Carl Maria von, *Euryanthe,* Angel, 1975.

Other

Christmastide, Philips, 1987.
Jessye Norman Live, Philips, 1988.
Jessye Norman Sings Duparc, Ravel, Poulenc, Satie, Philips, 1977.
Lieder (various composers), Philips, 1988.
Lucky to Be Me, Polygram, 1992.
Sacred Songs, Philips, 1981.
Spirituals, Philips, 1979.
(With Kathleen Battle) *Spirituals in Concert,* 1991.

With a Song in My Heart, Philips, 1984.

Sources

Books

Greenfield, Edward, Robert Layton, and Ivan March, *The New Penguin Guide to Compact Discs and Cassettes,* Penguin, 1988.

The International Encyclopedia of Music and Musicians, 10th edition, edited by Oscar Thompson, Dodd, 1975.

Periodicals

Chicago Tribune, July 7, 1992.
Ebony, March 1988; July 1991.
Life, March 1985.
Los Angeles Times, February 2, 1986; April 27, 1992.
Musical America, January 1991; July 1991; September/October 1991; November/December 1991.
Music and Musicians, August 1979.
Newsweek, December 6, 1982.
New York, April 1, 1991; April 29, 1991; May 20, 1991.
New Yorker, April 1, 1991; May 20, 1991.
New York Times, January 21, 1973; January 23, 1973; December 15, 1982; September 18, 1983; September 27, 1983; November 24, 1983; January 26, 1986; August 25, 1987; February 20, 1988; March 6, 1989; September 22, 1989; March 19, 1990; February 11, 1992.
Opera News, June 1973; February 18, 1984; February 16, 1991; July 1991.
Stereo Review, October 1989; February 1991; July 1991; August 1991; September 1991.
Vanity Fair, February 1989.
Washington Post, August 7, 1972.

Norman was profiled in the documentary film *Jessye Norman, Singer: Portrait of an Extraordinary Career,* Malachite Productions, 1991.

—Michael E. Mueller

Julius Nyerere

1922—

Former president of Tanzania

When he stepped down as president of Tanzania in 1985, one of the few African rulers ever to relinquish power voluntarily, Julius Nyerere cemented his reputation as one of the continent's greatest leaders. The first African from his former British colony, Tanganyika, to attend a university in the mother country, he returned to spearhead his nation's struggle for independence, becoming its first president. Re-elected four times, he also earned the right to be called Mwalimu, the Teacher, by his countrymen, Nyerere's 24-year leadership was highlighted by the peaceful union of Tanganyika and neighboring Zanzibar into Tanzania and his commitment to remake the nation into a self-sufficient egalitarian socialist society based on cooperative agriculture.

Though his economic policies fell short of his far-sighted goal, Nyerere managed to introduce free and universal education, greatly raising the nation's literacy rate, and vastly improved health care for the majority of the population. He also instilled a sense of national pride among Tanzania's diverse tribes, sparing it the vicious tribal conflicts of so many other African countries. Besides being a major force behind the modern Pan-African movement, Nyerere helped found the Organization of African Unity, united five African nations to successfully pressure the white-supremacist government of Rhodesia into becoming black-ruled Zimbabwe, and ousted Idi Amin, the tyrannical dictator of Uganda, from power. His accomplishments and stature have led many to call him "the conscience of Africa" and have made him one of the Third World's most prominent statesmen and spokesmen.

It was raining so hard the day Nyerere was born in March of 1922 that he was named Kambarage after an ancestral spirit who lived in the rain. Home was the village of Butiama, southeast of Lake Victoria and west of the Serengeti Plain in the British colony of Tanganyika. Years later, when he was baptized a Catholic, he took the name Julius. Nyerere's father, Nyerere Burito, was village chief of the Zanaki, one of the smallest of Tanganyika's 126 tribes. Young Nyerere, one of eight children from his father's fifth marriage, had a traditional tribal childhood—growing up in a leaky mud hut, having his teeth filed in the Zanaki manner, and spending much of his younger years hunting. Being the son of the chief, he went to school at 12 for instruction in Catholicism, Swahili, and English. He scored first in the 1936 territorial examinations and was enrolled in the Tabora Governmental School, originally built for the sons of tribal chieftains.

On graduating, he entered Makerere College in neighboring

At a Glance. . .

Born Kambarage Nyerere, March of 1922, in Butiama-Musoma, Lake Victoria, Tanganyika; took the name Julius when baptized a Catholic; son of Nyerere Burito (village chief of the Zanaki tribe) and Mugaya; married Maria Gabriel Magige (a teacher), January 24, 1953; children: five sons, two daughters. *Education:* Makerere College, Uganda, graduated in 1945; Edinburgh University, Scotland, M.A., 1952. *Politics:* Chama cha Mapinduzi (Revolutionary Party). *Religion:* Catholic.

Biology and history teacher at St. Mary's College, Tabora, Tanganyika, 1946-49; history teacher at St. Francis' College, Pugu, Tanganyika, 1953-55. Elected president, Tanganyika African Association (TAA), 1953; transformed TAA into Tanganyika African National Union (TANU), and served as president, 1954-77; appointed to temporary position on Tanganyika Legislative Council (TLC), 1954; addressed United Nations Trusteeship Council, 1955; elected member of TLC, 1958-60; chief minister of TLC, 1960; prime minister of Tanganyika, 1961-62; president, Tanganyika Republic, 1962-64; president, the United Republic of Tanzania, 1964-85; founder and chairman of Chama cha Mapinduzi, 1977-90.

First chancellor, University of East Africa, 1963-70; chancellor, University of Dar es Salaam, 1970-85, Sokoine University of Agriculture, 1984—; chairman, Organization of African Unity, 1984.

Awards: Third World Award, 1981; named Distinguished Son of Africa, 1988; honorary degrees.

Addresses: *Home*—Dar es Salaam, Tanzania. *Office*—P.O. Box 71000, Dar es Salaam, Tanzania.

Uganda, where he organized the campus chapter of the Tanganyika African Association (TAA), begun years earlier as a social group for African civil servants. After his 1945 graduation from Makerere, he taught history and biology by day at St. Mary's College, a Catholic school in Tabora, and English to the townspeople during the evening. Many nights he stayed up late discussing politics and Tanganyika's future with his friends.

With a grant from St. Mary's and a government scholarship, Nyerere traveled to Scotland in 1949 to attend Edinburgh University, becoming the first Tanganyikan to study at a British university. During his years abroad, he became enthralled with the socialist ideology of the British labor movement. Returning home with a master's degree in history and economics in 1952, he married Maria Magige the following year and began teaching history at St. Francis' College in Pugu, just outside Dar es Salaam, the colonial capital and largest city of Tanganyika.

Architect of Independence

Small, unpretentious, soft-spoken, and quick to laugh, Nyerere impressed his less-educated countrymen with his willingness to talk and work with them as equals. In addition, he was a dynamic orator and unusually politically perceptive. Three months after arriving at St. Francis', Nyerere was elected president of the TAA. Shortly thereafter, in July of 1954, he transformed the TAA into a political party, the Tanganyika African National Union (TANU), and began agitating for Tanganyikan independence. Under his leadership, the organization espoused anticolonialism but stressed peaceful change, racial harmony, and social equality for all.

Recognizing his growing stature, Tanganyika's British governor, Sir Edward Twining, appointed Nyerere to a temporary vacancy on the colony's Legislative Council in 1954. The following year TANU sent Nyerere to New York to address the United Nations Trusteeship Council. Granted a hearing, he asked that the UN set a date for Tanganyikan independence and recognize the principle that the colony's future government be led by Africans. Though the British government rejected his demands, the debate established Nyerere as his country's preeminent nationalist spokesman.

Returning to Tanganyika, he resigned his teaching post to devote himself fully to campaigning for independence. For the next several years he tirelessly toured the countryside preaching anticolonialism without racial strife while building TANU into a powerful political organization, the membership of which grew from 100,000 in 1955 to a half million in 1957.

This hard work paid off in 1958 when TANU candidates won all the seats available to them on the Legislative Council in the colony's first free elections. In the unrestricted election of 1960, TANU candidates won 70 of the total 71 seats, and Nyerere became chief minister. The understanding and mutual trust that developed between Nyerere and the new British governor, Sir Richard Turnbull, during independence negotiations helped make the bloodless transition period one of the most peaceful of any African nation. Other key factors were the large number of tribes in Tanganyika, which made it difficult for any one to dominate affairs, and the relatively small number of whites living in the colony.

Nyerere became prime minister in May of 1961 when Tanganyika achieved self-government; complete independence came that December. Six weeks after independence, Nyerere resigned his post to devote himself to fortifying TANU to aid "the creation of a country in which the people take a full and active part in the fight against poverty, ignorance, and disease," he was quoted as saying in a biography by William Edgett Smith. Within six months, the new TANU-led government had abolished the powers and salaries of the country's hereditary chiefs.

President of the Republic

But Nyerere could not stay away long. He was elected president of the new republic in November of 1962, receiving 98.1 percent of the vote. Pondering the meaning of a one-party democracy, he wrote a pamphlet, "Democracy and the Party System," explaining that parties like TANU "were not formed to challenge any ruling group of our own people; they were formed to challenge foreigners who ruled us. They were not, therefore, political parties, i.e., factions, but nationalist movements."

Following the election, TANU opened party membership to non-Africans and began the "Africanization" of the country's civil service. Several hundred British employees were cashiered with severance pay and left Tanganyika so that by the end of 1963, roughly half of the senior- and middle-grade posts were held by Africans, many insufficiently trained. Western nations stepped up their criticism of Tanganyika's one-party system. "Africanization" officially ended in 1964.

The new president turned his attention to African affairs, seeking means to better unite the continent's newly independent nations. He was one of the founders of the Organization of African Unity (OAU) in 1963 and the driving force behind Tanganyika, Kenya, and Uganda forming the East African Community in 1967, a common market and administrative union that operated a wide range of shared services for the three countries.

Meanwhile, trouble was brewing at home. Zanzibar, an island 24 miles off the coast of Tanganyika, received its independence from Great Britain in December of 1963. One month later, the island's African majority successfully revolted, seizing power from the traditional ruling Arab minority. Scarcely a week later, in January of 1964, a small group of Tanganyikan soldiers mutinied, causing Nyerere to flee the State House. Simultaneously, similar military coups erupted in neighboring Kenya and Uganda. All three

governments immediately called on Great Britain for military assistance against their own armies. With British help, the attempted coups were quickly extinguished.

But Zanzibar's continued instability worried Nyerere. Its new government quickly accepted aid from China, East Germany, and the U.S.S.R., becoming in the eyes of the West the "Cuba of East Africa." In April of 1964, Tanganyika and Zanzibar merged to form a new country, the United Republic of Tanzania, with Nyerere as its president. The union was widely interpreted as a victory for Western interests in the region.

President of Tanzania

Nyerere was re-elected president in 1965 with 96 percent of the vote. On a state visit to China that year, he was impressed by its progress since liberation and struck by the relevance of Chinese problems to those of Tanzania. Close relations ensued between the two countries, and the Chinese agreed to finance and build a new railroad to connect the Tanzanian capital and major seaport, Dar es Salaam, with the neighboring, landlocked country of Zambia.

Nyerere's shift toward the East continued when he broke off diplomatic relations with England in 1965 over Rhodesia—Britain had allowed white settlers in that African

> Nyerere's accomplishments and stature have led many to call him "the conscience of Africa" and have made him one of the Third World's most prominent statesmen and spokesmen.

colony to declare independence, thereby thwarting the wishes of the black majority. Nyerere organized five African nations to officially oppose white-minority rule in that runaway colony as well as in South Africa, Namibia, and the Portuguese colonies of Mozambique and Angola. To that end, Tanzania became the home base for nationalist freedom movements in those lands. By 1992, all but South Africa were independent and governed by black leaders.

Condemning white racism, oppression, and misrule while ignoring similar actions by black rulers was not within Nyerere's conscience; in 1972 he denounced Uganda's Idi

Amin when the brutal dictator expelled all Asians from that country. When Ugandan troops invaded and annexed a small border area of Tanzania in 1978, Nyerere appealed to the OAU for action, without success. The following year, 45,000 Tanzanian troops supported Ugandan exiles seeking to liberate their homeland. Within months Amin was toppled and former Ugandan president Milton Obote returned to power. Africa had successfully policed itself.

Ujamaa

From the beginning, Nyerere's goal had been to build his largely rural, impoverished country into an egalitarian socialist society based on cooperative agriculture. His 1967 Arusha Declaration set out the principles by which he meant to accomplish this. It collectivized village farmlands, established mass literacy programs, instituted free and universal education, and nationalized the country's banks, commerce, and major industries. At the same time, the declaration established a strict code of ethics for political leaders, prohibiting them from receiving more than one salary, owning rental property, or holding shares in private corporations. Nyerere also stressed that Tanzania must become economically self-sufficient, depending on its own peasant agricultural economy rather than foreign aid and investment.

Calling his experiment in African socialism *ujamaa* (Swahili for familyhood), Nyerere emphasized economic cooperation, racial and tribal harmony, and self-sacrifice. But his dream came at a cost: More than 13 million peasants were resettled, sometimes forcibly, into 8,000 cooperative villages so that medical services, water, and schools could be more easily provided. State-run corporations, called *parastatals,* set and controlled imports, exports, agricultural production, and ran the newly nationalized industries.

Results were discouraging. Agricultural production plummeted, with the yield of some crops like sisal and cashews declining by 50 percent. Food became scarce, and agricultural imports skyrocketed in order to feed the growing population. Peasant farmers were never able to accept the new collective farms, and by 1985, nearly 85 percent of them had returned to subsistence farming. Of the 330 companies nationalized, in industries ranging from clothes to cloves, nearly half went bankrupt; the survivors were working at only 20 percent of capacity. Declining government revenues coupled with increasing expenditures caused inflation-producing budget deficits. The national currency fell in value, per capita income was $250—one of the lowest in the world—and Tanzania's gross national product (GNP) decreased annually. Only the infusion of $10 billion in foreign aid from 1970 to 1990 kept the economy afloat.

Critics blamed poor management and a bloated, inefficient state bureaucracy, which controlled the failed *parastatals,* for turning the country into "an economic basket case," according to an international banker quoted in a 1985 issue of *Time.* Supporters ascribed the failure of *ujamaa* to collapsing world market prices for Tanzanian agricultural exports like coffee, tea, tobacco, and cotton, while prices for the country's imports, including oil and machinery, rose sharply. The dissolution of the East African Community in 1977 and war with Uganda two years later also greatly taxed the national treasury.

His Legacy

Yet in many ways Nyerere's policies vastly improved the lives of his countrymen. Tanzania has one of the highest adult-literacy rate in Africa, primary school enrollment has jumped from 25 percent of the child population at independence to 95 percent, 50 percent of the population now has clean water, the number of hospitals and rural health centers—as well as doctors—has zoomed, infant mortality has declined, and life expectancy has increased from 35 to 51 years. Tanzania's citizens possess national pride, there is little tribal strife, and the country remains politically stable, a rarity on the African continent.

Though his dreams of a Pan-African union and *ujamaa* did not materialize, Nyerere remained a popular figure in Tanzania and throughout Africa. Re-elected president in 1970, 1975, and 1980, he retired in 1985 but continued as chairman of the Chama cha Mapinduzi (Revolutionary Party), created by the merger of TANU and Zanzibar's ruling party, until 1990. Being one of the few African rulers to voluntarily relinquish power only reinforced his moral stature and worldwide perception of his personal integrity. And typical of Nyerere's overriding commitment to Tanzania was his choice of successor, Ali Hassan Mwinyi, former president of Zanzibar, a move designed to preserve the unity of the nation.

Nyerere's 24-year rule was unsullied by scandal or corruption, a rarity on the African continent, and his devotion to egalitarian ideals was never seriously questioned. Apparently uninterested in seeking personal wealth, he maintained modest housing and had earned a presidential salary lower than that of his cabinet ministers. "He is above corruption," stated a political opponent quoted in *Time* on Nyerere's 1985 retirement. "He never sought power for power's sake. He is a real man of the people."

Selected writings

Uhuru na Umoja (Freedom and Unity), 1967.
Uhuru na Ujamaa (Freedom and Socialism), 1968.
Ujamaa (Essays on Socialism), 1969.
Uhuru na Maendeleo (Freedom and Development), 1973.

Also author of the pamphlet "Democracy and the Party System"; translator of *Julius Caesar* and *The Merchant of Venice* into Swahili.

Sources

Books

Smith, William Edgett, *We Must Run While They Walk:* *A Portrait of Africa's Julius Nyerere,* Random House, 1971.

Periodicals

Christian Century, March 1, 1972.
Current History, April 1985; May 1988.
Economist, June 2, 1990; August 24, 1991.
Harper's, July 1981.
Newsweek, October 26, 1981.
New Yorker, March 3, 1986.
Time, November 4, 1985.
U.S. News & World Report, March 26, 1979.

—James J. Podesta

Olusegun Obasanjo

1937—

Nigerian politician and retired military officer

Throughout the early 1990s, voters in Nigeria, the most populous nation in Africa, were negotiating a precarious transition from military to civilian rule. The *Journal of West Africa* reported in November of 1992 that the completion of this transition—one of several attempts at a conversion to a democratic form of government—would be postponed another year. In light of the challenges facing the country, the experiences of former Nigerian head of state General Olusegun Obasanjo, designer of Nigeria's Second Republic (1979-1984), take on particular relevance. Obasanjo is credited with holding to his word in the late 1970s and delivering Nigeria to civilian rule, although his Second Republic survived only five years. More recently, Obasanjo has assumed leadership in analyzing the problems and challenges facing Nigeria—a country rife with religious and tribal tensions—at the dawn of the twenty-first century.

Nigeria is located on the eastern end of the west African coastline. A former British colony, the country experienced extreme nationalist agitation before finally gaining its independence in 1960. Obasanjo was a student during Nigeria's tumultuous conversion from a colonial territory to an independent state. He attended both elementary and secondary school in his hometown of Abeokuta in Ogun State, where he

was born on May 5, 1937. Having enlisted in the Nigerian Army in 1958, he trained at Mons Officers' Cadet School in Aldershot, England, and was commissioned in the Nigerian Army in 1959. He then enrolled in a variety of military courses abroad and began a long series of promotions in the Nigerian Army.

In England, Obasanjo attended the Royal College of Military Engineering in Chatham, the School of Survey in Newbury, and the Royal College of Defence Studies in London. Tunde Adeniran noted in *Africa Report* that Obasanjo won first prize and a citation as "the best Commonwealth student ever" at the British Royal Engineers' Young Officers School in Shrivenham, England. In addition, Obasanjo engaged in further study at the Indian Defence Staff College and the Indian Army School of Engineering in the mid-1960s.

While taking these various professional training courses, Obasanjo advanced through the ranks of the Nigerian Armed Forces. In 1958-1959, he served in the 5th Battalion in Kaduna and the Cameroons. He was commissioned second lieutenant in 1959 and lieutenant the next year, when he served in the Nigerian contingent of the United Nations Force in the Congo (now Zaire). Obasanjo joined the only Engineer-

At a Glance...

Born May 5, 1937, in Abeokuta, Ogun State, Nigeria; married Oluremi Akinbwon; children: two sons, four daughters. *Education:* Attended Mons Officers' Cadet School, Aldershot, England, 1958; Royal College of Military Engineering; School of Survey, Newbury; Indian Defence Staff College; and Royal College of Defence Studies, London.

Enlisted in the Nigerian Army, 1958; served in 5th Battalion, Kaduna and the Cameroons, 1958-59; commissioned second lieutenant, 1959; promoted to lieutenant, 1960, and served with U.N. force in the Congo (now Zaire); became captain and commander of Nigerian Army's Engineering Unit, 1963; became major and commander of Field Engineering Unit, 1965; became lieutenant-colonel, 1967, and commander of Ibadan Garrison, 1967-69; became colonel, 1969, and commander of 3rd Infantry Division, 1969-70; commander of 3rd Marine Commando Division, South-Eastern State, 1970; accepted Biafran surrender ending Nigerian civil war, January 13, 1970; appointed federal commissioner for Works and Housing, January-July 1975; led bloodless coup with Murtala Muhammed to overthrow head of state Yakubu Gowon, July 29, 1975; appointed chief of staff, Supreme Headquarters, Lagos, 1975-76; member, then chairman, Supreme Military Council, 1975-79; head of state and commander in chief of the Nigerian Armed Forces, 1976-79; retired from Nigerian Army as general, October 1979; member of advisory council of state. Founder, Obasanjo Farms Nigeria Ltd., 1979, and Africa Leadership Forum, 1988; member of several peace and disarmament commissions.

Selected awards: Grand Commander of the Order of the Federal Republic of Nigeria, 1980; Africa Prize for Leadership for the Sustainable End of Hunger, 1990; several honorary degrees.

Addresses: P.O. Box 2286, Abeokuta, Nigeria.

Civil war broke out in Nigeria in 1967. The Nigerian Army—previously regarded as a brutal enforcer of colonial policy—maintained its militant stance even after the country gained independence in 1960. When in 1966 the military seized power from the First Republic (the corrupt and disintegrating civilian government in place at the time), it interrupted a deluge of strikes, work-to-rule actions, demonstrations, and riots by the workers and peasants. Protests arose against the unrestrained use of police force on civilians, the inability to maintain public services, and the flagrant show of wealth by politicians in the midst of mass poverty, illiteracy, unemployment, and hunger.

According to historians Toyin Falola and Julius Ihonvbere in their book *The Rise and Fall of Nigeria's Second Republic, 1979-1984,* Major Nzeogwu, the leader of the 1966 coup, employed populist rhetoric in support of the enraged people and targeted against "all the big wigs" in government. While he termed it a "revolution" for an undefined "Nigerianism," within six months a second coup deposed him and his populist rhetoric; Nzeogwu's philosophy of government action in the interest of the common people proved empty, since it embodied no specific plans to change the essentially colonial economic relationships still in force in Nigeria. It also failed to offer an alternative to the still top-heavy government supported by money from those colonial relationships. No action was taken to alleviate the structural poverty and inequity existing throughout the country. While the first coup succeeded in suspending popular outrage, neither of these two coups could stabilize the regional conflicts within the moneyed, ruling class itself. A year later, a civil war broke out in Nigeria; the country's Eastern Region of Biafra, with its Christian populace, seceded from the central government.

Became Leading Civil War Commander

During the civil war, Obasanjo distinguished himself as a leading general, assuming command of the Nigerian 3rd Marine Commando Division. Under his lead, federal troops split the Biafran Army into two enclaves, making possible the final Biafran surrender less than one month later on January 13, 1970. Obasanjo described the maneuver in his book, *My Command,* a story of personal and national achievement in bringing the conflict to a close and reuniting the nation. He noted in the preface: "Within a space of six months I turned a situation of low morale, desertion and distrust within my division and within the Army into one of high morale, confidence, co-operation and success for my division and for the Army. . . . A nation almost torn asunder and on the brink of total disintegration was reunited and the wound healed."

Following the civil war, Obasanjo returned to his pre-war position of chief of army engineers. In 1972, he was promoted to brigadier, after which he enrolled in an

ing Unit of the Nigerian Army and became its commander in 1963, at which time he was also promoted to captain of the Nigerian Army. Two years later he advanced to major, and by 1967 he had become lieutenant-colonel.

advanced training course for two years at the Royal College of Defence Studies in London. Upon returning to Nigeria, Obasanjo was appointed federal commissioner for Works and Housing.

Rise to Power and Head of State

In 1974 Nigerian head of state Yakubu Gowon announced that the 1976 target date for a return to civilian rule was unrealistic. He postponed the transition indefinitely. Consequently, opposition to his regime mushroomed in newspaper editorials and features. Gowon responded with coercion to silence his critics. The crusade to oust him from office merely intensified, however, and top military officials openly criticized his administration. On July 29, 1975, Murtala Muhammed and Olusegun Obasanjo led a bloodless coup that overthrew Gowon. Muhammed became the new head of state and enjoyed wide popularity in his reaffirmation of the promise to return to civilian rule. However, his five-stage transition program toward that goal was halted by an unforeseen turn of events. On February 13, 1976, Muhammed was assassinated.

Obasanjo was subsequently appointed head of state and commander in chief of the Nigerian Armed Forces. He assured Nigerians that he would carry forth Muhammed's program of transition on time. His efforts culminated in the formation of Nigeria's Second Republic in 1979. At the end of his three years in office, Obasanjo successfully implemented the return to civilian rule, handing power over to elected president Shehu Shagari on October 1, 1979, as planned.

Plagued by endemic and violent corruption within its ranks and mounting protests, however, the Second Republic collapsed after only five years. In 1984, under the leadership of General Muhammadu Buhari, the military seized control of the state to prevent its fall to protesting students, workers, peasants, and the unemployed. In *The Rise and Fall of Nigeria's Second Republic, 1979-1984,* Falola and Ihonvbere remarked that "once again, the struggles of workers and peasants was practically 'hijacked' by a fraction of the armed forces with interests congruent to those of the custodians of state power in the Second Republic."

While in office, Obasanjo had overseen the writing of a new constitution for Nigeria. His government added seven new states, bringing the total to 19 states to better reflect Nigeria's ethnic diversity. He reformed the system of local government by setting up a one-tier system and by specifically defining its shape, functions, and sources of revenue. But as Falola and Ihonvbere pointed out, the democratic nature of the civilian constitution was limited by provisions that curtailed the registration of certain political parties. Also, no process existed to recall officials seen as inefficient, ineffective, or corrupt.

The most fatal limitation of the new constitution, however, was that it left unchanged the colonial-based international economic relations and the stark division of wealth within Nigeria that both stems from and reinforces those economic relations. During Obasanjo's administration in the late 1970s, income from the export of oil steadily increased. On the other hand, though, as historian Okello Oculi demonstrated in *Review of African Political Economy,* Nigeria also virtually ceased producing its own food; imports of food subsequently rose, as did food prices. As noted in *The Rise and Fall of Nigeria's Second Republic, 1979-1984,* overinflated costs of construction contracts with foreign firms and the heavy importation of machinery, spare parts, and weaponry meanwhile created a trade deficit and a government deficit. Those individuals involved with the sale of oil or with the importation of goods, however, continued to become enormously wealthy. Hence, colonial economic relations continued.

The division of wealth within Nigeria accompanying these trade relations also continued. The wealthy few who controlled state power remained unaccountable to the impoverished majority they supposedly represented. Falola and Ihonvbere recounted that within four years after the beginning of the Second Republic, the civilian government employed its police force without regard to law to suppress its citizens. Protest against the government once again climaxed. And once again, the military stepped in to restore order.

Having retired from the armed forces as a general in 1979, Obasanjo joined the advisory council of state and started a company called Obasanjo Farms Nigeria Limited in Otta, Ogun State, Nigeria. He also became a fellow at the University of Ibadan's Institute of African Studies. In the early 1980s he began writing and advising prolifically about Africa's contemporary crises.

By the mid-1980s, Obasanjo recognized that the government he brought into being had failed. That recognition led the former head of state to renew efforts to contribute to stable civilian rule in Nigeria. By founding and working for a variety of policy research and advisory committees throughout the 1980s and early 1990s, including co-chairing the Commonwealth Eminent Persons Group on South Africa in 1985 and founding the Africa Leadership Forum in 1988, Obasanjo continued to study Africa's problems and advise courses of action to relieve them.

Nigeria's Future

Addressing Africa's place in the world in his 1990 book *Challenges of Leadership in African Development,*

Obasanjo expressed a fear of a "new colonialism." Pointing to indicators of recent African decline, such as the enormous problem of malnutrition, the rising infant and child mortality rates, and a fragmenting agricultural and industrial base, Obasanjo described the debt burden as "the gravest problem yet to face Africa since the onset of independence." While over 30 African nations implement structural adjustment programs sponsored by the World Bank and the International Monetary Fund, officials from those international institutions assume powerful positions in the economies, central banks, customs departments, and ministries of finance and planning. Obasanjo warned of the power wielded by these officials, stating: "Thus ensconced, no major decision or initiative on the economy can be taken without their acquiescence at the very least. Unless we can summon the necessary resolution to resist it successfully, I fear a new dependence not unlike the old colonialism in content is upon us."

African historians such as S.O. Osoba argue that economic dependence and underdevelopment will continue to plague Africa even after decades of independence. In his article "The Transition to Neo-Colonialism," a study of decolonization in Nigeria that was published in *Britain and Nigeria: Exploitation or Development,* Osoba observed that Britain had fostered the growth of an indigenous elite through last-minute powersharing that would protect the "colonial economic bequest." From independence, Osoba argued, the British meant to "dismantle their formal colonial empire while at the same time . . . strengthening their informal colonial powers." Oculi has shown how Obasanjo's own agriculture policies while head of state reinforced Nigerian dependence. In his reflection in 1990, Obasanjo described the latest intensification of economic dependence that the industrialized world imposes upon Africa through the essential cooperation of the indigenous African elite.

In *Africa Today,* Pita Ogaba Agbese, a critic of the current transition to democracy in Nigeria, claimed that Nigeria's Third Republic would become one more exercise in futility before the military reclaimed power with a renewed lease of legitimacy. In this political context in the most populous nation in Africa, Olusegun Obasanjo's experiences as head of state and designer of the Second Republic become a crucial precedent in any understanding of the contemporary Third Republic.

Selected writings

A March of Progress: Collected Speeches, Federal Ministry of Information, 1979.
My Command: An Account of the Nigerian Civil War, 1967-1970, Heinemann Educational Books, 1980.

(With others) *Mission to South Africa: The Commonwealth Report,* Penguin Books, 1986.
Africa in Perspective: Myths and Realities, Council on Foreign Relations, 1987.
Nzeogwu, Spectrum Books, 1987.
Africa Embattled, Fountain Publications, 1988.
Constitution for National Integration and Development, Friends Foundation Publishers, 1989.
Not My Will, Ibadan University Press, 1990.
(Coeditor) *Challenges of Leadership in African Development,* Crane Russak, 1990.
(Coeditor) *Elements of Development,* ALF Publications, 1991.
(Coeditor) *The Leadership Challenge of Economic Reforms in Africa,* Crane Russak, 1991.
(Coeditor) *The Challenges of Agricultural Production and Food Security in Africa,* Crane Russak, 1992.
(Coeditor) *The Impact of Europe in 1992 on West Africa,* Crane Russak, 1992.

Founder and editor of magazine *Africa Forum,* 1990. Contributor to periodicals, including *Foreign Policy, Foreign Affairs, Review of International Affairs,* and *New Perspectives Quarterly.*

Sources

Books

Falola, Toyin, editor, *Britain and Nigeria: Exploitation or Development,* Zed Books, 1987.
Falola, Toyin, and Julius Ihonvbere, *The Rise and Fall of Nigeria's Second Republic, 1979-1984,* Zed Books, 1985.
Kirk-Greene, Anthony, and Douglas Rimmer, *Nigeria Since 1970: A Political and Economic Outline,* Hodder & Stoughton, 1981.
Obasanjo, Olusegun, *My Command: An Account of the Nigerian Civil War, 1967-1970,* Heinemann Educational Books, 1980.
Obasanjo, Olusegun, *Challenges of Leadership in African Development,* Crane Russak, 1990.

Periodicals

Africa Report, May/June 1976.
Africa Today, Number 3, 1990.
Journal of West Africa, November 1992.
Review of African Political Economy, May/December 1979.

—*Nicholas S. Patti*

Willie O'Ree

1935—

Retired professional hockey player

Canadian native Willie O'Ree was the first black man ever to skate for a team in the National Hockey League (NHL). O'Ree made his debut in typical modest fashion for the Boston Bruins on January 18, 1958, and played right wing for the team through 45 games between 1958 and 1961. In a sport dominated by white athletes then and now, O'Ree never received much media coverage; he thought less about his race than about perfecting his ability. "Being the first black didn't even enter into my mind," O'Ree told the Orlando *News and Sun-Sentinel*. "The NHL was the league and I knew it would only pick the best players. That's what I tried to be."

According to *Rocky Mountain News* correspondent Marty York, O'Ree faced an uphill battle from his first moments in the NHL until his premature consignment to the minor leagues in 1961. "Suffice it to say that, while O'Ree desperately tried to establish himself as an NHLer in the 1950s and 1960s, he was a victim of blatant racism, of the sort of human degradation that you and I might be able to comprehend only with the help of Hollywood," wrote York. "Few spared O'Ree from torment. Not opponents. Not fans. Not the men who governed hockey. It was hell on ice."

Indeed, O'Ree only played one full season of hockey in the NHL, and that year was punctuated by constant fighting, cheap shots, and racial slurs hurled by opposing players after the whistle. "People just wanted a piece of me, maybe because they viewed me as different, so I had to defend myself," O'Ree admitted in the *Rocky Mountain News*. In the *Oregonian* he added that he fought "sometimes every game, sometimes to the point where I felt like I had my gloves off more than I had them on. It wasn't, understand, that I wanted to fight. But I was determined to play, and if I had to fight to prove it, I would."

O'Ree broke the color barrier in hockey the same way Jackie Robinson did in baseball, but few blacks have followed in this pioneer's footsteps. In the more than seven-decade existence of the National Hockey League, only thirteen blacks have played in its ranks. As Joe Sexton put it in the *Oregonian*, "The careers of most of the black players have generally been short, their achievements marginal, their experiences mixed. The environment they played in has throughout been a charged one, for hockey games are played overwhelmingly and attended almost exclusively by whites." And, Sexton added, "the NHL, as well as its minor league affiliates, plays a brand of the game that tolerates and arguably promotes violence."

At a Glance...

Born William Eldon O'Ree, October 15, 1935, in Fredericton, New Brunswick, Canada; married; wife's name, Deljeet; children: Chandra. *Education:* High school graduate.

Professional hockey player, 1956-80. Began playing hockey as a child in Canada; played wing in Canadian Juniors, 1953-55; signed with Quebec Aces, 1956; made National Hockey League debut as first black player, January 18, 1958, with the Boston Bruins; returned to minor leagues for 1959 season; promoted again to Bruins for 1960-61 season; traded to Hull-Ottawa Canadiens, 1961; spent next nineteen years on minor league teams, including San Diego Gulls and San Diego Hawks; retired permanently, 1980. Later employed with Strategic Security Inc., a private security company in San Diego, CA.

Addresses: c/o New Brunswick Sports Hall of Fame, P.O. Box 6000, 502 Queen St., Fredericton, New Brunswick, Canada E3B 5H1; or New Brunswick Filmmakers' Cooperative, P.O. Box 1537, 51 York St., Fredericton, New Brunswick, Canada E3B 4Y1.

Witness one incident that happened to O'Ree during his stay with the Bruins: One night in 1961 at Madison Square Garden in New York City, O'Ree crashed hard into the endboards in the defensive zone of the New York Rangers. The wire mesh between the fans and the ice gave way, and the helpless O'Ree was yanked into an angry, drunken mob. Fortunately, he was pulled back onto the ice by his teammates, although by that time he had been showered with beer and taunted ruthlessly. "I don't even like to think now what might have happened had they got me up there," he told the *Oregonian.* "I just came to the conclusion at the time that the only safe place was on the ice."

The Right Climate for a Skater

William Eldon O'Ree was born in Fredericton, New Brunswick, a Canadian province just north of Maine. New Brunswick suffers long, ice-cold winters, and hockey is the favorite sport of almost any child who can walk. "I started skating when I was 'bout 3 years old and started playing organized hockey when I was 5," O'Ree told the *Los Angeles Times.* "I used to skate down the street and skate

to school. I was constantly on the ice. I was fortunate to be born and raised in cold country. . . . In the wintertime, my dad just turned a hose on out in the backyard and, boom, instant rink."

The O'Ree family was prosperous enough to afford the rather expensive equipment required for hockey games. Willie grew up playing in ever more competitive leagues, including Canada's Junior League, a recruiting ground for future professionals. A *Chicago Tribune* reporter commented: "O'Ree was a fast, tricky skater whose form probably would have fit perfectly into the successful European style currently used by the Edmonton Oilers." A rarity among hockey players, O'Ree suffered relatively little damage to his knees or his ankles—the two injuries that can end a career.

He did not escape injury, though. In 1954, while still with the Canadian Juniors, he was struck in the right eye with a puck. He lost 95 percent of his vision in that eye, but he kept right on playing. "I was out of commission for about ten weeks," he remembered in the *Los Angeles Times.* "I still had another eye. So I switched over from left wing and played right wing for the remainder of my career."

NHL Debut

O'Ree turned professional in 1956, signing with the Quebec Aces. Two years later, he would earn a spot in the majors with the Boston Bruins organization and gain a reputation for speed and ability at right wing. "They said I was one of the fastest skaters in hockey," he told the *Los Angeles Times.* "I played with guys who were just as fast as me, but the one thing that was a big asset for me was I could be standing still, take about four strides and be at top speed, while other guys may take seven or eight to get going."

Growing up, O'Ree had felt little prejudice. He was almost always the only black player on his various teams, and the more tolerant Canadians saw only his ability, not his skin color. Still, he was proud and felt that he was doing something for his race when he became the first black man to skate with an NHL team. He made his debut with the Bruins on January 18, 1958, and was warmly greeted by the fans. The Bruins beat Montreal that night 3-0. "It was a nice feeling," O'Ree admitted in the *News and Sun-Sentinel.*

The warmth soon faded. After only two games, O'Ree was sent back down to the minors. He stayed there one more season before finally making the Bruins' regular roster in 1960. Then the trouble began. "I wanted dearly to be just another hockey player, but I knew I couldn't be," O'Ree told the *Rocky Mountain News.* "No matter how hard I played or how fast I skated, people just kept making references to my color." The Boston fans were friendly, but elsewhere he was heckled with racial slurs. On the road he stayed at the same hotels as the other team members, but hospitality was noticeably lacking. "And there were always racial remarks made to me by other players after the whistles," he said. "I knew I was going to have to face all this, but I just felt like I had to keep going. That's how much I loved hockey."

Fights were numerous and prolonged for O'Ree. Not aggressive by nature, he had to answer challenge after challenge during his stay in the NHL. "I was always being tested on the ice, but that may have just gone along with being a new player," he said in the *Chicago Tribune*.

A Lengthy Stay in the Minors

By 1961, O'Ree had played 43 games with the Bruins and had scored four goals. The team management seemed high on him, as did the fans and his teammates. "I thought I had it made," he told the *Rocky Mountain News*. Then, to his surprise, he found that he had been traded in the 1961 off-season to the Hull-Ottawa Canadiens, a so-called "farm team" of the Montreal club. He was not even notified by the Bruins. The news came to him from a sportswriter who telephoned him for his comments. O'Ree was crushed. He knew the trade meant a long stay in the minors, at best. "I still think someone, somewhere, didn't want me in the NHL because of my color," he said.

Other black players in hockey have met similar fates. Today, only Grant Fuhr and Tony McKegney can be said to have had substantial careers as blacks in the sport. As for O'Ree, he spent the rest of a long career on various minor league teams. He finally settled in San Diego, California, with the San Diego Gulls and played with them until 1974. When that team folded he retired briefly, but came back to play with the San Diego Hawks. O'Ree retired permanently in 1980.

During the course of his career, O'Ree sustained almost all of the injuries hockey players can be expected to receive. In addition to the permanent eye damage, he suffered broken ribs and thumbs, a shoulder dislocation, broken teeth, and numerous cuts to the face. He still wears a metal pin in his shoulder, and he has undergone surgery several times for damage to his knees that occurred later in his career. Nevertheless, he played hockey professionally for twenty years, twice the length of an average hockey career.

Blacks in Hockey

Thirteen years passed between O'Ree's debut with the Bruins and the next NHL debut of a black player. Even in the 1990s, the sport was not attracting many black athletes. For his part, O'Ree is doing what he can to change that by appearing at clinics for young black skaters and promoting the sport in such places as New York's Central Park, where he held a teaching clinic for the Ice Hockey in Harlem program. O'Ree blames financial factors for the lack of black involvement in hockey. "I think blacks have just said, 'Hey, this is too hard to get into,'" he told the *News and Sun-Sentinel*. "Baseball can be played in any area, but with hockey you need to get on to the ice. It costs $150-$160 just for the equipment. That's a big factor."

"People say I paved the way," O'Ree told the *Los Angeles Times*. "Back then, it really didn't dawn on me that I was a pioneer, because it was no big deal. When I stepped on the ice, I wanted to be just accepted as another hockey player." In his best year as a hockey professional, however, Willie O'Ree earned only $17,000. Today, although he admits to being proud of his groundbreaking achievement, he is somewhat sorry that it has been so overlooked by the National Hockey League. "I've been honored in my home province [in Canada] and in San Diego for being a pioneer, but I've never gotten recognition from the NHL," O'Ree said in the *Chicago Tribune*. "I always thought it would be good for at least a ring or a plaque."

Sources

Associated Press wire report, July 2, 1991.
Boston Globe, February 8, 1991.
Chicago Tribune, January 23, 1983; April 17, 1987.
Ebony, February 1989, p. 84.
Jet, December 3, 1990, p. 48.
Los Angeles Times, December 17, 1989.
News and Sun-Sentinel (Orlando, FL), February 13, 1985.
New York Times, February 25, 1990, sec. 8, pp. 1, 9.
Oregonian, March 11, 1990.
Philadelphia Daily News, January 24, 1983.
Rocky Mountain News, November 4, 1990.
St. Paul Pioneer Press, January 14, 1992.

An independently produced film documentary titled *Echoes in the Rink: The Willie O'Ree Story,* directed by Errol Williams for the New Brunswick Filmmakers' Cooperative of Canada, is scheduled for completion in the fall of 1993. Additional information for this profile was taken from a press kit on the film.

—*Mark Kram*

Edward Perkins

1928—

U.S. diplomat

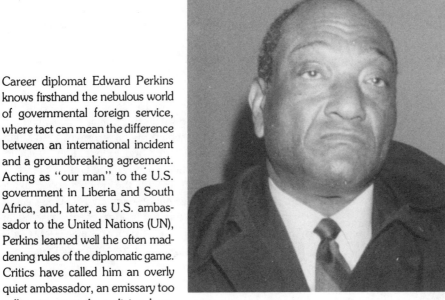

Career diplomat Edward Perkins knows firsthand the nebulous world of governmental foreign service, where tact can mean the difference between an international incident and a groundbreaking agreement. Acting as "our man" to the U.S. government in Liberia and South Africa, and, later, as U.S. ambassador to the United Nations (UN), Perkins learned well the often maddening rules of the diplomatic game. Critics have called him an overly quiet ambassador, an emissary too willing to spout the policies, however backward, of the U.S. administration employing him. And yet, he has, on occasion, strayed from official U.S. policy, only to find his remarks "clarified" by his bosses, who claimed the ambassador had spoken incorrectly or had been misunderstood. But Perkins understands that rebukes and catcalls are unavoidable on the diplomatic roller coaster ride that has brought him to the rarefied heights of foreign service.

The man who would one day be a pivotal force in changing American policy toward the brutally racist apartheid regime of South Africa was born into the segregated South of the United States on June 8, 1928, in Sterlington, Louisiana. Perkins attended a black-only, two-room school and later served in the segregated branch of the U.S. Army Quartermaster Corps in Tokyo and Korea. The army provided Perkins his early jobs, including a stint as the chief of personnel and administration of the Army and Air Force Exchange Service in Okinawa, Japan.

Compared to others bitten by the foreign service bug, Perkins came to the diplomatic establishment late. He was nearly 40 years old before he found the time and resources to receive a bachelor's degree in political science from the University of Maryland. He worked in the foreign service's Near Eastern and South Asian bureaus, and at the U.S. State Department in Washington, where, among other positions, he was director of the Office of West African Affairs.

Perkins's diplomatic dream was realized in 1985, when President Ronald Reagan appointed him ambassador to Liberia, where Perkins had served in a mid-level capacity a few years earlier. While he would only stay in the west African country for approximately one year, his experience there would deliver lasting lessons on the political forces—both internal and external—at work throughout Africa.

Perkins inherited an assignment in a country whose peace had been shattered by the rise of a dictator. Samuel K. Doe seized power in a 1980 coup, when Liberians were growing increas-

At a Glance...

Born Edward Joseph Perkins, June 8, 1928, in Sterlington, LA; son of Edward Joseph Perkins, Sr. and Tiny Estella Noble Holmes; married Lucy Chen-mei Liu, September 9, 1962; children: Katherine Karla Shih-Tzu, Sarah Elizabeth Shih-Yin. *Education:* University of Maryland, B.A., 1968; University of Southern California, M.P.A., 1972, Ph.D., 1978.

Served with Army and Air Force Exchange Service in Taiwan and Japan, 1958-66; Agency for International Development (AID), U.S. Department of State, Far East Bureau official, 1967-70; assistant director for management, U.S. Mission to Thailand, 1970-72; Office of the Director General of the Foreign Service, U.S. Department of State, staff assistant, 1972, personnel officer, 1972-74; administrative officer, Bureau of Near Eastern and South Asian Affairs, 1974-75; management analysis officer, U.S. Department of State, 1975-78; counselor for political affairs, Accra, Ghana, 1978-81; deputy chief of mission, Monrovia, Liberia, 1981-83; director of the Office of West African Affairs, U.S. Department of State, 1983-85; U.S. ambassador to Liberia, 1985-86; U.S. ambassador to South Africa, 1986-89; director general of the Foreign Service, U.S. Department of State, 1989-92; U.S. ambassador to the United Nations, 1992; named ambassador-designate to Australia by the Clinton administration, 1993. *Military service:* U.S. Army, 1954-58; served in Tokyo and Korea.

Awards: Eastern Region Award, Kappa Alpha Psi, for achievement in foreign affairs, 1985; Presidential Honor from George Bush, 1989; plaque from the Judicial Council of the National Bar Association for "integrity and courage" during diplomatic service in South Africa, 1990; numerous honorary degrees.

Addresses: *Office*—U.S. Department of State, Washington, DC 20520.

ingly disenchanted with the government of William R. Tolbert, Jr. But Doe, who in the aftermath of the coup had bayoneted Tolbert in front of television cameras, was less concerned with the stagnating economy that was frustrating Liberians than with safeguarding his own power.

By 1984 Doe had begun censoring newspapers and restricting the activities of opposition political parties and student groups. As U.S. ambassador, Perkins was charged with promoting economic reform and democratization in Liberia and, at the same time, protecting America's huge strategic and technical assets in the African country. While other industrialized nations were publicly disavowing the Doe government's vicious hold on power, the Reagan administration, echoing its policy in South Africa, was more openly conciliatory—an approach that cast America as Doe's chief apologist.

Strategy for Dealing with Liberian Dictator

When Perkins and his staff arrived in the Liberian capital city, Monrovia, their principle task was to convince Doe not to seek the presidency in the October 1985 general elections. The leverage Perkins used was financial; if Doe were elected, the United States and other countries, despite their interests in Liberia, would cut off aid and technical and military assistance. But Perkins's diplomatic finesses were no match for the egomaniacal Doe, who threw his hat in the political ring and claimed victory in an election that, despite his statements to the contrary, was largely regarded as rigged.

After the election, opposition forces attempted a coup, but Doe, enjoying a firm grip on the military, prevailed and instigated a period in which his government readily employed the tools of violence and intimidation to silence those who sought political change. The United States, as Perkins promised Doe, cut off the much needed aid to Liberia, and the African nation—which 140 years earlier had been born from the noble idea of establishing an African settlement for freed American slaves—entered a dark time of bitter fighting and economic collapse.

Won Over Blacks in South Africa

In 1986 Reagan appointed Perkins ambassador to South Africa, a position that had been offered to and rejected by two black foreign service veterans, including Terence Todman, who became ambassador to Argentina. Whereas in Liberia Perkins had faced the evil of one man, in South Africa he confronted the demon of an entire racist political system, apartheid, which denied the country's black majority the most basic human rights. At the time of his appointment as the first black ambassador to South Africa, worldwide condemnation of the stark unfairness of apartheid was at a fever pitch, and the Reagan administration was coming under increasing fire for its policy of "constructive engagement," which favored friendliness over antagonism as a tool for pushing reforms in Pretoria, the South African capital.

Perkins's first challenge was dealing with the resentment that greeted his arrival. "As a black representing a conservative Republican Administration in white-ruled South Africa, Perkins received a generally negative reception when he landed in Pretoria," William R. Doerner wrote in *Time*. "His appointment was regarded by many whites as a symbolic snub and by blacks as insulting tokenism." Black South African newspapers condemned Perkins for accepting what they called a transparently racist appointment, and a spokesman for the United Democratic Front, the largest antigovernment group, said that Perkins would be unwelcome in South Africa and that he should have turned down the job.

But Perkins, aware of the symbolic power of small actions, succeeded in turning around public perception among blacks to a far greater degree than his predecessor, Herman Nickel, had done. Ducking the press and avoiding publicity, he traveled to black townships and squatter villages and met with black opposition groups, winning over those who had earlier dismissed him as a token black apologist for a Reagan policy perceived as soft on the fight against apartheid. In the building housing the U.S. Embassy in Pretoria, Perkins used the elevator reserved for whites. He ordered all embassy functions to be multiracial, and he urged his staff to visit the black areas so that they could better understand the devastating effects of the country's politics on people of color. "There's no way any visitor to South Africa can travel in the country and not realize the disparity—the agonizing differences," he was quoted in *Jet* as telling his workers.

Went Further than Other Reagan Officials

The low-profile ambassador, who was reportedly told by the White House to shun the limelight, came out from under cover in April of 1987. In the wake of a South African government decree banning any public call to release people detained without charge—an estimated 30,000 people, including perhaps 10,000 children—he attended a black church service called to pray for the prisoners' release. Perkins joined the other churchgoers in rising to sing "Nkosi Sikelele Afrika," the country's black nationalist anthem, and, minutes later, the embassy issued a statement blasting South Africa's new sweep of repression in terms far stronger and impassioned than any that thus far had come out of the Reagan administration. "Ambassador Perkins, largely invisible since his arrival last November, has now become forcefully visible," the *New York Times* editorialized. "His symbolic gesture offers a new and welcome example for the Reagan Administration.

There may be hope yet that Pretoria will have to stop looking to Washington for comfort."

Perkins made another big splash—again, bigger than that made by any other Reagan official—when he published an article in *Leadership,* an influential current affairs journal, arguing that a black majority government is the only palatable political arrangement for South Africa. Up until that point, Reagan officials had skirted around articulating such a belief, fearful of the political fallout that would be generated by such direct and unequivocal language. Perkins further distanced himself from the administration when he claimed that economic sanctions, which the Congress had passed over Reagan's veto in 1986, had—without question—been a success. The State Department quickly "clarified" Perkins's remarks, saying the ambassador had been referring to the success of the sanctions in conveying the public abhorrence for apartheid; their economic impact, the department claimed, had not yet been determined.

Saw Dynamic Future for United Nations

After leaving his South African post, Perkins served as director general of the State Department, where he supervised thousands of foreign service officers and department employees. Then, in 1992, he was appointed U.S. ambassador to the United Nations by President George Bush. Perkins replaced Thomas Pickering, who was reportedly forced out because Secretary of State James Baker believed Pickering had displayed a showy, grandstanding relationship with the press during the Persian Gulf War.

While Perkins was perceived as a soft-spoken ambassador, in South Africa he had demonstrated—to the delight of liberals opposed to Reagan policies—his boldness in running against the political grain. Still, an editorial printed in the *New York Times* suggested that Perkins had "yet to demonstrate the risk-taking initiative needed for the U.N. job."

Perkins's tenure at the U.N. was short—the new president, Bill Clinton, replaced him with Madeleine Albright—but he wasted little time in once again taking a position at odds with the administration that had appointed him. Testifying before the Senate Foreign Relations Committee in July of 1992, Perkins said that the Bush administration would seek a new U.N. resolution sanctioning the enforcement of an existing resolution that called on Iraq, in the wake of the Gulf War, to respect the human and civil rights of the Shiites in the south of the Middle Eastern country and the Kurds in the north. But a senior Bush official quickly applied spin control to this statement, saying that Perkins had been mistaken and that there was a consensus within the administration that no further resolution was needed for the establishment, for example, of a no-fly zone to protect Iraqi minorities.

From his dealings with the United Nations, Perkins joined others in concluding that the world body will play a more prominent role in international affairs now that the Cold War between the United States and the former Soviet Union is over and there are no longer polarized superpowers to keep smaller political hot spots from boiling over. Rather than being intimidated by or resentful of the U.N.'s growing potency, the United States, according to Perkins, should recognize that its national interests, in terms of human rights and economic reforms, coincide with world interests. Perkins concluded in an interview with *Emerge,* "It's my view that as the U.N. becomes a much more accepted instrument of conflict resolution, not just in war but in economic and social justice, the United States will find itself more in tune with the U.N.'s program."

In the summer of 1993, Perkins was named ambassador-designate to Australia by U.S. president Bill Clinton. As of August of that year, the ambassador was still awaiting confirmation to that post.

Sources

Boston Globe, August 1, 1992, p. 14.
Christian Science Monitor, June 25, 1987, p. 14; November 2, 1992, p. 14.
Emerge, March 1993, p. 11.
Jet, April 18, 1988, p. 33; May 22, 1989, p. 37; October 12, 1992, p. 11.
Los Angeles Times, February 4, 1992, p. A8; April 27, 1992, p. E1.
New York Times, April 15, 1987, p. A26; December 9, 1987, p. A15; February 15, 1992, p. 22.
Time, February 23, 1987, p. 58; December 21, 1987, p. 50.
USA Today, July 30, 1992, p. A4; October 12, 1992, p. A13.

Additional information for this profile was obtained from the U.S. State Department.

—*Isaac Rosen*

Alvin F. Poussaint

1934—

Psychiatrist, educator, writer

Alvin F. Poussaint is considered an expert on a wide range of issues involving the black community. As a young medical school student, he was captivated by the study of the psychological effects of racism. As a psychiatrist and academic, he has fought to have the unique social and emotional needs of African Americans recognized.

Poussaint is dedicated to the eradication of racist myths. His writings for both specialized audiences and the general public—including articles in *Essence* and *Ebony* magazines and the books *Why Blacks Kill Blacks, Raising Black Children, and Black Children: Coping in a Racist Society*—effectively bash racial slurs and stereotypes. And during his years as production consultant for the hit television program *The Cosby Show,* Poussaint oversaw the formation of one of the first positive images of an upper-middle-class black family as a role model in America.

A bright and studious child, Poussaint grew up in Harlem, where he excelled in school. After junior high, he was able to enroll in the prestigious Stuyvesant High School, a predominantly white school for gifted students in Manhattan. He was interested in many subjects, including math, science, language, and music. Poussaint remembered his insatiable desire

for knowledge in George Metcalf's *Up from Within:* "I was very active in school, wanted to learn everything about everything. A lot of things I just took up on my own. I taught myself to play the clarinet, the saxophone, and flute. I started writing, too. I became associate editor of the literary magazine and received the creative writing award upon graduation."

After high school, Poussaint was accepted at Yale University but acceded to his father's wish that he attend a local school. He enrolled at Columbia University, an institution he found academically challenging but socially disappointing: "Social situations were awkward, there being a prevalent feeling among whites that blacks shouldn't come to social events," he told Metcalf. "They didn't expect you to show up at the dance."

After graduating from Columbia in 1956, Poussaint entered the Cornell Medical School as the only African American among 86 students. The racism he encountered there—as well as his past experiences at Stuyvesant and Columbia—led him to study the psychological effects of racial bias. He chose to specialize in psychiatry, and from 1961 to 1964 he interned at the Neuropsychiatric Institute of the University of California at Los Angeles Medical Center. He was named

At a Glance...

Born Alvin Francis Poussaint, May 15, 1934, in East Harlem, NY; son of Christopher and Harriet Poussaint; married Ann Ashmore, 1973 (divorced 1988); children: Alan. *Education:* Columbia College, B.A., 1956; Cornell University Medical College, M.D., 1960; University of California, Los Angeles, M.S., 1964.

Southern field director, Medical Committee for Human Rights (a division of the Student Nonviolent Coordinating Committee [SNCC]), 1964-65; Tufts University School of Medicine, senior clinical instructor, 1966, assistant professor, 1967-69; associate dean of students and associate professor of psychiatry at Harvard Medical School, 1969—; health consultant to the Congressional Black Caucus; production consultant, *The Cosby Show*, 1984-1992; chairman of Select Committee on the Education of Black Youth, beginning 1985; author.

Member: National Medical Association, American Association for the Advancement of Science (fellow), American Psychiatric Association, American Academy of Child Psychiatry.

Awards: Honorary degree from Wilberforce University, 1972; American Black Achievement Award in Business and the Professions, 1986; John Jay Award for distinguished professional achievement, 1987; Medgar Evers Medal of Honor, Johnson Publishing Company, 1988.

Addresses: *Office*—Judge Baker Guidance Center, Harvard Medical School, 295 Longwood Ave, Boston, MA 02115.

chief resident during his final year at the institute.

In 1965 Poussaint joined the civil rights struggles in the South, becoming the southern field director of the Medical Committee for Human Rights, a division of the Student Nonviolent Coordinating Committee (SNCC). His experiences in the South taught him much about the dynamics of racism. As the Reverend Jesse Jackson wrote in his introduction to Poussaint's book *Why Blacks Kill Blacks:* "Dr. Poussaint is no ivory-tower psychiatrist. . . . He is no armchair academician espousing theories and reaching conclusions from afar."

Poussaint developed some of his most influential theories during his time in the South, but, disillusioned by problems within the SNCC, he resigned from his post with the committee in 1966 and accepted a position as assistant professor of psychiatry at Tufts University School of Medicine. In 1969, he moved to Harvard Medical School, where he continues to work as an associate professor of psychiatry.

A Psychological Approach to the Study of Racism

Dr. Poussaint has investigated the complex issues of racism from several different angles and has written much on the psychological effects of discrimination. In articles such as "Why Black Kill Blacks," published in his 1972 collection of the same name, and *Black Children: Coping in a Racist Society*, published by the University of Michigan in 1987, he addresses not only the blatant forms of racism, but the more subtle and insidious forms as well. In essays like "Black Parents: What Shall I Tell My Child" and "White Parents: How to Raise your Child Free of Prejudice," both included in *Why Blacks Kill Blacks*, he discusses ways of fighting racism through early education. And the 1993 publication *Raising Black Children*—an update of 1975's *Black Child Care*, written with noted child psychiatrist James P. Comer—stresses the importance of instilling black pride and self-esteem in children of color.

Through his writings and his activities, Poussaint has prompted experts in psychiatry to rethink existing theories of racism. In articles such as "A Rap on Self-Hatred with Jesse Jackson," published in *Why Blacks Kill Blacks*, he debunks racist psychological theories made by whites in the field. Instead of subscribing to the theory of racial self-hatred, he developed the "aggression-rage" theory to explain the various psychological issues that challenge African Americans: "Much of black self-hatred is in reality repressed rage and a manifestation of being conditioned by fear to be docile and self-effacing," he wrote in the essay. "[The theory of racial self-hatred] allows whites to feel that [blacks] are psychologically deranged while [whites are] posing as models of mental health. In fact, it must be whites who are insecure and filled with self-hatred, since they are the ones who need to oppress blacks in order to cope with life."

Poussaint has also fought for professional equality within the field of psychiatry. In the late 1960s, he was instrumental in forming the first Black Caucus of the American Psychiatric Association and electing the first black officer of the group in 1969. He has loudly attacked studies and treatments with racist biases, such as the outrageous suggestion in 1973 that psychosurgery be used to curb urban violence. He told *Ebony* magazine that this frightening idea "assumes . . . black people are genetically damaged—that they're so animal and so savage that whites have to carve on their brains to make them into human beings. The whole concept is vicious."

Gained Nationwide Recognition

In addition to writing about issues specific to African Americans, Poussaint has explored national issues and their impact within the black community. For instance, in "An Honest Look at Black Gays and Lesbians," published in *Ebony,* he discusses the problems of homophobia and AIDS and their impact within the black community in the United States.

Poussaint's writings and activities have garnered him national recognition and, in turn, afforded him further opportunities for remedying racial injustice. In 1976, he became the health consultant for the Congressional Black Caucus. He has also advised the U.S. Department of State, the Department of Health, Education and Welfare, and the Federal Bureau of Investigation. And Poussaint's political reach extended into the presidential arena in 1984, when he codirected the Reverend Jesse Jackson's Massachusetts presidential campaign. That same year, he became a pivotal figure in the effort to dismantle old racial stereotypes on television, becoming a production consultant for the long-running series *The Cosby Show.* As Poussaint explained in *Ebony, The Cosby Show* "dramatically altered the image of blacks as poor, downtrodden, yet happy-go-lucky clowns. The Huxtable family [the fictitious clan headed by Cosby] help[ed] to dispel old stereotypes and to move its audience toward more realistic perceptions. Like whites, blacks on television should be portrayed in a full spectrum of roles and cultural styles."

Offered Solutions to Youth Crises

Poussaint's influence as a psychiatrist and educator crosses racial, economic, and social lines. With the election of Bill Clinton as U.S. president in the November 1992 elections, Poussaint saw an opportunity for change among the nation's disadvantaged youth. As he stated in the *Detroit Free Press,* we need to find ways to "teach parenting [and] conflict negotiation." "I'd put it in the junior high and high school curriculums," he added, suggesting that informed parents can better battle the ills of violence, drugs, and discrimination in society and therefore contribute to the physical and psychological health of their children.

Selected writings

Why Blacks Kill Blacks, Emerson Hall Publishers, 1972.
(With James P. Comer) *Black Child Care: How to Bring Up a Healthy Black Child in America,* Simon & Schuster, 1975, published as *Raising Black Children,* Plume, 1993.
Black Children: Coping in a Racist Society, University of Michigan School of Social Work, 1987.
(Author of introduction and afterword) Cosby, Bill, *Fatherhood,* Doubleday, 1986.

Contributor to additional books and to periodicals, including *Psychology Today, American Journal of Psychiatry, Essence,* and *Ebony.*

Sources

Books

Metcalf, George R., *Up from Within: Today's New Black Leaders.* McGraw-Hill, 1971.
Thomas, Arthur E., *Like It Is,* edited by Emily Rovetch, Dutton, 1981.

Periodicals

Black Scholar, May-June 1987.
Boston Globe, January 13, 1989; July 30, 1989; November 23, 1989; January 31, 1990.
Christian Science Monitor, September 23, 1991.
Detroit Free Press, February 16, 1993, pp. B1, B8.
Ebony, February 1973; November 1992, pp. 202-205; February 1993, pp. 86-89.
Jet, September 26, 1988.
Los Angeles Times, June 10, 1990.
Newsweek, January 25, 1993, p. 55.
New York Times, July 17, 1990.
Time, May 17, 1993, pp. 48-49.

—Robin Armstrong

Jerry Rice

1962—

Professional football player

In 1992 Jerry Rice, the star wide receiver for the San Francisco 49ers, grabbed the record for most touchdown receptions in a professional football career, with 101. That milestone—coming as it has during the prime of his career—assured Rice a future berth in the Pro Football Hall of Fame. *San Francisco Chronicle* correspondent Ron Thomas described Rice as "a ballet dancer in cleats" whose "dazzling runs leave defenders grasping at air and gasping for breath. Even when Rice doesn't have the ball, he can dominate a game."

Rice has been a mainstay on a football team that is never far from Super Bowl contention. The San Francisco 49ers dominated professional football in the late 1980s and advanced to the playoffs each year throughout the early 1990s. Rice is part of the reason for that success. He is tall, fast, and obsessively determined to catch passes and score. *Washington Post* columnist Thomas Boswell praised Rice for "the range of creative expression" in his performance, which is almost always carried out under double-team pressure. Boswell continued: "The way Rice moves while a ball is in the air, gliding like a hawk on an air current, and what he does after he grabs that ball, changing direction as suddenly as a snake in water, takes the breath from those who watch him and steals the heart from those who try to defend him."

Sports Illustrated correspondent Ralph Wiley claimed that Rice is "running his name into the record books with a smooth and impeccable stride." Wiley also offered a tongue-in-cheek warning to Rice's opponents: "You're dealing with a cold executioner. You must study Jerry Rice—what he does, when he does it, how he thinks, what he doesn't like. You must find the flaw in his character. You must know him as well as you know yourself. Why? So you won't embarrass yourselves or the cities and the institutions you represent when Rice comes to terrorize you and tread on your painted end-zone grass."

Wiley noted that Jerry Rice "grew up simon-pure. No street lights, or sidewalks, or traffic signs, or stadium concerts. No drugs, or crime, or sirens. No distractions." The reporter is referring to life in tiny Crawford, Mississippi, an all-black rural community where Rice was born in 1962. As a youngster the athlete saw few paved roads and even fewer of the luxuries that are now part of his life. His father was a bricklayer who built a home for the large family on the edge of a pasture. Rice and his five brothers amused themselves by playing sports, including a favorite pastime of chasing the horses in the

At a Glance...

Born October 13, 1962, in Crawford, MS; son of Joe Nathan (a bricklayer) and Eddie B. Rice; married, wife's name Jackie; children: Jacqui (daughter). *Education:* Attended Mississippi Valley State University.

Selected in the first round of the 1985 NFL draft by the San Francisco 49ers. Wide receiver for the 49ers, 1985—.

Awards: Numerous, including NFL Most Valuable Player, 1987, and Super Bowl Most Valuable Player, 1989. As of early 1993, held record for most touchdown receptions in a professional career.

Addresses: c/o San Francisco 49ers, 4949 Centennial Blvd., Santa Clara, CA 95054.

pasture until one could be caught and ridden. When work was plentiful, Rice helped his father by carrying bricks and mixing mortar. "I always did have good work habits," he told *Newsday.* "I guess it's from my parents. I take a lot of pride in everything and try to be the best in what I'm doing. Every time I step on the football field, it's not like a job to me; I really enjoy it. Working with my father taught me the necessity of hard work. On my mother's side, I'm a caring person. I guess that's why I've been successful."

His work ethic notwithstanding, Rice was not above some pranks in high school. In fact, he says, he owes his whole career to an attempt to play hooky from school one warm afternoon. As he tells the story, he was sneaking out of the school building when the vice principal saw him and told him to stop. Rice didn't stop—he ran, with the vice principal in hot pursuit. He was caught, whipped, and sent to the gym for football practice. Remembering the incident in the *Los Angeles Times,* Rice said that the principal "made me go out for the [football] team, and that's how I started playing this game. Until the day I played hooky, I had no intention of playing football."

In high school Rice played just about every position, from quarterback to tackle. He showed promise, but only one college coach made a recruiting trip to Crawford—Archie Cooley, then with tiny Mississippi Valley State in Itta Bena. According to Wiley, coach Cooley "took one look at Rice and began devising all manner of bizarre formations designed to spring Rice loose." A graceful, speedy, and nearly unstoppable wide receiver was born. Wiley wrote: "Rice helped put Mississippi Valley State . . . on the map. . . . [He] caught more than 100 passes in each of his last two seasons. As a senior he

had 28 [touchdown] receptions. He has faced constant double-teaming since he was an 18-year-old freshman." With Rice's help the Delta Devils ran up a 24-6-1 record in their conference, a feat that drew the attention of 49ers coach Bill Walsh.

Fitting into a Game Plan

Walsh came to the 1985 pro football draft determined to win Rice's services for the 49ers. So sold was the coach on Rice that he traded up in order to select the young man sixteenth pick in the first round. Immediately Walsh took some heat for the decision, because Rice had not proven himself in the high-stakes arena of Big-Ten or Pac-Ten football. Walsh explained his reasoning in a *Los Angeles Times* feature. "Jerry's movements were spectacular for a pass receiver, no matter the level," the coach said. "Even a casual fan looking at him on that [Mississippi] team would have asked, 'Who is that?' We also knew about the long exposure he'd had as a receiver. He'd been catching 100 passes year after year. We felt that if they'd throw to him that much, and if he'd catch that many, he must have the basic instincts for the job."

Rice's rookie season had a rocky start. He dropped a record fifteen passes, a feat not lost on the press or the fans. In retrospect, Rice blamed his early failures on the complex offense that Walsh ran. He simply had to learn the moves, he said, to the point where he could run a play without thinking about it. It is not at all uncommon for rookie professional players to stumble a bit, especially those who have not seen much top-level competition in college. Rice recovered quickly. Even before his first season ended he had set a team record with 241 receiving yards in one game. He was a unanimous choice for the 1985-86 all-rookie team and a new favorite—despite his shyness—in the San Francisco area.

Rice turned in two stellar seasons in 1986 and 1987. In 1986 he scored an impressive fifteen touchdowns and averaged 18.3 yards per carry. The following year was one of his best. Eyebrows everywhere were raised as he set NFL records for receiving touchdowns (22) and touchdown catches in consecutive games (13). His regular season scoring total of 138 points led the league and set a team record as well. At season's end Rice garnered Most Valuable Player honors from the Pro Football Writers of America, the *Sporting News, Pro Football Weekly,* and the Maxwell Club. The recognition was unsatisfying, however. In 1987 the 49ers took a playoff loss to the Minnesota Vikings that deprived Rice of a trip to the Super Bowl. Asked how he felt at the end of that season, Rice told the *San Jose Mercury News:* "I don't think about how many touchdowns I scored. I don't think about the yardage. I guess a lot of people sit down and look at stats. But not me. I just want to go to the Super Bowl.''

On Top and Staying There

Rice finally got his Super Bowl wish in 1989, when the 49ers met the Cincinnati Bengals and won a dramatic 20-16 last-minute victory. Just prior to the game, Rice sprained his ankle so badly that he was listed as ''questionable'' for the contest. He played, and he was voted Super Bowl Most Valuable Player after a series of stunning catches and slippery runs that saved his team from defeat. Boswell described the action: ''Rice shagged posts in traffic, like a 27-yarder in the final minute to set up the winning score . . . like his touchdown that tied the game, 13-13. He shook deep up the sideline for 30 yards with a defender in his lap. He caught hitches when cornerbacks laid off him in fear . . . when linebackers couldn't spin their heads fast enough to find him. . . . What Rice did this windy evening . . . warps the imagination and redefines what is possible.''

Until that Super Bowl moment, Rice had been relatively unknown outside the San Francisco area. The 49ers had many other stars, from the white-haired coach to the riveting quarterback Joe Montana, and the team had won two Super Bowls in the 1980s without Rice. Super Bowl XXIII changed the determined receiver's status. Suddenly he was able to renegotiate his contract from a position of power, and his performances were chronicled in glowing sports features in print and on television. Nevertheless, within days of his first Super Bowl win, the Most Valuable Player was complaining that he had been ignored by the press and passed over for commercial endorsements. ''I really don't want all the recognition, but I feel like I deserve to get some of it,'' he told the *San Francisco Chronicle*. ''Right now you read the newspapers, there's nothing about Jerry Rice being MVP. If it was Joe Montana, Dwight Clark there would be headlines all over. I'm really just speaking from my heart. I think everybody in the Bay Area feels that way.''

The matter might seem insignificant, but it isn't. Professional sports superstars can quadruple their multi-million dollar salaries with contracts for product endorsements. Montana, for instance, has earned vast sums with television commercials for Hanes underwear. When Rice did not receive the attention he felt he deserved, he suggested that race was the reason. In recent years he has been featured in some national advertising, but his endorsements still lag behind any number of NFL quarterbacks, most of them white.

Rice tried to diffuse his remarks on his celebrity by telling the *Washington Post:* ''You won't hear that from me

again. I guess I matured a little.'' Indeed, as the 1980s ended, Rice matured on the field as well as off. Still dogged by ankle problems, he turned in another outstanding season in 1989 and went with the 49ers to yet another Super Bowl—a 55-10 rout of the Denver Broncos—in 1990. Rice did not play as decisive a role in that Super Bowl win as he did in the one prior to it. However, his very presence on the field helped to confound the Bronco defense and assured a lopsided 49er victory. As early as the next season, the countdown began for Rice's record-breaking touchdown reception.

Going for the Record

The record stood at 100, an impressive number compiled by Steve Largent, a former Seattle Seahawks receiver who had played more than ten professional seasons. Observers were amazed that Rice was closing in on the record after only six years in the league—and while still in his early thirties. The pressure mounted as Rice became a premier superstar on the 49ers with the injury-related benching of Montana and the retirement of Walsh. Meanwhile, the talented receiver had to contend with injuries of his own.

Notoriety in the NFL can be quite hard on a receiver, as defenders exert themselves doubly to catch and hit. It is remarkable that Rice has never been sidelined for long. He tends to play through injuries and nurse himself back to health in the off-season. He has a number of weapons in his arsenal with which to confound defensive backs. First,

---

''I'm not going to say I'm the greatest ever to play the game.''

---

he is fast even when hobbled by leg injuries. He is also agile, at times seeming to move in two directions at once to slip by a lunging opponent. He has a good head for the game and a well-rehearsed list of proven moves. At six-foot-two he can make towering leaps for lofted passes, and he is strong enough to hold up under a hit and force his way for extra yardage. Rice's most distinguishing feature, though, is his determination. He has a passion for football and plays for the sheer joy of it. He simply craves the end zone. ''You see a lot of receivers . . . they're satisfied once they catch the ball and they fall to the ground,'' he told the *San Francisco Chronicle*. ''I'm not satisfied until I get into the end zone.''

That bald obsession with scoring brought Rice to the brink of the receptions-for-touchdowns record in 1992. During the fourth quarter of a rain-soaked game against the Miami

Dolphins on December 6, 1992, Rice ran a z-slant into the end zone and caught a twelve-yard reception. The catch was his 101st for a touchdown, breaking Largent's record. The sodden 49ers fans and players erupted in an ovation that lasted several minutes, and Rice ran to the stands to embrace his wife, Jackie. After the game, which San Francisco won, 27-3, Rice told the *San Francisco Chronicle* that he was relieved. "I've tried to downplay the record and focus in on football, but it's something I've been chasing for a long, long time," he said. "There is a lot of pressure off me now."

San Jose Mercury News reporter Bud Geracie was present when Rice scored his 101st touchdown. "Rice couldn't say what The Record meant to him, just that it meant 'a whole lot,'" Geracie recalled. "He credited his teammates, his coaches, his luck. He praised Largent. In his greatest moment, Rice was humble, classy and just happy to win the game."

Rice may have several more prime seasons ahead of him. The 49ers continue to look strong under coach George Seifert, and Rice is still considered a pivotal part of the offense. "I love to score touchdowns," the receiver told the *Los Angeles Times.* "There's nothing like the feeling you get in the end zone. When you score a touchdown, it feels like winning $6 million in the lottery."

During the off-season, Rice, his wife, and daughter Jacqui live in Crawford, Mississippi. Having broken one of football's toughest records—and played his entire career with a championship team—Rice is not likely to be passed over for those product endorsements anymore. The player once commented in the *Los Angeles Times:* "My goal is to be the best receiver to ever play pro ball." Today he can bask in the glory of his accomplishments and look forward to future seasons. "I'm a modest guy," Rice said in 1992. "I'm not going to say I'm the greatest ever to play the game."

Sources

Fresno Bee, January 28, 1990.
Los Angeles Times, December 13, 1987.
Newsday (New York), January 28, 1990.
San Francisco Chronicle, January 26, 1989; January 28, 1989; November 7, 1989; January 25, 1990; December 7, 1992.
San Jose Mercury News, September 2, 1988; December 7, 1992.
Sports Illustrated, September 28, 1987.
Washington Post, September 1, 1989; January 22, 1989; January 23, 1989.

—*Mark Kram*

Marlon Riggs

1957—

Documentary filmmaker

Marlon Riggs has made his name in a previously neglected field in film: the production of documentaries from a black gay male sensibility. Praised for their balance and style, his films display a technical skill and imaginative flair that have earned the respect of the filmmaking community at large. In addition, his treatment of controversial issues in a straightforward, documentary format have inspired considerable debate. Riggs's willingness both to be ''out'' about his sexual identity and to confront racism and homophobia through film strikes audiences differently according to their opinions about homosexuality and racial politics.

Like many children in military families, Riggs spent much of his childhood outside of the United States. Born in Fort Worth, Texas, in 1957, he lived there until the age of eleven, when his family moved to Georgia; soon after that, they relocated to West Germany. Riggs returned alone to the United States in 1974 in order to begin college at Harvard University in Cambridge, Massachusetts. At Harvard, he began the process of accepting his sexuality, a process known in gay communities as ''coming out.''

According to Riggs, learning to view his sexuality in a positive light was complicated for him as an African American man in a racist culture. Riggs described his experiences in a poetic essay published in *Out/look,* a gay and lesbian quarterly magazine: ''As an undergraduate at [Harvard], I was as much a prisoner as a student. Like most others, I had come there to learn, but foremost, I had come in search of community, of people like myself—the young, gifted, and Black. . . . I awakened, after I arrived, to the realization that I was also gay. And the reflection of myself that this new me suggested, this reflection I found nowhere. Worse, I believed it existed—nowhere. . . . Most days, at lunch and dinner, over the course of my freshmen year, I self-consciously surveyed the dining hall, steered a course beyond the anonymous rows of young white animated faces, among whom I clearly did not belong: moved further still beyond the cluster of 'Black Tables,' where I knew deep down, no matter how much I masqueraded, my true self would show and would be shunned; and sat, often alone, eating quickly, hurrying my exit from a room where all eyes, I felt, condemned me with unspoken contempt: misfit, freak, faggot. . . . Beneath such judgment I did as millions have done before me and since: I withdrew into the shadows of my soul; chained my tongue; attempted, as best as I could, to snuff out the flame of my sexuality; assumed the impassive face and stiff pose of Silent Black Macho. . . . I was serving time. For what crime I didn't

At a Glance. . .

Born in 1957 in Fort Worth, TX; son of a career officer in the U.S. military; domestic partnership with longtime companion, Jack, beginning 1980. *Education:* Harvard University, B.A., 1978; University of California at Berkeley, M.A., 1981.

Worked for television station in Texas, 1978-79; moved to Berkeley, CA, 1979; produced master's thesis *Long Train Running,* University of California at Berkeley, 1981; worked for various producers and directors in documentary film, with particular focus on public television production, 1981-87; began producing, writing, and directing original films, 1987; produced *Ethnic Notions* and *Tongues Untied,* 1989; continued producing films such as *Color Adjustment* and *No Regrets,* despite suffering complications from AIDS virus. Also part-time faculty member, School of Journalism at the University of California at Berkeley.

Member: Association of California Independent Public Television Producers, Bay Area Video Coalition, Black Gay Men United (Oakland, CA), Gay Men of African Descent (New York City).

Awards: Outstanding merit award and best experimental video, both from Black Filmmakers Hall of Fame, 1989, for *Tongues Untied;* best performance award from Atlanta Film Festival, 1989, for *Tongues Untied;* best documentary award from Berlin Film Festival, 1989, for *Tongues Untied;* Individual Craft Award of Outstanding Achievement in Research in the national news and documentary category, National Academy of Television Arts and Sciences, 1989, for *Ethnic Notions;* National Endowment for the Humanities grant; National Endowment for the Arts grant.

Addresses: *Office*—School of Journalism, University of California at Berkeley, Berkeley, CA 94720.

that would give him a sense of history and a sense of identity. Again, he described this change in *Out/look:* "When nobody speaks your name, or even knows it, you, knowing it, must be the first to speak it. When the existing history and culture do not acknowledge and address you—do not see or talk to you—you must write a new history, shape a new culture, that will." This self-creation took the form of a dissertation about "the evolution of the depiction of male homosexuality in American fiction and poetry," which he wrote under the guidance of a graduate student teaching assistant, since none of the professors at the university were willing to take on the project.

Chose a Career in Documentary Film

After he graduated with honors from Harvard in 1978, Riggs returned to Texas to work at a television station. In an interview for *Brother to Brother,* he told Professor Ron Simmons: "My parents and grandparents expected me to become a preacher. I didn't. I became a filmmaker and that's my platform, my podium, the pedestal from which I preach these days." Of the choice to make films per se, he said: "I didn't know anything about filmmaking when I decided to become a filmmaker. What drew me to film and video was that I wanted to communicate so much of what I was learning at Harvard. I was shocked by all the discoveries I came across when I studied American history, particularly when I found out about race relations and our legacy of black cultural achievement. It was shameful that I had never been exposed to such information before. It was a shock to realize that only a privileged few could get that kind of information, that kind of education. I didn't want to teach. . . . That's good work, but I wanted to communicate to the broadest possible audience and for me that was [through the medium of] television."

The job at the television station in Texas, however, didn't work out well because Riggs found himself confronted with immobilizing racism. He left Texas for California, where he earned a master's degree in journalism at the University of California at Berkeley in 1981. Immediately after, he began apprenticing himself to documentary filmmakers— particularly those working in public television—in order to learn his craft. By the time he began producing his own works in 1987, he had nine films to his credit, on which he had served variously as production assistant, editor, associate editor, post-production supervisor, and/or sound effects director.

know. . . . I served, in rage, pain, and bitter, needless solitude, for three and a half of my undergraduate years, ignorant that there could be any other way."

In the middle of his senior year, despite the resistance he found among the faculty, Riggs pursued a dissertation topic

Earned Acclaim for Original Films

Having already established a name for himself among producers and technicians in documentary film, Riggs continued to build on that reputation as he produced, directed, and wrote his own films, six of which appeared between 1987 and 1989. Two of these films—*Ethnic Notions* and *Tongues Untied*—have earned the highest regard and praise from filmmakers, black activists, and gay audiences. Simmons called *Ethnic Notions* a "masterpiece" and noted that it "establish[ed] Riggs as one of the foremost contemporary producers of historical video in documentary."

Although *Ethnic Notions* is a brutally challenging look at the images that have been used in American culture to reinforce racism from legal slavery through the late twentieth-century, it has been received with respect by white and African American audiences alike. In 1989, it won a series of prestigious awards, including the Individual Craft Award of Outstanding Achievement in Research in the national news and documentary category from the National Academy of Television Arts and Sciences. Showings at the San Francisco International Film Festival and at the American Film and Video Festival also brought awards.

Confronted Homophobia with *Tongues Untied*

Having confronted racism in *Ethnic Notions,* and having established a practice of voicing the concerns of communities that he felt had been silenced for too long, Riggs moved into even more controversial territory with *Tongues Untied.* In the words of Revon Kyle Banneker for *BLK,* the experimental *Tongues Untied* "unleashes the blackened voices of suppressed hunger, anger and aloneness." The frank discussion and portrayal of a black gay male identity kept the film from being aired on most public television stations and limited Riggs's funding to non-government sources. The film has, however, enjoyed broad distribution at film festivals—gay, black, and mainstream—and has earned its maker still more awards, including an outstanding merit award from the Black Filmmakers Hall of Fame film/video competition. After its premiere at the American Film Institute's 1989 Video Festival, *Tongues Untied* also showed at the Berlin International Film Festival and the Cleveland International Film Festival. Since 1989, it has appeared at countless festivals and series around the country and has managed to air, usually in censored versions, on some public television stations.

Although *Tongues Untied* features no explicit sex, it has inspired controversy among white conservatives and black activists alike. While both racist and homophobic responses were predictable, the latter evoked more concern from Riggs. He told Banneker, "Straight blacks are willing to give me an award, but they don't want to talk much about homosexuality." But it is precisely this discussion, he asserts, that "they need." In another essay from *Brother to Brother,* Riggs explained why this discussion is needed: "I am a Negro Faggot, if I believe what movies, TV, and rap music say of me. Because of my sexuality, I cannot be Black. . . . I cannot be a Black Gay Man because, by the tenets of Black Macho, Black Gay Man is a triple negation. I am consigned, by these tenets, to remain a Negro Faggot. And as such I am game for play, to be used, joked about, put down, beaten, slapped and bashed, not just by illiterate homophobic thugs in the night, but by many of Black American culture's best and brightest."

Since earning his degree at Berkeley in 1981, Riggs has continued to live in the San Francisco area, making a home with his lover, Jack, whom he met in the late 1970s. A

> "I am game for play, to be used, joked about, put down, beaten, slapped and bashed, not just by illiterate homophobic thugs in the night, but by many of Black American culture's best and brightest."

part-time position on the faculty of the University of California at Berkeley, in the same department that granted him his master's, has paid his living expense while he raised money to fund his films.

Appealed to Even Broader Audience

In 1989, while making *Tongues Untied,* Riggs tested positive for HIV—which means that he had contracted the virus that can cause AIDS, not that he had AIDS yet. He continued his filmmaking, turning out a documentary about the experiences of HIV+ gay black men entitled *No Regrets* in 1992, despite the onset of complications from the infection. He also produced *Color Adjustment* in 1991, the long-awaited sequel to *Ethnic Notions. Color Adjustment* was broadcast by PBS-TV in the summer of 1992 as part of the network's independent documentaries series *P.O.V.* Deeming the work "a thoughtful, engrossing essay on the history of television's portrayal of black people," Associated Press reporter Scott Williams noted that "there won't be any controversy over [*Color Adjustment*] simply because [Riggs] presents the virtually inarguable case that TV has ignored, distorted, assimilated and beatified black people but rarely depicted them honestly."

Ultimately, Riggs's voice is stronger than any prejudice or any virus. He explained the importance of the persistence of his black gay voice in *Out/look*: "Whenever we speak the truths of our lives, our words must be more than mere words: Every time we speak, we must engage in the most radical—as in fundamental—form of self-affirmation. As communities historically oppressed through silence, *through the power of Voice* we must seize our freedom, achieve our fullest humanity."

Selected filmography

Director and writer

Open Window: Innovations from the University of California, 1988.
(And editor) *Visions Toward Tomorrow: Ida Louise Jackson,* 1989.

Producer and director

(And editor) *Warring Ideals: A Portrait of Henry O. Tanner,* 1989.
Affirmations, 1990.
No Regrets, 1992.

Producer, director, and writer

(And editor) *Changing Images: Mirrors of Life, Molds of Reality,* 1987.
Ethnic Notions, 1989.
(And editor) *Tongues Untied,* 1989.
Color Adjustment, 1991.

Early film work

(Production assistant) *Two Parents, Two Homes,* 1981.
(Associate editor and sound effects director) *How Much Is Enough: Decision Making in the Nuclear Age,* 1982.

(Assistant editor) *The State of the Language: In Other Words,* 1983.
(Associate editor and sound effects director) *In Our Defense,* 1983.
(Editor) *A Traveling Jewish Theatre,* 1983.
(Editor) *Susan Noon Profiles,* 1983-84.
(Associate editor and post-production supervisor) *The First Fifty Years: Reflections on U.S./Soviet Relations,* 1984.
(Assistant editor) *Fighting Ministers,* 1985.
(Associate editor and post-production supervisor) *Faces of War,* 1986.

Selected writings

"Tongues Untied" (poem) and "Black Macho Revisited: Reflections of a SNAP! Queen" (essay), both published in *Brother to Brother: New Writings by Black Gay Men,* edited by Essex Hemphill, Alyson Publications, 1991, pp. 200-205 and 253-57.

Sources

Books

Brother to Brother: New Writings by Black Gay Men, edited by Essex Hemphill, Alyson Publications, 1991, pp. 189-205 and 253-257.

Periodicals

Ann Arbor News, Associated Press report, June 15, 1992.
BLK, April 1990, pp. 10-19.
Out/look, spring 1991, pp. 12-19.

—Ondine E. Le Blanc

John W. Rogers, Jr.

1958—

Investment firm manager

Once his father gave him shares of stock as a 12th birthday gift, John W. Rogers, Jr., was hooked on Wall Street. He secured the services of his own broker at age 18 and four years later, in 1980, became a broker himself. Raising $180,000 from family and friends, Rogers started his own investment firm, Ariel Capital Management, with one other employee in 1983. By 1992 Ariel had 16 employees, managed nearly $2 billion for individuals, corporations, university endowments, and some of the nation's largest public and private pension funds, and was one of the largest black-owned investment firms in the country. In addition, Rogers created the only two mutual funds in the United States managed by African Americans.

Rogers was born into a prominent Chicago family in 1958. His mother, Jewel Lafontant, senior partner in a Chicago law firm and longtime figure in national Republican politics, was named ambassador-at-large and U.S. coordinator for refugee affairs by President George Bush in 1989. John Sr., a circuit court judge, instilled early business sense in his son by giving him shares of stock as Christmas and birthday gifts and allowing him a checking account where he could deposit the dividends and his allowance.

Except for one bounced check, John Jr. learned his early financial lessons well. Soon he was following the newspaper stock tables and watching the stock ticker prices race along the bottom of the television screen on Chicago's local business channel. He also spent a lot of time after school in the office of his father's broker, Stacy Adams, one of the first black stockbrokers in Chicago. At the age of 16, Rogers was hawking hot dogs, peanuts, and soft drinks during White Sox games at Comiskey Park, putting the earnings into more stocks and phoning Adams to check on their progress during his work breaks.

Wall Street Smarts

Rogers graduated from the highly regarded University of Chicago Laboratory School in 1976, the same year he played on the Illinois Class A, All-State Hall of Fame basketball team. Attending Princeton University as an economics major, he quickly found a local broker whose enthusiasm convinced him that he, too, could be successful in the field. While in college, Rogers flew to the West Coast to appear on the *Wheel of Fortune,* winning $8,600 in prizes that he immediately invested with his broker.

At a Glance. . .

Born March 31, 1958, in Chicago, IL; son of John W. Rogers (a judge) and Jewel S. Lafontant (an attorney and government official); married Desireé Glapion (director of Illinois Lottery), 1988; children: Victoria. *Education:* Princeton University, B.S., 1980. *Politics:* Republican.

William Blair & Company, Chicago, broker, 1980-1983; Ariel Capital Management, Chicago, founder and president, 1983—. Member of the board of Chicago Symphony Orchestra and University of Chicago Laboratory School; trustee, Princeton University, Rush-Presbyterian-St. Luke Medical Center of Chicago, and La Rabida Children's Hospital and Research Center of Chicago; director of Chicago Urban League and Family Focus, Evanston, IL.

Awards: Entrepreneur of the Year, Arthur Young and *Venture* magazine, 1988; Mutual Fund Manager of the Year, *Sylvia Porter's Personal Finance Magazine,* 1988; Minority Small Business Person of the Year, U.S. Small Business Administration District, 1989; distinguished alumni award, Association of Black Princeton Alumni, 1991.

Addresses: *Home*—Chicago, IL. *Office*—Ariel Capital Management, Inc., 307 N. Michigan Ave., Suite 2014, Chicago, IL 60601.

After graduating from Princeton in 1980, Rogers went to work as a stockbroker for William Blair & Company, a Chicago investment banking firm. Besides being the first person hired directly out of college by the company in more than four years, he was the first black professional ever to work at the 400-employee firm.

For Rogers, it was the perfect place to learn his trade. The company had everything under one roof—corporate finance, public finance, trading, money management, mutual funds, and research—and specialized in small-company stocks. With experience and omnivorous reading of financial newsletters, magazines, and investment classics like *Security Analysis* and *A Random Walk Down Wall Street,* Rogers quickly began to develop his value-oriented investment strategy.

Less than three years later, at the age of 25, he left William Blair & Company to form Ariel Capital Management,

named after the fleet and nearly extinct African and Asian mountain gazelle. Starting with only one major account—$100,000 worth of Howard University's endowment fund to invest—within six months Rogers and an employee had raised an additional $190,000 in investment capital. From then on Ariel Capital moved nearly as swiftly as its namesake, growing to $45 million in managed assets by 1986.

Family ties helped Rogers's rapid rise in the financial world. His mother was an early investor and remains part-owner of Ariel. More importantly, her business connections helped open doors. She was a trustee of Howard University, and two other corporations where she served on the board of directors, Revlon and Mobil, later became Ariel clients. The firm also landed such accounts as the retirement funds of city employees in Chicago, Detroit, Los Angeles, and the District of Columbia. But, connections aside, the bottom line is results. "Our private clients can judge us by just one thing," Rogers told *Forbes,* "growth of assets."

Investing Over the Long Haul

To that end, Rogers quickly perfected a creative but conservative investment style best summed up by Ariel's motto, borrowed from Aesop's fable about the tortoise: "Slow and steady wins the race." His overriding philosophy is one of patience, timing, and making the most out of a down market. Unlike many investors, he has no sophisticated computerized trading programs. Rogers avoids buying into the current "hot" stock trends of any given moment, and he does not look for potential takeover targets with share prices that might quickly jump. Instead, he seeks out lesser-known, undervalued companies that produce quality products, then invests long-term in their stock.

Intensive research is the key to finding these companies. Rogers devotes several hours a day to reading five morning newspapers, nine business magazines, and more than 80 newsletters, including his own entitled *The Patient Investor.* He likes to concentrate on smaller companies with market capitalization of $50 million to $1 billion and good earnings records that "do one thing very, very well, and have a well-established niche," he told *Financial World.* Many of these firms are too small to be followed by the bigger Wall Street investors.

Rogers also looks for companies in currently unpopular industries, companies experiencing a temporary setback in earnings, or companies newly created by spinoffs and asset sales, and he aims to find them before they are discovered by other investors. Other criteria are effective and committed management, a clean, simple, and easily-understood balance sheet, good cash flow, and a low debt-to-capital ratio.

"A lot of our work is really tire kicking," he explained in *Black Enterprise,* "going out and visiting the companies, getting to know the employees and management, and talking to the customers, competitors and suppliers. The final judgment is whether there will be long-term demand for that product." Rogers expects the earnings of the companies he invests in to grow at a consistent 12 percent to 15 percent annually.

There are several types of companies, however, that Rogers never invests in. He stays away from cyclical industries like heavy machinery, steel, and automobiles because of their frequent ups and downs. He avoids all start-up companies, regardless of their business, because they have no track record. Commodity stocks like precious metals, gas, and oil are too volatile for his taste, while trucking, airline, banking, and other recently deregulated industries are, in his mind, still working themselves out in their new environments and, therefore, are not good buys. "We don't make exceptions," Rogers said in *Changing Times.* "We're very rigid."

Socially Conscious Investments

Even more important to Rogers is his strict code of socially conscious investing. He will not buy the stock of any company that does business with South Africa. Nor will he invest in defense contractors, nuclear utilities, cigarette manufacturers, and companies that make weapons or harm the environment.

"The principles just make investment sense," he told *Fortune* magazine. "Many defense companies are too reliant upon big government contracts. This reliance pressures management into doing unethical things to get and keep those contracts," he explained. "I don't own nuclear utilities because I don't like investing in companies that the courts might put out of business. The same goes for cigarette makers: I don't want to invest in a business everyone is trying to outlaw." In fact, when Kraft, one of Rogers's corporate clients, became a part of tobacco manufacturing giant Philip Morris Companies Inc., he terminated business with them.

Documented Success

Rogers's patient, disciplined approach has worked. Some of his earlier successes included investments in companies that manufacture toothbrushes, hospital uniforms, desktop stacking trays, plastic binders, baseball cards, and milkshake machines. And he has also been known to take advantage of a down market, investing, for instance, $9 million in Caesar's World, the hotel and gambling casino

firm, when its stock hit a low of $17 per share during the October 1987 stock market crash. By July of 1992 Caesar's price per share had risen 80 percent.

"Ariel is one of the few managers dealing with the middle-size, unknown, basic-business type of company, and those companies are the ones that have led the [stock market] charge since the crash," Edward G. Lloyd, former senior vice-president of the United Negro College Fund (UNCF), said in *Business Week.* The UNCF was one of Rogers's early clients, joining Ariel in 1984 and seeing its initial investment grow by 140 percent over the next four years.

Rogers claims similar results for his other 50 big-money institutional clients, which have included Chrysler, Ford, Procter & Gamble, AT&T, Pillsbury, Sara Lee, and the

> "The fortress of finance was one of the last to give way, but not a week goes by without the press reporting the creation of a new firm by minorities."

Stroh Brewing Company. In fact, from 1987 to 1990 Rogers's clients saw their total assets rise more than 53 percent, compared to the nearly 29 percent gain posted by Standard & Poor's index of 500 stocks.

"We were successful during the '80s because we picked some good, reasonably priced small stocks," he told *Black Enterprise.* "We avoided the go-go, glamorous small stocks that soared in 1980 and then plunged by 1985. Instead, we stuck with low-expectation stocks that didn't go up as much, but also didn't suffer as much."

Mutual Funds Attracted Smaller Investors

Ariel's institutional clients have average investment accounts of $30 million. To attract smaller investors, Rogers organized two mutual funds distributed by Calvert Securities, a Washington, D.C., firm that markets socially responsible investments. The Calvert-Ariel Growth Fund, started in 1986, invests in small companies. From its inception to 1992 the Fund appreciated 15.1 percent annually, growing to $260 million in assets, placing it sixth among 53 small-company funds followed and ranked by Lipper Analytical Services. His newer fund, the Calvert-Ariel Appreciation Fund, buys stock in companies as large as $3 billion. It grew to $140 million and gained 10.7 percent in value annually from its start in 1989 to 1992.

But Rogers's very success has caused problems and forced a change in the way he prefers investing. So much new money has flooded his firm and his mutual funds that he can no longer specialize in the small-company stocks that made his reputation. Back in 1986, when he managed only $45 million, Rogers could put 5 to 10 percent of Ariel's total capital in 10 or 20 carefully targeted small companies without disturbing their share price or ending up with too large a percentage of their stock. When their share prices rose, Ariel's total return appreciated accordingly.

However, as a multibillion-dollar money manager since the early 1990s, Rogers can no longer operate this way. His total assets are too large to permit such a concentrated investment strategy among selected small firms without severely jolting their share price. As a result, he must either scatter his investment portfolio among hundreds of small companies, diluting his overall return, or focus on much larger firms.

Rogers has tried to steer a middle course. Telling *Forbes* in 1991, "We can't take on any more new cash and still preserve our focus," he stopped seeking institutional clients and closed the Calvert-Ariel Growth Fund to new investors. This has allowed him to continue pursuing small companies while simultaneously investing in larger, more well-known firms like Clorox, Hasbro, and the Fleming Companies.

Thoughts on Minority-Owned Businesses

But the spotlight will be on Rogers as he tries to walk this investment tightrope because of the performance standards he has set and the pioneering role model Ariel has become as one of the black leaders in the financial world.

"The fortress of finance was one of the last to give way," he told *Changing Times* in 1990, "but not a week goes by without the press reporting the creation of a new firm by minorities."

Still, only a small fraction of all United States pension assets is managed by firms owned by blacks, women, Hispanics, Asian-Americans, Native Americans, and other minorities. Ariel and W. R. Lazard & Company in New York account for more than $3.2 billion of that amount, nearly half of all the assets managed by black-owned firms.

To maintain this pacesetting status, Rogers continues his workaholic six-day weeks to find the necessary time to keep up with all his managerial duties and research responsibilities. Yet people continue to underestimate him, Justin F. Beckett, senior vice president of NCM Capital Management in Durham, North Carolina, told *Black Enterprise*. "They see a mild-mannered, soft-spoken person, but he is a pure competitor who is out to win."

Sources

Black Enterprise, April 1992.
Business Week, July 11, 1988.
Changing Times, September 1990.
Financial World, April 18, 1989.
Forbes, September 2, 1991.
Fortune, July 16, 1990.
World Press Review, May 1989.

CBB spoke with John Rogers's office on October 14, 1992.

—*James J. Podesta*

Leah J. Sears-Collins

1955—

State supreme court justice

Judge Leah J. Sears-Collins is the first African American woman justice to serve on the State Supreme Court of Georgia. Upon her election to a regular judicial term in 1992, she also became one of the youngest high court jurists in the nation. Sears-Collins's fast-track career has included experience as a trial lawyer, a traffic court judge, and a superior court judge—all since earning her law degree in 1980. She was appointed to the state supreme court by Georgia governor Zell Miller, but in the summer of 1992 she earned a permanent seat by winning a statewide election. Since then she has sought to bring a fresh perspective to the predominantly white, male high court.

Sears-Collins told the *Atlanta Constitution* that she felt her age was the most important asset she brought to the Georgia Supreme Court. "I thought it was time to diversify the court, not just by race and sex, but in age as well," she explained. "I could be the voice of people who grew up [in the] post-civil rights era." The justice also noted that she had not achieved such a prominent position by chance or by virtue of her race. "I've worked my butt off," she said. "I come in at 7 or 7:30 every morning, and I work late whenever I have to. I don't shy from the difficult cases; those are the ones I love."

Sears-Collins was born June 13, 1955, in Heidelberg, Germany. Her father was a U.S. Army colonel whose work took the family all over the world; she had circled the globe twice before she turned sixteen. Throughout her academic career, Sears-Collins strove to do well in her schoolwork. Both of her parents stressed education, but the youngster seemed highly self-motivated as well. "She was a very studious child," Sears-Collins's mother told the *Atlanta Constitution*. "Many nights I'd go into her room and find her asleep and take the glasses off her face and the book off her chest. I used to have to insist she go outside and play sometimes."

As a child, Sears-Collins had a burning ambition: she wanted to be a judge. When she was only eight years old, she began ordering law school catalogues from prestigious institutions like Yale and Harvard universities. Paging through them, Sears-Collins wondered why all of the law students pictured in the catalogues were white men. Even then, she knew she would have to overcome the hurdles of gender and color in order to achieve her goals. Times changed as Sears-Collins grew, and she and her siblings were afforded educational opportunities that might well have been denied them in a previous era. Both of her brothers graduated from the U.S.

At a Glance...

Born June 13, 1955, in Heidelberg, Germany; daughter of Thomas J. (a U.S. army officer) and Onnye Jean (Rountree) Sears; married Love Collins (a business executive), July 3, 1976; children: Addison, Brennan. *Education:* Cornell University, B.A. (with honors), 1976; Emory University, J.D., 1980; additional graduate studies with National Judicial College, Reno, NV.

Alston & Bird Attorneys at Law, Atlanta, GA, lawyer, 1980-85; City Court of Atlanta, traffic court judge, 1985-88; Fulton Superior Court, Atlanta, judge, 1988-92; State Supreme Court of Georgia, justice, 1992—. Founder of Battered Women's Project of Columbus, GA.

Member: National Association of Women's Judges, Georgia Association of Black Women Attorneys (founding president), National Association of Alcoholism and Drug Abuse Counselors.

Selected awards: NAACP award for community service.

Addresses: *Office*—Administrative Office of Courts, 244 Washington St., Suite 550, Atlanta, GA 30334.

Naval Academy and became pilots. Later they earned law degrees and took jobs in California.

For her part, Sears-Collins feels that she benefitted from the rootless upbringing she experienced as a military officer's child. "When you grow up around people of all different nationalities, you learn to feel at ease with people of every kind," she said in the *Atlanta Constitution*. "You really have to learn to live, work and play with people who aren't like yourself."

Set High Goals

When Sears-Collins was in her teens, her family settled in Savannah, Georgia. She attended Savannah High School, where she was the first black student to make the cheerleading squad. The justice remembered that she tried out for cheerleading because she saw the color barrier as a challenge. She wanted to be the first to break it. After high school Sears-Collins entered the Ivy League as a student at Cornell University. She graduated from Cornell in 1976

with honors and was accepted to law school at Atlanta's Emory University.

"Leah has always recognized that the civil rights movement opened doors that we, as the next generation, can charge through," Sears-Collins's husband told the *Atlanta Constitution*. "Doing that, she has often been first." Sears-Collins earned her law degree in 1980 and landed a position with the Atlanta law firm of Alston & Bird. For five years she worked there as a trial lawyer. Then, at the tender age of 30, she achieved the dream she had held since childhood. She became a judge.

Early Court Experience

Her first judicial appointment was to the Atlanta Traffic Court, a position that might seem tedious and far removed from the high-stake cases of a state supreme court. But her days in traffic court gave her considerable experience in courtroom administration. She then moved on, in 1988, to Fulton County Superior Court. At 32, she was the youngest person ever elected to a superior court seat in the state of Georgia. There, Sears-Collins established herself as "a magistrate of special distinction," according to an unsigned editorial in the *Atlanta Constitution*. The editorial went on to note that lawyers who pleaded cases before Sears-Collins praised "her preparation, her grasp of the law and her practical sense of how to apply it." Often Sears-Collins worked ten-hour days and right through the weekend to keep abreast of the cases before the superior court.

One of the highly publicized cases Sears-Collins decided for the Fulton County Superior Court concerned the deescalation of life support for a terminally ill child. When the child's parents objected to the proposed termination of the support system on religious grounds, the judge—in a well-balanced and skillfully written decision—denied the Scottish Rite Hospital the right to withhold life support.

Became Georgia State Supreme Court Justice

Early in 1992, Governor Zell Miller began interviewing candidates for a position on the Georgia Supreme Court. The court hears about 1,700 cases a year, including appeals in death penalty sentences, constitutional issues, equity cases, election contests, cases involving public revenues, divorce and alimony, wills, and titles to land. Literally the court of last resort in the state, the seven justices on the high bench also hear appeals on decisions from the Georgia Court of Appeals.

Several women were called to interview for the position, as were a few men, and Sears-Collins was among them. She was 36 at the time and felt that her chances of winning the seat were slim. Still, she made a convincing argument that diversity on the high court bench should include age as a criterion. She also could point to her service as a judge on two quite different Georgia courts. "Many people thought I was appointed by Governor Miller only because I'm black or a woman," she told the *Atlanta Constitution*. "But Robert Benham (the first African American to serve on the Georgia Supreme Court) was already on the court and there were four other women that the governor could have chosen. I think the high ratings I am getting from my peers tells me I have overcome that hurdle."

In order to retain her seat, Sears-Collins had to win a July election against a popular challenger, Clayton County Superior Court judge Stephen Boswell. Sears-Collins crossed the state to win voters, and she received the endorsement of *Atlanta Journal* columnist Jim Wooten. Wooten called her a "refreshing change" and "wonderfully different," a high court judge who is "not afraid to lead." On July 23, 1992, Sears-Collins won the close race to retain her position on the Georgia Supreme Court. Almost immediately thereafter, *Ebony* magazine named her among fifty black women of highest achievement in the nation.

The justice was not chosen on the basis of some static political ideology. She describes herself as a moderate who judges each case before her on its own merits. As a member of the Georgia high court, Sears-Collins will serve a six-year term at a salary near $93,000 a year. She may be re-elected or re-appointed—the method of choosing justices in Georgia is under litigation—until she is 75 years old.

Committed to Hard Work

Sears-Collins's work load is phenomenal. She has never-

theless managed to raise two children with the help of her husband, Love Collins, an executive helping to organize the 1996 Olympic Games in Atlanta. The Collins family lives in a large old house in Ansley Park, once among Atlanta's most rigidly segregated neighborhoods. (The justice's father-in-law in particular is said to enjoy strolling through the streets of a neighborhood he was once not allowed near after six in the evening.) In her rare moments of free time, Sears-Collins enjoys bikeriding and rollerblading. She has little leisure, though. *Atlanta Constitution* correspondent Mark Curriden described Sears-Collins as "the court's hardest worker," adding, "She comes to work early, stays late, is there on weekends, and takes piles of work home."

Sears-Collins told the *Atlanta Constitution* that she gets angry when people try to make her a symbol because she is female and black. "I want to be known as a scholar and a hard worker," the justice said. "I know that as a woman and as a woman of color, I'll have to work very hard. But I think I've done that here. That won't be anything new."

Sources

Atlanta Constitution, February 18, 1992, pp. A1, D1, D4; February 24, 1992, p. A12; March 6, 1992, p. A1; July 6, 1992, p. C3; July 22, 1992, p. C3.
Atlanta Journal, July 8, 1992, p. A10.
Ebony, October 1992, p. 118.
Emerge, June 1992, p. 18.
Jet, March 9, 1992, p. 24.
Working Woman, November 1992, p. 20.

—*Anne Janette Johnson*

Moneta Sleet, Jr.

1926—

Photojournalist

Moneta Sleet, Jr., has been taking pictures of people all of his life, capturing on film the exuberance, sorrow, steadfast determination, and introspection of his various subjects—celebrities and unknowns alike. Working exclusively for the black press, he continues to exhibit a strong commitment to showing slices of black life that might otherwise be missed by the white-dominated media. This commitment, together with his natural sensitivity and gentleness, has made him a prize-winning photojournalist and artist.

Sleet's parents sparked his interest in photography when they gave him a box camera as a child, and his hobby grew throughout his high school and college years. Sleet studied business at Kentucky State College, interrupted by a couple of years in the U.S. Army, and after graduating in 1947 he began pursuing photography as a career. In 1948 he was invited to set up a department of photography at Maryland State College. After a year, he left to engage in postgraduate study in New York. Sleet briefly attended the School of Modern Photography, and in 1950 he received a master's degree in journalism from New York University.

Sleet's first journalism job was as a sportswriter for the

Amsterdam News, a black newspaper in New York, in 1950. Several months later, he secured a position with the black picture magazine *Our World* and worked there until it folded in 1955. That same year, he joined the staff of the Johnson Publishing Company and began shooting pictures for *Jet* and *Ebony* magazines.

In four decades as a staff photographer for Johnson Publishing, Sleet has documented the struggles and triumphs of people of color throughout the world. In addition to traveling extensively in the United States, he has been to Liberia, Libya, the Sudan, Ghana, the Gambia, Kenya, Nigeria, Norway, Russia, South America, and the West Indies. He has photographed former African heads of state such as Ethiopian emperor Haile Selassie, Ghanaian prime minister Kwame Nkrumah, Liberian president William Tubman, and Kenyan president Jomo Kenyatta. His celebrity photos include memorable shots of singers Billie Holiday and Patti LaBelle; jazz musician Thelonius Monk; actors Bill Cosby, Phylicia Rashad, and Sidney Poitier; and the late tennis great Arthur Ashe.

But Sleet has also taken pictures of the less famous in various settings from civil rights marches to beauty contests. He recorded the woes of the less fortunate in such places as death

At a Glance...

Born Moneta J. Sleet, Jr., February 14, 1926, in Owensboro, KY; son of Moneta J. and Ozetta L. Sleet; married Juanita Harris; children: Greg, Michael, Lisa. *Education:* Kentucky State College, B.A., 1947; New York University, M.A., 1950.

Taught photography at Maryland State College, 1948-49; sportswriter for *Amsterdam News,* New York City, 1950; photographer for *Our World,* 1951-55; Johnson Publishing Company, Chicago, staff photographer for *Ebony* and *Jet* magazines, 1955—; first one-man show in St. Louis and Detroit, 1970; second one-man show in New York City, Newark, Chicago, Washington, D.C., and other U.S. cities, 1986. *Military service:* Served in the U.S. Army, 1944-46.

Member: National Association for the Advancement of Colored People, Black Academy of Arts and Letters.

Awards: Citation for excellence, Overseas Press Club of America, 1957; Pulitzer Prize for feature photography, 1969; photojournalism awards from the National Association of Black Journalists, 1978, and the National Urban League; named to Kentucky Journalism Hall of Fame, University of Kentucky, 1989.

Addresses: *Office—Ebony* Magazine, Johnson Publishing Company, Inc., 820 South Michigan Ave., Chicago, IL 60605.

row, a West Virginia mining town, and Miami, Florida, in the aftermath of a riot. Traveling so much has been difficult on his family. As he told *Ebony,* "It's not an easy life, so it's important to have a family who understands. I have been very fortunate."

Documented the Fight for Civil Rights

Sleet's major contributions to photojournalism and world history are his pictorial chronicles of both the American civil rights movement and the emergence of independent South African States. He has recorded such major events as the famous 1963 march on Washington, D.C.; the 1965 Selma, Alabama march for voting rights; and the

independence day celebrations in Nairobi, Kenya—a former British colony—in 1963.

Over the years, his efforts—and the contributions of *Jet* and *Ebony* magazines—were often overshadowed by the white media. As a black artist, his works have not enjoyed the wide exposure often afforded the works of white artists. He has, however, been able to bring his experience as an African American to his photography of black subjects. Sleet's photographs illustrate a great sense of commitment: "I must say that I wasn't there [at major civil rights demonstrations] as an objective reporter," he told the *New York Times.* "To be perfectly honest I had something to say, or, at least hoped that I did, and was trying to show one side of it—because we didn't have any problems finding the other side. So I was emotionally involved. That may not be a good school of journalism, but that's the way I felt."

Because of his personal and professional interest in the civil rights movement of the 1960s, Sleet came to know Dr. Martin Luther King, Jr., well and produced one of the largest collections of candid shots of King and his family. He took one of his first shots of the Kings in 1956—a photo of Dr. and Mrs. King with their infant daughter, Yolanda, on the steps of the Dexter Avenue Baptist Church in Montgomery, Alabama, at the very beginning of the King crusade. He traveled with the family to Oslo, Norway, when King received the Nobel Peace Prize. Sleet grew close to the family over the years. "It's kind of a peculiar position to be in," he told the *New York Times,* "because, on one hand, you are there as [a photographer], but people soon forgot that."

Pulitzer Prize Winner

Following the assassination of King in 1968, Sleet attended the slain leader's funeral and received a Pulitzer Prize for his picture of Coretta Scott King comforting her young daughter, Bernice, during the service. In explaining the compassion shown in this picture to *American Photographer,* he said simply, "He was my leader, too."

Sleet's Pulitzer Prize for photography was the first awarded to an African American, as well as the first bestowed upon anyone working for a black publication. Sleet has also received a citation for excellence from the Overseas Press Club of America, awards from the National Urban League and the National Association of Black Journalists, and induction into the Hall of Fame at the University of Kentucky.

Some observers—and Sleet himself—credit his success more to his sensitivity and patience than to his practical technique. As the photographer explained in the *New York Times:* "You've got to know when to intrude and when not to intrude and when to pull back. You have to be very patient, a thing that's good for me because I have a lot of patience and don't mind waiting." And in *An Illustrated Bio-Bibliography of Black Photographers,* Sleet commented: "You try to develop the sensitivity and the 'eye' to see that very special mood of the moment. You develop the discipline to block out everything but you, the camera and the subject, and you develop the tenacity to stick with it, to have patience. The picture will happen—that very special picture will happen."

Successful Retrospective in the Mid-1980s

Although Sleet's photographs have been shown at the prestigious Metropolitan Museum of Art, he saw only one solo exhibition of his work during the height of the civil rights movement. This showing was sponsored by the Alpha Kappa Alpha sorority and toured St. Louis and Detroit in 1970. For more than a decade and a half after that, Sleet's works were not displayed in formal one-man exhibitions. But in 1986, the Philip Morris Companies and the Johnson Publishing Company cosponsored Sleet's second one-man retrospective exhibit, which opened first at the New York Public Library.

Initially set to run for two years and visit four cities, the show received so much attention and so many requests for bookings that its schedule was expanded. In addition to New York, the retrospective was shown in Chicago; Milwaukee; Newark, New Jersey; Frankfort, Kentucky; and Washington D.C. Highlights of the exhibit included many of his most famous shots of the King family, other political leaders, and celebrities. The photographs ranged in mood from heart-rending sadness to triumph; included was a strikingly poignant photograph of blues great Billie Holiday, wearily resting her head on her needle-scarred arms, as well as a shot of an unknown, exultant woman tramping and singing through the rain during the 1965 Selma march.

Sleet's body of work serves as a permanent reminder of the richness of black history and culture while providing a pictorial legacy of the key figures in the burgeoning civil rights movement. As he stated in the *New York Times,* "A lot of people have forgotten those days and I don't think they ever should."

Sources

Books

Crawford, Joe, editor, *The Black Photographers Annual: 1973,* Black Photographers Annual, 1972.
Willis-Thomas, Deborah, editor, *An Illustrated Bio-Bibliography of Black Photographers, 1940-1988,* Garland Publishing, 1989.

Periodicals

American Photographer, July 1988.
Chicago Defender, May 2, 1987.
Ebony, February 1969; June 1969; August 1971; January 1987.
Jet, October 13, 1986; March 2, 1987; June 5, 1989.
New York Times, October 19, 1986.

—*Robin Armstrong*

Franklin A. Thomas

1934—

Philanthropist, administrator, attorney

Franklin A. Thomas is president of the Ford Foundation, a vast and self-perpetuating trust originally endowed by car manufacturer Henry Ford and his son Edsel. With a reported $5.8 billion in assets in the early 1990s, Thomas and his Ford Foundation staff use strategic sums of money—more than $200 million annually—to help needy communities, finance educational and cultural institutions, support civil rights in the United States and around the world, and strengthen and empower policy influencing organizations. His priorities help set the American agenda and his decisions often leverage billions of government dollars.

Born in 1934 in the Bedford-Stuyvesant section of Brooklyn, Thomas is the youngest child of a proud but poverty-wracked West Indian family. When Thomas was just eleven years old, his father, James, a laborer, became disabled and later died. Left to support six children, Thomas's mother, Viola, worked as a housekeeper until World War II when she landed a job as a machinist at American Can. The stoic Viola returned to housekeeping at the end of the war when the availability of returning soldiers allowed manufacturers to again raise racial and gender barriers to hiring.

Despite living in a poor West Indian neighborhood that was

riddled with the violence of gang wars, Thomas was raised in a family atmosphere that fostered pride and an upward-looking mindset. "We were taught," he told *Ebony,* "that there were no limits on what you could do in life except the limits that you set on yourself." Thomas was a good student, a superior basketball player, and a leader in the Concord Baptist Church Boy Scouts. "He was something of a hero in my neighborhood," Dr. Bernard Gifford, who also grew up in "Bed-Stuy," told *Black Enterprise.* "Teachers held him up as a model because he was a student as well as a basketball player and that was important."

At 6 feet 4 inches in height, Thomas, a star center at Franklin K. Lane High School, was offered basketball scholarships by several major universities. He refused the scholarships and instead—on the advice of his mother who felt that others would question his intelligence if he accepted a sports scholarship—accepted an academic scholarship from Columbia University.

At Columbia, Thomas nevertheless continued his basketball career. He became the first African American to captain an Ivy League basketball team and was twice voted the league's most valuable player. In addition, he became involved with the

Born Franklin Augustine Thomas, May 27, 1934, in Brooklyn, NY; son of James (a laborer) and Viola (a housekeeper and machinist; maiden name, Atherley) Thomas; married Dawn Conrada (divorced, 1972); children: Keith, Hillary, Kerrie, Kyle. *Education:* Columbia University, B.A. 1956, L.L.B. 1963.

Federal Housing and Home Finance Agency, New York office, attorney, 1963; Southern District of New York, assistant U.S. attorney, 1964-65; New York City Police Department, deputy police commissioner in charge of legal matters, 1965-67; Bedford-Stuyvesant Restoration Corporation, Brooklyn, president and chief executive officer, 1967-77; attorney in private practice, 1977-79; Ford Foundation, New York City, president, 1979—. Member of the board of directors of the Aluminum Company of America, CBS Inc., Cummins Engine Co., Inc., Citicorp/Citibank, and AT&T; chair of the Study Commission on United States Policy Toward Southern Africa; member of the Secretary of State's Advisory Committee on South Africa, 1985-87. *Military service:* U.S. Air Force, Strategic Air Command navigator, 1956-60; became captain.

Awards: Honorary degrees from Yale University, Fordham University, Pratt Institute, Pace University, and Columbia University; award for contribution to the betterment of urban life from the Lyndon B. Johnson Foundation, 1974; medal of excellence from Columbia University, 1976; Alexander Hamilton Award from Columbia College, 1983.

Addresses: *Office*—Office of the President, The Ford Foundation, 320 East 43rd St., New York, NY 10017.

NAACP's (National Association for the Advancement of Colored People) drive to increase black admissions at the university. But what was perhaps most important about his Columbia experience were the relationships he developed with others who would later become movers and shakers in the fields of business, law, and politics.

After graduating in 1956, Thomas took advantage of his ROTC training and did a four-year hitch with the Air Force, where he worked his way up to captain and flew missions as a navigator with the Strategic Air Command. In 1960 he returned to Columbia for his law degree. He opted for a career

in law after seeing a con man swindle his mother out of a down payment on a house she wanted to buy.

Joined Government Ranks

Upon receiving his law degree in 1963, Thomas moved into a series of high-powered government jobs. He worked as an attorney for the Federal Housing and Home Finance Agency, was admitted to the New York State Bar the following year, served as an assistant U.S. attorney in New York from 1964 until 1965, and then worked for three years as New York's deputy police commissioner in charge of legal matters. Asked later how he made the remarkable transition from economic impoverishment to positions of leadership in the legal arena, he told the *New York Times Magazine*, "I grew up in a family that just assumed that one, you were smart and capable; two, that you were going to work hard, and three, the combination of these two meant that anything was possible."

In 1967 Thomas caught the attention of New York senator Robert Kennedy. Kennedy was looking for ways to improve living conditions in Bedford-Stuyvesant and wanted to create a nonprofit community development agency to raise and coordinate public and private redevelopment funds. To head up the agency, Kennedy sought a "Bed-Stuy" resident. On the advice of staff member and future *Black Enterprise* publisher Earl Graves, Kennedy met with Thomas. Impressed with the 33-year-old lawyer, in May of that year he appointed Thomas president of the newly created Bedford-Stuyvesant Restoration Corporation.

Impressive Tenure as President of Bedford-Stuyvesant Restoration

Thomas soon acquired the reputation of a man who gets the job done. During his ten years as president, the Restoration Corporation raised some $63 million in public and private funds—including a significant amount from the Ford Foundation. It built three apartment complexes and erected a 200,000 square foot shopping center. It rehabilitated 400 brownstone units, established the Billie Holiday Theater, helped to start or expand 120 businesses in the area, and developed a $21 million mortgage pool. Under Thomas's leadership, the Restoration Corporation lured an IBM facility into the neighborhood, placed 7,000 residents in jobs and helped engender a positive feeling among the neighborhood's residents. Perhaps most importantly, Thomas's Restoration Corporation became a model for the hundreds of community-based redevelopment corporations that would later come into being around the country.

During his tenure at Bedford-Stuyvesant Restoration

Corporation, Thomas also became well known in public and private circles. CBS, Citicorp/Citibank, AT&T, and the Cummins Engine Company all paid him handsomely to serve on their boards of directors. He was a trustee of the Ford Foundation, and in 1976, then president-elect Jimmy Carter even asked him to serve as secretary of Housing and Urban Development. A flattered Thomas refused, telling Carter that the only federal job he wanted was the one Carter was about to occupy.

Thomas left the Restoration Corporation in 1977, worked in private practice for a time, and for nine months filled in as head of New York's John Hay Whitney Foundation. Early in 1979, Rockefeller Foundation head Dr. John Knowles convinced him to lead a year-long study of apartheid—a policy of political and economic discrimination against blacks practiced by the oppressive white minority government of South Africa. Several months later, officials at the Ford Foundation asked if he would take on the foundation's presidency following the retirement of longtime Ford head McGeorge Bundy. Thomas agreed, stipulating that he be allowed to honor his commitment to the Rockefeller Foundation. He served as chairman of the Study Commission on United States Policy Toward Southern Africa and wrote the forward to the commission's 1981 report *Time Running Out*.

Became Ford Foundation Head

Reaction to Thomas's appointment as president of the Ford Foundation was enthusiastic. Vernon Jordan, former National Urban League president, hailed it as "the most significant black appointment in my time . . . the first real example of a case where whites have turned meaningful power over to a black," according to *Black Enterprise*.

Ebony reported that Thomas viewed the Ford Foundation as "one of the few places that has social purpose as its objective and . . . controls the resources with which to do something about it." But while his appointment represented honor and opportunity, it was not without its downside. The foundation was hitting hard times. Declining stock prices and overextension during the previous administration had shrunken assets to $2.2 billion from a mid-1960s high of $4 billion. Annual spending was down to $108 million from $220 million. In addition, the Ford Foundation was committed to too many programs.

Among his first actions upon occupying the foundation's New York offices was the creation of the Local Initiative Support Corporation (LISC). Funded by Ford and six corporations, the LISC would help existing community development groups—like the one Thomas had run in

Bedford-Stuyvesant—move from successfully managed small projects to major neighborhood revitalization efforts.

Changed the Face of the Ford Foundation

But while LISC was important, Thomas's main inaugural task was an exhaustive review of all of the foundation's administrative and grant-making activities. In order to turn things around financially, Thomas had to be a tough manager; changing the institution would mean confronting the entrenched staff. Each officer had to undergo a performance review and justify the worth of his or her program. Longtime staffers resented the review. They reportedly saw Thomas as aloof and unwilling to talk to them on a personal basis. Siobhan Oppenheimer-Nicolau, a program officer with Ford for 14 years, told *New York* magazine, "There was a very drastic change in style after Frank arrived. This had always been a very collegial operation, with a great deal of feedback, of exchange. Much of that stopped because he isolated himself and people had no way of knowing whether or not he had any confidence in them."

Early in 1981 Thomas completed his review and began making changes at the foundation. He told *New York* his mandate was to address problems of overextension, to reduce the ratio of management costs to program dollars, and to reorganize the staff in order to break up the largely separate divisions and encourage staff interaction. As a

> "The weak partner in community revitalization in the last decade has been the federal government."

result of the reorganization, 16 senior staff members left of their own accord and another 16 were laid off. By the end of his third year, Thomas had trimmed the entire Ford staff from over 442 to about 324.

Many staffers were angry at being forced to leave. Four older employees filed age discrimination complaints with the U.S. Equal Employment Opportunity Commission (EEOC). Thomas responded that he had the right to let these people go and that they should have known better than to expect lifetime employment at the Ford Foundation. "The foundation has hired people on term contracts in order to reinforce the fact that there is no tenure here," he told *New York*. "Besides, there is always the desirability of having a somewhat regular rotation of significant parts of your staff. . . . Age was just not a factor in the decision of retention or non-retention."

While most critics recognized that Thomas was acting in the interest of the organization, some questioned his tactics. As quoted in *New York,* Oppenheimer-Nicolau noted that Thomas "chose to make a drastic turnaround rather than an evolutionary one, and this necessarily created more of a sense of threat than would normally have been the case."

Along with the staff cuts, Thomas made many important changes in the foundation's organization and priorities. He phased out Ford's heavy involvement in population control, environmental protection, school-finance reform, public-interest law and some other areas, while allocating more than half the foundation's budget for urban poverty and rural poverty and resources. In terms of grant-making, he moved the foundation away from providing routine operating expenses for local groups and toward concentrating on broader programs with the potential to impact large groups of people. Finally, Thomas reorganized the institution's three nearly autonomous divisions into six thematic areas: human rights and social justice; urban poverty and the disadvantaged; rural poverty and resources; education; international, economic, and political issues; and governance and public policy.

In contrast to Thomas's detractors, some observers acknowledged the president's serious-minded approach to his work—especially at a time when the government was pulling back in its commitment to all sorts of programs. "Frank is very analytical, careful and deliberate," Ford staffer Susan Beresford told *Ebony.* "In a period of diminishing resources, the kind of care he brings is all the more important. And he brings freshness."

By 1990 Thomas had in many basic ways changed the operation of the world's largest charitable foundation: the previously sagging endowment reached the $5.8 billion mark. The grant-making focused more on issues of domestic poverty, with an emphasis on results-oriented programming rather than on studies.

Offered Commentary on Pressing Social Issues

In many ways Thomas had worked to bring the experience he gained at the Bedford-Stuyvesant Restoration Corporation to the hundreds of community redevelopment agencies the Ford Foundation was supporting through the LISC. "I would argue community development is emerging as a major revolution in the country," he told the *New York Times,* "one that engages people in ways that affect their lives and their localities. It may not be glamorous, but it should stimulate an excitement in all of us regardless of our politics or background."

Though not known for his public persona, Thomas was coaxed out of his quiet ways by the 1992 riots in Los Angeles. He blamed the riots at least partially on the U.S. government. "The weak partner in community revitalization in the last decade has been the federal government, which has retreated from participation," he told the *New York Times.* "The events in Los Angeles tell us we cannot continue to fail investing in our neighborhoods and our people. We are spending the capital invested years ago, and that capital needs to be renewed."

Sources

Black Enterprise, September 1980; February 1982; July 1990.
Ebony, October 1982.
Los Angeles Times, February 14, 1992.
Newsweek, September 7, 1981.
New York, September 28, 1981.
New Yorker, August 31, 1981.
New York Times, January 30, 1979; February 8, 1981; October 10, 1982; May 26, 1992.
U.S. News & World Report, March 31, 1981.
Wall Street Journal, February 15, 1979.

—*Jordan Wankoff*

Henry McNeal Turner

1834-1915

Clergyman, activist, author

Henry McNeal Turner was for many years the leading advocate of black migration to Africa as the only permanent solution to the problem of race discrimination in the United States. As bishop of the African Methodist Episcopal Church (AME), Turner was a highly vocal and vehement critic of white America's continued oppression of its black citizens, and he became natural heir to nineteenth-century abolitionist Frederick Douglass as chief spokesman for black pride and self-determination. Turner's firsthand experience of white resistance to equality among the races led him to embrace the cause of African migration even before the rise of black nationalist leader Marcus Garvey in the 1920s. His "back to Africa" campaign never won effective support from a majority of African Americans, but Turner remained one of the most powerful black leaders during the difficult years of widespread economic distress and segregation enforced by Jim Crow laws.

Turner was born to a family of free blacks in South Carolina in 1834. Although not slaves, the impoverished Turners found it necessary to put their children to work picking cotton side by side with slaves, and Henry's earliest memories were of hard labor under the hot Carolina sun. Already of a proud and defiant temperament, Turner ran away from home as a young teenager and found work as an office boy with a law firm. He swept floors and washed windows for a few pennies per day, but some of the law clerks noticed Turner's unusually bright and curious mind and offered to teach the young man how to read and write. (In most parts of the South, this was a criminal act.) Turner responded quickly to their help and soon became not only literate, but a powerful speaker as well. While still in his teens, the broad-shouldered, powerfully built Turner was offered a position as an itinerant minister by the Methodist Episcopal Church—South, beginning a career in the church that would continue for the remaining sixty-five years of his life.

Preacher and Politician

Throughout the 1850s Turner traveled widely in the deep South, preaching to slaves and free blacks under the auspices of the white-controlled Methodist Episcopal Church. Though himself a free man, Turner everywhere encountered the humiliations and restraints placed upon people of color in the prewar South, and he was not of a nature to suffer such indignities in silence. In 1858, Turner

At a Glance...

Born in 1834, near Abbeville, SC; died in Windsor, Ontario, Canada, May 8, 1915; buried in Atlanta, GA; son of Hardy and Sarah (Green) Turner; married four times, in 1856, 1893, 1900, and to fourth wife, Laura Pearl Lemon, in 1907. *Education:* African Methodist Episcopal (AME) training in theology, 1858-60. *Religion:* AME. *Politics:* Republican during Civil War; later, black nationalist.

Traveling preacher for Methodist Episcopal Church—South, 1851-57; joined African Methodist Episcopal Church, 1858, became deacon, 1860, and elder, 1862; pastor of Union Bethel Church, Washington, DC, 1862-65; appointed first black U.S. Army chaplain by Abraham Lincoln, 1863; worked briefly as an agent of the Freedmen's Bureau following the Union victory to the Civil War; organized AME churches and missions in Georgia, 1865-67; delegate to Georgia constitutional convention, 1867; member of the Georgia state legislature, 1868; church pastor in Savannah, GA, 1870-76; business manager, AME Book Concern, Philadelphia, 1876-80; elected AME bishop, 1880; established Morris Brown College, Atlanta, c. 1890, and served as president for twelve years; traveled to Africa four times, 1891-98; organized national convention of African Americans, Cincinnati, OH, 1893; headed Georgia Equal Rights Association, 1906.

Author of *The Genius and Theory of Methodist Policy,* 1885; founder of *Southern Christian Recorder, Voice of Missions,* and *Voice of the People;* author of editorials.

Member: American Colonization Society (elected president, 1876).

first heard of a Christian denomination run by and for blacks, the African Methodist Episcopal Church, and he immediately joined its mission in Baltimore.

The AME had been founded in Philadelphia in 1794 and was extensively represented in the northern half of the United States, but the threat posed to southern slaveowners by any all-black organization had prohibited its growth in the South. At the church's training mission in Baltimore, Turner studied Latin, Greek, Hebrew, and theology with professors from nearby Trinity College. He was appointed

deacon in 1860 and two years later elevated to the rank of elder.

Upon completion of his training, Turner was named pastor of the Union Bethel Church in Washington, D.C., the capital's largest black church. Turner was outspoken in his support for President Abraham Lincoln's general emancipation of the slaves in 1863, and equally so in his call for the use of black troops in the Union Army during the Civil War. Once this became federal policy, the first black troops from the Washington area were mustered in the Union Bethel churchyard, and President Lincoln named Turner the first black chaplain in the history of the United States. Turner served his soldiers with great distinction, accompanying them into the field of battle while carrying out his duties as chaplain. The successful completion of the Union victory filled Turner with high hopes for the future of black Americans, and he joined the government's Freedmen's Bureau in Georgia to help blacks make the transition from slavery to freedom.

Turner soon found that racial discrimination was as strong as ever in Georgia, and he resigned from the Freedmen's Bureau after a short tenure to return to the AME. As would be true throughout his life, Turner preferred to work within all-black organizations rather than endure the insults faced by blacks in an integrated setting. As head of the AME's new mission in Georgia, he proved himself a tireless organizer, dispatching AME ministers to the remotest corners of the state, taking on the burdens of administration, and defending the AME and himself from the hostility of whites resentful of this new source of black independence. In the tense atmosphere of the postwar South, Turner's aggressive manner earned him the hatred of many whites, but under his direction the AME flourished as never before.

At the same time Turner was asked to help organize Georgia's blacks under the banner of the Republican Party (the party of Lincoln, and for many years of all African American leaders). He was elected as a Republican to the state constitutional convention in 1867, where he adopted a surprisingly conciliatory position on most questions of race and equal rights. At this point in his career, Turner was still optimistic about the future of race relations in America, and he believed that changes in race relations would evolve inevitably as whites and blacks learned to live together as fellow citizens.

When elected to the state legislature in 1868, however, Turner quickly learned otherwise: Georgia's white legislators passed a bill forbidding blacks from holding elected office, so enraging Turner that he led a delegation of African American representatives in a walkout from the capitol building. Before leaving the legislative chamber, Turner unleashed the full fury of his wrath in a speech that amazed whites and encouraged blacks everywhere. As quoted in a record of the Georgia state legislature, he proclaimed: "I am here to demand my rights and to hurl thunderbolts at the man who would dare to cross the threshold of my manhood. . . . Never in the history of the world has a man been . . . charged with the offense of being of a darker hue than his fellow men."

Proponent of Black Pride and Colonization

Turner's disillusionment with the political process was redoubled the following year when he was forced to resign a federal appointment as postmaster of Macon, Georgia, after protests by local whites. His Washington connections did manage to secure Turner a minor job in the customs office of Savannah, Georgia, where he resumed full-time church duties as well; but his frustrations in the political arena had permanently altered his thinking about race relations in the United States. As early as 1862 the young clergyman had been impressed with the idea of African emigration for black Americans, and after his firsthand experience of the depth of white racism in the Reconstruction era, Turner returned to the dream of an African nation for blacks. The idea of African emigration was not new—as early as 1817 the American Colonization Society had begun the settlement of black Americans in Liberia, on the west coast of Africa—but Turner would become its most articulate and passionate nineteenth-century proponent.

Elected bishop in the AME in 1880, Turner used both pulpit and press to argue for the necessity of an African homeland for black Americans. He viewed as hopeless the efforts of blacks to achieve a decent life in the United States; racism was so ingrained in the American character, Turner believed, that people of color would never gain respect while living on American soil. Even if whites were to treat blacks with the best of intentions—which in the post-Reconstruction era they most emphatically did not—blacks would still suffer the psychic damage of living in a society founded, ruled, and defined by white culture. As cited by John Dittmer in *Black Leaders of the Nineteenth Century,* Turner wrote in 1898: "As long as we remain among the whites, the Negro will believe that the devil is black . . . that he [as a black person] is the devil . . . and the effect of such sentiment is contemptuous and degrading." It was his insistence on black pride and black nationalism that set apart Turner from earlier proponents of emigration, many of whom were southern whites hoping to purge the country of its black population.

Turner's black nationalism was equally emphatic in the religious arena. "God is a Negro," he often repeated, pointing out that every culture had always imagined God as one of its own. Such statements were infuriating to segments of white society, but Turner's brilliant oratory and message of black pride won him a huge following among the majority of southern blacks, for whom life as "free men" had become nearly unendurable in the face of continued white oppression. As bishop in the AME, Turner traveled constantly throughout the southern states and Indian territories, preaching his doctrine of African migration and openly scorning those many black leaders who thought him too radical for the times. Indeed, Turner was always at the center of controversy, whether for his firebrand proclamations ("Negro, Get Guns" was the title of one of his editorials) or for such irregularities as ordaining a woman deacon in 1888 or marrying for the fourth time at the age of 73.

Africa: Dream and Reality

African emigration remained the polestar of Bishop Turner's life and thought. African Americans needed "an outlet, a theater of manhood and activity established somewhere for our young men and women," he noted in an 1883 edition of *Christian Reporter.* "Until we have black men in the seat of power, respected, feared, hated, and reverenced, our young men will never rise." To further his dream of an African homeland, Turner urged the United States government to provide funds for the transportation of "5 or 10,000" blacks to Liberia every year, and he himself made the first of four trips to Africa in 1891.

Believing that the conversion of Africa to Christianity was part of God's plan for black Americans, Turner busily established churches and schools in Liberia, Sierra Leone, and later in South Africa. Everything he saw in Africa reaffirmed his belief in emigration for blacks, and back in the United States Turner organized a national convention for African Americans to meet in Cincinnati in 1893. The

> "Until we have black men in the seat of power, respected, feared, hated, and reverenced, our young men will never rise."

convention was attended by more than 800 delegates from around the country, Turner delivering a keynote speech which touched on the subject of emigration; but his plea for Africa as "the only hope of the Negro race" was rejected by the gathering, and Turner was forced to admit that his program was not acceptable to the majority of educated black Americans.

An even more serious blow to Turner's campaign was the bad publicity generated by the sending of two ships of black Americans to Liberia in the mid-1890s. Although reports varied, it appears that most of the colonists did not like or could not survive Liberia's tropical climate and backward economy. Many of the emigrants died of fever or made their way back to the United States, where their stories of hardship were widely publicized by the black press as proof of the folly of Bishop Turner's ideas. Turner reacted to the criticism with his usual scorn, referring, as quoted by Dittmer, to the failed emigrants as "shiftless no-account Negroes . . . accustomed to being fed and driven around by white men." The mismanaged expeditions effectively ended any real hope for a large-scale emigration to Africa by black Americans.

In 1895 Booker T. Washington seized black leadership with his speech at the Atlanta Exposition, in which he promised African Americans that if they remained patient and hard-working, they would eventually be accepted as equals by white society. Washington respected Bishop Turner as a powerful leader, especially among lower-class blacks, and the two men did not openly clash; but Washington's philosophy of accommodation had clearly prevailed.

Turner spent the balance of his life as an unapologetic and still virulent critic of America's social injustices. Though yielding to Booker T. Washington the title of national spokesperson for blacks in the United States, Turner remained a man of considerable power in both religious and political affairs. He was not above making alliances with southern white politicians of every variety, since he held all white leaders in similar contempt; and, as elder bishop of the AME for the last twenty years of his life, Turner's was the dominant voice in a church of some quarter million members. His last significant public role was as head of the Georgia Equal Rights Association, formed in 1906 by Turner, W. E. B. Du Bois, and other leading black figures. Turner's dream of African emigration already seemed outdated to younger men like Du Bois, but no one could deny the seventy-two-year-old bishop the courage of his words when he addressed the Georgia Equal Rights Association convention: "I used to love what I thought was the grand old flag, and sing with ecstasy about the stars and stripes," Dittmer quoted him as saying, "but to the Negro in this country the American flag is a dirty and contemptible rag." Turner died nine years later, his funeral attended by 25,000 mourners.

Sources

Books

Angell, Stephen W., *Bishop Henry McNeal Turner and African-American Religion in the South,* University of Tennessee Press, 1992.

Dittmer, John, essay included in *Black Leaders of the Nineteenth Century,* edited by Leon Litwack and August Meier, University of Illinois Press, 1988.

Drago, Edmund L., *Black Politicians and Reconstruction in Georgia: A Splendid Failure,* Louisiana State University Press, 1982.

Redkey, Edwin S., *Respect Black: The Writings and Speeches of Henry McNeal Turner,* Ayer Company Publications, 1971.

Wilmore, Gayraud S., *Black Religion and Black Radicalism: An Interpretation of the Religious History of Afro-American People,* Orbis Books, 1983.

Periodicals

Christian Reporter, 1883.
Ebony, February 1993.

—*Jonathan Martin*

Derek Walcott

1930—

Poet, playwright

Caribbean poet Derek Walcott is the recipient of the 1992 Nobel Prize for literature, one the world's most prestigious awards. Walcott won the prize on the strength of his many works of poetry and his plays about island life in a post-colonial era. He is the first native Caribbean writer ever to win a Nobel for literature. His poetry confronts his own mixed ethnic legacy—Walcott is of African, Dutch, and English descent—as well as the multi-ethnic character of the West Indies in general. In the 1981 biography *Derek Walcott,* Robert D. Hamner wrote: "Nurtured on oral tales of gods, devils, and cunning tricksters passed down by generations of slaves, Walcott should retell folk stories; and he does. On the other hand, since he has an affinity for and is educated in Western classics, he should retell the traditional themes of European experience; and he does. As inheritor of two vitally rich cultures, he utilizes one, then the other, and finally creates out of the two his own personal style."

Walcott's central preoccupation has concerned the union between two racial and social strains that has produced the unique Caribbean culture. He has worked from the "schizophrenic" point of view of an islander raised to respect and appreciate the culture of an enslaving colonial force. Hamner noted that Walcott "is a living example of the divided loyalties

and hatreds that keep his society suspended between two worlds." Likewise, *New Yorker* correspondent Jervis Anderson claimed that in ancestry and cultural heritage, Walcott "epitomized the composite New World culture in the Caribbean—roughly half black and half white—and he had no desire to elevate one component above the other. The two were reconciled in his view of himself as an artist and a 'divided child.'" In one of his best-known poems, Walcott perhaps spoke for himself when he wrote: "I'm just a red nigger who love the sea, / . . . I have Dutch, nigger, and English in me, / and either I'm nobody, or I'm a nation."

Walcott and his twin brother, Roderick, were born January 23, 1930, in Castries, a colonial town on the small eastern Caribbean island of St. Lucia. At the time of Walcott's birth, St. Lucia was part of the British protectorate, but its past as a French colony was evident in the creole dialect and religious practice of its citizens. Both of Walcott's parents were schoolteachers. His father died when Walcott was only a year old, but his mother compensated for the loss by nurturing her two sons' love of reading and study. She surrounded her children with English literary classics, recited Shakespeare to them, and encouraged them to appreciate poetry and drama.

At a Glance. . .

Born Derek Alton Walcott, January 23, 1930, on Castries, St. Lucia, West Indies; immigrated to United States, late 1950s; son of Warwick (a civil servant and teacher) and Alix (a teacher) Walcott; married Fay Moston, 1954 (divorced, 1959); married Margaret Ruth Maillard, 1962 (divorced); married Norline Metivier (actress and dancer; divorced); children: one son, three daughters. *Education:* University of the West Indies, B.A., 1953.

Poet and playwright, 1953—. Founding director of Trinidad Theatre Workshop, 1959; visiting professor at Columbia University, 1981, Harvard University, 1982, and Boston University, 1985—. Has given lectures and readings at numerous colleges in the United States and abroad; fund-raiser for international center devoted to the arts and the study of economics, to be based in the Caribbean.

Selected awards: Rockefeller Foundation grant, 1957-58; Obie Award, 1971, for *Dream on Monkey Mountain;* John D. and Catherine T. MacArthur Foundation grant, 1981; Nobel Prize for literature, 1992.

Addresses: *Office*—Department of English, Creative Writing Program, Boston University, 236 Bay State Rd., Boston, MA 02215.

In those days Castries was a picturesque town with large, ornate Victorian homes nestled among bright tropical gardens. Anderson noted that, as a youth, Walcott spent little time admiring the displays of affluence in the city. "His attention was drawn more strongly to the shanties of the poor, in Castries and elsewhere on the island, occupied by fascinating characters, some of whom later appeared in his book-length autobiographical poem, 'Another Life,'" Anderson commented. "Beyond the sociology of the land, young Walcott's imagination was transfixed by the sea: its sounds; its fishermen and schooner men; its far horizon of limits and possibilities; the dangerous seductions of its calm and stormy moods; its record of local drownings; its legends of shipwreck and isolation." This youthful fascination with St. Lucia's seafaring class would one day be translated into powerful poetry in the Homeric tradition. Walcott told the *New Yorker:* "Islands are great places to live in because the sea is close and there is the elemental feeling of things that are bigger than you are."

Early Interest in the Study of Literature

In school, Walcott learned English as a second language and became captivated by the works of Great Britain's best poets. At the same time he was well aware that England was the seat of the colonial rule that encouraged slavery during previous centuries. He therefore approached the European canon with an ambivalent attitude that would remain with him—and shape his own writings—through the decades to come.

"Walcott's growth into a free-spirited artist clashed on occasion with the island's religious establishment, and around the age of nineteen he began thinking of leaving St. Lucia," Anderson reported. Walcott rebelled against the rigid Catholicism of his homeland and sought a more congenial atmosphere for continued studies elsewhere. In 1950 he departed for the University of the West Indies in Kingston, Jamaica. The institution had only been established for a few years, but already it was "a virtual laboratory of regional integration," to quote Anderson. Islanders from all parts of the Caribbean descended on the University of the West Indies, and their close association helped to forge a sense of regionwide community. In the *New Yorker,* Walcott described Jamaica as "amazingly exciting. There was good theatre, good Jamaican painters, fine galleries, gifted poets and prose writers, most of whom I came to know very well."

A New Caribbean Voice

Walcott lost little time in making his own contribution to Caribbean arts. His first play, *Henri Christophe: A Chronicle,* was written and produced in St. Lucia while he was still an undergraduate. Another piece, *Henri Dernier,* played on radio in 1950. He also began to publish poetry, art criticism, and essays in periodicals such as the *Trinidad Guardian* and Jamaica's *Public Opinion.* After earning his bachelor's degree in 1953, he returned to St. Lucia to teach at St. Mary's College, the high school he had attended.

By 1954 Walcott was spending substantial time in Trinidad. His plays *The Sea at Dauphin* and *Ione* premiered there in the mid-fifties, and he became deeply involved with the establishment of a resident theater project on the island. In 1957 he received a Rockefeller Foundation grant to study theater arts in New York City. There he worked with Off-Broadway directors and companies, appropriating the skills he would need to establish a repertory group in Trinidad. "The New York experience was an unhappy one for Walcott," claimed Anderson. "He felt terribly alone in the city, an alien in its racial and theatrical communities—repelled, almost, by its segregated sensibilities. Neither Broadway nor Off-Broadway seemed the right model for the kind of theatre he had envisioned for the West Indies."

Walcott returned to Trinidad and founded the Trinidad Theatre Workshop in the capital city of Port of Spain. The group performed some of Walcott's plays and others that explored the myths, rituals, and superstitions of West Indian folk life. The workshop eventually folded, but Walcott found an audience for his plays in New York City at the Off-Broadway Public Theatre. There, in 1971, his most famous drama, *Dream on Monkey Mountain,* drew enthusiastic reviews and an Obie Award as best foreign play of the year.

Poetry drew more and more of the writer's energies as the 1960s began. At first he published primarily in magazines, but in 1962 his verse came to the attention of editors at the British publisher Jonathan Cape. Cape released Walcott's first major collection, *In a Green Night,* in 1962. The volume was well received; in fact, poet Robert Lowell was so impressed that he visited Trinidad to meet Walcott. "I remember sitting on the living-room floor while Lowell showed me some of the poems he was working on," Walcott told the *New Yorker.* "I was so flattered to hear this great writer asking me what I thought of his work. When he returned to New York, he called up Roger Straus and urged him to sign me on as a new writer. I've been with [publisher Farrar, Straus] ever since."

Having found a congenial publisher, Walcott turned out numerous books of verse. His work was hailed for its expressive language—"an old-fashioned love of eloquence, an Elizabethan richness of words and a penchant for complicated, formal rhymes," to quote *New York Times* reviewer Michiko Kakutani. Critics also commended Walcott for his brave exploration of the question of cultural ancestry. In the *New York Review of Books,* poet Joseph Brodsky called the Caribbean "the place discovered by Columbus, colonized by the British, and immortalized by Walcott."

In the early 1970s Walcott began to spend part of the year in the United States, teaching creative writing at universities such as Columbia, Rutgers, Yale, Harvard, and Princeton. Farrar, Straus published volumes of his poetry regularly, including *The Gulf* (1970), *Another Life* (1973), *Sea Grapes* (1976), *The Star-Apple Kingdom* (1979), *The Fortunate Traveller* (1981), *Collected Poems* (1986), *The Arkansas Testament* (1987), and *Omeros* (1990). In 1981 Walcott received a sizeable sum of money from the John D. and Catherine T. MacArthur Foundation—a no-

strings-attached award that has come to be called the "genius grant."

Winning the Nobel

The *New Yorker* reported that Walcott was in the running for a Nobel prize for years before he received it. Walcott tried not to be distracted by the politics of the prize. "Look at some of the great writers who died without winning the Nobel Prize—[James] Joyce, [W. H.] Auden, Graham Greene, Jorge Luis Borges," the author told the *New Yorker.* "Why should my chances be any better than theirs?. . . It got to the point where I learned to put the whole business out of my mind." Walcott kept busy writing and teaching at Boston University, where he began holding a part-time position in 1982.

The Nobel committee announced Walcott's selection on October 8, 1992. The date is doubly significant since 1992 marked the 500th anniversary of Columbus's landing in

> "The Caribbean is the place discovered by Columbus, colonized by the British, and immortalized by Walcott."
> —*Joseph Brodsky*

the Caribbean. From Sweden came the announcement that Walcott had been chosen for his "poetic oeuvre of great luminosity, sustained by historical vision" and his "multi-cultural commitment." In Walcott, the committee stated, "West Indian culture has found its great poet." Perhaps nowhere was the joy more visible than on St. Lucia, where the weekly newspaper in Castries devoted an entire 40-page issue to its native son.

The 1992 Nobel Prize for literature came with a cash award of $1.2 million. Its effects are far more lasting than mere dollars, however. Walcott's stature in the literary community is assured, and his opinions on everything from poetry to politics will be sought and valued. Most certainly, Walcott has earned the distinction—long held by some critics and fellow poets—of being among the very best writers in the English language. For his own part, Walcott accepted the acclaim with humility. His work, he told the

New Yorker, "had already been written in the mouths of the Caribbean tribe. And I felt that I had been chosen, somehow, to give it voice. So the utterance was inevitable. . . . I was writing it for the island people from whom I come. In a sense, I saw it as a long thank-you note." Walcott's future projects include collaborating with American folk-rocker Paul Simon on a Broadway musical.

Selected writings

Henri Christophe: A Chronicle (play), Advocate, 1950.

The Sea at Dauphin (play), University College of the West Indies, 1954.

Ione: A Play with Music, University College of the West Indies, 1957.

In a Green Night (poetry; includes "A Far Cry from Africa"), J. Cape, 1962.

Selected Poems, Farrar, Straus, 1964.

The Gulf (poetry), Farrar, Straus, 1970.

Dream on Monkey Mountain and Other Plays, Farrar, Straus, 1970.

Another Life (autobiographical poetry), Farrar, Straus, 1973.

Sea Grapes (poetry), Farrar, Straus, 1976.

The Star-Apple Kingdom (poetry), Farrar, Straus, 1979.

The Fortunate Traveller (poetry), Farrar, Straus, 1981.

Collected Poems, 1948-1984, Farrar, Straus, 1986.

The Arkansas Testament (poetry), Farrar, Straus, 1987.

Omeros (poetry), Farrar, Straus, 1990.

Sources

Books

Black Literature Criticism, Gale, 1992.
Black Writers, Gale, 1989.
Hamner, Robert D., *Derek Walcott,* Twayne, 1981.

Periodicals

Ebony, February 1993, p. 46.
Jet, October 26, 1992, p. 14; December 28, 1992, p. 24.
Newsweek, October 19, 1992, p. 73.
New Yorker, June 26, 1971, p. 30; December 21, 1992, p. 71.
New York Times Magazine, May 23, 1982, p. 32.
New York Review of Books, November 10, 1983, p. 39.
New York Times, March 21, 1979; August 21, 1979; May 30, 1981; May 2, 1982; January 15, 1986; December 17, 1986.
New York Times Book Review, September 13, 1964; October 11, 1970; May 6, 1973; October 31, 1976; May 13, 1979; January 3, 1982; April 8, 1984; February 2, 1986; December 20, 1987.
Time, October 19, 1992, p. 65; April 5, 1993, p. 13.

—*Anne Janette Johnson*

Frances Cress Welsing

1935—

Psychiatrist, activist, author

Washington, D.C.-based psychiatrist and race theorist Frances Cress Welsing rocked the fields of cultural and behavioral science with her 1970 essay *The Cress Theory of Color-Confrontation and Racism (White Supremacy)*. This striking theory of the origins of racism is rooted in the effects that varying degrees of melanin—the color-producing pigment in skin—can have on racial perception and development. "The quality of whiteness is a genetic inadequacy or a relative deficiency or disease based upon the inability to produce the skin pigments of melanin which are responsible for all skin color," she explained in the essay, adding, "The majority of the world's people are not so afflicted, suggesting that the state of color is the norm for human beings and [its] absence is abnormal."

In her essay, Welsing contends that because of their "numerical inadequacy" and "color inferiority," white people may have defensively developed "an uncontrollable sense of hostility and aggression" towards people of color which has led to "confrontations" between the races throughout history. Repressing their own feelings of inadequacy, whites "set about evolving a social, political and economic structure to give blacks and other 'non-whites' the appearance of being inferior."

The second of three girls, Welsing was born on March 18, 1935, in Chicago, Illinois, into a family that had already produced two doctors. Her father, Henry N. Cress, now deceased, was a medical doctor, as was her grandfather. After receiving her bachelor's degree at Antioch College in Yellow Springs, Ohio, in 1957, and her M.D. at Washington D.C.'s Howard University College of Medicine five years later, Welsing pursued a career in general and child psychiatry. Her *Cress Theory* essay was published while she was an assistant professor of pediatrics at the Howard University College of Medicine. According to Welsing, it caused such a stir that her tenure at the university was not renewed in 1975.

In addition to her role as an educator, Welsing spent nearly two and a half decades of her long and distinguished career working as a staff physician for the Department of Human Services in Washington, D.C., and served as the clinical director of two schools there for emotionally troubled children. A specialist in both child and general psychiatry, she began her private practice in the district in 1967 and has gained particular acclaim for her work with young people.

For Welsing, the world's most pressing problem is the disturb-

Born Frances Luella Cress, March 18, 1935, in Chicago, IL; daughter of Henry N. (a physician) and Ida Mae (a teacher; maiden name, Griffen) Cress. *Education:* Antioch College, B.S., 1957; Howard University College of Medicine, M.D., 1962.

Cook County Hospital, Chicago, intern, 1962-63; St. Elizabeth Hospital, Washington, DC, residency in general psychiatry, 1963-66; Children's Hospital, Washington, DC, fellowship in child psychiatry, 1966-68; Howard University College of Medicine, Washington, DC, assistant professor of pediatrics, 1968-75; District of Columbia Government, Department of Human Services, staff physician, 1967-91, clinical director of Hillcrest Children's Center, 1975-76, and of the Paul Robeson School for Growth and Development, North Community Mental Health Center, 1976-90; private practice of psychiatry, Washington, DC, 1967—; author.

Member: National Medical Association, American Medical Association, American Psychiatric Association.

Addresses: *Office*—7603 Georgia Ave. NW, Suite 402, Washington, DC 20012.

ing issue of white supremacy, or racism. "I put the discussion of melanin on the board in order to [describe how pigmentation] was a factor in what white supremacy behavior was all about," Welsing noted in an interview with Michael Eric Dyson for *Emerge*. "If I had my way, there wouldn't be all the discussion about melanin. I would say, Discuss white supremacy."

Expressed Views on Global White Supremacy

Welsing laid the foundation for her ongoing discussion of white supremacy in her groundbreaking 1970 essay *The Cress Theory of Color-Confrontation and Racism*. In it, she reasoned that because whiteness is a color deficiency and white people make up only a small percentage of the earth's population, they tend to view people of color as a threat to their survival and therefore treat them with hostility. She stated that their defensive reaction has been to impose white supremacy, or racism, on people of color throughout history.

Basing part of her argument on observations by Neeley Fuller in his 1969 *Textbook for Victims of White Supremacy*, Welsing focused on his view of racism as a "universally operating 'system' of white supremacy rule and domination" in which the "majority of the world's white people participate." He suggested that economic forms of government such as capitalism and communism were created to perpetuate white domination and that the white "race" is really an "organization" dedicated to maintaining control over the world. In addition, he argued that people of color have never imposed "colored" supremacy on anyone.

Using Fuller's contention that "most white people hate black people [because] whites are not black people," Welsing went on to suggest that "any neurotic drive for superiority," in this case, the white drive, is based on a "deep and pervading sense of inadequacy and inferiority." Welsing cited journals, diaries, and books written by whites as examples of their "initial hostility and aggression" towards people of color and particularly towards black people "who have the greatest color potential and therefore are the most envied and the most feared in genetic color competition." She added: "That whites desire to have colored skin can be seen by anyone at the very first signs of Spring or Summer when they begin to strip off their clothes, often permitting their skins to be burned severely in an attempt to add some color to their white, pale, colorless bodies, rendering themselves vulnerable to skin cancer in the process."

Psychological Causes and Ramifications of Racism

Welsing asserted in *The Cress Theory* that many whites are unable to peacefully live among or attend school with people of color because it explodes "the myth of white superiority" and forces them to face their "psychological discomfort" and "color inadequacy." She also stated that "the difficulty whites have in according 'non-whites' sociopolitical and economic equality stems . . . from the fundamental sense of their own unequal situation in regards to their numerical inadequacy and color deficiency." To compensate for this inadequacy, Welsing judged, whites strive to maintain a superior social position and manipulate non-whites and themselves into thinking that they are a worldwide numerical majority instead of the minority. In support of this conclusion, she cited statistics indicating that birth control is rarely emphasized for whites, while a great emphasis is placed on controlling the birthrates of people of color.

She concluded her *Cress Theory of Color-Confrontation* by arguing that people of color must gain a better understanding of the "behavioral maneuverings" of whites in order to avoid being "manipulated into a subordinated position." In her view, people of color need to "liberate" themselves psychologically from various forms of white domination. She also suggested that whites need to understand the motivation behind their behavior and explore with an open mind the emotional and psychological foundations of racism.

Published *The Isis Papers*

The issue of white supremacy is discussed in depth in Welsing's 1990 book *The Isis Papers: The Keys to the Colors,* a virtual fixture on the Blackboard African American Bestsellers List. In the book, the author uses America's preoccupation with sports to illustrate what she perceives to be white supremacist behavior in action: "The whole of white culture," she wrote in *The Isis Papers,* "is designed to say that whites have [certain] qualities. Everything possible is done to demonstrate this. First, you have [only] white players, then blacks come in, but a white has to be the quarterback. Western culture has to project white supremacy." Welsing further contended that when blacks succeed athletically, whites are forced "up against the psychological wall" because white youngsters are "brought up to believe a white has to be superior."

Theory Generated Controversy

Not surprisingly, Welsing's views about global white supremacy and racism in contemporary society have provoked controversy and stimulated debate in and outside of the black community, as well as on national television. Her theory has also challenged former definitions of racism put forth by social and behavioral scientists. Despite the controversy surrounding her, Welsing was praised in the *Los Angeles Times* for being "the first scientist to psychoanalyze white racism" in the history of Western psychiatry, rather then focusing on the victims of racism. She is sought out by the media for her provocative view of race relations and lectures about racism at colleges and universities in the United States and England.

Back in 1974, Welsing debated Dr. William Shockley, the author of a theory of black genetic inferiority, on national public television. She is responsible for generating public discussion throughout the United States about the possible effects of melanin on behavior and culture. Black authors, psychiatrists, and lecturers have written studies and books on this subject, and a series of conferences about it have been held on the East and West Coasts.

In the early 1990s Welsing's theory caused a stir in the media after a publicist for the popular rap group Public Enemy sent music reviewers copies of her 1970 essay along with advance tapes of the group's new album, *Fear of a Black Planet.* Their publicist, Harry Allen, said in the *Washington Post* that Welsing's paper "should be seen as some of the inspiration" for the album, the title song of which deals with racial purity and miscegenation (racial mixing).

In reply to those who have called her theory racist, Welsing commented in the *Washington Post* that her philosophy is "a challenge to white behavioral scientists to help white

> "We must create mature, mentally developed parents. Then we will be able to produce children with self-respect and a high-level functioning pattern."

people become comfortable with their numbers and their color, because if they become comfortable with their minority and genetic recessive status and stop getting upset about it so they're really in a posture of respecting themselves, then they can be in a posture to respect other people."

Still, Welsing drew skeptical comments from some Washington journalists over her reported statement in 1989 on ABC-TV's *Nightline* that drug trafficking is an effort by "genetically recessive" whites fearing "genetic annihilation" to kill a large part of the young black male population which poses "the greatest threat to white genetic survival." Welsing advocated the use of force to stop warring drug dealers in Washington, D.C.'s most dangerous neighborhoods. She also suggested in the *Washington Post* that more attention should be paid to "what is happening to black men, a large segment of whom are in a state of frustration and hopelessness." Linking drug-related homicides to personal history, she stated: "I'll bet if we examined the lives of these drug killers, we'd find a mother who started having babies as a teen-ager [and] a kid who had no self-esteem and a fatalistic expectation of a short, violent and jobless life."

Called for Strong African American Family Structure

Welsing suggested that African American families must operate more effectively if they are to produce "strong-minded" children who can "challenge" white supremacy. In an interview in *Essence,* she told Karen Halliburton, "No Black female should have children before the age of 30, and no Black man should become a father before the age of 35. Before child rearing, we should be going to school, going to the library, educating ourselves. We must create mature, mentally developed parents. Then we will be able to produce children with self-respect and a high-level functioning pattern."

Welsing theorized in the *Chicago Tribune* that many black children have received too little "lap time" or cuddling from their parents and that this "later propelled them into premature sex, alcohol and drug abuse." In private practice and in visits to schools, she observed that these children become parents without learning how to "satisfy emotional needs"; a resulting condition of "dependency deprivation" has perpetuated itself in black families since the days of slavery.

Ultimately Welsing believes that the key to eradicating racism lies in self-respect, discipline, and education. "We must clean up our neighborhoods," she told Halliburton. "We must revolutionize ourselves. . . . Whether white people are consciously or subconsciously aware of it, they are behaving in a manner to ensure white genetic survival. We must know this truth. And the truth is the first step toward real strength."

Selected writings

The Cress Theory of Color-Confrontation and Racism (White Supremacy), 1970.
The Isis Papers: The Keys to the Colors, Third World Press, 1990.

Sources

Books

Biographical Dictionary of the American Psychiatric Association, Bowker, 1977.
Negro Almanac: A Reference Work on the African American, 5th edition, Gale, 1989.
Welsing, Frances Cress, *The Cress Theory of Color-Confrontation and Racism (White Supremacy),* 1970.
Welsing, Frances Cress, *The Isis Papers: The Keys to the Colors,* Third World Press, 1990.

Periodicals

Black Scholar, May 1974.
Chicago Tribune, June 28, 1985.
Daily Illini, November 9, 1990.
Ebony, March 1991.
Emerge, February 1992.
Essence, May 1987.
Los Angeles Times, May 20, 1990.
Penn State Daily Collegian, April 18, 1988.
Washington Post, May 1, 1989; May 3, 1989; May 2, 1990.
USA Today, December 19, 1991.

—*Alison Carb Sussman*

Cornel West

1953—

Scholar, educator, social critic, writer

Professor of religion and director of Afro-American Studies at Princeton University, Cornel West has dazzled a vast array of audiences from scholars and activists to students and churchgoers with his analytical speeches and writings on issues of morality, race relations, cultural diversity, and progressive politics. A keeper of the prophetic African American religious tradition, West taught the philosophy of religion at both Union Theological Seminary and Yale Divinity School before landing his position at Princeton.

As a scholar, activist, and teacher of religion, West juggles his theological concerns with his political convictions. While teaching religion at Yale, for instance, he was arrested for participating in a protest rally. West's blend of philosophy and an "on-the-streets" politics reflects his passion and commitment to his main goal: namely, "uphold[ing] the moral character of the black freedom struggle in America," as he was quoted as saying in *Emerge.*

Thought of as "our black Jeremiah" by Henry Louis Gates, Jr., chair of Harvard University's African American Studies Department, West serves dual roles as prophet and intellectual both within and beyond the black community in the United States. His writings, which reflect the theories of early American historian Sacvan Bercovitch, combine a dual castigation for moral failure with an optimism that insists on the possibility—through struggle—of making real a world of higher morality.

In a 1991 book written with West, African American social critic bell hooks wrote that "the word 'prophetic' has emerged as that expression which best names both West's intellectual project, his spiritual commitment, and his revolutionary political agenda." Their book, *Breaking Bread: Insurgent Black Intellectual Life,* draws its title from West's own model for an effective—and sorely-needed—relevant black intellectual community.

West envisions the most effective role for the black intellectual as a "critical, organic catalyst" in what he calls the "insurgency model." In this model, intellectuals would challenge the status quo, voicing opposition to an inherently racist civil authority. The rebellion would then lead to the creation in the long term of a "post- (not anti-) Western civilization" and the revitalization in the short term of institutions that foster insightful critical thought and serve the cause of black insurgency. West defined his vision in *Breaking Breading,* noting, "The central task of postmodern black intellectuals is to

At a Glance. . .

Born Cornel Ronald West, June 2, 1953, in Tulsa, OK; son of Clifton L., Jr. and Irene (Bias) West; divorced twice; married third wife; children: Clifton Louis. *Education*: Harvard College, A.B., 1973; Princeton University, M.A., 1975, Ph.D., 1980. *Politics*: Democratic Socialists of America (DSA). *Religion*: Baptist.

Assistant professor of philosophy of religion at Union Theological Seminary, 1977-83 and 1988, Yale Divinity School, 1984-87, and University of Paris VIII, spring 1987; director of Afro-American Studies and professor of religion at Princeton University, 1989—. Involved in Theology in the Americas movement. Joined Democratic Socialists of America, 1982; served on national political committee for seven years; became honorary chairperson.

Addresses: *Office*—104 Dickinson Hall, Princeton University, Princeton, NJ 08544. *Publisher*—Beacon Press, 25 Beacon St., Boston, MA 02108.

stimulate, hasten, and enable alternative perceptions and practices by dislodging prevailing discourses and powers."

Early Life: Family, Church, and Friends in Struggle

In his autobiographical introduction to his book *The Ethical Dimensions of Marxist Thought,* West describes the various academic, political, and personal influences on his life, attributing most significance to his experience in "my closely knit family and overlapping communities of church and friends."

West was born on June 2, 1953, in Tulsa, Oklahoma, the grandson of the Reverend Clifton L. West, Sr., pastor of the Tulsa Metropolitan Baptist Church. West's mother, Irene Bias West, was an elementary school teacher (and later principal), while his father, Clifton L. West, Jr., was a civilian Air Force administrator. From his parents, siblings, and community, young West derived "ideals and images of dignity, integrity, majesty, and humility." These values, presented in Christian narratives, symbols, rituals, and moral examples, provided him "existential and ethical

equipment to confront the crises, terrors, and horrors of life." West suggests that the basis for his "life vocation" lies in three essential components of that Christian outlook, which he viewed most clearly in the example of Martin Luther King, Jr. These were "a Christian ethic of love-informed service to others, ego-deflating humility about oneself owing to the precious yet fallible humanity of others, and politically engaged struggle for social betterment."

In *Ethical Dimensions*, West examines his own experiences and those of his ancestors against a broad historical backdrop. His views on what he calls the "Age of Europe" are informed by his descent from seven generations of Africans who were "enslaved and exploited, devalued and despised" by Euro-Americans, and three more generations who were "subordinated and terrorized" by the legal racist practices of Jim Crow laws in the South. He recounts that both of his parents were born into a place and time—Louisiana during the Great Depression—when Jim Crow laws of segregation were thriving. West views himself, however, as the product of the post-World War II eclipse of this "Age of Europe," when European cultural domination of the world ended. Still closer to home, West sees himself as a child of the "American Century"—what American editor and publisher Henry Luce defined as the period of unprecedented economic prosperity in the United States—and a youth of the time that witnessed the overturning of discriminatory segregationist laws in the United States.

West's community of friends and family participated actively in the struggle to overturn these racist laws. His earliest political actions included marching with his family in a Sacramento civil rights demonstration and coordinating with three other Sacramento high school students a strike to demand courses in black studies. In his youth, West admired "the sincere black militancy of Malcolm X, the defiant rage of the Black Panther Party, and the livid black theology of James Cone [a noted writer and professor of religion at Union Theological Seminary]."

Robert S. Boynton highlighted in the *New York Times Magazine* the role the Panthers played in refining West's progressive international perspective: they taught him the importance of community-based struggle; introduced him to the writings of Ghanaian anticolonial philosopher Kwame Nkrumah; and acquainted him with the principles of critical Marxist thought, which calls for the achievement of a classless society. Still, West recalls in his introduction to *Ethical Dimensions* that he never fully agreed with these groups and thinkers, since he longed for more of the self-critical humility found in the life and work of Martin Luther King, Jr. In addition, he considers himself a "non-Marxist socialist," since he champions his Christianity over Marxism and believes that religion and socialism are reconcilable doctrines.

Developed Skills of Critical Thinking and Political Action

At age 17, West enrolled in Harvard as an undergraduate. By taking eight courses per term as a junior, he was able to graduate one year early, achieving magna cum laude in Near Eastern languages and literature. While there, he once wrote a spontaneous 50-page essay to work through the differences between Immanuel Kant and George Wilhelm Friedrich Hegel's conceptions of God. He even dreamed of philosophical concepts taking form and battling one another. According to Boynton, government professor Martin Kilson called West "the most intellectually aggressive and highly cerebral student I have taught in my 30 years [at Harvard]."

West credits his time at Harvard with fueling a reexamination of his world views; over those three years, he surveyed his own thoughts and actions and pursued a rigorous study of new ideas. In class, he developed a passionate interest in the effects of time and culture on philosophical thought and historical actions. Outside of class, he participated in a "breakfast program" group in the Massachusetts village of Jamaica Plain, took weekly trips to Norfolk State Prison, and worked with the Black Student Organization, which was responsible for the 1972 takeover of Massachusetts Hall to both protest Harvard's investments in Gulf Oil and show support for liberation forces operating in the southwest African country of Angola. But West attributes his greatest intellectual influences on political matters to a variety of philosophers such as nineteenth-century Serbian political writer Svetozar Markovic. He continued, however, to recognize the limits of "book knowledge" and to value dedication in action.

After Harvard, West began pursuing a doctorate in philosophy at Princeton University. There, he discovered that the values most precious to him were those of individuality and democracy. In the introduction to *Ethical Dimensions,* he defines individuality as "the sanctity and dignity of all individuals shaped in and by communities," and explained democracy as a way of living as well as a way of governing. The work of Richard Rorty, a philosopher at Princeton, also impressed West. West called Rorty's attention to history "music to my ears" and subsequently developed his own vision of Rorty's favorite philosophical tradition—American pragmatism—in his 1989 book *The American Evasion of Philosophy: A Genealogy of Pragmatism.* In this book, West defines his own version of pragmatism, called "prophetic pragmatism," which he believes is vital in promoting the formation of a democracy that both recognizes and extols the virtues of individual morality, autonomy, and creativity. Philosopher K. Anthony Appiah, writing in the *Nation,* considered the book "a powerful call for philosophy to play its role in building a radical democracy in alliance with the wretched of the

earth" and deemed West possibly "the pre-eminent African-American intellectual of our generation."

Into the Limelight: A Career in Teaching and Writing

West's books began to be published in the early 1980s, but he wrote many of them in the late 1970s. During his mid-twenties, he left Princeton, returned to Harvard as a Du Bois fellow to finish his dissertation, and then began his first tenure-track teaching job as an assistant professor of philosophy of religion at Union Theological Seminary in New York City. While a Du Bois fellow, West married and had a son, Clifton. Both this marriage and a later one ended in divorce.

While teaching at Union, West concerned himself with "the major national progressive multiracial and religious activity in the country in the 1970s." He also traveled to Brazil, Jamaica, Costa Rica, Mexico, Europe, and South Africa, where he saw and involved himself with intellectual and political progressive movements "reminiscent of our 1960s." In the early 1980s, West encountered Michael Harrington's Democratic Socialists of America (DSA), an

> "America's massive social breakdown requires that we come together—for the sake of our lives, our children, and our sacred honor."

organization that shaped the version of democratic socialism he would subsequently promote. West described the DSA in *Ethical Dimensions* as "the first multiracial, socialist organization close enough to my politics that I could join."

West wrote *The Ethical Dimensions of Marxist Thought* during his time at Union, but it wasn't published until 1991. In the book, he traces Karl Marx's intellectual development to reveal how Marx incorporated the growing consciousness of history in modern thought with values of individuality and democracy. West combined his interests in Marxism and religion in his 1982 book *Prophesy Deliverance! An Afro-American Revolutionary Christianity,* in which he shows the potential in prophetic Christianity—and especially in aspects of the black church—for meaningful opposition to racism and oppression.

In 1984, West assumed a post at the Yale Divinity School that eventually became a joint appointment with the institution's American Studies Department. He participated in a campus drive for clerical unionism and against Yale's investments in South African companies and was arrested and jailed during one campus protest. West viewed his political actions at Yale as "a fine example for my wonderful son, Clifton," who had become a progressive student body president in his predominantly black middle school in Atlanta. The Yale administration punished West by canceling a planned leave and requiring him to teach a full load of two courses in the spring of 1987.

Before his leave was canceled, West had already arranged to teach African American thought and American pragmatism at the University of Paris, so in order to fulfill his responsibilities to both schools, he commuted to Paris for his three courses there while teaching his two courses at Yale. He also served as the American correspondent for *Le Monde diplomatique* at Yale. In 1988, West returned to Union; one year after that move, he accepted a position at Princeton University as professor of religion and director of the Afro-American Studies program.

West continued to write and edit books on philosophy throughout the 1980s and early 1990s. In his 1985 publication *Post-Analytic Philosophy,* which he edited with John Rajchman, West reflects on the crisis in American philosophy. *Prophetic Fragments,* an essay collection published in 1988, is considered a tome of contemporary cultural criticism, addressing such subjects as theology, sex, suicide, and violence in America today. In 1991's *Breaking Bread: Insurgent Black Intellectual Life,* co-authors West and bell hooks limit themselves to the problems of creating black male-female dialogue and an effective black intellectual community while suggesting practical solutions to communication problems.

The Power of Diversity

West's impassioned and insightful writings make a resounding appeal for cross-cultural tolerance and unity, while urging individuals to recognize the power of diversity within a society. As a member of the editorial collective for the journal *Boundary 2: An International Journal of Literature and Culture,* West draws on his research to relate Marxist thought to cultural politics of difference, including differences in race, gender, sexual orientation, and age. And out of a desire to contribute to the building of coalitions across different communities, he writes a column for the progressive Jewish journal *Tikkun.* Finally, in an effort to reach out to still wider audiences, West provides commentary on contemporary subjects for popular journals, such as his essay on the 1992 Los Angeles riots for the *New York Times Magazine.*

West continues his exploration of race relations and cultur-

al diversity in his 1993 book *Race Matters,* which his publisher, Beacon Press, promotes as a "healing vision for the crisis of racial politics today." Appealing to a "broader audience" than some of his earlier works, West's message "remains . . . uncompromising and unconventional," according to Ellis Cose in *Newsweek.* "He sees salvation in a renewal of love, empathy and compassion, in a radical redistribution of power and wealth—and in facing difficult truths."

As Boynton indicated, West's inimitable drive to keep on teaching and writing is so strong that West feels as though if he were to stop, he would "just explode." Resolute in his belief that people of color must struggle now for a better future, he persists in his quest to create an effective, black, progressive leadership. West ends his introduction to *Ethical Dimensions* with a call to action: "The future of U.S. progressive politics lies in the capacity of a collective leadership to energize, mobilize, and organize working and poor people. Democratic socialists can play a crucial role in projecting an all-embracing moral vision of freedom, justice, and equality, and making social analyses that connect and link activists together. . . . America's massive social breakdown requires that we come together—for the sake of our lives, our children, and our sacred honor."

Selected writings

Black Theology and Marxist Thought, Theology in the Americas, 1979.
Prophesy Deliverance! An Afro-American Revolutionary Christianity, Westminster Press, 1982.
(Coeditor) *Theology in the Americas,* Orbis Books, 1982.
(Coeditor) *Post-Analytic Philosophy,* Columbia University Press, 1985.
Prophetic Fragments, Eerdmans, 1988.
The American Evasion of Philosophy: A Genealogy of Pragmatism, University of Wisconsin Press, 1989.
(Coeditor) *Out There: Marginalization and Contemporary Cultures,* 1990.
(With bell hooks) *Breaking Bread: Insurgent Black Intellectual Life,* South End Press, 1991.
The Ethical Dimensions of Marxist Thought, Monthly Review Press, 1991.
Beyond Eurocentrism and Multiculturalism, Common Courage Press, 1993.
Race Matters, Beacon Press, 1993.

Contributor of articles to periodicals, including *Monthly Review, Yale Journal of Criticism: Interpretation in the Humanities, Critical Quarterly, Nation, October, Tikkun, New York Times Book Review,* and *New York Times Magazine.* American correspondent for *Le Monde diplomatique,* 1984-87; member of editorial collective

Boundary 2: An International Journal of Literature and Culture.

Sources

Books

Bercovitch, Sacvan, *The American Jeremiad,* University of Wisconsin Press, 1978.
hooks, bell, and Cornel West, *Breaking Bread: Insurgent Black Intellectual Life,* South End Press, 1991.
West, Cornel, *The American Evasion of Philosophy: A Genealogy of Pragmatism,* University of Wisconsin Press, 1989.

West, Cornel, *The Ethical Dimensions of Marxist Thought,* Monthly Review Press, 1991.

Periodicals

Commonweal, December 20, 1985, p. 708.
Emerge, March 1993.
Nation, April 9, 1990, pp. 496-8.
Newsweek, June 7, 1993, p. 71.
New York Times Magazine, September 15, 1991.
Religious Studies Review, April 1992, p. 103.
Voice Literary Supplement, December 1988, pp. 3-4.

—Nicholas S. Patti

Michael R. White

1951—

Mayor of Cleveland

In 1965, Carl Stokes was elected mayor of Cleveland, becoming the first African American to hold this office in any major U.S. city. Michael White was only 14 years old at the time, yet even at this young age he knew he wanted to follow in Stokes's footsteps. Twenty-four years later, White's goal was realized when he became Cleveland's second black mayor.

White took over the leadership of Cleveland at a crucial point in the city's history. His predecessor, George Voinovich, had helped rebuild Cleveland's financial base and national reputation after the disastrous term of Dennis Kucinich, during which the city went bankrupt. Yet Voinovich's focus on investments in the downtown area had left a dichotomy between a thriving central business district and poverty-stricken neighborhoods rampant with drugs and crime. In spite of Cleveland's recovery from economic collapse, when White was elected in 1989 a full 40 percent of the city's population lived at or below the poverty line. Yet, White's political savvy, experience, and energy made him a symbol of hope and change for many of Cleveland's poor; as one East Side resident told the *Chicago Tribune* a few days before the election, "I feel Mike White is the person who can bring this city together racially and economically."

Michael White was born in Cleveland in 1951 and was raised in the East Side neighborhood where he still makes his home. He was educated at Ohio State University, first earning a B.A. in education and a year later a master's degree in public administration. He began his political career in 1974 by becoming a special assistant for the mayor's office in Columbus, Ohio. He then became an administrative assistant for the Cleveland City Council and, from 1978 to 1984, served on the council itself. White spent over four years in Columbus as a state senator, and then, in the fall of 1989, entered Cleveland's mayoral race.

White's emergence as a top candidate in Cleveland's October primary caused a considerable stir. Before his entrance in the arena, the race for mayor had been seen mainly as a contest between controversial black City Council president George L. Forbes, White's senior by 20 years, and three white candidates. Forbes, a longtime fixture on Cleveland's political scene with 27 years of experience on the council, had won the support of much of the city's black population but had alienated many white voters with his volatile temper and strong, often profane language—shown in incidents such as his throwing of a chair at a fellow councilman while calling him a "mulatto punk." According to the *New York Times,* former

At a Glance. . .

Born Michael Reed White, August 13, 1951, in Cleveland, OH; son of Robert and Audrey (Silver) White; married Tamera Kay (third wife). *Education:* Ohio State University, B.A., 1973, M.P.A., 1974. *Politics:* Democrat. *Religion:* Baptist.

Special assistant, mayor's office, Columbus, OH, 1974-76; Cleveland City Council, administrative assistant, 1976-77, city council member, 1978-84; sales manager, Burks Electric Company, 1982-85; partner, Beehive and Doan Partnership, 1983-84; state senator from 21st District in Ohio Senate, Columbus, 1984-89; mayor of Cleveland, 1990—. Former fellow of the Academy for Contemporary Problems, Columbus; member of board of directors, Glenville Development Corporation, beginning 1978; writer on issues of urban renewal.

Awards: Named outstanding young leader, Cleveland Jaycees, 1979; service award, East Side Jaycees, 1979; named an outstanding young man of America, 1985; outstanding service award, Cleveland Chapter of the National Association of Black Veterans, 1985; community service award, East Side Jaycees.

Addresses: *Home*—1057 East Boulevard, Cleveland, OH 44108-2984. *Office*—601 Lakeside Ave. E., Cleveland, OH 44114-1012.

Cleveland mayor Stokes once called Forbes a "foul-mouthed, uncouth, unregenerated politician of the most despicable sort." White, on the other hand, was, according to the *Washington Post,* "the only candidate with support across racial lines." When the dust settled after the October 3rd primary, the two black candidates, both Democrats, remained to square off against each other.

The 1989 mayoral campaign became one of the ugliest in Cleveland's history. Just a few days after the primary the Forbes camp accused White of abusing his wife and ignoring housing codes on some of his inner-city property. White denied the charges and countered the attack by claiming that Forbes had used his office for personal gain and had used his wife, Mary, as a "front person" for improper investments. White also began to undermine Forbes's support in the black community by portraying him as an elitist who favored tax breaks for downtown developers while ignoring the poorer neighborhoods. The Forbes campaign was then dealt a severe blow when outgoing mayor Voinovich—considered an important ally in the older candidate's campaign—refused to endorse either nominee.

Became Unexpected Front-runner in Mayoral Race

Ultimately Forbes's abrasive personality was his undoing. Although he tried to soften his image in TV commercials and justify his antics as being, as he told the *New York Times,* "all show-biz," the election became, as Cuyahoga County Republican party chairman Robert E. Hughes told the *Chicago Tribune,* "a referendum on George Forbes." Voters flocked to the polls not so much because they liked White but because they disliked his opponent; in the end the younger candidate was easily elected.

In his inaugural address—as quoted by the *Christian Science Monitor*—White focused on a topic that would become a central issue for his administration: the future of Cleveland's young people. "We can spend our money on roads and bridges and sewer systems as we must," the new mayor said, "but we can never afford to forget that these children remain the true infrastructure of our city's future." In keeping with this commitment, White has worked hard to upgrade public education and has supported the development of new jobs programs. As he told *Fortune,* "We should create a work program and show every able-bodied person that we have the time and patience to train them. And we should start people young. In Cleveland we want to guarantee every kid graduating from high school a job or a chance to go to college."

Cleveland's New Mayor Stressed Economic Balance

The White administration has also focused on creating a balance between Cleveland's prosperous downtown area and its deprived inner-city neighborhoods. "We do not accept that ours must be a two-tier community with a sparkling new downtown surrounded by vacant stores and whitewashed windows," he pledged in his inaugural address. White feels that Cleveland's business community must shoulder much of the responsibility for unifying the city; he told the *Christian Science Monitor:* "You can't have a great town with only a great downtown. I've said to corporate Cleveland over and over again that I'm going to work on the agenda of downtown Cleveland, but I also expect them to work on the agenda of neighborhood rebuilding." To this end White has supported the development of the Lake Erie waterfront and the completion of the Rock and Roll Hall of Fame, predicted to become one of Cleveland's major tourist attractions.

An enthusiastic White bestows soon-to-be President Clinton with a Cleveland Cavaliers jacket in honor of an Ohio coalition's mayoral endorsement of the candidate.

The safety of Cleveland's residents has also been an important focal point of White's program. "Safety is the right of every American," he told the *Christian Science Monitor.* "A 13-year-old drug pusher on the corner where I live is a far greater danger to me and this city than [Iraqi strongman] Saddam Hussein will ever be. What are America's priorities?"

A City Divided by Race

White has also tried to address head-on Cleveland's longtime difficulties with racial tension. With a population fairly evenly balanced between blacks and whites, the city has always endured periodic outbursts of racial violence. White's approach to the problem has been to focus on solidarity; he noted in the *Christian Science Monitor,* "We are a multicultural, multiethnic, multireligious community. It is a strength and not a weakness." White has

portrayed himself as a "unifier" in the tradition of Mayor Curt Schmoke of Baltimore, and, as he told the *New York Times,* he envisions a city "free of division, free of hatred, free of bickering, one Cleveland for blacks, whites and Hispanics." Indeed, one of his earliest campaign promises was to revise Cleveland's controversial busing laws, a failed attempt by the U.S. District Court to desegregate Cleveland schools in the late 1970s.

White's administration has not been without its difficulties. In April of 1991, while hosting a meeting of the nation's black mayors in Cleveland, White learned that he had been summoned to appear before a county grand jury on charges that, eight years earlier, he had improperly used his position as chairman of the City Council's community development committee to aid the development of real estate projects in which he was an investor. Although the charges were later dropped, the timing of the subpoena was an embarrassment to White and his administration and led other black mayors to speculate that the incident might have been racially motivated. As Emanuel Cleaver, the mayor of Kansas City, told the *New York Times,* "I thought the timing of the subpoena was as tacky as it gets. Every black mayor I have talked with, and many of my white supporters, have told me enough about black officials becoming targeted for investigation that I have become as paranoid as I can get." However, White has been able to put the incident behind him and focus on the immediate concerns of his city.

Clinton Supporter

The election of Bill Clinton as U.S. president in November of 1992 was greeted by White with particular enthusiasm. Long a critic of the federal government's apparent lack of support for the rebuilding of the nation's troubled cities, White had frequently lashed out against the administration of former President George Bush; for example, when he learned that the Persian Gulf War was costing the United States $500 million a day, he was outraged. "I'm the mayor of one of the largest cities in the country while we have an administration that is completely oblivious to the problems of human beings in this country," he told the *Washington Post.* "I sit here like everyone else, watching CNN, watching a half-billion dollar a day investment in Iraq and Kuwait, and I can't get a half-million increase in investment in Cleveland or any other city." White became an outspoken supporter of Clinton, and, as he told the *Los Angeles Times,* saw the new administration as an opportunity to "turn the boat around and get it going in the right way."

White was especially optimistic about Clinton's plans to abolish the existing welfare system. Two years earlier he had told *Fortune* that "our welfare system doesn't teach people to be independent or think for themselves. It just teaches them how to read the calendar and leads nowhere but back to the welfare office at the first of the month. In the years ahead, government must assist, cajole, and force these people back into the mainstream and give them a stake in society." He strongly praised Clinton's plans to substitute job training, child care, and other reforms to bring welfare recipients back into the work force.

White has also supported other elements of Clinton's domestic policy plan, which the president titled "Putting People First." Along with other mayors, he is anxious to see Clinton follow through on his promises to restore the economic vitality of the nation's cities by increasing funds for the building and maintenance of urban roads, bridges, and sewage treatment plants; building a network of community development banks to loan money to entrepre-

neurs; and putting more city police officers on the beat. Although, as he told the *Los Angeles Times,* White considers himself a "pragmatic idealist" and knows that "it won't happen overnight, or even in one term," he intends to do what he can to hold Clinton to his pledges. "If Bill Clinton put 'Putting People First' into a bill," White continued, "we would support it and I don't mean just support it like, 'Dear Senator, we support it.' I mean down there in Washington, in their face, saying, 'gentlemen, ladies, we support this and you've got to do it.'"

Advocated Progress at Local Level

Yet, though White has remained hopeful about an increase in support by the federal government, throughout his administration he has held the philosophy that state and city governments must in many ways fend for themselves. He commented in *Fortune* that "the answer to our problems doesn't lie in Washington. It lies in state capitals and city halls. While I'd like to have a stronger partnership with the federal government, I recognize that we're going to have to improve our quality of life ourselves, or it's not going to happen."

The city of Cleveland faces many challenges as it moves toward the twenty-first century. In spite of its renewed vitality in recent years, the city continues to be seen by many Americans as something of a cultural and economic wasteland. With the dedication and enthusiasm of its mayor, as well as that of the city's population at large, it may one day win the recognition it deserves; until that time White will continue to work toward building a thriving and harmonious urban center. "We're a scrapper city," he told the *Christian Science Monitor* with characteristic self-confidence. "We don't know the meaning of failure."

Sources

Chicago Tribune, October 29, 1989.
Christian Science Monitor, August 12, 1991.
Ebony, February 1990.
Economist, November 11, 1989.
Fortune, March 26, 1990.
Los Angeles Times, November 21, 1992.
New York Times, October 23, 1989; April 27, 1991; May 16, 1991.
Washington Post, October 2, 1989; January 24, 1991; June 9, 1992.

—Jeffrey Taylor

John Edgar Wideman

1941—

Writer, educator

John Edgar Wideman is one of the leading chroniclers of life in urban black America. An author who intertwines ghetto experiences with experimental fiction techniques, personal history with social events, Wideman is the only artist who has won the prestigious PEN/Faulkner Award for literature twice. His provocative works depict the widening chasm between the urban poor and the white power structure in the United States, as well as the deep cultural conflicts engendered in African Americans who succeed in penetrating that power structure. *Washington Post Book World* reviewer Jonathan Yardley noted that Wideman makes clear in his books that "moving out of the ghetto into the white world is a process that requires excruciating compromises, sacrifices and denials, that leaves the person who makes the journey truly at home in neither the world he has entered nor the world he has left."

Wideman is a prolific writer who has been publishing books since he was twenty-six. His body of work includes novels, short story collections, and nonfiction. Much of his fiction explores events and personalities from the Homewood section of Pittsburgh, the all-black neighborhood where he grew up. His stories reveal several generations of Homewood residents, including those who have left the area in triumph or

tragedy. Indeed, suggests Wideman, the "triumph" of leaving home is hollow unless one retains the spirit and the culture of the community left behind. For Wideman, an Oxford-trained scholar, that process of absorbing a community and relating its history artistically has provided grist for complex revelations on family relationships, isolation, and the search for self.

Wideman told the *Washington Post:* "My novels and the essays attempt to exploit the inherent tension between what is fictional and what is factual, and to illuminate how unsteady and unpredictable the relationship is. I'm trying to remind people of what Ralph Ellison [famed black author best known for his novel *Invisible Man*] said about the uncertainties that lie within your certainties." This tension between fiction and fact is a hallmark of Wideman's writing. It has helped him to address his own personal tragedies, including the life-term prison sentences of his son and his brother. In interviews the author says little about his brother, Robby, who is serving time in Pennsylvania as an accessory to murder, or about his son Jacob, convicted in 1988 in the stabbing death of another teenager. The dual tragedies loom large in Wideman's art, however, as he seeks to understand life's bitter twists of fate. "I'm not putting up my life as material to explain anything to anyone," the author told the *Washing-*

At a Glance...

Born June 14, 1941, in Washington, DC; son of Edgar and Betty (French) Wideman; married Judith Ann Goldman, 1965; children: Daniel Jerome, Jacob Edgar, Jamila Ann. *Education:* University of Pennsylvania, B.A., 1963; New College, Oxford, B. Phil., 1966.

Writer, 1966—; professor of English and creative writing, 1967—. University of Pennsylvania, Philadelphia, 1966-74, began as instructor, became professor of English, 1974, director of Afro-American studies program, 1972-73; University of Wyoming, Laramie, professor of English, 1974-86; University of Massachusetts at Amherst, professor of English, 1986—. Visiting professor and lecturer at numerous colleges and universities; National Humanities Faculty consultant; member of "Agenda for Black Power" panel sponsored by Knopf Publishing Group, February 1993; guest on *Frontline,* "L.A. Is Burning," broadcast on PBS-TV, April 1993, examining the 1992 Los Angeles riots.

Selected awards: Rhodes Scholar, Oxford University, 1963; Kent fellow, University of Iowa, 1966; Young Humanist fellow, 1975; PEN/Faulkner awards for fiction, 1984, for *Sent for You Yesterday,* and 1991, for *Philadelphia Fire;* John Dos Passos Prize for Literature from Longwood College, 1986; honorary degree from University of Pennsylvania, 1986.

Addresses: *Office*—Department of English, University of Massachusetts at Amherst, Amherst, MA 01003.

ton Post. "I'll put it this way. It's a formulation. My life is a closed book. My fiction is an open book. They may seem like the same book—but I know the difference."

Life as a "Symbol"

Wideman, the oldest of five children, was born in Washington, D.C. in 1941. When he was not yet a year old, his family moved to Pittsburgh, where his great-great-great grandmother, a fugitive slave, had settled in the mid-nineteenth century. Wideman's father, Edgar, worked hard at several jobs simultaneously but was unable to provide economic security for the growing family. As Chip Brown noted in *Esquire* magazine, "Edgar earned a living as a

paperhanger, a welder, a waiter in the cafeteria at Kauffman's department store; for all his doubling up on jobs, he was never able to break the barriers of class and race and economics, and his ambition to be a dentist fell by the wayside." His own perilous fortunes notwithstanding, Edgar Wideman encouraged his children to pursue excellence in everything they did. John became an honor student and an athlete, with dreams of playing professional basketball.

John Wideman's youth was spent in the Homewood district of Pittsburgh, a neighborhood that included many members of his extended family. From a young age he delivered newspapers on upper class Negley Avenue, a "lily white" region where he felt like an "intruder," according to a Wideman essay in the *New York Times Book Review.* If he was an intruder, he was determined to make his presence known. During his high school years, his family moved to a suburb called Shadyside so he could attend highly ranked Peabody High School. There he earned top grades and became class president and captain of the basketball team. He graduated first in his class in 1959.

"When my family moved to Shadyside so I could attend 'better' schools and we were one of only three or four black families in the neighborhood, I learned to laugh with the white guys when we hid in a stairwell outside Liberty School gym and passed around a 'nigarette,'" Wideman recalled in the *New York Times Book Review.* "I hated it when a buddy took a greedy, wet puff, 'nigger-lipping' a butt before he passed it on to me. Speaking out, identifying myself with the group being slurred by these expressions, was impossible. I had neither the words nor the heart. I talked the talk and walked the walk of the rest of my companions."

Wideman continued his conformist ways at the University of Pennsylvania, which he attended on scholarship from 1959 until 1963. One of only six black students at the Ivy League college, he became well-known for his basketball skill *and* for his exposition talents. *Washington Post* correspondent Paul Hendrickson pointed out that, as a Penn basketball star, Wideman "made All-Ivy, he made Big Five Basketball Hall of Fame. He was among the last of the great 6-foot-2 forwards, before forwards became 7-footers—a leaper who could mix it up underneath and take rebounds off players three and four inches bigger than he was." Wideman excelled off-court as well, winning the university's creative writing prize and being elected to Phi Beta Kappa.

During his senior year at Penn, Wideman applied for and won a Rhodes Scholarship to Oxford University. He was the first African American in more than a half-century to earn the important academic award. National recognition came from *Look* magazine, where a profile of Wideman ran in 1963. A professor quoted in the article warned that

Wideman would have to be "careful," that now he was a "symbol." Many times over the ensuing years, John Edgar Wideman would ask himself just what it was he symbolized.

The Evolution of an Artist

In his 1984 memoir *Brothers and Keepers,* Wideman wrote of his student days: "Just two choices as far as I could tell: either/or. Rich or poor. White or black. Win or lose. I figured which side I wanted to be on when the Saints came marching in. . . . To succeed in the white man's world you must become like the man and the man sure didn't claim no bunch of nigger relatives in Pittsburgh." As his family's circumstances forced them back into Homewood, Wideman persevered at Oxford. He studied English literature and philosophy and wrote a thesis on eighteenth-century narrative techniques. In 1966 he returned to America for a year's fellowship study at the Iowa Writers' Workshop, the nation's best-known proving ground for would-be novelists. He also married Judith Goldman, a fellow Penn graduate.

While still in his twenties Wideman began publishing fiction. His first novel, *A Glance Away,* appeared in 1967, followed by *Hurry Home* in 1970 and *The Lynchers* in 1973. All three books deal with black protagonists who are confused and controlled by their pasts, and who are, at the very least, highly ambivalent about white society. As early as *Hurry Home* Wideman began to explore the importance of cultural history to self-awareness and the role that family ties and friendships serve in promoting peace of mind.

Throughout the period when his first three novels appeared, Wideman was teaching literature at the University of Pennsylvania. There he was asked to present a course on black writing, and he delved deeply into black literature for the first time. The experience was enlightening—a catalyst to his own work—and eventually the course became the nucleus of the university's Afro-American studies program, which Wideman chaired in 1972 and 1973. Another catalyst to Wideman's work was the death of his grandmother, back in Homewood, in 1973. After the funeral, Wideman and his family reminisced about the history of the family in Homewood, going back many generations, almost to the founding of the neighborhood. From that conversation and others remembered from his childhood, Wideman fashioned his best-known work to date.

Wideman wrote most of his books and stories about Homewood while living in the prairie town of Laramie, Wyoming. He accepted a teaching position at the university there in late 1974. "It was hard to admit to myself that I'd just begun learning how to write," he commented in the *Atlanta Constitution.* "I realized that the core of the

language and culture that nurtured me had hardly been touched by my writing." A creative explosion occurred while he was in Laramie, and by the mid-1980s Wideman had released *Damballah, Hiding Place,* and *Sent for You Yesterday,* a series of interrelated stories and novels now known as the "Homewood Trilogy." Ranging from the nineteenth century to the present, the Homewood Trilogy explores the various lives of descendants of Sybela Owens, a slave who ran North to Pittsburgh with her white husband.

Enthusiastic reviews followed the publication of each of the Homewood Trilogy installments. "Mr. Wideman has used a narrative laced with myth, superstition and dream sequences to create an elaborate poetic portrait of the lives of ordinary black people," wrote Mel Watkins in the *New York Times Book Review.* "He has written tales that can stand on their own, but that assume much greater impact collectively. The individual 'parts,' or stories, as disparate as they may initially seem, form a vivid and coherent montage of black life over a period of five generations. . . . These books once again demonstrate that John Wideman is one of America's premier writers of fiction." In the

> "I'm not putting up my life as material to explain anything to anyone. . . . My life is a closed book. My fiction is an open book. They may seem like the same book—but I know the difference."

American Book Review, Wilfred D. Samuels concluded: "By going home to Homewood, Wideman has found a voice for his work and consequently a means of celebrating Afro-American culture and further validating the Afro-American experience in literature."

Sent for You Yesterday, the third part of the Homewood Trilogy, was awarded the PEN/Faulkner fiction prize in 1984. The work is yet another Wideman treatment on the themes of creativity, imagination, and cultural bonds as means to transcend despair and socially-sanctioned economic discrimination.

A Brother, a Son: Two Tragedies

The novel *Hiding Place* deals with a young boy on the run from a petty robbery that turned deadly. The situation is very similar to the circumstances surrounding the incarceration of Robby Wideman. Robby, the author's younger brother, was sentenced in 1976 to life in prison for his part in a larceny/murder case. Wideman sought to understand his brother's plight, publishing *Brothers and Keepers,* in 1984. The book, Wideman's only major nonfiction piece to date, attempts to address the difficult questions of "success" and "failure" on white society's terms as well as the sense of guilt Wideman felt about his brother's fate. Nominated for the National Book Critics' Circle Award, *Brothers and Keepers* brought Wideman national notoriety. He was profiled on *60 Minutes* and became a sought-after essayist and commentator on the particular dilemmas faced by black artists.

Tragedy struck again in 1986. Wideman's second son, Jacob, fatally stabbed a fellow camper during an outing in Arizona. Both boys were sixteen. Facing the death penalty, Jacob Wideman agreed to plead guilty and was sentenced to life in prison. John Wideman has steadfastly refused to comment on the case in interviews. "I don't like to talk about it," he said. "On the advice of lawyers, I don't talk about it. I've had all kinds of unpleasant experiences because, of course, the journalists smell the blood and feel it is their responsibility to go after it. . . . I don't talk about it." Not surprisingly, however, the theme of an incarcerated or missing son has permeated Wideman's fiction since the tragic events in 1986.

Wideman won his second PEN/Faulkner Award for the controversial novel *Philadelphia Fire,* an angry extrapolation on the 1985 bombing of a black religious cult's Philadelphia headquarters. The actual bombing, ordered by W. Wilson Goode, then mayor of Philadelphia, killed a dozen people and incinerated several blocks of low-income housing. The incident occurred on Osage Avenue, where Wideman had lived while teaching at Penn. The author told the *Washington Post* that he wanted to "pry the event loose from that collective amnesia that's settled on it. . . . I want people to re-imagine it, rethink this goddam fire." Wideman's imaginative re-telling of the fire includes direct references to Jacob in prison and an oblique, unfulfilled search for a child seen running from the blaze. A *Washington Post* reviewer called the book "199 pages of conflagration, a lyric and confusing and riveting and ragged work of fiction that does and does not concern the 1985 . . . disaster, in which a bomb from a state police helicopter was dropped on a back-to-nature cult." In the *Bloomsbury Review,* Mark Hummel concluded of *Philadelphia Fire:* "Despite the tough questions and the deep-rooted pain, the novel is about survival. While hope is distant, Wideman asks us to hold on. And while his own words seem—to him—heavy, even cumbersome, all he has left, they bring meaning to events apparently beyond meaning."

Currently a professor of literature and creative writing at the University of Massachusetts at Amherst, Wideman at mid-life has wrestled with more dilemmas—artistic, personal, and social—than most people encounter in a lifetime. Hendrickson wrote: "You keep wondering how he can even function in this unspoken, surreal, Kafka walking dream, let alone get the garbage out on Tuesdays and compose beautiful sentences." In fact, Wideman's prolific career has continued in recent years with two new story collections and a number of essays for mainstream periodicals like *Esquire.* His pieces in the 1990s offer a pessimistic view of race relations and a warning that the widening gap between white society and the minority underclass may result in serious social disruption. In an interview with the *Washington Post* the author said he hopes to wage "a little war against . . . a little war to beat back the direction the culture is going."

Concerning his fiction writing, Wideman concluded in the *New York Times Book Review:* "When I write I want to show how simple acts, simple words can be transformed to release their spiritual force. This is less a conscious esthetic to be argued or analyzed than a determination to draw from the unique voices of Homewood's people the means for documenting the reality of their attitudes and emotions. I want to trace the comings and goings of my people on the invisible plane of existence where so much of the substance of black life resides."

Selected writings

A Glance Away (novel), Harcourt, 1967, reprinted, H. Holt, 1985.

Hurry Home (novel), Harcourt, 1970, reprinted, H. Holt, 1986.

The Lynchers (novel), Harcourt, 1973.

Damballah (short stories), Avon, 1981.

Hiding Place (novel), Avon, 1981.

Sent for You Yesterday (novel), Avon, 1983.

Brothers and Keepers (nonfiction), H. Holt, 1984.

The Homewood Trilogy (includes *Damballah, Hiding Place,* and *Sent for You Yesterday*), Avon, 1985.

Reuben (novel), H. Holt, 1987.

Fever (short stories), H. Holt, 1989.

Philadelphia Fire (novel), H. Holt, 1990.

The Stories of John Edgar Wideman, Pantheon, 1992.

(With others) *Malcolm X: In Our Own Image* (essays), edited by Joe Wood, St. Martin's, 1992.

Sources

Books

Bell, Bernard W., *The Afro-American Novel and Its Tradition,* University of Massachusetts Press, 1987, pp. 281-338.

Black Literature Criticism, Gale, 1992.

O'Brien, John, editor, *Interviews with Black Writers,* Liveright, 1973, pp. 213-23.

Periodicals

American Book Review, July-August 1982, pp. 12-13.

Atlanta Constitution, December 3, 1989, p. L1.

Atlanta Journal, June 7, 1992, p. N8.

Bloomsbury Review, March 1991, p. 1.

Boston Globe, June 14, 1992, p. B40.

Chicago Tribune, July 9, 1992, p. TEMPO-1.

Esquire, August 1989, pp. 122-32; September 1992, pp. 149-56.

Nation, October 4, 1986, pp. 321-22.

New York Times, July 21, 1992, p. C15.

New York Times Book Review, April 11, 1982, pp. 6, 21; May 15, 1983, pp. 13, 41; January 13, 1985, p. 1.

North American Review, June 1988, p. 60-61.

People, February 11, 1985, p. 121.

Publishers Weekly, November 17, 1989, pp. 37-38.

Washington Post, May 12, 1984, p. C1; October 15, 1990, p. B1; May 3, 1991, p. B1; August 9, 1992, p. 15.

Washington Post Book World, July 3, 1983, pp. 1-2; October 21, 1984; November 15, 1987, p. 7; October 7, 1990, pp. 6, 12.

—*Anne Janette Johnson*

Joe Williams

1918—

Singer

His name is not as well known to the general public as those of jazz legends like Louis Armstrong, Duke Ellington, or Ella Fitzgerald, but Joe Williams is nevertheless counted among the masters of jazz and blues singing; he has, in fact, earned the title "Emperor of the Blues." His singing style, which he developed over a long and consistently successful career, contributed to the success of the Count Basie Orchestra and influenced the style of many younger singers. And he has also dabbled in acting, playing the role of Claire Huxtable's father on *The Cosby Show.*

Joseph Goreed was born in the small farming town of Cordele, deep in the heart of Georgia, on December 12, 1918. His father, Willie Goreed, vanished before Joe could even know him, but his mother, Anne Beatrice Gilbert, who was no older than 18 when she had her only child, provided a strong emotional bond until her death in 1968.

Soon after Joe was born, his mother moved them in with his grandparents, who had enough money to support an extended family. During this time, Anne Gilbert was saving up for a move to Chicago, Illinois. Once she had made the move—alone—she began saving the money that she earned cooking for wealthier white Chicagoans so that her family could join

her. By the time Joe was four, he and his grandmother and his aunt were on a train to Chicago, where they would live for many years afterward.

Probably most important to Joe's later life was the music scene—fueled largely by African American musicians—that thrived in Chicago in the early 1920s. Years later, he recalled going to the Vendome Theatre with his mother to hear Louis Armstrong play his trumpet. Chicago also offered a host of radio stations that featured the then-rebellious sound of jazz, exposing Joe to the styling of Duke Ellington, Ethel Waters, Cab Calloway, Joe Turner, and others. By his early teens, he had already taught himself to play piano and had formed a quartet, known as the Jubilee Boys, that sang at church functions.

In his mid-teens, Joe began singing solo at formal events with local bands. The most that he ever took home was five dollars a night, but that was enough to convince his family that he could make a living at it; at sixteen, he dropped out of school. After a family conference, the name "Williams" was chosen as a better last name for a singer, and Joe began marketing himself in earnest to Chicago clubs and bands. His first job was a kind of compromise—not unusual for a young singer—at a

At a Glance. . .

Born Joseph Goreed, December 12, 1918, in Cordele, GA; raised in Chicago, IL; changed surname to Williams, c. 1934; son of Willie Goreed (believed to be a farm laborer) and Anne Beatrice Gilbert (a cook); married Wilma Cole, 1942 (divorced, 1946); married Anne Kirksey, 1946 (divorced, c. 1950); married Lemma Reid, 1951 (divorced, 1964); married Jillean Milne Hughes-D'Aeth, 1965; children: (third marriage) JoAnn, Joe, Jr.

Began singing in his early teens with church quartet the Jubilee Boys; solo singer for Chicago bands during the early 1930s; sang and toured with several different bands, including those of Jimmie Noone, 1938-39, Les Hite, 1939-40, Coleman Hawkins, 1941, Lionel Hampton, 1942-43, Andy Kirk, 1946-47, and Red Saunders, 1951-53. Worked briefly as Fuller Cosmetics door-to-door salesman in late 1940s; treated for nervous breakdown at Elgin State Hospital, 1947-1948; sang with the Count Basie Orchestra, 1954-1961, touring Europe in the late 1950s; began solo career, 1961; recording artist and singer on soundtracks for films, including *Jamboree,* 1957 (with the Count Basie Orchestra), *Cinderfella,* 1960 (with the Count Basie Orchestra), and *The Moonshine War,* 1969.

Awards: *Down Beat* magazine's New Star Award, 1955, international critics' poll award for best male vocalist, 1955, 1974-78, 1980, 1981, 1983, 1984, and 1989-91, and readers' poll award for best male vocalist, 1955, 1956, 1990, and 1991; *Rhythm and Blues* magazine plaque for top song for "Every Day (I Have the Blues)," 1956; *Billboard* magazine's disc jockeys' poll award for best male vocalist, 1959; Grammy Award for *Ballad and Blues Master,* 1992; *Ebony* Lifetime Achievement Award, 1993.

Addresses: *Agent*—Abby Hoffer Enterprises, 223 East 48th St., New York, NY 10017-1538.

clarinet and saxophone master Jimmie Noone invited him to sing with his band. Less than a year later, the young singer was earning a reputation at Chicago dance halls and on a national radio station that broadcast his voice from Massachusetts to California. He took a tour of the Midwest in 1939 and 1940 with the Les Hite band, which accompanied the likes of Louis Armstrong and pianist Fats Waller. A year after that he went on a larger tour with the band of saxophonist Coleman Hawkins.

Williams didn't have to wait long before a national name in big bands asked for him: in 1942 jazz great Lionel Hampton hired him both for the band's home performances at the Tic Toc Club in Boston and for their cross-country tours. His work with Hampton ended when the band's regular male singer was able to return, but by that time Williams could return to his burgeoning fame in Chicago.

Personal Upheaval

Williams's first marriage—to Wilma Cole in 1942—set in motion a pattern of marital difficulties that he wouldn't be able to break until the 1960s. The emotional relationship quickly became painful for both partners, although the union remained legal until 1946. That same year, he married Anne Kirksey, with whom he also had a briefly happy relationship; they separated in 1948 and divorced in the early 1950s. It was during his second marriage that Williams experienced his one serious bout with depression. Following a nervous breakdown in the spring of 1947, he spent a year in Elgin State Hospital, where he received now controversial "treatments" such as electroshock therapy.

His marriage to Lemma Reid, which survived from 1951 until 1964, produced Williams's two children, JoAnn and Joe, Jr. The union wasn't, however, any more resilient than the first two had been: Lemma returned to her mother's home in Cincinnati soon after JoAnn's birth. Williams finally met Jillean Milne Hughes-D'Aeth, the Englishwoman who could make a relationship last with the hardworking vocalist, in 1957. Their first meeting, which was very brief, wasn't followed by an opportunity for a lengthier meeting until two years later, when the Basie band was touring in England. Before Williams left Europe, he knew that he was in love. In May of 1960, he and Jillean moved into a New York apartment together, but it wasn't until January 7, 1965, that they were able to be married, since Lemma did not divorce Williams until the fall of 1964.

Basie and Beyond

In the early 1950s, Chicago disc jockey Daddy-O Daily secured for Williams an opportunity to sing with the band of one of the most powerful bandleaders of the era—Count

club called Kitty Davis's. Hired to clean the bathrooms, Williams was allowed to sing with the band in the evening and keep the tips, which would sometimes amount to twenty dollars a night.

Williams's first professional break came in 1938 when

Basie. After the gigs, Williams returned to his floating solo career style, but by 1954 Basie wanted him on contract. Williams would stay with the "Basie machine" until 1961, making New York his home base and securing the best exposure a blues singer could have. National tours were interspersed with long spells in a number of America's musical capitals, when the band would play at one club for three or four weeks at a time. After 1955, the band stopped every year at the Newport Jazz Festival, one of the biggest events on the jazz calender. The years 1956, 1957, and 1959 also found the Basie band touring Europe, where the popularity of jazz had skyrocketed.

Williams developed his essential repertoire while he was with Basie, including standards such as "Every Day (I Have the Blues)," "Five O'Clock in the Morning," "Roll 'em Pete," "Teach Me Tonight," "My Baby Upsets Me," and "The Comeback." The recordings that he made with the Basie band cemented his popularity, selling in droves from record shops and earning airplay at major radio stations across the country. Williams became an important name in *Down Beat* magazine as early as 1955, when he won their New Star Award. In the same year, he won their international critics' poll for best new male singer, as well as their readers' poll for best male band singer—citations he would continue to accumulate throughout his career. In 1958, he lost only to Frank Sinatra, and he held second place on the rhythm and blues charts as well, right behind the multi-talented Ray Charles.

Despite his tremendous success with Count Basie, Williams eventually began to feel that the position was limiting his potential as an artist. By 1960 he was planning the beginning of a solo career that would allow him to pursue a broader range of material in blues and jazz. Initially, Basie's manager, Willard Alexander, set Williams up with a group of strong musicians and a tour schedule that would take him across the United States for six months. The bookings increased; Williams toured for almost all of 1961. By the late 1960s, he was on the road performing between thirty and forty weeks each year.

Williams continued to produce albums and received overwhelmingly positive reviews for both his recordings and his performances. Even after his 70th birthday in 1988, Williams continued touring and recording. He has been particularly sought after to sing at tributes to his peers, including Sarah Vaughan, Ella Fitzgerald, and Louis Armstrong. As ever, his performances spark laudatory reviews in magazines and newspapers; a *New Yorker* interviewer described a 1986 performance: "Williams has an enormous bass-baritone. It is lilting and flexible. It moves swiftly and lightly from a low C to a pure falsetto. It moves through glottal stops and yodels and delicate growls, through arching blue notes and vibratos that barely stir the air."

Williams was, of course, continually called back to sing at Count Basie "reunions," even after the Count's death on April 26, 1984; only a year earlier, the singer had his star placed beside Basie's in the "gallery of stars" on the sidewalk in Hollywood. In 1991 Williams finally attended his own gala tribute, entitled "For the Love of Joe," to call attention to the contribution that he had and was still making to music. The next year, he won a Grammy Award for his release *Ballad and Blues Master,* and he was later honored by the Johnson Publishing Company with its prestigious *Ebony* Lifetime Achievement Award.

Selected discography

Count Basie Swings, Joe Williams Sings (includes "Every Day [I Have the Blues]," "The Comeback," "Teach Me Tonight," and "Roll 'em Pete"), Clef, 1955.
A Man Ain't Supposed to Cry, Roulette, 1957.
Memories Ad-lib, Roulette, 1958.
Joe Williams Sings About You, Roulette, 1959.
A Swingin' Night at Birdland—Joe Williams Live, Roulette, 1962.
Joe Williams at Newport '63, Victor, 1963.
The Heart and the Soul of Joe Williams, Sheba, 1971.
Joe Williams With Love, Temponic, 1972.
Joe Williams Live, Fantasy, 1973.
Big Man, the Legend of John Henry, Fantasy, 1975.
Prez and Joe, GNPS/Crescendo, 1979.
Then and Now, Bosco, 1984.
every night: Live at Vine St., Verve/PolyGram, 1987.
The Overwhelming Joe Williams, RCA, 1988.
Ballad and Blues Master, Verve/PolyGram, 1992.
Joe Williams: A Song Is Born, VIEW, 1992.
Jump for Joy, Bluebird/RCA, 1993.

Sources

Books

Grouse, Leslie, *Everyday: The Story of Joe Williams,* Quartet, 1984.

Periodicals

Entertainment Weekly, November 20, 1992.
Jet, September 9, 1985.
Los Angeles Times, June 14, 1991.
New Yorker, October 27, 1986.
New York Times, June 22, 1989; June 27, 1991.
Washington Post, October 16, 1991.

—*Ondine E. Le Blanc*

Dave Winfield

1951—

Professional baseball player

Dave Winfield has been a top-performing professional baseball player for two decades. His turbulent career has included multiple seasons with the San Diego Padres and the New York Yankees, but he earned his first World Series victory as a member of the 1992 Toronto Blue Jays. A *Sports Illustrated* correspondent wrote: "Winfield has been around so long he can remember when kids came up to ask him for his autograph just to keep it. At 39 he became the oldest man to hit for the cycle. . . . He still has that royalty to him, that unmistakable grace and fluidity. He has won seven Gold Gloves. At an age when most guys take a commercial and a half to get from the fridge to the couch, Winfield still has a move from first to third that can bring tears to the eye of a track coach."

Indeed, Winfield has overcome serious injury and the inevitable encroachment of middle age to perform at his best in the twilight of his career. During mid-season of the year when he would find himself on a winning World Series team, he told *Sports Illustrated:* "For the last few years people have seen me and acted surprised that I'm still playing. Still playing? I'm kicking butt."

Winfield ranks among the top twenty all-time leaders in runs batted in, extra bases, and home runs. He was named to the All-Star game a dozen years in a row and won seven Gold Glove Awards for defensive play in the outfield. Impressive though his records are, Winfield contends they might even have been better. His prime years were spent in the New York Yankees organization, in the steely grip of Yankees owner George Steinbrenner. The strife between the two began almost upon Winfield's arrival in New York and lasted literally for years, because Winfield had the power to veto proposed trades to other teams. Worse, Winfield found his private life dragged into court—and the headlines—by a woman who claimed to be his common-law wife, and even his charitable organization, the David M. Winfield Foundation, was scrutinized by the media. Through it all, Winfield pressed on, playing in more than 2600 games and hitting well over 400 home runs. Still he could not hide his frustrations, telling *Sports Illustrated:* "Only I know how much better I could have been without all the distractions."

Childhood in St. Paul

David Mark Winfield was born October 3, 1951, in St. Paul, Minnesota. His father, Frank, worked as a waiter on

At a Glance...

Born David Mark Winfield, October 3, 1951, in St. Paul, MN; son of Frank (a waiter) and Arline (a public school system employee) Winfield; married Tonya Turner, February 18, 1988; children: (by previous relationship) Lauren Shanel. *Education:* Attended University of Minnesota, c. 1970-73.

Professional baseball player, 1973—. Played for San Diego Padres, 1973-80, New York Yankees, 1981-89, California Angels, 1990-91, Toronto Blue Jays, 1992, and Minnesota Twins, 1993—. Founder of David M. Winfield Foundation, a charitable organization.

Selected awards: Elected to All-Star lineups from San Diego and New York 12 times, 1977-88; winner of Gold Glove Award for defensive play 7 times; YMCA Brian Piccolo Award for humanitarian services, 1979; named "Comeback Player of the Year" by the *Sporting News,* 1990.

Addresses: *Home*—Peaneck, NJ. *Office*—c/o Minnesota Twins, Metrodome, 501 Chicago Ave. S., Minneapolis, MN 55415.

passenger trains. When Winfield was three, his parents separated. His mother took a job in the St. Paul public school system and endeavored to raise Dave and his older brother Steve alone. As a *Sports Illustrated* reporter noted: "The family of three living on Carroll Avenue in St. Paul turned their row house into a fortress. They learned to rely on one another, to need nobody else. So attached was David to his mother that, when it came time to go to college, he enrolled at [the University of] Minnesota so that he could live at home. . . . David was the kind of boy who took his mother's elbow as she walked, the kind who revered her every step."

As Winfield remembered it in a *Sport* magazine interview, his youth was quite ordinary. "Considering that we grew up in a broken home, we had a happy childhood because of the love and affection our mother gave us," he said. When the Winfield brothers did venture out, they usually strayed no farther than the Oxford Playground in the next block. There they were befriended by Bill Peterson, the playground director, who encouraged them to play basketball and baseball. "Bill Peterson was a white man in the black community," Winfield recalled in the interview, "but he gave more to that community than anyone I know. To me, at different times, he was coach, friend, father, all rolled

into one." The guidance he received as a youngster was not lost on Winfield. When he became a top-earning major league baseball player he founded an organization to help needy children, especially those in San Diego and New York City.

Hard as it may be to believe, Winfield—who now stands 6 foot 6 inches—was small for his age as a teen. He did not even try out for the varsity baseball team at St. Paul's Central High School until he was a junior. A phenomenal growth spurt helped him to catch up with his peers, and by his senior year he was All-City and All-State in both basketball and baseball. His talent attracted baseball scouts, and upon graduating from high school he was offered a contract with the Boston Red Sox. He decided to go to college instead, because he had heard that blacks were treated harshly in the smaller towns where minor league baseball was played.

The University of Minnesota offered Winfield a scholarship, and he declared a double major in political science and black studies. Trouble found him after his freshman year. He was arrested as an accomplice in the theft of a snowblower from a Minneapolis store, and he was taken to jail. The experience changed him for life. "My mother came to the jail and there were tears in her eyes," he said in *Sport.* "I pledged to my mother that I would never do anything like that again, ever. I was lucky. They let me go. But I was on probation the rest of my time in college. I feel that shame burning through me again, just by telling the story now for print. But I do it so that kids can know what a terrible feeling it is to do something so stupid and wrong and how awful it is to hurt someone who has loved you and cared for you."

As a college sophomore Winfield became a starting pitcher for Minnesota, winning 8 of 11 outings. He moved to the outfield the following year after an arm injury. By his junior year Winfield was playing both basketball and baseball. In his senior year the Gophers won both the Big Ten basketball championship *and* the Big Ten baseball championship. Returning to the mound, Winfield had a 13-1 season while hitting .385. He was named Most Valuable Player in the National Collegiate Athletic Association tournament and received collegiate All-American honors.

Drafted in Three Sports

The decision to attend college proved immensely fruitful for Winfield. In 1973 he was drafted in three major sports: baseball (by the San Diego Padres), basketball (by the Atlanta Hawks in the NBA and the Utah Stars in the ABA), and football (by the Minnesota Vikings). The attention from the Vikings was particularly astonishing, because Winfield had never played football in college. Even so, the NFL coaches felt he might excel as a receiver. But Winfield chose the Padres baseball team and embarked for California. He never spent a day in the minor leagues. His starting salary was $18,000 with a signing bonus of $50,000.

A franchise that struggled in those days, the Padres allowed Winfield to improve his talents in the big league arena. His pitching aspirations were quickly put to rest, and he became an outfielder. The club management found his ability as a hitter quite encouraging. During his rookie season he batted .277, and over the next four years he never batted below .260. At first he was plagued by streaks—brilliant hitting followed by long slumps at the plate. Coaches worked with him consistently, and he learned the art of prolonged concentration. In 1978 he batted .308, went to his second All-Star Game, and was named Padres team captain. The following year he again batted over .300 and won his first Gold Glove Award.

In the late 1970s Winfield became acquainted with a retired businessman named Albert S. Frohman. Frohman began to advise Winfield on money management and then offered to be his agent. Winfield accepted. *Sports Illustrated* described the unlikely friendship that would lead Winfield into trouble: "An odder pair of friends you couldn't invent. Winfield was tall, sleek and gorgeous. Frohman, who was short and wrinkled, looked like 10 pounds of Malt-O-Meal stuffed into a five-pound bag. Frohman ate badly, blew his stack readily and had had his tact removed surgically. Everybody, or so it seemed, took an instant dislike to him, just to save time. Everybody, that is, except Winfield."

Frohman helped nurture the idea that Winfield's talents were being wasted in San Diego. In 1979, when Winfield became eligible for free agency, the abrasive agent engineered a deal with the New York Yankees. At the time the Winfield contract broke all the records. It was a ten-year deal with cost-of-living escalators, a million dollar signing bonus, and a built-in $300,000 yearly contribution to the David M. Winfield Foundation, Winfield's charity for inner city children. The whole package would cost George Steinbrenner close to $25 million. Everyone was happy when the deal was announced and the contract was signed on December 15, 1980. But the troubles began almost immediately.

Yanked About by the Boss

Steinbrenner claimed that he did not understand the cost-of-living increases Frohman had written into the contract. Winfield was caught in a crossfire between his agent and the irritable Yankees owner, who began trading insults in the mass media. "After less than a year of Winfield/Frohman, Steinbrenner was trying to bum rush them both out of the Big Apple," noted a *Sports Illustrated* corre-

spondent. "He started trashing Winfield in the papers, especially after Winfield led the Yankees into the 1981 World Series and then went 1 for 22." Comparing Winfield to former Yankee Reggie Jackson—called "Mr. October" for his stellar postseason performances—Steinbrenner dubbed Winfield "Mr. May" and accused him of choking. The following year Steinbrenner quit making contributions to the Winfield Foundation. Winfield sued.

The tension filtered down into the locker room, where fearful managers dared not praise Winfield to reporters, and other players tried to avoid taking sides. One year the Yankees did not even submit Winfield's name for the All-Star ballot, although he was one of the team's biggest stars. "There is no way to fathom what was being done to me," Winfield told *Sports Illustrated*. "It was immoral, improper and reprehensible. It was a battle for everything, your performance, your credibility. Do you know what it's like to have people fooling with your career?" Steinbrenner tried to trade Winfield repeatedly, but a clause in Winfield's contract allowed the player to veto the trades. "I have had to fight adversity and animus, and I've answered: one, by the way I play, two, by speaking up when nobody else would, and three, by taking [Steinbrenner] to court and winning the money he owes the Winfield Foundation," the player stated in 1984.

Winfield had strong allies among Yankee fans, especially at first. After all, he was the first Yankee since Yogi Berra to get at least 100 runs batted in every year for five consecutive years. In 1984 he ran a tight race for American League batting champion and lost—to fellow Yankee Don Mattingly.

> "If my career had ended before Toronto, I wouldn't have been really happy with what baseball dealt me."

By the mid-1980s, however, his popularity had begun to erode. First he was taken to court by a woman who claimed to be his common-law wife. She was awarded a settlement and support for her daughter, whom Winfield has never denied parenting. Then independent auditors began to examine the finances of the Winfield Foundation, casting a shadow on a charity that had sent more than a half million children to ballparks, zoos, and plays for free. And in 1985, the mother-in-law of former heavyweight champion Mike Tyson sued Winfield on the charges that he had given her a venereal disease. Winfield denied the charge and settled the case out of court.

Throughout all the years of screaming headlines, scandals,

and bitter disputes with Steinbrenner, Winfield somehow managed to maintain his cool on the baseball field. He was blessed with stamina and a body not prone to injuries, enabling him to start almost every day, year after year. In 1988, for instance, his .322 batting average was fourth highest in the American League. He continued to be known as a power hitter who could knock long balls in a home ballpark with one of the deepest outfields in the major leagues. Still, the stresses of life began to tell on the aging star. He began to question Frohman's management of his assets and the Foundation's top-heavy bureaucracy. Then, in what amounted to a last blast at Steinbrenner, he published an autobiography, *Winfield: A Player's Life*. The book enraged Steinbrenner and alienated some of the other Yankee players.

Rebounding in California and Toronto

In 1989 Winfield suffered the first major injury of his career. He underwent surgery to remove fragments of a herniated disk from his back and missed an entire season of baseball. When he returned to the field in 1990, he was finally traded—to the California Angels. There he led the team in runs batted in (78), finished second in home runs (21), and batted .290 after the All-Star break. The *Sporting News* named him "Comeback Player of the Year." In 1991 he batted only .262 but hit 28 home runs.

Winfield signed with the Toronto Blue Jays as a free agent in the winter of 1992. Married and developing a relationship with his natural daughter, he seemed finally to be enjoying baseball, enjoying the new city, and especially enjoying the prospects of advancing to the World Series. He told *Sports Illustrated:* "I've been thinking about this. If my career had ended [before Toronto], I wouldn't have been really happy with what baseball dealt me. I would have had no fulfillment, no sense of equity, no fairness. I

feel a whole lot better now about the way things have turned out." Winfield's happiness turned to open enthusiasm in the 1992 World Series, when his double in the 11th inning of Game Six drove in the winning runs and gave the Jays the crown.

Dave Winfield finally has the World Series victory he always yearned for. He has played long enough to see former teammates become big league managers, and his long years of turmoil in New York are now the stuff of history. In 1993 he began his 20th major league season—having signed with the Minnesota Twins—remarkably spry and free of injuries. It is fitting that Winfield's singular career has brought him full circle, back to the region from which he launched himself years ago. Now in the twilight of his playing days—and a certain candidate for the Baseball Hall of Fame—Winfield can look back with satisfaction. "Always wanted to live that 3-D life," he told *Sports Illustrated*. He has done exactly that.

Sources

Books

Winfield, Dave, *Winfield: A Player's Life,* Avon, 1989.

Periodicals

New York Times, June 1, 1975, p. 3.
New York Times Magazine, March 29, 1981, p. 25.
Sport, December 1975, p. 69.
Sports Illustrated, September 10, 1984, p. 20; April 11, 1988, p. 36; May 30, 1988, p. 62; June 29, 1992, p. 56; November 2, 1992, p. 18; December 28, 1992, p. 12.

—Mark Kram

Granville T. Woods

1856-1910

Inventor

Within the landscape of the American Industrial Revolution, in the field of urban electrification and communication, stand prominent inventors such as Thomas Edison, George Westinghouse, and Alexander Graham Bell. Their place is recognized, their achievements heralded. But they are not alone. Obscured by the shadows of history, and even more by the dark denial of recognition, is the figure of Granville T. Woods, a contemporary of Edison, Westinghouse, and Bell and one of that era's most prolific and substantive inventors.

At the time of his death in 1910, Woods had been granted approximately 60 patents, mostly relating to electrical subjects. His inventions revolutionized railway and telegraph communication and ironically helped in the growth of his competitors' companies—General Electric, Westinghouse Electric and Manufacturing, and American Bell Telephone. At the time of his death, though, Woods was virtually penniless.

"Before the Civil War, slavery and racial sentiments did much to hamper the recognition of black inventors," Michael C. Christopher explained in the *Journal of Black Studies.* "Slaves were not allowed to receive patents or assign them to others. Because slaves were not citizens, they were not allowed to enter into contracts with the government or private citizens." The end of the U.S. Civil War in 1865 provided black inventors legal recognition, but it failed to foster complete social acceptance. Bound by legal restrictions to acknowledge black inventors after the war, white society merely altered its view of these individuals: adhering to the racist notion that blacks lacked the higher capacity to create and invent, many whites attributed black ingenuity to the white bloodlines so frequently present in people of color. This flagrant altering of personal history was further perpetuated by some black inventors themselves who "refused to acknowledge they were black because they feared a decline in the commercial value of their inventions if their ethnic background was publicized," Christopher pointed out. Following the war, then, the identity of black inventors was accepted, but their past—who they really were—was not.

Woods was born into this culture of division on April 23, 1856, in Columbus, Ohio, five years before the start of the Civil War. But he was born a free black because the Northwest Ordinance of 1787 prohibited slavery from the territory that included the future state of Ohio. Beginning shortly after its admission to the Union in 1803, however, Ohio adopted "Black Codes," or laws that restricted the participation of

At a Glance...

Born April 23, 1856, in Columbus, OH; died January 30, 1910, in New York City; son of Tailer and Martha Woods. *Education:* Studied mechanical and electrical engineering at an East Coast college, 1876-78.

Apprenticed as a machinist and blacksmith in Columbus, OH, 1866-72; worked as a fireman and then as an engineer for the Iron Mountain Railroad in Missouri, 1872-74; worked in a rolling mill in Springfield, IL, 1874-76; part-time machine shop worker in New York City, 1876-78; engineer aboard the British steamer *Ironsides,* 1878-80; ran a steam locomotive on the Danville and Southern Railroad in Cincinnati, OH, 1880-84; founder, with brother, Lyates, of the Woods Electric Company in Cincinnati, 1884; worked as an inventor in New York City, 1890-1910.

Granted first patent, June 3, 1884, for a steam boiler furnace; received approximately 60 additional patents (over 35 dealing with electrical systems), including 15 in the field of electric railways. Major inventions included an improved telephone transmitter, 1884; an electrical apparatus for transmitting messages, 1885; an induction telegraph system, 1887; a galvanic battery, 1888; an automatic safety cut-out for electric currents, 1889; a re-electric railway supply system, 1893; a regulator for electric motors, 1896; an egg incubator, 1900; and an automatic air brake, 1902. Many of Woods's patents were assigned to General Electric Company, American Bell Telephone Company, Westinghouse Air Brake Company, and American Engineering Company.

Awards: Elementary Public School No. 335, Brooklyn, NY, was dedicated in Woods's name, 1969; Governor John J. Gilligan of Ohio issued a proclamation recognizing Woods's achievements in science and invention, October 11, 1974.

blacks in the state militia, in public education, and in certain legal matters. By the time Woods began attending school, the state had modified its ban on public education, but the lives of blacks were still severely regulated: at the age of ten, Woods was forced to leave school and apprentice as a machinist and blacksmith in a machine shop. Child labor laws would not come into effect for another seventy years.

Overcame Lack of Formal Education

Woods's lifelong interest and education—mostly self-taught—in electrical and mechanical engineering began in this machine shop. He absorbed as much information as he could about the workings of a machine he ran. Others he learned about simply by watching. And still other times, so deep was his desire for knowledge, he used his own earnings to pay the master mechanic at the shop for private instruction. With each subsequent job, Woods learned more, and his increased knowledge gained him more skilled positions.

In 1872, at the age of sixteen, Woods left Ohio and, in what can be best described as his travel-and-study period, worked various jobs around the country, augmenting the practical knowledge gained from those positions with readings at night. His first stop was at the Iron Mountain Railroad in Missouri, where he worked as a fireman and, later, an engineer. His interest in electricity and its application to railroads began there. In 1874, he moved to Springfield, Illinois, to work in a rolling mill.

Woods's study and working knowledge of mechanics and electricity enabled him in 1876 to qualify to take courses in mechanical and electrical engineering at an eastern college. Working during the day in a New York City machine shop, Woods attended classes at night for two years. He left school in 1878 and signed on as an engineer aboard a British steamer, the *Ironsides,* embarking on a two-year tour that took him to nearly every continent in the world. In 1880 he returned to the United States to work as a steam locomotive engineer for the Danville and Southern Railroad in Cincinnati, Ohio, a position he held for four years.

Although his work record and his education should have entitled him to more responsible positions, he was constantly denied them. "Not only did he have to face a lack of advancement in his jobs because of his color," Jim Haskins wrote in *Outward Dreams,* "but there was no means by which he could ever achieve a position of influence while working for others." The Civil War had been over for almost twenty years, but the climate in the country had hardly stirred. Fortunately, his knowledge of mechanical and electrical applications gained from his years of journeyman work proved fruitful for Woods. In 1884 he received his first patent, for a more efficient version of a steam boiler furnace. That same year, along with his brother Lyates, Woods opened the Woods Electric Company in Cincinnati to produce and market his own inventions. He had begun his defining career as an inventor.

The legalities of patent assignment and regulation did not work to Woods's advantage. The U.S. Government grants patents for any new or useful machine or process or manufacturing method, or for an improvement of any previous machine or process or method. A patent gives its owner, the patentee, the sole right to manufacture, use, and sell that particular invention. Patents are, in a sense, recognized as personal property. If others try to make, use, or sell a patentee's invention, they are guilty of patent infringement and may be sued by the patentee. There are two instances, however, when an inventor may lose his right to a patent for his invention. First, if an inventor does not have enough money to manufacture and market his invention, the patent is then assigned, or sold, to another individual or company that has the necessary capital. Second, the inventor may simply wish to sell his patent outright. In either case, once the patent is assigned to someone else, the inventor gives up all legal and monetary claims to that invention.

Early Electrical Inventions Transformed Sound Transmission

Woods's first two electrical inventions dealt with sound transmission. In December of 1884 he was granted a patent for a telephone transmitter, an apparatus that conducted sound over an electrical current. Alexander Graham Bell had already developed a telephonic device almost a decade earlier, but Woods's instrument far surpassed any models then in use, carrying a louder and more distinct sound over a longer distance. The physical properties by which the device operated are still employed in modern telephones. Despite Woods's visionary achievement, patent guidelines dictated that the patent be assigned to a company that had the mechanical and monetary means to manufacture such a device. The patent was assigned to the American Bell Telephone Company.

Less than a year later, Woods was granted a patent for a mechanism he called a "telegraphony," a combination telegraph and telephone, which could transmit both oral and signal messages. Prior to Woods's invention, the telegraph could only send messages over an electrical current utilizing a combination of short and long pulses (commonly referred to as dots and dashes) that represent letters of the alphabet. Developed by Samuel Morse in 1838, this "Morse code," as it came to be known, became the language of the telegraph. It therefore demanded that operators on either end of a telegraphic transmission be fully versed in both Morse code and in the operation of the sending key apparatus.

Woods's invention, however, gave almost everyone, regardless of their knowledge of telegraphs, the chance to send messages. If a person were unfamiliar with Morse code, he simply could flip a switch on the telegraph and speak near the sending key. The message would then be heard on the receiving end as articulate speech. Because of the understandable great demand for such an invention, Woods decided to sell his patent, allowing a larger compa-

ny to manufacture the device. He was paid generously for the patent by the American Bell Telephone Company.

Over the next 25 years, Woods's inventions were numerous and varied, from an incubator that provided a constant temperature for the hatching of chicks to a series of tracks used by motor vehicles at amusement parks. "Woods also invented an improved system for transferring electric current to street cars," Portia P. James explained in *The Real McCoy*. "He designed a grooved wheel that allowed the car to receive the electrical current while reducing friction. This wheel, called a troller, is the source of the popular name for a street car, trolley car." Woods held over 35 patents on electromechanical devices, a dozen of which improved the electric railway system. But his greatest invention improved electrical communication between trains.

Changed the Course of Railway Travel

On November 29, 1887, Woods received a patent for his Induction Telegraph System, also called the Synchronous Multiplex Railway Telegraph. Communication between moving trains and between a moving train and a railroad station had previously been poor. In a telegraph system, a continuous wire must exist between a sending key and a

> "He has left us the rich legacy of a life successfully devoted to the cause of progress."
> —Henry E. Baker, U.S. Patent Office

receiving sounder. Ordinary telegraph wires were usually run along railroad tracks, but for a telegraph system to work aboard the train, part of the train had to have been in constant contact with these wires. Because of the jostling movement of trains, most messages sent or received were incomplete. Numerous times, warnings of washed-out bridges, rock slides, and other obstructions failed to reach a train in time. Still other times, trains learned too late—or not at all—of the location of other trains on the same track.

Woods's Induction Telegraph invention changed the course of railway travel, dramatically decreasing the number of lives lost in accidents. To realize his invention, he applied Faraday's Law of Electromagnetic Induction: an oblong coil was suspended beneath a train, and an electrical current was passed through it. In turn, a magnetic field developed around the train. When the train moved, the field moved with it and induced a similar current in the telegraph wires that ran along the tracks, allowing telegraphic messages to be sent and received uninterrupted.

Woods was greatly heralded for this invention, but he received even greater renown when Thomas Edison and another inventor, Lucius Phelps, challenged Woods's rights to the patent, claiming in separate legal suits that they each had developed a similar telegraph system before Woods. In both cases, Woods was declared the prior inventor. Nonetheless, his legal troubles did not end there. In 1892 Woods was sued for criminal libel after he claimed that a manager of the American Engineering Company stole his patent for an electric railway. He was jailed briefly when he could not post money for bail.

His payment of large legal fees, both in the challenge and defense of patent rights, and his loss of income from his inventions left Woods in poverty at the end of his life. As the owner of a small company, he could hardly compete with the larger corporations like those of Edison and Bell. And as a black inventor, Woods could not hope to receive the deserved public recognition his white counterparts did.

All this, however, did little to diminish his intellectual and creative output. Three years after Woods's death, Henry E. Baker, second assistant examiner at the U.S. Patent Office and an African American, wrote a telling epitaph in his book *The Colored Inventor:* "Mr. Woods is, perhaps, the best known of all the inventors whose achievements [add to] to the credit of our race; and in his passing away he has left us the rich legacy of a life successfully devoted to the cause of progress."

Sources

Books

Baker, Henry E., *The Colored Inventor,* Crisis Publishing Company, 1913, reprinted, Arno Press, 1969.
Current, Richard N., T. Harry Williams, Frank Freidel, and Alan Brinkley, *American History, a Survey—Volume 1: To 1877,* 6th edition, Knopf, 1983.
Haber, Louis, *Black Pioneers of Science and Invention,* Harcourt, 1970.
Haskins, Jim, *Outward Dreams: Black Inventors and Their Inventions,* Bantam, 1992.
Hayden, Robert C., *Eight Black American Inventors,* Addison-Wesley, 1972.
Jackson, W. Sherman, "Granville T. Woods: Railway Communications Wizard, 1856-1910," in *American Black Scientists and Inventors,* edited by Edward S. Jenkins, National Science Teachers Association, 1975.
James, Portia P., *The Real McCoy: African-American Invention and Innovation, 1619-1930,* Smithsonian Institution Press, 1989.

Periodicals

Essence, March 1993.
Journal of Black Studies, Volume 11, Number 3, March 1981.

—Rob Nagel

Richard Wright

1908-1960

Author

As a poor black child growing up in the Deep South, Richard Wright suffered poverty, hunger, racism, and violence—experiences that later became central themes of his work. Wright stands as a major literary figure of the 1930s and '40s, his writings a departure from those of the Harlem Renaissance school. Steeped in the literary naturalism of the Depression era, Wright's work expresses a realistic and brutal portrayal of white society's oppression of African Americans. Anger and protest served as a catalyst for literature intended to promote social change by exposing the injustices of racism, economic exploitation, and imperialism. Through his art, Wright turned the torment of alienation into a voice calling for human solidarity and racial advancement.

Wright was born on September 8, 1908, in the backwoods of Mississippi, on a plantation 25 miles north of Natchez, to a farmer and a schoolteacher. Descended from a family lineage of black, white, and Choctaw Indian, he spent the early years of his life playing among the "moss-clad" oaks along the Mississippi River. After failing to make a profit on his rented farm, Wright's father decided to move the family to Memphis, Tennessee. Upon arrival by paddleboat steamer in 1911, the Wrights took residence in a two-room tenement not far from Beale Street. To Wright, the concrete pavement appeared

hostile and dreary compared to the pastoral serenity of his former home. In a city filled with brothels, saloons, and storefront churches, Wright encountered the terrors of violence, vice, and racism.

The increasing absence of his father fueled Wright's growing sense of anger and estrangement. By the time the boy was six years old, his father had deserted the family to live with another woman. At first, he was elated to be free from his father's abusive behavior, but he soon realized that this newfound freedom brought severe poverty. "The image of my father became associated with the pangs of hunger," wrote Wright in his autobiography *Black Boy.* "Whenever I felt hunger, I thought of him with a deep biological bitterness." Left with two children to support, Wright's mother went to work as a housemaid and cook. After a brief period in an orphanage around 1915, Wright attended school for a short time at Howard Institute. "This period in Memphis was the beginning of adult suffering," wrote poet Margaret Walker in her book *Richard Wright, Daemonic Genius,* "the beginning of a terrible rage that he himself did not always understand."

Around 1919 the failing health of Wright's mother forced her to take the children to live with relatives in Arkansas. A year

At a Glance. . .

Born September 8, 1908, in Adams County, MS; died of a heart attack November 28, 1960, in Paris, France; son of Nathan "Nate" (a farmer) and Ella Wilson (a schoolteacher) Wright; married Rose Dhimah Meadman, 1939; married Ellen Poplar, 1941.

Published first story, "The Voodoo of Hell's Half Acre," 1924; worked variously as a dishwasher, busboy, porter, street sweeper, and group leader for a Chicago Boys Club; worked for U.S. Postal Service, Chicago, beginning in 1932; wrote poetry for leftist publications; attended American Writers' Congress, New York City, 1935; prepared guidebooks for Federal Writer's Project, mid-1930s; worked for Federal Theater Project, 1936; wrote for the *Daily Worker,* late 1930s; published *Uncle Tom's Children,* 1938; published *Native Son,* 1940; published autobiography *Black Boy,* 1945; lectured, appeared on radio and television, and contributed to periodicals, late 1940s; attended Bandung Conference in Indonesia, 1955.

Awards: Guggenheim Fellowship, 1939; Works Progress Administration award, late 1930s; Spingarn Medal, NAACP, 1941, for *Native Son.*

later, the Wrights moved to Richard's devoutly religious grandparents' home in Jackson, Mississippi. The household was dominated by Wright's grandmother and Aunt Addie, both of whom were Seventh-Day Adventists. Because of his rebellious attitude toward evangelical teachings, Wright lived as an outsider within the family. Although nonreligious literature was forbidden, he managed to acquire pulp magazines, newspapers, and detective stories. Inspired by local folklore, country sermons, and popular literature, Wright's first story "The Voodoo of Hell's Half Acre," was published in 1924 by a local black newspaper. Undaunted by the family's criticism of his work, Wright aspired to become a writer.

Memphis: Gateway to the North

To pursue this dream, Wright shifted his attention northward, to a place where he could escape the hostility of southern rural evangelical culture. With only a ninth-grade education and little money in his pocket, Wright fled to Memphis at the age of 17. There he became acquainted with the work of H. L. Mencken. In the fiery prose of Mencken, Wright learned that words could serve as weapons with which to lash out at the world. Soon afterward, Wright discovered such naturalist writers as Theodore Dreiser, Sherwood Anderson, and Sinclair Lewis. As Arnold Rampersad stated in the introduction to Wright's *Lawd Today,* the author's avid study of serious literature in Memphis became "the most effective counter to both his profound sense of isolation and the dismal education he received as a boy in Mississippi."

Unfortunately, Wright did not find the atmosphere of Memphis as enlightening as his private studies. Violence and hatred perpetrated by whites reinforced his dim view of the South. In November of 1927, Wright boarded a train bound for Chicago. His departure symbolized the end of a stay in an alien land where he existed as a "non-man" within the chasm of the black and white worlds.

Chicago: The Promised Land

Wright's family soon joined him in Chicago. Together they lived in a cramped apartment on the city's South Side. Bored with his studies, Wright left high school to help support the family. He took a number of odd jobs, working as a dishwasher, porter, busboy, street sweeper, and group leader at a South Side Boys Club. In 1932 Wright worked as a clerk at the Chicago post office. Nicknamed "the University," the post office employed numerous radical intellectuals, some of whom invited Wright to attend the meetings of the John Reed Club, a revolutionary writers' organization. While exposing him to Communist literature and Marxist ideology, club members encouraged Wright to pursue a professional writing career. Inspired by their support and enthusiasm, Wright began to write poetry for various left-wing publications.

Around this time, Wright's interest in race relations and radical thought led him to join the Communist party. Within the Communist ranks, he found, for the first time, a formidable peer group sharing a common goal of promoting racial and social equality. "It seemed to me that here at last, in the realm of revolutionary expression," Wright stated in his contribution to the book *The God That Failed,* "Negro experience could find a home, a functioning value and role." For a brief period, Wright's sense of loneliness subsided. Communism appeared to offer an alternative that could not only quell his own inner conflict, but the threat of poverty and racism confronting the disinherited peoples of all nations.

In 1935, after the Communist party disbanded the John Reed Clubs, Wright hitchhiked to New York, where, along with prominent writers like Langston Hughes, Malcolm Cowley, and Dreiser, he attended the American Writers' Congress. Back in Chicago that year, he found employment preparing guidebooks for the Federal Writer's Project, a New Deal relief program for unemployed writers. Early in 1936, Wright was transferred for a short time to the Federal Theater Project. Wright also wrote for the *Daily Worker* and started work on a collection of short stories and a novel, posthumously published as *Lawd Today* in 1963.

Wright's burgeoning literary career, however, soon conflicted with his membership in the Communist party. In Chicago, his study of sociology, psychology, philosophy, and literature led him to question the rigid policies of Stalinism and the aesthetic aspects of socialist realism. He found that recruiting, organizing, and distributing party literature interfered with his writing assignments. Moreover, the expulsion of many fellow members and the constant questioning concerning his loyalty alerted Wright to the duplicitous and paranoid nature of the organization. Accused of betraying the party by several Chicago Communists in 1937, Wright—tired of the Chicago scene—decided to leave for New York.

New York: Capital of Art and Literature

Not long after arriving in New York City, Wright won a Works Progress Administration award for his collection of novellas, published as *Uncle Tom's Children* in 1938. Based on Wright's Mississippi boyhood, "these stories were almost unbearable evocations of cruel realities," explained poet Arna Bontemps in *Anger and Beyond*. "His purpose was to force open closed eyes, to compel America to look at what it had done to the black peasantry in which he was born."

For the better part of a year, Wright took time off from his jobs at the Writer's Project and the *Daily Worker* to work on a novel. Published in 1940, *Native Son* became a Book-of-the-Month Club selection, selling over a quarter of a million copies in six months. By far Wright's most famous and financially successful book, *Native Son* is a militant racial manifesto exposing the evils of racism and the capitalist oppression of blacks in urban society. Based on the actual criminal case of convicted killer Robert Nixon, the book describes the story of Bigger Thomas, a street-hardened black youth who murders the daughter of a well-to-do white family while working as their chauffeur. Hunted down by white society, Bigger is sentenced to death by the very power structure responsible for his alienation, subjugation, and ultimate impulse to commit murder.

In 1941, the National Association for the Advancement of Colored People awarded Wright the Spingarn Medal for *Native Son*. Another great honor was bestowed on Wright when actor-producers John Houseman and Orson Welles mounted a stage adaption of *Native Son,* featuring the outstanding actor Canada Lee in the role of Bigger. Also in 1941, Wright published his third book, *Twelve Million Black Voices,* a folk history featuring photographs by Edwin Rosskam. Following his formal break with the Communist party in 1944, Wright wrote an essay for the *Atlantic Monthly* entitled "I Tried to Be a Communist,"

> "It seemed to me that here at last, in the realm of revolutionary expression, Negro experience could find a home, a functioning value and role."

explaining his reasons for leaving the party. Wright's finest work of the decade, however, was his autobiography *Black Boy*. Published in 1945, *Black Boy* is a harrowing record of Wright's early years in the South. In a review in the *Nation,* noted literary scholar Lionel Trilling described *Black Boy* as a "remarkable book" of great "distinction" and "purpose." Social scientists and historians continue to study the book's impact on black and white society long after its publication.

Paris: Avant-Garde City of Lights

Encouraged by avant-garde writer Gertrude Stein, Wright expressed an interest in visiting France. In the spring of 1946, he embarked for Paris on an ocean steamer. The city's colorful streets and cultured citizenry greatly impressed Wright. Stein introduced him to a number of leading French intellectuals, including Claude Magny and Maurice Nadeau. Wright went back to New York in January of 1947. He intended to resume work there, but rampant racism and the anti-radicalism of the Cold War era made him restless to return to France. In May of 1948, Wright moved into an apartment on Paris's Left Bank.

In permanent exile in Paris, Wright enjoyed celebrity status. He spent a great deal of time lecturing throughout Europe and appearing on radio and television. Besides his close association with existentialist philosopher Jean-Paul Sartre and the members of the Les Temps Modernes group, Wright became an active member of the Pan-African organization Presence Africaine. His 1953 novel, *The Outsider,* exemplifies the increasing influence of existentialism on his work. *Black Power,* completed following his trip to Ghana in 1954, presents a Pan-African perspective. After attending a 29-nation gathering of representatives of African and Asian countries at the Bandung Conference in Indonesia, Wright wrote *The Color Curtain,* which appeared in 1956. A year later, he produced a travelogue,

Pagan Spain, based on his observations of Spanish culture, politics, and religion. Up until his death from a heart attack in Paris in 1960, Wright continued to work on several literary projects, including a collection of short stories, *Eight Men,* published posthumously in 1961.

From the depths of the Mississippi Delta to the cities of Europe, Africa, and Asia, Richard Wright emerged an international literary figure championing the cause of social and racial justice. Poet, writer, social critic, and journalist, Wright authored about a dozen books and numerous poems and essays, most of which address the evils of racism and man's inhumanity to man. "Wright's unrelentingly bleak language was not merely of the Deep South or Chicago," commented writer James Baldwin in an essay titled "Alas Poor Richard," "but that of the human heart." It was Wright's destiny, as he himself wrote in *The God That Failed,* "to hurl words into the darkness and wait for an echo . . . no matter how faintly." Decades after his death, Wright's words still reverberate across the world—their dark and ominous tone embodying a message of hope for all humanity.

Selected writings

Uncle Tom's Children: Four Novellas, Harper & Brothers, 1938.
Native Son, Harper & Brothers, 1940.
Twelve Million Black Voices: A Folk History of the Negro in the United States, Viking, 1941.
Black Boy: A Record of Childhood and Youth, Harper & Brothers, 1945.
The Outsider, 1953.
Black Power, Harper & Brothers, 1954.
Savage Holiday, Avon, 1954.
The Color Curtain, World, 1956.
Pagan Spain, Harper & Brothers, 1957.
White Man Listen, Doubleday, 1957.
Long Dream, Doubleday, 1958.
Eight Men, World, 1961.
Lawd Today, Walker, 1963.

(Contributor) *The God That Failed,* edited by Richard Crossman, Books for Libraries Series, 1972.
American Hunger, Harper & Row, 1977.

Sources

Books

Alexander, Charles C., *Nationalism in American Thought: 1930-1945,* Rand McNally, 1969.
American Writers: A Collection of Literary Biographies, Vol. IV, edited by Leonard Unger, Scribner's, 1974.
Anger and Beyond, edited by Herbert Hill, Harper & Row, 1966.
Baldwin, James, *Nobody Knows My Name: More Notes of a Native Son* (includes "Alas Poor Richard"), Dial Press, 1961.
Bell, Bernard W., *The Afro-American Novel and Its Tradition,* University of Massachusetts Press, 1987.
Crunden, Robert, *From Self to Society: 1919-1941,* Prentice Hall, 1972.
The God That Failed, edited by Richard Crossman, Books for Libraries Series, 1972.
Richard Wright Reader, edited by Ellen Wright and Michel Fabre, Harper & Row, 1978.
Walker, Margaret, *Richard Wright, Daemonic Genius: A Portrait of the Man, A Critical Look at His Work,* Warner Books, 1988.
Wright, Richard, *Black Boy: A Record of Childhood and Youth,* Harper & Brothers, 1945.
Wright, Richard, *Lawd Today,* introduction by Arnold Rampersad, Northeastern University Press, 1986.
Wright, Richard, *Native Son,* Harper & Brothers, 1940.

Periodicals

Nation, April 1945.

—*John Cohassey*

Cumulative Indexes

Cumulative Nationality Index

Volume numbers appear in **bold**.

American

Aaron, Hank **5**
Abernathy, Ralph David **1**
Ali, Muhammad **2**
Allen, Byron **3**
Anderson, Marian **2**
Andrews, Raymond **4**
Angelou, Maya **1**
Armstrong, Louis **2**
Asante, Molefi Kete **3**
Ashe, Arthur **1**
Baker, Ella **5**
Baker, Josephine **3**
Baldwin, James **1**
Baraka, Amiri **1**
Barkley, Charles **5**
Basquiat, Jean-Michel **5**
Bearden, Romare **2**
Belafonte, Harry **4**
Belle, Regina **1**
Bennett, Lerone, Jr. **5**
Berry, Halle **4**
Bethune, Mary McLeod **4**
Bing, Dave **3**
Bluford, Guy **2**
Bond, Julian **2**
Bradley, Ed **2**
Bradley, Thomas **2**
Brandon, Barbara **3**
Braun, Carol Moseley **4**
Brimmer, Andrew F. **2**
Brooks, Gwendolyn **1**
Brown, Lee P. **1**
Brown, Les **5**
Brown, Ron **5**
Brown, Tony **3**
Brunson, Dorothy **1**
Bumbry, Grace **5**
Bunche, Ralph J. **5**
Busby, Jheryl **3**
Callender, Clive O. **3**
Carson, Benjamin **1**
Carter, Stephen L. **4**
Carver, George Washington **4**
Cary, Lorene **3**
Catlett, Elizabeth **2**
Chambers, Julius **3**
Chenault, Kenneth I. **4**
Chisholm, Shirley **2**
Clark, Joe **1**
Clark, Kenneth B. **5**
Clayton, Constance **1**
Clayton, Xernona **3**
Cleaver, Eldridge **5**
Cleaver, Emanuel **4**
Clements, George **2**

Cole, Johnnetta B. **5**
Collins, Marva **3**
Cone, James H. **3**
Conyers, John, Jr. **4**
Cornelius, Don **4**
Cose, Ellis **5**
Dandridge, Dorothy **3**
Dash, Julie **4**
Davidson, Jaye **5**
Davis, Angela **5**
Davis, Benjamin O., Jr. **2**
Davis, Benjamin O., Sr. **4**
Davis, Miles **4**
Davis, Ossie **5**
Dellums, Ronald **2**
Dinkins, David **4**
Dixon, Sharon Pratt **1**
Dixon, Willie **4**
Dove, Ulysses **5**
Drexler, Clyde **4**
Du Bois, W. E. B. **3**
Duke, Bill **3**
Dunham, Katherine **4**
Dutton, Charles S. **4**
Edelman, Marian Wright **5**
Edley, Christopher **2**
Edwards, Harry **2**
Ellington, Duke **5**
Evers, Medgar **3**
Farmer, Forest J. **1**
Farmer, James **2**
Farrakhan, Louis **2**
Fielder, Cecil **2**
Fishburne, Larry **4**
Flipper, Henry O. **3**
Foreman, George **1**
Foxx, Redd **2**
Franklin, John Hope **5**
Franks, Gary **2**
Freeman, Morgan **2**
Gantt, Harvey **1**
Garrison, Zina **2**
Gaston, Arthur G. **4**
Gates, Henry Louis, Jr. **3**
Gaye, Marvin **2**
Gayle, Helene D. **3**
Gillespie, Dizzy **1**
Gist, Carole **1**
Givens, Robin **4**
Glover, Danny **1**
Goldberg, Whoopi **4**
Goode, W. Wilson **4**
Gordy, Berry, Jr. **1**
Gravely, Samuel L., Jr. **5**
Graves, Earl G. **1**
Gray, William H. III **3**

Green, Dennis **5**
Gregory, Dick **1**
Guillaume, Robert **3**
Guy, Jasmine **2**
Guy, Rosa **5**
Haley, Alex **4**
Harris, Patricia Roberts **2**
Hayes, Roland **4**
Height, Dorothy I. **2**
Henderson, Gordon **5**
Hendricks, Barbara **3**
Henson, Matthew **2**
Hill, Anita **5**
Hinderas, Natalie **5**
Hines, Gregory **1**
Holiday, Billie **1**
Holland, Endesha Ida Mae **3**
hooks, bell **5**
Hooks, Benjamin L. **2**
Horne, Lena **5**
Houston, Charles Hamilton **4**
Hughes, Langston **4**
Hurston, Zora Neale **3**
Ingram, Rex **5**
Innis, Roy **5**
Jackson, Isaiah **3**
Jackson, Jesse **1**
Jackson, Mahalia **5**
Jackson, Maynard **2**
Jacob, John E. **2**
Jemison, Mae C. **1**
Jenifer, Franklyn G. **2**
Johnson, Beverly **2**
Johnson, Charles **1**
Johnson, Earvin "Magic" **3**
Johnson, James Weldon **5**
Johnson, John H. **3**
Johnson, Robert **2**
Johnson, Robert L. **3**
Johnson, William Henry **3**
Jones, Bill T. **1**
Jones, James Earl **3**
Jordan, Barbara **4**
Jordan, Vernon E. **3**
Joyner-Kersee, Jackie **5**
Just, Ernest Everett **3**
Kelly, Patrick **3**
Kincaid, Jamaica **4**
King, Bernice **4**
King, Coretta Scott **3**
King, Martin Luther, Jr. **1**
Kunjufu, Jawanza **3**
Lafontant, Jewel Stradford **3**
Lane, Charles **3**
Lane, Vincent **5**
Latimer, Lewis H. **4**

Cumulative Occupation Index

Volume numbers appear in **bold.**

Art and design
Basquiat, Jean-Michel **5**
Bearden, Romare **2**
Brandon, Barbara **3**
Catlett, Elizabeth **2**
Gantt, Harvey **1**
Johnson, William Henry **3**
Kelly, Patrick **3**
Lawrence, Jacob **4**
Lee-Smith, Hughie **5**
Ringgold, Faith **4**
Serrano, Andres **3**
Simpson, Lorna **4**
Sleet, Moneta, Jr. **5**
Tanner, Henry Ossawa **1**

Business
Baker, Ella **5**
Bennett, Lerone, Jr. **5**
Bing, Dave **3**
Brimmer, Andrew F. **2**
Brown, Les **5**
Brunson, Dorothy **1**
Busby, Jheryl **3**
Chenault, Kenneth I. **4**
Clayton, Xernona **3**
Cornelius, Don **4**
Farmer, Forest J. **1**
Gaston, Arthur G. **4**
Gordy, Berry, Jr. **1**
Graves, Earl G. **1**
Henderson, Gordon **5**
Johnson, John H. **3**
Johnson, Robert L. **3**
Kelly, Patrick **3**
Lane, Vincent **5**
Lawson, Jennifer **1**
McDonald, Erroll **1**
Morgan, Garrett **1**
Parks, Gordon **1**
Perez, Anna **1**
Rhone, Sylvia **2**
Rogers, John W., Jr. **5**
Simmons, Russell **1**
Sullivan, Leon H. **3**
Thomas, Franklin A. **5**
White, Walter F. **4**
Williams, Walter E. **4**
Winfrey, Oprah **2**

Dance
Baker, Josephine **3**
Dove, Ulysses **5**
Dunham, Katherine **4**
Guy, Jasmine **2**

Hines, Gregory **1**
Horne, Lena **5**
Jones, Bill T. **1**
Miller, Bebe **3**
Mitchell, Arthur **2**
Vereen, Ben **4**

Education
Asante, Molefi Kete **3**
Baraka, Amiri **1**
Bethune, Mary McLeod **4**
Callender, Clive O. **3**
Carver, George Washington **4**
Cary, Lorene **3**
Catlett, Elizabeth **2**
Clark, Joe **1**
Clark, Kenneth B. **5**
Clayton, Constance **1**
Clements, George **2**
Cole, Johnnetta B. **5**
Collins, Marva **3**
Cone, James H. **3**
Davis, Angela **5**
Diop, Cheikh Anta **4**
Dove, Ulysses **5**
Edelman, Marian Wright **5**
Edley, Christopher **2**
Edwards, Harry **2**
Franklin, John Hope **5**
Gates, Henry Louis, Jr. **3**
Harris, Patricia Roberts **2**
Hill, Anita **5**
Holland, Endesha Ida Mae **3**
hooks, bell **5**
Houston, Charles Hamilton **4**
Jenifer, Franklyn G. **2**
Johnson, James Weldon **5**
Jordan, Barbara **4**
Just, Ernest Everett **3**
Kunjufu, Jawanza **3**
Lawrence, Jacob **4**
Leffall, LaSalle, Jr. **3**
Massey, Walter E. **5**
Patterson, Orlando **4**
Poussaint, Alvin F. **5**
Ringgold, Faith **4**
Soyinka, Wole **4**
Sudarkasa, Niara **4**
Thurman, Howard **3**
Walcott, Derek **5**
Washington, Booker T. **4**
Welsing, Frances Cress **5**
West, Cornel **5**
Wilkins, Roger **2**
Williams, Walter E. **4**
Woodson, Carter G. **2**

Fashion
Berry, Halle **4**
Campbell, Naomi **1**
Davidson, Jaye **5**
Henderson, Gordon **5**
Iman **4**
Johnson, Beverly **2**
Kelly, Patrick **3**

Film
Baker, Josephine **3**
Belafonte, Harry **4**
Berry, Halle **4**
Brown, Tony **3**
Campbell, Naomi **1**
Dandridge, Dorothy **3**
Dash, Julie **4**
Davidson, Jaye **5**
Davis, Ossie **5**
Duke, Bill **3**
Dunham, Katherine **4**
Dutton, Charles S. **4**
Fishburne, Larry **4**
Foxx, Redd **2**
Freeman, Morgan **2**
Givens, Robin **4**
Glover, Danny **1**
Goldberg, Whoopi **4**
Gordy, Berry, Jr. **1**
Guillaume, Robert **3**
Guy, Jasmine **2**
Hines, Gregory **1**
Horne, Lena **5**
Iman **4**
Ingram, Rex **5**
Johnson, Beverly **2**
Jones, James Earl **3**
Julien, Isaac **3**
Kunjufu, Jawanza **3**
Lane, Charles **3**
Lee, Joie **1**
Lee, Spike **5**
Lincoln, Abbey **3**
McDaniel, Hattie **5**
Murphy, Eddie **4**
Parks, Gordon **1**
Pryor, Richard **3**
Riggs, Marlon **5**
Rock, Chris **3**
Singleton, John **2**
Snipes, Wesley **3**
Taylor, Meshach **4**
Townsend, Robert **4**
Van Peebles, Mario **2**
Vereen, Ben **4**
Warfield, Marsha **2**

Cumulative Subject Index

Volume numbers appear in **bold.**

Biology
Just, Ernest Everett **3**

Black Consciousness movement
Biko, Steven **4**
Muhammad, Elijah **4**
Ramaphosa, Cyril **3**

Black Enterprise
Brimmer, Andrew F. **2**
Graves, Earl G. **1**

Black Entertainment Television (BET)
Johnson, Robert L. **3**

Black History Month
Woodson, Carter G. **2**

Black literary theory
Gates, Henry Louis, Jr. **3**

Black Muslims
Ali, Muhammad **2**
Farrakhan, Louis **2**
Muhammad, Elijah **4**
X, Malcolm **1**

Black nationalism
Baraka, Amiri **1**
Carmichael, Stokely **5**
Farrakhan, Louis **2**
Garvey, Marcus **1**
Innis, Roy **5**
Muhammad, Elijah **4**
Turner, Henry McNeal **5**
X, Malcolm **1**

Black Panther Party
Carmichael, Stokely **5**
Cleaver, Eldridge **5**
Davis, Angela **5**
Newton, Huey **2**
Seale, Bobby **3**

Black Power movement
Carmichael, Stokely **5**
McKissick, Floyd B. **3**

Black theology
Cone, James H. **3**

Blues
Dixon, Willie **4**
Holiday, Billie **1**
Smith, Bessie **3**
Wallace, Sippie **1**
Williams, Joe **5**

Blues Heaven Foundation
Dixon, Willie **4**

Booker T. Washington Business College
Gaston, Arthur G. **4**

Booker T. Washington Insurance Company
Gaston, Arthur G. **4**

Boston Bruins hockey team
O'Ree, Willie **5**

Botany
Carver, George Washington **4**

Botswana Democratic Party (BDP)
Masire, Quett **5**

Boxing
Ali, Muhammad **2**
Foreman, George **1**
Louis, Joe **5**

Brazilian Congress
da Silva, Benedita **5**

Broadcasting
Allen, Byron **3**
Bradley, Ed **2**
Brown, Les **5**
Brown, Tony **3**
Brunson, Dorothy **1**
Clayton, Xernona **3**
Cornelius, Don **4**
Davis, Ossie **5**
Johnson, Robert L. **3**
Lawson, Jennifer **1**
McEwen, Mark **5**
Robinson, Max **3**
Shaw, Bernard **2**
White, Bill **1**
Williams, Montel **4**
Winfrey, Oprah **2**

Brooklyn Academy of Music
Miller, Bebe **3**

Brotherhood of Sleeping Car Porters
Randolph, A. Philip **3**

Brown v. Board of Education of Topeka
Clark, Kenneth B. **5**
Franklin, John Hope **5**
Houston, Charles Hamilton **4**
Marshall, Thurgood **1**

Cabinet
See U.S. Cabinet

Cable News Network (CNN)
Shaw, Bernard **2**

California Angels baseball team
Winfield, Dave **5**

California State Assembly
Waters, Maxine **3**

Calypso
Belafonte, Harry **4**

Cancer research
Leffall, LaSalle, Jr. **3**

Caribbean dance
Dunham, Katherine **4**

Cartoonists
Brandon, Barbara **3**

Catholicism
See Roman Catholic Church

CBC
See Congressional Black Caucus

CBS
See Columbia Broadcasting System

CDC
See Centers for Disease Control

CDF
See Children's Defense Fund

CEDBA
See Council for the Economic Development of Black Americans

Celebrities for a Drug-Free America
Vereen, Ben **4**

Centers for Disease Control (CDC)
Gayle, Helene D. **3**

CHA
See Chicago Housing Authority

Challenger
McNair, Ronald **3**

Chama cha Mapinduzi
Nyerere, Julius **5**

Chamber of Deputies (Brazil)
da Silva, Benedita **5**

Chanteuses
Baker, Josephine **3**
Dandridge, Dorothy **3**
Horne, Lena **5**

Che-Lumumba Club
Davis, Angela **5**

Chemurgy
Carver, George Washington **4**

Chicago Bears football team
Singletary, Mike **4**

Chicago Eight
Seale, Bobby **3**

Chicago Housing Authority (CHA)
Lane, Vincent **5**

Chicago Tribune
Page, Clarence **4**

Child abuse prevention
Waters, Maxine **3**

Children's Defense Fund (CDF)
Edelman, Marian Wright **5**

Child Welfare Administration
Little, Robert L. **2**

Choreography
Dove, Ulysses **5**
Dunham, Katherine **4**
Jones, Bill T. **1**
Miller, Bebe **3**
Mitchell, Arthur **2**

Chrysler Corporation
Farmer, Forest **1**

Church for the Fellowship of All Peoples
Thurman, Howard **3**

Defense Communications Agency
Gravely, Samuel L., Jr. **5**

Def Jam Records
Simmons, Russell **1**

Democratic National Committee (DNC)
Brown, Ron **5**
Dixon, Sharon Pratt **1**
Jordan, Barbara **4**
Waters, Maxine **3**

Democratic National Convention
Brown, Ron **5**
Jordan, Barbara **4**
Waters, Maxine **3**

Democratic Socialists of America (DSA)
West, Cornel **5**

Denver city government
Webb, Wellington **3**

Desert Shield
See Operation Desert Shield

Desert Storm
See Operation Desert Storm

Detective fiction
Mosley, Walter **5**

Detroit city government
Young, Coleman **1**

Detroit Lions football team
Sanders, Barry **1**

Detroit Pistons basketball team
Bing, Dave **3**

Detroit Tigers baseball team
Fielder, Cecil 2

Diamond mining
Masire, Quett **5**

Diplomatic Corp
See U.S. Diplomatic Corp

DNC
See Democratic National Committee

Documentary film
Dash, Julie **4**
Davis, Ossie **5**
Julien, Isaac **3**
Riggs, Marlon **5**

Drug prevention
Brown, Les **5**
Clements, George **2**
Rangel, Charles **3**

DSA
See Democratic Socialists of America

Dunham Dance Company
Dunham, Katherine **4**

Ebenezer Baptist Church
King, Bernice **4**

Ebony
Bennett, Lerone, Jr. **5**
Johnson, John H. **3**
Sleet, Moneta, Jr. **5**

Economic Community of West African States (ECOWAS)
Sawyer, Amos **2**

Economics
Brimmer, Andrew F. **2**
Brown, Tony **3**
Masire, Quett **5**
Sowell, Thomas **2**
Sullivan, Leon H. **3**
White, Michael R. **5**
Williams, Walter E. **4**

ECOWAS
See Economic Community of West African States

Edmonton Oilers hockey team
Fuhr, Grant **1**

EEC
See European Economic Community

EEOC
See Equal Employment Opportunity Commission

Egyptology
Diop, Cheikh Anta **4**

Emmy awards
Ashe, Arthur **1**
Belafonte, Harry **4**
Bradley, Ed **2**
Brown, Les **5**
Clayton, Xernona **3**
Foxx, Redd **2**
Goldberg, Whoopi **4**
Guillaume, Robert **3**
Jones, James Earl **3**
Parks, Gordon **1**
Robinson, Max **3**
Williams, Montel **4**

Energy studies
Cose, Ellis **5**

Epidemiology
Gayle, Helene D. **3**

EPRDF
See Ethiopian People's Revolutionary Democratic Front

Equal Employment Opportunity Commission (EEOC)
Hill, Anita **5**
Thomas, Clarence **2**

Essence
Parks, Gordon **1**

Ethiopian People's Revolutionary Democratic Front (EPRDF)
Meles Zenawi **3**

Eugene O'Neill Theater
Richards, Lloyd **2**

European Economic Community (EEC)
Diouf, Abdou **3**

Exploration
Henson, Matthew **2**

Famine relief
See World hunger

FCC
See Federal Communications Commission

Federal Communications Commission (FCC)
Hooks, Benjamin L. **2**

Federal Reserve Bank
Brimmer, Andrew F. **2**

Fellowship of Reconciliation (FOR)
Farmer, James **2**
Rustin, Bayard **4**

Film direction
Dash, Julie **4**
Davis, Ossie **5**
Duke, Bill **3**
Julien, Isaac **3**
Lane, Charles **3**
Lee, Spike **5**
Riggs, Marlon **5**
Singleton, John **2**
Townsend, Robert **4**
Van Peebles, Mario **2**

Finance
Rogers, John W., Jr. **5**

Flouride chemistry
Quarterman, Lloyd Albert **4**

Football
Edwards, Harry **2**
Green, Dennis **5**
Rice, Jerry **5**
Sanders, Barry **1**
Sanders, Deion **4**
Shell, Art **1**
Singletary, Mike **4**
Walker, Herschel **1**

FOR
See Fellowship of Reconciliation

Ford Foundation
Thomas, Franklin A. **5**

Foreign policy
Bunche, Ralph J. **5**
Rice, Condoleezza **3**

40 Acres and a Mule Filmworks
Lee, Spike **5**

French West Africa
Diouf, Abdou **3**

FRONASA
See Front for National Salvation

Front for National Salvation (Uganda; FRONASA)
Museveni, Yoweri **4**

Fusion
Davis, Miles **4**

Genealogy
Dash, Julie **4**
Haley, Alex **4**

Georgia state government
Bond, Julian **2**

Georgia State Supreme Court
Sears-Collins, Leah J. **5**

Cumulative Name Index

Volume numbers appear in **bold**.